Governing Without Consensus

An Irish Perspective

GOVERNING WITHOUT CONSENSUS

An Irish Perspective

by RICHARD ROSE

1933 -

Ireland is a small country where the greatest questions
of politics, morality and humanity are fought out.

GUSTAVE DE BEAUMONT, 1839

BEACON PRESS
Boston

TO THE CONELYS

OF

MACON COUNTY, ILLINOIS

Acknowledgments

When this book was planned in 1965 as a sequel to a short study of legitimacy in England, it seemed at most it would have only an academic interest. By the time the fieldwork was half-finished, Irish life once again seemed to be imitating art. The people of Northern Ireland have since demonstrated in the most palpable fashion possible that questions about the acceptance of Constitutions and basic political laws are more than matters of academic interest. They are issues agitating both loyal subjects and determined rebels. Unfortunately, dozens of people have had to die for this point to become clear to people in London and Dublin who claim sovereignty in Northern Ireland.

It is entirely appropriate that funds for research in Ulster came from both the United States and Britain. The American Social Science Research Council provided money for an extensive series of pilot interviews in 1966–67, and much needed support for travel. The Loyalty survey was financed by a grant from the British Social Science Research Council. Sampling and fieldwork were supervised by M. Douglas Scott Jr., who ably combined an American's concern with modern technology and an Irishman's interest in establishing the particularities of each thing in hand. Mrs. George Davis of Ulster Opinion Surveys, Belfast, was unfailingly helpful in managing a staff of 47 interviewers. A special debt of gratitude is owed to these women, because of the patience and care with which they painstakingly recorded individual remarks in very lengthy interviews. Opinion Research Centre and National Opinion Polls generously made available surveys conducted in Northern Ireland for secondary analysis. A variety of colleagues and staff in the Survey Research Centre of the University of Strathclyde have contributed time, labour and thought to the very considerable amount of data processing and statistical analysis involved in the survey.

In writing a book which touches upon many sensitive problems of politics, an author is particularly grateful for the readiness of people

Acknowledgments

to talk freely and at length about the reasons for their support or opposition to the regime, and also about their hopes and fears for the future. None of the several hundred interviews used as background for writing Chapter IV and Part Three was in a form suitable for analysis by computer. This does not make them less valuable. In pursuing what I hope was the right question, much pleasure and benefit was derived from comparing notes with fellow academics and journalists also working in Northern Ireland. Because the book concerns seriously disputed matters of constitutional and extra-constitutional politics, it is better that none of these persons be thanked by name here.

Within the academic world outside Ireland, serious and full criticism of draft manuscript was received from J. Bowyer Bell Jr., Val R. Lorwin, W. J. M. Mackenzie, Nicholas Mansergh, Eric Nordlinger and Derek Urwin. Mrs. M. McGlone, Mrs. C. Ryburn and Mrs. R. West typed several times the length of this manuscript as successive drafts were written, discarded and rewritten. In formulating ideas at successive stages of planning and writing, it was helpful to give talks based upon the research at Stanford and Harvard universities in America, and within Britain at Glasgow, Lancaster, Liverpool and London universities, and also at the Institute of Advanced Studies, Vienna. Chapter I draws heavily upon material that was initially published under the title 'Dynamic Tendencies in the Authority of Regimes', *World Politics* XXI:4 (1969). The ideas therein were formulated while the author was a visiting fellow at the Institute of Political Studies, Stanford University, in 1967. Chapter II reprints, with abridgment and some revision, materials originally published under the title *The United Kingdom as a Multi-national State*, Occasional Paper No. 6 of the Survey Research Centre of the University of Strathclyde. Materials from a first draft of Chapter IV were initially published under the title, 'The Dynamics of a Divided Regime', *Government and Opposition* V:2 (1970) and, in revised form, in a paper presented to the VIIth World Congress of the International Sociological Association, Varna, Bulgaria, 1970. Where percentage figures from the Loyalty survey differ slightly from those printed in earlier journalistic accounts, those contained herein are authoritative, because they show the removal of clerical errors that inevitably arise in any large-scale survey.

In view of the moral as well as empirical complexities of Northern Ireland politics, the author must emphasize that he is solely respon-

Acknowledgments

sible for all errors of fact. The author is also responsible for any interpretive remarks that may be deficient in understanding or charity.

To a native of Missouri, a border state in the American Civil War, it is no surprise to find in Northern Ireland evidence that all the problems of the past have yet to be resolved. Going back to study relations between whites and blacks in my native city of St. Louis during a hot summer in 1964 made it clear that there is no easy answer to America's great unfinished problem. Watching the English try to cope with their colour problem demonstrates that Ulster people with two passports and nationalities are perhaps better off than unwanted subjects of the Crown with none. Solutions to another country's problems are most easily offered by those farsighted persons who find it easier to see the mote in the eye of their neighbour over the water than the beam in their own. Years of contemplating Northern Ireland–that strange fruit hanging from the Union Jack–have made it clear to the author that what is most needed is knowledge and understanding of all who live there.

The one regret about this book is that its concentration upon a pathological feature of Northern Ireland may give readers unfamiliar with the land a misleading picture of life and people there. Except for problems arising from conflict about the existence of the state, Northern Ireland people are happy in their lives. They are also generous and hospitable to strangers. I only hope that the reception their relatives received when they came off the boat in my native land was as welcoming as mine from the time I disembarked in Belfast.

Fortunately, the survey results presented herein afford the people of Northern Ireland a chance to give collective voice to their view of their world. They and their ancestors have a right to be heard, for some have experienced political discord for 350 years, others for more than a millennium. To 1,291 people of Belfast and Londonderry, of Antrim and Down, of Armagh, Tyrone and Fermanagh, I am particularly indebted for their patient and frank responses to survey questions. Of them and their neighbours, one can only repeat the words that William Faulkner used to describe subjects in his mythical but real land of Yoknapatawpha County, Mississippi: *They endured.*

RICHARD ROSE

Helensburgh, Scotland
January 21, 1971

Contents

Ireland is not an exceptional country but
England is. Irish circumstances and Irish ideas as
to social and agricultural economy are the general
ideas of the human race; it is English circumstances
and English ideas that are peculiar. Ireland is in
the mainstream of human existence and human
feeling and experience; it is England that is in one
of the lateral channels.

JOHN STUART MILL, 1866

1 The Parliament Building at Stormont outside Belfast

2 Burned out Catholic houses in Belfast

3 Woman shopping, Catholic area, Belfast, *Thomson Organisation*

4 Catholic barricade in West Belfast, *Thomson Organisation*

5 Woman shopping, Protestant area, Belfast, *Belfast Telegraph*

6 Football Grounds, Belfast, *Belfast Telegraph*

7 Street scene in West Belfast, *Thomson Organisation*

8 Street scene in the Bogside, Derry, (B. McK.)

9 Captain Terence O'Neill in an Orange parade, *Belfast Telegraph*

(*above left*) "I'm not against force" — Bernadette Devlin at Derry, *Associated Newspapers*

(*above right*) Bernadette Devlin in custody, after Derry, *Belfast Telegraph*

(*opposite above*) "Thank God I am a menace to Popery" — Rev. Dr. Ian Paisley MP, *Belfast Telegraph*

(*opposite below*) "We are Protestants and British" — Rev. Dr. Ian Paisley MP, *Belfast Telegraph*

14 The Labour
Exchange, Derry,
*Thomson
Organisation*

15 The burial of a veteran IRA man, Jimmy Steele, at Milltown Cemetery,
Belfast Telegraph

16 Civil rights march, Belfast to Derry via Burntollet, 1970, *Belfast Telegraph*

17 At Burntollet, *Belfast Telegraph*

18 Police firing teargas, The Bogside, Londonderry, *Belfast Telegraph*

19 Bogsiders charge police, *Thomson Organisation*

20 Police charge demonstrators, *Belfast Telegraph*

21 The morning after — sweeping rubble and black flags in the New Lodge
Road, Belfast, *Belfast Telegraph*

Introduction

*Industrial Ulster is a social 'optimum' between rural Scotland
on the one hand and barbarian Appalachia on the other.*

A. J. TOYNBEE

Crises of authority are nothing new to the Irish. They could almost
claim to have discovered them. Irish people have been living matter
of factly, if not always peaceably, with regimes divided against themselves ever since recorded government first appeared in the land. At
times, the force of conquest or exhaustion has made the challenge
recessive, not dominant. But the absence of political violence is no
guarantee of political consensus. The events in Northern Ireland in the
past decade are a reminder that this crisis of authority continues still.

It is true that Northern Ireland is neither the largest nor the wealthi-
est of countries. Yet few would dismiss it as Neville Chamberlain
dismissed Czechoslovakia in 1938: 'a far away country of whom we
know nothing'.[1] Size is not the only reason why a country should
merit our attention, as citizens or as social scientists. The accidents
of history and geography may leave a small country with more
interesting political problems than can be found, say, in Australia, a
country that covers a continent. Within the confines of Northern
Ireland, people suffer simultaneously from conflicts of religion, of
nationality and of class. A trip of less than 150 miles will show contrasting ways of life from the era before the Industrial Revolution to
the present. Everywhere there are churches; on Sundays, many are
full. The fervent display of Union Jacks and Irish tricolour flags
betrays insecurity rather than security of national identity. The hill
farmers of Fermanagh and Tyrone live in the penumbra of an older
Celtic world. By contrast, Belfast was built upon shipbuilding and
textiles, two primary industries that helped launch the Industrial
Revolution. This results in a country which has had in microcosm
the problems that at one time have troubled most Western nations.

To say that Northern Ireland is not typically English is not to dismiss it from the study of British politics. The same reasoning would
imply that because the Deep South is not typically American, studying Mississippi tells one nothing about the authority of American
government. The contrary is the case: understanding how a regime

operates when problems are unusually difficult–or even insoluble–defines the limits of a regime's authority. Moreover, it is difficult to argue that the people of Northern Ireland are outside the mainstream of the Anglo-American world. The Protestant population of Ulster insists upon its Britishness by flying Union Jacks and toasting the Queen with a frequency and fervour found nowhere else in the United Kingdom. As the people are a mixture of the descendants of the ancient Irish, plus English and Scottish settlers of the seventeenth century, they could claim to be more typical of the composite British than are the exclusively English people of the Thames valley.

The contribution of eighteenth-century Ulster immigration to the initial population of America makes these people almost prototypically white Anglo-Saxon Protestant Americans. The outlook initially gained in settling Ulster against opposition from native Gaels was peculiarly appropriate to the circumstances of their second settlement. Theodore Roosevelt went so far as to assert that the West was won by 'that stern and virile people . . . whose forefathers had followed Cromwell and who had shared in the defence of Derry, and in the victories of the Boyne and Aughrim'.[2] Eleven American Presidents, from Andrew Jackson to Richard Nixon, have had Scotch-Irish forebears. The massive migration of Irish Catholics to America a century later has made them the prototype of successful and easily assimilated post-revolutionary immigrants.[3] This is most of all true in politics. If one stands in the lobby of Belfast airport in the summertime, when recent migrants and the descendants of immigrants return for visits, then one might believe that here, at least as readily as in New York, London, Ottawa or Sydney, could be found the nearest thing to the median citizen of the Anglo-American world.

The political history of Northern Ireland is a record of centuries of violence. The regime was founded by civil war and still lives in the shadow of the gun. Its leaders must now contend with new types of protesters, employing methods that are illegal but technically non-violent, to express in extreme form their rejection of the regime. How different the history of Northern Ireland is from that comfortable Anglo-American perspective that Arnold Toynbee recalled from his late Victorian childhood:

> Here we are on top of the world, and we have arrived at this peak to stay there–forever! There is, of course, a thing called history, but history is something unpleasant that happens to other people. We are comfortably outside all that.[4]

Toynbee adds that his sentiments would have been the same had he been in New York. But if he had grown up in the American South, 'I should not have felt the same. I should then have known from my parents that history had happened to my people in my part of the world.'[5] A similar qualification applies to the westernmost part of the United Kingdom. The 'something unpleasant' that happened in Ulster occurred just after the First World War, when 26 of the 32 counties of Ireland gained independence from Britain by force of arms. Some fear – or hope – that something unpleasant is about to happen again.

Because Northern Ireland politics differs so from the Anglo-American ideal, it may provide better insights into worldwide problems of authority than does a study of England, America or New Zealand.[6] Most Afro-Asian regimes were founded, like Northern Ireland, in less than ideal circumstances. Their peoples often lack internal unity, except that experience of Imperial rule has given them a common desire to seize authority for themselves as Irish Nationalists and Ulster Unionists did half a century ago. The leaders of these regimes, like the men in Stormont Castle outside Belfast, rest uncertainly in authority today. These parallels do not mean that the experience of Northern Ireland can easily be transferred to the far corners of the earth. They do suggest that viewing the non-Western world through orange-and-green spectacles is, *prima facie*, at least as sensible as viewing it through lenses tinted red, white and blue. Moreover, until Western social scientists can encompass such hard cases as Northern Ireland in their theories of politics, only modest claims should be made on behalf of putative general theories.[7]

If authority is a generic problem of politics, why study only one country? The conventional objection to a case study is that one case never proves anything. At best, it disproves a sweeping generalization, or illustrates with detail a more *or* less typical set of relationships between political cause and effect. Yet general theories of authority, devoid of careful reference to particular historical cases, prove or disprove even less. If case studies suffer from the defect of too much detail, general theories suffer from the defect of too little evidence of historical reality. Neologistic general terms may be incapable of withstanding the shock test of application to a particular situation, thus making hypotheses using them incapable of empirical proof or disproof. General theories, like case studies, are at best suggestive, not definitive in their conclusions. At a time when the

Introduction

challenge to 'authoritative' social science theories is almost as great
as the challenge to the authority of regimes, there is much to be said
for an approach that at least fits the one case at hand.[8]

This book is intended to be an extroverted not an introverted case
study, relating the problems of Northern Ireland to a wide range of
nations. Hopefully, this will lead to a better understanding of both
particular and general problems. If the concluding generalizations
are correct, they will at least be true of one country and capable of
projection elsewhere. To ensure a measure of generality in this study,
the first chapter provides a conceptual framework appropriate for
the study of political authority comparatively; concluding chapters
consider why the authority of regimes differs from place to place.
The presentation of survey data about popular attitudes is useful to
describe states of mind, but its primary value is in testing social
science theories that purport to explain why some people accept
political authority and others do not. One can then consider alternative ways to govern without consensus in Northern Ireland and
elsewhere in the Western world. The use of general concepts is no
more a guarantee of original thinking than the use of everyday
English ensures that a writer has risen above prosaic generalities.
Fortunately, the Irish have recurringly demonstrated how the
English language can be used to incarnate all manner of things
political.

A variety of materials and techniques have been necessary for this
study; no one can begin to provide answers for every relevant question about political authority. The materials range from an armchair
and time for thinking to computer print out. A considerable mass of
historical literature about all parts of the United Kingdom has been
sifted to discern persisting and unique features of Northern Ireland
politics. The data from a survey of public opinion provide a reliable
cross-section view of popular attitudes toward the regime. Equally
important have been informal and repeated discussions with a variety
of people active in Northern Ireland politics, both leading defenders
and leading opponents of the regime. Listening to them talk about
their perceptions of the authority or lack of authority of the regime
has been as illuminating as the analysis of survey data. In the course
of research, the author has observed many different kinds of political
activities: election meetings, Orange parades, parliamentary debates,
and the barricading of the Bogside of Londonderry on August 12,
1969. Being stoned by Catholic rioters and teargassed by the Royal

Ulster Constabulary has given the author a bipartisan perspective upon political violence.[9]

The political activist and the political optimist may wonder why this book does not conclude by propounding a clear and final solution to the Northern Ireland problem. The reason is simple. In the foreseeable future, no solution is immediately practicable.[10] This conclusion has been tested in prolonged discussions with politically active Northern Ireland people. Some have confirmed it by voicing the same view. For example, after reading a draft of the first portion of this book, a Northern Ireland politician of moderate outlook wrote:

> In the past I have been unduly optimistic about the prospects of setting the people of Northern Ireland on the path of rational democracy. On the other hand, until I read your draft it had seemed to me that while there were many practical reasons why rational democratic politics were difficult in Northern Ireland, there were no theoretical ones, and I comforted myself with the thought that in theory at least it was always possible that a new and reasonable generation would arise. I am afraid your thesis has now demonstrated all too convincingly that there are theoretical reasons as well as practical ones against this.

Others give confirmation by endorsing solutions that gain plausibility by pretending that the problem is very different from what is recorded here. Would that it were! The predicament is like that of the traveller who asks directions to the nearest town from an old farmer in a field. After several halting attempts to answer, the farmer pauses, throws up his hands, and declares: 'If that's where you want to go, I wouldn't start from here.'

To insist upon the immediately irrefragable character of the problem of authority in Northern Ireland is not to assert that individual actions are meaningless or blameless. In politics, men must always act. Doing nothing is a significant choice with major consequences. The conclusion of Chapter XIII lists 12 possible courses of action that Ulster politicians might follow. The fact that none of these is likely to create a fully legitimate regime does not mean all are equally unattractive alternatives.

Part One

I · The Dynamics of Political Authority

> Turning and turning in the widening gyre
> The falcon cannot hear the falconer
> Things fall apart; the centre cannot hold;
> Mere anarchy is loosed upon the world,
> The blood-dimmed tide is loosed, and everywhere
> The ceremony of innocence is drowned;
> The best lack all conviction, while the worst
> Are full of passionate intensity.
>
> W. B. YEATS, *The Second Coming*

The presence or absence of agreement about political authority is of central importance in every political system. Anglo-American political history is usually written as if authority is unchallenged, by constitutional stipulation or by quasi-divine intervention. From this comfortable, somewhat absentminded perspective, insurrection and political disorder are things that happen to other peoples.[1] The maintenance of authority by coercion is also alien to Anglo-American thought. It too is something that happens elsewhere: in Stalin's Russia, in Nazi Germany, or in some remote contemporary despotism. In more fortunate places, by common consent the rule of law prevails.

If nothing else, the violent political events of the 1960s have shown that it *can* happen here. No government is permanently immune from a challenge to its authority, even though it may come from groups that are small in number among millions of subjects. The sight of massed crowds of demonstrators confronting police is now familiar to every television viewer. In parts of America and the United Kingdom, the sight of soldiers patrolling with rifles is also familiar; occasionally, these rifles are put to use. In view of the reputation of France for political trouble, it is remarkable to note that fewer people were killed there during the events of May, 1968, and in the two years subsequently, than have been killed in the same period in racial and student troubles in America, and in sectarian conflict in Northern Ireland, the most turbulent part of the United Kingdom.

In order to study political authority, one must first be clear about

25

the meaning of terms. Unfortunately, authority is a word that is familiarly used in many contexts, describing everything from child-rearing to military relationships.[2] Defining the term in the language of political science is no easy task, because the word can only be understood in relation to a number of other familiar, but not necessarily precise terms, such as regime, government, and state. Hence, one must first clarify the meaning of basic terms frequently used with great casualness in many discussions of contemporary politics. This then makes it possible to compare and contrast the nature of political authority in modern Western countries.

A political *regime* is here defined as the institutions co-ordinating the civil administration, the police and the military within a state. The institutions may be endowed with an aura of legality by a written Constitution, or they may operate without regard to or in spite of formal provisions of a Constitution. In short, the description of a regime is an empirical matter, free from the moral overtones and confusion that often bedevil studies of a legal title to authority.[3] Defining a regime in relation to institutions of administration and coercion makes it relatively easy to identify it in particular contexts. A country is likely to have only one civil administration, police force and army, and only one formal means of co-ordinating their actions. The political activities of a regime will differ greatly from society to society, depending upon the ideology of those in power. The only necessary act stipulated in this definition is an effort to monopolize the organization of force. Many different theories of politics emphasize the claim to monopolize force as a unique feature of the state.[4] The use of force is not the most frequent, the most economical or the nicest way to govern. Even in totalitarian societies, the complexities of social life constrain the extent to which a regime can succeed in compelling people to do all that is wished.[5] Yet any set of politicians, if challenged, will call upon the police, and, if necessary, the army to defend their position against internal subversion. The regimes differ only in the way in which civil and coercive institutions are combined; all regimes will make some use of both.

The *government* is that group of people who occupy the most important positions within a regime. In societies such as Britain and America, a change of government leaves the institutions of the regime virtually unaffected. In a regime built around a dictator, such as Fascist Italy, the departure of the dictator from government can mean the end of the regime. In Northern Ireland, the empirical distinction between the regime and government is difficult to establish, for a single party, the Unionists, has been continuously and exclusively in power since the regime was established in 1921. A regime claims to control a *state*, a legal entity with geographical boundaries recognized by other regimes. A state is expected to be responsible for everything that happens within its boundaries. This expectation is not, however, a statement of fact. Within the boundaries of a single state, more than one *political system* can exist, i.e., sets of persons making decisions about the allocation of resources and values.[6] Political systems can cut across state boundaries too, as in the European Common Market or in border disputes. There is no necessity for the *de jure* boundaries of a state to be identical with the *de facto* boundaries of a single political system. The failure of these boundaries to match calls into question the authority of a regime. Irish history, like German history, is a particularly good illustration of this point.

People resident within the territorial boundaries of a state form its *population*. This is the maximum number of individuals from whom a regime legally claims support and compliance. People who live within a state are not necessarily under its authority. Only persons actually affected by the actions of a regime should be described as its *subjects*. In many states of the non-Western world, a significant fraction of the population is not subject to the authority of the regime. The central authority is isolated in a capital city: it must engage in long and often difficult campaigns to subjugate those on the periphery who are unaware of its commands or unwilling to follow them. In America, this process is familiarly known as the Winning of the West. Not only did it involve the colonization of lands formerly held by the Indians, but also the replacement of *ad hoc* frontier authorities, such as vigilante committees, with more respectable and settled forms of authority.[7] The process of integrating the peoples of the British isles into one state began in Wessex in the ninth century. The peoples of Wales, Scotland and Ireland were incorporated much later, with varying degrees of success.

Collectively, the population of a state might be referred to by the awkward but neutral title of 'a social aggregate'. The more euphonious word *society* will be used henceforth in this restrictive sense. Dorothy Emmet defines a society as a categoric group of people who do not necessarily have mutual relationships in a social system.[8] In so far as a group of people have the feeling that 'they belong together', then this group can be referred to as a *community*.[9] Many communities, such as philatelists or supporters of a football team, have no political consequences. Politically, such groups become important only if those who share a sense of community begin to demand special treatment or independence from a regime by virtue of their common feeling.[10] The existence of a *nation* is not dependent upon the existence of a state. For centuries, Germans, Poles and Irish maintained many of the characteristics of a nation, while lacking a state of their own. Reciprocally, the existence of a state does not depend upon its population forming a single national community. Switzerland has long been an example of how successful a multi-national state might be. In view of the demonstrated difficulties of nation-building, not least in Northern Ireland, the indiscriminate use of the term 'nation-state' must be avoided.

To say that a regime has authority says nothing itself about the pattern of relations between the regime and the population. Its authority may be fully legitimate, non-existent or something in between. To avoid the use of a universal concept as if it discriminated between different types of authority, one must descend the ladder of abstraction. The *authority* of regimes can be measured and differentiated by two characteristics: the extent of diffuse support for the regime among intended subjects, and the extent to which its population complies with basic political laws.[11]

In this study, the concept of *support* refers to a diffuse feeling that the institutions of a regime merit positive endorsement. The attitude is diffuse, because it does not refer to specific characteristics, such as the personality of the chief executive, the procedures of the legislature, or the activities of tax collectors. An individual may dislike a specific feature or personality in his regime, yet still maintain that overall it is good, or even the best in the world. The motives that lead an individual to support a regime will reflect a mixture of values, beliefs and emotions. An aggregate indicator of support for a regime might be the failure of anti-regime parties to secure many votes in free elections. For example, the derisory vote of the British Communist Party and the absence of other anti-regime parties in England indicates that support for the regime is very high there. In Northern Ireland, the relatively high vote for anti-regime parties indicates that support is less than unanimous there. In states where there are no free elections, one way of assessing support is to note whether there are any organizations or social groups that the regime defines as *ipso facto* disloyal, as Zionists are so defined in Russia. Where political and social conditions make attitude surveys practicable, then the extent of support for a regime may also be assessed by interviewing a sample of the population.

Compliance refers to the ability of a regime to secure the obedience of its nominal subjects to basic political laws. Basic political laws are only a small portion of the totality of laws promulgated in the name of a regime. They are laws which, if broken, will lead their violators to be treated as subversives committing a crime against the state.[12] By contrast, the violation of ordinary criminal laws is considered anti-social, not a crime against the state. Anti-social behaviour does not necessarily correlate with anti-regime behaviour. For instance, motoring offences or income tax evasion is unlikely to reflect political opposition to the regime. Even criminal acts that involve a political figure may not be interpreted as an anti-regime activity. In the United States, the murder of a President may be regarded as an anti-social act, rather than as a purposeful attempt to subvert the regime. Many activities are not unambiguously criminal, whether in a social or political sense. A study of police behaviour stresses, '*The normal tendency of the police is to underenforce the law*', ignoring many misdemeanour offences on the grounds that enforcement would do less to maintain order than would benign neglect.[13] The power to determine whether a particular act is a sign of political non-compliance rests with the officials of the regime. They decide what laws are basic, i.e., necessary to the survival of their regime. The area of discretion is very great. For instance, race riots in American cities are sometimes considered anti-regime activities by black power militants but defined by white public officials as irrational and purposeless hooliganism. The policies that follow from the latter definition are very different from those that would follow from diagnosing a riot as an act of political subversion.[14] As a regime moves toward totalitarianism, there is a great increase in the proportion of social activities defined as violations of basic political laws. Even drunkenness or abstract painting can be considered anti-regime activity.

Statistics of violence are the most frequently cited evidence of a regime's failure to ensure compliance with basic political laws. This is understandable, because violence is a visible, dramatic and threatening form of behaviour. It is inevitably anti-social. It need not be anti-regime, unless those who commit the violence intend to threaten the regime by their actions. Intent is crucial. As the traditional song notes, 'the wearing of green' could be construed as a mark of rebellion in Dublin in 1798. By wearing green prominently, a person could symbolize sympathy for James Napper Tandy and others involved in the plot by the United Irishmen to repudiate the authority of the English Crown. Reciprocally, substantial public violence can occur without any sign of intent to overthrow a regime. The American race riots of 50 years ago involved many deaths, but there is no evidence that those engaged meant to force change in the regime. They were seeking to control social relationships.

The vast majority of differences within a society do not challenge a regime, because they are unlikely to be translated into political issues. For instance, sex differences are not today the basis of differences about the authority of a regime. Most political disagreements are differences of opinion that can be handled by the existing institutions of the regime without loss of support or fear of non-compliance. Even in a society in which political violence occurs, it is usual to find that only a small proportion of statutory laws are a matter of *discord*, i.e., they involve differences concerning the authority of the regime. In a state where the authority of the regime is unchallenged, there will be recognized means to end discord peacefully and legally. In America, the Supreme Court is the institution formally charged with ultimate responsibility for resolving discordant views about the constitutionality of acts of Congress and the executive. The decisions of the Court are by no means final. The constitutional clauses that the Court cites as justification for its decision may subsequently be modified by constitutional amendment, if not by later judicial re-interpretation.[15] Yet the decision of the Court does provide a *pro tempore* resolution of conflict; only in race relations has it conspicuously failed to gain acceptance for its dicta. In England, the House of Commons functions as the 'court of the last resort' for political disputes. Even in instances such as the Suez War, when MPs disagreed about the legality of Sir Anthony Eden's measures, MPs of all parties complied with the government's decisions, when Britain was attacking Egypt and when it withdrew.[16] In such instances, diffuse support for the regime and habitual readiness to comply with its laws are sufficiently great to cause people to accept authority, even though they may differ profoundly about what the government of the day is doing.

The less individuals are inclined to accept the authority of their regime or the more strongly they are committed to specific courses of political action, then the greater is the likelihood that discord will result in a refusal to comply with basic political laws. In this study, the term *protest* will be reserved for expressions of disagreement that do not violate basic political laws. The term *demonstration* will refer to peaceful actions that do challenge such laws. Civil rights activists in America and in Northern Ireland have shown that legal protests may end in violence, just as illegal demonstrations can be peaceful. Yet there is always the possibility that demonstrations will lead to violence, whether by accident, by the initiative of the demonstrators, or by acts of police charged with controlling them. When violence is used in a conscious effort to repudiate the regime, this is an act of rebellion. Collectively, non-compliant actions can be referred to as *disorder*. In short, the most extreme forms of political action are not those that are violent, but those in which violence is used with the intent to express defiance of basic political laws. As war is the continuation of diplomacy by another method, so disagreement escalating to demonstration and rebellion is the continuation of politics by another form of bargaining. The fact that the bargaining encounter takes place in the streets, rather than around a conference table, does not mean that politics has ceased. People who have turned to extralegal acts are still pursuing the same goal and still confronting the same opponents.[17] Violent action is rational in a means-ends sense if the aim of a political group is to overthrow a regime. The reasoning is the same whether the rebellion is successful, as in the case of the American revolution against the English Crown, or unsuccessful, as in the case of the Jacobite rebellion against the English Crown only 30 years before.

The authority of a regime can be described by assessing its degree of support and the extent of compliance with its basic political laws. Each of these characteristics can vary along a continuum, ranging from very high to very low. This means that there are four very different directions in which regimes can tend; there is also an intermediate category. Regimes near the middle in support and compliance can be described as 'divided' in their authority. (See Figure I.1.)

The names given to each of the four corner categories describe ideal types. No regime, whether it is called fully legitimate or fully coercive, ever succeeds in securing full compliance from all its subjects. This is a goal that regimes approach as a limit. One category is clearcut: the repudiated regime, which loses support and compliance from subjects until it no longer exists. The Third Reich in Germany or the Spanish Republic of the 1930s are examples. The category of an isolated regime follows logically from the analytic scheme. In a modern Western context, it seems inconceivable that a regime could be fully supported, yet low in securing compliance with its basic political laws. But in the non-Western world it is possible to conceive of a regime that nominally receives support from its population, yet fails to secure compliance with its laws, because its administrative and communications networks are so poor that these laws are inadvertently disobeyed. A regime with divided authority perfectly fits its label. Yet even here it is possible to note that regimes can be more or less divided; as the ratio of support to non-support or compliance and non-compliance changes, then the regime moves toward full legitimacy, coercion or repudiation.

Figure I.1   A typology of the authority of regimes

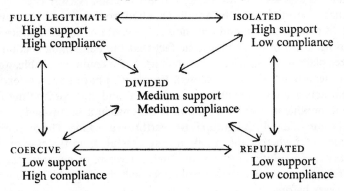

FULLY LEGITIMATE ⟷ ISOLATED
High support   High support
High compliance   Low compliance

DIVIDED
Medium support
Medium compliance

COERCIVE ⟷ REPUDIATED
Low support   Low support
High compliance   Low compliance

Using a continuum rather than a dichotomy for classifying each aspect permits an infinite number of distinctions to be made concerning levels of support and compliance. For instance, one can discriminate among Communist regimes according to the degree of popular support that they enjoy. The regime in the Soviet Union would appear to enjoy more support than that in Czechoslovakia. Similarly, one can discriminate among regimes by the degree of compliance that they can secure. The difficulties in America in enforcing Supreme Court orders concerning desegregation indicate that it is less successful in securing compliance with basic political laws than regimes in Norway or Sweden. Using two dimensions to classify regimes avoids confusing authorities that share one attribute but not the other. Both Hungary and New Zealand, for example, have regimes that obtain compliance from their subjects. Yet, judging by

32

the security measures of the former and their absence in the latter, the two differ greatly in the degree of popular support enjoyed. One gains compliance because it is coercive, and the other because popular attitudes diffusely favour the regime.

Loyalty is the correlative concept to authority in discussing individual outlooks. An individual's loyalty can be defined as the extent to which he has a diffuse positive attitude supporting the regime and shows a predisposition to comply with basic political laws. Understanding individual predispositions to act is as important as noting past behaviour. The latter information tells how much non-compliance has occurred in the recent past, or is occurring at the moment. In societies that are not in continuous disorder, the important point to note is the willingness of individuals to disobey basic laws at some future time. This calculation is important to regime officials trying to estimate the possible reaction of subjects to new laws; it is also important to rebels trying to estimate the reaction of subjects to actions intended to spark off widespread non-compliance and the repudiation of a regime.

Cross-classifying people on two dimensions in a manner analogous to Figure I.1. creates five ideal-type individual outlooks. Three are familiar figures: the fully allegiant person, the repressed individual giving compliance but not support, and the rebel. The individual who favours the regime but refuses compliance is less familiar but very formidable. This person is an *Ultra*, an individual who supports a particular definition of the existing regime so strongly that he is willing to break laws, or even take up arms, to recall it to its 'true' way. In Southern Rhodesia, for example, the Ultras have maintained their regime since 1965 in defiance of orders from Her Majesty's Government in London, nominally sovereign there. Similarly, during the war in Algeria in the 1950s, an Ultra view led French settlers to take up arms against the Fourth Republic. Individuals may fall in between the four corner categories for two very different reasons. Some will be ambivalent, seeing arguments for and against their regime and its basic political laws. Others will be uncertain; these are the people whose apathy is such that they don't know whether to give the regime support and compliance. Ambivalent subjects will behave unpredictably because of tensions within themselves; uncertain subjects are likely to go along with the prevailing views of those around them.

Statements about the authority of a regime and about the loyalty of its nominal subjects necessarily imply descriptions of each other. Yet there is no necessary one-to-one relation between the two. A regime can be classified as fully legitimate for practical purposes without the full support and compliance of every one of its millions of inhabitants. Reciprocally, it can avoid full repudiation, for a time at least, even if it has low support and compliance from a high proportion of its subjects, as occurred in South Vietnam in the 1960s. Since the maintenance of a regime is not ordinarily decided by electoral majorities or referenda, there is no specific proportion of the population that can be invoked as a threshold of compliance or support, such as 50 per cent or two-thirds. The National Socialist Party managed to overthrow the Weimar regime, even though it secured less than a majority of the votes–33 per cent–at the November, 1932 German general election and 44 per cent in the March, 1933 ballot. Social scientists have given little attention to the minimum level of loyalty or disloyalty necessary to maintain or repudiate a regime. The presence of a small handful of rebels within a society can cause a reaction out of all proportion to numbers. Rebels depend upon their actions *and* the regime's reactions multiplying their following. The difficulty of determining how big the small group of rebels must be to trouble a regime is dramatically illustrated by tables on the small proportion of blacks participating in urban American disorder.[18]

Classifying regimes in two dimensions guards against the simplistic assumption that all regimes are every day becoming more and more legitimate. It also guards against the simplistic assumption that all regimes that are not fully legitimate are heading straight toward a successful rebellion. A display of force may be the first stage in a movement toward coercion. For example, the shooting of 69 Africans at Sharpeville in 1960 was followed by years of coerced peace in the Republic of South Africa. The middle regime in Figure I.1 shows discord about authority. The majority of positions are intermediate and thus, by implication, transition points; all political authority is intrinsically changeable in nature. At a given point in time, we not only need to know what authority a regime enjoys, but also in which direction it is most likely to change.

Logically, there are four directions in which a regime can move–legitimation, isolation, coercion or repudiation. Only one category, a fully repudiated regime, is final; it belongs to the historical past. A fully legitimate regime may appear to be 'locked in' to full legitimacy. In the 1950s this assumption seemed to fit America and Britain. The rise of black and student militancy in America casts a shadow upon such an assumption today; doubts arise in Britain because of disorder in Northern Ireland and nationalist activities in Scotland and Wales. A regime isolated from its subjects might try to move toward full legitimacy or coercion by improving its capabilities to ensure compliance. In default of this, it might lose support and move to repudiation. Viewed at a single point in time, coercive regimes appear very durable, for a regime resting on bayonets is not lightly challenged. Yet it would be rash in theory and in practice to assume that no changes are likely in a coercive regime. In the course of two or three generations, the cumulative effect of coercion might lead to the legitimation of the regime, as an ever increasing proportion of its adult subjects know no other than that to which they have been conditioned by coercion. Some accounts of the Soviet Union suggest that this process is already in train. Yet, other countries in Eastern Europe, such as Hungary and Czechoslovakia, have demonstrated that a coercive regime could be quickly repudiated, if it relaxed reliance upon force even after two decades of coercion.

In trying to get a sense of the direction in which most regimes move, time is crucial, for the only information that can be gained quickly about the dynamics of a regime is negative: it can be overthrown soon after foundation. Few regimes achieve fully legitimate status in a short time. England, for example, faced its civil war a century and one-half after the Tudors created a centralized kingdom. The American Civil War began 72 years after the adoption of the Constitution. For generations in such major European states as France, Germany and Italy, regimes have risen and fallen. In practice, no regime might be said to be moving away from repudiation unless it has survived long enough to have been the predominant influence upon the political memories of more than half of its present adult population from childhood onwards.[19] Applying this criterion in 1970 means suspending judgment about the long-term course of change in any regime founded since the Second World War. In short, it is premature to speak with confidence of the direction of regime movements in nearly all African, Asian and Middle Eastern countries, for most regimes and states were founded there after 1945.[20]

Europe–defined broadly as the area from Iceland to the Soviet Union–provides a sufficient number of old-established states to allow generalization about changes in the authority of regimes. Of the 29 states existing in Europe at the outbreak of the Second World War, only eight, Britain, Ireland, Sweden, Switzerland, Russia, Spain, Portugal and Iceland, have had their regimes survive intact throughout the period. In five more states—Norway, Denmark, the Netherlands, Luxembourg and Belgium—regimes were displaced by the German army, but restored afterwards. In the first four of these countries, no regime change appears to have occurred in consequence of this. Changes in Belgium have been noteworthy, involving the rise and demise of a right-wing movement between the wars, the deposition of a reigning monarch, and latterly, intense nationalist agitation by Flemish-speakers.[21] In three of the 16 places where regimes have been unambiguously repudiated, Latvia, Lithuania and Estonia, the states themselves have ceased to exist. In the remaining 13 countries, civil wars and/or internal coups succeeded in overthrowing established regimes; in France and Greece, such upheavals have occurred more than once. In Eastern European countries, foreign invasion was an immediate cause of the repudiation of a regime. Yet it is implausible to assert that regimes in places such as Albania, Bulgaria, Hungary, Poland, Yugoslavia or Roumania were previously moving toward full legitimacy. Their postwar inheritors have been moving toward coercion. Past patterns need not recur, but given events in Western as well as Eastern and Southern Europe in the 1960s one might best conclude that there is no single direction in which European regimes tend to change. Some move toward full legitimacy, some toward coercion and some to repudiation.

The pattern of political change in Europe can usefully be compared with Latin American experience, to see whether the continental wars that have twice engulfed European states in this century are the cause of the repudiation of so many regimes. Latin American states are all more than a century old. They have been remarkably free from external military attack and their boundaries have remained much more stable than those of European countries. Yet Latin American regimes are notorious for their inability to maintain support and compliance. According to Martin Needler, successful insurrections have occurred 56 times in these 20 countries during the period 1935–1964. In 17 of these countries, there has been a successful coup against the regime at least once since 1945.[22] In short, the normal expectation of a Latin American regime would be that it is heading for repudiation. It could be argued that political protest and the disorderly change of leadership is so common in Latin America that an unconstitutional change of government is as unexceptionable as a general

36

election in a European country; altering the personnel of a regime by force need not mean the repudiation of a regime. The theoretical point is a valid one. Yet, sooner or later, such coups are likely to change institutions of government. At a minimum, regimes with a limited capacity to maintain compliance will be less than fully legitimate.[23]

Contemporary evidence of support and compliance in Western or non-Western regimes is not of equal character or validity for every regime. For instance, in East European and Latin American countries lacking free elections, it is impossible to draw inferences about the absence of support from electoral data. The use of such data in Western nations may produce difficulties too, in so far as opponents of the regime do not rely upon the ballot box as the principal channel of demonstrating their views of a regime. In so far as the occurrence of disorder is regarded as an indication of non-compliance with basic political laws, then it is clear that substantial opposition to regimes is still widespread in the Western and non-Western worlds. One researcher, Harry Eckstein, was able to document more than 1,200 such challenges to authority in the period 1946–59. In an analysis of civil strife during the period 1961–65, T. R. Gurr found that 104 of the 114 states studied had had some experience of political disorder. The majority of European states were in the bottom quarter of this ranking, but this did not mean that they were entirely trouble-free. Moreover, some Eastern European countries, such as Hungary, were low in civil strife in the early 1960s because of coercion successfully applied shortly before.[24]

The clear implication of this evidence is that regimes are as likely to be repudiated as to survive for many decades. According to Dankwart Rustow, the median contemporary regime is unable to show the basic requisite of longevity, the ability to carry out peacefully a change in the group controlling the government: 'In all three parts of the world–democratic, Communist and developing–changes of regime have been more frequent than have orderly changes of government within a continuing regime.'[25] Thus, in approaching the study of particular regimes, one should give at least as much attention to movement in the direction of repudiation and coercion as to movement toward full legitimacy. Unfortunately, much social science writing concentrates exclusively upon the restricted problem of making or maintaining fully legitimate regimes.

The record of the recent past and the present shows that any theory of political authority must explain why regimes differ in their character at one point in time and why they change in different directions. Comparing a number of regimes at one point in time makes it possible to understand some of the correlates of full legitimacy, coercion, or divided authority. It does not tell in what direction a regime is heading, for a study at a single point in time cannot comprehend change. Moreover, such an approach cannot consider whether the techniques suitable for developing support and compliance differ from those maintaining them once full legitimacy is achieved. A century ago Bagehot argued that this was the case, and events since have supported his thesis.[26] Put simply, this means that it would be easier to maintain the legitimacy of an established regime such as Switzerland or Sweden than it would be to achieve full legitimacy for a new regime founded in a society such as France or Spain. To understand the dynamics of authority, one must consider a regime across a lengthy period of time.

The chief purpose of this book is to examine intensively the dynamics of the regime in Northern Ireland. In order to understand the general implications of a process of movement, it is first desirable to outline briefly the general character of the process that all regimes undergo, whether heading toward survival or repudiation.[27]

In searching for an explanation of how and why regimes change, the logical place to start is at the beginning. This is not the date at which a regime is born, but the time of its conception. Regimes are not conceived without an inheritance,[28] nor are their new subjects devoid of prior political values and beliefs. In fact, the only criteria by which subjects can evaluate a new regime are those learned under another, sometimes inimical regime. To emphasize the importance of precursive conditions is not to suggest that the study of contemporary regimes need be transformed into the study of medieval history. Most regimes in Western nations are less than a century old. England and America are exceptional in their longevity.

Precursive conditions affect a new regime at the date of its foundation, and remain as constraints thereafter. The geographical situation of a country is a persisting constraint, even though the significance of geography may be altered by political treaties or changes in transportation. The traditional culture is not a fixed physical fact, but the founders of a new regime must treat it initially as a given, seeking to reduce its influence gradually through time. The social and economic conditions of a society must similarly be treated initially as givens. Even the most elaborate and optimistic plan for economic growth must start from somewhere. Another important initial constraint is the size of the pool of administrators from a previous regime. Without a sufficiency of field administrators, both civil and coercive, a regime risks isolation. The one thing that new men can most influence is the range and number of political skills that they bring to their task of managing authority.

At the foundation of a new regime, leaders can exercise considerable influence upon political events that follow. A cross-national study indicates that while precursive conditions outside the control of the regime can cause turmoil, depriving a regime of full legitimacy, the actions of the regime are likely to be of major significance in determining whether the level of protest reaches such a stage of violence that the regime is repudiated.[29] They also have a wide choice of aims. On *a priori* grounds, at least four different strategies can be identified. A popular strategy places equal value upon support and compliance. A confederal strategy values support so highly that requests for compliance are limited. Its opposite is an authoritarian strategy, in which a regime seeks to maximize compliance without regard to the effects of its actions upon support. In non-Western countries, a government may act in an arbitrary manner, without regard for the response of its subjects under either heading, because its leaders are interested only in the short-term exploitation of their position.

The tasks that face the leaders of a new regime are sometimes described by social scientists as necessary functions. A few functions are universal in all regimes: e.g., the recruitment of leaders, the aggregation of interests, and the implementation of decisions. Because these terms are high-level abstractions, they are of little use in explaining variations of political authority. To say that a regime has failed to perform its necessary functions is simply another way of saying that it has been repudiated. Moreover, a regime may be repudiated even though it performs most of these functions. A single failure in dealing with an insurgent nationalist group can be sufficient for repudiation.

The causes of the repudiation of regimes appear to vary greatly from country to country and continent to continent. Sometimes these difficulties are described as crises of authority.[30] The choice of terms is unfortunate, because a crisis is of limited temporal duration and its resolution is usually reckoned to have removed the difficulty associated with it. Yet in the politics of regimes, particular difficulties can recurringly cause crises. For instance, France has had crises of

authority repeatedly since the Revolution of 1789. Often, new difficulties have closely paralleled those from an earlier period in time;
they have not been dissolved by a temporary solution. If such difficulties are called problems this is reasonable, as long as it is recognized that it is a moot point whether the existence of a problem also
implies the existence of a solution.

Comparative studies of social structure and politics in Western
nations by S. M. Lipset, Stein Rokkan and others have emphasized
the importance of four major social differences as potentially threatening discord about the regime.[31] In point of time, the first potential
source of discord arises from differences between individuals identifying with the central community of the regime, and those whose
identification is with a peripheral community. If the regime is to avoid
nationalist challenges, then these differing communal loyalties must
be integrated into a new loyalty appropriate to a nation-state, or a
multi-national state. The second potential source of discord is a
difference of religion, whether between Protestant churches and the
Roman Catholic Church, or between an established Church and dis-
senting denominations or secular and anti-clerical groups. A third
potential source of discord arises from differences between urban
dwellers and rural inhabitants. These may concern the prices at
which they exchange their goods, or contrast the styles of life of
peasants and a landed gentry with an urban bourgeoisie and manual
workers. Differences between manual workers and those in the middle
class within urban industrial centres are last in order of historical
occurrence but not necessarily least in the difficulties that they are
expected to cause regimes.

Although these difficulties have often arisen at different points of
time in the European past, they can persist simultaneously into the
present or last longer than the life of a regime. As such difficulties
threaten repudiation, they are the first priorities of the leaders of a
regime. At any given time, the leaders of such a regime are, in Richard
Neustadt's phrase, 'The prisoners of first-things-first, and almost
always something else comes first.'[32] In such circumstances, one would
hypothesize that leaders who wish to maximize the chance of their
regime for survival would give greatest priority to those *ad hoc*
strategies designed to meet immediate difficulties threatening repudiation. After all, if politicians are assumed to maximize short-term
electoral benefits in fully legitimate regimes, the argument for maximizing short-term considerations is even more compelling in a regime

in which the penalty for failure is far greater. Maximizing political security is very different from maximizing economic development. Economic growth is unlikely to occur quickly enough or powerfully enough to resolve immediate challenges to authority. In some instances, it may even intensify challenges to the regime.[33]

To emphasize the importance of the authority of regimes is not to argue that the survival or the repudiation of a regime is the only thing that matters in politics. It only asserts that the subject is of sufficient political importance to merit a book on its own. This claim is specially strong when Northern Ireland provides the primary illustrative material. Moreover, the topic helps increase understanding of what other important political concepts do and do not involve. For example, it is implicit in the preceding discussion that the authority of a regime is not necessarily determined by the possession of such democratic institutions as competitive political parties and free elections. Regimes may be fully legitimate while lacking such institutions or they may possess such institutions yet have divided authority. The effectiveness of a regime is also not synonymous with its type of authority. Both coercive and fully legitimate regimes may make claim to effective action. It is an open question whether one or the other is likely to be more effective in mobilizing resources from its society. Studying the dynamics of a regime avoids the assumption that because a regime is peaceful at one point in time it is inevitably stable.[34] It emphasizes the need to consider what makes authority change, and what forces resist change. This is true whether the regime studied is moving toward full legitimacy, toward repudiation or, like Northern Ireland, is agitated at some point in between.

II · The United Kingdom as a Multi-national Regime

Despite the many attributes of the English, a peculiar talent for solving the problems of Ireland is not among them.
ROY JENKINS, Home Secretary 1967

In a world in which challenges to political authority are frequent and often violent, England stands as a great exception. The last successful challenge to authority in England was the short and glorious revolution of 1688. Yet it does not follow from this that today the regime is fully legitimate, since legally there is no such thing as an English regime. In international law, as in the title of the Queen, the regime is the United Kingdom of Great Britain and Northern Ireland, a composite of jurisdictions joined into one state. Because of the prolonged and continuing refusal of some Irish people to give allegiance, at no time in history has this regime been fully legitimate everywhere in the realm. Any analysis of the authority of the regime in a part of the United Kingdom must commence by considering the nature of the whole.

Unfortunately, many who write about the subject confuse England, the largest part, with the whole of the United Kingdom. Alternatively, they ignore any possibility of differences within the United Kingdom. Conceivably, England rather than Northern Ireland may be the exception to many familiar generalizations about British politics, or each of the parts of the Kingdom could differ from instead of resembling all the others. To avoid a cumbersome phrase and, even more, to avoid an awkward reminder of history, reference is often made to a nominally simple entity, 'England' or 'Britain'. Walter Bagehot's study of *The English Constitution*, published in 1867, gave no hint of the constitutional problems that followed the Fenian rising in Ireland in the same year. Latterday writers have also ignored differences between English and United Kingdom politics. L. S. Amery, an active politician during the Irish troubles, gave careful attention in his *Thoughts on the Constitution* to the integration of colonies into the British Empire and Commonwealth, but none to the

The United Kingdom as a Multi-national Regime

problem of the integration and disintegration of parts of the United Kingdom. To American writers such as Harry Eckstein, the terms England and Britain are also interchangeable. Eckstein writes of a period when Scotland had its own King and Ireland was unsettled, 'Britain emerged from the Middle Ages with a consensus upon the most basic of all elements of political culture.'[1] Recognition is sometimes given to differences of peoples within the United Kingdom, but these are then treated as of little or no political significance. For instance, Jean Blondel begins a discussion of social structure by asserting, 'Britain is probably the most homogeneous of all industrial countries', and S. E. Finer lists regional differences as the first of 'factors that assist consensus'.[2]

In this study words often used loosely to refer to institutions and peoples will be given restricted meanings. Ireland and Britain (or Great Britain) are geographical terms referring to the two major islands that once were totally within the United Kingdom. Because of historical associations, they will collectively be referred to as the British isles, as this is much clearer than the Irish phrase, 'these islands'. England, Wales and Scotland refer to geographical subdivisions of the island of Britain. Ireland is here used only as a geographical concept, without prejudice to political boundaries or questions of national identity. The regime that rules 26 of its 32 counties will be referred to as the Republic of Ireland. The remaining six counties are most conveniently described by the British title, Northern Ireland; this is not recognized by the Republic, which refers to the Six Counties. For the sake of euphony and convenience, Northern Ireland is also referred to as Ulster, or simply as 'the Province', a phrase that aptly connotes its measure of integration in a larger entity–whether that be considered Britain or the Republic.[3] (The traditional Province of Ulster includes three counties now within the boundaries of the Irish Republic–Donegal, Cavan and Monaghan.) The population of Britain can be subdivided into the English, Welsh and Scottish peoples. While residents of the Republic readily accept the identification of Irish, those who live in Northern Ireland might neutrally be referred to as Ulstermen, without prejudice to any other identity–legal or social psychological–that these individuals may prefer to claim.

Once these terminological difficulties are recognized, then it is possible to speak precisely of the extent to which a group within the United Kingdom forms a community, a single group of people who

feel that they belong together, or a nation, a community demanding political institutions recognizing its distinctiveness within the state. If no such distinctive institutions are found, then it is proper to speak of the United Kingdom as a nation-state, with Wales, Scotland or Ulster of no more than regional significance. In so far as distinctions are found, then the United Kingdom is a multi-national state. The concept of a British people would then become a second-order abstraction, lumping together the peoples of the English, Scottish and Welsh nations, almost as the term the English-speaking peoples aggregates Americans, Australians, and the parts of the British isles.

The United Kingdom as a Multi-national Regime

In theory, social relationships between the major communities of the United Kingdom might have followed any of three different courses.[4] The first is Anglicization, the assimilation of non-English peoples to English values, beliefs and emotions. A second model of change is that of the melting-pot, in which the distinctive communal characteristics of each group would merge in something that mixed parts of each, thereby becoming different from each. This would mean that English people would lose distinctive characteristics in the course of becoming British. A third pattern of communal adjustment is structural pluralism, in which peoples who live in different parts of a state (or in the same area) retain distinctive communal characteristics but establish stable relationships with those who differ from them. If a society has undergone pervasive penetration by one communal group or if a melting-pot process produces a new communal identity, then the result is a nation-state, with no immediate potential for challenge to its regime on nationalist grounds, because the society is totally homogenized. Where structural pluralism has prevailed, then there is, potentially at least, ground for a nationalist challenge to the regime. Challenges vary greatly in intensity, from requests for minor decentralization or symbolic gratification to demands for substantial autonomy or independence as a separate nation-state.

Characteristically, political scientists treat the United Kingdom as a nation-state. This makes it impossible to conceive of a nationalist challenge to the regime, because only one nation, Britain, is cognized. A variety of explanations are offered to explain why the British regime should be fully legitimate, notwithstanding its composite origins. Leslie Wolf-Phillips describes the Constitution of the regime as the result of the passage of Acts of Parliament claiming effect everywhere in the United Kingdom.[5] The assumption that Acts of Parliament are the means of assuring support and compliance is found in Westminster too. A variety of authors have posited that the British people have become a single nation because class differences are similar or identical in England, Wales, Scotland and Northern Ireland. Robert Alford, the one writer to attempt a systematic comparison of class and national differences within Great Britain, concluded that class differences are pre-eminent politically.[6] The presence of Conservative and Labour party candidates in all parts of the Kingdom and even the permeation of opinion surveys everywhere also lead social scientists to conclude that Britain is a homogeneous nation with a fully legitimate regime.[7]

The United Kingdom as a Multi-national Regime

The composition of society offers an alternative explanation for the authority of a regime. Challenges to the authority of a regime depend upon the numerical strength of different groups composing the population of the state. At one extreme, if the population of a state is entirely homogeneous in social characteristics, then people will have no basis for disagreeing in ways that will challenge authority. For example, if every subject speaks the same language or has the same skin colour, then there can be no challenge to the regime in the name of linguistic or racial groups. As a population divides into approximately equal social groups with contrasting or mutually exclusive goals, then the potential for challenge to a regime becomes greater; other influences can intervene between the numerical distribution of a population and the mobilization of people for political action. The compositional theory is especially useful in analysing the structure of the United Kingdom, for it draws attention to the importance of the relative size of the nations that compose it.

A third general theory concerning the relationship of the parts of society emphasizes the importance of relative deprivation: the more a group has a common identity and the more its members regard themselves deprived in relation to other groups within society, then the more likely it is to challenge the authority of a regime. The most familiar example of this theory is found in the literature of class conflict. Yet it is equally applicable to relationships between nationalities within a state, or to any groups with a sense of communal distinctiveness, whether religious, linguistic, racial or agricultural.[8]

Any attempt to measure the real or potential bases of political discord within a society immediately raises the question: What social differences are most likely to be important politically? If, for instance, the drinking habits of the population of the United Kingdom differ,[9] it does not follow that different tastes in drink will correlate with different tastes in regimes. The Lipset-Rokkan approach provides a parsimonious framework for assessing the strength and intensity of major social differences concerning centre-periphery relations, religion, and urban-rural and industrial class differences within the United Kingdom. To substantiate the proposition that the United Kingdom is a multi-national state, one must show that such differences in community feeling as exist are translated into political differences between the parts of the United Kingdom. Alternatively, to prove that the United Kingdom is a homogeneous nation-state, one must show that the same social differences are of equal political significance in all parts of the Kingdom and are treated equally. To determine whether such political differences as exist challenge the authority of the regime, one must consider the quality as well as the quantity of political issues. For example, a difference in the proportion of Scottish and English youths entering university may not be a political issue; if it is, it can be met by a marginal adjustment in the provision of university places. By contrast, a dispute about whether children should be taught in public or church primary schools, or in English or in Welsh, raises an issue where compromise is much more difficult.

To test the hypothesis that changes in the composition of the United Kingdom affect politics, an historical perspective is necessary. Extending historical analysis back in time also makes it possible to consider how industrialization and consequent changes of social conditions have affected the authority of the regime. Conceivably, increasing contacts between different communities might increase friction rather than reduce differences. Or industrialization could lead to greater regional or national inequalities because of internal colonization or problems arising from 'unbalanced' growth.[10]

*

The distinction between centre and periphery fits the British context well given the undoubted political predominance of England and, within it, of London. Some writers even explain the existence of a politically homogeneous Britain in terms of its geography.[11] Yet the evidence by no means fits this assertion. The principal island of the United Kingdom is divided into three nationality groups. England is only one part of an island; its land area is only 41 per cent of the British isles and 55 per cent of the United Kingdom as currently constituted. In so far as territorial contiguity is of political significance, one might expect a state to occupy an island to itself, or a pair of islands. Irish nationalists have always argued that geography compels the existence of two island states, Ireland and Britain, a position always rejected by the regime.[12] Since 1922, the international boundary of the United Kingdom has cut across a portion of Ireland, the one arrangement that is not implicit in insular geography. It is also the boundary that has caused the most political disorder within the contemporary United Kingdom.

The United Kingdom as a Multi-national Regime

The 4,900 miles of coastline around Britain and the 2,200 miles of coastline around Ireland have been of major importance, for they permitted easy access to these islands of successive waves of Celts, Romans, Angles, Jutes, Danes and Norsemen. The invaders came from different parts of the European continent, entered Britain and Ireland at a varied number of points, and settled and adapted themselves to pre-existing customs in different ways. The result was that Britain, at least at the time of the Norman conquest, was 'a Balkans'.[13] The Romans, by dominating England but no other part of the British isles, introduced another major difference, pushing the Celts out of England. The east coast of Britain, including Scotland, was most vulnerable to migration from the Continent. The people who gave their name to England, the Angles, were first known to history as a tribe living in what is now northern Germany. The west coast, especially where the mainland of Scotland and the North of Ireland are only 12 miles apart, was convenient for people moving back and forth across the Irish sea. The Scots were known in Ireland before migrating east in about the sixth century A.D. The flood climaxed with the invasion of the Normans in 1066.

The term Britain is derived from the name of a Celtic group that came to these islands before Roman times. Originally, it referred to people who were distinctly un-English. Linguistically, the British isles divided into three groups of peoples: the q-Celts (Irish, Manx and Scottish Gaelic); the p-Celts (Welsh, Cornish and, in France, the Bretons); and those who spoke Anglo-Saxon tongues that are the basis of modern English. These distinctions survive today, not only in differences of place names, but also in blood groups of the population. Blood group A is dominant in England, and blood group O in Ireland, whereas the population of other parts of the British isles is a mixture of blood groups.[14] It is likely that the only time at which the population of the British isles formed a reasonably homogeneous group was prior to the Roman invasion, when it was heavily Celtic.[15]

The insular geography of the United Kingdom meant that the natural routes of transportation were by water until the introduction of the railway 150 years ago. Nearly all the first cities were port cities, for the sea was a better trade route than roads or waterways into the hinterland. Viewing the United Kingdom in terms of water routes immediately questions the position of London as the centre. The pre-eminence of London is in spite of geography, for it lies in the south-east extremity of the United Kingdom. It is central only with reference

48

to Ireland and France; medieval kings of England claimed dominion over both these places. A theory of centralization in terms of communication might lead to the conclusion that Liverpool, not London, is the natural centre of the United Kingdom, for it is convenient by water to Wales, Scotland and Ireland, and is located where Northern England and the Midlands meet. Viewing Ireland in terms of water transport emphasizes the ease of movement between coastal parts and places outside Ireland, and the difficulty of movement within the island because of its large central land mass. A Dutch geographer, M. W. Heslinga, has argued that it is reasonable to think of the West of Scotland as the region closest to Ulster, and Leinster and parts of Munster as closest to England and Wales. Similarly, it could be argued that parts of Munster and Connacht are closest to America. In the last half of the nineteenth century, 48 per cent of total Irish emigration to America came from six of the most western Irish counties.[16]

Industrialization and the development of modern means of travel—the eighteenth-century canal system, the railway, the automobile and the airplane—has affected movement in the United Kingdom in three ways. It has brought the people of each part of the United Kingdom closer to their fellow nationals; it has brought the non-English parts of the United Kingdom closer to London; and it has brought people in each of the four nations closer to the world outside the United Kingdom. The result is something very different from centralization. Instead, it represents a multiplication of relationships. For example, people in a Scottish village in Fife may feel peripheral to Edinburgh in one context, but to London, New York, Hollywood or Zürich in another.

Prior to industrialization, the peoples of all the nations of the United Kingdom were widely dispersed in the villages of an agricultural society. Given the land area and population of Scotland, Wales and Ireland, there were few towns or cities of any size. Industrialization drew people into cities and concentrated industry regionally in Central Scotland, in South Wales and around Belfast. Thus the centres increased in numerical strength within each of the four nations (Table II.1). Centralization occurred *least* in England, for the development of industry in the North and Midlands created counterweights to the South-East that had no counterpart elsewhere.

Railway transportation developed greatly within less populous parts of Scotland, Wales and Ireland in the nineteenth century,

The United Kingdom as a Multi-national Regime

as in industrialized England.[17] In the twentieth century, the automobile has similarly eased travel *within* each nation. The road distance between the first and second city in each nation is: Edinburgh–Glasgow 45 miles; Cardiff–Swansea 45 miles; London–Birmingham 113 miles; Belfast–Londonderry 75 miles or Belfast–Dublin 103 miles.

Table II.1   Regional dominance in the British Isles, 1801–1961

	1801		1966	
	Pop'n 000s	% of nation	Pop'n 000s	% of nation
ENGLAND				
London and 6 Home Counties	1,880	22·6	13,163	30·3
WALES				
Glamorgan and Monmouth	116	19·8	1,668	63·1
SCOTLAND				
8 central counties, Ayr to Fife	616	38·3	3,213	62·0
NORTHERN IRELAND				
County Antrim	271*	19·6	712	47·9
REPUBLIC OF IRELAND				
County Dublin	335*	6·2	795	27·6

* Irish figures for 1821, the first Irish census.
Source: Census data.

By comparison, the road distance between capitals is much greater. London is 154 road miles from Cardiff, 386 miles from Edinburgh, and 401 road miles plus a boat journey from Belfast. The development of the railways brought the nations closer to London, because the lines of railway companies tended to converge there. The railway did not abolish all sense of distance, however, nor did it abolish differentials within the United Kingdom. Cardiff is the only major city outside England from which it is possible to travel by train to London and back within a day, and still have time left for business there. Edinburgh, Belfast and Dublin are all further in travel time than Newcastle-upon-Tyne, the most distant of the English regional centres. The development since the 1950s of air travel has finally made it possible for a person living almost anywhere within the United Kingdom to travel to London and return home on the same day. Air travel is also significant, in that it links the different nations with London, and not with each other: the radial pattern of the railways is repeated. But air travel also abolishes water as a barrier to movement. Travel to the European continent has become as easy as travel within the British isles for the first time since the eighteenth century. With 27 daily flights to Paris, London has better air links with France than with any city within the United Kingdom. London is the chief destination of Scottish and Ulster flights, but some passengers use it only as a transit point to a journey outside the British isles.

The invention of modern means of communication–the rotary printing press, the telegraph and telephone, radio, television and motion pictures–has, like the airplane, served to multiply the communications alternatives of people within the United Kingdom. Mass circulation London-based daily newspapers, available almost everywhere each morning, provide a link between London and the peripheral parts. Similarly, radio and television broadcasting makes it possible for nearly everyone to hear or see major public events while they are occurring. Yet the media are not entirely London-centred. Television and films are especially noteworthy for the amount of imported materials offered to British audiences. Most national daily newspapers print outside London as well as in London, and commercial television companies are based on regions, with a commitment to provide regional news programmes.

London-centred media complement or compete with local media: they do not supplant them. Local evening newspapers and local weeklies exist throughout the United Kingdom. In 1970, there were 146 weeklies in Scotland, and 45 weeklies in Northern Ireland. Large circulation daily papers are also published in Scotland, Wales and Northern Ireland. In Northern Ireland, nearly everyone who reads newspapers reads a daily Ulster paper; 38 per cent read British papers too, and 6 per cent papers from Dublin. Even in Wales, which is relatively integrated with England, 28 per cent read a regional morning newspaper, and 46 per cent a regional evening daily.[18] The fact that people have a choice between and within news sources is important, for audience studies emphasize the extent to which individuals select from a wide range of media offerings only those items that they are predisposed to be interested in. This point is often overlooked in studies of the 'national' press in Britain.[19] In the absence of intensive studies of the use that viewers and readers make of the media in Scotland, Wales and Northern Ireland, one cannot confidently conclude whether people are more interested in news from London, in news about their own nation or locality, or in the media as a means

The United Kingdom as a Multi-national Regime

of escaping to remote lands. All one can say for sure is that a person in Birmingham, Edinburgh, Cardiff or Belfast has a wide range of choices set before him.

The openness of the British peoples to the world outside these islands has long been evidenced by patterns of migration. One might hypothesize that a person strongly attached to a British way of life, if leaving his native locality, would move within Britain, e.g., to the South-East of England, rather than leave the British isles entirely. Historically, movement has been in the latter direction. The Irish are the extreme example, for emigration was very much to the United States. In 1852, 84 per cent of Irish immigrants went to America; fifty years later the proportion was 85 per cent. There were also large-scale movements of Scottish and Welsh people out from the British isles.[20] Contemporary figures of emigration indicate that prospects of a job, conditioned by fluctuations in economies, may greatly affect whether non-English Britons decide to migrate within the United Kingdom or leave it for America, Canada or Australia, an indication of indifference to place outside the national home.[21]

The movement of peoples within and outside the British isles does not make the population that remains within each nation more cosmopolitan. The vast bulk of people in each nation were born there. Those who remain in their native locale are the least cosmopolitan or most nationalist in outlook.

Table II.2   Native-born population in the British Isles, 1851–1966

Born and living in:	1851 %	1901 %	1921 %	1966 %
England	95·5	96·8	97·4	90·5
Wales	88·2	84·7	84·4	82·9
Scotland	91·2	97·4	93·9	90·8
Northern Ireland	94·4	91·9	90·0	90·5
Republic of Ireland	99·3*	97·6*	97·7*	97·5

* Refers to 32 counties of Ireland.

Sources: Hechter, 'Regional Inequality and National Integration', Table 2; 1966 Summary Tables, *Census of Great Britain*, but figures of both parts of Ireland from the 1961 censuses.

Census data from the past century (Table II.2) show that there has been little change in the extent to which the different nations have remained homogeneous. Moreover, the Irish figures underestimate homogeneity, for movements between the six and 26 counties are counted as migration. With its long land border with populous parts of England, Wales is proportionately most subject to in-migration. In absolute terms, England has the largest number of non-native residents, but it also has the largest native-born population to act as an absorbent.

As in most of Europe, the centralization of political power in the state now called the United Kingdom resulted from colonial settlement, good and bad political judgments, forced depopulation, and fortuitous dynastic succession. In medieval times, kings of England were interested in enlarging their territories in every direction possible. France was not abandoned until the withdrawal from Calais in 1558. (The formal claim to rule in France was not abandoned until the Treaty of Amiens in 1801.) Wales, the nation closest to the political centre of England, had union furthered by accident of dynastic succession: the Welsh-born Henry Tudor gained the English throne in 1485 as Henry VII, thus uniting in his person authority in the two lands. The incorporation of the two nations as 'England and Wales' was institutionalized by Act of Parliament in 1535. The position of Scotland was then very different. It was independent with its own king and a foreign policy sometimes antagonistic to the English crown; proximity brought enmity and border wars. England and Scotland were also joined by an accident of dynastic inheritance. James VI of Scotland gained the English crown upon the death without issue of Queen Elizabeth in 1603, and ruled England as James I. With the unity of two kingdoms under one monarch, the term Great Britain first gained currency. The regime remained a dual monarchy for more than a century, with separate Parliaments in London and Edinburgh. The whole island became unambiguously integrated in a single state only with the passage of the Act of Union between England and Scotland in 1707, and the defeat of the Jacobites at Culloden in 1746. In the eighteenth century an attempt was made to popularize the term Britain. Differences between the parts were treated as regional differences. Scotland was referred to as North Britain, and England as South Britain. The usage received official endorsement, but not popular endorsement. Older forms persisted, labelling Britain as one state but not one nation.

At no time was Ireland ever treated as if it were part of Britain. During the middle ages and Tudor and Stuart times, Ireland was nominally under English jurisdiction, but the regime did not have support and compliance in most of the territory. In the eighteenth century, British kings ruled a dual monarchy, for an Irish Parliament sat in Dublin. The United Kingdom was not established until the merger of the British and Irish Parliaments in 1801. Although Britain and Ireland were thus formally integrated into one state, a sense of Irish distinctiveness continued in England as well as in Ireland. Many prominent Victorians endorsed the idea that the English and the Irish were two separate races, with the latter inferior to the former. Optimists considered it Britain's duty to maintain British rule in Ireland for the sake of the natives, as was done in India. Pessimists considered the Irish a corrupting influence in England, and welcomed home rule as removing inferior Celts from that most noble of Anglo-Saxon institutions, the Westminster Parliament.[22]

The contemporary structure of the state is relatively recent. It dates only from the signature of the Anglo-Irish Treaty of 1921. Today, the institutions of the regime reflect both the diversity of the peoples of the United Kingdom, and the confusion of things English and things British. Formally, the regime is a unitary state. Yet Northern Ireland has a separate Constitution, Parliament and Cabinet at Stormont with very substantial powers granted to it. Scotland lacks a separate Parliament, but much of the *de facto* responsibility for governing Scotland is concentrated in the Scottish Office. Edinburgh, like Belfast, is therefore a major administrative centre of government outside London. The Secretary of State for Scotland, by virtue of his position in a British Cabinet, is able to advance claims for separate legislation for Scotland, and to supervise separate administration and an independent legal system. To a lesser extent, special provision is also made for Wales. A separate Minister of State was established for Wales in 1962, and a Secretary of State was named to the Cabinet in 1964.

A variety of contemporary surveys have found that both in Scotland and Wales people favour changing the structure of the regime, albeit by measures of devolution stopping short of independent home rule. For example, a study undertaken on behalf of the BBC in May, 1968, indicated that the median Scottish respondent was in favour of creating a regional [*sic*] government with responsibility for internal Scottish affairs; the median Welshman favoured a lesser measure of devolution of authority to Wales. Only 10 per cent of the Scots and 25 per cent of the Welsh said that they wished no change.[23] English attitudes toward devolution dominate a 1967 all-Britain survey which found that 53 per cent considered it a bad idea for every region to have its own government, as against 35 per cent approving. The opposition to decentralization within England was strongest in London and the South-East, where 64 per cent disapproved.[24]

In party politics, the great nationalist challenge to the authority of the regime came from Ireland after the 1867 franchise reform made it practicable for Irish Nationalists to elect a bloc of MPs opposed to rule from Westminster. This challenge was ultimately met by an alteration in the boundaries of the United Kingdom. Today, the chief locus of nationalist politics is still Northern Ireland, where the major parties contest the boundaries of the state; party politics there also involves less respect for established authority than anywhere else in the United Kingdom. At the 1970 general election, the vote for parties challenging the regime in Ulster was nearly one-third of the total vote; this has been the pattern in past elections too. In Scotland and Wales, electoral support for Nationalist candidates has not been so high, but it did grow significantly in the 1960s. At the 1959 general election, Scottish Nationalist candidates polled 0·8 per cent of the vote in Scotland, fielding only five candidates; in 1970, the party polled 11·4 per cent of the vote with 65 candidates. In Wales in 1959, Plaid Cymru took 5·2 per cent of the Welsh vote with 20 candidates. In 1970, this nationalist group contested all 36 Welsh seats and polled 11·5 per cent of the vote. In both nations, the Nationalists have now supplanted the Liberals as the third party in terms of votes; within the confines of their territory, they gained a better percentage poll than the Liberals did in England in 1970.

Within the parts of the United Kingdom, the strength of the two major parties differs greatly too, reflecting the influence of distinctive national issues. In this century, the Conservatives have always won the great bulk of Ulster seats at Westminster. They have never won a majority of the seats in Wales. Labour has been the majority party without interruption since 1922; prior to that the Liberals dominated. In Scotland, there has been two-party competition between the Conservatives and Labour. None the less, Labour has carried the majority of Scottish seats at the last four general elections, even though overall it has lost two of these elections. The results in England tend to approximate the United Kingdom average only because it contains 511 of the 630 parliamentary seats. If one looks at election results in London and the South-East, the most 'central' part of the United Kingdom, the pattern found is exactly opposite to that in most peripheral parts. The Conservatives have won an absolute majority of seats in the central area at every general election since 1906, with the exception of the 1945 Labour landslide.[25] The differences in the strength of the major parties cannot be explained by class differences, for survey data show that within the middle and working classes, the proportion favouring the parties varies significantly from area to area, and nation to nation.[26]

Legally, the United Kingdom makes no distinction in citizenship between persons native to the four parts of the United Kingdom:[27] all are regarded as British subjects. Psychological identifications do not correlate exactly with legal categories. An individual British subject may even identify with two politically relevant communities, just as an American may consider himself a Texan or a New Yorker as well as a citizen of the United States. The Union Jack symbolizes a melting-pot process, for the flag contains a cross for St. Andrew of Scotland, for St. Patrick of Ireland, and a cross of St. George for England and Wales [sic.] Language use shows another form of change, Anglicization. The issue has been most noteworthy in Wales. When language-use statistics were first collected there in 1891, 53 per cent of the population was Welsh-speaking; in 1961, the figure had fallen to 27 per cent. In Scotland, language has never been such an issue because Gaelic, the language of the Western Highlands, is confined to one region. Elsewhere in Scotland Anglo-Saxon tongues have been predominant for more than a millennium. In 1891, seven per cent of Scots spoke Gaelic; by 1961, the figure had fallen to two per cent. Within the six counties of Ulster, the recorded proportion of Irish speakers was one per cent in the 1851 census; available evidence indicates that it has not changed much since then. The proportion of Irish speakers in the 26 counties of the Republic was 29 per cent in 1851, falling to 18 per cent in 1911, and rising to 27 per cent, with strong government support, by 1961.[28] Within the United Kingdom, language is a substantial issue only in Wales. It is also a major issue in the Republic of Ireland, because it too has a bilingual population subject to strong inducements to become Anglicized in speech. The acceptance of English as the standard language everywhere in the British isles required an aggressive policy of Anglicization by the British regime in nineteenth-century Welsh and Irish schools.[29] Only in Scotland did the Anglicizing of speech follow independently of directives from London.

In response to direct questions from survey interviewers, residents of Scotland, Wales and Northern Ireland identify themselves with their particular nation, rather than with Britain or the United Kingdom. In Wales, 69 per cent of a sample described themselves as Welsh, as against 15 per cent considering themselves British. In a Glasgow survey, 67 per cent said they were Scottish, as against 29 per cent choosing a British identification. In Northern Ireland, 43 per cent identified themselves as Irish, 21 per cent as Ulster, and 29 per cent as British.[30] Undoubtedly, the great bulk of people in England similarly think of themselves as English, rather than British. They would almost certainly be identified by Scots, Welsh and Irish people as English in any of the non-English parts of the United Kingdom.

The political differences between England and other parts of the United Kingdom are sufficient to justify recognizing the differences in community as differences between nations. To note that the United Kingdom is a multi-national state is not to imply anything about the resulting character of the regime. The politics of accommodation in a structurally plural society can take many different forms. One group can dominate another, or there can be exchanges to the mutual advantage of all national groups. Whatever the basis of accommodation, the authority of the regime is always potentially vulnerable to challenge, for disagreements that occur between national groups not only threaten the position of the government of the day, but also may threaten the regime's authority within its existing boundaries.

*

Historically and today, religion is the other characteristic that most strongly differentiates the nations of the United Kingdom. The Reformation came to these islands first of all as a political issue. For centuries after the Reformation, while the Crown was gradually increasing authority at the centre, groups of the King's subjects were dividing–often violently–about matters of religious belief and practice. Henry VIII wished to establish a national church, with bishops subject to his temporal authority, as against the supranational authority of the Pope. The conflict was not theological, for the Church of England then had little doctrinal disagreement with the Roman Catholic Church. Because the conflict was political, those who refused to adhere to the new ecclesiastical authority were regarded as potentially or *ipso facto* disloyal. Pope Pius V counterattacked, founding a seminary at Douai to train missionaries for the conversion of England. In 1570, he excommunicated Queen

The United Kingdom as a Multi-national Regime

Elizabeth, absolved her subjects from allegiance to her authority, and called upon France and Spain to depose the heretic authority.

Political history cannot be understood until one appreciates the extent to which the Pope, his church and his secular allies were seen as a military and political threat to the regime throughout the British isles. Until the rise of Imperial Germany at the beginning of the twentieth century, England's major enemies – the Spanish, and then the French – were Catholic powers. The insular position of the Kingdom meant that it was potentially vulnerable to the attack of a foreign armada, aided by disaffected Catholic co-religionists within Britain, stirred up by foreign-educated priests and Jesuits working within Britain for the return of a Roman Catholic monarch. The regime pursued repressive measures against Catholics within its jurisdiction. In the middle of the twentieth century, the sentiments seem remote; parallels with the American fear of communism at home and abroad are illuminating.

The response to the Tudor establishment of a national [*sic*] church varied greatly around the British isles. In Wales, Catholicism was readily abandoned although the instrument of conversion – the translation of the Bible into Welsh – helped maintain the language there. In Scotland, the creation of a Presbyterian Church, under the leadership of John Knox, entrenched anti-episcopal as well as anti-Romanist values. In Ireland, the attempt to transfer the allegiance of the mass of the peasant population from the Church of Rome to the regime's Church of Ireland failed almost entirely.

The main danger of rebellion came from Ireland, the second largest part of the Crown's jurisdiction. The flight of the Catholic, Gaelic, earls from Ulster in 1607 made it easy and inviting to encourage the plantation there of Protestant settlers from Scotland and England. The process of encouraging Protestant immigration and driving the native Irish out of Ulster by force of arms continued throughout the century. Within Britain, the civil war of the seventeenth century also emphasized religious divisions, with the Romanizing tendencies of the Stuart kings opposed to the anti-episcopal bias of Cromwell's Parliament and Army. The Civil War challenge to the monarchical regime was not only about religion, but religion played an important part in the controversy. Religion was also important in the final establishment of a fully legitimate regime in England at the end of the seventeenth century. In the language of the Bill of Rights of 1689, the deposed James II 'did endeavour to subvert and extirpate the

Protestant religion and the lawes and liberties of this kingdome', and his successor, William of Orange, was described as a man 'Whome it hath pleased Almighty God to make the glorious instrument of delivering this kingdome from popery and arbitrary power'. The Glorious Revolution settled in no uncertain terms the Protestant nature of the Crown. This was done by including in the coronation oath a long and explicit rejection both of Catholic doctrine and of papal authority.[31]

For more than a century thereafter, Catholics suffered substantial disabilities, both legal and practical. In Ireland, penal laws were 'successive enactments, challenging religious faith, material security, professional advancement and the unity of family life, which deliberately sought to depress the Catholics to the lowest level of society'.[32] When a measure of toleration of Catholic worship and Catholic rights was shown later in the eighteenth century, the reaction was great. The anti-Catholic Gordon Riots in London in 1780 led to 285 deaths by violence, and 25 hangings after subsequent trials.[33] In the nineteenth century Catholic toleration became established by law, along with toleration for other religious minorities, such as nonconformists and Jews. The changes were fiercely resisted.

The Catholic Emancipation Act of 1829 was the start of the era of Reform. Once this occurred then other changes such as the 1832 reform of the franchise could follow; the inviolable authority of the Old Constitution had been breached. The fear of Catholicism was shown in that Act, with clauses reaffirming the Protestant bias of the regime, notwithstanding the formal willingness to accept individual Catholic office-holders.[34] The Pope's re-creation of a Roman Catholic hierarchy in England in 1850 stimulated more anti-Catholic reaction. Lord John Russell, writing as Prime Minister, stated:

> There is an assumption of power in all the documents which have come from Rome; a pretension of supremacy over the realm of England, and a claim to sole and undivided sway, which is inconsistent with the Queen's supremacy, with the rights of our bishops and clergy and with the spiritual independence of the nation.[35]

Mr. Gladstone, though a firm adherent of the episcopal church and of religious toleration in Ireland, none the less held traditional views about Catholicism as a political enemy. In 1874, he wrote, 'The Rome of the Middle Ages claimed universal monarchy. The modern Church of Rome has abandoned nothing, retracted nothing . . . No one can now become her convert without renouncing his moral and mental freedom, and placing his civil loyalty and duty at the mercy of another.'[36]

Within Britain, unity in defence of Protestantism was not matched by unity in accepting a single established church. The civil disabilities placed upon non-conforming Protestants were relaxed early in the eighteenth century, but other marks of discrimination were not removed until the latter half of the nineteenth century. In nineteenth-century England, as in many Roman Catholic countries, debates about the introduction and expansion of compulsory education often became debates about whether religious education in the schools should be controlled by the established church. This remained notably so as late as the debate leading up to the Education Act of 1902.[37] Non-conformists had substantial grounds for pressing their case against the Anglican establishment, for the non-conformists had about as many church-going members as did the Church of England. At the time of the 1851 census, moreover, there was also a third religious group of great significance: those who did not go to church or chapel.[38]

During the nineteenth century, the continuance of the episcopal church as the established church of Wales and of Ireland was a source of persisting political protest. In 26 counties of Ireland, 89 per cent of the population were Roman Catholic. The Church of Ireland was disestablished in 1869, thus removing one of the Irish grievances against the regime. In Wales, the position was similarly anomalous. In the 1851 census, non-conformists outnumbered those who attended the Church in Wales by a margin of about four to one. By 1905, the reported strength of the two churches showed non-conformists nearly three times as numerous as those in the still established church. The fight for disestablishment was a major issue for three generations in Welsh public life, uniting Welshmen against their English and Anglicized governors. At times the militia was needed to suppress demonstrations against establishment. Disestablishment was finally achieved in 1920. In Scotland, the establishment of Presbyterianism as the state church removed the grounds for controversy between Scots and English. The great disruption of the Church of Scotland in 1843 involved evangelicals withdrawing to form a Free Church independent of the regime's influence. It quickly gained worshippers equal to that of the established Presbyterian Church. The divisions within Presbyterianism were linked with party politics. In the Scottish universities constituency at the general election of 1868, a tabulation of

The United Kingdom as a Multi-national Regime

ballots cast by open voting showed that 95 per cent of established clergy voted Conservative and 5 per cent Liberal; non-established clergymen divided 97 per cent Liberal and 3 per cent Conservative. The schisms gradually became less significant, and a major reunion occurred in 1929. By this time, Irish emigration to Scotland had raised the proportion of Catholics among church members in Scotland to the status of a substantial minority of 16 per cent.[39]

In consequence of centuries of religious divisions, each of the parts of the British isles today shows a very distinctive pattern of religious identification (see Table II.3). England is the most homogeneous of the nations, because of the nominal strength of the Church of England. Northern Ireland is most divided, for no denomination has a majority of the population and the Catholic minority is substantial. In Wales, Protestants are divided. Among Welsh-speakers, non-conformity is strong: 72 per cent are non-conformists, and 27 per cent episcopal.

Table II.3   Religious identification in the British Isles

	Episcopal C. of E.	Presb'n C. of S.	Other Prot	Roman Catholic	Other; None
	%	%	%	%	%
England	69	1	10	10	10
Wales	45	—	45	7	4
Scotland	3	68	3	16	9
Northern Ireland	24	29	10	35	2
Republic of Ireland	4	0·5	—	95	0·5

Sources: England and Scotland: Gallup Poll, 1964, N = 10,336; Northern Ireland and the Republic, Censuses, 1961; Wales: Opinion Research Centre, 1968, N = 1,381.

Religious issues rarely become prominent in British politics today. For example, the debate about the reorganization of secondary education in the 1960s involved very little discussion about the continuation of compulsory religious instruction in the schools. The influence of religion upon politicians in the Labour Party also appears to be declining.[40] None of the Prime Ministers of this century has shown a particular interest in church affairs. Earlier in the twentieth century, when religion was still important, men such as David Lloyd George and Ramsay MacDonald could serve as Prime Ministers, notwithstanding their ostentatious distance from the established church. The chief reminder of the bitterness that religious matters raise is found in the fact that legislative matters which touch upon religion, e.g., abortion and divorce law reform, are shunned by both political parties. Backbench MPs are left to take the initiative in incurring ecclesiastical wrath and clerical criticism. In Scotland and in Northern Ireland, there is recognized separation of children into state-financed Protestant and Catholic schools.

The decline in the political significance of religion in British politics illustrates the importance of changes in the composition of a society. The episcopal church has gradually become more secure by the growing domination of England in the population of the United Kingdom, for only in England is it the church of the majority. Relatedly, disestablishment of the Church of Ireland and of Wales was made easier because this occurred at a time when their contribution to the total episcopal strength in the United Kingdom was small and declining. The absolute fall in the population of Ireland similarly reduced the size of the Catholic 'threat' to the Protestant majority. If this had not occurred, then in the great disputes of the late nineteenth century about church and state in the United Kingdom, the established church would have been supported by only a limited minority, with Irish Catholics about twice as numerous in proportion to the population as blacks are in America today.

A second and equally great change has been the growth of secularization, i.e., 'the process whereby religious thinking, practice and institutions lose social significance'.[41] Persons regular in church attendance are much more likely to experience conflicts between religious and political laws. By contrast, those with only a nominal religious preference (especially for the state church) are unlikely to question basic political laws on religious grounds. While church-going was never universal in this century there has indubitably been a substantial decline in church-going. E. R. Norman argues, 'The Church had not "lost contact" with modern society and its peculiar problems and needs, as is so often said. Contact had never been established in the first place.'[42] Only 26 per cent of a 1963 British sample claimed that they went to church at least once a month. The largest group, the Anglicans, were those most likely to be non-attenders. The more or less regular church-goers divided into three groups: 42 per cent Anglican, 33 per cent Church of Scotland or non-conformist, and the remainder Roman Catholic.[43] Only in Northern Ireland, where religious differences are much involved in challenges to the regime, is the majority of the population still church-going.

*

The United Kingdom as a Multi-national Regime

Before the advent of the Industrial Revolution, all the peoples of the United Kingdom had one thing in common: they lived in the countryside. Except for London and, latterly, Dublin there was no place that would be recognized as a city of size. Political life was dominated by London because of the scattered rural population.[44] Political divisions were not strictly along town and country lines. The patronage system gave the government of the day ample opportunities to influence or bribe rural electors, and the system of rotten boroughs added to landowners' influence. The tendency of politically active people to divide their time between country estates and London further strengthened the ties between London and the rural parts of the British isles. Moreover, the concentration of landownership and management in few hands meant there was nothing comparable to the European peasant proprietor.

The enclosure of land and the introduction of grazing in place of labour-intensive agriculture in Scotland and Wales proceeded more or less in step with the development of industry. At the time of the first census in 1801, agriculture was the chief occupation, including 35·9 per cent of the British labour force, but its proportionate significance was declining.[45] In the development of industry, England and Scotland moved at much the same pace; Wales lagged slightly behind (Table II.4). As the absolute numbers in agriculture did not decline, this lessened the dislocation of workers. By the turn of the twentieth century, farm labour accounted for only one-tenth of the work force, except in Ireland.

Table II.4   Labour in agriculture in the United Kingdom, 1831–1966

	1831	1851	1881	1911	1966
	(Per cent of workers in agriculture)				
England	31	27	10	8	3·2
Wales	40	34	13	10	6·3
Scotland	30	30	14	10	5·9
Ireland	64*	53*	54	40	35·5
Northern Ireland	—	—	—	—	13·4

* Families engaged in agricultural work; 1831–1911 data for 32 counties

Sources: 1831–1911: Hechter, 'Regional Inequality and National Integration', Table 5; Irish figures for 32 counties. 1966: Census, Economic Activity Tables.

The shift from farm work to industry was not a peaceful one. Some agricultural labourers and those who lived by a mixture of farming and cottage industry resented the change. The reaction against innovation during and after the Napoleonic wars was viewed by contemporary officials of the regime as a major challenge to their authority. According to Briggs, the government 'employed an army against them [i.e., the Luddites] as large as that which Wellington was leading in the Peninsular War'.[46] There was less industrialization and agitation in Wales. In Scotland, the great trauma had come in the Highland clearances of the eighteenth century. In Ireland, the great conflicts between farm tenants and authority came in the late nineteenth-century agitations in Southern Ireland. In Northern Ireland, tenants for the most part had security of tenure. A commitment to reduce the importance of agriculture was implied in the repeal of the Corn Law in 1846, and confirmed later in the century by a refusal to reintroduce tariffs for cheap imported foodstuffs.

In the contemporary United Kingdom, nowhere is agriculture the major employer of labour, as it still remains in the Republic of Ireland. There are, however, differences in its relative place in the four nations. Farming is most important in Northern Ireland, and least important in England. Given the difference in population between them, the total number of people in agriculture in England is greater than the total elsewhere. The politics of agriculture is thus a matter in which English and non-English farmers both press claims. The small numbers of marginal farmers and crofters outside England –in relative and absolute terms– make it easier to provide special legislation and subsidies for them, since the aggregate cost is low, though the *per capita* cost per farmer can be high.

At the time of the first census in 1801, there were only eight cities in the United Kingdom with populations of 50,000 or more: London, Birmingham, Bristol, Liverpool, Manchester, Edinburgh, Glasgow and Dublin. In Wales, Merthyr Tydfil was the largest city with a population of 7,704.[47]

Urbanization has progressed much more quickly and to a much greater extent in England and Scotland than in Wales and Ireland (Table II.5). Moreover, the resulting cities are larger. Glasgow, the largest city in Scotland, is about four times the size of Cardiff, the largest city in Wales, and more than twice the size of Belfast. Politically, the cities are the point at which the two-party system is most strongly entrenched. In Scotland, Wales and Northern Ireland, rural areas show disproportionate support for Liberal or Nationalist candidates.[48]

The United Kingdom as a Multi-national Regime

Table II.5   The growth of cities of more than 50,000, 1801–1966

	1801	1851	1881	1911	1966
	(As % of total population of nation)				
England	17	31	39	51	52
Wales	0	0	13	27	36
Scotland	10	24	34	40	43
Republic of Ireland	4	9	10	15	21
Northern Ireland	0	6	16	31	33

Sources: Michael Hechter, 'Regional Inequality and National Integration', Table 6, and census data.

The growth of cities involved radical changes in the character and institutions of political representation. New centres of population required new parliamentary constituencies, and the new urban middle class sought the right to vote. These changes resulted in the abolition of electoral practices that facilitated aristocratic influence. The creation of a sizeable urban electorate after the Reform Act of 1867 meant that personal connections–whether of deference or intimidation–could no longer be strong as in rural constituencies, for urban voters and their MPs could not know each other personally. The decline in personal influence was matched by the rise of party machines in cities such as Birmingham.[49] By 1906, the two major parties–the Conservatives and Liberals–were competing for votes in nearly all British constituencies. Universal suffrage was granted in 1918. In Britain, these changes came peacefully. In Ireland, the consequences were not pacific. In the 1918 British election Sinn Fein won 71 of the 101 seats. The party did not, however, come to Westminster to advance claims in Parliament. Instead, it remained in Ireland, seeking to repudiate the regime.

*

The development of an urban class structure in the United Kingdom involved the common experience of industrialization in varying national contexts. In England, it involved the disruption of a rural society with a basis in feudalism, but little else.[50] In Wales, industrialization brought English-speaking workers into the mining valleys to work side by side with Welsh-speaking Welshmen, greatly increasing the use of English in Wales. In Scotland, some migrants to industrial

The United Kingdom as a Multi-national Regime

Clydeside came from the Highlands or from Ireland, where clan society and the privations of previous existence made the new working class less readily amenable to an orderly, urban life. In Ireland, the development of Belfast as an industrial city gave Protestants a counterweight in national influence to predominantly Catholic Dublin. In Belfast, religious differences were more disturbing than class differences. From the beginning of the nineteenth century, the city was the scene of recurring communal disorder and violence between Protestants and Catholics.[51]

Within each of the four nations, standards of living rose with industrialization. The longer the time-span involved the greater the rise. Hechter's analysis of tax assessments in the old United Kingdom provides a rough guide to differences in wealth. By industrializing, Scotland achieved much the same *per capita* standard of wealth as England by the end of the First World War. In 1801, Scotland's *per capita* wealth was 46 per cent that of England; in 1921, it was 110 per cent. Wales had its absolute *per capita* wealth increase more than five times but altered its relative position very little: in 1801, its *per capita* wealth was 56 per cent that of England, and in 1921, 66 per cent. Ireland gained in *per capita* wealth but its relative position deteriorated. In the 1850s, its wealth per head was about 27 per cent that of England; in 1921, it was 20 per cent. Each nation became wealthier in absolute terms, but relative standards moved in different directions between the nations of the United Kingdom.

Many social scientists reckon that the coexistence of wealth and poverty poses the greatest of all challenges to the authority of regimes. The term 'class conflict' is regarded as something more than a metaphor, implying demonstrations, disorder and the possibility of overthrowing one regime and establishing another. In fact, nothing like this happened in Britain. The great crises of the regime shortly before the First World War concerned Ireland, the aristocratic House of Lords, women's suffrage and, only incidentally, industrial unrest.[52] The non-violent nature of the General Strike and of labour conditions generally between the wars is further evidence of the compatibility of economic deprivation and full legitimacy. The absence of challenge to the regime in Wales and Scotland is especially striking, for in the inter-war period unemployment was especially bad in both nations.[53]

In the contemporary United Kingdom,[54] differences in economic well-being exist between the nations of the United Kingdom, but their magnitude is often exaggerated (cf. Table II.6). Within Great Britain

66

The United Kingdom as a Multi-national Regime

during the 1960s, Scottish earnings for male manual workers were consistently below the United Kingdom average – but only by a few per cent. Earnings in Wales were slightly above the average. In most of the period Scottish and Welsh earnings were higher than those of a number of English regions.[55] The major disparity is between Northern Ireland, with wages one-sixth below average, and all parts of Great Britain. Moreover, a lower proportion of Ulster men work in manufacturing industries.

Table II.6   Personal wealth in the United Kingdom, 1803–1967

	1803	1851	1871	1891	1921	1966–67 Average income per worker £
	(£ per capita *tax assessments* – Schedules A, B and D)					
England	10·2	11·0	15·2	18·1	45·8	1,180
Wales	5·7	7·2	9·5	11·7	30·2	1,103
Scotland	4·8	7·9	12·0	15·1	50·5	1,093
Ireland – 32 counties	*	3·0	4·9	8·4	9·2	—
Northern Ireland	—	—	—	—	—	975

* Income tax was not introduced in Ireland until 1855; the first figure given is for that year.

Sources: 1803–1921: Michael Hechter, 'Regional Inequality and National Integration', Table 7. 1964–65: and *Abstract of Regional Statistics*, No. 6 (London: HMSO, 1970), Table 59.

More substantial differences between the nations arise in the incidence of unemployment. In 1968, when English unemployment was 2·2 per cent, the Welsh figure was 4·0 per cent, the Scottish, 3·8 per cent, and that for Northern Ireland, 7·2 per cent. Differentials between the nations are of long standing. The gap has been gradually reduced between Wales and Scotland and England in the period since 1951. In Northern Ireland, however, the rate for unemployed men has ranged between 6·4 per cent and 8·7 per cent, without showing any tendency to decline on a secular basis.[56] While persisting, these differences are of limited magnitude within Britain. Fluctuations around such levels can cause votes to shift from one party to another at elections. It does not follow that people are equally likely to swing in their allegiance to a regime.

The United Kingdom as a Multi-national Regime

Facts about the relative standard of living in the different parts of the United Kingdom are always capable of diametrically opposite interpretations, one favouring the existing regime and another favouring great changes or repudiation. The above figures can be interpreted as indicating that there is very little difference in living standards within Britain as it now exists. A nationalist could therefore argue that changing the institutions of the regime would increase a nation's standard of living, and a centralist that it would make it fall. A 1968 survey found that an absolute majority of Scottish respondents thought their standard of living would rise with the major devolution of power to Scotland, and a clear plurality thought the same would happen if Scotland became financially independent. Welsh respondents were less certain, and divided about the financial consequences of devolution and home rule.[57] In Northern Ireland too, Protestants and Catholics divide when asked to assess the economic implications of unification with the Catholic Republic. The issue cannot be resolved by citing economic statistics because it concerns future change, not past or present performance.

Theories of class conflict stress the consequence of conditions of employment as well as wages and living standards. Industrialization created a once-for-all change in occupations. Today, the class structure of the United Kingdom is relatively stable, with marginal changes occurring on a decade to decade basis. Nationalist support in Britain and anti-regime activities in Northern Ireland are so volatile that they cannot be explained simply by reference to changes in class structure. Moreover, United Kingdom census data emphasize the similarity in class structure in all parts of the state. At the 1966 census, 20.2 per cent of the population of England was assigned to unambiguously middle-class status, 19·4 per cent of the Welsh, 16·9 per cent of the Scots, and 25·3 per cent of the people of Northern Ireland. The high Ulster proportion reflects its relatively large proportion of farmers. The overall difference in the class profiles of the four nations is otherwise trivial.[58]

Class relations might vary within the United Kingdom if minority status in language, religion, or a rural way of life makes it difficult for an individual to think of himself in class terms. The most striking feature of Table II.7 is the relatively large proportion of people in Northern Ireland who do not place themselves in a class. In part, this reflects the fact that they were not prompted with the names of different classes, as were British respondents. But it may also indicate that

The United Kingdom as a Multi-national Regime

class distinctions are less strong than in Britain. This inference is strengthened by the fact that the plurality of Ulster respondents identify with the middle class. Within Britain, the most notable difference is the relative strength of working-class identification in Scotland and Wales, as against England. In part, this reflects the greater numbers of people in the Registrar-General's Classes IV and V in these two parts of the United Kingdom. It is noteworthy that discord about the regime is greatest where working-class consciousness is lowest. Where consciousness is highest, nationalist parties rather than left wing parties pose the greater challenge to the political *status quo*.

Table II.7   Subjective class assessment in the United Kingdom

	England	Wales	Scotland	Northern Ireland
	%	%	%	%
Upper class	1	—	—	1
Upper-middle	3	2	2	1
Middle class	28	28	22	44
Lower-middle	11	9	9	2
Working class	50	54	60	31
Don't know, other	6	7	7	22

Sources: Great Britain: Gallup Poll, 1964 Survey; Northern Ireland: Loyalty survey, 1968.

A third potential source of class conflict is trade union membership. A worker who is not in a trade union will be less likely to develop ideas inimical to the economic interests of his employer than a man who belongs to an organization devoted to improving his working conditions. By extension, it could be argued that non-unionized workers would be more likely to accept the authority of a regime. Sample survey data make it possible to judge to what extent trade union membership differs within the United Kingdom. England is the nation where trade union membership is lowest: 35 per cent of respondents reported that the family head was currently a union member, as against 47 per cent in Wales and 45 per cent in Scotland. In Northern Ireland 46 per cent said that the head of the house is or was a union member. In short, the non-English parts of the United Kingdom are not backward in their degree of unionization.[59]

*

The United Kingdom as a Multi-national Regime

The thesis of the social homogeneity of the United Kingdom is clearly rejected by the foregoing array of data. There are very considerable cultural differences concerning religion and identification with a peripheral community rather than the centre of the United Kingdom. This cultural distinctiveness is particularly noteworthy notwithstanding the fact that Scotland, Wales and, to a lesser extent, Northern Ireland show very great economic similarities to regions within England.[60] The thesis of political homogeneity must also be rejected on institutional and behavioural grounds. Distinctive political institutions exist for the government of Northern Ireland, Scotland and Wales. The extent of autonomy differs from nation to nation. It is specially noteworthy that in the 1960s there have been moves initiated by London to increase autonomy in both Wales and Scotland. In part this is because of a desire to decentralize administration from an overloaded Whitehall, and partly a response to nationalist agitation.[61] The multi-national character of the non-unitary United Kingdom is most aptly illustrated in Acts of Parliament, because they differ in their territorial scope. Legislation sometimes applies solely to England or to England and Wales, with a separate measure passed at Westminster for Scotland, and Stormont making another decision about Northern Ireland legislation. Occasionally, legislation may differ in each of the four parts of the United Kingdom: this is notably the case with laws about drinking.

Within the multi-national United Kingdom, major challenges to political authority have occurred in the past. In nineteenth-century Wales, demonstrations followed discord about the established position of the episcopal and Anglican church in a predominantly nonconformist nation. In Scotland, only the accident of the establishment of the Presbyterian Church under an earlier dynasty avoided similar discord. In both the North and South of Ireland, religion and disagreement about national identity led Protestants and Catholics to take up arms to settle matters outside Parliament. In recent generations, the cultural distinctiveness of Wales and Scotland has not led to serious challenges to the authority of the United Kingdom. But the election of a single Nationalist MP in Wales in 1966 and in Scotland in 1967 were reminders that even a peaceful protest on behalf of a peripheral loyalty presents far greater difficulties to pro-regime parties than does any other kind of political competition. In Northern Ireland, differences have never been confined solely to party competition: the political battle has also been waged by violence in the streets.

The United Kingdom as a Multi-national Regime

The challenges to authority within the United Kingdom cannot be explained by differences of political institutions, inasmuch as the Parliament at Westminster has always retained sovereign power throughout the Kingdom. Even in Northern Ireland and the Republic, the forms of Westminster government are usually accepted with little disagreement.[62] To explain discord in terms of differences in political cultures does no more than change the label of the thing to be explained from disorderly relationships to inharmonious cultural norms. To purport to explain discord in terms of relative deprivation is to beg the question: what can be valued so much that people cannot tolerate being deprived of it? The foregoing review suggests that loss of economic wellbeing is not the answer, for decades of relatively high unemployment and forced migration from Wales and Scotland in the inter-war years did not encourage any substantial challenge to a London-based regime. Subsequent chapters will explore the possibility that the things most valued by people are their religion or national identity. In so far as this is so, then to subject people to deprivation on religious or nationality grounds would go furthest to undermine the full legitimacy of a regime.

The most parsimonious explanation for the virtual legitimation of the United Kingdom regime is provided by evidence on the changing composition of its population. As the peoples of Ireland, both North and South, have always presented the greatest challenge to the regime, then it follows that if their proportion of the population declined, the legitimacy of the regime would rise. Fortuitously, census data for the United Kingdom are available from 1801, the year in which the United Kingdom of Great Britain and Ireland was created. Within Great Britain, the proportion of English in the population has been virtually static; in 1801 England contributed 79 per cent of the population, and in 1966, 85 per cent. Nearly all of the growing preponderance of England within the United Kingdom can be explained by the decline in the population of Ireland. When the first census was compiled, England had only a bare majority of the population of the United Kingdom (Table II.8). The limited size of England was concealed in the pre-1832 unreformed Parliament by the fact that representation was in no sense proportionate to population. With 53 per cent of the population, England had 74 per cent of the seats in the House of Commons. Ireland, with one-third of the Kingdom's population, had only 15 per cent of the seats.[63] Moreover, open voting and intimidation of many Catholics kept Irish constituencies in 'loyal'

The United Kingdom as a Multi-national Regime

hands until late nineteenth-century electoral reforms incidentally made possible the election of Catholic and Nationalist MPs from Irish seats. By the time that seats in the British House of Commons began to be allocated according to population, Ireland no longer contributed so large a part to the population of the United Kingdom.

Table II.8 The distribution of population in the British Isles, 1801–1966

Proportion living in:	1801	1851	1901	1951	1966
	%	%	%	%	%
England	52·9	61·2	73·5	77·3	78·8
Scotland	10·2	10·6	10·8	9·6	9·0
Wales	3·7	4·2	4·9	4·9	4·6
Ireland:					
26 counties of Republic	26·6 est.	18·7	7·8	5·6	5·0
6 counties of N. Ireland	6·6 est.	5·3	3·0	2·6	2·6
Total population (millions)	16·0 est.	27·3	41·4	53·5	57·6

Source: Census data.

The causes of the decline of Ireland's population are rarely mentioned in accounts of the legitimation of the regime. The earliest censuses showed massive emigration in consequence of poverty and a high birth rate. In the decade of the 1830s, an estimated half a million people left Ireland. Heavy emigration continued throughout the century. Famine was the second and more dramatic cause of Ireland's loss of population. In the 1840s approximately one million people died of starvation because of the failure of potato crops, and another million emigrated;[64] while nearly every other country in the world has had its population rise in the past 150 years, Ireland has experienced an absolute decline in numbers. At the first census of 1821, the island had 6,081,000 people. In 1921, at the time of the establishment of the Republic and the Northern Ireland regime, the population was approximately 4,228,000 in the 32 counties; it has remained relatively stable since.

Had the population of Ireland grown in proportion to that of England, at the time of the 1916 insurrection against the Crown it would have had about 12 million people. One-third of all United Kingdom MPs would have been Irish, and about 190 of them Irish Nationalists, pledged to protest and demonstrate against the regime. In such circumstances, a Cabinet wishing to govern with a majority independent of Nationalist votes would have needed at least 70 per cent of the remaining United Kingdom seats in order to have a constitutional majority; to govern without the votes of Ulster Protestants too would have required an even larger majority. Calculating a majority by excluding a major party is alien to English politics. It is, however, a familiar and necessary procedure in societies such as France and Italy, where those who govern must face the fact that they do so without the allegiance of all parties in the state.

The Irish challenge to the regime was resolved in 1921 by a treaty between the United Kingdom government and an 'illegitimate' revolutionary force in Ireland. The solution proposed was simple: a change in the composition of the regime. A total of 26 of the 32 counties of Ireland were allowed to secede from the United Kingdom, thus reducing the challenge to authority by reducing the regime's claim to allegiance. One portion of Ireland remained within the United Kingdom: six counties of Ulster. It did so because the Protestants there had demonstrated by force of arms that they wished to remain in union with Britain. Because the composition of Ulster was not exclusively Protestant, it left within Northern Ireland and thus, within the United Kingdom, a minority of disaffected subjects.

It can be argued that the political outlooks of a very small part of the population of the United Kingdom are of little or no practical significance to its politics. This is true, as long as political controversies avoid issues that concern the constitution of the regime. The taxes raised and the money spent in Ulster are of limited importance in the grand account books of the British Chancellor of the Exchequer. Account must be taken, however, when discord leads to massive violation of basic political laws, to arson, to politically inspired sabotage and murder. All of this has happened in Northern Ireland in the 1960s. It has happened there in times before too.

To argue that the people of Northern Ireland are not 'really' part of the United Kingdom is only to support the hypothesis that the composition of a regime's population is a major determinant of its legitimacy. It implies that if the composition of the United Kingdom were altered by notionally excluding its most awkward part, then the regime's legitimacy would be greater. Convenient as such an assumption is for hard-pressed politicians as well as for academic students of politics, it is an assumption that is contrary to the British Constitution and to public international law. British politicians from the time of Oliver Cromwell and William of Orange to that of Harold Wilson and Edward Heath have always insisted that Northern Ireland is indubitably a part of their regime.

III · The Development of a Divided Regime

Believe we dare not boast,
Believe, we do not fear –
We stand to pay the cost
In all that men hold dear.
What answer from the North?
One Law, one Land, one Throne.
If England drive us forth
We shall not fall alone.

RUDYARD KIPLING, *Ulster 1912*

What need you, being come to sense,
But fumble in a greasy till
And add the halfpence to the pence,
And prayer to shivering prayer, until
You have dried the marrow from the bone?
For men were born to pray and save:
Romantic Ireland's dead and gone,
It's with O'Leary in the grave.

WILLIAM BUTLER YEATS, *September 1913*

Northern Ireland is neither a nation nor a state. Legally it is a subordinate part of the United Kingdom. Historically, it is an insubordinate part. Even in name it is an anomaly, for the northernmost part of the island is Donegal in the Republic. Anomaly or not, Northern Ireland indubitably exists as a fragment of larger societies.[1] It is a fragment because its Protestant forebears broke off from the mainstream of English and Socttish society to colonize Ulster in the seventeenth century. It is doubly a fragment, because its Catholic population was separated from the mainstream of Irish society as a result of Protestant settlement, and, latterly, by the creation of the Northern Ireland regime. Because of this one can find in Northern Ireland features of Scottish and English life that were long ago abandoned in Britain. Because Northern Ireland is a fragment of two societies, not one, it must be seen from an Irish as well as from a British perspective. Viewed from the perspective of Irish history, many anomalous features of Northern Ireland life become understandable, even if not entirely predictable.

74

Ireland is almost a land without a history, because the troubles of the past are relived as contemporary events. The influence of precursive events is still present today, as in the Protestant wall slogan: Remember 1690. The recurrence of violence is also an important fact: the killings in Belfast in August, 1969, followed patterns well known in its narrow streets for more than a century.[2] Three themes of particular significance to political authority are found in reviewing Irish history. The first is that the inhabitants of the island have not shared a single national identity for nearly a millennium, or even longer. In the period after St. Patrick, people with a common religion still tended to be particularistic, even parochial in their political outlook. The coming of English overlords in the twelfth century encouraged communities to coalesce along lines of difference recognizable everywhere in Ireland. From the late sixteenth century, religion raised a distinction that Protestants met by denying or qualifying their Irishness. A second theme is that the peoples of Ireland have never been effectively united under a single independent regime. Thirdly, there has never been a period of Irish history when a fully legitimate regime ruled all the people of the island.

The peoples of Ireland, in the South as well as the North, are descended from successive waves of immigrants and invaders. The oldest finds of human life date from the middle stone age around 6000 B.C. They are of people who crossed from Scandinavia and Britain, settling primarily in what is now Ulster. The Celts became established in Ireland about two centuries before the birth of Christ. They came as small groups of invaders, and not, as the Romans came to Britain, with a unified army representing a central political authority. The natives with whom they mingled also lacked anything resembling a central authority. In Celtic times, the island was divided into at least 150 small kingdoms. These small kingdoms were linked by payment of tribute and the exchange of gifts.[3] Later, Norsemen invaded the east coast of Ireland as well as Britain, founding Dublin in the middle of the ninth century.

Christianity was introduced in the fifth century, and quickly gained adherents. During the Dark Ages in Europe and Britain, Irish scholarship flourished and Irish monks gained their land a reputation for saints and scholarship. Active involvement in what was then considered a universal church took Irish Catholics abroad, beginning with missionary efforts directed at the conversion and settlement of heathen Scotland. Significantly, within Ireland the Catholic Church

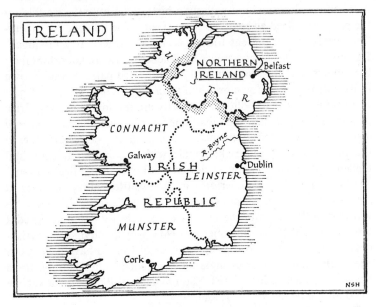

was organized by monasteries administered by abbots, rather than on a diocesan basis. Heslinga notes, 'This loose organization reflected – in fact, was adapted to the loose political organization of Gaelic Ireland.'[4] Brian Boru became famous as one of the first high kings of Ireland about A.D. 1000. After his death, while the title remained, there was a series of continuing struggles among different claimants to the honour. The conflicts of the time are aptly signified by the title of *ri co fresabra* ('king with opposition'), given to a provincial leader who aspired to the high kingship. A multiplicity of tribal groups existed within the island, each with its own king.[5]

The Anglo-Norman invasion of 1169 both complicated and simplified political allegiances. The invading army introduced yet another alien group and set of institutions. Because the differences were great, there was a clear distinction between the Anglo-Norman invaders and the 'mere' Irish. Henry II of England was proclaimed Lord of Ireland, beginning 800 years of English attempts to maintain authority in Ireland. In medieval times, the English-dominated regime never secured full support and compliance in all of Ireland. Few English kings showed much interest. In more than six centuries between the visit of Henry II in 1171 and the Union of 1801, reigning sovereigns

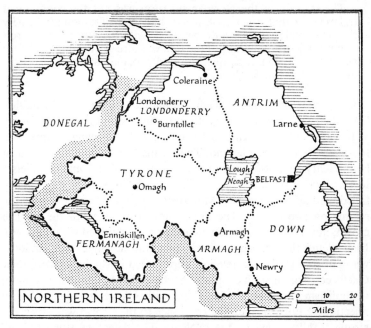

NORTHERN IRELAND

spent nine months in the land.[6] Within the Pale, an area extending out from Dublin, compliance with the laws of the English Crown was more or less general. A large portion of the island was ruled through the 'degenerate English', Anglo-Norman lords who detached themselves from their culture, marrying and assimilating to the native Gaelic-speakers. These territorial lords were strong in their own interest, not that of their nominal superior. In the West and in Ulster, native Gaelic customs and political leadership were predominant. The English regime sought to maintain communal divisions within the island. The mere Irish were not allowed to plead in the courts that the Crown established. The statutes of Kilkenny of 1366 were intended to prevent assimilation of Anglo-Norman settlers into Gaelic society. The division was also recognized by the Church; *inter Anglos* clergymen were English or Anglo-Norman, whereas *inter Hibernicos* the Church was in the hands of the native Gaels. In England, the Norman conquest created a strong, centralized monarchy with an army capable of subduing the whole land; gradually, from Norman French and Anglo-Saxon influences a new 'English' nation was created. In Ireland, as Father F. X. Martin comments:

The Development of a Divided Regime

The tragedy of the Norman invasion was not the conquest of Ireland–for that never took place–but the half-conquest. . . . By the year 1300 there was a drawn battle with the Normans controlling most of the country but the tide was already beginning to turn against them. The Irish question had become part of the heritage of Ireland and of England.[7]

In the sixteenth century, Tudor monarchs sought to end isolation from their nominal Irish subjects and gain coercive authority. Henry VIII was proclaimed King of Ireland in 1541, showing an intention to govern Ireland as England. The means was to be confiscation of land. Henry VIII also sought to convert the people from Catholicism to a Church of Ireland subject to the English Crown. The latter policy failed, and failed abysmally. Moreover, it increased opposition to the regime on two counts. The Pope, previously allied to the English crown, now became an opponent and priests identified with the native Irish against the English overlords. In addition, Anglo-Norman lords who adhered to the old religion were forced into alliance with their Gaelic co-religionists, a people with whom they had little in common. Catholicism thus became identified with Gaelic Ireland, and with rejection of English rule. The resistance to the Crown was especially strong in Ulster, led by the O'Neills. The defeat of Hugh O'Neill and peace in 1603 marked a victory for the English campaign to achieve coercive authority throughout Ireland. The flight to the Continent of the Ulster earls and their retainers in 1607 marked the end of Gaelic political authority in Ireland. It also left leaderless Ulster ripe for occupation by persons loyal to the established regime.

The policy adopted by the English Crown to solve the Ulster problem was similar to that adopted for the American colonies: plantation. The argument for introducing colonists into Ulster was far more immediate than that for introducing them into Virginia or Pennsylvania. Ireland was of great strategic importance. In the hands of a Continental enemy it could isolate England both from Europe and America. The point had occurred to the Spaniards at the time of the Armada, and was later noted by French and German enemies. The same King who chartered Jamestown, Virginia, in May, 1607, later that year approved plans for the settlement of the majority of the Ulster counties by Scottish and English colonists. In all, an estimated 150,000 Scots migrated, and about 20,000 English.[8] A party from Dublin, accompanied by soldiers, surveyed the territory and proposed that 23 towns be dotted throughout the Province, in what was, 'beyond doubt, the most important scheme for the building of new towns to be carried out in these islands before the end of the Second World War'.[9] Because settlement proceeded by the grant of specific estates to undertakers, rather than by a gradual movement of settlers from east to west as in America, the native Catholic Irish, while subject to loss of title to land, were not systematically forced out of the country. In America, settlers achieved a final solution of the Indian problem by force, and Protestant Ulstermen who migrated there were pre-eminent in the vigour with which they pursued wars of elimination against Indians.[10] In Ulster, Catholics remained near the settlers, a standing challenge to the property of the new settlers and to their regime. There also remained an alarming 'political element in Irish brigandage'. In 1609 it was calculated that there were more than 10,000 swordsmen in the country with no occupation but military service to the lords and gentlemen they followed.[11] This encouraged among settlers a mentality appropriate to a state of seige, and they armed themselves accordingly.

During the troubled reign of Charles I, the Anglo-Norman and the Gaelic Catholics rose against the Protestant regime in 1641, claiming allegiance to the Crown, but not to all of its agents. In the Ulster rising, Catholic peasantry took vengeance upon Protestant settlers. The civil war that followed was brought to an end when Oliver Cromwell, after establishing Parliamentary and Protestant ascendancy in England, landed in Ireland in 1649. In nine months Cromwell's army established military supremacy in a campaign of vigour and cruelty. The consequences were lasting, because Cromwell confiscated large areas of lands previously held by Catholic gentry and awarded it to Protestants. By 1703, the proportion of land owned by Catholics was less than 14 per cent of the whole of Ireland. In the Province of Ulster, more than 95 per cent of the land in eight of its nine counties was in Protestant hands, and in County Antrim, more than half.[12] When trouble again arose in England between the Catholic King James II and Parliament, the Catholic Irish once again saw an opportunity to gain independence. In alliance with the French, they rose in arms to support James's claim. At the Battle of the Boyne, near Drogheda, on July 12, 1690, James was defeated by the armies of the Protestant William of Orange, husband of Mary, Queen of England.[13] The victory firmly established the Protestant ascendancy in Ireland. The war ended in 1691 with the Treaty of Limerick.

The Development of a Divided Regime

Military victory altered but did not solve the problem of political authority. How were the rebel Catholics to be treated? What kind of regime could be established? The English Crown adopted a policy of coercion: it sought compliance from its Catholic subjects while abandoning hope for their support. Control of the new Irish Parliament established in Dublin was placed in Protestant hands, with ultimate authority remaining with the Crown in London. Ireland had one regime, but three classes of citizens. A series of penal laws not only banned Catholics from public office, but also from purchasing land or holding it except on short leases; it also prohibited Catholics from establishing schools or sending their children abroad to be educated. At its most severe, the law turned Catholic priests into outlawed enemies of the regime. Because the priests suffered the same deprivations as their people, the attachment of the Irish peasantry to the Catholic Church was unusually strong. Because the deprivation of power and property applied to the Catholic Church as well as to its adherents, both were poor. There was thus less basis for anti-clericalism to develop among Catholics, as occurred in Continental countries. As in a colonial situation, the natives were treated as inferior subjects, and the economy managed for the benefit of absentee landlords and alien landlords. Gradually, the regime began formal abandonment of its anti-Catholic legislation: in part, this was recognition of the fact that it had failed to secure full compliance with its penal laws. Abandoning these laws did not remove the consequences of treating Catholics as disloyal and inferior subjects.[14]

The advantages of rule by the Crown were shared unequally by Presbyterian and Church of Ireland settlers. Protestant tenant farmers had, according to the Ulster custom, considerable security on their land; they could sell their tenancy and benefit from their improvements. This encouraged a tenant farmer to invest in agricultural improvements. By contrast, Catholic tenants had short leases and the value of their improvements could be lost by landlords increasing rents. This custom of rack-renting continued until the late nineteenth century in Munster, Connacht and Leinster. Politically, the Presbyterians were objects of discrimination. The major powers of the regime were exclusive to members of the Church of Ireland. Presbyterians suffered disabilities similar to those imposed on nonconformists in England in the eighteenth century. This, combined with rising rents in Ulster, and stories of free land and freedom of worship in America, led many Ulster Presbyterians to migrate again.

From 1718 until the outbreak of the American Revolution, an estimated 200,000 'Scotch-Irish' emigrated during the eighteenth century.[15]

Both Protestants and Catholics continued to hold to the old Irish tradition of relying upon localized armed forces to ensure compliance with the laws that they thought right, without regard to the laws or the officers of the nominal regime. Such self-reliance is explicable in circumstances long antedating a national police force or rapid means of moving troops. In Ireland, it was carried far beyond the limits of localized disorder and vigilantism known in England. In the seventeenth century, there were rapparees, 'country people armed in a kind of hostile manner with half-pikes and skeins and some with scythes or muskets'.[16] In the eighteenth century violence first took the form of attacks of agrarian 'whiteboys' against landlords and agents who sought to exact unpopular Church tithes and enforce enclosure. Sometimes these bands formed and fought along sectarian lines, and sometimes along economic lines. During the American Revolution, the formation of Volunteer regiments in lieu of a militia put arms into the hands of Irishmen, mostly Protestants, and gave official sanction to drilling in the countryside by 40,000 men. As war with France approached in the 1790s, both Catholics and Protestants believed this meant another rising in Ireland. An attack by a Catholic group upon a Protestant inn in Loughall, County Armagh, in 1795 resulted in the death of about 30 Catholics. Protestants, afraid of more attacks, formed the Orange Order, to uphold the King and his heirs '*as long as he or they support the Protestant ascendancy*'. One of their earliest actions was to intimidate Catholic tenants to leave homes in Protestant areas; about 700 Catholic families were thus expelled from Armagh and fled to Connacht.[17]

Dissatisfaction with the Ascendancy Parliament in Dublin finally culminated in a rising against the regime by the United Irishmen in 1798. The United Irishmen, founded in Belfast by Wolfe Tone, emphasized parliamentary reform, religious toleration and redress of agrarian grievances. The organization was non-sectarian, and Tone as well as many of his associates were Protestant. The rising of the United Irishmen with French support alarmed the established regime. The failure of the rising was followed by the suicide of Wolfe Tone and in 1803 the hanging of another Protestant rebel, Robert Emmet. The last fully ecumenical Irish rebellion against the Crown was over.[18]

On January 1, 1801, the kingdoms of Ireland and Great Britain

The Development of a Divided Regime

were formally merged into a single United Kingdom. The Act of Union, passed after the usual machinations of the days of Old Corruption, provided that the two countries would 'forever be united'. The precedent of Scotland, united with England a century previously, was favourable. Ireland was no longer to be a colony of England but a partner in a larger and grander state. In addition to economic advantage, this promised the extension of English reforms to Ireland. It was easier for Protestants in London to grant concessions to Catholics over the water than for Protestants in Dublin to grant concessions to their more numerous neighbours. From a Protestant point of view, the creation of a single Parliament for the whole of the British isles guaranteed a permanent Protestant majority, whatever reforms might prevail. Legally, Irish agitators would have as little claim to secede as Cockneys or Yorkshiremen, or as Pennsylvanians or Mississippians. By putting the sanction of law behind the argument that the two islands were a single entity, the British offered Irish subjects two alternatives: to deny their nationalist aspirations or to reject the established regime.

The history of nineteenth-century Ireland, as viewed from the South, is a story of the alternative appeal of two substantive goals— good government and self-government. Good government meant the reform of the existing regime, especially as it operated in Ireland. The policy had much to recommend it, since the nineteenth century was by European standards an era of great liberal reform in Britain. British governments were not, however, as quick to perceive the need for reform in Ireland as in England. The two leading statesmen of the century had little first-hand knowledge of Ireland. Gladstone only once visited a country but a few hours by boat from his birthplace and country residence. Many public figures who visited only found their stereotypes of Irish inferiority confirmed.[19] Disraeli never visited Ireland at all. The legislation that successive governments passed at Westminster often involved substantial exceptions for Ireland, not always to the advantage of the Irish.[20] The goal of self-government meant the repudiation of the regime, whatever reforms it adopted, because only self-government was good government. The proposition was widely voiced in Europe; it was supported by many English MPs in debates about Greece and Italy. The case for good government was linked with the case for constitutional action. On moral and pragmatic grounds, reformers argued that only by working within the constraints of the United Kingdom could the condition of

82

the Irish people effectively be improved. Violence would only lead to death and further coercion. Against this, the proponents of self-government argued that the regime would never peacefully accept the secession of Ireland; only force would be effective in gaining independence, and independence was a great enough blessing to give moral justification to the use of force.

The use of force and the use of parliamentary means were not mutually exclusive strategies. Centuries of internal disorder, conquest and insurrection made Irish politicians view as normal many tactics that English parliamentarians thought violated the spirit as well as the letter of the regime's laws. In the early nineteenth century, Daniel O'Connell sought, by parliamentary means and outdoor protest meetings, to increase Catholic rights. Simultaneously, agrarian secret societies, religious societies and local factions continued their disorderly activities 'in the field' in Ireland. Lord Grey told the House of Commons that in Ireland in 1832 there were 242 homicides and more than 300 attempted homicides. An historian of the period notes that this was 'the last occasion during which the agrarian secret societies were able to control sizeable areas of rural Ireland for considerable periods of time'. The establishment of the Royal Irish Constabulary was meant to make this impossible.[21] Reforms of the British Constitution from 1832 gave the Irish hope of exercising influence through Parliament in London. The activities of a Nationalist movement in the 1880s under the leadership of Charles Stewart Parnell made Home Rule for Ireland a major issue in British as well as Irish politics. Parnell's activities were kept within constitutional bounds, but his language was less bridled.[22] From the 1880s until the First World War, bills for Irish Home Rule passed from the House of Commons to the House of Lords and limbo.

Simultaneously, advocates of repudiating the regime by demonstrations and armed rebellion began organizing the institutions of revolt. The Fenians, founded in 1858 in Dublin and New York, were not discouraged by the failure of their abortive rising of 1867. The later success of the Fenians in attracting popular support, not withstanding explicit Papal condemnation in 1870, reflects the intensity with which the regime was rejected by many of its subjects.[23] The successful boycott campaign of the Irish Land League in the 1880s showed that voting at elections was not the only way to influence Acts of Parliament. The foundation of the Gaelic League in 1893 was an attempt to increase Irish self-respect and emphasized alienation from things English. The foundation of Sinn Fein (Gaelic for 'Ourselves Alone') in 1898 was an attempt to use parliamentary institutions to attack the regime directly. Arthur Griffith, its progenitor, held that as Union in 1801 was immoral and illegal, Sinn Fein should nominate candidates for Westminster who would refuse to attend Parliament if elected. They would instead constitute a new regime in Ireland. An eight-month strike in Dublin in 1913–14 led to disorder in the capital, described as the poorest in Europe,[24] and James Connolly organized the Irish Citizen Army, as an urban working-class group dedicated to class and nationalist goals. Throughout the period there was the spectre of action by the Irish Republican Brotherhood, founded in 1858 with the aim of repudiating the regime by force.

From a Northern Ireland perspective, the nineteenth century saw a growing apart of the North and the South. In the first instance, the process was economic. Belfast grew from a town of 37,000 in 1821 to a city of 349,000 in 1901. The existence of a handloom linen industry encouraged the introduction of textile factories, and the port facilities of Belfast harbour made it easy to import cotton. Shipbuilding boomed too, notwithstanding the need to import iron and coal, neither of which was found in Ireland's boggy soil. Simultaneously, Dublin remained an administrative centre. The contrast between Georgian Dublin and Victorian Belfast is still visible in the architecture of the two cities; it is a contrast mirrored in many countries, e.g., in the difference between Washington and Pittsburgh, or Edinburgh and Glasgow. The bulk of the industrial capital was in the hands of Protestants. The contrast in the wealth of the two communities in the North was often interpreted as a sign of innate Irish inferiority. In the words of a modern Ulster economist, Professor Thomas Wilson, Catholics 'were made to feel inferior and to make matters worse they often were inferior, if *only* in those personal qualities that make for success in competitive economic life'. In reaction, some Nationalists seized upon the appearance of differences as evidence that the rural, Celtic culture of the native Irish was superior to that of the industrial North, and a further justification for repudiating rule by an industrialized Britain.[25]

The rise of industry made Belfast an attractive place for thousands of rural labourers, forced from the land by the decline of agriculture and, especially in the South, by the Famine of the 1840s. Catholics as well as Protestants came to work in the new factories. The proportion of Catholics in the city grew from about ten per cent to about 30 per cent; the absolute number of Catholics also grew as the city increased in size.[26] Industrially, Belfast was integrated with Britain, for its principal manufactures were exchanged or in competition with those of Clydeside and Lancashire, both easily accessible by short sea journeys. Industrialization thus further reinforced a pattern of communication dominant for more than a millennium: the movement of people in Northern Ireland across the Irish Sea to Scotland and England rather than into the Irish hinterland.

Politically, the distance between North and South was widening throughout the century. The Orange Order survived despite repeated attempts of the British government to ban it. Following rumours of Orange intrigue in Britain, involving the King's brother, the Duke of Cumberland, the Orange Order was dissolved under Parliamentary pressure in 1836, and remained so for a decade.[27] Orange demonstrations were unpopular with the British government because they often ended in violence. Moreover, the oathbound character of the organization was seen as a potential challenge to the Orangeman's allegiance to the British regime. Notwithstanding a series of Acts of Parliament intended to stop Orangemen and Catholic Ribbonmen from provocative parades, processions continued, and so too did violence, not least in Belfast.[28] The temper of Protestants was shown when William Johnston of Ballykilbeg was jailed for leading a banned march of more than 20,000 Orangemen on the Twelfth of July, 1867. Johnston gained such popularity that he was promptly elected to Parliament, where he helped secure the repeal of acts restricting parades, and represented South Belfast for 30 years.

A chasm opened between North and South in the 1880s. The extension of the franchise, accompanied by increasing Nationalist organization, brought about the return of 85 Irish Nationalists to the Westminster House of Commons in 1885, giving them the balance of power between Liberals and Conservatives. Irish Home Rule thus became a major issue in British politics, and a grave concern of Ulster Protestants. Home Rule meant that instead of being part of an overwhelmingly Protestant regime, Ulster's Protestants would be a minority in a predominantly Catholic state. Rightly or wrongly, Protestants reckoned that a Catholic majority would take vengeance upon them for previous wrongs, and that the Roman Catholic Church would restrict their religious rights. Nationalist assertions that the people of Ireland were one nation, united by geography if not by religion, were countered by Protestant claims that they were one

The Development of a Divided Regime

nation with Britain, united by law if not by geography. The problem was simple, even elemental. The alternatives were simple but hard. As in war, victory for one side was defeat for the other.

The Ulster response to the threat of Irish Nationalism was to organize resistance. As in the South, resistance took two paths— opposition by peaceful, Parliamentary means, and opposition by resort to force. The Unionist movement was founded in 1886 to organize Parliamentary resistance to Home Rule. Previously, Ulster had returned both Liberal and Conservative MPs to Westminster. The Liberals lost support as the party of Home Rule and the Unionists were assured of pre-eminence among Protestant electors. It also forestalled the growth of the nascent Labour Party in Belfast. Belfast businessmen and landed gentry joined with leaders of the Orange Order in making the new party. The businessmen and aristocrats provided funds and leadership in Westminster. The Orange Order provided a ready-made organization in the countryside, and masses of militant Protestant supporters of all classes.[29] The Ulster Unionists allied themselves with the British Conservatives in the Westminster House of Commons, while retaining autonomy in Northern Ireland. Lord Randolph Churchill summed up their view in 1886 by proclaiming, 'Ulster will fight and Ulster will be right.' The defeat of Gladstone's Liberal government in 1886 because it espoused Home Rule gave the Unionists 20 years to organize, before the issue again became immediate with the return of a Liberal government in 1906.

Fenian sentiment in the South and Protestant defence organizations in the North developed concurrently. Marching and the practice of marksmanship were sports that united all Ireland. In the South, this was rebellion, for Fenians neither supported nor wished to comply with Britain's regime. In the North it was *Ultra-ism* for loyalists supported their regime so much that they were prepared to refuse compliance to laws that they deemed inconsistent with that to which they had given allegiance. The leader of the Unionists, Sir Edward Carson, proclaimed in Belfast on September 23, 1912, 'We must be prepared–and time is precious in these things–the morning Home Rule passes, ourselves to become responsible for the government of the Protestant province of Ulster.'[30] The following Monday, a small group of Unionists and Orangemen met to prepare plans for the creation of an Ulster Volunteer Force, armed and ready to defend a Protestant regime in Ulster, even in opposition to a British Act of Parliament. Carson said in a public address in Newry, 'I am told it

86

will be illegal. Of course it will. Drilling is illegal . . . The Volunteers are illegal and the government know they are illegal and the government dare not interfere with them . . . Don't be afraid of illegalities.'[31] The stand of the Unionist leaders was supported in their threatened nullification of Acts of Parliament by the Conservative Party in England. By a fluke of history, its leader during these troubled times was Andrew Bonar Law, the son of a Presbyterian clergyman from Coleraine. Bonar Law, though born in Canada and raised in Scotland, had never lost his close personal ties with Ulster.[32] Intransigence was visibly popular in Ulster. The most formidable evidence of this was the success of the Ulster Covenant. In a country with approximately 500,000 adult Protestants, a total of 447,000 people signed the following statement:

> Being convinced in our consciences that Home Rule would be disastrous to the material well-being of Ulster as well as the whole of Ireland, subversive of our civil and religious freedom, destructive of our citizenship, and perilous to the unity of the Empire, we, whose names are underwritten, men of Ulster, loyal subjects of His Gracious Majesty King George V, humbly relying on the God whom our fathers in days of stress and trial confidently trusted, do hereby pledge ourselves in solemn Covenant throughout this our time of threatened calamity to stand by one another in defending for ourselves and our children our cherished position of equal citizenship in the United Kingdom, and in using all means which may be found necessary to defeat the present conspiracy to set up a Home Rule Parliament in Ireland. And in the event of such a Parliament being forced upon us we further solemnly and mutually pledge ourselves to refuse to recognise its authority. In sure confidence that God will defend the right we hereto subscribe our names. And further, we individually declare that we have not already signed this Covenant. God Save the King.

By the end of July, 1914, when a Home Rule bill had passed in Parliament, Ulster Protestants had a stock of more than 40,000 rifles, with ammunition and men organized ready to use them.[33]

The outbreak of war in Europe in August, 1914, drew the attention of the British government from the Irish problem. An act to suspend operation of the Home Rule bill reached the statute book before the bill itself. Many of the Ulster Volunteers joined the British Expeditionary Force: on almost the eve of Orange Day, 1916, 5,500 members of the Ulster Division were killed at the Battle of the Somme.[34] In the South, the parliamentary Nationalists agreed to a truce in their battle, in anticipation of the enforcement after the war of a Home

Rule bill approved in principle by Parliament in 1914. The adherents of Sinn Fein regarded the involvement of England in Europe as an invitation to act: 'England's difficulty is Ireland's opportunity.'

The settlement of the land question and concord between the regime and the Catholic Church had still left unresolved one issue—the constitution of the state. On Easter Monday, 1916, a group of armed men entered the General Post Office in Dublin and proclaimed the Irish Republic 'in the name of God and of the dead generations from which she receives her old traditions of nationhood'. The proclamation described the constitutional regime as a 'usurpation'. By the end of Easter Week the rebels had surrendered. The leaders of the Rising were executed by the British early in May in Dublin. The executions caused a revulsion against the British, and turned the rebels into martyrs. John Dillon, a Nationalist MP committed to Home Rule by peaceful means, told the British House of Commons, 'You are washing out our whole life-work in a sea of blood.' The British Prime Minister, H. H. Asquith, soon admitted as much, telling the House of Commons, 'The government has come to the conclusion that the system under which Ireland has been governed has completely broken down.'[35] A long guerilla war followed. The 'Troubles', as the time is euphemistically known, are usually described from the point of view of the victors in the South. The Protestant majority in the North wrote a different conclusion to events there. Because they were ready and willing to defend their independence from Dublin rule by force of arms, they too were victors. The strength of the rebels in the South meant that Unionists such as Carson, a Dubliner by birth, had to abandon the hope of retaining a British regime in all 32 counties of Ireland. The abandonment of Leinster, Munster and Connacht to the rebels was of little concern to the political leadership of Ulster. They sought simply to hold what they had.

By 1920 guerilla war was endemic all over Ireland. The Republican and Protestant forces, as well as some British troops hastily drafted in for service, fought with limited regard for the protocols of war as it was supposed to be conducted by well organized armies representing sovereign states. An unofficial history of the Protestant defence forces emphasizes the casual use of firearms, and the ferocity of guerilla war: 'Vendetta shootings were a commonplace in that grim period.' In Belfast in 1922, there were 97 cases of murder and 96 reported attacks upon life; the city was under curfew, except for two brief intervals, until Christmas, 1924. During these troubles in the North, 232 people were killed, including two Unionist Members of Parliament, nearly 1,000 men injured and property valued at £3,000,000 was destroyed.[36] Granted the difference in population, the causalty list was the equivalent of 40,000 injuries from political vio- lence in Britain, or 160,000 injuries in modern America. By the stan- dards of Irish history, casualties were substantial, but not unprece- dented.

The political objective of the British regime was, characteristically, a compromise, because in most of Ireland their interest was limited, and once land had been sold to the peasantry, not in fixed assets. Compromise was necessary, instead of withdrawal on the pattern of later colonial challenges, because seventeenth-century Ulster settlers had become immovably attached to their place of settlement, like other settlers in the old Dominions. In recognition of this, Westminster passed the Government of Ireland Act of 1920, proposing separate Parliaments in Dublin and Belfast, with a Council of Ireland given limited responsibilities for the 32 counties. Both parts of Ireland were to continue to have representation at Westminster, which would reserve such powers as defence, foreign affairs, and coining money.[37] Eventually, the Council might become a single all-Ireland Parliament federated to the Westminster Parliament. While not accepted *in toto*, the Act provided the basis of the resulting constitutional settlement. The Ulster Unionists were willing to accept the division of Ireland – something not previously regarded as desirable – because it gave them a secure redoubt. By excluding the three heavily Catholic counties of Ulster from the boundaries of the new state, Northern Ireland became two-thirds Protestant, a simple and striking example of solving a constitutional problem by controlling the composition of the state (cf. Table III.1).

The strength of the rebels in the South made partition, while not ideal, acceptable to Ulster Unionists, provided that the new boun- daries were regarded as 'a *final settlement*'.[38] The new Northern Ireland Parliament met for the first time on June 27, 1920. Its 40 Unionist members took their seats, but neither the six Nationalists nor the six Sinn Fein MPs appeared to take the oath and recognize the regime. King George V, addressing the new Parliament in June, 1921 asked 'all Irishmen' [*sic*] to join in making for the land they love a new era of peace, contentment and goodwill'.[39]

In Southern Ireland, the rebels rejected the proposed settlement. They wished a Republic free of subjection to Westminster, and would

Table III.1   The religious composition of the historic nine counties of Ulster, 1911 and 1961

| | Protestants | | | | Catholics | | | |
| | 1911 | | 1961 | | 1911 | | 1961 | |
	N 000s	%	N 000s	%	N 000s	%	N 000s	%
Belfast	293	75·9	302	72·6	93	24·1	114	27·4
Antrim	154	79·8	207	75·5	39	20·2	67	24·5
Down	140	68·6	191	71·5	64	31·4	76	28·5
Armagh	66	55·0	62	52·5	54	45·0	56	47·5
Londonderry – City	18	43·9	18	33·3	23	56·1	36	66·7
County	58	58·6	64	57·1	41	41·4	48	42·9
Fermanagh	27	44·3	24	47·1	34	55·7	27	52·9
Tyrone	63	44·4	61	45·5	79	55·6	73	54·5
Total 6 counties	819	65·7	929	65·1	427	34·2	497	34·9
Donegal	35	20·8	15	13·3	133	79·2	98	86·7
Cavan	17	18·7	6	10·7	74	81·3	50	89·3
Monaghan	18	25·4	7	14·9	53	74·6	40	85·1
Total 3 counties	70	21·2	28	13·0	260	78·8	188	87·0
Total 9 counties	889	56·4	957	58·3	687	43·6	685	41·7

Sources: Official Census Returns, 1911, Province of Ulster; 1961, *Northern Ireland* and *Republic of Ireland* census. Column totals reflect rounding.

not endorse the exclusion of Ulster from their state. The integrity of an island state was as much a fact to them as the integrity of Britain was to the English. A Treaty was finally signed between Sinn Fein representatives and the British government in December, 1921. The Northern Ireland Parliament was given the right to contract out of this new regime. This was promptly done. The Irish Free State was given dominion status. The Northern Ireland regime, by contrast, was denied the same formal autonomy. Sir James Craig was prepared to accept dominion status for Northern Ireland, but Lloyd George rejected it on the grounds that it would 'stereotype a frontier based neither upon natural features nor broad geographical considerations'.[40] The men who signed the Treaty returned to Dublin to find themselves repudiated by a substantial section of their associates because dominion status did not break completely the connection with the Crown. The pro-Treaty men argued that it gave *de facto* independence, and further bloodshed would be avoided. Notwithstanding the merits of the first point, the second was proven false. A civil war followed between pro-Treaty and anti-Treaty Republicans, leading to the death of many leaders of the war against England. In the first ten months of this war, approximately 665 men were killed and 3,000 wounded.[41] A truce was finally agreed in 1923. The consequence is aptly summed up by T. W. Moody:

> Both Northern Ireland and the Irish Free State thus owed their origin not to the force of argument, on which the national movement from O'Connell to Redmond had relied, but to the argument of force, and their history bears the marks of that tragic but inescapable fact.[42]

The precursive inheritance of the new Northern Ireland regime was mixed. Geographically, the new state was compact. Belfast provided both a secure capital and easy access to Scotland and England for trade. Except for the city of Londonderry, which was isolated from its natural hinterland in Donegal, the communities on the border were small and of little consequence. The predominance of British-oriented Protestants, the lack of absentee landlords and industrialization meant that Ulster, of all the parts of Ireland, was more like Britain than it was a dominion or colony. In economic terms, Northern Ireland was well endowed by Irish standards, for it had the island's only industrial city as well as much good farmland. By British standards, the land was poor in natural resources and its major industries, shipbuilding and textiles, peculiarly subject to trade fluctuations. The civil service that had chosen to work in Belfast rather than Dublin was loyal. Because it was trained to British standards, it was of reasonable quality. The regime could also call upon thousands of Protestants to defend it, men who had gained experience in the hard school of civil war from 1916 to 1922. The political leaders of the new regime, including the Prime Minister from 1921 to 1940, Sir James Craig (later Lord Craigavon), had proven their ability as self-sufficient politicians, by organizing resistance both to Irish Republicans and to the British Parliament. The North had lost by violent death fewer leaders and potential leaders than had the South. Only one precursive condition was unambiguously threatening to the regime. Until Partition, both Protestants and Catholics could consider themselves Irishmen, albeit Irishmen who disputed whether they should be ruled from Dublin or London. After Partition, Belfast became part of Britain, and any Ulsterman who wished for Dublin rule was *ipso facto* disloyal to the new regime.

The Development of a Divided Regime

The problems that faced the new regime were several and persisting. The most immediate was that of physical security against external attack or subversion from within. If Irish Catholics were prepared to shoot each other, what would they do to Ulster Protestants? The civil war in the South ended when the anti-Treaty side laid down their arms, but peace brought also the commitment by all parties in the Republic to the unification of the 32 counties of Ireland under a single regime, based on Dublin. Eamon de Valera, leader of the anti-Treaty forces, became Premier in 1932, further increasing anxieties. De Valera's reduction of links with Britain throughout the 1930s and his domestic policies further emphasized the alien and enemy nature of Northern Ireland's closest and larger neighbour.[43] The boundaries of the new regime were in theory subject to review by a Boundary Commission established by the Anglo-Irish Treaty of 1921. Fearful of the loss of Fermanagh and Tyrone (cf. Table III.1), Craigavon was adamant against any review. The six counties were reckoned to be viable, but a further reduction in territory would make absorption into the Republic much more likely. Craigavon's motto—Not an inch—was an appropriate successor to the seventeenth-century Protestant motto: No surrender. Craigavon warned that if the Boundary Commission advised changes, he would resign as Prime Minister and put himself at the head of an Ulster Volunteer Force pledged to maintain Protestant authority in the six counties.[44] The Commission ended its work without reporting, when the Dublin regime in 1925 agreed to recognize the existing boundary on a *de facto* basis in exchange for financial assistance from London. It has never recognized the boundaries on a *de jure* basis, and the 1937 Constitution explicitly affirms in Article 2 claims to the 'lost' counties of Ulster.

The threat from within and without gave the leaders of the regime a strategy for maintaining some support as well as full compliance: identification with the Protestant majority. This the leaders of the regime were glad to do. Lord Craigavon himself spoke of the regime as 'a Protestant government' and called it 'a Protestant Parliament for a Protestant people'.[45] The language aptly summarizes the Unionist point of view. Protestants had been loyal to the British Crown; therefore, only Protestants were deemed worthy of participation in government. As long as Catholics resided in Northern Ireland, they would be expected to comply with the regime's laws; their support was neither sought nor obtained. This caste division was simple, easily understood and entirely consistent with the Orange version of Irish history. The regime could rely on support at the ballot boxes. From the first election in 1921 until the present, the Unionist Party has always won a large majority of seats in the House of Commons at Stormont, the regime's administrative centre on the outskirts of Belfast. In twelve elections in nearly half a century, the strength of the pro-Union parties has fluctuated between 40 and 42; the anti-Partitionists have seen their numbers vary between 10 and 12 (cf. Table III.2). The stability of party strengths is particularly surprising in view of the number and the fluidity of the party labels under which candidates fight.[46]

Whether the Unionist policy be viewed as cause or consequence of Catholic disaffection is a matter of faith, not historical scholarship. The important point is that the Unionists, from the very foundation of the regime, did not seek to make it fully legitimate by attracting the support of Catholics. Protestant solidarity sufficed to give the Unionists a permanent hold on office and to leave the Nationalists a permanent minority without hope of gaining power–at least, by peaceful constitutional means. To establish and maintain a regime with full compliance and mixed support may seem a less than ideal solution. But Northern Ireland was, in the eyes of both Protestants and Catholics, a less than ideal regime. To the regime's leaders, partial legitimacy was better than complete repudiation.

The Nationalist Party in Northern Ireland was in an impossible position. The party had always been anti-Sinn Fein. In 1918, the leader, Joe Devlin, defeated de Valera in a Belfast contest for election to the Westminster House of Commons, taking 73 per cent of the votes. But the Nationalists could not accept as permanent a settlement which meant abandoning their *raison d'être*, the unity and independence of the 32 counties of Ireland. It was not until the end of 1927 that a full complement of Nationalist MPs regularly appeared at the Stormont House of Commons. They disdained the title of Loyal Opposition. Yet Devlin also announced rejection of unconstitutional measures, even though these were the actions that had heretofore advanced the Republican cause. The failure of the Nationalists to organize effectively on a constituency basis throughout Ulster meant that their supporters were liable to break away to support more extreme candidates. Sinn Fein candidates sporadically fought and won election to Parliament, pledged to abstain from attendance there.

Table III.2 General elections in Northern Ireland, 1921–69

Date	Unionist	Ind. Unionist	Lib.	Lab.	Ind.	Nat.	Eire Lab. Rep. Lab. Soc. Lab. Ind. Lab.	Sinn Fein abstention	For Union	Anti-Partition
24 May 1921	40	—	—	—	—	6	—	6	40	12
28 April 1925	33	3	—	3	1	10	—	2	40	12
22 May 1929	37	3	—	1	—	10	—	1	41	11
30 Nov. 1933	36	2	—	2	1	9	—	2	41	11
9 Feb. 1938	39	3	—	1	—	8	1	—	43	9
14 June 1945	33	2	—	2	3	9	3	—	40	12
10 Feb. 1949	37	2	—	—	2	9	2	—	41	11
22 Oct. 1953	38	1	—	—	1	7	3	2	40	12
20 Mar. 1958	37	—	—	4	1	8	2	—	42	10
31 May 1962	34	—	1	4	1	9	3	—	40	12
25 Nov. 1965	36	—	1	2	2	9	2	—	41	11
24 Feb. 1969	36	3	—	2	3	6	2	—	40	12

Classification based on data in D. E. Butler and J. Freeman, *British Political Facts, 1900–67*, p. 254.

The world depression of the 1930s intensified the economic diffi-culties resulting from civil war. Unemployment increased by more than two and a half times between 1929 and 1938, reaching a peak of three in ten. The dependence of Northern Ireland upon the British Exchequer for subsidies gave it no funds of its own to use in fighting unemployment. It did, however, have other means of attacking the problem–at least as far as Protestant workers were concerned. Sir Basil Brooke (later Viscount Brookeborough) endorsed the campaign of the Ulster Protestant League against the employment of Catholics. In 1933 the future Prime Minister said, 'Many in the audience employ Catholics, but I have not one about my place. Catholics are out to destroy Ulster with all their might and power. They want to nullify the Protestant vote, take all they can out of Ulster and then see it go to hell.'[47] The chief troubles in Belfast in the 1930s were not demon-strations by unemployed workers but sectarian riots. The worst occurred in July 1935 when 11 people were killed and 574 reported injured. There were few arrests, and juries often refused to convict Protestants.[48]

During the Second World War, the existence of Northern Ireland was of great advantage to Britain and America. Londonderry became the major Anglo-American naval base protecting the Western approaches to Britain. The relative inaccessibility of Belfast to Ger-man aircraft made it an important centre for war production, and Ulster's agriculture helped feed Britain too.[49] Conscription was not introduced in Northern Ireland, for fear it would cause civil disorder, as efforts to conscript had done in the First World War in Ireland. The Republic maintained its neutrality throughout the war. The regime there refused the United Kingdom the use of ports in Cork and Donegal which had once been earmarked for Britain to use to defend Atlantic convoys against German submarines. Moreover, it maintained diplomatic relations with Nazi Germany up to the end of the war. The IRA caused little trouble in the North, but the regime exercised special precautions against it. At the height of the emer-gency in 1940, 302 persons were interned under the Special Powers Act. The number of rebel suspects interned reached a low of 12 in 1944.[50]

Ironically, the major blow that the Republic aimed at British sovereignty after the war has strengthened the legal position of the Northern Ireland regime. In 1949, the Irish Republic withdrew from its previous limited association with the British Commonwealth. (It still retained many anomalous privileges and is a party to bilateral agreements that have no counterpart between Britain and other independent states.) In consequence of this symbolic gesture, the British government had to amend various items of legislation. In passing the Ireland Act of 1949, it included a specific pledge of Ulster's position.

> That Northern Ireland remains part of His Majesty's Dominions and of the United Kingdom and it is hereby affirmed that in no event will Northern Ireland or any part thereof cease to be part of His Majesty's Dominions and of the United Kingdom without consent of the Parliament of Northern Ireland.[51]

The measure received an unusual amount of opposition when passing through the British House of Commons; 63 Labour MPs voted against it at a committee stage. The Unionists welcomed the measure as one more buttress of a regime where authority could not be taken for granted.

Violence was once again used to challenge the regime when the Irish Republican Army began a series of armed raids in 1954. On December 12, 1956 it issued a formal declaration of war on the regime, modelled after the proclamation of the Irish Republic in 1916. The declaration was explicitly non-sectarian, calling for the unity of Protestants and Catholics, just as it was uncompromising in opposition 'to British political control in the North and to British economic domination in the South'. Although the Republican forces were divided among themselves, this did not make their campaign any the less violent. In consequence of armed attacks upon police, military installations and other targets, 19 people were killed between 1956 and 1961. About 200 men were interned in the North, and another 100 in the South, where the IRA was an illegal organization. The 'legal' branch of the Fenian movement, Sinn Fein, won 23·5 per cent of the vote in Northern Ireland at the 1955 British general election. Two Sinn Fein candidates were victorious, but neither returned to Westminster; both were in Crumlin Road Jail, Belfast, for their part in a raid at Omagh. The campaign formally ended with a communiqué of February 26, 1962, announcing that 'all arms and other materials have been dumped'. They were not destroyed.[52]

Viscount Brookeborough's retirement as Prime Minister in March, 1963, after 20 consecutive years in office, meant the departure of a man who sought to maintain the regime as partially legitimate. Lord Brookeborough, a landowner in the border county of Fermanagh, had played a prominent part in organizing the Ulster B Special Constabulary as a Protestant defence organization during the Troubles. While in office, he invited Protestant Ulstermen to treat Catholics as disloyal. Critics were told, in the words of Professor T. Wilson, 'They [i.e., Catholics] have less to complain about than the US Negroes and their lot is a very pleasant one as compared with that of the nationalists in, say, the Ukraine.'[53] Professor J. C. Beckett summed up the record from 1923 to the early 1960s by noting:

> Though the settlement left a legacy of bitterness issuing occasionally in local and sporadic disturbances, it inaugurated in Ireland a longer period of general tranquillity than she had known since the first half of the eighteenth century.[54]

The installation of Captain Terence O'Neill as Lord Brookeborough's successor in 1963 began a new phase in Northern Ireland politics. In family background, the new Prime Minister could claim descent from the legendary O'Neills of the Gaelic past, as well as descent from Plantation aristocracy. By virtue of age, O'Neill was too young to have experienced the Troubles first hand. Because his early family life was primarily spent at school in England, abroad and in the Army, he lacked the intensely parochial outlook conventionally found among politicians in the Province. Instead of looking in and back, he looked forward and out. From an international perspective, O'Neill's programme was hardly novel. In Northern Ireland terms, however, Terence O'Neill was an innovator, even a revolutionary, for he sought nothing less than a fully legitimate regime in which Catholics would support the Constitution as well as comply with its basic laws.[55]

In common with the rest of the British isles, the Northern Ireland regime began to show an active interest in economic planning in the early 1960s. This concern was by no means inevitable. Previous Unionist governments had no electoral need to make economic policy the main feature of the party's programme, as it was inevitably successful in appealing for votes on constitutional grounds. A policy of 'step-by-step' legislation in welfare matters meant that the Northern Ireland regime adopted British welfare programmes shortly after the Westminster Parliament approved such measures for Great Britain. Commitment to this principle was tested by the actions of the 1945 Labour government. Notwithstanding their conservative economic bias, the Unionists adopted Socialist legislation. The British Treasury paid the resulting budget deficit. In 1962, there were local economic circumstances requiring attention. A committee led by Sir Robert Hall, economic adviser to the British government, gloomily forecast that unemployment in Northern Ireland was likely to rise during the decade because of the decline of older industries and agriculture. In reaction, O'Neill commissioned Professor Thomas Wilson of Glasgow University to prepare a report on economic development. In 1965, the Wilson Report appeared. Not only did it point to the weak features of Ulster's economy, but it also contained positive recommendations to improve the location of industry, transport, tourism and recreation, manpower training, agriculture and capital investment in industry. The Wilson Report, along with a series of other reports on such matters as regional development around Belfast and siting a new university, both induced and reflected change.[56]

In Northern Ireland, no economic plan could be without implications for Protestant-Catholic relations. Difficulties arose in various ways. The new town planned as a centre for expanding industries outside Belfast was named Craigavon, hardly an attraction to potential Catholic residents. Protestant militants protested when a new bridge across the River Lagan in Belfast was not named the Carson Bridge, after the co-founder of the Northern Ireland regime. Naming the new structure the Queen Elizabeth II Bridge was not considered loyal enough by these Protestants; but it was hardly a name congenial to Catholics. Both Protestants and Catholics in Londonderry protested about the recommendation of the Lockwood Committee to site the New University of Ulster in Coleraine. The Londonderry protest was but one token of resentment by people living west of the River Bann against the concentration of economic growth around Belfast. Catholics, a disproportionate part of the population of the western counties of Londonderry, Tyrone and Fermanagh, alleged that the location of new industries had less to do with economics than with the religious composition of the counties.

Judged in purely economic terms, the development plans showed substantial signs of success in the 1960s, relative to previous conditions and the probable alternative of continued economic decline. Numbers in employment rose from 457,000 in June, 1963 to 479,000 in June, 1968, notwithstanding a loss of almost 12,000 jobs in agriculture, shipbuilding and textiles, traditionally the chief occupations of the Province. Population grew by three per cent in the five-year period, an encouraging sign in a land where emigration by unemployed younger people has normally been the means of keeping the population constant. The number of houses built in 1968 was 12,120, as against 8,842 in 1963 and 4,938 in 1958. The index of money wages which stood at 100 in April, 1960 was 118 in 1963 and 173 in 1968.[57] Unemployment rates fell by only 0·3 per cent, however, and the absolute number of people out of work was constant.

Politically, the emphasis on economic issues implied risks as well as gains. If the policy succeeded, then the Unionist Party, by attracting Catholic support, would no longer be a Protestant defence organization, a change that Orangemen could hardly welcome. If the economy had downturns as well as prosperous periods, then Unionists might sometimes lose seats that they would hold if contests were always fought on the Constitution. To quiet criticism, O'Neill sought approval for his policies at a snap general election in November, 1965. The result was success. Instead of losing ground, the Unionists won two seats from the Northern Ireland Labour Party in industrial Belfast.

Terence O'Neill's policy toward the Republic of Ireland was an even greater novelty, in an island where the two regimes had historically viewed each other as enemies. No Northern Ireland Prime Minister had ever had official conversations with his opposite number in the Republic, nor had successive Prime Ministers there shown themselves ready to set aside their commitment to the eventual unity of the 32 counties, for the sake of improved diplomatic relations in the present.[58] Hence, the decision of O'Neill to meet with Sean Lemass— a one-time rebel and then the Republic's Taoiseach (Prime Minister) —had all the overtones and anxieties, in Irish terms, of a summit meeting between Russian and American leaders. Their public meeting in Belfast in 1965, taken without consultation with Parliament, was followed by further public emphasis of the advantages of cross-border co-operation. In O'Neill's eyes, the border could never be abolished, but it could be banished as a major issue in Ulster politics. The Nationalist Party, led by Eddie McAteer, took half a step toward co-operation within Ulster in 1965 by accepting the title of official Opposition.

While the Northern Ireland regime was limited by the response from the Republic in what it could do to improve North-South relations, it did have great formal powers to influence Protestant-Catholic relations within Northern Ireland. O'Neill sought to encourage toleration. The climate for doing this seemed favourable everywhere else in the Western world. The accession of John XXIII to the Papacy in 1958 had encouraged liberal tendencies within the Roman Catholic Church. Within Protestantism, the World Council of Churches and other bodies were endorsing ecumenical measures designed to reduce ancient divisions within it and between Protestantism and Rome. Admittedly, Rome was a long way from the residence of the Catholic Primate of All Ireland in Armagh, and the World Council of Churches is spiritually even more remote from the Orange lodges of Ulster. To encourage conciliation, O'Neill avoided the familiar charge that Catholics, *en masse*, were disloyal. Secondly, the Prime Minister visited a variety of Catholic institutions and organizations to give positive evidence that he did not regard this third of his subjects as 'outside the Pale'. Toleration is not to be confused with integration. At no time did the Prime Minister encourage the appointment of Catholics to prominent positions in the regime, let alone within the Unionist Party. While he was able to increase Catholic representation on statutory committees and boards a survey in 1966 found that out of 102 members, only nine were Catholics.[59]

Viewed from afar, the policies associated with Terence O'Neill hardly seem original or dangerous. They are consistent with the ideals, if not the practice, of liberal people throughout the Anglo-American world. Yet this was a world that did not exist when Protestant planters went into the Gaelic fastness of Ulster more than three centuries ago. It was also a world that leading Republicans had always attacked as alien to Irish civilization. Thus, Terence O'Neill's programme proposed radical changes in the practice of Ulster politics. Because it threatened this, to some it betokened hope, to others hypocrisy; to yet a third group, it made O'Neill a traitor to the regime. The result was that a policy intended to lead to the full legitimation of the regime threatened its repudiation.

The challenge came first from within the Protestant community; it was led by the Rev. Dr. Ian K. Paisley of the Free Presbyterian Church in Ulster. Opponents of O'Neill accused him of undermining the regime by seeking friendship with the Republic, and by treating Catholics as potentially loyal subjects. Dr. Paisley first became prominent politically during the October, 1964 Westminster general election, when he organized demonstrations against a Republican candidate. In 1966, Paisley organized demonstrations against the 'Romeward' trend in the Presbyterian Church. The demonstrations affronted both Presbyterian dignitaries and Belfast Catholics. Paisley was convicted for unlawful assembly. When he and two of his clergy-men refused to be bound over to keep the peace, they went to prison for three months. During this summer, three people were killed in Belfast in incidents intended to intimidate Catholics. Terence O'Neill denounced Paisley and his followers for using the tactics of 'a Fascist movement'. The issue raised was simple, 'Who is to rule in Northern Ireland?' Dr. Paisley answered the question by declaring, 'My voice will not be silenced by all the police at the command of the Prime Minister.' *A propos* the efforts of the Prime Minister to build bridges to the Catholic community, he commented, 'A traitor and a bridge are very much alike, for they both go over to the other side.'[60]

Signs of Catholic dissatisfaction with O'Neill's programme were slower to appear. Initially, Nationalists gave tacit support to the bridge-building efforts of the government. But the two ends never met. Nationalists hesitated to support policies that might strengthen the Unionist Party by drawing Catholic voters to it. They had no immediate incentive to support the policies, for no patronage was offered them, collectively or individually, in return for muting their criticisms of the regime. The Prime Minister's declarations of good-will were 'non-political', i.e., they excluded his partisan opponents. Republicans could see no attraction in amelioration, for if successful, it would only strengthen the Border that divided the North from the Republic. Many Catholics did not regard economic growth as their only or prime concern. Catholics waited and waited in vain, for the reformist Prime Minister to take steps to give Catholics, whether or not loyal supporters of the regime, more effective rights as citizens, especially in local government.[61] The reaction of Unionists in Parliament and Paisleyites in the streets emphasized that little could be expected.

The first stirrings of interest in civil rights came almost concurrently with the accession of Terence O'Neill to the Prime Ministership. As is often the case, action was sparked by a particular case in a single locality—the housing of Catholics in Dungannon, County Tyrone. In 1963, Mrs. Patricia McCluskey, wife of a doctor in the town, was incensed by the unwillingness of the Protestant-dominated council to move Catholics from very overcrowded housing to a group of empty post-war utility homes far superior to their existing accommodation. She organized a Homeless Citizens League in the town and, after protests at Stormont as well as a direct action 'squat in', the Catholics were granted the tenancies they desired. In January, 1964, she and her husband, Dr. Conn McCluskey, founded the Campaign for Social Justice to collect and publicize information about cases of injustice in Northern Ireland. The Campaign was intended to remain independent of party politics, but not to refuse co-operation with individual politicians with common interests. The other founders of the group were professional people relatively free from electoral ambitions and economic pressures. Its main effort was the preparation and distribution of leaflets and pamphlets attacking discrimination against Catholics in Northern Ireland. Recourse to the duplicating machine and the post made it unostentatious within Ulster. By the same token, it gave the McCluskeys access to a wide audience in Britain. By postal efforts, the McCluskeys established contact with a number of Labour supporters who were later to become MPs. They were also active in anti-Unionist affairs in Mid-Ulster. The Campaign affiliated to the National Conference of Civil Liberties in London in 1965. With the help of the NCCL, the Northern Ireland Civil Rights Association was formed in 1967.[62]

The protest that sparked the civil rights demonstrations was undertaken by Austin Currie, a young Nationalist MP from County Tyrone. Currie was frustrated by the refusal of the Unionists to help him secure a council house in Caledon for a Catholic family living in squalor; the local council intended to let it to an unmarried 19-year-old Protestant secretary of a Unionist politician. Unionists at Stormont said they were powerless to intervene; housing was a local authority responsibility. Currie reckoned, 'If I waited a thousand years, I'd never get a better case than this one.' He organized a 'squat in' at the house on June 20, 1968. The publicity for this gesture led to a civil rights march at nearby Dungannon on August 24. It was peaceful. Its success in turn led to the scheduling of a civil rights march in Londonderry on October 5, 1968.

Londonderry, Northern Ireland's second largest city, was a crucial site for a march. From the time of the successful defence of the city against a Catholic siege in 1689, Derry* has been a symbol of resolute Protestantism. The creation of the Northern Ireland regime and partition isolated it from its natural hinterland in Donegal, three miles away at the border with the Republic. Blatant gerrymandering

---

* Derry (Gaelic, *doire*=the oak wood) was renamed Londonderry when it became a Plantation settlement under the proprietorship of the City of London in 1613. In this book, the two names are used interchangeably as appropriate for euphony and emphasis, without regard to the political implications of nomenclature.

and restrictive franchise laws resulted in a Protestant council governing a predominantly Catholic population. The civil rights group decided that their march in Derry would avoid Republican and Catholic symbols: it would concentrate instead upon claiming rights nominally those of every British subject. The decision of the Minister of Home Affairs, William Craig, to ban the march, gave its sponsors two choices–to abandon their protest or to demonstrate their refusal to accept all laws of the regime. The latter course was chosen. The Royal Ulster Constabulary reacted by treating the demonstrators roughly, including three Labour MPs from Britain present as observers. In the words of a later official enquiry, 'The police broke ranks and used their batons indiscriminately' and with 'needless violence'.[63] A total of 77 people received medical treatment. The violence of the police stimulated more demonstrations against the regime in Belfast as well as in Londonderry. On November 22, the government admitted that some grievances had validity. It announced the suspension of the Protestant-dominated local authority; the city's government was placed in the hands of a special development commission. It also pledged to establish an Ombudsman to investigate grievances against Stormont administration and to recommend new principles for allocating council houses.

Protestant Ultras promptly reacted against this concession to Catholics. At the Cathedral town of Armagh on November 30, Dr. Ian Paisley led hundreds of his supporters in a day-and-night vigil designed to prevent about 5,000 Catholic civil rights protesters from conducting a march along a route accepted by the police. Searches of Protestant counter-demonstrators at the scene found two revolvers and 220 weapons such as scythes and cudgels studded with nails. No weapons were found by police on civil rights marchers.[64] Paisley was later sentenced to a three-month prison term in consequence of the Armagh disorder.

In an effort to calm the disorder, Terence O'Neill dropped William Craig from his post as Minister of Home Affairs, and made a television appeal on December 9, 1968, for what he described as 'a continuing programme of change to secure a united and harmonious community'. He told civil rights demonstrators that they could secure change without further demonstrations; he warned that demonstrations could only lead to bloodshed. O'Neill told Protestants that 'Unionism armed merely with strength' would be less secure than 'Unionism armed with justice'.[65] The broadcast stimulated messages and petitions of endorsement bearing the signatures of approximately 150,000 people in the Province. The Unionist Party in the Stormont House of Commons gave O'Neill an overwhelming vote of confidence. A desire for party unity rather than reform motivated many Unionist MPs.

The reform measures that the Prime Minister announced in the face of two months' demonstrations contained more concessions to Catholics than had been won in 47 years of attendance and non-attendance at Stormont. Yet the measures announced did not meet the majority of the grievances enunciated by civil rights protesters. For example, there was no promise of one man, one vote, one value in local government. Most civil rights groups decided to call a truce on demonstrations at Christmas. But a group of Young Socialists, led by Michael Farrell, Kevin Boyle, and Louden Seth said they would 'break the truce' by holding a protest march from Belfast to Londonderry, starting January 1. The march was also endorsed by the People's Democracy, a group of students and former students of Queen's University, Belfast. The challenge in the march did not arise from the violation of any statutory law or ministerial order. Farrell was aware, from studying an account of Martin Luther King's march at Selma, Alabama, of the dramatic nature of exercising legal rights in parts of Northern Ireland where Protestant Ultras were known to be strong. The Minister of Home Affairs sought to talk the group out of proceeding, but he did not deem it sufficiently dangerous to ban the march.

The march to Derry began to be harassed shortly after it left Belfast. The Royal Ulster Constabulary did not regard the legality of the march as sufficient reason to exert themselves on its behalf, when militant Protestants appeared outside towns and villages, threatening their progress. The climax of the People's Democracy march occurred at Burntollet Bridge outside Londonderry. There the marchers were ambushed by an organized crowd of Protestant Ultras armed with stones and cudgels. No one was killed, but many marchers were injured as they ran the gauntlet or fled into the river for protection. RUC policemen and members of the Ulster B Special Constabulary talked congenially with the Ultras as they waited in ambush.[66] When the marchers reached Londonderry, they were again assaulted by Protestants waiting in ambush. In the weekend that followed, Royal Ulster Constabulary men entered the Catholic Bogside area of Derry, batoning men, women and children on the streets and inside their houses. In the antiseptic words of a Commission of Inquiry:

> A number of policemen were guilty of misconduct which involved assault and battery, malicious damage to property in streets in the Catholic Bogside area giving reasonable cause for apprehension of personal injury among other innocent inhabitants, and the use of provocative sectarian and political slogans. (E.g., 'Come out you Fenian bastards and we'll give you one for the Pope.')[67]

In an attempt to prove that the mass of the people of Ulster were behind his policies, Terence O'Neill called a general election in February, 1969. The result was a failure. The Prime Minister could not purge anti-O'Neill candidates in his party. The Unionists returned to the new House of Commons were divided about his leadership and about concessions to the civil rights movement. Catholic voters did not swing behind O'Neill's men. Moreover, two leading civil rights workers—John Hume and Ivan Lee Cooper—were elected in place of Nationalist MPs who had not encouraged demonstrations. In the Prime Minister's constituency of Bannside, contested for the first time in 24 years, Terence O'Neill secured re-election by a minority vote: he took 47 per cent of the poll, against 39 per cent for the Rev. Ian Paisley, and 14 per cent for Michael Farrell. In April, 1969, another marcher, Miss Bernadette Devlin, an undergraduate at Queen's University, was elected a Westminster MP at a by-election in Mid-Ulster. Further demonstrations and disorder occurred after Easter, including the dynamiting of a major public utility station outside Belfast, an act emphasizing the regime's inability to prevent disorder. On April 28, 1969, Terence O'Neill announced his resignation as Prime Minister.

The new Prime Minister (and distant cousin of Terence O'Neill) was Major James D. Chichester-Clark, who had been involved with his Protestant constituents in efforts to 're-route' the march to Londonderry. Bernadette Devlin described him as 'the nigger in the Unionist woodpile'.[68] Chichester-Clark began by seeking to conciliate the badly divided Unionist Party. An amnesty was announced in May. The new government also said that it accepted the principle of one man, one vote, one value for local government elections.

The change in Prime Ministers did not alter the persisting challenges to authority. One climax of disorder came in August, 1969. The annual march of the Apprentice Boys of Derry, commemorating the relief of the city from the siege of 1689, was scheduled to occur on August 12. It raised Catholic fears of a Protestant 'invasion' of the Bogside with the assistance or connivance of the RUC. To prevent a recurrence of this, the residents of the Bogside began making barricades with builders' supplies near at hand. Youths manufactured petrol bombs from readily available ingredients, milk bottles and petrol drained from cars or taken from storage tanks. For 48 hours, Bogsiders threw stones and petrol bombs at the Royal Ulster Constabulary. The police retaliated with teargas. The RUC was apparently under instructions from Stormont not to use 'all measures necessary' (i.e., gunfire) to force the barricades and enter the Bogside. They could and did enter the area through side streets, but they could only move about by remaining within armoured cars, required for protection from stones and petrol bombs. The exclusion of the police led people within to proclaim 'Free Derry'. The Republic's tricolour flag, the Plough and the Stars of James Connolly's Irish Workers' Republic and the American Stars and Stripes flew at various times from the tallest block of new council flats. Notwithstanding the scale of disorder, no one was killed and only a few shots were fired. The estimated bill for property damage was £1,416,000. The local dairy lost an estimated 43,000 milk bottles.[69]

News of events in Derry led Catholics in Belfast to fear that another pogrom would be launched against them. Reciprocally, Protestants feared a rising by Catholic rebels. Tension was greatest in the Falls and Shankill roads area of West Belfast. Catholics there began building barricades at street corners, even stealing doubledecker buses to use for this purpose. IRA men were asked to provide arms, but had little to offer. Protestant groups began to congregate between the Shankill and Falls roads. A relatively small number of Royal Ulster Constabulary men, armed with rifles, fully automatic weapons and armoured cars patrolled there, supported by armed members of the B Special Constabulary. Max Hastings, a British journalist at the scene, described it thus:

> The chaos grew as some lights were knocked out by stones, the fires grew bigger, and the engagement more and more widely spread out over an area more than a mile square. It will probably never be established for certain who fired the first shot.[70]

Chief Inspector David Cushley of the RUC later testified that 'a state of war' existed with Catholics in the Falls Road. The RUC opened fire. Protestant crowds surged forward, intimidating Catholics from their homes and burning groups of houses left by the Catholics. Catholics counter-attacked and fought defensive actions, but they were literally 'outgunned' by their opponents. As Mr. Justice Scarman commented later at the Tribunal of Inquiry, 'Speaking in material terms, the real burden and impact of this war fell on Catholics.' Five Catholics and two Protestants were killed in Belfast. One Catholic victim was a nine-year-old boy; he was fatally wounded by an RUC bullet that penetrated into his family's modern council flat. At a press conference afterwards, the Prime Minister blamed 'a Republican or sinister element' for the troubles. The Minister of Education, Captain Long, suggested that Catholic houses must have been burned out by their co-religionists. Catholics blamed the Prime Minister and his regime.[71]

The disorder in Londonderry and the killings in Belfast brought yet another challenge to the authority of the regime, this time from London. A contingent of 6,000 British Army troops was sent into action in the Province. A 'peace line' of corrugated iron and barbed wire was later stretched for three-quarters of a mile between Protestants and Catholics in West Belfast. Soldiers patrolled it with automatic weapons ready for use against anyone who made the first move. Major James Chichester-Clark went to London to visit the British Prime Minister and the Home Secretary, James Callaghan. Two communiqués were issued, pledging a series of reforms embracing the franchise, anti-discrimination legislation in public employment, and the allocation of houses by a central housing authority. The British Army became responsible for internal security. A three-man committee of British experts chaired by Lord Hunt advised that the RUC be disarmed and the locally commanded B Special Constabulary replaced by a new defence regiment responsible to the British Army. An independent commission headed by Lord Cameron, a Scottish judge, issued an official report that blamed the regime, rather than the demonstrators, for the original demonstrations. It concluded that civil rights grievances had a 'substantial foundation in fact and were in a very real sense an immediate and operative cause of the demonstration and consequent disorders'.[72]

The reform programme of August, 1969 represented a major development in the laws and institutions of Northern Ireland. The major assumption underlying the reforms that London recommended was that Northern Ireland had previously not been British enough in its laws. From this it was deduced that adopting more 'British-type' laws would make government in Ulster more nearly resemble that in England. The reform communiqués did not explain why Northern Ireland has previously failed to govern itself in a British manner, nor was attention given to the kind of politicians who would be responsible for the interpretation and administration of these laws, or to the political demands that would be made upon them by supporters and opponents of the regime. The reform proposals did not go into 'political' matters. The measures had to be put together in great haste after the disorders of mid-August. There were no contingency plans at hand. Even if the British government had known more about 'un-English' features of Northern Ireland politics, these were relatively unamenable to short-term change.

In sum, British policy assumed that reforms would make the system work because most people were predisposed to give allegiance to the regime. This was an act of faith, not an empirical assessment. When asked for evidence of this assumption, government spokesmen would retreat into moral exhortations or stress the impossibility of taking any other course than that they were pursuing at the moment. To doubt the efficacy of the 1969 reform programme was to be a pessimist. Oliver Wright, Downing Street's representative in Northern Ireland, emphasized the importance of optimism in an interview in March, 1970: 'The only suggestion I would make to people here is quite simply to cheer up–it is really very much better than you think.'[73] As the British Army's presence had stopped the disorder of August, 1969, there was, in his view, much to be cheerful about.

Stormont's formal endorsement of the reform programme incidentally provided Westminster with a simple argument against the introduction of direct rule from London in the most ungovernable part of the United Kingdom. It also meant that those who continued to attack the regime that endorsed the reform programme became suspect. Reginald Maudling, in his first speech as Conservative Home Secretary on July 3, 1970, told the House of Commons that in his recent trip to Northern Ireland he had met no one 'who would deny that once the programme had been completed any grievances arising from discrimination in these matters would really have been dealt with'. James Callaghan guardedly endorsed these sentiments from the Labour side. Stormont politicians put the matter more starkly. In October, 1970, the Prime Minister endorsed a speech by his Cabinet colleague, Roy Bradford, in which Bradford stated, 'When it comes to asserting the integrity of this province against attack, moderation must go hand in hand with the mailed fist.'[74] The mailed fist could be brought to bear against opponents of the regime in a matter of hours. The 1969 reform legislation inevitably requires years before its effects could be experienced and evaluated in the land.

The Stormont regime had reason to move with 'all deliberate speed' because of Protestant opposition to the 1969 reform programme. Ultras saw it as a first step toward the repudiation of the Protestant basis of the regime. Ultra reaction promptly showed itself on the Shankill Road when the disbanding of the B Specials was announced in October, 1969. There was a rising on the Shankill in which two Protestants and one policeman were killed; 16 British soldiers were wounded by thousands of rounds of Protestant gunfire directed at the defenders of the regime. The gunfire from the Protestants was also heard in Whitehall. If anything, distance magnified the effect. London realized that gunfire directed against Catholics in August, 1969 could be turned on them. Westminster wished to avoid a frontal confrontation with Protestant Ultras at all costs. The appearance of this Ultra challenge gave the Unionist Prime Minister a strong bargaining card in discussing the tempo of reforms with Whitehall. If he proceeded hastily and fell from office as a result, would Westminster like to confront his Ultra successor? In the late spring and summer of 1970 the Ultra threat grew in intensity. In April by-elections, the Rev. Ian Paisley and a fellow clergyman were elected to the Stormont House of Commons in competition with official Unionist candidates. Paisley won the seat formerly held by Terence O'Neill. In the June Westminster election, Paisley was elected to the British House of Commons too, unseating the Unionist MP, a relative of Terence O'Neill. The killing of six Protestants by Catholics in fighting in Belfast at the end of June increased the demand for 'tough' measures against the rebels. A Prime Minister concerned with keeping his party united had no choice but to conciliate 'hardline' Unionist MPs. The appearance of Protestant MPs outside Unionist ranks reduced the amount of support that Chichester-Clark could afford to lose within his diminished ranks and still remain Prime Minister.

The armed attacks upon Catholics in Belfast in August, 1969, greatly altered the character of Catholic challenges to the regime. In effect, the Royal Ulster Constabulary brought the gun back into Northern Ireland politics. Much Catholic energy that had formerly gone into civil rights activities was redirected to citizens' defence groups under other leaders. These groups sought guns from IRA contacts and from the Republic of Ireland. The point of view was clearly expressed by Samuel Dowling, the Chairman of the Newry and District Civil Rights Association, at his trial in the Republic for being in possession of three sub-machine-guns, a ·303 rifle, a bomb, three and one-quarter pounds of gelignite and sundry other arms.

> Those weapons were in our possession, were at that time in my possession, through the work of officers and agents of the Irish Government. I myself negotiated with some of those agents, and it was made clear between us that such arms would be used only for defence of those minority communities in the North when under attack. . . .
>
> I submit to the court that to fail to provide us with these weapons for these limited purposes would have been a crime. For us not to have disciplined and trained ourselves in their use would have been a crime.[75]

Dowling spoke freely about the source of arms for by the time of his arrest and trial a Dublin court had already acquitted four men–two of them Irish government officials–for their involvement in attempts to import £100,000 of arms to the North. Dowling was acquitted too.

Catholic protests against the reformed but still exclusively Protestant Chichester-Clark regime were expressed in parliamentary and extra-parliamentary ways. At the June, 1970 Westminster general election, Bernadette Devlin was again elected MP for Mid-Ulster, and Frank MacManus, the brother of an IRA man killed in the 1950s, was elected MP from Fermanagh and South Tyrone. Later in the summer civil rights MPs joined together to form a Social Democratic and Labour Party, to provide a 'British-type' opposition at Stormont The appearance of the SDLP did not, however, eliminate the old 'Irish-type' issues from their concern. The accession of new recruits to the IRA and splits within the IRA encouraged extra-parliamentary groups to turn to direct-action methods of creating disturbances. The truce between Catholics and the British Army was first breached on April 2–3, 1970, by riots at the Ballymurphy council house estate on the edge of West Belfast.[76]

It was clear by April, 1970, that the British Army's duty of keeping peace in Northern Ireland gave no indication of ending. The General Officer Commanding, Lieutenant-General Sir Ian Freeland, showed his irritation in a television interview warning that the people of Northern Ireland would have to start trying to solve their own problems, because the Army could not remain there forever. In the same period, he announced a 'get tough' policy, threatening to shoot demonstrators throwing petrol bombs. An IRA spokesman promptly issued a statement threatening to shoot British soldiers in reprisal if Irishmen were killed. The Protestant Ulster Volunteer Force, not to be outdone, offered to shoot a Catholic in return for every British soldier shot by the IRA.[77]

A joint Army-RUC raid for arms in the Lower Falls Road area on July 3, 1970, gave the British Army a chance to demonstrate its new approach. Previously, the Army had been attacked as being 'neutral for the Catholics' just as the RUC was regarded as 'neutral on the Protestant side'. The Army found 50 pistols, 26 rifles, 5 sub-machine-guns and 25,000 rounds of ammunition in its house-to-house search of approximately 3,000 homes. Protestants were pleased with the demonstration that 'law and order' was once again being enforced against Catholics. The methods used showed Catholics the Army's power. In response to Catholic stoning, the Army initially threw teargas and refused to negotiate with local priests who offered to act as intermediaries to calm the situation. A total of 2,000 troops were committed against an area containing approximately 15,000 Catholics. After shooting started, the Army declared a curfew. Ironically, the previous August, General Freeland had dismissed the idea of a curfew with the remark, 'What do you do if people disobey it ? Shoot them ?' In the Lower Falls a year later, his soldiers killed four people.[78] Catholics were shocked and angered by this indication that the British Army was now 'neutral on the Protestant side'.

Continued disorder disturbed Protestants fearful for the future of their regime. But perceptive supporters noted that after passage of the 1969 reforms, there need be no weakening of the Unionists' monopoly of power—as long as the party remained united electorally. Moreover, the reduction in the duties of local authorities would actually enhance the power of Stormont. The regime would decide which Catholics would sit as minority members of the post-reform housing and police authorities; it would also determine which Catholics would be excluded as 'undesirable' if not 'unrepresentative'. Once the reforms were enacted, Catholics would no longer appear as an aggrieved minority in the eyes of Westminster; they might remain an ineffective minority. The actions of frustrated and fissiparous Republican groups made Westminster aware that there might also remain a dangerous minority. In the first ten weeks of 1971, 21 people were killed in political violence; most were Protestants. IRA groups, using machine guns, rifles, and bombs, killed British soldiers, RUC men, civilians, suspected informers and, upon occasion, each other.

The period since the arrival of the British Army to maintain peace had thus become the bloodiest time in Northern Ireland since the end of the Troubles in the 1920s. In the five years of Terence O'Neill's government, only three persons died in disorder; none died during ten months of civil rights demonstrations from October, 1968. In summer, 1969, 15 people were killed. In nine months after the return of violence in late June, 1970, at least 39 persons have died, nearly all men of fighting age. Both sides have had ample cause to mourn their dead and each can point the finger of accusation at the other. Of the first 54 dead, 30 have been Protestants and 24 Catholics. MPs at Westminster have had a taste of Northern Ireland trouble too. In July, 1970, a visitor at a debate threw CS teargas canisters onto the floor of the Commons, shouting, 'Now you know what it's like in Belfast'.[79]

In 1971, exactly 800 years from the date that Henry II came from England to assert personally his claim to the Lordship of Ireland, the land contained the most ungovernable territory of the Crown. Perhaps the most apt comment about the place of Northern Ireland was made by Sir Edward Carson, one of its founding fathers. In a speech in 1914 in opposition to Home Rule, Carson told Westminster:

> I know very well that the motto of every government – it is pasted outside every Department – is 'Peace in our time, O Lord'. But you do not get rid of the difficulty – be it today or tomorrow or a year hence, or be it six years hence. The difficulty will remain, and Ulster will be a physical and geographical fact.[80]

IV · Institutions of Discord

It is quite plain that ordinary laws calculated for civilized communities are not applicable to a country so circumstanced.
EARL OF RODEN, *Report of Select Committee on the State of Ireland, 1835*

Anyone who isn't confused here doesn't really understand what is going on.
BELFAST CITIZEN, *The Times, 1970*

In a fully legitimate regime, civil administration, the law and coercive institutions will all contribute to the same result–popular allegiance–because by definition there is no opposition to the regime. In a regime that lacks full legitimacy, the effect of each institution is problematic. The institutions of law may encourage disorder, civil administration can be ignored in the absence of coercive threats, and coercion may fail to coerce. In Northern Ireland, the chief political institutions are such institutions of discord.

The extent of discord in Northern Ireland is most dramatically demonstrated by the regime's lack of a monopoly of powers of coercion. If a monopoly of force is regarded as a defining characteristic of the state, the absence of a monopoly would mean that there is no state, but only a congeries of institutions competing for recognition as the regime. The Royal Ulster Constabulary (the RUC) is responsible to the Stormont regime. The British Army, which undertakes the 'heavy' work of coercion, is responsible to Westminster. Armed Ultra groups owe allegiance to the doctrine of Protestant supremacy. Members of the several Irish Republican Armies impartially repudiate the claim of both the Stormont and Dublin regimes to allegiance, in the name of 'the people of Ireland'.

To anatomize the institutions supporting and opposing the Stormont regime risks both oversimplification and over-elaboration. For example, it is an oversimplification to describe groups as Protestant or Catholic, in so far as churches usually refrain from explicit political statements. None the less, churchgoers continue to undertake political action in sectarian groups. In such circumstances, the

The historical present tense in this chapter refers to Northern Ireland at the beginning of the 1970s. Only exceptionally are there references to events occurring after January 21, 1971.

113

use of religious labels has at least as much justification and relevance as references to 'right' and 'left' in societies where economic issues predominate. To generalize about a political institution also means overlooking differences among individuals who belong to it. Disagreements concerning short-term tactics as well as long-term goals are endemic in any political group. In some instances, differences may arise from conflicts of personality and ambition. Terence O'Neill, for example, was particularly vulnerable to challenge from his most able Cabinet minister, Brian Faulkner, because O'Neill had little personal following within his Cabinet and Faulkner had ambitions to succeed O'Neill. When institutional goals and activities persist for decades or generations, it is impossible to dismiss them as reflecting *ad hoc* personal considerations. Long-lived groups themselves 'institutionalize' values and beliefs influencing those who become members.

Describing a collection of people by reference to an institutional label may make the group appear much more elaborate and powerful than it actually is. This is particularly likely in Northern Ireland, for the small population of the land reduces the scale of all institutions, by comparison with Britain or America. For example, the Northern Ireland Liberal Party launched its manifesto for the 1965 Stormont election at a meeting held in a vacant house in Belfast attended by two Liberals and three reporters. If all the active members of the Irish Republican Army were ever assembled in one place at one time, an unlikely event, they would not require a massive parade ground. They could almost certainly fit in less than half a football field. For that matter, the Cabinet of the Stormont regime could be contained in two taxis. Smallness of size is no guarantee of simplicity. As long as an organization has at least two members there is always the possibility of two different points of view being put forward in its name, or even more if one of the pair is changeable in his outlook.

The politics of the Province is carried on in a society so small that many important political relationships can be based upon an extended network of personal ties. The population of Northern Ireland is one-third less than that of metropolitan Glasgow or St. Louis. In times of trouble, Catholics in the Falls Road area of Belfast can turn to friends, neighbours and relations for leadership and help; the total census population of the ward is 34,840, and it is 91 per cent Catholic. Similarly, Protestants in the adjoining Shankill Road area can also turn to their neighbours to decide informally what to do.

The census population of the Shankill is 31,932 and it is 91 per cent Protestant.[1] In such circumstances, a group can assemble to build a barricade or throw stones and petrol bombs on very short notice, without regard to the wishes of their nominal representatives and leaders. Intimacy is specially important in violent activities directed against the regime. A pub or a house can be burned out by a single individual under cover of darkness. A bombing attack upon a public building requires no more than gelignite and wiring, a man to set the fuse, another to drive the car and perhaps a third to act as a lookout.

Institutions are none the less of great importance in the politics of a divided regime because they give meaning and direction to political activity. The chief institutions of Northern Ireland politics set the alternatives within which an individual must act, if he wishes to extend his personal influence beyond his friends and neighbours. The alternatives that the institutions represent are not complementary in character. Instead, they offer Ulster people the choice of competing regimes.

Stormont and Westminster

The institutions inherited from the past provide a mixture of advantages and disadvantages in governing Northern Ireland. The most conspicuous inheritance has been a tradition of separate and distinct institutions for the government of Ireland. Until the merger of the Kingdoms of Ireland and Great Britain in 1801, there was an entirely separate Irish state, joined with Britain by real and coerced allegiance to a common crown. Even when the Parliament of Westminster was the sole legislative authority for Ireland in the nineteenth century, there was a separate administrative headquarters for Ireland at Dublin Castle, responsible to the British Cabinet through the Chief Secretary for Ireland. Ireland thus enjoyed substantial autonomy far later and to a far greater extent than Scotland, which had experienced a legally analogous Union a century before.[2] Many of the distinctive legislative and administrative measures introduced in Ireland were pioneering and progressive, whether they concerned planning, welfare, the abridgment of rights in property or the maintenance of public order.[3] In general, the major features of British government prevailed. As a consequence, the institutions of government in Northern Ireland today, as in the Republic, usually resemble their British counterparts. In view of the attention given the pathology of the regime in this volume, it is important to empha-size that most of its political institutions and procedures are familiar throughout the Anglo-American world.[4] Whatever their political outlooks, Ulster people do not desire authoritarian rule or the dis-orderly advent of a charismatic leader. Opposition is not directed at parliamentary institutions, but at the conception of the regime. The challenges are justified by appeal to what one constitutional lawyer has described as 'higher considerations than legality'.[5]

The constitutional status of Northern Ireland is anomalous, even within the context of a Commonwealth of Nations that contains many anomalies. Formally, Northern Ireland is a part of the United Kingdom. It has a written constitution, the Government of Ireland Act, passed by Westminster in 1920. That Act presupposed a com-plicated tripartite arrangement of governments in Belfast and Dublin, plus a Council of Ireland for both. The fact that Stormont was the only one of the three sets of institutions to be established is a remin-der that the intent of the framers of its Constitution was never achieved. One might alternatively argue that stillbirth at least avoided death of the proposed federal institutions in infancy, for one expert comments, 'Among all the uncertainties embedded in the tortuous history of Anglo-Irish relations, one thing seems certain: none of the Liberal Home Rule bills would have worked in Ireland.'[6]

By the terms of Stormont's Constitution, it lacks the formal status of a traditionally independent state, a British Dominion, or an ex-colonial country such as the United States of America. The Government of Ireland Act explicitly states in section 75, 'the supreme authority of the Parliament of the United Kingdom shall remain unaffected and undiminished over all persons, matters and things in Ireland and every part thereof'. The Anglo-Irish Treaty of 1921 diminished the Crown's power in 26 counties of Ireland. Decisions of the Privy Council in the 1920s further confined the powers of Westminster. The Privy Council ruled, in effect, that the Governor, the Queen's representative in Northern Ireland, could not issue orders in response to instructions given by the Crown on the advice of the Prime Minister of Great Britain.[7] The implication of the ruling was that while the Westminster government retained the power to suspend or abolish the Northern Ireland regime, it did not have the power to give it legally binding executive directives about matters delegated there. In this respect, Stormont enjoys greater legal inde-pendence than Scotland of Wales, or a colony in which the Governor has a variety of emergency powers. This narrow construction of the Governor's powers has been maintained by the appointment to the post of men who have no wish to exercise an independent influence upon Stormont. It has been further reinforced by rulings of the Speaker of the British House of Commons, holding that most political matters concerning Northern Ireland, such as charges of religious discrimination, may not be discussed at Westminster because they are the responsibility of the Northern Ireland Parliament.[8] They may only be raised at Stormont. These rulings have left Westminster with the 'blockbuster' power of abolishing the Stormont regime, but with few other formal powers.

Because the United Kingdom has never been a federal government, there is no corpus of law governing relationships between Stormont and what is known in Ulster as the 'Imperial Parliament' at Westminster. In Canada, Australia and the United States, the federal character of the whole of government requires a clear explication of the respective rights and duties of the several parts, and the position of the subject in relation to each part of the federal regime. The absence of any other part of the United Kingdom like Northern Ireland has meant that its relationships with Westminster have evolved with limited attention at Westminster. History and convenience have both argued strongly for the removal of as much responsibility as possible to Ulster. The Stormont regime not only enjoys a substantial block of transferred powers, but also powers of administration for the majority of services directly affecting the lives of Ulster people. This means that even if Westminster legislates on matters for Northern Ireland it will lack the means to carry out its will through its own officials. In the formative decades for developing conventions regulating relations between Westminster and Stormont, the Imperial regime sought to retain only a few powers affecting external affairs and money. This allocation of responsibilities was acceptable to Stormont, because these were not the powers that most interested the government of Northern Ireland.

The desire of Westminster to control the external affairs of Northern Ireland arose from the traditional British wish to prevent Ireland from falling into an alliance with an enemy power. Both World Wars emphasized the value of Ulster ports and latterly, air bases for patrolling North Atlantic waters and protecting Allied shipping from German submarines. Stormont had no desire to negotiate with far-off foreign powers. Its most important external relationship concerned the close-at-hand Republic of Ireland. It is not an exaggeration to describe the meeting between the Prime Ministers of the two regimes in 1965 as a summit conference. In terms of antiquity, the Cold War between Belfast and Dublin is far older than that between Washington and Moscow. The Ireland Act of 1949 gives Stormont an assurance that its boundary with the Republic will not be altered by unilateral negotiations between London and Dublin; the Stormont Parliament retains a veto power over any agreement that London might reach. It also has some overseas programmes, principally to increase trade. In efforts to develop tourism and attract industry, Stormont has opened offices in London and New York. In travels abroad, Northern Ireland ministers receive attention and enjoy plenipotentiary powers far beyond that of an English local government figure.

The interest of Westminster in the tax policies of Stormont comes from a desire to ensure that no customs barrier could arise within the United Kingdom, nor could Northern Ireland be a tax haven for British subjects or foreign manufacturers. Westminster therefore retained the bulk of taxing powers, and itself collects the great bulk of taxes paid in Northern Ireland. (The Inland Revenue and the Post Office are the chief 'Imperial' administrative agencies in Ulster.) Stormont has relatively minor taxing powers, covering such things as death duties and motor vehicle licences. Powers of expenditure are held by the Stormont regime, which has its own Ministry of Finance, annual budget and, when things are going badly, its own emergency budgets too. These powers are exercised in accordance with the principle that the economy of Northern Ireland should be integrated with that of Britain. One implication of this is that Stormont accepts commitments to Welfare State expenditure on the same scale as Britain, passing such legislation on a 'step by step' basis. A second basic principle is that Northern Ireland has obligations and privileges in the budget of the United Kingdom. The obligation of the Stormont government is to make a contribution to the United Kingdom exchequer representing the Province's share of Imperial services, such as defence and the national debt. The privilege is that Stormont can draw upon United Kingdom resources to compensate for sub-standard tax revenues, as would any other depressed area of the United Kingdom, whether in Scotland, Lancashire or the East End of London. Northern Ireland is the net beneficiary from this financial arrangement; its claim for financial assistance far outweighs the notional sum it is charged for Imperial services. Northern Ireland economists refer to these arrangements as the maintenance of parity; others less favourably disposed to the regime call it a subsidy.[9]

It is often mistakenly stated that Northern Ireland is financially dependent upon Britain. This misstates the case. To be precise, one must say that the present standard of living of the people of Northern Ireland depends in part upon financial grants from the British government. The sum is substantial by any reckoning, but it is not in a literal sense 'vital'. Even without British grants, the *per capita* income of Ulster would be higher than that in the Republic of Ireland. (This would be true *a fortiori* if a Stormont regime without British financial assistance curtailed welfare expenditure at the expense of disaffected Catholics.) In 1968–69, Stormont put the value of British financial assistance at £78·1 million, i.e., £52 a person. Much of this money is allocated for payments to farmers, the unemployed and recipients of welfare benefits. In the same year, the Prime Minister, Terence O'Neill, publicly estimated the value of aid at £100,000,000. Other estimates of Stormont's financial aid from Britain range as high as £140,000,000 annually.[10] Even at its highest, the transfer payment is less than that which the British Treasury claims is given, notionally if not in fact, to Scotland.[11] Just as Northern Ireland's beneficial dependence upon London is not unique within the United Kingdom, so the London-based economy is itself interdependent with America and Europe, and sometimes in receipt of benefits therefrom.

The institutional arrangements linking Stormont and Westminster were simple and slight because prior to 1968, 'there was little inclination on the part of London to intervene when the financial aspect was of minor importance'.[12] Economic matters could be reviewed annually when financial payments had to be negotiated. The General Department of the Home Office was technically responsible for liaison with Northern Ireland. Northern Ireland was not the only or the primary concern of successive Home Secretaries. In the 1960s, for example, Home Secretaries were primarily concerned with problems of coloured immigration and race relations as well as with a range of issues of crime and punishment. Northern Ireland was one of the Secretary of State's minor concerns, like the regulation of London taxis and the Crown's relations with the Channel Islands or Isle of Man. The distance between London and Belfast was a formidable barrier to communication for the first two generations of

Stormont's existence, since Belfast was then a lengthy train and boat ride away, rather than an 80-minute flight. There was little demand in the House of Commons for Ministers to involve themselves in Ulster affairs. Northern Ireland has always sent an overwhelmingly Unionist group of MPs to Westminster. They had no wish to question their regime away from home. Opponents of the regime often refused to recognize the claim of the Crown to Northern Ireland, and thus disqualified themselves from attending Parliament. The disinterest of London in the affairs of the Stormont regime is shown by the fact that even as late as September, 1968, the Home Office had no civil servant devoting fulltime attention to Northern Ireland affairs, and by October, 1969, its complement had only risen to two fulltime men.

After initial anxieties arising from a fear of abandonment, Ulster Protestants have come to regard Stormont as an ideal form of government. In its 1970 submission to the Royal Commission on the United Kingdom Constitution, the Ulster Unionist Council stressed that Stormont provided for greater accessibility of MPs and civil servants to constituents by virtue of the size of the Province. The Unionists also emphasized the promptness with which Stormont could act on matters of particular concern to Northern Ireland, and vary legislation, administration and economic policies in keeping with local needs. The only reference to discord about the regime came in an oblique historical reference, stating that adverse comments about Stormont often reflect an 'under-estimation of the gravity of those factors . . . which are unlikely to have effect anywhere else in the United Kingdom'.[13] The formal submission also neglected to emphasize other features that make it popular with Northern Ireland Protestants, such as the autonomy traditionally granted Stormont in dealing with rebels against its authority, and the financial benefits derived from being an integral part of the United Kingdom. In consequence of all this, Northern Ireland Protestants appear to regard Stormont more than Westminster as 'their' government. In colloquial speech, reference to the government usually implies the Northern Ireland regime. Its permanence is symbolized by the massive stone buildings at Stormont, where Parliament and Cabinet meet. The most prominent feature of the mile-long approach to the buildings from the main road is a massive statue of Sir Edward Carson in a posture evoking the Ulster motto: No surrender.

The return of a British Labour government in 1964 brought to Westminster a group of backbench Labour MPs interested in Ulster affairs and sympathetic to the Catholic minority. The Campaign for Democracy in Ulster was founded in 1965, under the chairmanship of a new MP, Paul Rose, to call public attention to civil rights issues in Northern Ireland. The group was handicapped in raising issues in the House of Commons by the Speaker repeatedly ruling that many matters were only appropriate to debate at Stormont. The Labour government showed no desire to reduce the autonomy of the Stormont regime. The reform orientation of Terence O'Neill made it politically plausible for Roy Jenkins, speaking as Home Secretary in October, 1967, to argue that trusting the O'Neill government was a desirable as well as necessary policy. In private, Harold Wilson hinted to the critics of Stormont that in the last resort Westminster could always act if it was deemed necessary.[14] This *laissez-faire* policy was entirely acceptable at Stormont. The civil rights demonstrations of October, 1968, supported by a few backbench Labour MPs, called attention to the distance that the Stormont regime would have to travel to meet British critics. O'Neill found it increasingly difficult to make statements that would satisfy both Protestant Ultras in Northern Ireland and Labour MPs in London. His failure to win electoral endorsement in February, 1969, undermined Labour's policy of trust in one man to resolve Ulster's problems. It also increased the risk that events might force London to intervene in Ulster against the wishes of the Labour government. Ministers sought to forestall involvement by issuing cautious statements and trusting the Stormont regime to avoid default. Civil rights MPs appealed to the Home Office to act, but their appeals were politely turned down. On August 12, 1969, when the Apprentice Boys paraded in Londonderry and the Bogside rose, the Prime Minister, the Foreign Secretary and the Home Secretary were all on holiday.

The rising in the Bogside and the killings and arson in Belfast so publicized disorder and disaffection in Northern Ireland that London's 'holiday' from involvement was abruptly ended. London was forced to act, and act without any contingency plans or staff experience in Northern Ireland affairs. 'At the request' of Stormont, London provided troops to maintain order in the Province. The despatch of the Army was not accompanied by a suspension of the Constitution. Instead, London sought to influence events by working through established institutions. There was intervention in civilian affairs too. On August 19, Major Chichester-Clark met in London with Harold Wilson; a joint communiqué affirmed Chichester-

Clark's commitment to reforms. Eight days later the Home Secretary, James Callaghan, made an official visit to Northern Ireland to meet a wide range of political figures, including Protestant Ultras and disaffected Republicans. In an unprecedented step, Callaghan met twice with the Northern Ireland Cabinet. At the end of the visit, the Stormont government issued a communiqué pledging a more extensive set of reforms.[15] British civil servants began to visit Belfast to see drafts of reform legislation and to supervise changes in the police. In addition, an Office of the United Kingdom Representative in Northern Ireland was opened, to keep watch on progress with reforms, and to provide political intelligence.

In consequence of its intervention in 1969, the British government became heavily committed to the reform of Northern Ireland government. The commitment was in its own interest, for it was reckoned that only the passage of the reform package would make it possible to withdraw or reduce the use of British troops in Ulster, by meeting Catholic grievances behind disorder. Simultaneously, London also became committed to defending Stormont with the full force of the British Army. Stormont welcomed this in so far as it provided manpower and weapons far superior to those of the RUC. Republicans reacted against a policy of 'mere reform'. By February, 1971, they sought to test how much force Britain would use to defend the Stormont regime. Reform had become *passé*.

The limited extent of London's intervention in Northern Ireland politics is shown by the size and character of the civil staff it has. The absence of an MP as Minister in residence is not of any consequence, for no senior British politician would wish to be assigned to the 'graveyard' of Northern Ireland politics. And on important matters, only a senior politician would be listened to in London. The choice of Foreign Office men (Oliver Wright, and then Ronald Burroughs) rather than home civil servants as the first London representatives in Northern Ireland symbolizes the extent to which the work is more analogous to that of an ambassador than to that of a district commissioner in a colony or a general during a state of martial law. Just as ambassadors have no legal authority to take decisions in their host country, so the United Kingdom representative has no power to issue directives to the Prime Minister and Cabinet of Northern Ireland. The representative has simply the right to be consulted on executive matters being considered by the Northern Ireland Cabinet. Freedom from a home civil service outlook means that the representative is almost encouraged to talk to a wide range of politicians and civic figures outside official channels, including persons opposed to the regime. Moreover, an ambassador need not hesitate in putting strongly his home government's point of view. Because Northern Ireland affairs not only concern the Home Office, but also directly affect the Treasury, the Foreign Office (the link with the Republic of Ireland) and the Ministry of Defence, a considerable amount of paperwork is involved in dealing with this disparate number of Whitehall departments. To supervise this, the Home Office in January, 1971 maintained a staff of 20, including one Under-Secretary and two assistant secretaries. At the Conway Hotel in Belfast, Britain had a staff of two, plus a secretary. The staffing ratios appropriately symbolize the desire of London to minimize involvement in Northern Ireland for the sake of the 'credibility' of the Stormont regime and, even more, to assure that its own responsibilities will not be further enlarged.

The absence of a large British staff in Northern Ireland does not mean that Whitehall takes no interest in what happens in Ulster. The intervention of British troops has made the whole of Whitehall more Northern Ireland conscious from the Prime Minister down. In some respects this is advantageous to Stormont. It means that they now have more people in London to give assistance, and their needs are more likely to get special attention. At times of crisis, Northern Ireland affairs 'jump the queue', with immediate and personal attention by the Home Secretary, a senior Cabinet committee, or the Prime Minister. Attention switched on quickly can also be turned off quickly, when senior individuals are busy elsewhere.

Even with information, the British government is legally powerless to act directly to affect events in Northern Ireland, short of the blunderbuss weapon of suspending the Constitution. It may offer advice, but Stormont may ignore its advice. The contrasting political pressures are neatly illustrated by the problems that arose in obtaining an official enquiry into the death of Samuel Devenney of Londonderry in July, 1969. The cause of death, according to the inquest, was a coronary attack. The fact that Devenney and other members of his family had been beaten by members of the RUC in an attack in their own home in April made his funeral a political event witnessed by 15,000 people. Civil rights groups in Ulster promptly demanded an investigation of the assault. In December, 1969, four months after London had become involved in Ulster matters, the RUC reported that it had 'carried out a wide-ranging investigation which had almost completely negative results' about the assault on Devenney. The finding was politically convenient for Stormont, in view of the low morale of the RUC at the time, and the importance of the police to Ultras. The decision of a Northern Ireland court to award three members of the Devenney family damages for injuries suffered from an RUC assault was announced on March 13, 1970. It was politically embarrassing both for Stormont and London. Stormont did not want to reopen the investigation, but London found it difficult to explain why no further action was taken. At Westminster, the Speaker refused to allow an adjournment debate on the subject and the Leader of the House said 'there is no ministerial responsibility here for that case'. In protest, Bernadette Devlin camped outside 10 Downing Street overnight, in the company of press photographers. Harold Wilson could only state publicly that 'there is adequate machinery' for dealing with complaints. It took additional lobbying by Westminster in Northern Ireland before the British Prime Minister could tell the House of Commons that 'on his own initiative' the head of the RUC had now asked for Scotland Yard to make a second enquiry.[16] Scotland Yard had no difficulty in finding evidence of police brutality.[17]

In balancing relationships between Westminster and Stormont, the chief power of the former is a weapon that threatens damage to its user: direct rule. Legally, Westminster could easily abolish the Northern Ireland Constitution, for it is an act of the British Parliament, and assume powers in Northern Ireland analogous to those in Scotland, Wales and England.[18] Politically, direct rule would alter and perhaps intensify, but not remove causes of discord. At all times both Conservative and Labour leaders have made avoiding direct rule a major object of their Northern Ireland policy. It often appears to be *the* major objective. Seen in this light, the delegated and discretionary powers given Stormont have the great advantage of keeping the Northern Ireland problem from the British Cabinet and Commons. The overwhelming majority of British politicians do not wish to devote their scarce time and political resources to a problem that touches only a very small part of the United Kingdom. The fact that the problem may be insoluble–or at the least, involves grave risks and difficulties–is a further disincentive for involvement. The existence of a Stormont Parliament, albeit one created by Westminster, is an additional political obstacle to direct rule. It would mean supplanting an 'elected' government by an authority that was primarily responsible to British not Ulster voters.

The commitment of the British government to the 1969 reform package has complicated Westminster's position. In August, 1970, the Home Secretary, Reginald Maudling, publicly warned that 'To go back on what has been done or to depart from the ideal of impartiality and reconciliation, would endanger the present constitutional arrangements under which Northern Ireland governs its own affairs.'[19] In short, repudiation of reforms by a Stormont government *could* lead to the suspension of the Northern Ireland Constitution. For this to happen, the Stormont Cabinet would have to repudiate reform measures openly and unambiguously. This, it should be noted, is not the only way by which reforms or their consequences may be subverted. For the British government of the day to decide in ambiguous circumstances that reforms had been abandoned would be to take the initiative to increase involvement in Northern Ireland. This is a step it has never willingly taken.

The desire to avoid confrontation with Stormont has been succinctly explained by James Callaghan. The maintenance of the Stormont regime, he said, permitted reforms to be carried out by 'the people of Ireland themselves'. The alternative would be for them to be 'enforced by British soldiers' against a million Protestants who 'wish to govern themselves'. This would have as its consequence 'bloodshed on the streets of Northern Ireland'. His Conservative successor, Reginald Maudling, concurred, describing direct rule as 'one of the last things that any British government would want to contemplate'.[20] As long as Protestants or Catholics, or both, are prepared to risk bloodshed and London is loath to accept this risk, then Northern Ireland rather than London institutions will always sound the dominant note amidst the discord. For London to dominate, it must be willing, if need be, to assert its claims by force.

Laws and Order

One responsibility that the Government of Ireland Act has placed unambiguously in the hands of Stormont is responsibility for law and law enforcement. Viewed from London, there are good reasons for these powers to be left in the hands of Stormont. The chief one is that

Institutions of Discord

Northern Ireland, since the creation of the United Kingdom in 1801, has always been governed by criminal laws formulated and administered for Irish conditions. Recurring sectarian, agricultural and insurrectionary activities required exceptional legal treatment from the time that Ireland joined the United Kingdom until new regimes were established in Dublin and Belfast. The delegation of this responsibility has had critics. For example, Professor Thomas Wilson, an economic adviser to the Stormont regime, suggests that there would be some truth in the assertion:

> Stormont has been free from interference in cases where interference would have been most justified (i.e., citizens' rights and law enforcement) but has been unduly restrained in dealing with certain other matters (e.g., financial policy) that should be the core of Provincial autonomy.[21]

Responsibility for law enforcement does not confer upon those responsible the means to enforce laws. Nor does it assure that the actions taken to secure enforcement will conform to 'the rule of law' as that term is used in discussions remote from the realities of Belfast. In a fully legitimate regime, there is no problem of political crime for hardly anyone is predisposed to violate basic political laws: there is a consensus about obedience and support for the regime. Any individual who breaks the consensus will be tried and punished by a regime secure in its position. In a divided regime, the law operates without consensus. By definition, there is no agreement about what political laws ought to be obeyed. In the eyes of rebels, the illegality of an act may even be a positive recommendation, expressing or intensifying their challenge to the regime. The Irish Republican Army, which does not recognize either the Stormont or the Dublin regimes as legitimate, provides an extreme example of welcoming discord. When arrested and tried, IRA members refuse to recognize the court. A judgment of guilty and punishment is accepted by IRA men as the logical response of an inimical and illegitimate regime.

In the adversary form of legal proceedings used in Northern Ireland, as elsewhere in the Anglo-American world, there are always two points of view–the view of the enforcer of the law and the view of the alleged violator. The procedures of the courts are based upon the assumption that there are two sides to any case. When the trial concerns a political offence, the jury may make up its mind in accordance with points of law and fact legally admissible in the court

Institutions of Discord

room. But there is no assurance that anyone else will use the same procedure to evaluate the case. Politically, the defendant is not the only person on trial. The agents of law enforcement are also on trial. In a fully legitimate regime, diffuse allegiance predisposes individuals to find in favour of the agents of law enforcement. But in a divided regime, some subjects will be predisposed to find the convicted person innocent and the courts guilty. This will especially be the case if the act treated as a crime by the regime, e.g., the wearing of 'the green', an Easter lily or some other symbolic gesture of Republicanism, is regarded as a proud and virtuous act by the disaffected.

In every society, the agents of the law to some extent act 'as a legitimizer or an illegitimizer of particular actions'.[22] The end actions and their consequences are contingent, not automatic, for an element of discretion enters into every stage of the legal process, from the drafting of a statute defining a crime through a policeman's decision to arrest a suspect to the verdict, sentence and the claim for clemency. One could hypothesize that agents of the regime will always give it the benefit of the doubt in cases of political crime, and opponents of the regime will never give the law the benefit of the doubt. Father Denis Faul, a Dungannon priest, has summed up the problem succinctly. 'Our people are afraid of the courts. They believe the judicial system as it operates in the blatantly sectarian conditions of life here is loaded against them.' What is even more striking is that he admits that 'whether this is based on fact or not' is less important than whether a substantial proportion of Catholics believe the law is politically biased.[23] Scepticism about the law's absence of bias in discretionary legal decisions is not confined to Catholics. Protestants such as the Rev. Ian Paisley also voice suspicion of the courts and other agents of the law. Put crudely, an Ultra is inclined to believe that any Catholic brought to court (and many who are not) are guilty of rebellion, whatever the charge, evidence, or verdict, and a rebel will be inclined to believe the same in reverse about an Ultra.

The extent to which the law enforcement agencies are institutions of discord can be demonstrated unequivocally by going through each stage of law enforcement and noting whether there are disagreements about the exercise of discretionary powers and whether these disagreements reflect discordant views of the Stormont regime. The stages include the following: the enactment of statutes defining crimes; the exercise of ministerial discretion in issuing statutory orders; decisions about whether a crime has been committed and about making an arrest; decisions to prosecute; the granting or refusal of bail; conduct of trial; judge's decision or jury verdict; problems of evidence; sentencing and provisions for remitting sentences. Any such review inevitably focuses upon unusual, even extreme cases. These *causes célèbres* are not representative of all criminal cases in Northern Ireland. Yet because they are celebrated, they gain in political significance.

Theoretically, there are an infinite number of things that Stormont might deem a crime by statutory enactment. In practice, controversy normally concerns Westminster laws that Stormont has failed to enact, and, reciprocally, measures that Stormont has passed that have no counterpart in a Westminster statute. Just as there are critics within Westminster of any bill passed or defeated there, so too there is criticism in Stormont of its legislative acts of omission and commission. In Northern Ireland, the argument has added piquancy, because there are those who argue that the value of devolution lies in the power of Stormont to vary legislation to meet local needs, just as their critics argue that the value of British citizenship is that residents of Ulster—whether fully allegiant or not—should enjoy the same legislation as citizens elsewhere. Among acts of omission, the most relevant here as a source of discord is the failure of Stormont to adopt for Northern Ireland provisions of the Race Relations Act applicable in Britain, extended to cover cases of religious discrimination. The policy of both Labour and Conservative governments at Westminster is that such a measure is the responsibility of the Northern Ireland Parliament.[24] At Stormont, Unionists have argued that such a measure is either not necessary or not appropriate in the circumstances of the Province.

Of all the statutes enacted in Northern Ireland, the most controversial has been the Special Powers Act, passed in 1922 and subsequently amended and extended. It was designed primarily to repress the IRA and Republican groups. The Act authorizes the Minister of Home Affairs 'to take all such steps and issue all such orders as may be necessary for preserving the peace and order'. It also provides that an action may be deemed 'prejudicial to the preservation of the peace or maintenance of order' even if not specified in the regulations. In law, the Special Powers Act removes any grounds for dispute about the exercise of discretionary powers by making large blanket grants of authority, including the power to intern a man for years without trial or relief of habeas corpus. The necessity for such an act has been argued strongly. A Northern Ireland constitutional authority, Harry Calvert, concludes, 'Whatever evil has been created by the Special Powers Act is a necessary evil, or even if not necessary, at least the lesser of two immediately obvious ones.' The Act has the endorsement of the British government too, for it is modelled upon earlier measures in force when Westminster was responsible for the whole of Ireland. Moreover, legal authority for much that the British Army does in Northern Ireland is found in the Act. Harold Wilson reaffirmed this endorsement in 1969, stating that 'not a government in the world' would do without its authorization 'until they were assured that there would be a period of law, order, peace, calm and quiet'.[25] Notwithstanding its broad powers and public endorsements, the Stormont regime has been hesitant to use some of its strongest provisions against civil rights demonstrators because of the criticism of the Act by Ulster opponents and by English libertarians.[26] To counter the novel non-violent tactics of the civil rights movement, Stormont passed a new measure, the Public Order (Amendment) Act, 1969. It provides legal powers to act against those involved in demonstrations and sit-in activities. At one point in the debate on the bill, Opposition MPs sat down on the floor of the House of Commons to demonstrate their protest, singing the civil rights song, 'We Shall Overcome'.

The exercise of discretionary statutory powers by ministers is by definition a matter of judgment. When a judgment is made by a politician, then his political opponents have every reason to question it, as they would question his judgment on matters that are not quasi-judicial in form. The Minister of Home Affairs has very substantial discretionary powers vested in him by statute. His use of these powers has long been a matter of discord. A classic example occurred in autumn, 1968, when the Minister, William Craig, used his discretionary powers to declare illegal the civil rights demonstration of October 5 at Londonderry. The Minister justified the decision on the grounds that a Protestant group had at the last minute also announced plans to parade; the concurrence of the two parades might lead to serious public disorder. Craig's ban did not prevent the march. By making it illegal, it became a challenge to the regime's authority. Instead of drawing several hundred protesters, the illegal demonstration drew more than 2,000 persons, including press and television from Britain. Serious public disorder resulted. In the tart words of the Cameron Commission, 'The effect of the Ministerial order was to transform the situation.'[27] But not in the manner the Minister intended.

The introduction of the British Army to Northern Ireland in recognition of a very serious breach of order introduced complex questions of powers and jurisdiction. The Army operates in Northern Ireland under the command of Westminster, and not under the Stormont government. Moreover, troops in action in Northern Ireland operate under Stormont statutory provisions so broad that they give little need to invoke powers of the common law, martial law, or the laws of war. The point is of political significance, for a declaration of a state of war or martial law would be *prima facie* evidence of the collapse of the Stormont regime. While Stormont and Westminster are both anxious to avoid the Army undermining the former's authority, some Republicans are very anxious to force the suspension of the Government of Ireland Act 1920, even if this would mean martial law. The legal status of the Army's activities provoked great controversy after the curfew in the Lower Falls area of Belfast on July 3–5, 1970. The Army orders used the word curfew; afterwards the Magistrate ruled that the ban on street movement was an act taken under common law powers. In the words of the Crown solicitor, 'The soldiers in so doing [i.e., restoring the peace by occupying the area] are acting as citizens although they have greater resources.'[28] The scope of discretionary Army powers is apparently very broad. At the time of its arrival the Army treated throwers of stones as a nuisance, or riotous group, but not as a lethal menace. At a press conference in November, 1970, an Army spokesman announced that stone throwers might be shot to prevent persons throwing home-made bombs or grenades. Anyone throwing *any* missile was to be classified as a 'potential bomber'.[29] The Army did not follow up its threat promptly. The hail of stones and an occasional bomb continued.

Whatever statutory or common law powers exist, those charged with enforcing the law must decide when they witness activities whether or not what they have seen is a crime. One of the most important legal charges used against persons for political acts does not assess what has happened, but rather, what *might* happen. This is a charge of disorderly behaviour by which a breach of the peace is likely to occur. This probabilistic type crime is familiar in the context of motoring offences: an individual who is exceeding a speed limit or driving carelessly may be charged with dangerous driving, that is, endangering life. A motorist does not need to kill a pedestrian to be convicted for behaviour that raises greatly the probability that he could do so. In the context of political crimes, assessing the probability of a breach of the peace occurring is more controversial than assessing dangerous driving. For example, in 1970, a Catholic docker was charged with action likely to cause a breach of the peace, convicted and sentenced to six months in jail. The overt act that constituted the crime was painting on the wall of a house in a Catholic district the slogan 'No tea here'. No disturbance followed. The police regarded this as a crime because 'it is a direction to the residents not to supply anything to the military'.[30]

When overt activities occur, it still must be left to the judgment of the policeman or the soldier on the spot whether a crime has been committed. For instance, RUC officials at the Burntollet ambush saw nothing in the assembly of Protestants with stones and cudgels that seemed 'likely' to break the peace, nor did they regard the subsequent assault upon the non-violent demonstrators as constituting a crime under the laws of the Northern Ireland regime. Reciprocally, they did not charge the demonstrators with a breach of the peace.

Often, decisions about the occurrence of a crime are taken with much regard for the difficulties in arresting those witnessed in what may be regarded as a criminal act. The problem arises in its most acute form when processions are held in violation of a government ban. For example, a Paisleyite demonstration attended by 2,000 persons in County Tyrone in July, 1970, was regarded by police as a 'walk' and not illegal, even though the clergyman in charge declared the event a breach of the ban on marches. Five hundred Orangemen wearing sashes proceeded a quarter of a mile along the highway. The 'walkers' outnumbered the police and Army by more than six to one.[31] Similarly, the RUC and the British Army have made no effort to arrest persons dressed in military-style uniforms when they parade with the tricolour at Republican funerals. In one flagrant challenge to the law in 1970, four IRA men fired a volley of shots in full view of 5,000 people at the grave of a veteran comrade, Jimmy Steele. While numbers are the most important consideration in whether a crime is recognized, the status of the potential culprit is also important. It is specially difficult for officials of the regime to investigate charges of misconduct against other officials of the regime. This was demonstrated in the case of Samuel Devenney, for the RUC enquiry found no case against policemen, whereas the enquiry conducted by an outsider from Scotland Yard did. Each of these decisions is bound to satisfy some subjects–those deemed not to have acted in ways meriting arrest. It will also be seen as an abuse of justice by political opponents, thus further contributing to discord.

The incidence of political crime in Northern Ireland from October, 1968 has been far greater than any police force or Army could witness. Literally tens of thousands of people have engaged in violence, breaches of the peace, banned marches and other actions contrary to laws. In one year of disturbance, the regime announced that it arrested 1,221 persons and convicted 942, with another 223 prosecutions pending.[32] This group is not the sum total of persons guilty of political crimes, but rather, a sample of those who could lawfully be charged for their actions. Decision of when to arrest and whom to arrest in a crowd of law violators is thus often highly discretionary. For instance, when a Belfast crowd of 30 Protestant youths coming home from a football match started singing 'Oh, they're only Fenian bastards over there', in passing a Catholic block of flats, the police seized one youth from the crowd and charged him with disorderly behaviour. The youth received a six-month sentence upon conviction.[33] In such circumstances, one must consider whether the grievance against the regime is likely to be felt more strongly by the one man in jail for an act for which others are unpunished, or by those who may be equally culpable but never charged, unlike their 'unfairly' treated mate.

Once an arrest is made, the decision about whether to prosecute and what charge to prosecute for is left in the hands of the police in the great majority of criminal cases in Northern Ireland. This procedure is also used in English law. It has come under criticism in England because it vests decisions about whether any prosecution should then follow in the hands of the men responsible for collecting the evidence, rather than transferring this evaluation to a legally trained public prosecutor. In Northern Ireland, the discord about the regime increases the burden of suspicion of the police, whatever decision is taken. For example, 66 persons arrested and held by the police for breaking the curfew in the Lower Falls were issued summonses to appear in court 18 weeks after the alleged offence. On appearance, they found that the Crown wished to withdraw charges against them because of the inadequacy of the evidence. The Hunt Committee on the Police recommended the introduction of independent public prosecutors, already in use in Scotland.[34] A lawyer appointed by the regime may be independent of the police, but not free of controversial discretionary powers. For example, the Attorney-General of Northern Ireland, a Unionist politician, has the authority to decide whether prosecutions will be undertaken under the Prevention of Incitement to Hatred Act. The Act, introduced as a reform measure, did not lead to prompt prosecutions, in spite of reference to the Attorney-General of cases deemed *prima facie* crimes by Catholic MPs. The Act thus becomes yet another stimulus to discord.[35]

After a person is charged with a crime, the next stage in law is a decision by the court about bail. Granting or refusing bail is a judgment of the seriousness of the crime alleged, the reputation of the accused, and the likelihood of his non-appearance at trial if released from jail. A judge, acting often upon police advice, has no formulae by which bail is granted or refused. In theory any Catholic charged with a political crime against the regime might be refused bail on the ground he could flee to the Republic where he would not likely be extradited. In practice, the courts exercise discretion in granting bail to Catholics as well as Protestants. Refusal of bail results in an individual being imprisoned, even though no assessment of guilt has yet been made, and trial may return a verdict of innocent. For example, five Protestants alleged to be members of the illegal Ulster Volunteer Force were held without bail for several months in the winter of 1969 because they were charged with blowing up a major Belfast public utility. The men were acquitted.[36] The regime did, however, succeed in restraining their actions for a few months just as effectively as if it had interned them under the Special Powers Act. A comparison of decisions to grant or withhold bail inevitably leads to complaints against discretionary decisions. For example in December, 1970, Austin Currie raised in the Stormont Commons information that a Catholic with rusty firearms had been refused bail whereas a Protestant with a large cache of arms had been granted bail. The Opposition MPs were so dissatisfied with the Minister's answer that they withdrew from the Commons for a day after Currie was ordered out for accusing the Minister of 'twisting like an eel'.[37]

Once a case comes to trial the judge becomes prominent. In Northern Ireland, the judges in the Superior Courts are appointed by the Crown, whereas the lower court judges are appointed by the Stormont regime. The selection of High Court judges by the Lord Chancellor does not make them free of all political connections.

Of the seven judges of the High Court in 1970, three were ex-Unionist MPs at Stormont, including one former party whip; a fourth was the son of a Unionist minister. The Stormont regime's power to appoint magistrates is particularly important, inasmuch as the bulk of 'political' crimes are tried at that level. As the judges are appointed by the regime, it is not surprising that opponents of the regime should reject their claim to impartiality. In the first two years after the Londonderry march, judges have been relatively free from criticism; they are only one link in a chain of law enforcement. The most egregious remark in the period was made by the President of the High Court in Dublin, Mr. Justice O'Keeffe. He publicly expressed concern about presiding at the Dublin arms trial as a one-time political associate of men accused.[38]

The actions of a jury at a political trial in Northern Ireland afford much scope for dispute. By virtue of their political outlooks, the opponents of the regime are unlikely to be over-represented upon jury panels. More important is the unlimited right of the Crown to challenge potential jurors. A Crown prosecutor could, if he wished, exclude from a jury all persons whose political opinions were thought to be at variance with the regime, whether Protestant Ultras or Catholic Republicans. Once chosen, jurors can hardly ignore extra-judicial considerations. No person can purge his mind of all prior political predispositions when hearing a trial in which the defendant may plead that 'his only crime was loyalty', whether to a purely Protestant regime or a United Ireland. In the nineteenth century, the right of jury trial was suspended for some political cases because juries were inclined to bring in verdicts contradicted by unchallenged evidence. In Northern Ireland today, the prudent juror is as likely to think of personal security as well as about political ideals. (Both considerations may point in the same direction.) For example, the jury sitting in the case of the Dunadry public utilities explosion of 1969 had a bomb go off in the courthouse during the trial. The jury acquitted the five accused men. The complexities of the law are such that James Callaghan, the British Home Secretary at the time, claimed eight months afterwards that the accused were in prison for the crime. Even a Home Secretary sometimes forgets that indictment, whatever the evidence, is not tantamount to conviction.[39]

The evidence that the Crown brings to court depends upon intrinsic characteristics of the case, the thoroughness with which evidence is sought and legal procedures governing the evidence required.

134

Defendants are under no such inhibition. In fact, the greater the evidence of guilt, then the greater the incentive to elaborate or invent evidence implying innocence. In hectic circumstances, such as a riot, it is sometimes difficult for victims of crimes to obtain evidence relating to specific individuals. For instance, following the British Army curfew in the Lower Falls, the Army's own investigating team reported that it found 58 instances in which there was evidence to suggest that soldiers had committed offences in house-to-house searches for arms. But, an Army spokesman said, 'No evidence emerged which would justify taking action against any individual.' In many political crimes, the search for evidence is made difficult because individuals are hesitant to risk retaliation for giving information to the police. For instance, a witness against a man accused of killing a policeman was assaulted in his house by a man who broke in, shouting 'I want to see you, you informing bastard.' Requirements of evidence create difficulties. For instance, to claim damages from the state for property destroyed in disorderly circumstances, proof must be offered that three or more persons are responsible for the destruction of property. Hence, the courts dismissed the award of £2,200 for the burning of a community hall in Armagh because the number of persons causing the arson was unknown. Lord Justice Curran told the claimants 'I have every sympathy because I have had my house bombed. I am sorry that I can't allow compensation.'[40]

The sentences given convicted persons reflect the maximum or fixed statutory penalties, plus judicial discretion. For instance, a London judge announced that he was giving two Belfast Catholics lighter sentences than three others involved in procuring arms for Northern Ireland because he believed the pair 'were activated by a desire to defend your community rather than by any idea of attack'. Often, the significance of discretion can only be seen by comparing the penalties that different judges give. For instance, in 1970 in Belfast courts one man was given two years for firing a revolver at a group trying to burn him out of his house, another was given six months for writing 'No tea here' while a person convicted of assaulting a Crown witness in an important case was sentenced to only six months.[41] To reduce anomalies in judicial discretion and to deter potential rebels, Stormont in June, 1970 enacted a minimum sentences act, requiring a six months' jail sentence for anyone convicted of such offences as threatening a breach of the peace during 'the period of the present emergency'. It applied to non-political crimes and to juveniles. The protests against the measure led the regime to amend the act. The measure did not have sufficient deterrent effect to end political disorder.[42] It became another ground of complaint against the regime.

Formal recognition is given to the possibility of legal error by provisions for the amnesty of persons who may have committed crimes, or the reprieve of persons sentenced for crimes. The most dramatic illustration of amnesty powers was given when Major James Chichester-Clark became Prime Minister in May, 1969. He announced an amnesty that dropped investigation, prosecution or quashed sentences concerning 230 persons, involved in demonstrations for and against civil rights in the preceding eight months.[43] The amnesty covered Protestants and Catholics as well as members of the RUC. Exceptionally, individuals have been released from prison when the regime has deemed punishment excessive. Malachy Grogan, a Belfast Catholic sentenced for two years for shooting at men trying to burn his home, was released after he had served five months of his sentence. Acts of mercy do not, however, remove discord. The release of Grogan was condemned by the Rev. Ian Paisley and by Protestant defence groups. There can be 'amnesty by anticipation' too. For instance, during the July, 1970 curfew in the Lower Falls Road area, 3,000 Catholic women and children marched toward the area, bringing food to persons confined therein. Technically, they were defying curfew and could have been arrested. An Army spokesman admitted that troops 'looked the other way'. When asked why, he replied, 'Well, we are human. Everybody just seems to think that we are ogres.'[44]

The regime has sought to avoid the limitations of the courts by establishing special commissions of a quasi-judicial kind to investigate major challenges to its authority. For example, in March, 1969, Terence O'Neill appointed a Scottish High Court judge, Lord Cameron, to enquire into the causes and character of civil disorder in Ulster since the Londonderry march and to assess the bodies involved in the demonstrations. The regime could hardly have anticipated the findings of Lord Cameron. Instead of being an attack upon irresponsible and subversive Republicans, the main burden of the Report was a criticism of the regime for giving grounds for disaffection. The Report was as unpopular with one group of Protestants as it was popular with Catholics. William Craig refused an invitation to meet the Commission, denouncing its appointment as 'the act of a weak inept government'. There was no necessity for Craig to appear, and the Commission did not have full judicial powers to compel his presence.

No sooner had the Cameron Commission reported than the regime appointed a different type of body, chaired by an Englishman, Mr. Justice Scarman, to enquire into the disorder and loss of life from April to August, 1969. Although dealing with events immediately subsequent to those of the Cameron Commission, the Scarman Tribunal had narrower terms of reference but fuller legal powers. It was able to compel the attendance of witnesses and, if it deemed suitable, offer immunity when questioning them about criminal activities. The Tribunal's hearings have thus produced masses of sworn and published testimony. Testimony of this sort supplements but cannot substitute for prosecution and punishment of guilty individuals. Moreover, the very openness of the Scarman Tribunal, provides both Ultras and rebels with sources of quotations to use against each other in their never-ending controversies.[45] In the world of Ulster politics, it could hardly change many minds.

While the Stormont regime is in part responsible for the extent of discord arising from legal procedures, an element of discretion and dispute is intrinsic in any process of law enforcement. Where the agents of the law are not perceived as neutral and impartial, then discretionary judgments are inevitably subject to dispute. The dispute is incapable of resolution by discussion, because there is no agreement about criteria of decision. From a commonsense point of view, the fact that a person has been shot dead in circumstances ruling out suicide is evidence that a crime has been committed. The question then arises: Who did the killing? Or is the death accidental? In law, no judgment can be rendered until the legal process has run its course, for the trial *is* the fact of the matter, as far as the courts are concerned. In law, a person not convicted of a crime is presumed innocent. For example, a man who is alleged to have thrown a petrol bomb cannot be said to be legally guilty of this criminal act until he is tried and convicted. Yet in riot conditions, the British Army can punish a man whom it believes to be throwing a petrol bomb. The punishment can be death by shooting, even though the act in question would not merit the death sentence in a law court. There is no means of seeking posthumous conviction or acquittal for the alleged crime. The soldier who has shot the man may show that he did so on the orders of an Army officer, who judged the riotous conditions sufficiently grave to warrant the act. Witnesses will be produced to state that the man shot was conducting himself in a way that gravely endangered the peace, just as friends of the deceased are likely to appear at an inquest and swear the contrary. In such circumstances, the insufficient and conflicting evidence is such that the man causing the death cannot be charged and convicted for his act. In law, he too must be presumed innocent. In particular instances, e.g., the deceased is a nine-year-old child, it is most improbable that he was guilty of a major crime. In such circumstances, inquests commonly bring in an open verdict, leaving the matter unresolved. The case is then out of the courts, but it is not out of public attention. Those who have no sympathy with the community of the deceased will assume that the fact of death is presumptive proof that the person was up to no good when he died. Those who sympathize with the deceased, will regard the slayer as the guilty party. For instance, the Belfast Citizens' Defence Committee has accused the British Army of acting as 'judges and executioners' when soldiers occasionally fire at demonstrators.[46]

In many instances, crimes can be attributed collectively to a group of people. It is easy enough for a citizen outside the courts to recognize situations in which 'they' killed a man. 'They' may refer to a group as vague or large as 'the Fenians' or 'the Orangemen', or as specific as a particular IRA or RUC unit. Given the intimate scale of life in Northern Ireland, it is possible for the suspect group to be defined with some precision, e.g., a group of Republicans in an area of a few streets, or men in a numbered patrol car at a specific point in time. A legal indictment on a charge as serious as murder can only be returned against identified and identifiable individuals. The presence of a corpse and a suspect group is not necessarily sufficient to sustain an indictment and conviction for murder. The Scarman Tribunal produced sworn evidence illustrating this point.[47] John Gallagher, a Catholic, was shot to death in Armagh the night of August 14, 1969, at the height of the disorder. A squad of 17 Ulster B Specials was at the scene of the death, some firing at the time he was fatally wounded. The B Specials failed to follow accepted procedures for reporting the crime; a number promptly and privately cleaned their rifles after the shooting. The fact that the men remained on duty for months afterwards could be interpreted by Protestants as evidence of the confidence that the regime had in their innocence, just as Catholics would interpret their later testimony to the Tribunal as evidence of collective guilt. In such circumstances few Ulster people need a court verdict to decide in their own minds who is innocent and who is guilty.

Force and Order

The ideal of the rule of law assumes that discretionary decisions taken by law enforcement officers will be accepted in mind and in fact by virtually everyone in society. When this happens, law prevails without resort to coercion. This is the most economical as well as the 'nicest' way to govern a society. The British have always had the ideal of maintaining the rule of law in those parts of Ireland where the Crown has been sovereign. Reginald Maudling, in his first speech as Home Secretary, affirmed this clearly:

> We must emphasize–and I do so with all the vehemence at my command–that force will not triumph and that the rule of law, not the rule of the gun, will be maintained throughout every part of the country for which this House is responsible.[48]

Unfortunately, all the people of Northern Ireland will not voluntarily comply with all the rules that a British Home Secretary is sworn to maintain. In such circumstances, the question then becomes: How does one rule by force as well as law? How are the means of coercion to be organized? And what kind of consequences will the use of force have? The consequences of force are variable–force will sometimes reduce disorder, but it will increase disorder when rebels or Ultras respond with counter-force.

The internal security requirements of any regime are multiple, not singular. Different levels of force will be required to meet at least four kinds of circumstances. The first need is for a 'watchman'-like surveillance of society. Secondly, force is needed to control large crowds that *might* become disorderly. When crowds have become disorderly, then greater force is required to repress them. In extreme circumstances, firearms are required for use against a riotous or insurrectionary group that resorts to the use of arms to attack the regime.

The simplest requirement, always undertaken in Northern Ireland by the Royal Ulster Constabulary, is the watchman task. The job of the watchman is to maintain surveillance of social actions and, by his presence, to deter law violations. When an individual violates the law, he is then expected to apprehend the violator. If the violator acts alone as a shoplifter or a drunken driver, then the only resource needed to make an arrest is a traditional nightstick or a fast police car. If the violator is armed, e.g., a bank robber in an isolated farmhouse, then the police will require arms too. The Stormont regime, like its Dublin Castle predecessor, has had little need to make special police provision for 'non-political' crimes. From 1864, when Irish criminal statistics were first presented in a form directly comparable to those in England, they have shown that, even with allowances for population differences, traditional crimes such as forgery, offences against property, or rape have been lower in Ireland than in England. It is only in the field of political crimes that Ireland and, latterly, Northern Ireland, has required much more policing than England. The pattern continues to the present.[49] When political disaffection is not evident then Northern Ireland, like the rural parts of many Western societies, is a relatively easy land to police.

The problem of social control is different in kind if large numbers of people collect in circumstances in which a breach of the peace is possible. In many circumstances, the probability of a breach of the peace is low, e.g., crowds of Christmas shoppers. In a divided regime, the possibility of a breach of the peace is always higher, for many casual incidents can be seized upon by those present as an instance of sectarian differences, and political disorder follows. A football crowd can become a political demonstration, for team loyalties parallel regime loyalties. (Catholics support Glasgow Celtic and Protestants support Glasgow Rangers. Matches between Catholic and Protestant teams in Belfast were abandoned decades ago because of recurring violence.) If the crowd is assembled for a legal parade, then the duty of the regime's force is to protect it. If a demonstration is illegal, then it becomes contingent whether an attempt to stop the parade will itself lead to a breach of the peace. Coercing a large crowd of disaffected subjects to obey the law requires large numbers of trained and uniformed men. In some demonstrations in early August, 1969, the RUC was trying to contain crowds of up to 3,000 with as few as 40 police.[50] In default of large numbers of men skilled in crowd control, a riot can ensue.

Confronted by a group that is numerous as well as disorderly, the regime requires force sufficient to repress a large and violent crowd.

In Northern Ireland demonstrations of the late 1960s, the usual weapons of resistance were stones and petrol bombs. While neither is likely to cause death, either is capable of causing a fatal injury. A stone can fracture a skull, and a petrol bomb may set fire to a building from which someone inside cannot escape. The force necessary to contain a rioting assembly is much more substantial than that needed to contain a potentially riotous crowd. Instead of night-sticks, law enforcement officials require riot shields and other protective gear, as well as weapons of offence. Upon occasion, the RUC and its predecessor used guns when rioting reached serious proportions. Police behaviour in firing more or less randomly in Catholic areas in West Belfast in August, 1969, was consistent with this practice. The British Army initially relied upon CS teargas and bruising rubber bullets to contain or disperse crowds. When the Labour Prime Minister was challenged about the use of teargas, Harold Wilson explained that it was employed in urban areas as the lesser choice of evils; the alternative, he pointed out, would be using gunfire to disperse crowds. Precisely because these instruments of force are not lethal, anti-regime demonstrators have come to accept their use, like the weather, as a minor hazard of Ulster life. In February, 1971, conflict escalated in Belfast. Republican groups resorted to machine guns and gelignite bombs to show their rejection of the regime. In such circumstances, the British Army replied with rifle fire. There were fatal results on both sides.

The IRA threat to the Northern Ireland regime is a threat of internal subversion as well as of military attack across the Border with the Republic. The terrain of the Border area makes it impossible to maintain a maginot line of defence installations, but the 'redoubt mentality' has been in evidence in the RUC. The IRA is as likely to attack the regime in the centre of Belfast as at a Border crossing. Moreover, because its numbers are small and its typical activity is a surprise raid by a dozen or so men, it can be counter-attacked by armed police. For this reason, RUC men were regularly armed, until the 1969 reforms. The force needed to subdue an armed gang that has robbed a bank to get funds to import guns for the Republican cause is, after all, no greater than that required to apprehend a non-political bank robber. In defending the regime against armed attack, the 3,000 men of the RUC prior to the 1969 reforms could call upon the 8,000-man Ulster B Special Constabulary. The Specials provided a well-dispersed and well-armed pool of manpower, albeit largely untrained in military or police work. They were mobilized for full-time duty or part-time night patrols whenever IRA raids were expected. Their chief duties were guarding public utilities, collecting intelligence, Border patrols, manning road blocks to check the movements of suspicious persons, and, at times, assisting in riot work. The importance of a prompt response to troubles in the countryside placed a premium upon the Specials working in small units with large amounts of discretion. To keep the men a ready reserve, B Specials often held their guns at home, including automatic weapons. Because rebels were overwhelmingly from the Catholic community, the Specials were an exclusively Protestant force.[52]

The Royal Ulster Constabulary, like its predecessor under the old Dublin Castle regime, was accustomed to undertaking a wide range of duties, from playing the part of a watchman against petty theft to participation in gun battles with terrorists and insurrectionary forces. Given the limited number of armed Republicans in the field against them and the unreadiness of the Army of the Irish Republic to attack over the Border, the RUC and the B Specials had sufficient force for traditional internal security work. Military considerations played a significant part in the training and equipment of the RUC. The tradition of combat was also reinforced by the list of policemen who have died from wounds inflicted by Republican assailants. As long as the only challenge to the regime came from the IRA, the RUC and the Special Constabulary were trained and able to meet it.[53]

The civil rights demonstrations presented a novel challenge to the Royal Ulster Constabulary. Instead of attacking the regime by the violent actions of a small number of men, the civil rights groups massed hundreds or thousands to protest under banners of non-violence. The illegal and public nature of their actions meant that the RUC could not ignore what was done. But its men had no special training in techniques of controlling large numbers of civilians. Upon occasion, their task was made even more difficult by the appearance of Protestant counter-demonstrators. The frequency of the demonstrations and their dispersion meant that the undermanned RUC worked many hours of overtime without rest in unfamiliar conditions. The employment of B Specials in these novel circumstances presented a further difficulty, because the Specials had little training and their equipment was designed for armed Republican attacks.[54] Yet never was the good judgment of the ordinary policeman more important for the security of the regime, for in police work, unlike most branches of government, the greatest discretion is given to the lowest-ranking man: the policeman who meets demonstrators in the front line of confrontation.[55] Whatever orders a Minister of Home Affairs gives can only be put into effect by the concerted actions of such men. Conversely, any actions that such individuals take become the responsibility of the regime, not only in law but also in political controversy.

The persisting and intense demands made upon the Royal Ulster Constabulary resulted in police behaviour that stimulated more disorder in the streets. The RUC's reactions were apparently based upon the assumption that the civil rights demonstrators were potential rebels, best treated by whatever measure of repression was appropriate to the task. Hence, from the first demonstration at Londonderry on October 5, 1968, the RUC were inclined to see their task as requiring batons, water cannons and similar instruments of coercion. The Cameron Report evaluated the political consequences of the RUC strategy thus:

> If the objective of this operation was to drive the civil rights movement into the ground by a display of force and firmness in the enforcement of the ministerial order, it signally failed.[56]

The RUC saw nothing wrong in Protestant groups assembling at the scene of officially permitted civil rights marches. The marchers did. The Cameron Report commented that repeatedly, 'The police did not take early and energetic action to disperse growing concentrations of persons who were obviously hostile to the civil rights demonstrations and were at least likely to resort to violence against them.'[57]

The RUC broke under the burden placed upon it in August, 1969. The collapse began in Londonderry, where the Bogsiders barricaded themselves in; they anticipated a combined assault by the RUC and Protestant mobs as the climax to the Apprentice Boys parade there. Ironically, the RUC gave little cause for grievance that day. Police defined their task as containing the demonstrators in the Bogside. This could be done from outside the area. As the Bogsiders' chief objective was to keep the police from breaching the perimeter, the aims of the two groups were complementary, rather than in conflict.

143

Institutions of Discord

The exchanges between the two combatant groups occurred at the perimeter, with the police keeping the rioters from breaking out to the centre of the city, and the demonstrators keeping the police from breaking in. The Bogsiders' weapons were stones and petrol bombs; the RUC fought defensively, using shields and returning some stones. As in trench warfare, the combatants rarely came close enough for batons or shillelaghs to be of any use. After eight hours of attack by missiles across barricades, the RUC played their strongest card short of guns–teargas. It failed to disperse the crowds or reduce the Bogside attack. The battle of the barricades thus became a test of endurance. The undermanned and overworked RUC had two alternatives–to make use of their firearms or retire from the field. The British Army was brought in to replace it 48 hours after fighting commenced. The Bogsiders underscored their rejection of the RUC by promptly ending their violence in acceptance of the Army's presence.[58]

In Belfast, the RUC reinforced by the B Specials reacted differently. In the midst of masses of Protestant and Catholic mobs fighting each other, the RUC turned heavy firearms against the Catholic population. A journalist eyewitness, Max Hastings, described the situation as follows:

> The police were involved in a battle under utterly false illusions, completely without understanding or direction or even acceptance of basic riot tactics. How could men only half-trained with firearms be allowed to attempt to pick off snipers with machine-gun fire in a crowded city area? How could Protestants be suffered among the police lines for every Catholic to see? How could Protestants wreak so much havoc among Catholic houses and business without interference or care from the police?[59]

The reporter then answers his own question, 'Their [the RUC] tragedy was that very often they were atrociously led and quite undirected.' After two days of death and widespread disorder, the British Army was called in to restore peace in Belfast too.

The failure of the RUC to prevent or repress widespread political disorder disturbed both officials and opponents of the regime. Opponents of the regime were anxious to bring to account individual policemen and B Specials whom they accused of crimes, including murder. When foreign journalists broached the subject of investigation at a Stormont press conference immediately after the violence, the Minister of Home Affairs assured them that any such complaints would be promptly investigated. He was asked by whom. By the police, he replied. 'Almost the whole hall burst into laughter.'[60] Defenders of the regime could not laugh off the problem of which particular crimes were only examples: the inability of the RUC and B Specials to cope with the internal security problems then before them. To seek an answer, Stormont appointed a special advisory committee chaired by Lord Hunt, the conqueror of Mount Everest, with two leading British policemen as its other members.

The Hunt Committee concentrated attention upon the existing institutions of force used by the regime. This approach meant that its recommendations inevitably concentrated upon the strengths and the limitations of the RUC and the B Specials. It did not examine in detail the political and security problems that had led to the creation of these two forces. In other words, the Hunt Committee's recommendations were not addressed to the entire range of questions concerning defence of the regime.

The principal finding stated by the Hunt Committee was that the functions previously assigned the RUC were too broad. It was expected to do everything from preventing non-political crime to maintaining Border stations against armed attacks. The Committee recommended that the RUC 'be relieved of all duties of a military nature as soon as possible'. Its duties should be limited to the enforcement of conventional statute law, providing bodyguards for important persons and gathering intelligence. The recommendation was based upon the belief that policing requires public consent to work well, and that 'any police force military in appearance and equipment is less acceptable to minority and moderate opinion than if it is clearly civilian in character'.[61] The most tangible symbol of de-militarization of the RUC was that it should forthwith abandon the practice of arming patrolmen. The Report noted that the B Special Force was primarily engaged in military work although it was part of the police arm of Stormont under command of the RUC. To replace the B Specials the Committee recommended that the necessary work of guarding key installations and assisting in security checks should be done by a locally recruited para-military force, under the General Officer Commanding the British Army in Northern Ireland. While this Ulster Defence Regiment would use part-time volunteers, its military direction would ensure better training for counter-insurgency work and also make available transport and radio communications on a scale unavailable to the B Specials. To supervise this very substantial reorganization, the Committee recommended the creation of a new central Police Authority for Northern Ireland, composed of representatives of local government, trade unions, universities, etc., subject to the Minister of Home Affairs.[62] A very prominent English police officer, Sir Arthur Young, was given a one-year appointment to head the RUC during the period of reorganization. His importation from London was meant to symbolize the fact that the 'civilian style' RUC should be like an English police force. The Committee reported in October, 1969 and its recommendations were promptly accepted by the Stormont regime.

As befits a 'non-political' body (that is, a Committee whose technical competence is meant to keep them from controversial issues) the Committee did not examine the character of the problems that had faced the old RUC and the B Specials. Because of this, the Report's recommendations were entirely prescriptive in character. The empirical basis of their prescriptions was not made evident. For instance, the Committee expected that its reforms would be 'widely accepted by reasonable men and women in Northern Ireland'. It did not estimate what proportion of the population was reasonable, nor did it suggest who would bear the burden of dealing with 'unreasonable' people, especially if their numbers were large. In so far as difficulties were recognized, the Committee sought to overcome them by exhortation:

> We believe that the recommendations in this report will call for outstanding qualities of leadership to carry them out. There must be a conviction of the need for the changes and a due sense of urgency. There must also be an ability to appreciate the problems of Northern Ireland and the sensitivities of its people combined with a determination to chart a course towards the future, undeflected by the events of the past.[63]

The reaction to Lord Hunt's recommendations was mixed. The Stormont regime and the British government promptly accepted them, and moved quickly to put them into force. Like other reform measures of the time, the Hunt Committee's recommendations were publicly presented as if they were sufficient as well as necessary. The Ulster Defence Regiment was established in April, 1970 to do guard duty and man road blocks. By autumn it had 3,800 men in its ranks; about one-sixth were Catholics.[64] Some Catholic politicians gave cautious endorsement to a number of specific measures. It was easier praising the negative recommendations, such as disarming the police or disbanding the B Specials, than praising the positive recommendations. None the less, some Catholic MPs and the Cardinal gave their blessing to the recruitment of more Catholics to the RUC. There remained considerable scepticism among Catholics, inasmuch as the new forces would inevitably include large numbers of men who had served in the pre-reform organizations. Protestant opponents of the regime reacted against the changes. Immediately after publication of the Report, a major riot occurred on the Shankill Road. An unarmed policeman was shot dead by Protestant Ultras. At every sign of Republican violence since, Protestants have not hesitated to call for the rearming of the RUC and its return to the task of repressing disorder by force. William Craig, former Home Affairs minister, summed up their criticisms succinctly when asked if he wanted the police to use their guns more.

> The forces of law and order–the police and the Army are entitled to, *must use their guns*, when that degree of force is necessary.[65]

Initially, the RUC and the B Specials were extremely demoralized by the carefully phrased but inevitably critical comments of the Hunt Report. As these demoralized men were both armed and Unionist sympathizers, the regime sought to treat them with consideration. Within a year, morale was improving. Former B Specials were being recruited in substantial numbers into the Ulster Defence Regiment, and Sir Arthur Young's successor was a career RUC man. Moreover, many policemen appreciated that the disarming of the force, whatever its symbolic overtones, had practical advantages. It meant they were no longer expected to do all the 'heavy' work of repressing political disorders. Support for the new civilian role of the RUC was shown by a poll organized by the Police Representative Body. It gave a majority of 1,196 to 1,085 in favour of remaining disarmed.[66] Sir Arthur Young aptly summed up the Hunt viewpoint by stating in a valedictory talk that the policemen in Northern Ireland should never need arms to do their job, because their duties were very circumscribed. 'It was not for the police to solve our problems. That was a matter for politicians.'[67]

The Hunt Committee could engage in the luxury of shedding responsibilities from the police because of the presence in strength of the British Army. The Army's entry into Ulster affairs in the emergency of August, 1969, quickly led to the stationing of more than 6,000 troops on active duty, principally in Belfast and Londonderry, the major centres of disorders. The decision to involve the Army was taken under great pressure to meet an urgent crisis. The initial communiqué emphasized London's desire that 'British troops can be withdrawn from the internal security role at the earliest possible moment'. Yet the Hunt Committee's recommendations effectively made the British Army the residuary legatee of all the duties shed by the old RUC and B Specials.

The British Army brings to the task of maintaining order resources vastly superior to those of the Royal Ulster Constabulary. Its first advantage is that of manpower. In its first 18 months on duty in Northern Ireland, the Army, depending upon the political situation, had a force about two to four times as large as that of the RUC, i.e., from 6,000 to 12,000 men. To maintain order during the Twelfth celebrations of 1970, it had more manpower than the old RUC and B Specials together could muster. Modern military air transport makes it possible for facilities initially designed to fly troops from the United Kingdom to emergencies elsewhere to fly troops back to the chief trouble spot of the United Kingdom. This can quickly bring the Army's strength to above 20,000 men in a grave emergency. The troops are free from the routine and dispersed watchman duties of civilian police and can be massed in great numbers at trouble spots and potential trouble spots within the Province. The communications and transport facilities of the Army provide tactical flexibility in moving men at short notice. The training of an infantry soldier makes him more disciplined in confused crowd conditions than a policeman accustomed to patrol alone in the countryside, and makes him accept violence as a normal part of his working conditions. Last and not least, there are few inhibitions about the level of force that soldiers may use when disorder becomes intense and widespread. But in its use of arms, the Army has been disciplined. For example, in the fighting on the Shankill Road in October, 1969, Protestant Ultras killed one man with hundreds of rounds of firing. The Army killed two demonstrators with 26 aimed shots.

The protection of Northern Ireland's Border from external attack is a novel duty for the British Army, for it is the only land boundary of the United Kingdom. The legitimacy of the regime within Britain has given the Army no experience in combating subversion within its home territory. The British Army is trained and ready to serve overseas, and regards its chief responsibilities as those abroad. At a time of greatly contracting manpower and resources, the Ministry of Defence in 1969 found itself with a new burden. In addition to forming part of the NATO tripwire in Germany, it was expected to act as the military tripwire between County Fermanagh and County Monaghan, and the Falls and the Shankill roads. The slight risk of military defeat by the Dublin regime or the IRA does not absolve the Ministry of a tedious amount of responsibility for every incident within its domain. Part-time soldiers in the Ulster Defence Regiment can do much of the patrol work and manning of road blocks, the most effective deterrent against a large influx of armed men into the Province from the Republic. Every time the IRA blows up an empty customs post the Army must investigate and the Secretary of State for Defence is responsible at Westminster for what has happened. In its work in Northern Ireland, unlike activities in the Middle East or Far East, the Army is seeking to subdue people who have MPs in the House of Commons at Westminster, ready to question their activities at each turn.

The British Army has also inherited full responsibility for repressing disorders. Once the stones begin to fly, disarmed RUC men leave the field to troops clad in riot gear. An armed soldier in battle dress is a more forceful symbol of authority and threatens the use of stronger weapons of coercion than those available to a policeman. Soldiers have an offsetting handicap. Because they are trained always to move as a group under orders from superiors, they cannot easily circulate in small numbers among a potentially disorderly crowd, seeking to quieten things by gentle directives and casual conversation, as a policeman might. They can only meet civilians by confronting them with their strength. Their stolid appearance and reputation for not using their strongest weapons promptly makes it possible for the crowd they face to test their strength and endurance with stones and petrol bombs. In such circumstances, troops can only soldier on, hoping to contain troubles by a show of force and superior endurance.

Within a year of the announcement of the Hunt reforms, the Army and the RUC had developed means to handle protests and demonstrations jointly, where a breach of the peace was possible but not inevitable. This can reduce the Army's immediate manpower commitments and, equally important, increase the credibility of the reformed RUC. The procedures adopted for a Republican-sponsored and officially illegal civil rights march in Enniskillen in November,

1970, illustrate how the Army, the RUC and the UDR can work together. A crowd of up to 3,000 strangers, including Protestant counter-demonstrators, was expected to come to this town of 7,400 people. In all, 2,000 uniformed men were assigned to the task of maintaining order–1,000 soldiers, 650 RUC men and 350 members of the Ulster Defence Regiment. The Army organized security checks; a reporter going to the rally from Belfast had his automobile stopped eight times *en route*.[68] At the site of the demonstration, the Army provided five helicopters, and radio communications. As an exercise in maintaining order, the effort was completely successful: the likely breach of the peace did not, in fact, occur. Politically, the security effort was only one more source of discord. Protestants criticized the Army and the RUC for allowing a flagrant breach of the law to occur. Republicans criticized the security forces for their 'cowardly' arrest of leading participants six weeks after the demonstration was over. A Westminster MP, Frank McManus, was sentenced to six months in jail for his part in the demonstration.

The creation of a 'No Go' land for the police in parts of Belfast and Londonderry has also given the British Army responsibilities for conventional watchman duties to forestall non-political crimes. Initially, the Army had no great difficulty in working in these areas, because of the co-operation of local citizens' defence groups, who had organized the demonstrations that led to the withdrawal of the police. The increased co-operation between the Army and the police led to a breakdown in arrangements. Protestant political pressures caused the return of a token RUC late in 1970.[69] But the Army has continued its involvement, providing protection for individual patrolmen. In the most troubled parts of West Belfast, policemen on foot have a pocket radio, so that in case of attack they can alert military police, no more than a minute away in a riot car. When Republican guns come out, the Army takes full responsibility for what follows.

The RUC continues to do intelligence work of major importance. It is not the only organization engaged in political intelligence work in Northern Ireland–the British Army, the Irish Army, the IRA and Protestant Ultras also have contacts that provide information secretly. The data that interest all of these groups concern subversive and counter-subversive activities. The police have several advantages in doing this work. Their network of men throughout Northern Ireland means that no part of the Province is without coverage. A policeman may come across evidence of subversive activities, e.g., the stockpiling of weapons or explosives, in a routine search for evidence of non-political crimes. RUC men also have, by comparison with British Army officers, great local knowledge of their area. Politically, this makes disaffected Catholics regard the Army as a committed agent of a rejected regime.

Collectively, the Army, the Ulster Defence Regiment and the disarmed and expanded Royal Ulster Constabulary provide a range and size of internal security forces far greater than that available in Northern Ireland prior to the disorder of 1969. The strength of the force can only be evaluated in relation to the challenge to the regime. In the period following the Hunt Committee's report, the challenges increased, reaching a degree of intensity greater than at any time since the Troubles of the early 1920s. This did not require the maximum of force that the Crown could muster. Demands made on British troops elsewhere in the world could, however, threaten the reallocation of men from Ulster to external security work. This would lower the number of men available for service within Ulster. There is virtually no ceiling on the number of places where disorder might occur in Ulster, and on the numbers of men that might be required to maintain order. The level of disorder in Northern Ireland can fall as well as rise. The long-term objective of the Ministry of Defence is that it should fall. Making the level of disorder fall requires something other than the repression of symptoms of disorder. It requires political action. For all its equipment, the Army has no device that will force rebellious Catholics to give full allegiance to the regime, or Protestant Ultras to change their views about Catholic subjects. The Army can only defend the regime as it is, warts and all.

The Ultra Loyal

The idea of loyalists attacking a regime sounds a contradiction in terms. Groups that call themselves loyal should support rather than oppose the regime claiming their allegiance. The paradox is resolved if one asks What are the people loyal to—the institutions of the regime or the policies that they believe it ought to stand for? In a fully legitimate regime, there is no inconsistency between the two kinds of allegiance. In a regime lacking full legitimacy, efforts to adapt the regime to accommodate disaffected subjects may require abandoning what some consider are the very things that the regime is meant to stand for. In Northern Ireland, any accommodation of Catholics may be viewed by some Protestants as a departure from the basic principle to which they give loyalty: Stormont as a Protestant government for a Protestant people. Those who refuse compliance to 'illegitimate' laws are the Ultra loyal.

Among Protestants in Northern Ireland, commitment to Ultra views is more a state of mind than a sign of membership in a particular organization. Ultras can be found almost everywhere–in the churches, in Orange lodges, among the Unionist MPs and at times, within the Cabinet itself. In addition, endorsement of the Rev. Ian Paisley's views is not confined to the few thousands who belong to the organizations he heads. So-called 'Paisleyite' views are held in many places. The complement of this is that fully allegiant Protestants can also be found in such organizations. Discord within the Protestant community does not occur between institutions but within them.

The Ultra state of mind recurringly appears in Northern Ireland history. The prospect of Home Rule stimulated the majority of Ulster Protestants to endorse Ultra sentiments. The intensity and dispersion of civil war during the Troubles from 1916 to the middle 1920s made popular resort to arms a necessary condition for the maintenance of the British connection and Protestant rule in Northern Ireland. So widespread was the arming of Protestants by the regime that official statistics report that the strength of the police force in Northern Ireland for each year from 1921 to 1926 'cannot be stated'.[70] Protestant farmers fearing attack in the countryside armed themselves and fought the enemy. For example, in Desertmartin, County Londonderry, in revenge for RUC men killed in ambush and mills burned, a group of Protestants took four Catholics from their beds one night and shot them a short distance from the village.[71] Armed groups of volunteers were later regularized, forming the core of the Ulster B Special Constabulary.

Civil rights demonstrations were viewed by some Protestants as a return to the days of the early 1920s. Protestants have been prepared to meet the threat of another Catholic rising, for the number of licensed firearms in the country has always been extremely high; in 1969 there was one licensed gun for every fifth man between the age of 20 and 60. Moreover, as a publicity release from the Northern Ireland Tourist Board has boasted, shooting 'is a popular sport in the countryside'. It added, 'Unlike many other countries, the out-standing characteristic of the sport has been that it is not confined to any one class.'[72] In a land where no organization has a monopoly of force, the regime's policy has been to avoid the build up of arms for use against it. This can be done by co-operation with those who wish to arm themselves as well as trying to disarm those who wish to keep arms. According to Wallace Clark, the historian of the B Specials and recipient of an M.B.E. from the Labour government in 1970, a latent and important function of the organization was to prevent or at least reduce 'the growth of numerous private armies, defence associations and vigilante bodies'. During the August, 1969, Troubles, Clark notes that the B Specials were less successful than at other times in restraining the initiative of Ultras.[73] After the dis-banding of the B Specials the regime was ready to defend a policy of issuing licences for the formation of private gun clubs made up of former B Specials. As one backbench Unionist MP said, it would encourage 'crack shots to keep their hands and eyes in'. Without benefit of official licensing, a variety of local groups in the Shankill and other troubled areas, have quietly collected money and bought guns for use in troubled times.[74]

The only organization actively pledged to the Ultra position is the Ulster Volunteer Force. The name asserts a link with the Covenanters who fought to keep Ulster under the Union Jack at the time of the Troubles. Because the UVF is pledged to use force to secure its aims, the Stormont regime declared it an illegal organization in 1966, after its members were implicated in three killings in Belfast. Legally, the UVF has the same status as the IRA. Politically, the only thing it has in common is a distaste for the Stormont regime. The slogan 'Up the UVF' painted on a wall off the Shankill Road is just as much a challenge to the authority of the regime as is the slogan 'Up the IRA'. Neither the O'Neill administration nor the Chichester-Clark administration was deemed worthy of support. These 'true Protest-ants' regard the country's Prime Minister as the traitor. The existence of the UVF makes the Stormont regime take security precautions against armed attacks from Protestant as well as from Catholic quarters.

Even by comparison with the IRA, the UVF lacks organization. No effort was made to keep the organization intact after the Troubles ended in the 1920s, because the UVF had won. Political events in the 1960s made some doubt the permanence of victory, and seek to revive the spirit of the Covenant by invoking an old and honoured name. The spirit is easy enough to find, but the institutions of the UVF are not a matter of public report. The Cameron Commission, for example, found out little about the UVF. It also declared that it had no evidence to confirm or reject the possibility of connections between the Ulster Protestant Volunteers and the UVF.[75] Some security officials regard the UVF as no more than a label, used by a collection of Belfast Protestants associated with 'non-political crime', and individuals with Ultra political convictions. Reported arms shipments from the Continent to Ultras suggests that there are at least a few UVF men who are sophisticated enough to engage in the difficult task of international arms smuggling.

Evidence of the existence of an armed Protestant Ultra group (or groups) can be found in the streets and cemeteries of Northern Ireland. The Ultras were the probable perpetrators of a major public utility explosion in April, 1969, designed to discredit the authority of the O'Neill government. In October, 1969, a uniformed UVF man died in Donegal, when an accident occurred when he was attempting to dynamite an electricity station in the Republic. The UVF has also claimed credit for the symbolic destruction of other monuments in the Republic, as well as bomb attacks upon the home of Opposition MP Austin Currie. Many Protestant acts of political violence can occur without central directives, for there are Protestants everywhere prepared to take the initiative in their own community to defend Protestant political power, if they fear that official security forces are not strong enough in defence of their regime.

Irishmen and Irishwomen

The institutions challenging the regime on behalf of Catholics in Northern Ireland are numerous and in conflict with each other. Political parties, direct action civil rights groups, armed bands of citizen defenders, and 'conventional' guerilla armies coexist uneasily within Northern Ireland. The association of the disparate groups results from their common opposition to the Stormont regime and Stormont's tendency to treat all who oppose the regime as equally outside the Pale. The groups can be referred to as acting on behalf of Catholics, even though most are formally non-sectarian and the IRA is anathema to the hierarchy, because few Protestants are members of any of these anti-regime groups. Moreover, each must develop a *modus vivendi* with the Catholic clergy, ranging from the co-option of priests to the exclusion of clerics from participation. In terms of the distinctions outlined in Chapter I, two main types of Catholic opponents of the regime may be distinguished, the rebels and the repressed. *Rebels* endorse the violation of basic political laws as means to the end of repudiating a regime they do not support. The *repressed* refuse to support the Stormont Constitution, but are unwilling to violate basic political laws. Together, the two groups can be described as *disaffected*. It is appropriate to treat the groups together, because the line between them is often blurred. The civil rights demonstrations and their aftermath have shown that there are degrees of political opposition between the passiveness of a repressed subject and the activity of an IRA gunman. In the period of civil rights demonstrations, as previously, Catholics giving full allegiance to the regime had no political institutions stating their distinctive point of view. In so far as such people are numerous and active within the Catholic community, they add to the discord within it, because they differ from both their repressed and rebellious co-religionists.

Political parties drawing massed votes from Catholics are disaffected but not rebellious. They express disloyal views by legal means. With the exception of Sinn Fein, all the Catholic parties speak of the unification of Ireland occurring peacefully. None of the parties endorses the Constitution, but they differ among themselves in the extent to which they emphasize rejection of the Constitution. The parties also differ about issues that they emphasize in addition to the Border, as well as exhibiting many local and personal differences (cf. Chapter VII).

Ironically, the historic Northern Ireland opponent of the regime, the Nationalist Party, has presented the least challenge to it. The Nationalists at Stormont are heirs of the parliamentary tradition in the Irish independence movement, and have remained loyal to this in the face of competition from 'physical force' Republicans. The Nationalists have always feared the consequences for the Catholic minority in the North of any attempt to unite Ireland by force. In the period of conciliation, the leader of the Nationalists, Eddie McAteer, accepted the title of leader of the Opposition at Stormont. The Nationalists resigned the role following police actions in August, 1969. In the 1960s, Gerry Fitt came forward in Belfast to lead the Republican Labour Party's challenge to the regime. It expressed a positive concern with social and economic issues, as well as endorsing traditional Republican ends. The party was opposed to rebellion as a means to their end. Fitt was moderate only in an Ulster context, for he participated in the Londonderry march and was the first person batoned by the RUC there. Subsequently, he has concentrated more upon attacking the regime at Stormont and Westminster Parliaments; he sits simultaneously in both. The Republican Labour Party split in 1970, and Fitt became leader of the newly formed Social Democratic and Labour Party, which brought together civil rights MPs of various party ties and none. As its name suggests, the SDLP emphasizes social and economic issues. Its members are also vociferous in attacking the regime in Parliament for its civil rights actions and inactions. It does not organize illegal street demonstrations against the regime. By contrast, Sinn Fein, the political counterpart of the guerilla force of the Irish Republican Army, has always eschewed attendance at Parliament in Dublin, Stormont or Westminster. Its main effort is propaganda for Republican views, as well as providing an organization in which less military-minded Republicans can advocate or criticize policies.

The civil rights demonstrations begun in 1968 posed a novel challenge to the regime, substantively and in tactics. The civil rights groups reversed the tactics of Sinn Fein. Instead of trying to change the regime by refusing recognition of British sovereignty, they sought to change it by claiming full rights as British citizens. The major planks of the 1968 campaign concerned one man, one vote, one value in local elections; anti-discrimination legislation covering public employment and public administration; allocation of subsidized public housing by objective measures of need; repeal of the Special Powers Act; and disbanding the Ulster Special Constabulary. By British standards, most of these demands seemed moderate, even elementary. Within a Northern Ireland context, however, the civil rights programme was revolutionary, i.e., an attempt to transform the regime by sharing political power among Catholics and Protestants within Northern Ireland. This made the proposals more difficult to deal with; the demonstrators could not have their requests rejected out of hand as a challenge to the borders of the state.

The commitment of civil rights groups to non-violent protests and demonstrations was a tactic that took the Stormont regime by surprise. A challenge to authority expressed in arms can easily be met by arms. Ulster Protestants have time and again shown that they are prepared to meet firearms with firearms – and likely to emerge victorious on whatever battlefield is chosen. But in contemporary Anglo-American societies, a challenge to authority that rejects the use of firearms is unlikely to be met by gunfire. This is especially true if the challengers take care that their defiance occurs in front of journalists and television cameramen. Yet a demonstration by thousands of people in a busy public thoroughfare on a Saturday afternoon cannot be ignored, especially when it occurs in spite of a ban by the Minister of Home Affairs. The strategy of the Northern Ireland civil rights groups thus had much in common with those of American civil rights demonstrations of a few years previously, even to the point of using 'We Shall Overcome' as a marching song. The song also had a second use: it avoided demonstrators singing songs of a Republican character.

The illegal status of some demonstrations was of little concern to those organizing the demonstrations, because they rejected the claim to legitimacy of the regime branding their acts illegal. Such a response could only be expected when discord was made public. Breaking a law even had the advantage of increasing the seriousness of the challenge to the regime. The violation of civil law by reference to a higher morality was publicly endorsed by the Catholic hierarchy in January, 1969. Cardinal Conway and his Northern bishops praised the civil rights movement as 'non-violent and non-sectarian in character; fidelity to these principles had been clearly and movingly demonstrated on many occasions'. Their statement also noted, 'The sad fact is that virtually nothing was done until the people took to the streets.'[76]

The use of the term 'movement' to describe the civil rights groups is appropriate, because it suggests activity. But actions can lead in many directions. Northern Ireland civil rights groups, like their American counterparts, have agreed more about what they are against than what they are for. Individuals and organizations acting in the name of civil rights differ about tactics as well as ultimate ends. Initially, the Northern Ireland Civil Rights Association, the co-ordinating council for civil rights activities, was meant to be inclusive. It was non-sectarian; one Unionist was even on its original council. It avoided discussing issues outside the field of civil rights, concentrating upon the few anti-regime issues that united its disparate membership. It was inevitably political, in the sense that its issues raised major differences of opinion and attracted people with interests beyond civil rights. At the beginning, the civil rights movement was multi-partisan, attracting members of all parties and none. It included ex-IRA men in its ranks as well as what the Cameron Report described as 'a ballast of moderate and earnest men and women'. The complexities of Northern Ireland politics are such that the Communist chairman of the CRA, Miss Betty Sinclair, was one of those most prominent in counselling moderation.[77] The February, 1969 general election showed the extent of political differences within the movement. Some activists thought that the CRA should nominate candidates, whereas others wished to keep it independent of party politics. The CRA did not sponsor candidates but a variety of persons nominated and elected owed their political prominence to participation in the movement.

As an association of affiliated civil rights groups, the Northern Ireland Civil Rights Association could not rely upon all its member groups acting in accord with its policy resolutions.[78] The CRA's initial success made it possible for regional councils to co-ordinate the stopping and starting of demonstrations for a period of about six months in 1969. But the disorder of August ended this. At all times, affiliated organizations have been free to follow their own line, not only in committee discussions but also in the streets. Because of this, local affiliates can influence events by making policy on the ground. Thus, the challenge to the regime does not come from a single cohesive organization, but rather from a series of local and special political groups, which tend to differ greatly about the desirability and tactical wisdom of any particular course of action.

The development of civil rights activities in Londonderry illustrates these complexities in a single community. Prior to the October 5, 1968 demonstrations, a small number of local Catholics had become increasingly dissatisfied with Catholic political leadership in Derry, because it had achieved nothing in opposition to the dominant Unionists, nor did it promise hope of better conditions for the city in the future. Because the established Nationalist Party leader, Eddie McAteer, represented a Derry constituency, there seemed no hope in working through existing political institutions. The desire for community improvement involved many things besides civil rights. For instance, in 1965 some Protestants and Catholics joined together to protest at Stormont against the government's decision to site the new second university of Northern Ireland at Coleraine, rather than in the city itself. A Catholic school teacher, John Hume, began organizing a credit union locally, to encourage poor people to save money and avoid exorbitant interest charges when buying goods on credit. Hume became president of the national (i.e., all-Ireland) association of credit unions in recognition of his work. There were also militant Socialist groups active in Derry, under the leadership of Eamonn McCann. Thus, there was no difficulty in finding people and local groups interested in planning a protest march there in autumn, 1968. The CRA initially encouraged the October 5 demonstration, but when the march was made illegal, it lost enthusiasm. There was sufficient enthusiasm in Derry to push ahead with the march.[79] Differences between Derry and the CRA in Belfast were matched by differences within Derry. At the 1969 general election, Hume and McCann fought each other as well as the Nationalist McAteer in the Foyle constituency. Hume won. In the crisis of August 12, 1969, Derry Catholics co-operated in barricading the Bogside, and Catholics in other towns and Belfast co-operated by attacking their local RUC stations to prevent police reinforcements from being sent to the Bogside.

The creation and growth of the People's Democracy shows how a civil rights group can be quickly formed independent of a local community. The People's Democracy, or PD, was started in autumn, 1968 by lecturers, students and ex-students of Queen's University, Belfast, arising from meetings at the students' union. At a time when student riots were disrupting campuses elsewhere in the Western world, it is entirely in character that events in Northern Ireland moved in the opposite direction. Student members left the university precincts in peace and concentrated attention upon the society around them. The PD has as its ultimate goal the replacement of both the Stormont and the Dublin regimes by an Irish Workers' Republic, in the tradition of James Connolly. Society's problems are defined as economic rather than sectarian or constitutional at bottom. Irish independence is desired, not so much as an end in itself, but as a means of freeing the land from the domination of British and foreign capital. Michael Farrell, one of the leaders of the group, has succinctly summed up the PD position by stating, 'Revolution not reform'. Bernadette Devlin, a founder member of the PD, has been most prominent in emphasizing that anti-regime demonstrations should be about something beyond civil rights. In December, 1970, she explained her absence from a civil rights demonstration against the regime by stating:

These things are important. But essentially they are 'fair play' issues and not for the first time let me make the point that fair play is not enough . . .

If we are going to march–and I have no dogmatic objections to breaking Tory bans–let us march for a programme which is in the interests of all the working-class people, that is, a Socialist programme and anti-capitalist programme. Let us demand more jobs as well as fair play in job allocation.[80]

The immediate aim of the PD is to radicalize the working class and small farmers. In efforts to do this, it has turned away from the narrow confines of university circles, recruiting ex-students and non-students. It organizes such things as protests against higher bus fares, or a 'fish in' on Lough Neagh against the privileges of the eel fishery. At the 1969 Stormont election, the PD nominated eight candidates for Parliament; they polled an average of 27 per cent of the vote in the rural constituencies they fought. The PD candidates fought the election with a promise that they would be back in the streets when the election was over. In the words of Michael Farrell,

The danger of being swallowed by parliamentarism required constant vigilance and a clearly worked out Socialist strategy towards a bourgeois Parliament, using Parliament as a sounding box and as only one section of an activity which is mainly extra-parliamentary.[81]

The PD has only been able to secure support from within the Catholic community. Its leadership mainly consists of young people from Catholic homes; many are no longer practising Catholics and strongly dislike anything with sectarian overtones. For example, when Farrell was once pressed to say how he would describe himself in a society divided along religious lines, he replied, 'People would call us Fenians.'

The loose alliance of groups and individuals forming the Northern Ireland Civil Rights Association was not strong enough to suppress internal differences of opinion. As disorder intensified in the streets in 1969, so too discord flourished within the CRA. By the time the association's annual general meeting occurred in Belfast in February, 1970, the individuals controlling the association were under attack from two sides. Dr. Conn McCluskey of the Campaign for Social Justice, Dungannon, and two others refused to stand for re-election to the executive, charging that there were substantial administrative irregularities in its affairs, and that the CRA since June, 1969, 'was being manipulated to suit one political ideology, that of International Revolutionary Socialism'. Simultaneously, Michael Farrell and Kevin Boyle of the People's Democracy refused to stand for re-election, on the grounds that the CRA executive had been taken over by people who were closer to the 'green and red' views of one faction of the IRA than they were to the 'pure red' of international socialism. Eamonn McCann tore up a membership card while walking out of a CRA meeting, protesting that Protestants would no longer be welcome in the CRA as it would not support such civil rights demands as a divorce law in the Republic.[82]

The events of August, 1969, radically altered the alternatives facing disaffected Catholics. The Bogside rising showed that rebellious activity could succeed, even in the face of police opposition. The intimidation, arson and shooting directed at Catholics in Belfast showed what could happen to those without guns. The range of possible political alternatives seemed infinite, from a successful Irish insurrection against British sovereignty to a successful Protestant pogrom against Catholics. These new possibilities reduced the attention Catholics gave to other goals. Parliamentary opposition became less credible, because opposition MPs, in spite of frequent efforts to prevent troubles, had been unable to influence the Protestant regime. Civil rights demonstrations also became of secondary importance. Manning barricades in riotous streets got higher priority than parading through peaceful streets. Patrick Pearse's comment on the situation facing Republicans in 1913 after the formation of the Ulster Volunteer Force once again became relevant:

> It is symptomatic of the attitude of the Irish Nationalist that when he ridicules the Orangeman he ridicules him not for his numerous foolish beliefs, but for his readiness to fight in defence of those beliefs. But this is exactly wrong. The Orangeman is ridiculous in so far as he believes incredible things; he is estimable in so far as he is willing and able to fight in defence of what he believes.
>
> It is foolish of an Orangeman to believe that his personal liberty is threatened by Home Rule; but granting that he believes that, it is not only in the highest degree common sense but it is his clear duty to arm in defence of his threatened liberty. Personally, I think the Orangeman with a rifle a much less ridiculous figure than the Nationalist without a rifle; and the Orangeman who can fire a gun will certainly count for more in the end than the Nationalist who can do nothing cleverer than make a pun.[83]

Institutions of Discord

While the context was unique, the situation was a recurring one in Irish history. Long before the police existed in any part of the British isles, Catholics had felt threatened by Protestant attacks and Protestants, in turn, felt threatened by Catholic attacks. The consequence was the formation of armed bands of men to provide communal protection. The best-known Protestant group was the Orange Order. Among Catholics at the end of the eighteenth century, there were three categories of armed groups—agrarian secret societies, religious societies and local factions. Their lack of central organization made it difficult for Dublin Castle to decapitate them. The agrarian societies were concerned with the redress of peasant grievances, primarily of an economic type. The major religious society was called the Ribbonmen; it was concentrated principally in Ulster as a counterweight to the Orange Order. The local factions fought at fairs and similar occasions, often with little motive beside a desire for a fight. As an historian of the period cautions, in words also true of the present:

> A degree of order can be introduced by ignoring the problems of regional distribution and identification by name and attempting instead to classify the groups by organisation and purpose. . . . The categories, however, tend to overlap. On occasion the Ribbon Society, a Catholic protection organisation, might turn away from its major concern and pursue economic goals similar to those of the agrarian secret societies. Local factions, formed to perpetuate peasant feuds by gang-fighting at markets and fairs, often resembled the Ribbonmen in their enthusiasm for clashes with Protestants. Where both agrarian secret societies and local factions existed in the same area, it is quite possible that the former drew most of their members from the latter.[84]

In one respect, Catholics saw their position in 1969 as worse than that at the end of the eighteenth century. In earlier times, Catholics might lack police protection from attack by an armed Protestant band. But at least, when the Protestants attacked, the Ribbonmen were fighting an enemy with much the same talents and weapons as those available to themselves. In the absence of an organized police force anywhere in the British isles, political violence was unmediated by the police, and troops were often several days distant because of poor communications and transport. In 1969, Catholics had to contend with the Royal Ulster Constabulary. Many Catholics did not view the police as a force providing protection, but as an organization that they required protection against.

In Belfast, where fears of a major pogrom were greatest, Catholics reverted to the old tradition of Ribbonmen, forming local defence associations based upon a parish or even smaller clusters of Catholic homes. The British Army provided a line of defence against an immediate repetition of the August, 1969 attacks, but the Army was at best seen as a stop-gap. Catholics preferred to assume the responsibility for their own defence rather than trust alien troops subject to a distant command. Local defence groups came together by electing representatives to a newly formed city-wide Central Citizens Defence Committee. The immediate problem facing the CCDC and the British Army was: What to do about the barricades? The creation of a 'no go' land was a palpable derogation of the authority of the Stormont regime. The Army was ready to negotiate with the CCDC about the removal of the barricades. Catholic clergy, such as Father Padraig Murphy, administrator of a large parish in the Lower Falls, became prominent in the negotiations. The CCDC leadership agreed to ask their neighbourhood groups to co-operate in the peaceful removal of the barricades, in return for an Army assurance that it would guarantee protection at all times for Catholics against attacks by Protestants.[85] Most home-made barricades came down in September, 1969. The Army provided portable barbed-wire barriers at vulnerable street corners, for quick use by soldiers in emergencies. The CCDC has continued all-night patrols by vigilante groups in sensitive areas and at times of trouble. The vigilantes are intended to provide a 'trip wire', rousing a neighbourhood in the event of attack by Protestant arsonists or gunmen, and dealing on the spot with law breakers within the Catholic community.

Defence requires guns. Broken paving stones, bottles, burnt-out automobiles and stolen buses can make barricades proof against unexpected attack from men in passing automobiles. But they could not be proof against the kind of armed attack that Catholics in Belfast feared might happen yet again. As a Bogside man told a court in the Republic, after being arrested for training in the use of firearms,

> We have been attacked by the RUC, by Paisleyites and by B Specials in and out of uniform. We have had enough. We will take no more.[86]

The citizens defence groups are not themselves organized along military lines. The task of securing arms, training men in their use and maintaining stockpiles near at hand is primarily the responsibility

163

of those involved in the military side of the Irish Republican movement. The very diffuseness of the Republican 'movement' has meant that individual Republicans are inevitably present in civil rights and citizens defence groups. Cathal Goulding, an IRA leader, has explained that such persons could act as 'members of the community' and not on 'a specific IRA assignment'. The Cameron Report praised known IRA members involved in civil rights demonstrations in 1968–69 as 'efficient stewards, maintaining discipline and checking any disposition to indiscipline or disorder'.[87]

The Irish Republican Army has a long, sporadic and unsuccessful history of using guns to attack the Stormont regime. Upon occasion, IRA men will use their guns against officials of the Dublin regime too. The dedication of IRA members is often considerable. Men have endured a decade or more of imprisonment, often under extremely harsh conditions in the Republic, for refusing to give symbolic recognition to the authority of the Dublin or Stormont regime. A few IRA men have literally starved to death in hunger strikes protesting against the existence of two regimes in Ireland. The military efficiency of members of the IRA is another matter. The greatest loss of life it has occasioned since the Second World War occurred in 1957 at Edentubber in the Republic. Five Republicans were killed by an accident when handling their own explosives.* The failure of the 1956–62 campaign against Partition had made some members of the IRA think again about their long-term objectives. Was the Army dedicated to the creation of a United Ireland without regard to what followed after? Or was it dedicated to achieving a particular kind of society within a United Ireland? In 1965, a special conference of the IRA Army Council produced a nine-point programme endorsing social revolution as well as political revolution. The Council also endorsed the abandonment of abstention from Parliament, so that 'guerilla activities' could be undertaken in the three Parliaments then claiming some authority in parts of the 32 counties of Ireland. In social terms, the recommendations meant a turn to the left, resurrecting the ideals of James Connolly and the language of Marxists. But the political implications were in the opposite direction – recognition of the Dublin and Stormont regimes, even if only tactically and temporarily. The Sinn Fein annual conference, representing the party political wing of

* Five Protestants were killed by an explosion at Brougher Mountain, Fermanagh, in February, 1971. The explosive charge was apparently not intended for them.

the Republican movement, refused to accept so drastic a change in policy. Republicans then apparently deadlocked on the issue of maintaining or abandoning their traditional abstentionist policy. By 1967, the movement was, in the words of its own chief of staff, 'dormant'.[88]

The civil rights agitation strengthened those Republicans who argued that the regimes in Ireland could be repudiated by non-violent as well as violent means. The Protestant reaction to the civil rights campaign in August, 1969, strengthened IRA men who argued that only force would resolve Ireland's difficulties. The use of private and police arms against Catholics in West Belfast caught the IRA completely unprepared; it had less than a dozen guns available for use. IRA men in the Lower Falls Road area held off Protestant crowds for three hours with revolvers, while their comrades sped to Dundalk to secure several machine-guns for use in defence of the parish church, the school and a block of expensive new council flats. Paradoxically, the reputation of the IRA among Protestants for storing arms appears to have made Protestant groups cautious about attacking their Catholic neighbours. Paddy Devlin, the MP for the area, expressed his constituents' views with English understatement, 'There was a certain amount of ill-feeling against the IRA for not having produced any' (i.e., guns).[89]

The absence of weapons when needed intensified recriminations within the IRA. In January, 1970, the split came into the open at the Sinn Fein annual conference in Dublin. One point of view is tersely stated by Dr. Roy Johnston, a Marxist computer analyst, 'There is no point in fighting unless you are going to win', i.e., achieve a regime with the 'correct' social and economic policies, as well as jurisdiction in all 32 counties of Ireland. A Belfast opponent states the opposite point of view, 'We are traditional Republicans fighting to free our people. When they are free they will decide what kind of government they want. But the communists in Dublin want to shove a ready-made workers' Republic down the people's throats.'[90] The split resulted in the creation of two IRAs and two Sinn Feins—the Red and Green or Official IRA under the leadership of Cathal Goulding, and the Provisional or Green IRA, under Ruairi O'Bradaigh of Sinn Fein and a military commander who prefers to remain anonymous. The IRA in Northern Ireland reportedly split at gun point. These two groups are not the only armed Republican organizations operating in Northern Ireland. Saor Eire (Gaelic for

Free Ireland) has maintained a nucleus of members. It is known for using force whenever possible, whether against the British or the RUC or to rob banks to secure money for guns and organization work. By the summer of 1970, a journalist making enquiries in Belfast and Dublin concluded that there were *five* IRAs, i.e., groups claiming to be the heirs to the tradition of ending British sovereignty in Northern Ireland by resort to force.[91]

Within Northern Ireland, both 'Ribbonmen' and IRA groups faced difficulties in getting arms and storing them without detection. Money was not the greatest problem. Gun purchases could be financed in many different ways – by house to house collections of a few shillings a week; by contributions from well to do people sympathetic to the Republican cause, or by robbing a bank. The problem has been a shortage of guns. Shotguns and revolvers, while reassuring, are inadequate if one wishes to fight the British Army. A few sub-machine guns and high-powered rifles have found their way into Republican armouries. Gelignite has also been in good supply. It is used to cause explosions in public buildings, and in home-made grenades thrown in street fighting. After the killings in August, 1969, Republicans faced new demands for training in arms from Catholics 'who would in normal circumstances run 40 miles from a gun'.[92] Supplies are always subject to loss in Army or RUC raids. Republicans complain bitterly that security forces make more raids against them than in search of Protestant arms.

In this time of trouble, the obvious place for Catholics to turn for arms was to the Republic. Constitutionally, the Dublin regime asserts a claim to govern Northern Ireland. Article 2 of the 1937 Constitution states, 'The national territory consists of the whole island of Ireland, its islands and the territorial seas.' Article 3 suspends application of its laws there 'pending the re-integration of the national territory'. This constitutional claim to sovereignty in the North has been a major source of discord between Stormont and Dublin since the foundation of the two regimes. (Westminster turns a blind eye to the clause, and treats the Republic with the consideration due a Dominion or even a remote and poor part of the United Kingdom.) The failure of the Dublin regime to do anything positive to achieve 'the re-integration of the national territory' creates discord between it and Republicans.

The events of August, 1969, had a powerful impact in Dublin as well as in the North. After an all-day Cabinet meeting on August 13, the Taoiseach, Jack Lynch, announced that Irish Army forces would move to Border areas near Derry to provide 'field hospital services'. He added enigmatically, 'The Irish Government can no longer stand by and watch innocent people injured and perhaps worse.' Arguably, the Taoiseach's broadcast intensified Protestant fears of a military attack across the Border, notwithstanding the small size, poor equipment and poor training of the Irish Army. The broadcast was an attempt to forestall pressures within his own Cabinet and from Republican elements in the Army and outside the Army that 'something' be done to aid Catholics under fire in the North.

Afterwards, there was discord in Dublin about what the regime there could and should do on behalf of its 'citizens' in Northern Ireland. Military attack by the 8,000-'strong' Irish armed services was out of the question, given the presence of a vastly superior British Army. Providing the IRA with sheltered bases inside the Republic to use as havens after operations within Northern Ireland was ruled out by virtue of the IRA's refusal to recognize the Dublin regime as well as Stormont. Furthermore, the leftward trend in the IRA made its members increasingly ready to criticize the Dublin regime where its social and economic policies were most vulnerable. Shipping arms of the Irish Army to the North was also ruled out because the source of the weapons would easily be identified if uncovered by the British or the RUC. Dublin is too dependent upon London for favourable treatment in bilateral trade negotiations to give overt offence. The arguments for taking some positive action were none the less strong. One argument was moral: Catholics threatened with attack by arson or gunfire had a right to arms in self-defence. A second was strategic: as Protestants were already armed, then Catholics required arms to maintain a balance of power. A third argument had immediate appeal in Dublin, because it was prudential: by supplying arms and training men in their use, the Irish government could see that guns got into the 'right' rather than the 'wrong' hands.

The positive steps taken by officials of the Dublin regime were several and collectively ambiguous. The following activities are matters of record. Immediately upon the outbreak of disorder, refugee camps were established for Catholics who were intimidated from their homes, and sought a temporary refuge in the South. In autumn, 1969, Catholic youths from the North were given military training at government camps in the Republic. The wings of the IRA also began organizing weekend schools in the Republic, with men from the North trained in the use of arms. Upon occasion, individuals were arrested, but they were not prosecuted energetically. In a case in Donegal, the state's attorney told the court, 'Let them go in peace and leave their arms behind.' The lethargy of Dublin's Special Branch police in moving against known IRA men was described by one Dublin weekly as 'the politics of "underkill" '.[93] £100,000 was appropriated for the relief of individual distress. An unknown but substantial 'special service' fund was opened to pay for arms shipments; an official of the Dublin regime made efforts to purchase arms on the Continent of Europe for possible use in the North. The Ministry of Defence in Dublin, caught unaware by the August, 1969 disorder, began drawing up contingency plans in the event of a 'doomsday' situation, that is, an armed attack on Catholics of such intensity that the Irish Army might be committed across the international boundary with the North, in an effort to forestall a massive pogrom.[94] As part of its active policy of following events in the North, the Ministry moved 500 rifles to Dundalk, near the border, in spring, 1970, when it appeared that there might be considerable disorder and bloodshed. In the event, they were not needed.

The major point of dispute is not whether the regime gave military aid to people in the North, but who was responsible. Were such actions taken with or against the authority of the Prime Minister and his Cabinet? Captain James Kelly of the Intelligence section of the Irish Army, has testified unambiguously about his efforts to buy arms to supply to the North. The Prime Minister was sufficiently convinced of the involvement of his Minister of Finance, Charles Haughey, and the Minister of Agriculture, Neil Blaney, to indict both for participation in arms deals. But the charge against Blaney was subsequently dismissed, and in October, 1970, a Dublin jury acquitted Haughey, Captain Kelly and two others after testimony that implicated individuals still within Lynch's Cabinet. John Kelly of Belfast, an active member of the Belfast CCDC and formerly interned for Republican associations, swore that at his trial. When defence committees came to Dublin, Kelly said:

> They did not ask for blankets or feeding bottles—they asked for guns and no one from the Premier, Mr. Lynch down, refused that request or told them that this was contrary to government policy.[95]

At a minimum, it appears that Lynch hoped circumstances, not excluding Northern subversive acts, might force the British government to suspend the Constitution of the Stormont regime. Once this happened, he might then negotiate better terms for the Catholics with a British Labour government or even negotiate a move toward the reunification of Ireland. This was the story he was said to tell delegations from the North.[96]

From a Northern Catholic perspective, the actions of the regime in Dublin were a source of discord, not harmony. The promise to give assistance was not fulfilled by large-scale shipments of arms. The bulk of the measures did no more than create cadres of trained men in the North whom Dublin might mobilize under Dublin's command, as and when an emergency made this policy necessary or desirable from Dublin's point of view. The decision of Lynch to indict those officials doing the most to give assistance to the North further alienated Catholics in Ulster, for it meant that their potential 'armoury' was unreliable. Subsequent to the Dublin trial, Haughey and Blaney supported a vote of confidence in Jack Lynch to maintain the unity of the Fianna Fail party. This was a sign to Ulster Catholics that even friends in the Republic were more interested in using them in a power struggle in the governing party than in acting from a sense of Republican idealism.

The Catholics of Northern Ireland have had no difficulty in maintaining discord without Southern intervention. Within the CCDC, the presence of representatives of both IRAs, plus Ribbonmen with more immediate and less grandiose concerns with self-defence, was one source of controversy. The uneasy relationship between the two IRAs and the absence of widespread public confidence in their capabilities, at times appeared to make both the Red and Provisional groups ready to take the offensive to show force. The dispersion of weapons and the will to use them had become so great that often neither of the IRA factions needed to give a command for shooting to begin and bloodshed to follow. A member of the Army Council of the Green IRA complained in August, 1970:

> There is an element in Belfast and other parts of the North which are neither under our control nor under the Goulding unit's control. Some of them could perhaps be loosely described as hooligans. There are gangs of youths who come out, they throw stones and bottles, and when the real trouble starts, they just disappear and run away, leaving the IRA and the Defence Committees to deal with the situation.[97]

Institutions of Discord

Three months later, after two men were shot dead in the street in Belfast, the Central Citizens Defence Committee denounced IRA groups that engage in or advocate militant offensives: 'Recent events and statements indicate that the *legitimate defence* of our people is no longer their only concern.' Almost coincidentally, Bernadette Devlin stated a third, 'all red' point of view upon emerging from prison in Armagh, 'The riots are terrible because they simply prop up the system. They make the majority of people more conservative.' She hastened to add that her rejection of Protestant-Catholic or Catholic-Army confrontations was not a sign of pacifism, 'I'm not against force. I don't even believe that force should only be used as a last resort to take power. I believe it should be used when it will work.' As the winter moved on, Republicans tested the hypothesis that the only argument that will work with Westminster is force. After six weeks of battles, six British soldiers, two RUC men and at least three IRA men were dead. Four IRA men were also shot when the Provisional and the Red and Green groups held a 'shoot out' with each other in the streets of West Belfast.[98]

Nations in Arms

Any anatomy of political institutions is likely to make the parts described look simpler, more clearly defined and more neatly interrelated than they are in life. A listing of political institutions also tends to suggest that each group discussed is equally organized and, perhaps, equal in consideration. This is palpably not the case in Northern Ireland. Nothing could be more organized, in a formal sense, than the British Army. Nothing could be less coherent than the fragmented IRAs or the Ulster Volunteer Force. The former moves impressively around Northern Ireland with all the power and paraphernalia of a modern Army. The latter move furtively in small groups under cover of darkness. The evidence that they are there at all is the detonation of an explosive or the firing of a gun; often, the violence inflicts more injury upon those starting it than upon those attacked.

The grouping of institutions under common headings, such as law enforcement or coercive forces, can also mislead. For example, seen from a distance, Westminster appears a monolith. Yet any analysis of its relations with Northern Ireland must take into account the different interests of the Home Office, the Ministry of Defence, the Treasury, the Foreign Office, the Shipbuilding Industries Board and other departments of state that, from time to time, will take decisions affecting Northern Ireland. The combined power of all these civil institutions is limited. For instance, within eight months of pledging the British government to uphold the rule of law, Reginald Maudling committed himself before the Stormont Parliament to the use of guns, i.e. lawful British Army weapons, to maintain the authority of the Northern Ireland regime.

The multiplicity of institutions and interests in play in Northern Ireland raises fundamental questions: What is government in Northern Ireland? Does a regime exist at all? In every Anglo-American society, especially those with federal forms of government, there is a sense in which government can never be seen as a whole.[99] The examination of its activities in a particular case may emphasize finance, the social service, the judiciary or the military side of a regime. This is very true in Northern Ireland. Many of the activities of the Stormont regime, such as health or agriculture, have little reference to issues raised in this chapter. In a complementary manner, many of the activities of the Republican regimes in exile hardly affect the activities of Stormont. The debates about policy within the IRA in the period 1965–68 attracted little attention in Northern Ireland. Yet all these institutions affect Stormont's authority.

The chief institutions defending the regime come together at meetings of the Joint Security Committee, the body formally concerned with co-ordinating the actions taken to prevent the regime's repudiation by force. It is a co-ordinating body because its members sit as representatives of independently important institutions. The membership as of January, 1971 included the Prime Minister; two of his senior Unionist Cabinet colleagues, Brian Faulkner and William Long; the General Officer Commanding the British Army in Northern Ireland, Lieutenant-General Sir Ian Freeland; the Chief Constable of the Royal Ulster Constabulary, Graeme Shillington; and the United Kingdom Government's representative in Northern Ireland, Ronald Burroughs. Others with relevant responsibilities are asked to attend the Committee to discuss particular problems concerning them. For example, John Taylor, the Minister of State for Home Affairs, handled day to day business under the general responsibility of the Prime Minister; he can provide specialist knowledge beyond that which would normally come from the Prime Minister. In early February, 1971, Taylor summarized his policy for dealing with Republicans thus: 'We are going to shoot it out with them. It is as simple as that.'[100]

The outlook of each member of the Security Committee reflects his institutional interests and role. The Prime Minister, for example, has an immediate interest in retaining the support of sufficient Unionist MPs to prevent his forced resignation. Similarly, his Cabinet colleagues will have an interest in maintaining their own status within the Unionist Parliamentary party. There is potential discord among these three men, for any minister important enough for inclusion in the Committee can see himself as a potential successor to the Prime Minister. All three will seek to make Committee decisions palatable to the Unionist backbenchers, even though they may differ about what must be done to achieve this goal. In the climate of 1971 dissident MPs within the party and Protestant Unionists pressing hard at its edges demand 'tougher' measures, i.e., a readier use of coercive force and the application of sterner and broader laws against Catholics rejecting the regime. The interest of the head of the disarmed Royal Ulster Constabulary will be in doing things to raise the morale of a force that has gone through hard times, and also increase public confidence in it. Traditionally, the head of the RUC gave the benefit of the doubt to the supporters of the regime, and withheld it from its opponents. As long as Orangemen and other Protestants assert that they will march, even in defiance of the regime, then the police have an immediate interest in supporting their request to parade. To ban a march that will occur anyway is sure to lead to a breach of the peace, with RUC men against Orangemen. To allow such a march to proceed may not breach the peace. The same argument will also appeal to many Unionist MPs, thus affecting the thinking of Cabinet ministers. If the threat to the peace comes from Republicans, then some Unionists are likely to think that repressing their parades in the long run is to preserve the peace. Where major parades are confined within the Catholic community the police can try to turn a blind eye to events, but Republicans can frustrate a strategy of non-confrontation by openly provocative acts.

The British civil and military members of the Joint Security Committee sit as fully participating members; they are not confined to the status of advisers, as often happens to British officials in their dealings with Stormont. The General and the United Kingdom 'ambassador' are responsible, ultimately, to the British Parliament, not the Stormont Parliament. Yet they must be acutely sensitive to local political conditions, inasmuch as a decision that is satisfactory to them but not to spokesmen for the Unionist government will lead to deadlock, and the political repercussions of deadlock on security matters would be grave. Each, in effect, wishes to claim a veto over the proposals of the other.

In considering a particular case, the Army's immediate interest is in assuring that if a breach of the peace occurs, it will have sufficient force at hand to contain and repress any disorder. This means that even seemingly innocuous matters, such as the return of a crowd from a football match, may require the Army to make contingency plans for troop movements, in case the supporters of a Protestant team begin to clash with Catholics. The general interest of the Army is to avoid a situation likely to create disorder so widespread that its troops could no longer repress violence everywhere in Northern Ireland. Positively, the Army's goal is to transfer day to day responsibilities for internal security to the RUC and reduce the Army's manpower in the Province to 2,000 to 3,000 troops in barracks with no internal security duties at all. This is the traditional strength of British troops in the Province in quiet times.

The immediate interest of any United Kingdom government in Northern Ireland is to pursue a policy that can be defended in its Westminster Parliament. The civil rights demonstrations and all that has followed since make the old policy of non-involvement unacceptable in a climate of greater British interest and awareness of Ulster affairs. The British government's diagnosis of a defensible policy is the 1969 reform programme. Hence, its representative must guard against measures contrary to these reforms, e.g., rearming the RUC. A second object is the maintenance of a separate Northern Ireland regime, so that the British government does not have to defend at Westminster all that happens in civil administration in Northern Ireland. At a given point of time, this object is likely to be reduced to a policy of maintaining the current Prime Minister in office, for fear that the alternative may mark a turn toward the Ultras. British support for the Premiership of Major James Chichester-Clark rested upon just this basis in 1970. As long as it is Westminster's policy that the incumbent is 'the best Prime Minster we've got', then risks of disorder must be weighed against political risks. In this balance, the political life of the Prime Minister weighs more heavily than any other. By a process of reaction, British policy has effectively shifted from that of a neutral guardian of the Queen's peace to that of a committed participant. Just as the IRA makes no apology for what is done in its name, so Westminster cannot be overly critical about the actions of the Stormont regime it defends. The Westminster view is that it is doing no more than supporting the lawfully established regime. The disaffected Catholic view is that it is supporting a Protestant regime. It can, in fact, do both.

Any problem that comes up to the Joint Security Committee threatens more discord. Men who agree about maintaining the Stormont regime can none the less disagree about how this would best be done in particular circumstances. Any decision taken is unlikely to satisfy all the objects of all parties to the discussion. Moreover, any decision is only a statement of intentions, based upon hypothesized responses by opponents of the regime. Opponents of the regime may not respond as expected. In the event, the consequences may be better than anticipated or worse. Such matters can be estimated in advance of an event, but demonstrations, by their nature, can unexpectedly go out of control, just as riots for which the police and Army prepare carefully may not, in the event, happen.

Incidents in the summer of 1970 illustrate how the outcome of Security Committee decisions can vary from what is expected. The approach of the Twelfth of July was carefully anticipated as a time of disorder in the streets. The Security Committee decided to allow the marches to proceed, with heavy police and military protection. Because of careful preparations for trouble, the marches took place without disorder. Yet a fortnight previously, the Security Committee had made a similar decision to allow much smaller Orange parades to occur on what is in effect a mini-Twelfth in Belfast. Fighting between Protestants and Catholics broke out as the Orangemen marched through West Belfast, and fighting later broke out in East Belfast. By the time the weekend was over, seven people were dead— six Protestants and one Catholic.[101] In terms of peace-keeping, the weekend was a disaster. Politically, the Cabinet avoided blame for restricting the rights of Orangemen to march by Catholic areas, and Unionist politicians wishing a more repressive policy against Catholics were given an issue which could only strengthen their case.

The Security Committee is fortunate when challenges to authority can be anticipated and discussed days or weeks ahead. Many actions must, by the immediacy of the challenge, be decided in a matter of hours or minutes by men on the spot. For instance, the Army reported taking on very short notice the decision to impose a 'curfew-type' order on the Lower Falls Road on July 3, 1970. The Army went there at 4.40 p.m., after receiving a reliable tip a half-hour previously that arms were stored in a particular house. It was afraid that arms might be shifted if it delayed. It found arms and removed them. While withdrawing, troops were stoned and teargas was thrown back. Then barricades began being built by the 'Red and Green' IRA, in retaliation for the loss of arms. The General Officer in Command at Lisburn, consulting by radio with the brigadier directly in control, had only minutes in which to decide how to respond to this escalation. The decision was made to surround the area with troops to prevent the arrival of IRA reinforcements from other parts of Belfast. This was done. By 7.17 p.m. the first man was dead. At 10 p.m. a curfew proclamation was read aloud from helicopters flying over the area. The largest Army operation of 1970 was thus mounted without time to consult any Committee.

Notwithstanding the subsequent attack upon the Army by Catholics for this curfew, at least the Army had the solace that what happened involved actions under their orders. The alternative is for disorder to turn to death without any involvement by institutions of the Joint Security Committee. This happened the last weekend of June, 1970, at Ballymacarrett in East Belfast. There, Catholic Ribbonmen and Protestant volunteers returned gunfire all night. When a journalist turned up on the scene at 11.30 p.m., two RUC patrolmen stopped him with the caution, 'I wouldn't go down that way. We are about to evacuate ourselves.' He saw them disappear and turned to view two crowds of people–Protestants and Catholics –directing heavy small arms fire at each other at short range across the Newtonards Road. Catholics were firing from the grounds of St. Matthew's Catholic Church and the Protestants were returning the attack. The sexton's house was burned, and the church door scarred, but the church itself survived. British soldiers who arrived on the scene after firing started were confined for hours to patrolling the main road in armoured cars.[102] They had insufficient men to leave the safety of these cars and force the two sides to separate and stop shooting. The firing between Protestants and Catholics continued, with the Army unable to stop it, until after dawn. Four men were killed.

The job of the Security Committee is an awesome task, in a land in which private citizens can turn out to fight fellow citizens with

Part Two

V · How People View the Regime

Bourgeois democracy and the national state are recent developments in Ireland and their traditions do not run deep, in contrast to the tradition of armed insurrection, or revolution as a means.

MICHAEL FARRELL, People's Democracy

Political authority is more than a problem of institutions: it is also a problem of popular opinion. The political structure of Northern Ireland encourages a close relation between governors and governed. Both social and geographical distances are limited. Unlike England, Members of Parliament are not drawn from a social stratum apart from the mass of the population. The bulk of MPs are middle class, not upper class. In other words, they have the same social standing as one-third of the population, and, apart from a slightly higher living standard, no special claims to high status or to deference. With the exception of a succession of Old Etonian Prime Ministers—Brookeborough, O'Neill and Chichester-Clark—Unionist MPs have almost always been educated within Ireland, and Opposition MPs invariably so.

In so far as ability is proportionate to numbers, then Northern Ireland, with its population of 1,500,000 might have the political talent of an English county such as Durham, Cheshire or Hampshire, or of an American state such as Nebraska, Oregon or West Virginia. If Northern Ireland were without its own Constitution, it might provide an occasional Cabinet minister for a United Kingdom government, but no more, judging by the record of Scotland and Wales.[1] The *de facto* exclusion of Catholics from office has reduced the pool of potential political leadership by one-third. Moreover, the loss of a significant number of able young men by emigration to London is not offset by an equal influx into politics of men born outside the Province. The small size of the government—14 ministers and junior ministers[2]—reflects the lesser demands of governing a small state, but the demands of office do not decline proportionate to size. Moreover, the pool of talent for office is limited. Because there are only 52 MPs, one-third or more of all Unionists *must be* given posts if the government is to be carried on. Mr. Harold Wilson's personal

179

representative in Northern Ireland, Oliver Wright, delivered the most succinct comment on the situation: 'Northern Ireland produces just as much talent in every field, proportionally, as you would expect anywhere else in the realm. It has got rather above average problems.'[3]

Viewed positively, an individual has much easier access to his elected representative because there is one MP at Stormont for every 18,000 registered electors. By comparison, an English elector lives in a constituency of about 58,000 voters, and in America, there is one Congressman for approximately 250,000 eligible voters. There is an expectation, common throughout Ireland, that MPs will interest themselves in the welfare and patronage problems of their constituency.[4] The distances within Northern Ireland are such that an MP can continue to live in his constituency, even if it is in the most remote part of the country. Stormont is little more than an hour by car from two-thirds of the population, and few places are more than 100 miles from Belfast. Most MPs live in or near their constituency, even though this is not a legal requirement. As the House of Commons sits only three afternoons a week and the salary is a part-time wage (£1,500 a year), there is an immediate financial incentive for MPs to retain their business interests locally and not become fulltime politicians.

The machinery for readopting the sitting MP as the official party candidate provides a further incentive for governing politicians to remain close to their constituents. Before each general election, the constituency association of the Unionist Party advertises for a prospective candidate. The sitting member must compete against all challengers to retain the seat he holds. Since nomination in the past has usually been tantamount to election, an MP cannot long ignore strong feelings among those active in his constituency. If defeated, and this happens often enough to be a real and present danger, he is unlikely to be adopted elsewhere. In many respects, political representation in Northern Ireland resembles a large American city, where councillors are close to those in their ward, more than it does the Imperial and sometimes imperious Palace of Westminster. Stormont might even be closer to the average voter than American big-city government, since the ratio of population to elected representatives is usually higher in major American cities than it is in the Northern Ireland Parliament.[5]

Despite close contacts with constituents, religious differences make

it impossible for an MP to try to represent the views of all his constituents. Bernadette Devlin, the MP at Westminster from Mid-
Ulster, no more represents the views of many of the Protestant
electors in her constituency than her Unionist predecessor represented
the views of many of the Catholics. Inasmuch as nearly all constituencies have a predictable political bias in their electorate, an MP
can safely ignore minority opinion. The Unionist politician, like a
white politician in the American Deep South, is threatened with
defeat if the majority suspects that he is willing to be the voice of the
minority too. In America, a strong correlation exists between white
voters' views about race and the actions of Southern Congressmen,
because the race issue concerns a difference immediately visible to
constituents. The same conditions are met in Northern Ireland by
differences about religion and nationality. Here too, opinions are
likely to be well defined, stable and immediately salient to political
leaders, because they can be linked to highly visible social groups.[6]
In short, the average Ulster elector with limited education need not
know much about abstract political theories, as long as he knows
who he likes or who he doesn't like close at hand.

Conceivably, the great bulk of Protestants and Catholics might
hold views very different from those of the political leaders mentioned
in the preceding chapters.[7] Alternatively, they might be apathetic
about constitutional issues. Yet people apathetic about casting ballots
may none the less be enthusiastic about casting stones or taking up
cudgels in opposition to the regime.

In Northern Ireland, the case for studying popular opinion is
irrefutable. The most straightforward way to do so is by a sample
survey of the general public. The techniques are the same as those
used in studies of voting behaviour, but the questions and objectives
are very different. The most difficult task in any survey is to ask the
right questions. The concepts discussed in Chapter I provide a specific
focus for study: nothing is required so comprehensive or diffuse as
analysis of the total political culture. A large body of social science
literature provides a suggestive list of topics worth asking about.
Reference to these ideas can ensure that each item in the questionnaire provides a test for a particular hypothesis.

A second difficulty is to see that the right questions are asked in the
right way. No survey of political opinion had been undertaken in
Northern Ireland when the research commenced in July, 1965, nor
had a questionnaire been developed elsewhere measuring properly

181

the crucial attitudes of support and compliance. Three major difficulties were anticipated in asking novel questions in a novel setting. (i) Theoretically important questions might be irrelevant or incomprehensible to most Ulstermen. (ii) Using colloquial language might impart sectarian bias or employ words meaning very different things to Protestants and Catholics. (iii) Important questions might fail to be asked. In the event, it took two and one-half years to develop a questionnaire that covered all the points of interest to the researcher and to the people being studied. Seven pilot surveys were conducted from June, 1966 until November, 1967. The questionnaire was rewritten and revised after each pilot study in the light of knowledge gained from previous interviews. By acting as the interviewer for the initial pilot, the author was immediately able to see how individuals responded in conversation to questions that were easy to pose in the abstract. At first, nearly all the questions were open-ended, that is, no preconceived list of alternative answers was given the interviewer or the respondent. The words that each individual used in reply were recorded to collect the most commonly used phrases. This procedure revealed unexpected alternatives. For instance, the fourth person to be interviewed in the first pilot said, when asked how he voted, 'I always spoil my ballot.'[8] Each pilot survey involved interviews with 16 to 40 people, with quota controls ensuring representation by religion, sex, region and class. Numbers were of little importance at this stage, for badly phrased questions show their faults in a dozen interviews. The replies to each questionnaire in each pilot were carefully read by the author to see to what extent the language of Northern Ireland people could be matched to the concepts of social science. Upon occasion, the answers not only revealed ambiguities in the questionnaire, but also ambiguities in social science concepts.

From the first, Ulster people showed themselves only too willing to talk about religion, politics, Ireland and much else.[9] Pilot interviews averaged two and one-half hours each. In short, the questions suggested by social science theories were immediately relevant to the lives of ordinary people. But length also posed practical problems, for one could not hope to conduct a thousand or more interviews of such duration with a reasonable expenditure of time and money. The questionnaire was continually revised to make it easier and faster to administer, and to eliminate questions that were of little or no significance to respondents or to theories. In November, 1967 a final 'dress-rehearsal' survey was held in Belfast to test all parts of the survey.

At this point, M. Douglas Scott of the Survey Research Centre of the University of Michigan came to the United Kingdom to take charge of sampling and fieldwork. A total of 176 households were selected for interview from a stratified random sample of the electoral register. The effective response rate was 87·7 per cent, indicating that there would be no difficulty in getting people to talk about political issues. The responses were then coded preparatory to putting the data on IBM cards for analysis. The coding revealed shortcomings in the phrasing of open-ended questions. Analysing the distribution of answers showed that some potentially interesting questions were of little value because nearly everyone gave the same answer, or had no interest in the topic. The questionnaire was once again thoroughly revised.

Interviewing for the Loyalty survey commenced in March, 1968. A pause was required at Easter because Easter Monday is the anniversary of the Dublin rising against the British in 1916. Nearly all the interviews were completed before the Twelfth of July, the Orange celebration of the Protestant victory at the Boyne in 1690. The final ones were done in August, 1968. The sample was a multi-stage stratified random sample of 1,500 households. In selecting areas for inclusion in the sample, there was stratification by religion, partisanship, and urban, semi-urban or rural character. In consequence, interviews were conducted in 30 of the 48 geographical parliamentary constituencies of Northern Ireland.[10] Within each constituency, interviews were scattered throughout a number of district election divisions, the smallest administrative unit, in order to ensure that a representative cross-section of each constituency was interviewed, and people were not drawn exclusively from a Protestant or Catholic ward. The basic listing of the population was the annual electoral register. It decays monthly in accuracy, as a proportion of persons alive and resident at an address at the time of compilation move on. Moreover, a number of people listed on the register are not always resident at the address given, because of the seasonal migration of workers to Britain. Hence, the electoral register was only used as a master list of households. When the interviewer called at the household drawn in the sample, her first task was to enumerate the persons living there at the moment and then, on the basis of random criteria of age and sex, to select a particular resident to interview. This selection technique improved the representativeness of the sample and the response rate for interviews.[11] As questionnaires were completed, they were sent via the Belfast field office to the Survey Research Centre of the University of Strathclyde, where a codebook was developed for classifying answers to open-ended questions. A team of coders laboriously classified and transcribed the data into a format suitable for punching on 16,783 IBM cards as a necessary preliminary to analysis.

Although Northern Ireland is a single, even if singular, political system, physical propinquity does not ensure identity of opinion. Protestants have always assumed that there is a great political gulf fixed between them and their Catholic neighbours. While willing to regard Protestants as fellow Irishmen, Catholics have emphasized their alienness from those who consider themselves British. The distinction is symbolized by the widespread use of the term 'community' to label people of the same religion. Northern Ireland people talk of 'the Protestant community' or 'the Catholic community'.[12] Even a village of less than a thousand people will still be divided into two communities, that is, social groups whose religion gives them a strong sense of belonging together–and of being set apart from those who differ in their religion. The study was initially conceived as a comparison of Protestants and Catholics and then, within each of these communities, a comparison of those who did and did not give full allegiance to the regime. Fortunately, Protestants and Catholics are so distributed that a design appropriate to a national sample yields two large and representative groups of respondents from each community.

In the final Northern Ireland survey, 757 Protestants and 534 Roman Catholics were interviewed. The two religions were thus represented in the proportions 58·6 per cent to 41·4 per cent. According to the 1961 census, the proportion of Catholics, calculated in relation to the total of known Protestants and Catholics, was 35·7 per cent. The higher figure in the 1968 survey reflects in part a real growth in the Catholic proportion of the population, arising from high birth rates and falling emigration. Since survey results are presented separately for Protestant and Catholic respondents, there is no risk that any slight over-representation of Catholics would affect comparative results.[13]

In conducting the survey, particular attention was given to interviewing difficulties that might arise from religious differences. Some points were easy to identify, such as variant forms of speech used to describe the act of going to church or mass. This was overcome by asking a very general question: How often do you go to church for services or prayer? In all, only 20 questions had to be phrased differently for Protestants and Catholics. These concerned such things as membership in the exclusively Protestant Orange Order, or the exclusively Catholic Hibernians. (Cf. Q. 7a–17a, Appendix.) No one broke off the interview with the accusation that the study was an Orange or a Popish plot, nor were there other accusations of bias. It was feared that people might not talk freely about politics to strangers whose religion was unknown to them. In America, where colour creates analogous problems, there is at least little difficulty in a respondent knowing whether his interviewer is also white or black.[14] In anticipation of difficulties, in the 'dress rehearsal' survey the name and address of each household was scrutinized by local staff and assigned to Protestant, Catholic or doubtful categories. Then an attempt was made to assign a co-religionist as the interviewer. After the respondent was asked his or her religion in the first five minutes of the interview, the interviewer indicated her religion, if she and the person interviewed had the same faith. If they were of different faiths, nothing was said, but suspicious looks or remarks were noted. In 71 per cent of these pilot interviews, co-religionists interviewed each other. The dress rehearsal demonstrated that there was no hesitancy or suspicion among respondents who did not know the religion of the interviewer. Therefore, in the final study, nothing was said by the interviewer about her religion to avoid the possibility of biasing responses toward conformity with a communal norm. Respondents showed more wariness about a letter the author sent to each household outlining the purpose of the study. It was sent on the stationery of the Institute of Political Studies, Stanford University, a collaborating institution. The United States Consulate in Belfast received six enquiries from persons uncertain whether Stanford was a proper university, or a front for some other kind of organization. Occasionally, interviewers were mistaken for missionaries from sects such as the Mormons and Jehovah's Witnesses.

Because of the controversial nature of questions concerning the Constitution and the violation of basic political laws, it is important to consider the credence that should be given answers. The most impressive indicator of the validity of the questionnaire is the proportion of people prepared to answer it. The effective response rate was 87·3 per cent, one of the highest ever recorded for a nationwide academic survey in the British Isles (cf. Table V.1). The response rate was significantly higher than that for the most successful of the three British voting surveys conducted in 1963, 1964, and 1966.[15] Most importantly, the proportion refusing to be interviewed at all – a major indicator of evasiveness – was lower in Northern Ireland than in Great Britain, notwithstanding the very different political environments in these two parts of the United Kingdom.

Table V.1   Response rate for Northern Ireland and British surveys

	Northern Ireland		Britain	
	N	%	N	%
Names issued	1,500	—	2,560	—
Premises empty or demolished	22	1·5	54	2·0
Respondent dead or moved away	(Not applicable)		195	7.6
Names added to substitute for removals	(Not applicable)		218	8·5
Total interviews attempted	1,478	100	2,529	100
Reasons for non-responses:				
Refusals	121	8·2	217	8·6
Ill, infirm	32	2·2	33	1·3
Failure to contact	34	2·3	259	10·1
Miscellaneous causes	0	0	11	0·5
Effective interviews:	1,291	87·3	2,009	79·4

Sources: Northern Ireland = Loyalty survey; Britain 1963 = David Butler and Donald Stokes, *Political Change in Britain* (London: Macmillan, 1969), p. 453.

In consequence of the high response rate, the total number of interviews – 1,291 – was the equivalent of the response that would be obtained in Northern Ireland by a survey of approximately 50,000 people throughout the United Kingdom. Because the handful of interviews obtainable in Ulster in a typical United Kingdom sample would be too few for reliable statistical analysis, it is normally omitted entirely from surveys by opinion polls or academic researches. The total of Northern Ireland respondents is larger than that from each of five nations in the landmark cross-national survey study of *The Civic Culture*.[16] The total number of Catholics interviewed, 534, was larger by 58 than the total number of middle-class persons interviewed in the major Butler-Stokes British voting study, and 375 larger than the total number of blacks interviewed in the major 1964 American presidential election study.[17] Relative size does not, of course, mean that survey data are free from sampling error. For most of the tables, figures will usually be within five to eight per cent of the true population figures. The error will be greater than this, according to probability theory, once in twenty times.

A second indicator of validity is the willingness of individuals to spend a substantial amount of time in being interviewed. This evidences their degree of interest in the subject, and willingness to think carefully about answers given. Lack of interest will greatly speed up an interview because nothing is quicker to say than 'I don't know'. Casual and unreliable answers may also be given quickly. The median interview lasted 75 minutes. Persons in both religions showed equal degrees of interest in talking. The median Protestants talked for 80 minutes and the median Catholics for 75 minutes. A total of 31 per cent talked for at least an hour and one-half, whereas only 10 per cent spoke for less than an hour. The willingness of people to give frank answers is also shown by the virtual absence of 'Don't know' replies to the most serious questions, those concerning the use of violence for political ends (cf. Tables V.4–6).

A final indicator of frankness was the report of the interviewer. After each interview, the person conducting it recorded whether there were any points at which the respondent was hesitant to answer, or an answer gave grounds for suspicion of evasiveness. (See Table V.2.)[18]

Table V.2   Incidence of hesitancy and suspicious vagueness

	Protestant %	Catholic %	Total %
No hesitancy, vagueness	79	75	77
Hesitancy, vagueness noted:			
At one point	13	13	13
At two points	7	11	9
At three points	1	—	1

In all, 77 per cent of persons interviewed showed no signs of hesitancy or vagueness in any of their replies to the long and detailed questionnaire. Among the quarter with some hesitancy or vagueness, a fraction were undoubtedly affected by advanced age, poor education or other non-political factors. The greatest hesitance was shown in replies to questions about class and income: 13 per cent appeared shy of giving details on these points. On political matters, 15 per cent of Catholics and nine per cent of Protestants sometimes hesitated or were vague in their answers; seven per cent of Catholics and five per cent of Protestants were vague in replies to religious questions. As no comparable figures are available from surveys elsewhere in the United Kingdom or in the United States, the comparative significance of findings in Table V.2 cannot be evaluated precisely.

How People View the Regime

All the indicators point to the same conclusion: the overwhelming majority of persons interviewed were glad to give their opinions freely about the main themes of this study. If anything, the subject matter and the novelty of the survey encouraged co-operation and thoughtfulness.

The truth about social action and social beliefs is inevitably situational. What a person believes in some metaphysically obscure 'heart of hearts' is not necessarily what he will say in public. Because truth is situational, one must therefore ask: What kind of a social situation is an interview? It is an informal semi-public discussion, in which the person interviewed is the centre of attention. On balance, the constant request to give opinions is more likely to make a person expansive and frank than to make him hide his views; this is especially so in a lengthy interview. The use of non-directive open-end questions about politically sensitive issues minimizes the risk of a person being prompted to give a particular reply. The fact that the interviewer is a stranger results in less social pressure to conform than in a discussion with friends, each of whose views is known. In so far as a person answers the question the way he believes he is expected to, then he shows susceptibility to social influence. This does not make such replies any less relevant. It simply indicates that the particular respondent is more a follower than a leader. Such replies also show what kind of leader he is predisposed to follow. The relatively peaceful circumstances of an interview may encourage a few individuals to endorse forms of protest that they would not undertake when faced with the opportunity and risks of doing so. The absence of extreme provocation might equally lead some people to underestimate their willingness to break basic political laws. It is ultimately sterile to debate whether 'secret' views are more significant than those professed in an interview situation. The important point is that the interview situation is similar to many political situations in which people are asked to state views that will be known to others, and may have undefined social consequences.

The most important questions in the survey were those designed to measure support for the Constitution and compliance with basic political laws. In a liberal democratic society, researchers may assume that the regime is fully legitimate, and only study *why* individuals give allegiance to the regime. In a society such as Northern Ireland, one must also ask *whether* allegiance is given. The political situation in Northern Ireland is such that there was no need to make respondents distinguish between views about the regime and about the party in office at the time of interview. This problem arises only where there is an alternation of parties in office. The identification of the Unionist Party with the regime from its beginning has meant that there is no distinction. After experimenting with a variety of ways of elucidating attitudes toward the regime, a decision was made to use a simple direct question: There has always been a lot of controversy about the constitutional position of Northern Ireland. On balance, do you approve or disapprove of it? The pattern of responses (Table V.3)[19] shows that among Protestants, supporters of the Constitution out-number overt opponents by a majority of 7 to 1. Catholics, by contrast, are divided into three almost equal groups—supporters, don't knows and opponents. Only one-third are explicitly prepared to endorse the Constitution. The high level of don't knows indicates in part confusion about the meaning of a complex, four-syllable word, especially among persons with a limited education.[20] The aggregate profile of opinion in the country is profoundly ambiguous. One can say that as much as 54 per cent of the people support the Constitution or that only 54 per cent support the Constitution.

Table V.3 Reasons for supporting or disapproving the Constitution

	Protestant %*	Catholic %*	Total %*
Supports because:			
Material benefits	21	11	17
Good government; okay as it is	16	10	13
British connection	18	2	11
General approval	9	10	9
Anti-Republic; anti-Catholic	6	2	5
Democratic, free	5	2	3
Protestant	1	0	1
Don't know	6	8	7
Total Supports:	68	33	54
Disapproves because:			
Prefers United Ireland	3	14	7
Unfair, anti-Catholic	3	13	7
Inefficient, impractical	2	6	4
General and miscellaneous	1	4	2
Don't know	7	9	8
Total Disapproves:	10	34	20
Don't know about Constitution:	22	32	26

* Figures can add to more than 100% for questions allowing more than one response.

How People View the Regime

A variety of reasons are given for approving or disapproving of the Constitution in response to a direct question (Table V.3). Both Protestants and Catholics see the material benefits it provides as the main thing favouring the regime. This tangible motive, while important, none the less suggests a conditional commitment, inasmuch as support that is bought can disappear as and when people think that it will pay to sell the regime short, or when the regime is no longer reckoned to be delivering the material goods. The British connection is an unalterable advantage of the regime to Protestants. But it is a disadvantage to Catholics, who are most likely to reject the regime because it prevents a United Ireland. The proportion who disapprove because it is anti-Catholic is about balanced by the numbers who support the regime because it is pro-Protestant and against rule from the Catholic Republic. (References to democracy and freedom by Protestants in Northern Ireland usually imply a contrast with the 'priest-ridden' Republic.) Catholics do not disapprove of the regime because it is inefficient and impractical in what it does. This objection is cited only once for every four times disapproval is voiced on patriotic or civil rights grounds.

One pervading feature of the replies is their vagueness and generality. A total of 41 per cent of people interviewed either had no opinion about the Constitution or could give no reason for the views they voiced. Among Catholics, 49 per cent were apathetic. The impression of apathy is further strengthened when one notes that more than one-sixth of the reasons given for supporting the Constitution are best classified as 'general approval'. The simplest interpretation to place upon the data is that even among those favouring the regime, there is a relatively shallow commitment to it, as shown by the lack of much factual, emotional or ideological content in the justifications given for it.

One major qualification to this indifference exists among Catholics who explicitly state disapproval of the Constitution. In this group – about one-seventh of the total population of Northern Ireland – there is a clearly defined sense of what the alternative is to a Stormont regime. When Catholics who disapproved of the Constitution were asked what they would like to see in its place, half said a united Ireland. Another quarter see the alternative as a radically transformed Stormont, with Catholics sharing power with Protestants. Only three per cent see closer ties with Britain as a suitable alternative to Stormont. By contrast, the largest group of Protestant critics of the regime did not know what they wanted in place of Stormont. The remainder divided into three equal and equally small groups, favouring closer ties to Britain, radical changes at Stormont, or a link with Dublin. This means that Catholics constitute four-fifths of the unambiguous opponents of the Constitution.

Asking people whether or not they would comply with basic political laws is hardly meaningful in a fully legitimate regime, for the great majority of persons may find the idea inconceivable. In Northern Ireland, a history of popular demonstrations and armed uprising makes the question realistic, and the replies meaningful. The arguments for and against compliance with the regime are complex, giving grounds for people to differ in their views. Among Catholics, moral arguments are often phrased in the language of inalienable rights, the language used in the rebels' proclamation of the Irish Republic in Dublin in 1916. Claims for civil rights are also stated in absolute moral terms, and not as requests for a little more justice or a little less injustice. The Protestant position is phrased in moral terms too. The descendants of settlers of three centuries ago claim a right to the land they have cultivated and enriched by their labour, as Americans claim land formerly occupied by Indians, and English claim soil earlier occupied by Celts. Religion too provides an absolute moral justification: rule from Dublin is reckoned to threaten the true (i.e., Protestant) faith with subjugation to doctrines of the false (i.e., Roman Catholic) faith.

In a fully legitimate regime, pragmatic arguments reinforce moral arguments for giving allegiance to a regime. The diffuse advantages that flow from accepting the rule of law are greater than the specific advantages that might arise from non-compliance. In a divided regime, the same calculus may lead an individual to rebellion rather than allegiance. The use of violence by a Catholic minority may be rejected simply on the grounds that it is impractical, because of the superior firepower of Protestant opponents. In so far as this assumption is correct, it then becomes a pragmatic justification for the use of arms by Protestants. Similarly, illegal demonstrations can be justified if the benefits they bring, e.g., reform legislation or a reduction in the regime's authority, are greater than the costs inflicted, e.g., police baton charges, or physical assault by Protestant Ultras.

The Republican rising and the arming of the Ulster Volunteers a half-century ago are classic illustrations of recourse to arms against a legally established regime in the name of a higher morality. More than two-fifths of the people interviewed were old enough to have at least childhood memories of the violence of the 1920s. The great bulk of Northern Ireland people think that the resort to arms by their co-religionists was justified. Among Protestants, 83 per cent said they thought it right that 50 years ago people took up arms to keep Northern Ireland British; only six per cent said that it wasn't right that this was done. Among Catholics, 60 per cent said they thought it right that 50 years ago people in the South took up arms to make the Republic, and 21 per cent said it was not right. Undoubtedly, Protestant endorsement of the past use of force is higher because Protestants have emerged victorious from trials by force. The burden of defeat explains the lesser degree of Catholic approval of civil war.

Table V.4   Protestant views of violent non-compliance

Approves 'any measures' to remain Protestant because: 52%

	%
Defend Protestant ways	58*
Anti-Catholic, anti-Republic	27
It's a good government now	6
Feels British	24
Protects material benefits	9
Don't know	3

Disapproves 'any measures' to remain Protestant because: 45%

	%
Dislikes use of force	49*
Live and let live	28
Discuss, negotiate	9
Protestantism not that important	9
Miscellaneous	2
Don't know	16

Uncertain, don't know about using 'any measures'   4%

* As a proportion of all persons in this category.

To measure the lengths to which Northern Ireland people are prepared to go in defiance of basic political laws of the established Stormont regime, each respondent was asked how he would respond if the regime was challenged in the name of substantive goals. Specifically, Protestants were asked whether they thought it would be right to take any measures necessary to keep Northern Ireland a Protestant country. Colloquially, keeping the country Protestant does not mean expelling the Catholic third of the population, but maintaining a Protestant monopoly of power in the regime. The reference to violence is clear, because the Ulster Covenant pledged Protestants to use 'all means which may be found necessary' to defeat Home Rule, and signers of the Covenant were the backbone of the Ultra force of Ulster Volunteers.

The pattern of replies in Table V.4 shows that there is no apathy when the Protestant regime might be endangered. Only four per cent are uncertain of their views. A majority, 52 per cent, endorse the use of violence to keep Northern Ireland Protestant. The reasons given are few, simple and unambiguous: defence of Protestantism and the British connection, and opposition to Catholicism and the Republic. Few Protestants refer to economic or conventional 'good govern-ment' justifications for taking up arms. The strength of the commit-ment to a Protestant regime is suggested by the fact that the most common reason given for favouring compliance is dislike of the use of force, and not toleration for Catholics. Only a tenth of those dis-approving of force do so because they feel little commitment to continued Protestant rule.

Table V.5   Catholic views of violent non-compliance

Approves 'any measures' to end partition because:		13%
	%	
Believes in United Ireland	74*	
Benefits of United Ireland	24	
Don't know	15	
Disapproves 'any measures' to end partition because:		83%
	%	
Dislikes use of force	81*	
Loss of economic benefits	17	
Anti-Republic	4	
Not practical	2	
Don't know	8	
Uncertain, don't know about using 'any measures'		4%

* As a proportion of all persons in this category.

The comparable question to ask Catholics is whether they think it right to take any measures necessary to end Partition. A big majority of Catholics disapprove of the use of force to bring Ulster into the Republic (Table V.5). Force is disliked in principle, and also rejected as impractical. The two views are neatly summed up by such answers as: 'Force does not help. It causes more trouble than it's worth', and 'We've had enough of bloodshed. Only innocent people get killed.' Among the small minority who are prepared to endorse the classical Fenian position, the motive is also simple: belief in a

193

How People View the Regime

United Ireland: 'The present system is unnatural', 'Union would prevent bitterness' and most simply, 'It's right'.

A striking feature of both Protestants and Catholics is that while many are apathetic about the Constitution, few are apathetic about the use of violence. Only four per cent of the people interviewed are don't knows or uncertain. The overwhelming number of Ulster people also give clear explanations justifying their views. The firmness of replies indicates attitudes that are unlikely to change easily or quickly. In aggregate, 36 per cent of the population endorse the use of violence in opposition to the regime, and 61 per cent disapprove of it

The authority of regimes can also be challenged by actions that fall short of bloodshed. In contemporary Ulster, this tradition has been kept alive among Protestants by the Rev. Ian Paisley and his supporters, who have demonstrated many times when 'disloyal' Catholic subjects were expected to appear.[21] Among Catholics, the traditional way to challenge the regime in a quasi-peaceful manner is to display the green, white, and orange tricolour flag of the Republic, especially on Irish holidays such as Easter Monday. These 'mildly' illegal actions are not intended to cause violence, but disorder may follow if the police decide to enforce the law, or if counter-demonstrators and demonstrators are not separated by the police. The civil rights demonstrations have greatly extended the scope and significance of illegal Catholic parades.

Table V.6   Attitudes toward illegal demonstrations

	Protestant %	Catholic %	Total %
All right to hold them	20	40	28
Disapproves	67	43	57
Depends	11	14	13
Don't know	2	3	2

To measure the extent of approval for these calculated non-violent challenges to the regime, Protestants were asked whether they thought it all right for Protestant groups to hold meetings or parades if the government banned them. Catholics were asked whether they thought it all right for Republican groups to hold meetings or parades banned by the government (Table V.6). At first glance, the replies to this question are unexpected: two-thirds of Protestants are unequivocally against illegal demonstrations by their co-religionists, whereas a majority of Catholics give unconditional or conditional approval to such actions. The reversal of attitudes appears to reflect a pragmatic evaluation of the costs and benefits of refusing to comply with laws. Protestants see illegal demonstrations as a cause of political confusion and uncertainty, with no attendant advantages. Catholics, by contrast, appreciate that flying the flag of rebellion is not likely to result in grave physical harm to themselves, yet provides the emotional gratification of repudiating an unpopular regime, at least symbolically. The salience of this form of political protest is indicated by the fact that only two per cent of those interviewed had no opinion about such parades.

The answers given to questions about basic political laws express no more and no less than predispositions to action. One must therefore consider to what extent the predispositions shown in an interview situation are likely to be valid indicators of subsequent actions. In logic, the answer must be moot. Just as predispositions cannot be equated with behavioural acts, so behaviour cannot exist without predispositions, especially where outlooks are historically conditioned, as is the case in politics. Current events provide a test of the aggregate validity of these findings. The organizers of the civil rights movements held their first illegal demonstration shortly after the final interviews were concluded. Thousands of Catholics responded by participating. Londonderry, the city that has given the most popular support to challenges to the regime, was also the area in Northern Ireland where Catholics interviewed were strongest in endorsing illegal demonstrations in the Loyalty survey. A 1969 Ulster survey by Opinion Research Centre five months after the Londonderry march, similarly found a plurality of Catholics favoured continued demonstrations.[22] A second and bloodier indication of the reasonableness of the findings appeared when Protestants began to oppose Catholic political activity by whatever means necessary. This climaxed in Belfast in August 1969, in a riot of gunfire, and intimidation with Catholics the chief victims. Subsequently, Republicans have shown, with fatal consequences for opponents and themselves, that though their numbers are limited, their resolution is intense.

The Loyalty survey found that the folklore picture of Northern Ireland as a society in which every person was ready for combat against Fenians or Orangemen is only partly true. Reciprocally, it also found that the optimist's picture of Northern Ireland as a society in which nearly every Protestant and Catholic was a fully allegiant subject 'except for a few troublemakers' is only partly true. There

How People View the Regime

are major differences in attitudes toward the regime *within* the Protestant and Catholic communities as well as between them. This variation in outlooks provides the basis for a systematic examination of the outlooks of Ulster people concerning the regime: Why do some people support the Constitution and others not? Why are some people willing to comply with basic political laws and others not?

The replies given to the direct question about approval of the Constitution show differences between Protestants and Catholics. The latter divide into three almost equal groups—supporters, opponents and don't knows. By contrast, most Protestants are in one group—supporters of the Constitution; don't knows are the second largest group, and critics the smallest. Detailed analysis of the views of Protestants expressing disapproval of the Constitution found only a very few who favoured a United Ireland, a group too small to regard as at all significant. The Protestant don't knows do not differ in their views of compliance from those voicing support for the Constitution. In the absence of any positive evidence of Protestant disapproval of the Constitution, it is best to treat the views of the community on this issue as an invariant characteristic, not a variable one. There is thus little point in presenting in detail tests of hypotheses about influences upon Protestant support for the Constitution.[23] Among Catholics, one cannot regard those with no views about the Constitution as inevitable supporters of the regime, given the political situation of Catholics generally and the fact that 43 per cent of the don't knows endorse illegal demonstrations against the regime. The safest strategy is to divide Catholics into three categories, and in testing hypotheses concentrate upon those Catholics who deviate from the group norm by positively endorsing the Constitution.

Many American studies of political disturbances imply that the greater the level of violence, the greater its political significance.[24] Northern Ireland people show by their replies that they pay more attention to the meaning of acts than to their intensity. Acts can be equivalent in political intensity even if they are not identical in levels of violence. Large numbers of Protestants and Catholics endorse breaking basic political laws; they differ in the ways in which they are prepared to break them. Protestants are readiest to endorse the use of 'any measures' to keep Northern Ireland Protestant. Violence is accepted as a necessary means to repress potentially violent Republicans. Because few Protestants give unclear or uncertain answers, there are hardly any whose answers cannot be analysed here.

196

The equivalent answer for Catholics is endorsement of an illegal demonstration, rather than a resort to violence. As the losers in repeated violent combats in Northern Ireland, Catholics have practical reasons for wishing to avoid violence. Those whose defeats have not cured them of defiance remain ready to endorse illegal demonstrations against the regime. The soldier or policeman exposed to a hail of stones and petrol bombs from a crowd will find it of little comfort to be told that most of his assailants are eschewing guns. Catholics who were uncertain or conditional about participating in a demonstration are excluded from intensive analysis, as they could not confidently be assigned to the ranks of the compliant or the rebellious.[25]

Together, the replies show ample variations in attitudes toward three of the four basic measures of outlooks. Catholics differ substantially among themselves in their readiness to support the Constitution or to comply with its basic political laws. Protestants divide almost evenly in their attitude toward basic laws, but overwhelmingly endorse the Constitution. Logically, these two pairs of responses can result in nine possible sets of replies, for allowance must be made for those who give the reply of 'depends' or 'don't know'. Among Protestants, the incidence of these intermediate groups is not a problem, for there are few in the intermediate group for compliance, and very few who actively reject the Constitution in favour of a Dublin regime. Hence, it is reasonable to regard as Ultras those Protestants who positively endorse the Constitution and endorse violating the law to keep the country Protestant. Those who are compliant will either actively endorse the Constitution or give passive support to it in conformance to their communal norm. Among Catholics, the greater dispersion of answers and the smaller numbers of respondents make it difficult to assign individuals neatly to the nine categories of the theoretical construct, because the resulting groupings are so subdivided as to lack substantial numbers for intensive statistical analysis (cf. Table XIII.1). Hence, hypotheses concerning Catholic outlooks will be tested separately in relation to support and compliance.[25] By doing this, one can inductively gain precise knowledge of the extent to which the same influences affect attitudes toward each of these primary components of political allegiance. After this is done, one can consider the inter-relationships of these attitudes and, equally important, the consequences of these inter-relationships for politicians who support and oppose the regime.[26]

How People View the Regime

To explain variations in regime outlooks, one must do more than catalogue statements given by individuals in response to a request to explain themselves. The replies to the question about the Constitution illustrate the difficulties that people sometimes have in formulating answers, let alone complex explanations for their views. The replies to questions about compliance show comprehension, yet precisely because the explanations are so close to the view stated, their standing as an explanation is diminished. To say that a Catholic is against political violence because he fears the consequences of invoking force only raises the question: Why does he fear these consequences? Similarly, to say that a person favours violence because he favours a Protestant regime at all costs begs the question: Why does he favour a Protestant regime at all costs? Hence, it is important to go beyond simple attitudinal correlates to search out underlying influences.

For centuries political philosophers have grappled with the problem of explaining man's willingness to comply with basic political laws. A. J. Ayer has identified 13 different answers that philosophers have given to the question: Why should I do what the government tells me to?

1. You ought to obey because you are forced to. (Hobbes.)
2. You ought to obey because you have promised to. (Hobbes, Locke, Rousseau and other believers in the social contract.)
3. You ought to because it is in your interest. (Plato, Hobbes, Bentham.)
4. You ought to obey because it is in the general interest. (Locke, Rousseau, Mill, Green.)
5. You ought to obey because it is you who are giving the orders. (Hobbes, Rousseau, Bosanquet and other believers in the General Will.)
6. You ought to obey because God wants you to. (Medieval writers.)
7. You ought to obey because the Sovereign is God's anointed. (Absolute Monarchists.)
8. You ought to obey because the Sovereign is descended from someone who had the right to be obeyed. (Legitimists.)
9. You ought to obey because people always have. (Traditionalists.)
10. You ought to obey because your government exemplifies the highest point yet reached in the spiritual development of man. (Hegel. This can hardly be true of all governments.)
11. You ought to obey because your government has history on its side. (Marx. Again, this may not be true of all governments.)

12. You ought to obey because you ought to obey. (Some English moralists.)
13. You have no obligation to obey. (Anarchists.)

After this review, Ayer concludes, 'This is not, to my mind, a very impressive list of answers'.[27] The formulations of philosophers emphasize ethical motives. Yet to decide how a man ought to act is not to describe how he does behave. Northern Ireland politics illustrates that ethical considerations may also be invoked to explain why a person should *disobey* basic political laws.

Social scientists have a battery of conflicting theories explaining why people differ in their basic political outlooks. The most immediately attractive explanation of discord about allegiance refers to political culture, i.e., a set of distinctive values, beliefs and emotions about the regime. In this study, however, the political culture cannot provide the explanation, for it is what requires explaining. Because attitudes toward the regime are an integral part of the culture, it is tautological to explain allegiance in terms of a holistic entity of which it is an integral part. To invoke other norms important in the culture as an explanation is to risk entering a closed circle, in which only attitudes are relevant, without regard to material and institutional considerations.[28] Similarly, to explain regime outlooks by reference to the influence of party also raises problems, because in Northern Ireland the major parties are so closely identified with conflicting positions about the regime.

Social psychologists have developed a variety of theories to explain how patterns of relationships between people – whether friends, enemies, relatives or strangers – can affect political outlooks directly and indirectly. Theories of political socialization can explain *how* attitudes from the past, even as far back as the seventeenth century, might persist into the present. To explain *why* these attitudes persist in Northern Ireland, but in few other places in the world, requires reference to historical and institutional influences not normally considered by social psychologists. The risk of ignoring such phenomena and concentrating exclusively upon a psychological explanation is illustrated by the efforts of Freud's biographer, Dr. Ernest Jones, to analyse the Irish troubles as a consequence of Ireland – represented in politics and poetry by a woman – being a symbol of womb security. Because of this, Dr. Jones believed the Irish were bound to react against the entry of Protestants, for 'the settlement of Ulster is an abiding rape'.[29]

How People View the Regime

Logically, it is possible that no theory will explain variations in political outlooks within a nation or cross-nationally. This idea is implicit or explicit in critiques of the very idea of social science. This all-encompassing 'anti-theory' might seem peculiarly relevant to Northern Ireland, given its seemingly unique concatenation of historical and contemporary influences. Even if one pronounces Northern Ireland *sui generis*, it does not follow that it is unique in *every* respect. One need only find one factor in common between Northern Ireland and one other country to disprove such a sweeping assertion. It is best to assume that general theories of politics can explain some but not all of the variation in political outlooks in Ulster. In other words, conditions in Northern Ireland are in part unique and in part like those elsewhere in the Western world.

Logically, it is also possible to assert that one theory might explain all of the variation found in political outlooks in Ulster. For an author to assert this at the beginning of a book is a grand act of arrogance, inviting the reader to suspect that the interpretation that follows is tendentious, making everything fit the scheme. It is also to deny that in the course of investigation the author may learn anything about the problem he is studying. Such an assumption is more appropriate to an age of faith than to an era of social science.

In this study, theories are used eclectically and pragmatically. The multi-dimensional form of social structure developed in the Lipset-Rokkan analysis of political change provides an appropriate framework for the organization of the next several chapters. Because the framework is more a means of classifying ideas and insights than it is an integrated theory, it does not inhibit reference to other ideas and theories. Within a given chapter, hypotheses are drawn from a variety of alternative and sometimes contradictory theories. The approach is appropriate because more than one type of social science theory is likely to be required for an understanding of a society as complex as Northern Ireland. Which ones are relevant is best determined after many are tested and found wanting.

The possible differences between Protestants and Catholics necessitates giving separate distributions for each item in the questionnaire. The assumption is adopted as a working hypothesis and not as an irrefutable truth. It would presumably apply less to the ratio of men and women among Protestants and Catholics than to the ratio of Unionists and Nationalist voters. Differences between religions in social characteristics and attitudes can be measured by taking the sum of the differences between the proportions of each religion giving a particular response and dividing by two.[30] The resulting difference index ranges from 0 when proportions are identical in both religions to 100 when no Protestant shares an opinion or attribute with a Catholic and vice versa. The lower the index, the greater the similarity between the two religions, and the higher the index, the greater the difference. For example, the difference in sex ratios among Protestant and Catholic is one per cent; the difference in party preference profiles is 74 per cent in the Loyalty survey. For each table, the difference index is indicated by the abbreviation D.I.

In testing hypotheses, it is important to measure degrees of relationship; in the social sciences, no relationship is likely to hold in every instance. Because data are analysed separately for Protestants and Catholics, each test always controls for the influence of religion. The use of percentages is a standard way of assessing degrees. In assessing the strength of a relationship, the first point to note is whether it is in the direction hypothesized. If so, one can say that there is a tendency for the items in question to be associated with each other. This will be true whether the tendency relates to a small proportion of the population, e.g., university graduates, or a large proportion, e.g., manual workers. To use statistical significance tests to determine whether differences in distributions are due to chance is to introduce an arbitrary threshold of significance into the analysis. It risks misleading the reader, for a finding that a difference is statistically significant depends upon the size of the sample group, as well as upon the size of the difference. The larger the sample, the smaller a difference that is called significant. Differences of less than ten per cent in the Loyalty survey will often be statistically significant. Frequent use of statistical significance tests might encourage readers to ignore an even more important point. An influence causing a ten per cent difference in political outlooks will account for very little of the total variation in the political attitudes of Northern Ireland people. For this reason, statistical tests of association are not reported, although some were calculated.[31] This is done so as not to mislead readers unfamiliar with the difference between measures of association and causation. In Chapter X a variety of complex multi-variate statistics are applied to influences previously considered singly in order to see which are independently important in association with the two major dependent variables.

To enumerate all is not to equate all. Important as individual attitudes are, they cannot by themselves be used to explain how a regime manages to lack full legitimacy yet avoid repudiation, nor why some regimes survive while others fall. The attitudes of individuals are not translated automatically into policies of government. To assume this is to be guilty of the individualist fallacy, i.e., to make inferences about complex institutions by summing individual preferences.[32] Men who govern, especially in regimes lacking full legitimacy, are not individuals passively responsive to a popular will. The difficulties of response are peculiarly great in divided regimes, because popular pressures are in opposing directions, and the alternatives are the survival or repudiation of a regime.

VI · National Identities

I'm not happy about being called an Irishman because of the 1916 rebellion.

                    VISCOUNT BROOKEBOROUGH

They (i.e., foreign Socialists) will never understand why I am here. They will forget I am an Irishman.
                    JAMES CONNOLLY, Kilmainham Jail, 1916

Defining a nation presents great difficulties to social scientists. It also presents great difficulties to politicians and subjects who live in a state where there is no agreed national identity. Social scientists must distinguish national identities from other group loyalties of little or no political significance. Politicians have the task of maintaining popular identification with *their* state, in competition with alternative states from the past, or a state that could be created by a nationalist revolution. The subjects of a multi-national state find theoretical disputes immediately relevant in seeking an answer to the question: Who am I?

At all times in history, men have identified with groups beyond the family, even if only such parochial entities as the clan or village. Identifications with groups beyond the family can generically be described as communal loyalties, the feeling of a collectivity of people that they belong together;[1] when a communal group claims distinctive political treatment for themselves, then they may be described as a *nation*. Nationality is thus a social psychological concept, defined by the way that people feel about each other and about their government. It is not defined by legal dicta. Nationalism is a set of doctrines justifying distinctive political institutions for a particular community of people. As Elie Kedourie notes, 'Nationalist doctrines introduced a new style of politics in which the expression of will overrode treaties and compacts, dissolved allegiances and, by mere declaration, made lawful any act whatever.'[2]

The development of nationalism in Ireland initially involved subtle distinctions of a social and political kind. At one extreme were the native Gaels, and at the other, persons only temporarily resident in Ireland by virtue of a posting from London. Between them were

203

several groups. In Ulster, Protestants were no longer British in the same sense as their kin over the water, by virtue of generations of removal from England or Scotland. Among Catholics in the North and South, the spread of English ideas and institutions distinguished those who, to some extent, assimilated from those who remained remote and untouched. The differences within Ireland prior to the troubles were reflected in varying views of what the Irish nation should demand from London. In the event, the Fenian view triumphed. Simply stated, it was 'No amount of good government could be a substitute for self-government.'³ In the North, Protestants often insisted that they were both Irish and British, i.e., their national identity was held in common with others in the 32 counties, but their political allegiance was first to Westminster and the Crown. The fate of the disunited Kingdom of Great Britain and Ireland was settled after the First World War, but it was not settled by the negotiations of the allies at the Peace Conference. Out of deference to Britain (and perhaps from prudence), the victors preferred to confine themselves to the nationality problems of Eastern Europe. From an Ulster point of view, the solution was a compromise, not the creation of a nation-state.

The confusion about national identity and political authority in Northern Ireland today is reflected in the fact that two states—the United Kingdom and the Republic of Ireland—claim the right to rule there. Natives of both parts of Ireland enjoy an anomalous legal status. Natives of the Republic effectively enjoy most of the rights of native-born Britons, including right of entry into the United Kingdom and participation in British politics, although they are subject to residence requirements before participation is allowed in Northern Ireland politics. Reciprocally, natives of Northern Ireland automatically qualify, under the Republic's Irish Nationality and Citizenship Act 1956, for citizenship there.⁴ For example, Gerry Fitt, a Westminster and Stormont MP, travelled to the United States in 1969 on a Republic of Ireland passport.

Conflicting citizenship claims present each resident of Northern Ireland with a psychological as well as a political choice. In addition to deciding which regime he obeys, on prudential or other grounds, he must also decide with which nation he identifies in a multitude of ways. The conflict involves matters of much deeper significance than whether to travel on a British or Irish passport. It concerns personal identity. In a land where everyone has the same nation, there is certainty and security in such an identity. In Northern Ireland, whatever choice an individual makes will create discord. This is true whether he acts consistently with his group norm–to be Irish if Catholic, and British if Protestant–or if he deviates, and thinks of himself as British though Catholic, or Irish though Protestant. The individual who deviates in his choice of identity embodies in himself the discord of society. The individual who adopts the national identification normal to his religious group has harmonized roles within his own person. His choice, however, contributes to the maintenance of discord between the two religious communities.

Because national identity is a variable not a constant in Northern Ireland, it is potentially an important influence upon political allegiance. In view of the long historical association of Irishness with disloyalty to the Crown, one would hypothesize that Ulstermen who identify most strongly with Ireland would be most likely to refuse support for the Constitution. Reciprocally, those who identify most strongly with Britain would be most likely to support the Constitution. Given the significance of revolutionary activities in Irish history, one would also expect that Catholics most identified with things Irish would be most ready to refuse compliance to a British regime. Among Protestants, those who feel themselves most strongly British would be most prepared to fight to stay as they are. Alternatively, Ultra views might be strongest among those Protestants who feel that Ulster is a place apart, neither British nor Irish.

In order to test these hypotheses, one must first determine how Northern Ireland people think of themselves. A resident of Ulster has a wealth of identities to choose from. Among Catholics, identification with Ireland has been regarded as normal. British settlers traditionally scorned the old Gaelic customs and manners of the 'mere Irish', as well as stigmatizing such people as disloyal. With the founding of the Gaelic League in the late nineteenth century, there was a conscious insistence that 'Irishness' was something very different from Britishness and from the dominant mode of life emerging in industrialized nations.[5] The Gaelic revival never became strong among Catholics in the North. The civil rights movement of the 1960s further complicated matters by advancing Catholic claims in the name of their British citizenship. Defenders of the regime saw the demand as a tactical device entirely characteristic of the politics of the 'dishonest and disloyal' Irish. The great majority of demonstrators for British civil rights avoided using Irish emblems–but they did not forswear their hope that a United Ireland might come about some day.

National Identities

Among Protestants, there is no nation with which the great majority may readily identify, if Britain is not regarded as a basis for communal loyalty. The ties of the seventeenth-century colonists with England and Scotland were broken long ago. The label Scotch-Irish was created in America, not Northern Ireland. Significantly, it was adopted by Ulster Protestant emigrants as a means of distinguishing themselves from the Catholic Irish.[6] The label Anglo-Irish is characteristically applied to those Protestants–south and north of the Border–who are sufficiently prominent to know who their English forebears were and/or sufficiently wealthy today to maintain a flat in London or educate their children in England. An Ulster Protestant may describe himself as British, but doing this does not necessarily mean he thinks as English, Scottish and Welsh people do when they identify themselves thus. For the residents of Great Britain, this label supplements their primary nationality. For the Ulsterman, it is a substitute for it. The regime itself has sought to popularize the use of the word Ulster, domestically and in public relations work in Britain and America. The term connotes a distinctive identity, but it is also a contentious one, for the historic boundaries of Ulster until 1921 consisted of nine counties, three of which were excluded from the Northern Ireland state because they were heavily Catholic in population. Its use by the regime can thus lead to elaborate protests from Republicans.[7] Republican references to the non-sectarian character of Irish identity are unlikely to appeal to Protestants, since they are often coupled with references to the valour of Protestants who died for Ireland, such as Wolfe Tone and Robert Emmet, leading figures in the rising of the United Irishmen against Great Britain. The confusion is aptly expressed in remarks made by prominent Unionist politicians. As Prime Minister, James Chichester-Clark had the following dialogue in 1970 with a German interviewer from *Der Spiegel*:

INTERVIEWER: You, Mr. Prime Minister, were born and grew up in this environment. Do you feel yourself Irish?
PRIME MINISTER: I consider myself British.
INTERVIEWER: You have a British passport, yes, but geographically speaking, it would be natural to call you an Irishman.
PRIME MINISTER: I consider myself an inhabitant of Ulster and British.
INTERVIEWER: Is an inhabitant of Ulster an Irishman?
PRIME MINISTER: Well now, he lives on the same island. I don't know.[8]

206

A few months later, his colleague, Dr. Robert Simpson, Minister of Community Relations, had a similar experience with an interviewer from the Catholic oriented *Irish News*:

> INTERVIEWER: Do you believe that the Northern Protestant suffers from a crisis of identity that, in fact, he is uncertain whether to regard his homeland as Ireland, Scotland or England? Ulster, after all, is an artificially created state.
>
> DR. SIMPSON: Our position may be ambivalent, but the facts are clear enough. Certainly we are Irish. When your forefathers have lived in Ireland for hundreds of years this is obvious. But we are also British. We are United Kingdom citizens paying United Kingdom taxes and electing representatives to the United Kingdom Parliament.[9]

Simultaneously, Brian Faulkner, a very senior minister, emphasized his Irish identity, but in a form that few of his Catholic fellow subjects or neighbours would accept. In commenting upon a move by the Taoiseach of the Irish Republic to establish in Dublin a study group on Northern Ireland, he said:

> I would hope that Mr. Lynch and his colleagues will have the courage to put into practice the lessons they will learn for the benefit of the population in the Republic. For we in the North, *as fellow Irishmen*, wish our Southern neighbours well and would be delighted to see them enjoy as high standards of living and the same measure of civil rights as we already do in Northern Ireland.[10]

A propos differences in the standards of welfare benefits between the North and the Republic, Faulkner added, 'This is part of the price the South has paid over the years for its separatism and we, for our part, must respect their right to make this sort of sacrifice, however slight a consolation that is to the families in need.'[11]

To bring order out of this confusion, each respondent was given a card with six alternatives and asked: Which of these terms best describes the way you usually think of yourself? Nearly everyone in Northern Ireland has a sense of national identity, but there is no collective agreement about what the nation is (Table VI.1). Only 15 per cent of Catholics identify with the nationality attributed to them by international law. Protestants divide into three groups – British, Ulster, and those who feel wholly or partly Irish. Because of uncertainty about their national identity, Ulster Protestants are more likely to assert it; 45 per cent claim a 'strong' rather than an 'average' sense

National Identities

of nationality. Among Protestants who think of themselves as Ulstermen, 59 per cent feel strongly about this loyalty. By contrast, only 28 per cent of Protestants who think of themselves as Irish identify strongly with this label, almost the same proportion as among Catholics. This further emphasizes the extent to which an Irish identity is natural to Catholics. Because it is perceived as normal, it does not require special emphasis. Statistically, there is no median identity; the modal group identifies with Ireland, a state opposed to the Stormont regime.

Table VI.1   National identities

	Protestant	Catholic	Total	
	%	%	%	
Irish	20	76	43	
British	39	15	29	
Ulster	32	5	21	
Sometimes British; sometimes Irish	6	3	5	
Anglo-Irish	2	1	1	
Don't know	1	—	1	D.I. = 55%

In terms of the Constitution, it would be expected that persons identifying themselves as Irish–especially as strongly Irish–would be least likely to support an 'alien' regime. The tendency is found most clearly among strongly Irish Catholics; 53 per cent actively disapprove of the regime, as against 22 per cent supporting it. Among the small group of Catholics who think of themselves as British, 55 per cent support the Constitution and 18 per cent disapprove of it. Among Protestants, however, 60 per cent who think of themselves as Irishmen favour the Constitution. This is consistent with the historic Unionist assertion that Ireland is an integral part of the United Kingdom. The association of Ulster symbols with resistance to Home Rule by a Catholic majority would lead one to expect that Protestants who think of themselves thus are most likely to be Ultras. This hypothesis is confirmed; 79 per cent of those who think of themselves as strong Ulstermen endorse a resort to arms if necessary, as do 57 per cent of those who feel themselves average Ulstermen. Catholics with a strong sense of Irish identity are not disproportionately inclined to endorse illegal demonstrations.

To explore further the meaning of national identity, each person was asked why he thought of himself as he did. The pattern of replies (Table VI.2) shows that the overwhelming majority of Irish and

Ulster people regard their identity as a simple consequence of being born and bred in Northern Ireland. But among those who think themselves British, a majority regard their nationality as a consequence of constitutional arrangements, a foundation less secure psychologically than custom and upbringing–especially in Northern Ireland. Interestingly, those Protestants who think that laws, not custom, determine their identity, are as willing to comply with the regime as any others, notwithstanding the fact that they would have least reason to feel secure. This suggests that a sense of Britishness correlates with a more general respect for legality, whereas Ulster identification, based on the naturalness of birth and upbringing, reinforces the readiness to resort to arms against legal but 'unnatural' political measures.

Table VI.2   Reasons for choice of national identity

	Irish	British	Ulster	Mixed	Total
		(As % of each group)			
Born and bred	93	41	81	28	71
Pride, sense of belonging	13	11	19	8	13
Under British rule	1	53	4	31	18
Economic ties	—	6	1	9	3
Miscellaneous and mixed	3	3	8	40	7
Don't know	2	3	4	4	3
Total	43	29	21	6	

The complex of identities makes most Ulster people willing to attend to the views of people outside Ulster. When asked whether or not they ought to take notice of what is said about Northern Ireland in other countries, 54 per cent reckoned that outside views should be attended to, and 38 per cent were for ignoring them. Protestants and Catholics showed virtually the same profile of opinions; the difference index is four per cent. One could hypothesize that those most interested in world public opinion among Protestants would be most likely to be fully allegiant, rather than endorse Ultra views. There is weak support for this hypothesis, for the two categories differ by only six per cent in their readiness to endorse the use of any measures to keep the regime Protestant. Among Catholics, one could expect that those looking outside would be most likely to be rebels or disaffected. Of Catholics regarding outside opinion as important, 41 per cent explicitly disapprove of the Constitution, as against 29 per cent supporting it. There is a slight tendency for the former group to be readier to endorse illegal demonstrations; 51 per cent take this view as against 46 per cent of the more introverted Ulster Catholics.

When Ulster people look outside their Province they can choose between alternative points of reference – the Republic or Britain. In so far as Catholics are primarily concerned with the Republic and Protestants with Britain, these conflicting ties could account for variations in basic political outlooks. The facts of physical geography call attention to the permeable nature of Northern Ireland, for both Scottish soil and that of the Republic can be seen from Northern Ireland. Road, rail, sea and air connections with other parts of the British isles are good too, and newspapers, radio and television easily cross the boundaries of the Province. In theory, cross-Border contacts could give rise to new political institutions, with pacifying consequences. For example, the more ties that Catholics had with Britain, the more likely they would be to give allegiance, and the more ties that Protestants had with the Republic, the less likely they would be to adopt Ultra views. The converse of this assumption is also possible: cross-Border ties might also increase political discord. Catholics with most ties to the Republic would then be most disaffected, and Protestants with fewest British ties most likely to endorse the go it alone position of the Ultra.

The most detailed knowledge of another country is gained by living there. Among Ulster people, 29 per cent have lived outside Northern Ireland; 73 per cent of Protestants and 69 per cent of Catholics have always lived within the Province. England is the second home of most of the mobile: 22 per cent of Catholics and 16 per cent of Protestants have lived at some time in England or Wales, as against five per cent of Protestants and seven per cent of Catholics at one time resident in the Republic. Lifelong residence in Northern Ireland appears, however, to have little influence upon basic political outlooks, i.e., attitudes toward the Constitution, or willingness to comply with basic political laws.

Holidays provide another opportunity for people to become familiar with other lands. Although Northern Ireland itself has a number of natural attractions for holidays, given the small size of the country it is hardly surprising that 87 per cent of the population say they have been outside the Province on holiday trips. The Republic is the most popular place to go: three-quarters of people interviewed have been there. The scale of movement across the Border is also shown by statistics of the Irish Tourist Board. In 1967, more than 15,000,000 day trips were made across the Border from the North to Southern Ireland, and 481,000 visits of more than one day. These visitors contributed £24,000,000 to the Republic's tourist earnings, 34 per cent of its total tourist revenue.[12] England is the second most popular place for travel, and then Scotland. The majority in both communities know the southern half of the British isles – both the Republic and England – from first-hand visits. One might hypothesize that travel is a moderating experience. There is, however, no relationship between travel and refusal to comply with laws among Protestants. Among Catholics, there is a slight tendency for more of those who visit the Republic to reject the Stormont regime and to approve of illegal demonstrations, but travel has even less effect than residence outside Northern Ireland upon basic outlooks.

The knowledge that a person has of politics in Northern Ireland, the Republic and London is a good indicator of attentiveness to events in different parts of what an Ulsterman may regard as 'his' nation. Because every Northern Ireland subject has an MP at Stormont and at Westminster it is easy to compare political awareness on this point. Knowledge of party labels is not comparable, because Westminster MPs are overwhelmingly Unionist. To measure knowledge of the Republic, people were asked to name the Prime Minister at a time when the incumbent, Jack Lynch, had held office for two years, and also to name the governing party. The dominant party, Fianna Fail, has a name that might easily be confused with that of its principal opponent, Fine Gael, by a person with little knowledge of things Irish.

The pattern of responses shows that both Protestants and Catholics have a miscellany of information about all three political systems but they are less well informed than a British voter. In Britain, 55 per cent of people asked the name of their MP knew it correctly, and 79 per cent knew his party. By comparison, in Northern Ireland 44 per cent knew the name of their Westminster MP[13] (Table VI.3). There is no sharp contrast between the political awareness of Protestants and Catholics; the difference index for seven questions averages 11 per cent. The openness to all three political systems is shown too by the fact that Protestants are more likely to know the name of the Prime Minister of the Republic than the name of their own Stormont MP. Similarly, Catholics are more likely to know the party of their Stormont MP than the governing party in the Republic, although Fianna Fail had been in office for 30 of the 36 years prior to the survey.

Knowledge of politics does not show any relationship to Ultra views among Protestants with different levels of political knowledge. Among Catholics, those most knowledgeable about the Republic are least likely to endorse the Northern Ireland Constitution, but the division is less than might be expected: 28 per cent approve of Stormont, and 44 per cent disapprove. Catholics knowledgeable about politics in the Republic are no more ready to demonstrate than those poorly informed about politics there.

Table VI.3 Knowledge of political systems

	Protestant %	Catholic %	Total %	D.I. %
For Northern Ireland, knows:				
MP's name	52	49	51	3
Party	78	65	74	13
Both	51	45	49	6
For Westminster, knows:				
MP's name	49	35	44	14
For Republic, knows:				
Premier's name	62	68	65	6
Party	29	48	37	19
Both	25	44	33	19

Limited knowledge about politics in the Republic does not necessarily mean that people avoid value judgments about the regime; ignorance can even be an aid to easy judgment. To assess stereotypes of the regime in Dublin, people were asked what they liked or disliked about the government there. The most striking feature of the response is the absence of any opinion—good or bad—about government in the South. In total, 82 per cent of Ulstermen found nothing that they liked about the Republic, and 84 per cent could think of nothing that they disliked about it. Only one respondent among 757 Protestants said that he disliked 'everything' about the Republic. Among the quarter of Catholics with favourable views of the Republic, disapproval of the Constitution in Northern Ireland was expressed by 59 per cent. Among the sixth who criticized the Republic, 53 per cent also expressed disapproval of Stormont. Among politically aware Catholics, there is thus a group that dislikes both regimes. But the bulk of Ulster people care little about the activities of the government in Dublin, although it is little more than an hour's drive from the border with Northern Ireland.

If Ulster people are apathetic about the politics of Dublin and Westminster, it would seem to follow that there is little popular support for the traditional controversies about the Border between politicians. To test this early in the survey each person was asked the question: What changes, if any, would you like to see concerning the Border? The replies show that this is still an issue that concerns people, for only 11 per cent had no view (Table VI.4). It is also an

Table VI.4   Attitudes toward the Border

	Protestant %	Catholic %	Total %
Merge with Britain	10	2	7
No change	45	21	35
More co-operation across the Border	12	9	11
Abolish: alternative vague	19	42	28
Abolish and unite Ireland	4	14	8
Don't know	11	12	12

D.I. = 34%

issue that divides the two communities; the difference index is 34 per cent. Among Protestants, the median and modal respondent desired no change on the Border. Among Catholics, the equivalent group wished to abolish the Border. Undoubtedly most Catholics who failed to specify explicitly the consequences of abolishing the Border had union with the Republic in mind, just as Protestants had in mind the reconstitution of the old United Kingdom, with all 32 counties of Ireland linked with Westminster. In short, even though Ulster people do not take a keen interest in the politics of the Republic, they are concerned about the Border that divides them from it. When asked what they think are the things that the government ought to do something about, few Protestants or Catholics mention the Border as of immediate importance.[14] The absence of immediacy in the issue suggests there is little that can be done in the first instance. It also suggests that among Catholics there is no expectation that the Stormont regime would ever do anything about the Border. To abolish the Border, one would not press demands upon the existing regime but seek a new regime in its place. As would be expected, Catholics most in favour of abolishing the Border are also most likely to be disaffected in their outlooks, and Protestants most in favour of the *status quo* are most likely to take an Ultra position.

Borders are ambiguous, not least when a source of political controversy. The case against the Border is that it divides Ulster from people with whom it has a community of interests, just as the case for the Border is that it unites Ulster with others with whom it has a community of interests. The proportion of respondents calling themselves Ulstermen is a reminder that the same line on a map may separate the Province from two groups, the English and the Irish. Conceivably, Protestants and Catholics within the Province might feel more of a community of interest with each other—however great their political differences—than with their neighbours. Differences of nationality do not imply an absence of contacts between those in differing groups, but rather a carefully defined set of customs and conventions, regulating relationships across such boundary lines.[15] These may be friendly, as in a fully legitimate multi-national state, or antagonistic, as in multi-national states moving toward repudiation.

To measure the psychological extent of communal identification, each person was asked whether in general he thought people in Northern Ireland were much different or about the same as people in England or as people in the Republic. Then, in another part of the questionnaire, each Protestant was asked whether he thought Catholics were much different or about the same as Protestants, and a complementary question was asked Catholics. The replies are surprising (Table VI.5). Among Northern Ireland Protestants, 66 per cent

Table VI.5   Scope of community identification

	Protestant %	Catholic %	Total %	D.I. %
English people about the same	29	30	29	1
Irish people about the same	45	44	45	1
Ulstermen of the opposite religion about the same	67	81	73	14

feel that their co-religionists in England are much different from themselves. Similarly, a plurality of Catholics feel that their co-religionists and co-nationals in the Republic are much different from themselves. This sense of alienness from Englishmen and Irishmen of the 26 counties is almost equally strong among Protestants and Catholics; the difference index approaches nil. The most surprising of all findings is that more than two-thirds of Protestants and Catholics think that Ulstermen of the opposite religion are about the same as themselves. That people of contrasting national identifications and religions think of each other as about the same is a reminder that national identifications are not the only things salient in relationships between people. Particularly in the small towns and villages that abound in Northern Ireland, residents not only have diffuse statuses as Protestant and Catholic, but also highly particularistic statuses, based upon individual and family characteristics. This kind of intimacy in social relations can lead to people refusing to generalize by reference to nationality or religion, e.g., 'There's good and bad everywhere', or 'People are much the same'.

Because there are differences within the Protestant and Catholic communities about the extent of identification, it is possible to test how such variations influence attitudes toward the regime. One might hypothesize that Catholics who feel close to people in the Republic would feel most disaffected, and that the Protestants feeling isolated from Ulster Catholics as well as from English and Irish people would be most likely to favour Ultra views. Statistical tests show that no such relationship exists between responses to any of the three questions and basic political outlooks.[16] The absence of any correlation emphasizes the predisposition of Ulster Protestants and Catholics to live together as long as politics is not involved.

Conventionally, Northern Ireland is treated as a conflict between two nationality groups. This view is implied by the British government's insistence upon maintaining sovereignty, and by the Republic's irredentist claims to the six counties. Both regimes reiterated these views, even after the killings of August, 1969 showed how un-English the people of Ulster are in politics, and also how little the Dublin regime would do when trouble occurs in the North. The evidence of the Loyalty survey questions the claims of both London and Dublin by showing that Ulster people have a well developed sense of their Province's distinctiveness.

This sense of apartness, based upon firsthand contacts with England and the Republic, implies that Ulster is truly a separate political system. It follows that the challenges to the regime arise from problems internal to Ulster, and not from British imperialism or troublemakers from the South. There is substantial historical evidence suggesting that this has long been the case. For example, there are no parallels elsewhere in Ireland to the sectarian riots that occurred in Belfast in the nineteenth century. Differences prior to partition have been intensified by a half a century of government from Stormont. Autonomy was reasserted dramatically in the disorders of 1969. The conflict was not fought between British and Irish troops; it was an internal though hardly civil war, with neighbour against neighbour in the streets of West Belfast.[17] If historical events and contemporary social psychology be regarded as sufficient to justify the creation of a nation-state, then Northern Ireland might claim complete independence of both Britain and Ireland. Yet this is the solution least mentioned in the politics of this troubled land.

Questions of communal similarity and dissimilarity are not controlling politically; differences in national identity need not lead to the political exclusiveness of a nation-state. If they did, Ulster Protestants would be least qualified to have their own regime for they are much divided among themselves about who they are. The crucial question is: On what political basis do different national groups live together? Ironically, the survey evidence suggests that the Province suffers more from a 'non-Irish' than from an Irish problem. An unambiguous identification with Ireland is expressed by 43 per cent of all residents, a mixed identification by 6 per cent, and a local or provincial identification by the 21 per cent who call themselves Ulster. Less than one-third identify with the land over the water, Britain.

The crux of the difficulty is the strong association between Irishness and Catholicism: 72 per cent of those who call themselves Irish are also Catholics. Protestants reject political identification with the 'mere Irish'. This act of rejection does not, however, give Protestants a positive sense of community focused on political symbols; instead, they fall back upon their religion for symbols of identity. The absence of a secure political identity like that enjoyed by the indubitably Irish Catholics can be a source of personal anxiety.[18] This interpretation is supported by the tendency of Protestants to feel more strongly than Catholics about their identity–whatever they choose–and for those who identify strongly to be more likely to hold Ultra views. The identification of the Ultras with Protestantism rather than nationality explains the success of the Rev. Ian Paisley politically. He voices fears arising from what ordinary people perceive as the common threat of clerical ecumenicism and British negotiation with the Republic about the Border.

Because Catholics see discord in nationality terms whereas Protestants see it in religious terms, politics in Northern Ireland involves ideologically unrelated conflicts. Disaffected Catholics claim that the appropriate solution is nationalist–to abolish the Border to create a 32-counties Republic of Ireland. Protestants tend to see their regime as a bulwark of religious faith against Catholics within the six counties, against the mere Catholic Irish outside their Provincial pale, and against the forces of error and darkness everywhere growing stronger in a threatening and increasingly ecumenical world. By their own standards, each side is right and uncompromisingly so.

Faced with such a conflict, there remains the possibility that leaders of the regime might try to establish a new national identity acceptable to Protestants and Catholics alike. Traditionally, leaders of the Stormont regime have stressed the British connection, and waved the Union Jack with unconcern or a positive desire to increase the disaffection of some subjects by invoking this symbol of disunity. Upon becoming Prime Minster, Terence O'Neill sought to reverse directions, by increasing community spirit at the local level, as an alternative to identifications cutting across national differences.[19] The approach assumed a local consensus. The programme to enlist the people collapsed with the rise of the civil rights movement and the recurrence of communal violence. The failure of this short-lived scheme to emphasize a common loyalty is hardly surprising in view of the centuries of prior differences. In a comparative review of the problem of nation-building, Eric Nordlinger remarks, 'Not only is it highly unlikely that a national identity can be created in a space of a few years, but the attempt to do so is likely to usher in the unhappy consequences of repressive rule and exacerbation of potentially violent divisions.'[20]

VII · Party Allegiance and Regime Allegiance

There is no floating vote on the constitutional issue.
PROFESSOR J. L. MCCRACKEN

Intrinsically, political parties are neither for nor against a regime. The main objective of a political party is to institutionalize loyalty for itself in order to gain control of government. Incidentally, its actions may help make a regime fully legitimate *or* increase disaffection. Which happens depends upon the goals of the parties as well as upon the activities of the regime. In a fully legitimate regime, party loyalties and regime allegiance, although different, are mutually reinforcing. In such circumstances, it is of no importance whether an individual's first loyalty is to a party or to the regime.[1] In a regime lacking full legitimacy, the point is crucial. To suppress such a conflict, the leaders of the regime may outlaw their opponents. Where party competition exists notwithstanding discord about authority, then elections become, in effect, referenda about the regime. Election results reflect the discord about authority. As long as pro-regime parties win, the regime is not upset by election results. But it is also not legitimated. Majority rule is not the same as unanimous consent.

Northern Ireland is a society in which party loyalties reinforce discord rather than allegiance to the regime. Political parties are not the only institutions challenging the regime, but they are the institutions making the widest claim to popular support. The two major parties have traditionally agreed that the Constitution is *the* major political issue in Northern Ireland. They have 'only' disagreed about whether it was desirable or fit for repudiation. Other parties cannot be neutral on such an issue, for to avoid endorsing the Constitution is to create the suspicion of disloyalty. The moderate line followed by groups such as the Northern Ireland Labour Party is to give little emphasis to the party's views about the regime. But moderation is itself suspect among persons with intensely held views about the Constitution.

In so far as the Constitution is a major issue, reflecting and re-inforcing religious differences, there is no motive for voters to change

218

their party allegiance at election time. The inelasticity of voting has traditionally been reflected in Stormont elections by the return of a large proportion of MPs without any contest. At the November, 1965 election, MPs were returned uncontested in 23 out of the 52 constituencies, the average figure for the preceding two decades.[2] The importance of constitutional discord does not, however, result in a two-party system. Groups divide into separate parties because of contrasting views about the best way to defend or oppose the Constitution. They also divide about the policies that a government should follow in the regime of their choice. Personality conflicts too cause individuals with generally similar political outlooks to compete for votes against each other. In consequence, Northern Ireland has a multi-party system operating within the framework of a dichotomous division about the Constitution.

The fragmentation of parties in Northern Ireland is extreme, and the ratio of parties to parliamentary seats is by far the highest in the Western world.[3] At the 1965 Stormont election, candidates from ten different parties were nominated for the 29 contested seats, and candidates of six different parties plus one independent were returned for the 52 seats.[4] At the 1969 Stormont election, fragmentation was even greater (Table VII.1). The election involved eight different parties, plus a variety of independents and five Unionist groups that differed in crucial ways. Six parties or factions succeeded in returning candidates to Stormont; three independents were also victorious. Subsequent to the general election new parties were formed and there were splits within established parties!

The fractionalization of the total vote was extremely high too. The most successful group–pro-O'Neill Official Unionists–took only 32 per cent of the total vote and the second most successful group, the anti-O'Neill Official Unionists, took 16 per cent. None of the eight non-Unionist parties secured as much as a tenth of the vote. The reason for this was not the electoral weakness of candidates nominated, but rather, the tendency of parties to nominate candidates in only a limited number of constituencies. Only the Unionist supporters of Terence O'Neill had candidates in as many as half the Northern Ireland constituencies. The median party nominated seven candidates for the 52 seats in the Commons. Fewness of candidates is not, however, tantamount to electoral weakness. In the constituencies contested, each group polled a substantial proportion of votes. Only eight of the 119 candidates failed to obtain one-eighth of the vote, thus forfeiting the £150 deposit required as a sign of earnestness. By contrast, at the 1970 British general election 22 per cent of candidates forfeited their deposits.[5]

Table VII.1 Electoral competition, 1969 Stormont general election

PARTY	Seats pre-election	No. of candidates	Returned un-opposed	Total seats	Votes cast	% of total
Official Unionist —						
Pro-O'Neill	22	31	6	24	178,973	32·0
Anti-O'Neill	15	13	—	12	90,617	16·2
Total Official Unionist	37	44	6	36	269,590	48·2
Ind. Pro-O'Neill U'st	—	15	—	3	72,120	12·9
Protestant Unionist	—	5	—	—	20,991	3·7
Unofficial Unionist	—	3	—	—	13,932	2·5
N.I. Labour Party	2	16	—	2	45,123	8·1
Nationalist	9	9	1	6	42,315	7·6
National Democratic	1	7	—	—	26,009	4·6
People's Democracy	—	8	—	—	23,645	4·2
Republican Labour	2	5	—	2	13,155	2·4
Independent	—	4	—	3	21,977	4·0
People's Progressive	—	1	—	—	2,992	0·5
Liberal	1	2	—	—	7,337	1·3
TOTALS	52	119	7	52	559,196	100

Source: Alf McCreary, 'Where the Votes Counted', *Belfast Telegraph*, March 11, 1969.

The fragmentation of parties occurs in part because of the importance of personal contact in Northern Ireland politics, as in the Republic. Constituencies are small enough so that a successful candidate can personally canvass a majority of his voters. An incumbent MP or a frustrated prospective nominee may stand as an unofficial or independent candidate, counting on his personal following to secure election; he may even stand as a 'one-man' party. In so far as voting is along religious lines, the sole candidate of a denomination is guaranteed a substantial vote by his religion alone. The return of six unofficial or independent candidates at the 1969 election demonstrates that individuals can successfully oppose major party candidates to a degree unknown in Britain. Another consequence is that a parliamentary party may have no members other than its leader and perhaps a deputy leader.

Party Allegiance and Regime Allegiance

Organizationally, only the Unionists and the Northern Ireland Labour Party have regularly had full-time paid officials.[6] The Nationalist Party has been no more than a loose alliance of local notables from different parts of rural Ulster, lacking even a national headquarters. Groups lacking formal organization might not be described as political parties by political scientists accustomed to such established institutions as the British Labour Party or the American Democratic Party; both, for all their factionalism, none the less maintain national committee headquarters and central organizations. Yet a one MP party cannot be ruled out of consideration as a minor party, when its policies are a threat to the regime. The return of MPs such as Gwynfor Evans, Winifred Ewing and Bernadette Devlin at by-elections after the 1966 British campaign illustrates how so-called minor parties can have major repercussions.

Survey techniques provide one way to establish the number of parties in a system. How many parties do people name when asked: Which would you say are the political parties that are now active in Northern Ireland? The replies show that the median voter conceives of Ulster as a three-party system: the average number of parties mentioned was 2·7. The difference index is nine per cent. The median Ulsterman does not see party politics as a simple conflict between the two communities: there is usually a third force, and for nearly one-fifth of the population a fourth force too. One could hypothesize that the more parties a Catholic perceived, the more likely he would be to support the regime, inasmuch as he would have a better chance of finding some group giving expression to his views. No such relationship exists. Similarly, one might hypothesize that those who perceived a greater multiplicity of alternative parties might also be more inclined to comply with basic political laws. This hypothesis too is rejected by the data.

A multiplicity of parties need not increase allegiance to the regime, if a substantial proportion are anti-regime parties. At general elections, Unionists and Nationalists have traditionally sought to identify each other with extreme positions to increase cohesion among their own supporters. One might expect Protestants to see politics in terms of a conflict between a moderate party representing co-religionists and Republican extremists. Similarly, Catholics might see the party system as a contest between moderate Nationalists and Paisleyite Unionists. The findings in Table VII.2 reject these hypotheses. Persons in both communities tend to see competition between parties that are

221

relatively moderate. It is particularly noteworthy, however, that the chief non-sectarian party – Northern Ireland Labour – is mentioned by only half the population.

Table VII.2   Parties cited as active in Northern Ireland

	Protestant	Catholic	Difference Prot–Cath	Total
	%	%	%	%
Extreme Protestants	3	3	0	3
Unionists	90	79	11	86
Liberals	16	15	1	16
Northern Ireland Labour	50	44	6	48
Communists	2	1	1	1
Nationalists	61	69	– 8	64
Republican Labour	9	17	– 8	13
Extreme Republicans	7	7	0	7
Don't know	9	15	– 6	12

D.I. = 20%

From a plethora of 29 different party labels mentioned, three stand out as specially visible to the mass of the electorate at the time of the 1968 Loyalty survey – the Unionists, the Nationalists and the Northern Ireland Labour parties. Yet within two years of the survey, all three parties were badly disrupted, with parliamentary candidates opposed and sometimes defeated by their upstart or breakaway groups. The splintering of the parties does not mean that the attitudes of Ulster electors had necessarily altered. The contrary is more likely the case. Most of the new parties can be readily located in terms of four major *tendances* of opinion: Unionism, Irish unity, Fabian Social-ism, and progressive Conservatism. Voters thus need have no diffi-culty relating pre-existing views to new proponents of Orange, Green, Red and Blue causes.* Labour and progressive Conservative parties belong in the same *tendance* in one respect, for they are secular parties.

The aim of the Ulster Unionist Party, according to Article III of the party constitution, is 'to maintain Northern Ireland as an integral part of the United Kingdom: to uphold and defend the Constitution and Parliament of Northern Ireland'. Commitment to the main-tenance of British ties thus makes the Unionists a 'nationalist' party,

* Analysing party support in terms of *tendances* guards against the diffi-culties that arise from frequent changes in party names. Parties are less likely to change their colour than their label.

albeit diametrically opposed to the nationalism of Irish Catholics. In intent, the Unionists are a single-claim party, advancing no distinctive principles or programme other than that of continued union with Britain. The party thus explicitly seeks support across class lines, and avoids doctrinaire statements on issues such as free enterprise vs. Socialism. Unlike the British Conservative Party, the bulk of Ulster Unionist MPs are not from a relatively exclusive stratum of expensive English public schools. Working-class Unionists have held Cabinet posts and a Unionist Labour Association seeks to mobilize working-class votes. The regime's step-by-step policy has meant that Unionist governments introduce to Ulster the welfare legislation of British Labour governments subsequent to passage in Great Britain. Unionist politicians align themselves with Conservatives on British issues, and British Conservatives have consistently supported the Northern Ireland regime in debates at Westminster.[7] The chief institutional link is at Westminster, where Ulster Unionists receive the Conservative Party whip. British Conservatives benefit from the addition of Unionist votes to their strength in the House of Commons. In 1951, Unionist numbers were sufficient to make the difference between a majority and a minority Conservative government, and in 1964 they denied the Labour government a manageable majority.

While inclusive on economic issues, the Unionist Party has traditionally been exclusive in religious terms. It does not explicitly exclude Catholics, but the affiliation of Orange lodges to the party at constituency and at central council level militates against Catholic participation. Representatives of the Orange Order constitute 122 of the 718 members of the Ulster Unionist Council. Three-fifths of the men who consider themselves 'strong Unionists' are members of the Order, and thus able to put an Orange point of view if they wish, at private as well as public party meetings. In a sense, the Unionists, like the British Labour Party, are a movement with several wings. An Ulster Protestant could argue that the Orange Order's place is no more anomalous than the Labour Party's requirement that its members, if eligible, belong to an appropriate trade union. For decades, all male Unionist MPs were members of the Orange Order. The ecumenical policies of Terence O'Neill were followed by a small breach in this practice. By August, 1969 there were five Unionist MPs who were not Orangemen, including one woman. However, Richard Ferguson, who resigned from the Order at that time, was promptly repudiated by his constituency association, and resigned his seat.[8]

Party Allegiance and Regime Allegiance

The Unionist Party has never nominated or elected a Catholic candidate to Stormont. At the 1969 general election, a Unionist association in County Down preferred not to contest the constituency rather than nominate a local resident, Louis Boyle, former president of the Queen's University Unionist Association. Boyle was a Catholic.[9] The party leadership said nothing about the incident.

The image that Ulster people have had of the Unionist party is simple. When asked what they think the party stands for, the majority with views stress its support for the British connection, the single claim that the party itself stresses (Table VII.3). The association of the party with Protestantism is its second major characteristic. Notwithstanding the efforts of Terence O'Neill to associate the party with economic progress, only four per cent saw the Unionists as standing for prosperity, although others may have had this in mind when they referred to such general virtues as 'good government'. The major components of the party's image are things that are virtues in Protestant eyes – the British connection and defence of Protestantism – and vices to Catholics.

Table VII.3 What the Unionist Party stands for

	Protestant	Catholic	Total
	%	%	%
Unity with Britain	55	35	47
Protestants	13	19	16
Economic benefits	4	2	3
Power; holding office	2	4	3
General virtues	17	6	13
General vices	2	6	4
Miscellaneous	1	1	1
Don't know	19	38	24

D.I. = 33%

Because the Unionist Party has always appealed to a broad cross-section of Ulster Protestants, it has always been peculiarly vulnerable to factional disputes and breakaway groups. The Loyalty survey found ample evidence of this, for among Protestants identifying with the Unionist Party, 58 per cent were Ultras in their commitment to a Protestant regime and 42 per cent were fully allegiant. Differences within the Protestant community are thus reflected in the ranks of the Unionist supporters. As the civil rights demonstrations of 1968–69 placed increasing pressure upon the Stormont regime to endorse or oppose reform, disagreements within the party heightened, leading to breakaway groups, as well as stimulating factional disagreement among Unionists at Stormont and in constituency associations.

As long as the Unionist Party has a majority in the Stormont House of Commons, then factionalism within the party is inevitably of prime importance. In the early days of the Prime Ministership of Terence O'Neill, differences within the party, while affecting claims to office, did not threaten party unity. The civil rights challenge was a major policy issue that split Unionist MPs, like Unionist voters, into at least three major groups. On the one hand were the Unionists who accepted or even welcomed reforms as a means of strengthening Stormont against criticism. Some Unionist MPs, however, saw it as threatening a breach in the Protestant monopoly of political power. A third group, by no means unimportant, were unaligned partisans. principally concerned with the threats to party unity arising from differences about the regime's response to the demonstrations.[10]

The Unionist opponents of Terence O'Neill, and latterly critics of Major James Chichester-Clark, have not formally organized themselves into a separate political party. For one thing, they have been sufficiently strong within the Unionist Party to give them hope of gaining a majority in the party. Within the party anti-reform Unionists press their views in bodies such as the West Ulster Unionist Council.[11] Former Cabinet ministers such as William Craig and Harry West have repeatedly criticized Major James Chichester-Clark's programme, and suffered suspension from the parliamentary party for doing this. Craig, Minister of Home Affairs at the time the civil rights demonstrations started, has been the major spokesman for the Ultra critics of Unionism. He succinctly stated his political philosophy while still a minister. Shortly after civil rights demonstrations began, he told a Belfast audience:

'There is all this nonsense about civil rights', he said. 'There are our old traditional enemies exploiting the situation. The civil rights movement is bogus and is made up of ill-informed radicals and people who see in unrest a chance to renew the campaign of violence.'

There was a fact that some people were scared to talk about and that was 'the difference between our concept of democracy and that of a Roman Catholic country'.

He had a great respect for people of other religions but he faced reality. Where you had a Roman Catholic majority you had a lower standard of democracy. 'The greatest civil right that they have in the Irish Republic is to leave it', Mr. Craig declared to great cheers.[12]

Party Allegiance and Regime Allegiance

Following the violence of August, 1969, Craig publicly recommended the use of firearms against Catholic protesters, 'so that Ulster could get back to normality', a prescription rich in historical irony and ambiguity.[13]

In reaction to opposition to the policies of Terence O'Neill within the Unionist Party, an *ad hoc* body of O'Neill's supporters was formed during the 1969 Stormont general election campaign. The group, which included Catholics as well as Protestants, called itself the New Ulster Movement.[14] At the election, the New Ulster Movement gave backing to independent Unionists running against official Unionist candidates who opposed the then Prime Minister. The result was inconclusive. The resignation of O'Neill left the group without an immediate *raison d'être*. In April, 1970 individuals from the NUM, the Northern Ireland Liberal Party and ex-Unionists came together to form an Alliance Party. The new party was both a challenge to the Unionists and an admission that the regime's historic governing party was unlikely to favour changes endorsed by the Alliance group. The new party endorsed the link with Britain, the 1969 reform programme, and 'complete and equal partnership in government and public life between Protestants and Catholics'. The Alliance Party ostentatiously attempts to maintain a cross-class appeal on socio-economic issues, favouring 'alliance between different political theories from conservative to labour, between all classes and religions'.[15]

Disagreements within the Unionist Party about the policies of the regime have reduced its traditional appeal to Ultras, previously sustained by a leadership that had never cast doubt upon the belief that the party stood for a 'Protestant country for a Protestant people'. At the 1969 general election, the Rev. Ian Paisley entered party politics to provide an unambiguous Orange alternative to Unionism. At that contest, his five candidates, standing as Protestant Unionists, polled an average of 28 per cent of the vote in their constituencies, and Paisley himself ran a strong second to Terence O'Neill in Bannside. In 1970 Paisley secured a double victory, winning election to the Stormont Parliament in a Bannside by-election, and winning election to the Westminster Parliament in June. Paisleyite candidates did not contest all the parliamentary seats held by Unionist MPs. Dr. Paisley said this was the result of a pact he made with Unionists at 'the highest levels'; the Prime Minister denied that any pact existed.

The Protestant Unionists have shown less interest in party organization than in ideology. The ideology of the Protestant Unionists is that of the traditional Orangeman. Dr. Paisley's own profession of faith makes this clear:

I am loyal to the principles of the great Protestant Reformation and refuse to barter my heritage for a mess of ecumenical pottage. I am loyal to the Queen and throne of Britain, being Protestant in the terms of the Revolution Settlement.
I am loyal to Ulster, the Ulster of our founding fathers.[16]

The Ulster of Paisley's founding fathers is a regime which will not countenance Catholic influence. The political implications of Paisley's position are stated clearly in the constitution of the Ulster Constitution Defence Committee and Ulster Protestant Volunteers, secular arms of his politico-religious movement:

The body of representatives pledge to maintain the Constitution at all costs. When the authorities act contrary to the Constitution the body will take whatever steps it thinks fit to expose such unconstitutional acts.[17]

The preamble states that Protestants should confine themselves to 'lawful methods ... as long as the United Kingdom maintains a Protestant Monarchy and the terms of the Revolution settlement'. But when this settlement is threatened, a member must pledge 'his first loyalty to the Society, even when its operations are at variance with any political party to which the member belongs'. The commitment of Dr. Paisley to this ideology has been demonstrated in the streets and courts of Ulster, as well as in the pulpit and on the hustings. In 1966 and again in 1969 after being charged with disruptive behaviour, he preferred to go to jail rather than give an undertaking to keep the peace for two years.

By contrast to Unionism, nationalist politics in Northern Ireland is that of a disorganized movement. People with a 'national' outlook meet together in a variety of contexts: in Catholic parish halls, in sporting activities of the Gaelic Athletic Association, or as students in Irish language classes. These people lack a single political party organized to fight the Unionists throughout Ulster. The absence of an organization reflects disagreements among Catholics about the best way to oppose Unionism and the most relevant issues to emphasize in addition to Irish unity. On economic issues, Catholic MPs range from the conservatism of Nationalists, called 'Green Tories' by their critics, through democratic socialism to revolutionary socialism. On constitutional tactics, Nationalists stress parliamentary

227

measures, while civil rights politicians have made their name by illegal demonstrations. Both reject the Sinn Fein faith in the contribution that violence can make to Irish unity.

United Ireland politicians have most frequently fought as Nationalists, and this is the party label that most Ulster voters recognize. The Northern Ireland Nationalist Party is the local descendant of the Irish parliamentary party at Westminster from 1885 until 1918. The moderate line of the Nationalists was always more popular in the North than in the South, because of the strength of Protestant opposition to Home Rule. Because nationalism appeals for votes in terms of an ascriptive characteristic, there is less need for organization than in a party competing against others with attributes that all can share. The Northern Ireland Nationalists have never had a central party headquarters. Until May, 1966 the party did not even hold an annual conference. Previously, moderate Catholics in each constituency would meet among themselves to agree a candidate: where

Table VII.4 What the Nationalist Party stands for

	Protestant	Catholic	Total
	%	%	%
United Ireland	55	48	52
Roman Catholics	14	11	13
Economic policies	1	2	2
Opposition	3	1	2
General virtues	1	3	2
General vices	3	5	4
Miscellaneous	1	1	1
Don't know	31	35	33 D.I. = 10%

Catholics were predominant, Stormont elections could be contests between Catholics differing on personal grounds or in the character of their opposition to partition. Successful Nationalist MPs had no incentive to create a party organization that might influence or supplant them. Instead, they preferred to build and maintain personal followings. (The phenomenon of 'clientelism' is also known in rural areas of Mediterranean countries.) In the words of one Londonderry councillor, 'Constituencies were like dioceses and the MPs like bishops, answerable to no one and answering no one.'[18]

Survey evidence shows that the Nationalists succeeded in establishing themselves as a one-issue party. The party in the 1968 Loyalty survey is seen to stand for a United Ireland even more strongly than the Unionists were seen to stand for the British connection (cf. Tables

VII.3 and VII.4). Catholicism is its other prominent characteristic. Very few general virtues are attributed to Nationalists. One-third of people interviewed do not know what the party stands for. Ignorance is not a reflection of the party's failure to contest seats everywhere. The proportion of those not knowing what the party stands for is as high in constituencies it contested as in seats it failed to contest.

In the 1960s, under the leadership of Eddie McAteer the Nationalist MPs at Stormont pursued a cautious policy. Nationalists agreed to act as an Official Opposition in response to gestures of conciliation from Terence O'Neill. At the 1966 party conference, the party discussed trying to formulate an alternative programme for government, but McAteer was hesitant about extending the party's commitments beyond the single demand for a United Ireland. He said it was 'not a time for hurling thunderbolts'.[19] The strength of the Nationalist commitment to parliamentary action was pointedly shown at its June, 1968 annual conference. Four months before civil rights demonstrations broke out everywhere in Northern Ireland, the conference voted to shelve a motion favouring civil disobedience. McAteer counselled:

> I detect a dangerous ground swell of resentment among our people – a dangerous feeling of disillusionment that we are not really wanted here, and that there is no real desire for this much sought holy grail of good community relations . . .
> We must not allow ourselves to be goaded into precipitate action which could only set the clock back a very considerable time, and which indeed might not be fully supported by the body of our people.[20]

Nine months later, McAteer lost his seat in Parliament to John Hume, a Derry civil rights leader. In his valedictory speech, he characteristically ignored civil rights issues and said 'The tricolour must be respected.' Even after the disorder of 1969, the Nationalist Party at its annual conference still concentrated attention upon an end to partition.[21]

Civil rights demonstrations presented a common problem to MPs of a Green tendency. As always in Ulster politics, more than one response was evoked. The complexities of the situation are reflected in the actions of two Catholic MPs from Belfast whose constituents were threatened by the killings of August, 1969. Prior to the event, Gerry Fitt and Paddy Kennedy sat at Stormont as the two representatives of the Republican Labour Party, a Belfast political group emphasizing conventional Socialist objectives as well as Republican goals. Following the killings of 1969, Kennedy increasingly emphasized the Republican element in the party label. (Another Republican Labour councillor in Belfast was arrested and charged with illegally possessing ammunition in troubled West Belfast.) Fitt, by contrast, emphasized the Labour element in his actions, pointing to the need to act against the unemployment, bad housing and social disorganization found in the most disorderly areas of Belfast. In consequence, there was a split in the Republican Labour Party.

In an attempt to draw Opposition MPs together in a party concerned with social measures as well as partition and civil rights, a Social Democratic and Labour Party was formed in August, 1970.[22] The founding group of six MPs, including Austin Currie, John Hume and Paddy Devlin, had been elected to Stormont 18 months earlier under four different labels—Republican Labour, Northern Ireland Labour, Nationalist and Independent. Gerry Fitt was named leader of the party. The cumbersome title emphasized the extent to which the new group's members differed among themselves about the extent to which Socialist policies should be promoted. Hume and Currie, for example, had previously been outside the ranks of the Labour movement. The title is also noteworthy for the omission of traditional Irish symbols. It could as easily be the label of a party in an ethnically homogeneous and secular Scandinavian society. The party's non-sectarian intentions were supported by the presence of Ivan Lee Cooper, a Protestant MP from Mid-Londonderry. But Cooper, like his associates, was returned in a predominantly Catholic constituency by Catholic votes. On one point, the new SDLP was united—the rejection of violence. This not only meant violence against Catholics, but also violence used by Catholics for the sake of uniting Ireland.

The civil rights demonstrations were also followed by a split in Sinn Fein, the political party wing of the Republican movement. (The Irish Republican Army is the other wing of the movement.) Sinn Fein's electoral activity has always been distinctive: its candidates have contested general elections with a pledge that they would not serve in Parliament if elected, because they refuse to recognize the legitimacy of Stormont or of the Dublin regime. Sinn Fein has not contested Stormont elections since the passage of an act in 1957 that compelled candidates to declare that they recognized the Stormont Parliament as a condition of having their names on the ballot paper. These Republicans have refused to make such a declaration. As no such declaration is required at Westminster, Sinn Fein has nominated candidates for these elections from time to time. In 1955, it contested all 12 seats in Ulster, winning 23·5 per cent of the vote. The party's two victors did not take their seats at Westminster; both were serving ten-year prison sentences for their part in an arms raid in Omagh the previous year. In 1970, Sinn Fein split on the issue of whether to continue its abstentionist policy. Those who favoured participation in Parliament also favoured left-wing social policies. The abstentionists continued to give sole priority to the unification of Ireland by any means necessary.[23] The division in the party matched the split of the IRA into two factions.

Labour politics in Northern Ireland has been as fissiparous as Nationalist politics, although for different reasons. The chief division among working-class parties has concerned national identity. One Labour tradition in Northern Ireland insists upon the solution of the Province's problems by closer integration within the United Kingdom, and the achievement of British welfare state standards under a Labour Government in London. The second mixes Irish Republicanism and Socialism, in the tradition of James Connolly, a leading trade unionist executed by the British in 1916 for taking part in the Easter Rising.[24] The British tradition emphasizes the efficacy of piecemeal achievements gained by parliamentary activity. The Republicans' variety of Socialism has a revolutionary bias, arising from Fenianism and Marxism. In 1970 this latter outlook was prominent in the 'Red and Green' IRA group and in one of the sections of the split Sinn Fein.

The Northern Ireland Labour Party, the most prominent of this group of parties in the 1960s, was formed in 1949, when the recurrence of the Border issue once again split Labour politicians. It endorsed maintaining the existing boundaries of the United Kingdom, as well as denouncing sectarianism in Northern Ireland life. The party won no seats at the 1949 and 1953 general elections, when partition was a major issue. In 1958, it secured the return of four MPs; this has been the height of its strength. At the 1969 election, two of its 16 candidates were successful.

While formally non-sectarian, the Northern Ireland Labour Party is better understood as an inter-confessional party, i.e., an organization bringing Protestants and Catholics together in pursuit of common interests, but still responsive to religious pressures. For example, the

Party Allegiance and Regime Allegiance

strength of fundamentalist Protestantism among the Belfast working class led to major disputes within the party in the early 1960s about children using playground swings on Sundays. Fundamentalist Socialists objected to the Sunday use of swings as a desecration of the Sabbath. Liberal and lapsed Protestant Socialists saw no objection to such recreation on Sundays. Catholics, free from any religious inhibitions about Sunday activities, saw Sabbatarianism as symptomatic of Orange tendencies among their working-class comrades. The opposite bias was shown at the April, 1968 party conference, when the creation of an all-Ireland Council of Labour was endorsed, bringing together Labour groups north and south of the border.

The confusing history of Labour politics in Northern Ireland would lead one to expect that its image would be less clear than that of the Unionist and Nationalist parties, and this is borne out by replies to survey questions (Table VII.5). The largest group of

Table VII.5 What the Northern Ireland Labour Party stands for

	Protestant %	Catholic %	Total %
Socialism: working class	36	43	39
British connection	3	5	4
Tolerance	3	4	3
United Ireland	7	3	5
Catholics	1	—	1
General virtues	1	2	1
General vices	10	4	8
Miscellaneous	4	4	4
Don't know	42	42	42

D.I. = 12%

respondents consists of people who don't know what the Labour Party stands for. Among those with some idea, the party has a single clear characteristic: it is the party of the working class and Socialism. Protestant antipathy is indicated by the emphasis given to the party's vices, a reaction stronger than that against the Nationalist Party (cf. Table VII.6). The third most frequently mentioned attribute, the alleged United Ireland bias in the party, is also a negative feature among Protestants. It is matched by the fact that Catholics are more likely to see Labour as standing for the British connection.

The intensification of anti-regime demonstrations in the late 1960s placed great strains upon the Northern Ireland Labour Party because the party drew support from both communities. The bulk of the

232

disorders were concentrated in working-class parts of Belfast and Londonderry; hence, there could be no doubt about the importance of the issue to the party's potential supporters, both Protestant and Catholic. The Loyalty survey found that among supporters the largest single group approved of the Constitution, but this was a minority of the party, 43 per cent; 31 per cent openly disapproved of the Constitution, and the remainder were don't knows. Labour supporters were also divided about complying with basic political laws: 35 per cent of its Protestants favoured an Ultra position and 43 per cent of Catholic Labour supporters endorsed illegal Republican demonstrations. The party's leaders played no prominent part in civil rights demonstrations, because of a desire to avoid the issue of religious discrimination in the name of non-sectarianism. In May, 1969, the Labour Party endorsed the civil rights campaign at its annual conference.[25]

The refusal of the Northern Ireland Labour Party to become involved in civil rights alienated a number of its Catholic supporters. Paddy Devlin, the Labour Party's Chairman and Catholic MP from the Falls Road, left the party, thus halving its parliamentary representation. Devlin's departure, to join the Social Democratic and Labour Party, was a major blow, because he had initially joined the party 'to talk to Protestants'. Eamonn McCann, a leading Derry Catholic civil rights worker and left-wing agitator, was expelled from the Northern Ireland Labour Party for endorsing Bernadette Devlin's candidacy.[26] The Northern Ireland Labour Party headquarters had previously refused to endorse McCann's candidacy for Derry in the Westminster election after he had been officially adopted by the local party to contest the seat.

The rejection of association with the Green-tinged SDLP was balanced by an attempt to draw closer to the British Labour Party, with which the Northern Ireland Labour Party has maintained fraternal associations but no integral link. The efforts of the Northern Ireland party to become a region of an expected United Kingdom Labour Party were not greeted with enthusiasm by Transport House in London, or by Labour MPs who had campaigned with Gerry Fitt for civil rights; they preferred a group less committed to the British connection.[27] At the end of 21 years, the Northern Ireland Labour Party had only one MP in the Stormont Commons, Vivian Simpson, and his committee rooms were burned out during the 1969 troubles in Belfast.

Party Allegiance and Regime Allegiance

Collectively, Protestants and Catholics agree about what the major parties stand for. Reference to the history and actions of the parties shows no misperception of reality. What people disagree about is the value that should be given to the party images. The very things that draw so many Protestants to the Unionist Party are the things that repel Catholics. To use terms such as 'like' and 'dislike' is to underestimate the force of the sentiments. The repulsion that exists is not of a kind that can be bridged by minor alterations or better public relations. There are great gulfs between the parties.[28] Moreover, the actions these parties take to maintain their own support sustain the discord that deprives the regime of full legitimacy.[29] Because *none* of the parties was seen to stand for civil rights, they failed to provide an institutional focus for grievances of part of the population. This provided an opening for extra-parliamentary civil rights groups to become strong in 1968. In 1969, the civil rights groups in turn lost popular appeal because they were associated with non-violent political action. The Protestant Ulster Volunteer Force and the IRA began to draw support because they stood for the use of force to achieve political ends.

The characteristics of Northern Ireland parties make them compete on issues that concern the survival of the regime. As long as the regime established in 1921 continues, the Unionist Party is expected to hold office. If the Nationalists or Republicans were to win, the chief change would not be in economic policies but in the boundaries of the state. In such circumstances, elections have a different function than in Britain or America.[30] To explore this further, each person was asked whether he usually voted, and why that would be. The replies show the importance of voting as a citizen duty. Even in a society where many citizens do not give full allegiance to the regime, 79 per cent of Protestants said that they usually voted, and 70 per cent of Catholics. These answers would not be literally true for every election, because of the large number of uncontested seats. None the less, they are psychologically true, reflecting the high value that people place upon the ballot. The act of voting is not seen as an instrument to change policies, but as a duty, or a means of expressing substantive loyalties. Protestants are much more likely than Catholics to see an election explicitly as a chance to vote for the regime (Table VII.6). Only six per cent see voting as a means of getting things done politically.

In many Western nations, social characteristics are not automati-

Table VII.6   Reasons for voting

	Protestant	Catholic	Total
	%	%	%
Duty to vote	41	36	39
Support party, candidate	18	20	19
Support regime, what it stands for	18	1	12
Oppose regime, what it stands for	—	6	2
Habit, social influences	6	8	7
Make changes, get things done	5	6	6
Don't usually vote	10	15	12
No regular chance to vote	11	12	11
Don't know	1	2	1

D.I. = 20%

cally translated into party loyalties.[31] In Northern Ireland, things are different, for regime outlooks reflect religious differences. Survey findings emphasize that religion is a barrier preventing voters floating between the two major parties. Among Protestants, 79 per cent support the Unionists, as against half of one per cent favouring Nationalists. Among Catholics, support for the Nationalists is nearly ten times greater than that for Unionists, who have secured only five per cent of the Catholic vote[32] (Table VII.7). The lesser degree of unity among Catholics arises from the failure of Nationalists to contest elections everywhere in the Province. The two major parties are exclusive on religious grounds: 95 per cent of Unionist supporters are Protestants, and 99 per cent of Nationalist supporters are Catholics. The importance of parties institutionalizing general political outlooks is also shown by the high sense of party identification. Without prompting by name, 86 per cent volunteered a party identification, notwithstanding the confusion about the structure of party competition in Northern Ireland. When asked whether they thought themselves strong or average supporters of their party, 28 per cent of

Table VII.7   Party identification in Northern Ireland*

	Protestant	Catholic	Total
	%	%	%
Unionist	79	5	49
Nationalist	0·5	51	21
N.I. Labour Party	11	27	18
Liberals and others	1	5	3
None; don't know	8	11	9 D.I. = 74%

* Where minor party names were given respondents are classified according to *tendance*; Republican Labour supporters are grouped with Nationalists.

Party Allegiance and Regime Allegiance

Protestants considered themselves strong partisans, as did 16 per cent of Catholics.

When party identification so closely follows religion, there is limited scope for it to correlate independently with attitudes toward the regime. As expected, Ultra Protestants are more likely to be Unionist than are fully allegiant Protestants; the difference, however, is only a matter of 14 per cent. What is more important to note is the fact that Ultra Protestants are 53 per cent of all Unionist supporters. Only eight per cent of Catholics who supported the Constitution also identified with the Unionist Party. Strong partisans are more likely to oppose the regime than are moderate partisans. Among Protestants, 67 per cent of strong partisans endorse the use of force if necessary, against 47 per cent of average partisans. Among Catholics, 41 per cent of strong partisans disapprove of the Constitution and 56 per cent favour illegal demonstrations.

Table VII.8 'Second choice' parties

As 2nd, 3rd or 4th choice:	Protestant %	Catholic %	Total %
Unionists	8	8	8
Nationalists	2	31	14
N.I. Labour Party	23	26	24
Liberals and others	15	10	13
No 2nd preference	59	49	55
No 3rd preference	93	87	90
No 4th preference	99	98	99

To test whether there is, potentially, a floating vote between the parties which might moderate inter-party differences, each respondent was asked to list additional parties that he would support, if his first choice did not have a candidate standing in his constituency. The question is particularly apt in Ulster, in view of the multiplicity of parties and the failure of most parties to contest most seats. In so far as religion is not an overriding concern, then one would expect that the party of the other community would receive a significant number of second, third or fourth preferences, reflecting the existence of marginal differences between the major parties. The test shows that Ulster people have very little inclination to cross religious lines in their voting, even when asked for their fourth choice party (Table VII.8). A majority said they had only a single party preference, and 35 per cent more had only a single reserve party. Only three per cent of Protestants could ever conceive of voting Nationalist, even as their fourth choice party, and only 13 per cent of Catholics could ever conceive of voting Unionist.

To confirm whether these attitudes reflected an opposition of principle or apathy in the face of a hypothetical problem, each person was also asked whether there was any party that he would *never* vote for. The replies again confirm the importance of partisan and religious ties. Only two per cent of Protestants said they would never vote Unionist, as against 56 per cent who said they would never vote Nationalist. Among Catholics, 45 per cent said they would never vote Unionist, with only six per cent expressing total rejection of Nationalists (D.I. = 57%). The relative intensity of partisanship in Northern Ireland is further underscored by comparison with France and Finland, two countries where Communist parties are strong and challenges to regimes have been recent. In both France and Finland, voters are much readier to indicate second, third and fourth preferences than in Northern Ireland.[33]

The foregoing findings show that those who criticize the Unionist Party because of alleged electoral gerrymandering and irregularities have missed the point. The nub of the difficulty is not the gerrymandering documented in places such as Londonderry or the disproportionate disfranchisement of Catholics at local government elections prior to reforms secured by the civil rights movement.[34] The fundamental problem – at least for the Catholic minority – has been the *undeniable majority supporting the Unionist Party*. At the time of the 1968 Loyalty survey, 54 per cent of all Ulstermen with partisan views were Unionists, giving the party a lead of 31 per cent over the second largest party, the Nationalists. The strength is also reflected in past and present elections to Stormont (see Tables III.2 and VII.1). Nowhere else in the Western world has a single party maintained such a hegemony for so long.[35] The pre-eminence of the party is based upon the identification of the Unionists with the regime. As long as elections are about constitutional issues, then the Unionists have been the natural majority party.

The electoral system used in Northern Ireland – the return of a single member by a simple plurality of the vote in a constituency – favours the largest party in Ulster as it would anywhere in the Western world.[36] The greater the disparity between the first and second party in size, the greater its advantage. In Northern Ireland, the bonus in seats provided by the system has been of the order of one-half; the Unionists have usually won about three-quarters of the seats at Stormont when supported by slightly more than half the electorate. The use of some type of proportional representation system would reduce the extent of the Unionist majority, but it would not *of itself* eliminate it. But proportional representation would encourage parties to multiply by giving greater representation in Parliament to lesser parties. The fear of this happening led the Unionist regime in 1929 to abandon the proportional representation method of electing MPs.[37] For the same reason, opposition groups such as the Social Democratic and Labour Party have favoured proportional representation. If the form of proportional representation permitted voters to express a preference between candidates of a single party, as occurs in the Republic, then such a change would also free sitting Members of Parliament from the fear of failure to gain renomination from their local party. In effect, an American-style party primary for candidates could be held simultaneously with a general election ballot. Almost inevitably, this would result in the creation of a House of Commons with a membership more nearly reflecting the wide and complex distribution of political opinions along several dimensions in Northern Ireland. Protestant Unionists, Marxist Republicans, anti-Marxist Republicans and other groups would all be assured of seats. If MPs who differed greatly in their views formed themselves into separate parties this could lead to such a multiplicity of parties that none would have an overall majority, and coalition government would follow. Such a development assumes that the threat of coalition would not, of itself, lead divided Unionists to unite in a single party to maintain their monopoly of office.

The workings of the British-style electoral system in Northern Ireland raise basic questions about majority (or plurality) rule. The doctrine is strongly defended by the majority party, the Unionists. For example, the 1969 Unionist election manifesto stated:

> The Ulster Unionist Party believes in an Ulster in which the obligations and rights of all citizens will be fully recognised. It expects of all citizens that loyalty toward the state which is due when the institutions of that state have the expressed support of a clear majority. . . .
> We shall resist every attempt to usurp the authority of Parliament or to substitute the rule of force for the rule of law. Our aim will be to create the fullest confidence in our democratic system. Parliament is the centre of that system and it is in Parliament by the process of debate and discussion that the answers to our problems must be found.[38]

In form, the sentiments could be repeated in good faith by the leader of any freely elected government. In Northern Ireland, majority rule has never had minority rights as its corollary. In most Western societies, such rights are safeguarded by the alternation of major parties between office and opposition. Moreover the opposition regards itself and is regarded as loyal. Neither of these conditions holds in Northern Ireland. Majority rule offers the prospect of permanent Unionist rule—as long as the party system retains its established form, votes are counted as in Britain and the regime retains its existing boundaries.

The close association between party and regime is not unique to Northern Ireland. Every regime begins with a nucleus of politicians who seek to make new institutions work in the face of some degree of opposition. The proponents of the regime have an advantage because they command substantial material and institutional resources. They command attention from subjects too, for they are more than a political party—they are also the government. In half a century, one would expect the actions of a 'party-regime' to have a considerable cumulative effect upon popular opinion. In Northern Ireland the fragmentation of the opposition gives even greater reason to hypothesize that the regime's resources can reduce disaffection and increase full allegiance.

The simplest model of a regime developing or maintaining support is that developed by David Easton.[39] This liberal model of legitimation posits that regimes develop support by responding to demands from their subjects. In turn, these responses stimulate subjects to give support. The logic of the model still holds if one thinks of regime leaders taking the initiative in providing benefits to stimulate subjects to respond with positive support for the regime. The latter model is particularly appropriate for a regime with divided authority, inasmuch as such a regime can hardly respond positively to the demands of disaffected subjects that they deconstitute the regime. It is also appropriate to Terence O'Neill's analysis of Northern Ireland, which hypothesized that if Catholics as well as Protestants perceived the regime as a source of benefits, then they would give it full allegiance.

If the actions of a regime are to influence individual political outlooks, at least three conditions must be met. First, individuals must perceive the regime's actions as relevant to their personal needs. Secondly, the benefits of the regime must be relevant to the demands that individuals make of government. Third and not least, the actions of the regime must be regarded as beneficial, by those who experience them. The obviousness of these conditions is not a guarantee that they are met; it is a reminder that Easton's theory assumes conditions which may–or may not–exist in Northern Ireland.

In any book about politics, the significance of government to the ordinary subject is likely to be overestimated. People have many roles in life, and that of citizen or partisan is only one among many. Yet in Northern Ireland, there is much reason to believe that government *is* important to the mass of the population, because of its use to maintain a particular power relationship between Protestants and Catholics. Moreover, a lower standard of living than England gives the welfare services of the regime a greater significance to a larger proportion of citizens. To assess the relevance of government to individuals, people were first asked: When you think of your own situation and that of your family, what problem concerns you most? The pattern of replies was virtually identical among Protestants and Catholics (D.I. = 6%). A total of 42 per cent mentioned the cost of living and economic problems; 24 per cent referred to worries about family matters, including their children; and 12 per cent to worries about housing and welfare services. Only four per cent of Protestants and five per cent of Catholics referred to worries about religion or politics. Moreover, 27 per cent said that they had no problems.

The concerns of Ulster people today are both personal and political. Unemployment, the education of children, the prospect of emigration, housing and health are all matters for which the Stormont regime accepts responsibility, as well as intimately affecting the daily lives of people. To see whether Ulster people regard the government as a source of help with their main family problem, each person was then asked who he thought most able to help him. In the total sample, 33 per cent of Protestants and 29 per cent of Catholics referred to the government, public agencies or politicians as a source of aid. Family and relatives were mentioned by 17 per cent. Only one per cent referred to help from churches. No source of help was perceived by seven per cent of those interviewed. Among those regarding the government as a source of assistance, 69 per cent of Protestants as against 34 per cent of Catholics approved of the Constitution. This shows that those who look to the regime for help are no more likely to support the Constitution than those who do not.

When people were asked to turn from personal problems and say what they thought were the most important problems that the government ought to do something about, the replies were much the same: 66 per cent said they wished the regime would act on economic problems, 62 per cent also referred to welfare measures and housing, and only 17 per cent made reference to religious or political problems. The pattern of replies varied little by religion: nine per cent of Protestants and ten per cent of Catholics could think of nothing that they wanted the government to do. In short, the demands of subjects upon the regime resemble those found elsewhere in the United Kingdom.

The governing party may not swing votes by meeting these demands, but it could do something even more important – build support for the regime itself. For the regime to do this, its actions must not only affect people, but also be perceived as beneficial. Otherwise, the regime would be an irrelevant or even malevolent institution.

Table VII.9   The effect of the regime

	Protestant	Catholic	Total	
	%	%	%	
A lot	24	25	24	
Some	26	15	22	
A little	31	28	30	
None	17	31	23	
Don't know	1	2	1	D.I. = 15%
(Among those saying it has any effect)				
Makes life better	53	37	47	
Makes life worse	7	18	12	
Depends	17	14	16	
Don't know	23	31	25	D.I. = 19%

When asked about the effect of the regime on their lives, nearly one-quarter of Ulster people said it had none, and another 30 per cent thought it had only a little effect (Table VII.9). There is little difference between Protestants and Catholics in the degree of impact that they attribute to the regime. A more significant difference emerges when those registering effect are asked whether they think the regime's actions usually help make their lives better or worse. In aggregate, 36 per cent of the population think that the regime usually makes their lives better; a majority have no views or are uncertain about the impact of the regime's actions on their own lives. The proportion seeing the regime's effect as great is lower than that revealed by a comparable question asked in Britain, America and Germany.[40]

Those who believe that the regime makes their lives better are more likely to support the Constitution. Among Protestants in this group, 77 per cent approve of the Constitution, as against 62 per cent of those who think that government activities harm their lives. The difference among Catholics is greater: 50 per cent who think the regime makes their lives better support the regime, as against 17 per cent among those who think it makes their lives worse. This suggests that Unionist politicians do not need to 'buy' support from Protestants, for the majority will stand by them in any event. Among Catholics, policies that positively influence the lives of subjects will raise regime support – but not to a level as high as that of deprived Protestants. The gain in support among Catholics is also matched by a gain in compliance: demonstrations are favoured by 35 per cent of those who think the regime makes their life better and by 65 per cent of those who think that Stormont makes their life worse.[41] Among Protestants, 58 per cent of those who think that the regime usually makes their life better are prepared to defend Protestant rule by force. So too are 42 per cent who think that the regime makes their life worse. In aggregate, the prospect of the regime's actions increasing allegiance is limited by the fact that the majority of Ulster people fit into neither of the foregoing categories.

A more complex analysis of regime actions and the allegiance of subjects is given by Max Weber, who emphasized the multiplicity of strategies that leaders could use in efforts to legitimate their regime. One is an appeal to calculating mentalities, offering benefits as a positive inducement to allegiance, or harsh sanctions as a calculated deterrent. A second strategy is to invoke absolute values as ends of overriding importance. In a Communist regime, the substantive goal of transforming the economy may be invoked. In an Anglo-American society, regimes might appeal by emphasizing procedural values, such as majority rule. An even more compelling motive to give allegiance is traditionalism, accepting a regime because the custom of support and compliance is so pervasive in a society that an individual cannot conceive of living under any other form of government. Last and not least, Weber stressed the emotional appeal of the charismatic leader, a man whose personal magnetism is such that he can overthrow an existing regime and gain allegiance – for a short time if not permanently – by his personal qualities.[42]

Cataloguing the strategies by which a regime can seek allegiance can be misleading, for the discount rate between that which is sought and that which is achieved is often extremely high. (A regime can, of course, cut its losses, as the Craigavon and Brookeborough

242

governments did, by refusing to seek full allegiance from all its subjects.) Weber's discussion of the means by which a regime *might be* legitimated did not stipulate that these means would be inevitably and equally effective. Unfortunately, students of political authority have often assumed that a politician's recourse to strategies of legitimation is *ipso facto* evidence of success; some have been more impressed by a given regime than its nominal subjects. It is possible that strategies intended to increase support or compliance, e.g., the banning of an anti-regime demonstration, might boomerang by causing rationally calculating subjects to conclude that the wisest thing to do in the circumstances is to rebel.

As a first step in testing this diffuse and general set of statements, Northern Ireland respondents were asked what they thought were the most important reasons for supporting the government in what it does. Notwithstanding the explicit request for a pro-regime response, 22 per cent of Catholics volunteered the opinion that they did not support the regime, and another 35 per cent said that they didn't know any reasons for supporting it. By contrast only five per cent of Protestants expressed no support, and 20 per cent were don't knows. Efforts to classify the free responses of individuals showed difficulties in applying Weber's distinctions. For instance, is a reference to welfare policies an absolute value, an economic calculation, or a belief in the processes of the welfare state? Is respect for the Queen the result of traditional influence or a charismatic response to authority? To avoid unreliability in classification, the answers given were placed under two broad headings: *instrumental* justifications for support (i.e., the regime as a means to an end, such as economic benefits, peace, or procedural fairness), and *expressive* justifications (i.e., the regime as an end in itself: e.g., it has good leaders, or stands for the Union Jack). Among Protestants, 56 per cent offered instrumental reasons for supporting the regime and 36 per cent expressive ones. Among Catholics, 36 per cent referred to instrumental reasons for supporting the regime, and 13 per cent expressive reasons. The limited range of the answers precluded more detailed analysis.

To test the multiplicity of appeals systematically, each respondent was then asked to say whether he agreed, disagreed or had no opinion about each of a series of eight statements offered as reasons for favouring the regime. The meaningfulness of the prepared statements is evidenced by the small proportion who do not give a clearcut opinion: on average, 87 per cent of the sample gave a definite answer to each statement. Four of the statements offered were instrumental arguments on behalf of the regime, and four were expressive ones (Table VII.10).

Table VII.10   Reasons for supporting the regime

	Protestant %	Catholic %	Difference %	Total %
Instrumental:		*Agree*		
It usually provides lots of benefits for people	85	75	− 10	81
It keeps things peaceful	82	58	− 24	72
Its goals are usually good ones	86	52	− 35	72
We've got to accept it whatever we think	67	74	+7	70
			Average D.I. = 19%	
Expressive:		% *Agree*		
It is good because it gives us a Queen to rule over us	82	37	− 45	63
It is good because it is what the people vote for	74	37	− 37	59
It is in the hands of men who are good leaders	73	47	− 26	62
It's good because it is traditional	51	23	− 28	40
			Average D.I. = 34%	

Responses show marked differences between Protestants and Catholics. A majority of Protestants agree with each of the eight reasons offered. By contrast, a majority of Catholics do not agree with any of the four expressive justifications. While a majority agreed with the four instrumental reasons, the proportion was always lower than Protestants, except for the statement: 'We've got to accept it whatever we think.' The intensity of Protestant support for the regime is suggested by the fact that when four of these reasons were advanced to an English community sample, none was accepted by so high a proportion of respondents.[43] In the society as a whole, the four expressive reasons are less favoured than the instrumental ones. It is specially noteworthy that Catholics see elections as offering little inducement to endorse the regime; only the monarchy and traditionalism are as unpopular.

It is also important to test the cumulative weight of a multiplicity of motives for giving allegiance, for the *number* of motives impelling a person to give allegiance may be more important than the content of any one. Each respondent can be assessed according to the number of times that he agrees with the four instrumental reasons for supporting the regime, and with the four expressive reasons. The replies show that the greater the number of positive justifications for support–without regard to content–the greater the likelihood that both Protestants and Catholics will approve of the Constitution (Table VII.11).

Table VII.11 The influence of multiple motives for allegiance

Total		SUPPORT		COMPLIANCE	
		Protestant	Catholic	Protestant	Catholic
%		%	%	%	%
Instrumental reasons endorsed:					
40	Four	69	46	39	63
31	Three	73	39	48	59
17	Two	62	24	60	42
8	One	54	17	68	33
4	None	56	22	53	45
Expressive reasons endorsed:					
28	Four	71	59	34	64
22	Three	72	43	44	69
15	Two	62	45	60	59
17	One	63	29	59	51
18	None	61	19	81	37

The effect of cumulative reinforcement is most noteworthy among Catholics responding to expressive arguments; the most responsive are nearly three times as likely to approve of the Constitution as the least. But Protestants who fail to endorse any reasons are still *more likely* than the most responsive Catholics to approve the Constitution. In aggregate, the effect is limited by the fact that those Catholics most affected by a multiplicity of appeals are also the least numerous group in the Catholic community. The cumulative scale also emphasizes the importance of expressive symbols in *decreasing* full allegiance to the established regime within the Protestant community. Among those responding positively to four expressive reasons, 66 per cent are Ultras; the proportion declines to 19 per cent among those responding to none of these justifications. Among Catholics, the tendency is in the opposite direction. A similar but less strong pattern is found in responses to instrumental appeals.

The justifications that leaders of the regime may use to develop allegiance in fact maintain discord. Instrumental justifications are of some effect, but they do not raise the level of Catholic support to that shown by the least impressed Protestant. The appeals that influence outlooks most are those concerning expressive symbols. Within the Protestant community, however, these cumulatively affect Ultras. Simultaneously, their effect on Catholics is likely to be negative, because Catholics do not like expressive symbols whether they be tokens of royalty or of electoral victory. In such circumstances, recourse to political symbols is a means of *decreasing* the authority of the regime, as these symbols erode allegiance among both Protestants and Catholics. This leaves the regime with whatever allegiance it can gain from its reputation as a source of benefits. This is less valuable than propounders of materialist social theories suggest. The response of the people of Northern Ireland is not unique. In the Republic, since the early 1930s the regime has enjoyed virtually full legitimacy, notwithstanding its instrumental shortcomings, including an economic policy forcing massive emigration. The regime there has remained secure by appeals to expressive symbols of nationalism, Catholicism and Gaelic culture. Moreover, the challenge to the regime in Dublin comes most immediately from those who invoke symbols too, the Republicans who refuse allegiance because they claim the regime has not gone far enough to achieve their valued ideal of Irish unity.

VIII · Two Bodies in Christ

> Since the coming of St. Patrick 1,500 years ago, Ireland
> has been a Christian and a Catholic nation. All the ruthless
> attempts made down through the centuries to force us from
> this allegiance have not shaken her faith. She remains a
> Catholic nation.
>
> EAMON DE VALERA

> INTERVIEWER: *What do you have against Roman Catholics?*
> BELFAST PROTESTANT: *Are you daft? Why, their religion,
> of course.*
>
> BBC-TV, 1970

Traditionally, kings and bishops saw church and state as partners.
Whichever was supreme, both agreed upon the need to reinforce the
church with the authority of the state, and the state with the authority
of the church. The Reformation rent this ideal of unity. Churches
and regimes began to compete for authority. Today in a world in
which Protestant and Catholic leaders endorse ecumenical efforts to
draw together Christians of all denominations, Northern Ireland remains a monument to an earlier age of faith and wars of faith. An
Ulsterman reading about the Thirty Years War might reckon that
seventeenth-century German victims of religious discord got off easy:
at least that war is now ended. Religious philosophies that elsewhere
emphasize the binding together of men in Ulster still sustain differences between them.

The introduction of religious differences into Ireland was the consequence of a conscious act of policy of the English Crown. When
Henry VIII broke with Rome, he expected his Irish as well as his
English subjects to convert to his new Erastian Church. When Irish
subjects failed to follow royal wishes loyally, successive monarchs
sought by force of arms and by plantation to create a society that was
loyal because Protestant. Throughout Ireland, the penal laws made
the Catholic Church, the church of the mass of the population, virtually outlaw, and treated Catholics attainted by their religion. The
resulting difficulties were not resolved until the creation of the Irish
Republic finally placed authority for the government of 26 counties
of Ireland in the hands of an overwhelmingly Catholic electorate. It

established a regime that, in the words of Article 44, Sec. 2 of the 1937 Constitution, 'recognises the special position of the Holy Catholic Apostolic and Roman Church as the guardian of the Faith professed by the great majority of the citizens'. Ironically, in Northern Ireland the constitutional settlement created, at least in appearance, a secular state. Stormont is prohibited by the Government of Ireland Act from making 'a law so as either directly or indirectly to establish or endow any religion or prohibit or restrict the free exercise thereof, or give a preference, privilege or advantage or impose any disability or disadvantage on account of religious belief or religious or ecclesiastical status'.[1]

In reality, Northern Ireland is best considered a bi-confessional society. It is bi-confessional because nearly everyone identifies himself as either a Protestant or a Catholic. In the 1961 census, only 384 of the 1,457,000 persons enumerated described themselves as free thinkers, atheists or humanists.[2] In the 1968 Loyalty survey, 1,280 of the 1,291 persons interviewed promptly gave a denominational identification when asked their religion, and seven more readily stated a preference for Protestantism or Catholicism when asked to do so.[3] Because the society is bi-confessional there are *two* versions of many things, a Protestant and a Catholic version.[4] Terence O'Neill, the most prominent advocate of bi-confessional co-operation in the 1960s, emphasized that this could only be based on an acceptance of differences in religious beliefs. Moreover, he told Catholics that there would be no bargaining in the name of religious goodwill about disagreements 'centred not around the activities of the state, but around its very existence'.[5]

Religion not only provides individuals with a way to orient themselves to another world, it can also influence their worldly outlooks in politically significant ways. Religious values and beliefs can sanction acceptance or rejection of political policies or regimes. Involvement in the affairs of a particular church may reinforce attitudes by bringing a person into regular contact with people who share a common outlook. Identification with a religion can sustain loyalties independently of church attendance. A man does not have to be a practising Catholic, Protestant or Jew to find that most of his friends and associates are co-religionists. American studies[6] have found a multiplicity of religious factors of some social significance; there is good reason to believe that these factors are at least as important in Northern Ireland.

In Northern Ireland, unlike America and England, religion symbolizes political discord.[7] Given the connection between the regime and Protestantism, those Protestants most influenced by their religion should be most likely to hold Ultra views. In the Catholic community, one would hypothesize that the greater the influence of religion, the less likely an individual would be to support the Constitution. It does not, however, follow that strongly Catholic Ulstermen would also be readiest to violate political laws, for the teachings of the Catholic Church, in Ireland as elsewhere, have traditionally emphasized acceptance of civil authority. As John Whyte notes, 'The Catholic Church in Ireland has always provided much of the opposition to revolutionary movements.'[8] For example, the hierarchy denounces membership in the oathbound IRA as a mortal sin. Hence, the most involved Catholics might be repressed subjects, refusing support to the regime but complying with its laws. Persons most distant from Catholic influences might be fully allegiant subjects, withdrawing from the Catholic community while entering into affairs of the dominant community. Alternatively, they could be rebels, rejecting the authority of the Catholic Church as well as that of the regime.

The study of religious influences can begin by considering churches as social institutions. Like any other social institution, a church institutionalizes values, beliefs and emotions. It conserves outlooks from the past, and not only the ancient past of Biblical times. Specific events in the past – the establishment of apostolic succession or the great upheavals of the Reformation – justify their existence today. They are peculiarly significant in Ulster, because of the relevance of past history to current discord about the regime. By teaching the importance of differing doctrines to successive generations, the churches transmit past differences into the present and future.

In institutional form, the Roman Catholic Church in Northern Ireland is much the same as branches elsewhere in the English-speaking world. It is the environment that makes it appear different. The Catholic Church, like its Protestant counterparts, does not recognize for ecclesiastical purposes the international boundary that separates the North from the Republic. The Primate of All-Ireland resides in the North at Armagh, as does the head of the Protestant and episcopal Church of Ireland. Northern priests usually go to a seminary in the South for training. In 1963, William Cardinal Conway became the first head of the Catholic Church in Ireland to

Two Bodies in Christ

be born in Belfast. In many contexts, the Catholic Church and its leadership are objects of verbal abuse in conversation, political speeches and wall slogans in Northern Ireland. The most polite of these slogans is: To Hell with the Pope. Physical assaults, when they occur, are usually directed at lay Catholics and their property. During the 1969 disorders, very little church* property was damaged, by comparison with the number of Catholics intimidated from their homes in Belfast. In a number of parishes, fear of attack led to the posting of firewatchers and guards around church property.

The first concern of the Catholic Church in Northern Ireland is the spiritual welfare of its communicants. To ensure this requires negotiations with political authorities about education.[9] The hierarchy opposes the mixing of Catholic and Protestant children in the same schools, because, in the words of Cardinal Conway, 'They do not think that they would grow up with a strong and virile faith if all they got at school was an agreed syllabus Christianity, watered down to the lowest common denominator of different persuasions and taught by persons who may not even be believing Christians themselves.'[10] The financial provisions for Catholic schools in Northern Ireland were not so favourable as in England until 1968. Because the bulk of running costs of Catholic schools are paid by the state, the position is far more favourable than that in America. The chief Catholic hospital, the Mater Infirmorum, receives no state subsidy; it is maintained privately under clerical control. Its position is thus less favourable than that of Catholic hospitals in Britain, but formally no different from that of Catholic hospitals in the United States.[11]

Officially, the Catholic Church (i.e., the senior officials in the hierarchy in Northern Ireland) takes no stand on constitutional issues. Given the divided authority of the regime, abstention from positive action can be taken as tacit disapproval of the Constitution. Terence O'Neill, supported by Church of Ireland and Presbyterian leaders, failed in his attempts to get the hierarchy to show positive approval of the regime.[12] Cardinal Conway has argued that by negotiating with Stormont on matters such as school subsidies, the Church has 'recognized' the regime. (Such action cannot, after all, be taken for granted in a land where the verb 'to boycott' originated.) Few

* In Northern Ireland, it is common to refer to a Catholic church as a chapel. The term emphasizes its non-established status and constricted position in earlier times.

250

signs of acceptance have been given, the Cardinal has explained, because: 'We do not think it right to go junketing at receptions and garden parties with a regime which has practised a very efficient policy of discrimination against Catholics ever since its inception.'[13] The nationalist inclinations of the hierarchy are reflected by parochial clergy too. A survey study in County Armagh in 1968 found that all the priests and curates interviewed identified themselves as Irish, and all disapproved of the Constitution.[14] Cardinal Conway has made it clear that he personally would like to see a United Ireland, but he would be 'appalled by the idea of a United Ireland brought about by force'. Pope Paul VI has also explicitly condemned the use of violence in Northern Ireland, while expressing sorrow at the disorders there in 1969.[15] The Catholic hierarchy's arguments against forceful political action combine moral and pragmatic considerations. In the words of Cardinal Conway in May, 1970, violence 'is morally wrong and that is doubly so in Northern Ireland at the present time because of what it may lead to. It could lead to great suffering and death.'[16] In short, the officers of the Catholic Church in Northern Ireland are disaffected but not rebels: they refuse support but give compliance to the regime.

The civil rights demonstrations created a novel situation for the clerical authorities. The Catholic hierarchy approved the technically illegal activities of the demonstrators because of what was regarded as the denial of natural law rights. In the words of Cardinal Conway, 'You cannot exact political conformity as the price of justice.' Priests have not, however, been openly involved in civil rights demonstrations; their silence has been neutral against the regime, as there is no shortage of lay Catholics to lead demonstrations. Benevolent silence has not been extended to those civil rights advocates, usually lapsed Catholics, who threaten the authority of the Catholic Church as well as that of the Stormont regime. Cardinal Conway has publicly expressed concern about 'ultra-left' and 'neo-Marxist influences' within the civil rights movement.[17] Parish priests undoubtedly reinforce this view, given their long association with the fortunes of the Nationalist party in Northern Ireland.[18] Individual priests retain the freedom to speak as they wish, so long as they are not explicitly ordered to be silent. For example, Father Denis Faul of Dungannon has denounced the Stormont regime for its abuse of the courts in terms so strong that the Cardinal repudiated them. Such remarks are not meant as rebellion to episcopal authority, for Faul has also delivered equally lengthy panegyrics praising the Pope's encyclical against contraception. Anti-clerical Catholics usually keep criticism of the Catholic hierarchy private, because public quarrelling would only dissipate energies better directed against the Stormont regime. Typically, Bernadette Devlin has published her views, 'Among the best traitors Ireland has ever had, Mother Church ranks at the very top, a massive obstacle in the path to equality and freedom.'[19] Notwithstanding such remarks, Bernadette Devlin has not refused the votes won by her status as the 'Pan-Papish' parliamentary candidate in Mid-Ulster. Carrying out constituency duties has led her to attend the funeral mass of a constituent who died in an unsuccessful attempt to burn an Orange Hall.

The disorder and killings of August, 1969, placed the Catholic hierarchy in a difficult position not of its choosing. The Cardinal and his five Northern Ireland bishops promptly denounced the armed attacks upon Catholic districts and regretted that 'the true picture of these events has been greatly obscured by official statements'.[20] As residents of the Falls Road and of the Bogside, clergy shared risks with their parishioners. For example, Clonard Monastery abuts on an area of Belfast where Catholic families were driven from their homes by arsonists, and have since been active in armed defence. Priests guarding church property or on the streets with their parishioners in troubled times have no desire to wait for a Stormont statement to tell them what protection they can hope to get from the Royal Ulster Constabulary in the event of another attack by armed Protestants. In such circumstances, to denounce the work of lay Catholics securing arms for the defence of their parish and their parishioners would be to counsel pacifism.

The Catholic hierarchy's respect for authority has never led it to oppose the use of force for rightful ends. Priests in the most troubled parishes denounce violence, when this is instigated by Catholics against the British Army or Protestant Ultras. But since 1969 priests have not denounced or threatened to excommunicate Catholics actively engaged in securing arms ready for use in defence against Protestant aggression, even though the names of the people principally responsible may be well known in the parish. Local defence committees have received the benevolent neutrality of the hierarchy. In West Belfast, the Central Citizens' Defence Committee has the blessing of the diocesan bishop. Father Padraig Murphy, administrator of the chief parish there, is active in its work, directing vigilantes and negotiating with the British Army in efforts to avoid gunfire and disorder, whichever side it may come from.[21] An active role in the Belfast CCDC incidentally involves Father Murphy with laymen active in the Republican movement. The executive committee of the group, in addition to priests, has also included activists in both of the quarrelling factions of the IRA. At another level, the hierarchy continues to denounce the IRA. The revolutionary Socialist commitment of one wing of the IRA makes it doubly anathema. None the less, the Catholic Church in Ulster is sufficiently large and complex so that it is even possible to find a priest who says that he prefers dealing with Cathal Goulding, the head of the Red IRA, to his own bishop.

In institutional form, Protestantism in Northern Ireland is much the same as Protestantism elsewhere in the English-speaking world: adherents are divided among many different churches. The 1961 Northern Ireland census reports by name membership in 55 different Protestant denominations. Of these, 42 have less than one thousand members; the two smallest enumerated – the Free Pentecostal and the Emmanuel Mission – had 11 members each. Only five denominations had a membership of more than one per cent of the total Protestant population: Presbyterians 46·9 per cent, Church of Ireland, 38·3 per cent, Methodists, 8·0 per cent, Brethren, 1·9 per cent, Baptists, 1·5 per cent, and Congregationalists, 1·1 per cent.

The two dominant Protestant churches – the Presbyterians and the Church of Ireland – reflect two very different historical traditions. The Presbyterian Church was brought to Ulster by Scots settlers in the seventeenth century and, although the state church in Scotland, it was not given equal recognition in Northern Ireland. Instead, the Church of Ireland, a product of the English break with Rome, was the state-established Church. In the North, there were initially two divisions. Presbyterians and Catholics were both excluded from the advantages of establishment, while Presbyterians and the Church of Ireland shared an abomination of popery. The latter proved stronger, especially after the disestablishment of the Church of Ireland in 1869. Today, there is no evidence of public controversy between the Presbyterian Church and the Church of Ireland. Both are organized on a 32-county basis, with the bulk of their members in Ulster. Both give strong support to the Stormont regime, and to the regime in the Republic. Protestants in the Republic do not complain of discrimination there.

Two Bodies in Christ

One could hypothesize that major differences in authority patterns between the episcopal Church of Ireland and the Presbyterian Church would influence attitudes toward the regime. The episcopal church places final authority in the hands of bishops, as does the Catholic Church, which emphasizes the importance of the clergy as interpreters of doctrine. By contrast, the Presbyterian Church places responsibility for church government in the hands of congregations of lay members, emphasizing the importance of individual responsibility for decisions of all kinds. If these differences carried into other spheres, then episcopal worshippers would be more likely to comply with basic political laws, and Presbyterians more likely to decide for themselves and refuse compliance. In fact, no significant relationship exists between Protestant denominationalism and endorsement of violence. The Ultra position is taken by 54 per cent of members of the Church of Ireland, 52 per cent of Presbyterians and 58 per cent in other Protestant denominations. Similarly there is no relationship between denomination and support for the Constitution.

The Rev. Ian Paisley's Free Presbyterian Church represents a viewpoint of substantial historical significance in Ulster. Its significance arises from Paisley's desire to maintain the connection between religion and politics that has for centuries characterized Irish politics. He does this not only in terms of traditional political values, but also in terms of Protestant fundamentalist values that he would argue are as relevant today as they were when Martin Luther nailed his 95 theses to the church door in Wittenberg in 1517. This fundamentalist, anti-ecumenical theology is not unique to Northern Ireland. Paisley's doctorate was conferred as an honorary degree by Bob Jones University, Greenville, South Carolina.

To suggest that Ian Paisley has created a religious base for Ultraism is to put the cart before the horse. It is more appropriate to say that he has voiced opinions and stimulated predispositions long found among Ulster people. The important question is: How many people have views similar to his? In institutional terms, the Free Presbyterian Church is no more than one among many small sects. It has 12 churches scattered through the Province and was credited with 1,093 members in the 1961 census. The 1968 Loyalty survey found three persons who identified themselves as Free Presbyterians, suggesting a membership still well below five figures. Supporters have been numerous enough to finance the construction of a new church in Belfast in 1969, costing an estimated £200,000, and to fill any auditorium at which Paisley preaches in Ulster.[22] A person who does not attend a Free Presbyterian church or subscribe to his news-sheet, the *Protestant Telegraph,* can still agree with much that is said therein and thus be regarded as a 'Paisleyite' in political if not church-membership terms. Defining Paisleyism at its broadest–at all costs to endeavour to keep Northern Ireland Protestant–would classify slightly more than half the Protestants in the Province as Paisleyites. Defining Paisleyism as support for the man as a potential political leader, shows a lower, but still substantial following. A survey by National Opinion Polls in 1967 found that 32 per cent of Protestants said that they usually agreed with what Paisley said, and 58 per cent usually disagreed. There was only a difference of one per cent in the views of members of the Church of Ireland and the Presbyterian Church. Hardly any Catholics had a good word to say about Paisley. A more detailed analysis of those with Paisleyite sympathies shows that there is a tendency for such persons to cluster in the Belfast working class. But Paisleyites are by no means confined to 'hardline' Protestant districts such as the Shankill Road district. There is some Paisleyite sympathy everywhere–among young and old, men and women, the middle class and working class, and in the towns and countryside as well as in the capital.[23]

Table VIII.1   Characteristics liked about churches

Likes	PROTESTANT CHURCHES			CATHOLIC CHURCH		
	Prot	Cath	Total	Prot	Cath	Total
	%	%	%	%	%	%
Freedom	29	2	18	(Not mentioned)		
Services; traditions	21	4	14	4	21	11
Fellowship, belonging	19	11	16	3	21	10
Doctrines	15	3	10	1	20	8
General approval	9	8	6	3	19	9
Actions of clergy, members	3	5	4	31	15	25
Tolerance	2	3	2	—	3	1
Nothing	5	11	8	15	4	10
Don't know	15	57	32	41	11	29
	D.I. = 59%			D.I. = 65%		

Because pilot interviews had called attention to the fewness of Free Presbyterians by contrast with sympathy for anti-Catholicism, the Loyalty survey sought to establish generalized images of the Catholic and Protestant churches. This also had the advantage of controlling

Two Bodies in Christ

for the influence of individual personalities, such as Paisley. Open-ended questions were asked about the things liked and disliked about both churches, to give each respondent the opportunity of volunteering uncomplimentary opinions about a church, while avoiding the risk of putting words into the respondent's mouth.

The replies show that Protestants and Catholics attribute much the same virtues to their own church, with one conspicuous exception (Table VIII.1). Protestants most like the 'freedom' of their church, a phrase that Catholics do not mention. In viewing the other man's church, neither group finds much good to say about doctrines or services, thus indicating substantial ideological opposition to ecumenical trends. Praise for the actions of Catholic clergymen and members primarily reflects a Protestant tribute to the regular attendance of Catholics at mass by contrast with Protestant church attendance. In all, there is a high degree of liking for one's own church; only five per cent found nothing to like about their own church. There is also a high degree of indifference toward the other church: 47 per cent said they couldn't think of anything they liked.

Table VIII.2   Characteristics disliked about churches

Dislikes	PROTESTANT CHURCHES			CATHOLIC CHURCH		
	Prot	Cath	Total	Prot	Cath	Total
	%	%	%	%	%	%
Doctrines, rituals	17	5	12	26	1	16
No freedom, authoritarian	(Not mentioned)			25	7	18
Actions of clergy, members	14	4	10	7	8	8
Intolerance; politics	6	9	7	5	2	4
General dislike	3	1	2	2	1	2
Nothing	57	61	59	30	79	50
Don't know	7	22	13	19	5	13
	D.I. = 23%			D.I. = 56%		

The pattern of dislikes shows greater Protestant antipathy toward the Catholic Church than Catholics show toward Protestant churches (Table VIII.2). The median Protestant could find something to say against the Catholic Church – especially against doctrines and the authority of priests. By contrast, five-sixths of Catholics said there was nothing they disliked about the Protestant churches.

The Catholic Church in Northern Ireland does not exist in isolation, politically or administratively. Every respondent was therefore asked what he thought of the position of the Roman Catholic

256

Church in the Republic (Table VIII.3). Significantly, more Protestants had views about the Catholic Church in the Republic than had views about it in Northern Ireland. Nearly all the Protestant answers amounted to variations on one theme: the power of the Catholic Church there. In other words, Protestants still see a Dublin-based regime as inevitably subject to strong clerical influences. (This remains true whether directives come from Rome or from indigenous clerics.) The majority of Ulster Catholics agree, although the value judgment implied is likely to be opposite to that of Protestants. Objective scholarly accounts of politics in the Republic confirm the secular power there of the Catholic Church.[24] There is no correlation between the views that Protestants have of the Catholic Church in the Republic and their basic political outlooks. This is further evidence that the outlooks of Northern Ireland people are predominantly formed within the Province, and not in response to external influences.

Table VIII.3 Characteristics of the Catholic Church in the Republic

	Protestant %	Catholic %	Total %
Too powerful	19	18	14
Powerful	39	44	41
Politically important	11	5	9
General approval	3	19	9
Same as here	1	10	4
Miscellaneous comments	2	3	3
Don't know	35	22	30 D.I. =31%

The equivalent Protestant symbol of institutionalized power is the Orange Order, a religious, fraternal and political body. The Loyalty survey estimates that the Order has a membership of 32 per cent of Protestant men in Northern Ireland, i.e., about 90,000 people. Positively, the Order favours strict Sabbatarianism, conservative interpretations of the Bible, and regularity in church attendance. Negatively, a member is pledged by his oath to 'avoid countenancing (by his presence or otherwise) any act or ceremony of Popish worship'. Throughout its history, the Order has seen itself as the primary institution opposing Catholicism and Catholic influence in Ulster.[25] The fraternal side of the Order is particularly important in the countryside, for Orange Halls are one of the few places besides

Two Bodies in Christ

257

pubs where people can meet. The Order's membership is dispropor-tionately rural; only 15 per cent live in Belfast.

Like other Masonic-type organizations, the Orange Order has rituals, regalia and elaborate titles. The most striking ceremony is an annual parade on the Twelfth of July, when Orangemen, wearing black bowler hats and orange collarettes, parade for hours through Belfast and other major centres, under banners commemorating major battles in the establishment of Protestant rule in Ulster three centuries ago. The spirit of religion and national feeling is neatly caught by a letter-writer to the *Belfast Telegraph*:

> Orangemen that day not only commemorate a very significant military and political victory, but a great deliverance from Roman slavery, in much the same way as the Jews each year commemorate their deliverance from bondage in Egypt.[26]

In an exclusively Protestant state, such a ceremony would be an occasion expressing communal solidarity, as Independence Day is in America or in any ex-colonial nation. In a regime with divided authority, however, the parades of Orangemen – especially when they march through Catholic quarters of towns – intensify discord, for Catholics regard the marches as a show of force by those who have conquered them. Given the character of the Order and of Northern Ireland politics, Orangemen are inevitably involved in politics. In the words of Walter Williams, secretary of the Grand Lodge, 'We have a strong constitutional basis, and if there is any attack on the Consti-tution, we have to get involved. In this sense it is impossible at times to stay out of politics'.[27]

The Orange Order has a clearly defined image. More people know what it stands for than know what the Northern Ireland Labour Party stands for. Two and only two characteristics are widely noted: the Order stands for the Protestant religion among 47 per cent, and for maintenance of a Protestant and Unionist regime among 26 per cent. Only one per cent see the Orange Order as a fraternal organiza-tion, standing for friendship and charity. Among Protestants, 56 per cent express approval of the influence of the Order upon Northern Ireland life, as against 14 per cent expressing clearcut disapproval. Catholics take the opposite view, with only 9 per cent approving and 51 per cent disapproving (D.I.=55%); there are also a substantial number of don't knows. One would expect that Protestants who approve most strongly of the Orange Order would also be most inclined to be Ultras. This hypothesis is confirmed, for 75 per cent of the Order's strongest supporters endorse the use of force if necessary. Reciprocally, among Catholics, those who disapprove most strongly of the Order are also most ready to endorse illegal demonstrations against the regime; 62 per cent take this position.

As the largest exclusively Protestant organization in Ulster, the Orange Order unites men of different denominations in defence of their common Protestant traditions. This commitment to religious exclusivism distinguishes it from the Stormont regime, which is not formally committed to the exclusion of Catholics from public office. Thus, as Prime Minister, Terence O'Neill could make a series of friendly gestures toward the Catholic community, visiting Catholic institutions, attending bi-confessional meetings and, most importantly, avoiding anti-Catholic rhetoric in his speeches. From a civil rights point of view, such actions did not make O'Neill a protagonist of their cause. They were sufficient to raise doubts in the minds of Orangemen about the future course of 'their' regime. New members are reported to have joined this defence league in increasing numbers. As expected, the Loyalty survey shows that 73 per cent of the members of the Order endorse using any measures to keep Ulster Protestant. Yet this also means that 27 per cent of Orangemen are not Ultras. In short, the Orange Order is no more a monolithic organization than is the Unionist Party. Any confrontation between the leaders of the Order and the Unionist Party would threaten to disrupt both organizations, because differences in political outlooks cut across institutional boundaries. In recognition of this problem, the Order has refused to condemn the regime's reforms, although from time to time it passes resolutions indicating disquiet. In turn, Unionist leaders, including the Prime Minister and the Attorney-General, have defended the continued links between the party and the Order.[28]

In view of the tendency to equate Orangeism and Ultraism, it is important to emphasize that membership in the Order is neither a necessary nor sufficient condition of endorsing the view that any measures are justified to keep the regime Protestant. In fact, three-quarters of Protestants who endorse the use of any measures are not members of the Order.[29] Belonging to an Orange lodge thus cannot be the principal cause of Ultra Protestant views. The Order is significant because it provides opportunities for people to express their political views and organize support for them. The political influence of individual Orangemen with Ultra views is enhanced by the fact that membership in the Order does not isolate them from the mainstream of Ulster political life. It is entirely consistent with it.

The Catholic community has no functional counterpart to the Orange Order. The nominal equivalent is the Ancient Order of Hibernians, the heirs of eighteenth-century Catholic defence organizations.[30] Its membership is confined to nationalist Catholics. The Hibernians stage parades in Catholic areas, principally on August 15, the date of the Assumption of the Blessed Virgin. Politically, its principles are nationalist, but they are considered outmoded by those who endorse campaigning for civil rights by appealing to non-sectarian libertarian principles. According to the Loyalty survey, the Hibernians' membership is small, 2·6 per cent of the Catholic population, i.e., 5,000 to 10,000 Catholic men. The real weakness of the Hibernians is indicated by the fact that 69 per cent of Catholics and 71 per cent of Protestants say that they don't know what the organization stands for. Those who do refer to its connection with anti-partition views and Catholic rights. The ineffectual nature of the organization is also evidenced by the fact that 48 per cent of Catholics and 54 per cent of Protestants offered no opinion about the Hibernians when asked whether or not they approved of its influence on Northern Ireland life.

Ulster churches have an institutional interest in propagating their distinctive doctrines because they provide an explicit and transcendental justification for the continued existence of each denomination. It is noteworthy that Protestants in Ulster have been as hesitant to merge denominations as they have been to endorse joint activities with Roman Catholics. Moreover, the influence that churches seek to exert is best achieved when individual communicants adopt as their own the values that clergymen seek to propagate. The direction of influence definitely flows from the institution to the individual, because the views adopted, whether Catholic or Protestant, are historically common to all of Western Europe. Because they do not originate in Northern Ireland – Ulstermen have been as uninventive in their theology as they are tenacious – the views can hardly be explained as an attempt to rationalize positions adopted on other grounds.

To measure the extent of doctrinal fundamentalism, each Ulster respondent was asked whether he agreed or disagreed with four propositions relating religious belief to public affairs. Two did so explicitly and a third, endorsing fatalism, has clear implications for compliance with authority. People were also asked whether they accepted Biblical miracles as literally true, since faith in such miracles might go with belief in political 'miracles', such as Irish independence. Since an American study has shown that Christians divided into doctrinal groups along denominational grounds, replies were analysed separately for three Protestant groups as well as for Catholics. In America, Episcopals have tended to hold liberal views, Presbyterians to be moderates, and Roman Catholics are consistently conservative.[31] In Northern Ireland, no such pattern was found (see Table VIII.4). There is very little difference between the two major

Table VIII.4 Endorsement of fundamentalist religious values

	All Prot	Presby.	C. of I.	Other Prot	Cath	Total
	(Per cent agreeing)					
The miracles in the Bible happened just as described	72	70	74	71	77	74
Preachers of false religious doctrines shouldn't be allowed in this country	63	63	62	62	60	62
Everything that happens must be accepted as God's will	56	55	57	55	68	61
The more active in politics a man is the harder to be a good Christian	41	38	42	44	38	40

Protestant communicants–the average is three per cent. Between all Protestants and Catholics the average difference is also low–three per cent. Doctrinal conservatism is very high in Northern Ireland by comparison with Britain. An Opinion Research Centre survey that asked identical questions about orthodox religious beliefs throughout the United Kingdom found that an average of 80 per cent of Northern Ireland respondents were definitely in agreement with five conservative theological doctrines, whereas only 49 per cent of British respondents thought the same.[32] Religious and political differences in Northern Ireland cannot be said to be generated by a handful of Paisleyite fundamentalists, for orthodox believers are in the majority.

Conservative doctrinal beliefs might lead people in either of two very different directions. They might indicate general ideological rigidity in thinking about problems, and hence lead to Ultraism among Protestants, and rebellion among Catholics. The content of fundamentalist religious beliefs might also justify a resort to political violence among Protestants or rebellion by Catholics. Yet the opposite could also be argued. Concern of believers with other-world matters might encourage a fatalistic willingness to comply with all political laws and to support any regime as ordained by God. In fact, statistical analysis shows that there is no substantial relationship between any of these four beliefs and support for the Constitution among Protestants or among Catholics. There is a small but regular tendency for Protestants who endorse fundamentalist religious beliefs to be readier to endorse the use of violence to keep Ulster Protestant.

As an additional test of the hypotheses, each person interviewed was ranked on an eight-point scale of religious fundamentalism, with those agreeing with all four statements in Table VIII.4 at the top, and those explicitly disagreeing at the bottom. A total of 19 per cent of Catholics and 16 per cent of Protestants endorsed all four fundamentalist doctrines, and an additional 34 per cent of Catholics and 32 per cent of Protestants endorsed three such doctrines. Only seven per cent rejected all four doctrines. There was virtually no difference between Protestants and Catholics (D.I.=5%). The only noteworthy relationship between doctrinal views and regime outlooks occurred among Protestants. In the most fundamentalist group, 62 per cent endorsed the use of violence against the regime. In the most liberal group, only 23 per cent took this position; together, the two extremes had only one-quarter of all Protestants, thus limiting the impact of the effect. The aggregate position is as in Gerhard Lenski's American study: '. . . *the irrelevance of doctrinal orthodoxy for most aspects of secular life*'.[33]

Proponents of ecumenical activities elsewhere in the Western world have emphasized the importance of interdenominational agreement among churches to concentrate Christian resources in opposition to secularism.[34] The similarity of values shown above suggests that Ulster believers may be readier to agree than is usually credited. Yet the strength of religion in Northern Ireland – even though there is agreement on many points – might also be a barrier to ecumenical reunion for, as Glock and Stark note, ecumenism makes most progress, in America at least, among 'the most secularized mainline denominations'.[35] Whatever else Northern Ireland is, it is not secularized. Moreover, centuries of religious history emphasize that people who agree on many things may none the less divide into separate denominations or even go to war about a relatively few points of doctrine.

As a straightforward measure of the perceived area of agreement between Protestant and Catholic churches, Ulster people were first asked in a non-directive manner what they thought of uniting the two churches into one. Among Catholics, 60 per cent said they thought it a good idea, 14 per cent disapproved on principle, and the remainder were uncertain. Protestants reacted oppositely: 40 per cent showed explicit disapproval, 27 per cent dismissed the idea as impractical, and only 19 per cent positively approved the idea. The replies are notable for the difference shown between Protestants and Catholics; the index is 42 per cent. By contrast, a similar question asked by the Gallup Poll in Britain in 1962 resulted in a difference of only ten per cent between Catholics and members of the Church of England, and 18 per cent between Catholics and Scottish Presbyterians.[36]

Ecumenicism can be dismissed as impossible in practice, or as undesirable in principle. When asked explicitly about both points, 69 per cent of Catholics said they thought it desirable to unite the churches, as against 27 per cent of Protestants (D.I.=45%). Among Protestants, 73 per cent said ecumenicism was impossible; Catholics were relatively optimistic with 43 per cent thinking such a change possible (D.I.=31%). Protestants who opposed ecumenicism in principle were also more likely to endorse violence to keep the regime Protestant: 63 per cent were in this category. Among Catholics approving of church unity in principle there was a slight tendency for more to reject the Constitution: 39 per cent were in this category. Similarly, 52 per cent were ready to endorse illegal demonstrations. Collectively, these replies indicate that the world ecumenical movement affords little hope for the amelioration of political discord in Ulster's part of Christendom.

Sociologically, there is much reason to expect that political outlooks will be more affected by differences in religious involvement than by differences in beliefs. Active participation in church affairs should encourage an individual to conform to the group norms of his co-religionists.[37] In Northern Ireland, involvement acquires a special significance as a worldly reinforcement of supernatural scrutiny; 86 per cent of Ulster people believe that God watches over what each person does and thinks, as against 49 per cent with this belief in

Britain.[38] One would therefore expect the most involved Protestants to be strongest in support for the Constitution, and readiest to violate basic political laws to keep Ulster Protestant. Similarly, the most involved Catholics should be strongest in refusing support to the regime. It is arguable whether they would also be more likely to take part in illegal demonstrations because of communal pressures or least likely to do so because of clerical admonitions against violence.

The simplest measure of religious involvement is church attendance. Church attendance in Northern Ireland is probably higher than anywhere else in the Western world–except the Republic of Ireland. Among Catholics, 33 per cent report that they go to church more than once a week, and another 62 per cent report weekly attendance at mass. By comparison, in Catholic countries such as France and Austria, only two-fifths to one-third of nominal Catholics are regular in attending mass. Similarly, among Protestants, seven per cent report attending church more than once a week, 39 per cent are weekly churchgoers and another 18 per cent attend at least once a month. By comparison, only 26 per cent of a British sample report that they go to church at least monthly, and 16 per cent are monthly church attenders in exclusively Protestant Sweden.[39] Only a third of the Protestants, that is, about one-fifth of the total Ulster population, are occasional churchgoers or never attend. Church attendance does not affect Catholic or Protestant attitudes toward compliance with basic political laws, and there is only a slight tendency for the most frequent Catholic churchgoers to be more likely to oppose the Constitution.

Another measure of religious involvement is subjective: how a person feels about his religion. There is good psychological reason to believe that people with an inward commitment to religion will be more strongly influenced by it than those for whom involvement is little more than conformity to the norm of church attendance. One way to measure this is to ask people whether they consider themselves a strong or an average Protestant or Catholic: 45 per cent of Protestants consider themselves strong adherents, and 38 per cent of Catholics. Catholics who strongly identify with their religion do not have distinctive views about the Constitution. Among strong Protestants, 67 per cent favour violent measures, if need be. Among strong Catholics, no such relation holds; 51 per cent of strong Catholics favour illegal demonstrations, but so do 46 per cent of those who consider themselves average Catholics.

264

Two Bodies in Christ

The certainty of a man's religious faith can encourage him to set
the laws of a regime aside, as he can confidently justify his action by
reference to a supernatural authority. This might particularly be the
case for Protestants, who formally acknowledge no external judge
beyond their own conscience but God. Sureness of religious belief is
high in Northern Ireland, both among Protestants and Catholics;
only 11 per cent confess themselves uncertain of their faith, and 71
per cent of Catholics and 54 per cent of Protestants are 'very sure' of
their faith. Among Protestants very sure of their faith, there is a
tendency to refuse compliance: 60 per cent endorse using violence to
maintain the political power of their faith. Among Catholics, only
one slight relationship is found; 51 per cent of 'very sure' Catholics
endorse illegal demonstrations, as against 40 per cent who are 'fairly
sure' of their faith.

The absence of strong correlations between Catholic involvement
and political outlooks can be explained on two grounds. The first is
that Ulster Catholics are a relatively homogeneous group; because of
this, there is insufficient variance to affect differences in political outlooks. The pervasiveness of anti-regime attitudes means that a higher
degree of involvement in religion would not alter a Catholic's outlook much, because he would not move into a different political
environment. Secondly, the religious norm for compliance is uncertain. The Catholic Church in Ireland could not repudiate all disobedience to civil authority without repudiating its own history,
when the Catholic religion was kept alive in Ireland by priests who
were technically outlaws. That there is some kind of a correlation of
religious involvement and Ultra views among Protestants arises from
the fact that church and state are seen as two aspects of one society,
incapable of separation. The fact that a substantial proportion of less
involved Protestants also show willing to fight is a reminder that
Protestants inclined toward secular beliefs do not, *ipso facto*, become
more favourable toward the militantly anti-secular Catholic faith.

Whatever the degree of an individual's involvement with religion,
it will not cause political problems unless two conditions are met:
there is a direct conflict between religious and political norms, and
primacy is given to religious values. The *a priori* grounds for discord
between clerics and politicians are fewer than might be expected. A
paradigm developed by a sociologist of law, Jack Gibbs, can illustrate this. Gibbs notes that every normative regulation may take one
of four forms: it may prescribe action, stipulate conditions under

265

Two Bodies in Christ

which action is necessary, make action entirely optional or proscribe
it. Logically, there are 16 possible relationships between two sources
of authority, such as a regime and a church. Only two of the 16 cells
imply necessary conflict, with one institution prescribing action and
the other proscribing it or vice versa. There are also two instances in
which both sets of norms reinforce each other, prescriptively or pro-
scriptively. In the majority of cases there is no basis for conflict. For
instance, the orthodox Jewish proscription of pork is not in conflict
with the regime's laws, for in every Western regime it is optional
whether a subject eats pork. This is consistent with the definitional
stipulation that institutions outside the political system are not
primarily political in their goals.

The primacy of politics is not to be taken for granted in Northern
Ireland. Ulstermen pay lipservice to the ideal of separating politics
from religion; for example, in the Loyalty survey, only 26 per cent
said that they thought everyone of their religion should vote for the
same political party (D.I.=4%). Yet the observed voting patterns of
Protestants and Catholics show that the two major parties are nearly
100 per cent sectarian in their support. The organization of churches
along territorial lines, especially noticeable in the parish system of
the Catholics, gives fulltime clergymen a potential for influence far
superior to that of a political party. Census figures show about 3,500
clergy and other religious workers in Northern Ireland, an establishment as large as that of the Royal Ulster Constabulary, which is also
concerned with maintaining regular contact with the population at
large. The status of clergymen further enhances their potential for
influence. A survey by Opinion Research Centre found that 70 per
cent of Northern Ireland people said they respected clergymen a
great deal, compared to 39 per cent giving the same answer in Great
Britain. By comparison, only 14 per cent in Ulster said they respected
MPs a great deal. Respect does not inhibit personal contacts; 66 per
cent of Ulster people say they find it easy to talk to members of the
clergy and 61 per cent say that they look forward to meeting them.
Only eight per cent say that they look forward to meeting MPs and
nine per cent find MPs easy to talk to.[40]

Because churches have a potential political influence, it does not
follow that this is consciously or regularly used for political ends. A
total of 67 per cent say that a clergyman *ought* to speak out on
public matters that he thinks important; there is very little difference
between Protestants and Catholics on this point (D.I.=3%). In

266

addition, 48 per cent say that their clergyman speaks at least occasionally about public matters (D.I.=3%). For example, the official leaders of all Northern Ireland churches speak out against political violence. It does not follow that their flocks will necessarily follow them. Among Protestants there is no tendency for those subjected to politics from the pulpit to be any more likely to reject violence. Among Catholics, the same is true about demonstrations. Moreover, Catholics who expect their priest to state political views are no more likely to support or reject the Constitution than those not exposed.

Two explanations might be offered for the absence of direct clerical influence upon regime outlooks. The first is that differences in political outlooks among clergymen tend to cancel each other out. This assumes that the political cues that are given from the pulpit vary from place to place, especially in Protestant churches where ministers are, if anything, subject to congregational not hierarchical influence. To argue this is to assume that clergymen do not have a common political outlook, and thus by implication to confirm the lack of the clergy's independent influence. An alternative explanation is that clergymen maintain a distance from political affairs. To test the assertion that clergy abstain from political involvement, an intensive pilot study was undertaken by P. A. Fahy in rural Catholic parishes in County Armagh.[41] The study, based on interviews with parochial clergymen, explored how priests managed the potential role conflict between their national identity; their sacramental role in an institution with an extra-terrestrial orientation; and their role as a community leader, seeking to assist parishioners with worldly needs and aims. It found that the priests avoided the potential conflict by limiting the scope of their involvement in community affairs. All the priests identified themselves as Irish, and none indicated doubts about the importance of his sacramental role. Politically, priests defined local problems as a shortage of housing and jobs. Bigotry and sectarianism were not mentioned as a *local* problem. In parishes with Catholic controlled local councils–a small minority in Northern Ireland as a whole–priests found housing no problem; in both Nationalist and Unionist council jurisdictions, employment was a continuing problem. Priests tended to define their social role in individualistic terms, seeking to alleviate the consequences of an individual's deprivation. Only one priest was exceptionally prepared to take a political initiative; he sponsored a housing association independently of Stormont, but did not make a frontal challenge to its

267

authority. The de-politicized character of the Catholic clergy is also shown by their absence from civil rights demonstrations. While their presence might have inflamed Protestants, it is none the less noteworthy that in civil rights demonstrations in America, both Protestant clergymen and Catholic priests have played a prominent role in organizing non-compliance to basic laws of local authorities and in resistance to the Viet Nam war.

Although belonging to a community need not make all persons within it identical, it does involve withdrawal from other groups within the larger society. One would expect exclusiveness or clannishness, to use a term specially appropriate in a land with many Scottish settlers, to be particularly strong in Northern Ireland. Ulster people who feel most strongly the need to stick together with their co-religionists would be most likely to hold Ultra views if Protestants, or disaffected if Catholics.

To measure the extent of clannishness, respondents were first asked whether or not they thought people with the same religion should stick together and do a lot to help each other. Protestants and Catholics both replied similarly (D.I. = 6%), with 58 per cent emphasizing sticking together. There was no correlation between this feeling and Catholic willingness to disobey laws. But among Protestants, two-thirds of those who believed in sticking together also believed in using any measures necessary against the regime. This implies that the remaining third (about one-fifth of the total Protestant community) would be under social psychological pressures to follow an Ultra course in a time of political crisis, when sticking together is important.

In addition to positive injunctions to stick together, groups can maintain their distinctiveness by imposing very strong social sanctions against leaving the group to join the other side. To measure constraints against 'crossing over', each respondent was asked what difference, if any, he thought it would make to his friends and family if he changed his religion or his politics (Table VIII.5). The replies show that four-fifths of Ulster people think it would make a substantial difference to friends and family if they changed their religion. There is no clear relationship between these perceptions and political outlooks. Those who challenge the regime do not do so because they are particularly sensitive to pressures from family and friends; something inside them makes them feel they ought to reject the symbols and laws of the established regime.

By comparison with the sanctions against changing religion, the social sanctions against crossing over parties are significantly weaker (Table VIII.5). None the less, the median Protestant and Catholic thinks it would make a difference to at least some of his friends and family if he 'turned' politically, and only 15 per cent assert that it would make no difference. These social psychological inhibitions against a floating vote reinforce the organizational and ideological tendencies of the major parties to look to their own kind, without hope of support from the other community. In such circumstances, speeches and actions increasing support from partisan followers might simultaneously increase the distance from other parties. To see whether Ulster people themselves believed in 'inner-directed' or 'other-directed' politics—that is politics that ignore or take notice of the opposite religion—Protestants were asked how much importance

Table VIII.5 Social sanctions against changing religion or politics

	CHANGE RELIGION			CHANGE POLITICS		
	Prot	Cath	Total	Prot	Cath	Total
	%	%	%	%	%	%
Big difference	47	43	45	35	26	31
Difference to some	35	38	36	28	25	27
Not much difference	12	10	11	16	19	17
No difference	5	7	6	11	21	15
Don't know	2	2	1	11	9	10
	D.I. = 5%			D.I. = 13%		

they gave to Roman Catholic opinion of government policies, and Catholics were asked about the importance of Protestant reactions to Nationalist activities. The replies show a considerable degree of other-directedness; 55 per cent of the total population think it at least fairly important to pay attention to the other community when adopting political policies. It is specially noteworthy that Protestants are more likely than Catholics to show some sensitivity to the view of the other side (D.I.=19%).

A composite measure of clannishness can be constructed from replies to four questions concerning communal differences and cohesion: questions about the strength of religious identity, the sanctions against changing religion, the need for co-religionists to stick together, and the extent of difference between Protestants and Catholics.[42] The range of possible scores on the resulting scale is from 12, signifying a clannish attitude on all four items, to four, indicating an explicit rejection of clannish views on all items. The median Protestant and the median Catholic both fall exactly in the middle of the scale. There is little tendency for levels of support to be affected by degrees of clannishness. There is, however, a distinct association between Protestant clannishness and the endorsement of an Ultra position. Among the most clannish Protestants, 83 per cent are prepared to use any measures necessary to keep political power in their own hands; among the least clannish, the proportion is 30 per cent. No such strong relationship exists among Catholics, for 43 per cent of the least clannish endorse illegal demonstrations, as do half the most clannish. It is noteworthy that psychological attachment to communal cohesion is more influential than such objective measures of involvement as church attendance.

In view of the distribution of Ulster people along a continuum ranging from extreme clannishness to extreme openness, it is important to consider how people of opposite religions think they should treat politics when they meet. To assess this, each person was asked whether in dealing with people of the opposite religion, a person should stand up strongly for his own religion, ignore these differences, or, in view of past troubles make a special effort to be friendly. Protestants and Catholics answered nearly the same (D.I.=6%): 31 per cent thought that they should stand up strongly for their own religion in relations with persons from the opposite community and 42 per cent thought a special effort of friendship should be made. The others said differences should be ignored. The validity of these answers is further confirmed by replies to a question about changes, if any, desired in relations between Protestant and Catholics in Northern Ireland. The desire for friendlier relations *between individuals* of different religions is strong: 76 per cent of all persons expressed this wish. In short, personal relationships do not reflect institutionalized discord.

One way to try to be friendly is to avoid controversial subjects such as politics. This practice, if followed widely, would encourage a false belief that Protestants and Catholics thought much alike about politics when this is not the case. In fact, Protestants and Catholics agree that talk should flow freely, including political controversy at mixed social affairs; 58 per cent hold this view, as against 33 per cent who think that controversial topics should be avoided. Those who are ready to talk about politics to people from the other side are a cross-section of Protestants and Catholics. This means that Protestants will be exposed to Catholics who reject the Constitution, and Catholics to Protestants with unmistakably Ultra views. The commitment of individuals for or against the regime is therefore made in the face of knowledge of the commitments of their opponents.

A full exchange of views is not *ipso facto* a fair or a satisfying exchange. Contacts between groups can be a source of friction or dispel the illusion of friendship, instead of creating co-operation. Religious discrimination is an example of this, for it results from one group meeting and rejecting members of the other on grounds that the latter regard as unfair. Discrimination against Catholics has been the most important issue of the civil rights movement. (The attempt to protest against economic disadvantages suffered by Protestants as well as Catholics has so far failed, for Protestants have not joined the nominally non-sectarian civil rights movement.) Charges of discrimination often involve allegations of discrimination by public authorities in allocations of jobs, council housing, local government electoral districting, etc., etc. When Protestants reply by charging that Catholics also discriminate against them, this only intensifies differences between the two communities.

Until the publication of the Cameron Report in September, 1969, the leaders of the regime had always been coy about discussing discrimination, or openly denied such allegations. The Commission's Report accepted that discrimination against Catholics had existed since the foundation of the regime, and presented evidence in support of its charges. The Report was not designed to reflect Ulster opinion. Therefore, it does not follow that the judgment of this semi-judicial body is consistent with that of Ulster Protestants or Catholics. In a social psychological sense, events are real if people think they are real; that is, discrimination is a political problem only if people think it exists.

To assess the perceived degree of discrimination against Catholics, each person was asked: People sometimes say that in parts of Northern Ireland Catholics are treated unfairly. Do you think this is true or not?[43] Those who said that they thought discrimination exists were then asked whether or not this belief was based on personal knowledge, or upon remarks made in conversations by others (Table VIII.6). The degree of polarization is extreme; nearly three-quarters of Protestants asserted that there is no discrimination, and three-quarters of Catholics that there is. The difference is particularly striking because discrimination necessarily involves both Protestants

Two Bodies in Christ

and Catholics. The replies show that there is a fundamental antagonism about the character of relations between the two communities. Moreover, according to the 1967 Belfast pilot survey, it is an issue that four-fifths of Catholics regarded as 'very important', a year before the civil rights demonstrations.

Table VIII.6   Perception of discrimination against Catholics

	Protestant %	Catholic %	Total %	
Discrimination exists				
Personal knowledge	4 ⎫ 19	36 ⎫ 74	17 ⎫ 41	
Indirect	15 ⎰	38 ⎰	24 ⎰	
No discrimination here	74	13	48	
Don't know	8	14	10	D.I. = 61%

The significance of discrimination as an issue challenging the regime was demonstrated in the streets of Northern Ireland by the civil rights movement in 1968–69. The campaign intensified political discord because of the high level of agreement within each community on this issue, and the high level of disagreement between them. The civil rights campaigners neither created discord nor did they increase the gulf between Protestants and Catholics on this issue. A survey in February, 1969 by Opinion Research Centre asked the same question about discrimination. It found no change in opinions after months of civil rights demonstrations. In the ORC survey, 76 per cent of Catholics said that discrimination existed, and 77 per cent of Protestants said it did not.

The depth and breadth of the dispute about discrimination is further evidenced by the fact that 77 per cent of Catholics who see discrimination as a problem think that something can and should be done to change things. Only eight per cent were defeatist before the civil rights campaign began. Two kinds of policies were recommended, government action and changes in the attitudes of individuals. The pattern of replies indicated that most Catholics expect the former to produce the latter; they were not willing to wait for popular Protestant opinion to alter as a prelude to anti-discrimination measures. Among Protestants, 58 per cent who thought there is no discrimination regarded talk about it as the work of trouble-makers in the Catholic community; another quarter simply rejected complaints as unfounded. Only 18 per cent reckoned that Catholics' minority status or previous experience had given them grounds to complain.

Protestant certainty of their rightness and righteousness is further evidenced by the fact that among those denying discrimination, 65 per cent thought that the complaints should be investigated rather than be ignored. They were fully confident that investigation would vindicate their position. In fact, the regime's own Commission refuted it.

Politically, the basic disagreement between Protestants and Catholics about discrimination in Northern Ireland suggests that the dispute may be less about the 'facts' of the situation than it is about the definition of what constitutes fair treatment. Protestant defenders of the regime believe that citizenship involves obligations as well as privileges. Because Catholics have not accepted the obligation of supporting the regime, then they have not been thought to deserve the privileges that the regime can confer: equality in voting, public jobs, housing and other benefits. The greater the value placed upon the regime by Protestants, the greater the sanctions justified in inflicting deprivations upon opponents of the regime. The outlook was aptly summed up by Viscount Brookeborough, a former Prime Minister, in a television interview shortly before the 1969 Stormont general election:

> Taking it by and large, the Protestant is a loyalist–that is to say he believes in the U.K. On the other hand, the Roman Catholic–and please take it that I am not criticising their religion whatsoever, it is their concern–they won't do anything about the Union Jack, they won't take their hats off, they won't stand up when 'God Save the Queen' is played, and naturally, with very severe frictions as a result.[44]

Asked about Catholic grievances, Lord Brookeborough said complaints were 'stirred up by the Irish Republican Army, admittedly by them, and by Communists'. In such circumstances, he said, it would be politically difficult to deal with charges of discrimination 'because of the antipathy of the Roman Catholics and the fact that they were backing the IRA. They were out to defeat Northern Ireland and shoot our people.'[45]

From a Protestant viewpoint, discrimination is not the fault of Protestants but of Catholics. The latter are credited with intelligence and freewill sufficient to be responsible for their acts. If they choose to align themselves with Nationalist and Republican groups opposed to the Constitution and in some cases to defy the law, then they should be prepared to accept the consequences of their actions.

Two Bodies in Christ

Similarly if individuals choose to follow the teachings of the Catholic Church and have large families that are difficult to support on their income, then this is their fault for believing false doctrines. It is not regarded as a problem that is the responsibility of the state. One Catholic reaction is to argue that the regime has its priorities and values wrong. Its values are wrong because it seeks to maintain an 'unnatural' connection with Britain. The regime's priorities are wrong, because it should first remove the disabilities of Catholics, and then Catholics *might* give allegiance to it. The conditional verb is important because Republicans favouring a United Ireland regard the removal of discrimination as a necessary but not sufficient precondition for allegiance. Their goal, in Wolfe Tone's words, is simply 'to break the connection with England'. Given conflict about facts, the burden of blame, and the next appropriate step, there is no reason to expect either side to accede to the other.

Analytically, one of the most surprising findings is the very limited relationship between *individual* regime outlooks and *individual* religious influences. Within each community, exposure to religious influences does not greatly differentiate one Protestant from another, or one Catholic from another. People who are more regular in church attendance, or stronger in their faith, or more fundamentalist in their faith are not much more likely to be Ultras, disaffected, or fully allegiant citizens. In Northern Ireland religion is less a variable that a constant. At the level of the *society as a whole*, there are major variations in political outlooks by religion. Protestantism and Catholicism have created and maintained a division into two communities. Yet, at a very high level of abstraction, agreement can be found; for example, 74 per cent of the people of Northern Ireland think it 'very important' that theirs should be a Christian country.[46] What they disagree about is whether it should be a Protestant Christian or a Catholic Christian country.

IX · The Political Salience of Economic Differences

Once the Irish Church is dead, the Protestant Irish tenants in the province of Ulster will unite with the Catholic tenants in the three other provinces of Ireland and join their movement.

KARL MARX

Ireland still remained the Holy Isle whose aspirations must on no account be mixed up with the profane class struggles of the rest of the sinful world.

FRIEDRICH ENGELS

Nineteenth-century visitors to Ireland invariably commented at length upon the economic conditions of the country. They did so because everywhere poverty was great. During the Hungry Forties, famine was an awesome scourge in most parts of the island. Even in the best of times, the contrast between the wealth of largely Protestant landowners and the poverty of mostly Catholic tenants was sufficiently marked to stir condemnation from men inured to the existence of 'two nations' within Industrial England.[1] Any visitor who concentrated his stay in Belfast, rather than in the rack-rented and congested Western counties, might have gained a different impression. In Belfast, industrialism had arrived beyond doubt. The establishment of industry in a port city without landward access to coal or iron ore was a special tribute to the enterprise and industry of its citizens.[2] Some saw in the emergence of an industrial working class the potential for a new form of politics in Ireland, setting worker against capitalist, rather than Protestant against Catholic. Others feared that industrialization in the predominantly Protestant North would only intensify differences along religious lines within the island. As the quotations from Marx and Engels illustrate, even then commentators differed about the extent to which the root of the Irish problem was economic. Successive Conservative governments, as well as Marx, believed that the 'fundamental' problem was economic. Agitation about the land question – the chief economic issue in an agricultural society – was ended by the Balfour government's act of

The Political Salience of Economic Differences

1903, which turned Ireland from a land of tenants into a land of peasant proprietors. It did not resolve constitutional questions.[3]

The creation of the Stormont regime enhanced the significance of comparison between local (i.e., Ulster) standards and living standards elsewhere. As a part of the United Kingdom, Northern Ireland has usually had the dubious distinction of appearing last among the regions in tables concerning economic prosperity. For example, in 1968 the unemployment rate in Northern Ireland was 7·2 per cent, almost three times the United Kingdom average, and more than half again as much as that in the worst-affected British region, Northern England.[4] Viewed in an Irish context, however, Northern Ireland people have been relatively prosperous, by virtue of their status as subjects in a relatively generous Welfare State.[5] Because substantial powers useful in promoting economic development are in the hands of Stormont, Northern Ireland has been well suited, by comparison with Scotland, Wales or an English region, to undertake economic planning and development programmes, including the provision of generous financial subsidies to attract new industry. The efforts of Stormont to find new industries to replace declining industries succeeded in the 1960s, for unemployment rates in Northern Ireland did not rise in proportion to those in England, when economic difficulties in the British isles intensified in the late 1960s. Even more striking is the fact that from 1960 to 1968 the index of manufacturing production rose 46 per cent in Northern Ireland as against 24 per cent in the United Kingdom generally. In the 1950s and 1960s, the growth rate *per capita* was also higher in Ulster than in the United Kingdom as a whole.[6]

Implicit or explicit in the minds of many concerned with economic planning is the hope or belief that economic development in Northern Ireland will lessen or end the sectarian differences that divide people about the regime. Terence O'Neill was the most prominent exponent of the hypothesis that good living standards would lead Catholics to give allegiance to the regime. O'Neill also sought to make Protestant Ultras comply with basic laws by threatening them with the loss of British economic benefits, if they refused to accept measures endorsed by Stormont and London. In a dramatic television appeal for support two months after the civil rights campaign had begun, the Prime Minister told his audience:

> We cannot be a part of the United Kingdom merely when it suits us. And those who talk so glibly about acts of impoverished

276

defiance do not know or care what is at stake. Your job, if you are a worker at Short's or Harland & Wolff; your subsidies if you are a farmer; your pension, if you are retired–all these aspects of our life, and many others, depend on support from Britain. Is a freedom to pursue the un-Christian path of communal strife and sectarian bitterness really more important to you than all the benefits of the British welfare state?[7]

The leaders of the People's Democracy group agreed with Terence O'Neill about the importance of external investment in Ulster. But the conclusion they have drawn is very different. In the words of Michael Farrell:

The Six Counties are economically unviable. The struggle for socialism would mean snapping the link with Britain, over-throwing the rotten capitalist system, discarding the Border and rooting out British and U.S. economic imperialism in both parts of Ireland. It would mean, in fact, the struggle for Connolly's Socialist Republic.[8]

Yet Farrell's own analysis of the *political* situation in 1969 emphasized sectarian rather than economic differences. In the middle of one of the Derry disorders he told an English interviewer: 'We have failed to get across at all to the Protestant working class. So there is now a more radicalized Catholic working class, while the Protestant proletariat is still as remote and inert as ever.'[9]

The presence of economic as well as constitutional issues has given politicians the option of responding in more than one way to the problems arising since the civil rights demonstrations of 1968 and the disorder of 1969. The Northern Ireland Prime Minister, Major James Chichester-Clark, endorsed the view that economic problems are basic and political reforms only superstructure.

Any package of political reform is merely scratching the surface. Deprivation can never justify violence, but it can explain it; and it is a plain fact that the seeds of riot and disorder, even if sown originally by politics or religion, have grown most alarmingly in the slums of our cities.[10]

The nineteenth-century Conservative view that the long-term solution of Northern Ireland's problem is an economic solution has also been endorsed by British Cabinet ministers. The commitment of thousands of British troops in Ulster has, however, made the long-term problems less significant than short-term problems of security.[11] Moreover, the increasing difficulties of the British economy have reduced the ability of the United Kingdom to provide greater subsidies to the Northern Ireland government for economic development.[12]

Divisions among civil rights groups have resulted from economic as well as political issues. Initially, the Northern Ireland Civil Rights Association emphasized *only* political rights, such as freedom of assembly and association. After the demonstrations began, demands for houses and jobs also became prominent. These can be construed as civil rights issues, in so far as poor housing and unemployment are seen as a consequence of discrimination against Catholics. But they can also be seen as a first step in the creation of a Socialist regime in the six counties, in the 26 counties, in all 32 counties of Ireland or in the entire British isles. Because civil rights demonstrators differ on economic issues, varying from conservatives to revolutionary Socialists, economic issues have fragmented the original civil rights alliance. Bernadette Devlin illustrates Socialism in an extreme form. After coming out of jail for participating in the Bogside rising, she spoke out against civil rights demonstrations, saying, 'The riots are terrible because they simply prop up the system. They make the majority of people more conservative.' She added that she no longer thought of herself as an Irish MP but as a Socialist MP. 'My commitment will be to the trade unions from the shop stewards down.'[13]

The political salience of economic differences is important to the Stormont regime, as well as having consequences for social science theories of the economic basis of political discord. In order to test this, one must first of all carefully specify and measure the many forms economic differentiation can take: type of work, income, unionization or psychological identification with a class. These several indicators of economic difference are likely to be related to each other, but there is no assurance of a perfect correlation. It is also important to note to what extent religious differences may be a misnomer for economic differences. This would tend to be true in so far as Protestants and Catholics differed greatly in their economic conditions. In a pure caste society, for example, all Protestants would have higher incomes than all Catholics. In so far as religious differences do not correlate with economic differences, then the economic profiles of the two religious communities will tend to be identical. The difference index is an appropriate measure of this phenomenon, for the higher it is, the greater the contrast in economic conditions between the two religions, and vice versa. In so far as differences are low, this would reduce the plausibility of the proposition that discord is a function of economic exploitation.

The general hypothesis tested in this chapter is that Northern Ireland people with economic advantages are most likely to be fully allegiant subjects. Disadvantaged Protestants, reacting against their conditions, would be expected to have an Ultra outlook to defend the advantage of their dominant religious group. Disadvantaged Catholics suffering both economic and non-economic deprivations from the existing regime would be most likely to reject the Constitution and approve illegal demonstrations. Reciprocally, middle-class Catholics, because of their economic advantages, might be expected to have a greater stake in the system than their working-class coreligionists, and thus be more likely to give allegiance to the regime.

Before testing hypotheses drawn from theories of modern industrial societies, it is important to determine to what extent Northern Ireland today is an industrial society, with all that is implied in terms of modern outlooks.[14] One could hypothesize that politics based on religion is only a stage in a land's development, to be replaced by class politics at some indefinite future date when Northern Ireland became properly industrialized. If characteristics of modern, industrial society are already widely diffused yet politically unimportant, then there is little basis for hoping that economic change will resolve existing political discord.

When the Ulster economy is compared to that of Britain, the relative significance of agriculture and of rural population lends plausibility to analysis in terms of stages of development. Yet, when Northern Ireland is compared to the Republic of Ireland, it appears relatively industrialized. The simplest indicator of industrialization is the proportion of the population employed in agriculture. The Northern Ireland Ministry of Agriculture reported a total of 70,100 adults working in agriculture in 1968, 12 per cent of the workforce. In response to market and government pressures to consolidate small land-holdings and employ more capital and less labour to produce food more efficiently,[15] the number working on farms has been declining steadily, falling by 30 per cent from 1960 to 1968. The level of agricultural employment in Northern Ireland is virtually the same as that in Sweden and West Germany, both of which would certainly be described as modern industrial societies.[16] Among farmers, 96 per cent own their own land. The Loyalty survey found that 51 per cent of farmers are Protestants and 49 per cent Catholics. The relative over-representation of Catholics among farmers does not mean that Catholics primarily work on the land: only 15 per cent are so employed, and 11 per cent of Protestants. Politically, farmers might be expected to be relatively traditional in their outlook. In the Northern Ireland context, they would therefore be disproportionately Ultra if Protestant, or disaffected if Catholic. Protestant farmers are more inclined to favour the use of force, if necessary to maintain 'their' regime: 63 per cent endorse this view. Among Catholic farmers, however, traditional nationalism is relatively weak; 41 per cent positively support the Stormont Constitution, as against 24 per cent who disapprove of it; 56 per cent disapprove of illegal demonstrations.

Table IX.1   Religion and class

	Protestant	Catholic	Total
	%	%	%
Business and professional	16	9	14
Lower middle class	29	24	27
Working class	48	58	52
Residual class	6	9	7

D.I. $= 13\%$

The decline of agriculture's significance in Northern Ireland makes it practicable to analyse class differences by placing farmers and those in industry in common occupational categories. (Such aggregation is neither attempted nor readily practicable in the Republic of Ireland.[17]) The single criterion most often used in assigning people to a class is occupation. The scheme for classifying people employed here is derived from that established by the British Registrar General's office. Respondents were classified into four groups according to the work of the head of the household—the business and professional middle class; the lower middle class; manual workers, and a residual class of miscellaneous persons such as elderly spinsters on a pension. The class profile of Northern Ireland shows a relatively small working class, with 52 per cent of the population in this category; the relatively large middle class includes four-fifths of all farmers (Table IX.1). The difference index of 13 per cent shows that there is a limited tendency for Protestants to have a higher occupational class than Catholics; the median Protestant, like the median Catholic, is a manual worker.

In so far as class differences are more important than religious differences, then Ulster people of the same class should have more similar regime outlooks than people of different classes but the same religion. The data from the Loyalty survey clearly reject this hypothesis. The difference between middle-class and working-class Protestants in support for the Constitution is four per cent, and three per cent in endorsement of an Ultra position. Similarly, among Catholics, there is only a two per cent difference across classes in support for the Constitution, and a five per cent difference in readiness to demonstrate against the regime. The differences between religions are much larger. Within the middle class, Protestants and Catholics differ by 36 percentage points in their readiness to support the Constitution, and manual workers differ by 30 percentage points. In refusal to comply with basic political laws, about half of each class group is ready to endorse extra-constitutional actions against others who share class but not regime outlooks. It is particularly noteworthy that there is no consistent tendency for middle-class Ulster people to be readiest to endorse the Constitution and refrain from extra-constitutional politics, notwithstanding their relative advantage in terms of status.

Trade unions are secular, industrial institutions. Union membership is something more than a label used by a social scientist with a penchant for classification. It represents affiliation to an organization that emphasizes economic calculations and solidarity among workers without regard to religion. A simple model of economic and political change in Northern Ireland might assume that as workers move into industry, they would downgrade religious attachments and instead become attached to a union. This, in turn, would make them class conscious and secular in political outlooks, since as Barritt and Carter note, the unions in Northern Ireland 'contain all shades of opinion–Communist and Catholic, Nationalist and Unionist–and do not fit into the neat divisions usually drawn across Ulster life'.[18] The trade union branches to which most Ulstermen belong are affiliated to unions with headquarters in Britain; a few have chief offices in Ulster or the Republic. Some British unions in Ulster also have branches in the Republic, a relic of the old United Kingdom. About five-sixths of Northern Ireland trade unionists are in organizations that also affiliate to the 32-county Irish Congress of Trade Unions, the heir of the Irish Trade Union Congress founded in 1894. The willingness of unions to co-operate across the Border for long made the Unionist regime suspect them on constitutional as well as economic grounds. Stormont did not recognize the Northern

The Political Salience of Economic Differences

Ireland Committee of the Irish Congress of Trade Unions until 1964, and at times has failed to enact in Northern Ireland British laws intended to safeguard or favour unions.[19]

A series of questions established the *de facto* secular character of trade unions in Northern Ireland: 82 per cent of union members said their union mixed the two communities, six per cent said members were mostly Protestants, four per cent mostly Catholic, and eight per cent said they didn't know the religious composition of the union's membership.[20] The secular character of unions is further evidenced by the fact that the difference index for membership is four per cent; 54 per cent of Ulster people have someone in their household a past or present trade union member. By United Kingdom standards or by those of other Western countries, Northern Ireland is definitely a land where unions have high membership.[21] In attitudes toward the Constitution, Protestant trade unionists are no more likely to favour the Constitution than are non-members of a trade union; among Catholics, 42 per cent disapprove of the Constitution, as against 26 per cent endorsing it. There is also no relationship between union membership and refusal to comply with basic political laws. The absence of a strong relationship between union membership and political outlooks is surprising and significant. It is surprising because of the extent to which union membership is strongly associated with political attitudes elsewhere. It is significant because the failure of unions to encourage a more secular approach to politics is not a function of weak union organization, but in spite of the well-established position of unions in Northern Ireland.

A person whose job brings him into contact with people outside Northern Ireland is also likely to be subject to secular, economic influences, whether or not he belongs to a trade union. For example, a bus driver in the countryside is much more subject to local cultural norms than is an airline pilot or an office worker in a modern industrial factory operated by an international company to international (and secular) standards. A total of 34 per cent of Northern Ireland people said that their work or that of the head of the house at least occasionally brought them into contact with people from outside Ulster (D.I. = 3%). Most of these contacts are with people from Britain. Exposure to cosmopolitan influences at work exerts no significant influence upon political outlooks. The proportion of Ultras is reduced by only seven per cent from the average for all Protestants. Catholics in contact with outsiders are more likely to

282

reject the Constitution and to endorse illegal demonstrations, but the size of the influence is very limited.

In so far as the Northern Ireland Labour Party is considered an instrument for encouraging secular class politics in Ulster, then one would expect its supporters to be most likely to give full allegiance to the regime, regarding questions of nationalism as irrelevant to the economic problems of Ulster. This hypothesis is consistent with the stated policy position of the Northern Ireland Labour Party. The survey findings show that the Northern Ireland Labour Party is truly a working-class party, and not a place of refuge for middle-class people seeking an alternative to parties divided along sectarian lines. More than three-quarters of its support comes from manual workers, a figure similar to that for the British Labour Party. Nearly two-thirds of its support has come from Catholics. This does not mean that the Labour Party is *the* party of Catholics in Northern Ireland; nearly twice as many Catholics prefer Green parties to Labour (cf. Table VII.7). Moreover, the Protestant section of the party has supplied a disproportionate number of parliamentary candidates and leaders. Unlike Labour parties elsewhere, in which members are agreed on religious or anti-clerical views,[22] the Northern Ireland Labour Party is *divided* by religious issues. Among Catholics favouring the party, the proportion ready to endorse the Constitution is 37 per cent, little different from the overall Catholic average. Protestant adherents to Labour are relatively less likely to endorse violence to retain Protestant rule: only 35 per cent take this position. Among Catholics, the proportion of Labour Party supporters prepared to endorse illegal demonstrations is 43 per cent. At the level of the individual, Labour Party sympathies tend to increase compliance with basic political laws but not support for the regime. In aggregate, there are major differences within the party; of its voters 43 per cent approve the Constitution, and 31 per cent explicitly disapprove it. Similarly, 60 per cent are willing to comply with basic political laws and 40 per cent are not.

The extent to which Labour Party supporters actively reject sectarianism can also be assessed by noting whether they would vote for sectarian parties in the absence of a Labour candidate. This question is particularly important inasmuch as both Labour and Nationalist candidates have fought less than half the seats at Stormont elections. About half of Labour's supporters display a second party preference for the Unionists or Nationalists, i.e., parties campaigning on religious and constitutional issues. Another measure of secularization is the extent to which Labour supporters agree on the principal enemy of the working class, i.e., the party they would *never* vote for. No agreement can be found. The Unionists are most often rejected by Catholic supporters of Labour, and the Nationalists are most often rejected by Protestant supporters. Religion more than economics determines who the enemies of the workers are thought to be. Only one-tenth of the electorate supports a secular Labour Party to the exclusion of sectarian values. The failure of any party but the Unionists to fight the majority of constituencies means that voters are compelled, if they wish to vote at all, to be prepared to shift from party to party, to try to keep their chief opponent out. The reciprocal of this is that in a number of seats that Labour fights, it too must receive votes from those who give it their support in the absence of other parties. Because it tends to take on Unionist opponents in constituencies without Nationalist candidates, it therefore has had a disproportionately large Catholic vote. This is not because in Northern Ireland (or anywhere else) Catholics are particularly inclined to Socialist and secular views of life. It is because Catholics are very strongly anti-Unionist. If offered a choice between Northern Ireland Labour candidates and those who favour a United Ireland as well as Socialist policies, Catholics appear to prefer the latter. For example, at the 1964 Westminster general election, Republicans outpolled Labour Party candidates in five of the ten constituencies in which they directly competed with each other, even though the former party drew votes from only one religion, and the latter from both.

Further evidence of the insulation of regime politics from economic issues is found in attitudes concerning the influence of 'big' business and trade unions upon life in Northern Ireland. Notwithstanding the fact that the bulk of the population lives in small towns or in the country, there is no rejection of large and modern economic institutions in the name of a parochial belief in economic individualism (Table IX.2). Moreover, although Catholics are more likely to be anti-big business than are Protestants, a plurality in both religions approve of trade unions and big business. If no other issues were important, there would thus be a ready market for conventional 'left-right' politics of economic issues along lines familiar in Britain, with substantial support for 'centre' policies too.[23] The absence of a correlation between economic attitudes and regime outlooks means

The Political Salience of Economic Differences

that there is no well-defined and stable base in Ulster society for a party that mixes pro- or anti-constitutional politics and class appeals.

Table IX.2 Attitudes toward business and unions

| | BIG BUSINESS | | | TRADE UNIONS | | |
	Protestant	Catholic	Total	Protestant	Catholic	Total
	%	%	%	%	%	%
Approves	54	39	48	41	41	41
Mixed views	16	11	14	17	15	16
Disapprove	13	23	17	25	21	24
Don't know	17	27	21	17	23	19
		D.I. = 20%			D.I. = 6%	

Ironically, the European Common Market shows the importance Ulster people give to non-economic issues. Within Britain, this issue is usually debated on economic grounds. Ulster people were asked about 'this country' joining the Common Market on the assumption that it is a non-sectarian issue in Northern Ireland too. In fact, replies were sectarian (D.I.=26%). A majority of Catholics favour joining the Common Market, and a plurality of Protestants are against. The differences in Northern Ireland on the Common Market are as great as that between Conservative and Labour supporters in Britain on industrial relations issues.[24] The reason for this is the belief among Protestants and Catholics that the lowering of national barriers between the United Kingdom and the Common Market countries would inevitably be followed by moves to unify Ireland. Moreover, four of the six nations signing the Treaty of Rome are overwhelmingly Catholic, and the Catholic Church is active politically. This interpretation is confirmed by the fact that among Catholics favouring entry into the Common Market, 44 per cent reject the Stormont Constitution, and 50 per cent favour illegal demonstrations. Reciprocally, among Protestants who are against joining Europe, 58 per cent are in favour of using violence to keep Ulster Protestant.

One possible explanation for the limited influence of class upon political outlooks is that Ulster people do not perceive economic distinctions noted by sociologists, because they structure society along religious lines. This explanation is also consistent with a theory of stages of development, for it implies that at some future date Northern Ireland people might be brought to see their society in class terms. Such a projection gives hope to groups as different as the Northern Ireland Labour Party and Republican Socialists. To test

The Political Salience of Economic Differences

this possibility, each person was asked what class he felt he belonged to (Table IX.3). In all, 81 per cent identified themselves with a group conventionally considered part of the industrial class structure. Only two of 1,291 people said that they belonged to Protestant or Catholic classes, and only two per cent rejected the idea of class identification; another 12 per cent were uncertain how to describe their place in the social structure of Northern Ireland. The degree of class awareness is relatively high by Anglo-American standards.[25] People who are Catholics are not particularly likely to think of themselves as lower class, nor are Protestants likely to upgrade themselves, for the difference values for self-perceived and objective class status are nearly identical (cf. Tables IX.1 and IX.3). Differences in subjective class assessment have no effect on attitudes toward the regime. In other words, a man's social status does not lead him to conform to any particular pro- or anti-regime norm.

Table IX.3 Self-perceived class

	Protestant	Catholic	Total
	%	%	%
Upper class	1	0	—
Middle class	52	41	47
Working class	29	34	31
Lower, poor class	2	4	3
Average, ordinary class	2	5	3
Don't believe in classes	2	2	2
Don't know, miscellaneous	12	14	12

D.I. = 12%

To explore further the meaning of class in Northern Ireland, each person was asked how he would describe people who were members of his class: 47 per cent gave a definition in occupational or income terms, 11 per cent said 'average', nine per cent evaluated their class in moral terms, and eight per cent as sociable or friendly; the remainder gave a miscellaneous answer or none. Respondents were also asked to enumerate and describe other classes that they thought existed in Northern Ireland today, to see whether people had simple models of class relations, divided into 'us' and 'them', or more complex models of three or more classes, with less clearcut distinctions between social strata.[26] Catholics might particularly be expected to see Northern Ireland in terms of two groups in conflict. The hypothesis is rejected. Replies showing a simple dichotomization were given by 21 per cent of Protestants and 25 per cent of

286

Catholics. The median and modal respondents, 47 per cent of the total, sees social structure differentiated into three classes. When asked to describe people in the various classes named, people chose neutral labels rather than emotive terms with religious overtones. Two-thirds of the labels are sociological terms, e.g., working class or lower middle class; 16 per cent status or prestige terms, and 12 per cent income terms. There is a complete absence of reference to farming groups, further confirming the assimilation of industrial class models in this partly rural society.

The existence of a clearly perceived class structure is not proof of class conflict. Relations between classes of people may range from amiable to extremely antagonistic. In view of the degree of religious discord in Northern Ireland, it might be expected that people would be less likely to perceive class conflict. A comparison of Northern Ireland and British survey responses shows that 33 per cent of Ulster people and 34 per cent in Britain think there is some conflict between classes, as against 54 per cent in Ulster and 57 per cent in Britain seeing classes getting along together. The difference index is very low between the two countries–four per cent–as well as between Protestants and Catholics in Northern Ireland–five per cent.[27] Among Catholics, there is a tendency for those who believe in class conflict to be more likely to reject the Constitution: 43 per cent take this view, as against 34 per cent who think that classes can co-operate. There is also a slight tendency for persons in both religions to favour non-compliance with basic laws as well as class conflict.

Another test of the importance of class concerns the extent to which class or religious differences inhibit social relations. People were asked whether they thought they had more in common with those of the same class but a different religion or with people of a different class but the same religion. The answers show that 39 per cent of Protestants and Catholics feel that they have more in common with those in the same class as themselves whatever their religion; only 15 per cent think they have more in common with co-religionists of a different class. In addition, 36 per cent are open-minded, saying neither class nor religion makes a difference in social relations (D.I.=6%). The replies reflect the limited scope of religious differences in Northern Ireland. In everyday social relationships class differences are more important than religion. It does not follow that this sense of community within a class also extends to political matters (cf. Chapter X). Catholics who feel most in common with persons in the same class are also less likely to support the regime; 45 per cent actively disapprove it. As expected, among the minority of Protestants who feel religious ties are strongest, 77 per cent were ready to fight for their group. There was no such relationship among Catholics.

It could be argued that the various measures of class show little or no correlation with basic political outlooks because none is by itself an accurate indicator of the ideal-type worker in industrial society. Four attributes in addition to occupation are regularly ascribed to prototypical manual workers: subjective identification with the working class, trade union membership, living in rented property, and a minimum of education. The more of these characteristics an individual has, then the more likely he is to reflect whatever influence class has in Northern Ireland. The proportion of ideal-type workers in Northern Ireland is 26 per cent of the working-class, the same as in Britain.[28] In a complementary manner, 36 per cent lack two or more typically working-class characteristics, as do 34 per cent in Britain. The cumulative intensity of working-class involvement does not, however, correlate consistently with attitudes toward the regime among Protestants or Catholics.

The above findings conclusively demonstrate that the people of Northern Ireland see themselves as part of an industrial society. Familiarity with the terminology of Socialism and of sociology is widely diffused, even in the rural parts of Ulster. There is a class structure which could and, according to some theories, should influence attitudes to the regime. Although the prerequisites for class politics exist, the influence does not.

Conceivably the foregoing has failed to find economic conditions significant because the criteria are not materialistic enough. A more materialistic model might posit that the regime can buy support and compliance by providing subjects with economic benefits. The approach is prominent in many studies of the relation of economic to political change. S. M. Lipset states the view succinctly, 'The more well-to-do a nation, the greater the chances that it will sustain democracy.'[29] Terence O'Neill attempted to apply this assumption in Northern Ireland. Thus, a social science theory is also a political theory with clear prescriptive and predictive implications: if one wants to increase allegiance to the regime, then raise living standards in absolute or relative terms.

The simplest way in which a regime might buy support is to

The Political Salience of Economic Differences

manage an economy producing high wages for everyone. Alternatively, it might seek to economize limited cash resources by ensuring high wages for Protestants but not for Catholics. Even if wages were not high by the standards of London or Birmingham, as long as Protestants had higher wages than Catholics, then they might endorse Ultra views for fear political change would threaten their living standards. Contrary to what is often alleged about major economic differentials among the communities, the Loyalty survey found that the median weekly family income of both Protestants and Catholics was between £16 and £20.[30] The difference index of reported earnings is 15 per cent (Table IX.4). Catholics are proportionately more numerous in the bottom income group, and less numerous in the upper income group. Given their larger numbers in the population, however, there are *more poor Protestants than poor Catholics* in Northern Ireland, just as there are more well to do Protestants. Income differences persist even when allowance is made for educational differences. Protestants who have some sort of qualification–whether a diploma, a degree or a certificate–are likely to enjoy higher wages than educated Catholics. The difference index is 18 per cent, a greater difference than for the population at large. This suggests that educated Catholics–a pool of potential political leaders for or against the regime–are more subject to relative economic deprivation than are manual workers.

Table IX.4 Reported weekly family earnings

	Protestant	Cumulative	Catholic	Cumulative	Total	Cumulative
	%	%	%	%	%	%
Up to £10	16	16	21	21	18	18
£11–15	18	34	23	45	20	38
£16–20	19	53	23	67	21	59
£21–25	16	69	13	80	15	73
£26–30	9	77	8	88	9	82
£31 per week +	18	95	7	96	14	95
Don't know; won't say	5	100	4	100	5	100

D.I. = 15%

In aggregate, the limited income difference between the two communities is evidence that the political conflict in Northern Ireland is not between rich and poor religious groups. In the case of individuals, one would expect the most prosperous to be the most allegiant, and the least to tend toward Ultra or disaffected views. No such pattern

The Political Salience of Economic Differences

is found. Well to do Catholics are as likely to be against the Constitution as are the poor. Similarly, there is little association between income and willingness to violate basic political laws. Only in the highest income brackets is opposition to illegal action relatively high; none the less, 39 per cent of the most prosperous Ulster Protestants say they would favour any measures to keep the regime Protestant; 35 per cent of Catholics favour illegal demonstrations.

The amount of money that a family receives each week is possibly less important than the relationship between the amount earned and the amount thought necessary or desirable for a fair standard of living. To measure subjective economic wellbeing, each person was asked to evaluate his family's standard of living. The replies show that three-quarters of the population are at least fairly satisfied with their standard; 21 per cent said their position was not very satisfactory and only four per cent regarded their economic position as poor. The small proportion who feel poor is particularly noteworthy, as it is less than the proportion of unemployed at the time of the survey. It suggests that a significant economically deprived group—those in receipt of welfare benefits–are not strongly dissatisfied with their resulting standard of living. Contrary to economic determinist hypotheses, economic dissatisfaction does *not* cause Protestants or Catholics to disapprove of the Constitution. Among satisfied Catholics, 35 per cent support the Constitution and 37 per cent disapprove of it; among the dissatisfied, 36 per cent support the Constitution and 31 per cent disapprove of it. The proportion of dissatisfied Catholics who favour illegal demonstrations is 51 per cent, but this is only marginally higher than the 46 per cent approving demonstrations among satisfied Catholics. Among satisfied Protestants there is a slight tendency for endorsement of Ultra views to be lower among very satisfied Protestants.

The regime directly influences standards of living by providing a wide range of cash benefits for people of all ages–family allowances, unemployment payments, national assistance and old age pensions. In 1967/68, the last fiscal year prior to the beginning of civil rights demonstrations, the total expenditure of the Stormont regime was £304,000,000, about £200 for every person in Northern Ireland, or £800 for every family of four. About 43 per cent of government expenditure is for welfare services of immediate use to the population, such as education, health and housing. In addition, £55,000,000 was paid in benefits from national insurance funds to old age pensioners, the unemployed and others in need. The benefits paid were three times the value of individual contributions; 44 per cent of the total payments came from Northern Ireland or British government contributions.[31] Thus, both directly and indirectly, standards of living in Northern Ireland are transparently linked to policies of the regime. Because most welfare benefits are paid as of right to anyone meeting minimum qualifications, such as a test of age, there is limited administrative discretion in application, and thus limited grounds for charges of discrimination. In fact, some Protestants complain that these benefits discriminate in favour of Catholics, because Catholics tend to have larger families and are also a disproportionate number of the unemployed; the fact of need is taken as evidence of moral irresponsibility or shiftlessness. When respondents were directly questioned about the level of welfare benefits, 34 per cent of Protestants replied that they thought them too high, as against 19 per cent of Catholics. The median person in both religions described the benefits as about right. The difference index of 22 per cent is substantial but less than that for the Common Market. There is no inclination for views about benefits to correlate with regime outlooks. Protestants who object to high welfare benefits are no more likely to be Ultras than others. Among Catholics, those who think benefits too low are but 10 per cent more likely to favour illegal demonstrations than those who think benefits too high.

The Stormont regime is also involved in two benefits with a very considerable discretionary element: public jobs and housing. In Northern Ireland as in the Republic, public jobs and public housing are more desirable than in England or America, given chronic unemployment and relatively poor housing. Persistently, Catholics have complained that the regime's officials have discriminated against Catholics in the allocation of these patronage benefits. The grievance is not only a complaint about the particular level of benefits provided, but also about being systematically deprived of benefits by comparison with Protestants. Social science studies in many different contexts have emphasized the importance of a feeling of relative deprivation. The concept of relative deprivation assumes that absolute levels of employment, earnings or housing are less important than any differentials that may appear along communal lines. In so far as Catholics feel relatively deprived by a regime, then they will be more likely to be disaffected. But in so far as Protestants see Catholics as deprived, then the greater might be their support for

The Political Salience of Economic Differences

institutions providing Protestants with advantages relative to other subjects in the state.[32] A sense of community between Protestants and Catholics would only result if both see advantages arising from peaceful, positive co-operation.[33]

Housing is an appropriate field for testing allegations of discrimination, because of the importance of government in building and letting new houses. The sub-standard condition of much housing in Northern Ireland reflects the heritage of early industrialization, as well as a disproportionate number of people living in the countryside. By comparison with areas in Britain, housing conditions are bad in Ulster. The 1961 census found that 51 per cent of all households lacked modern amenities such as a fixed bath and a hot-water tap. In the 1960s, the regime began a major programme to clear slums and build new houses. In the first instance, local authorities have had the responsibility to build and let houses at subsidized rents. The Northern Ireland Housing Trust has acted in areas where local

Table IX.5   Types of housing in Northern Ireland

	Protestant	Catholic	Total	
	%	%	%	
Home-owner	45	37	42	
Private landlord	21	23	22	
Local authority	20	26	23	
N.I. Housing Trust	10	9	9	
Not classified; lodgers	4	5	4	D.I. = 9%

authorities were unable or unwilling to make adequate provision for subsidized council houses. In the post-war period, 37 per cent of all new houses have been built by local authorities, 36 per cent by private enterprise, and the remaining 27 per cent by the Northern Ireland Housing Trust or other public agencies. About seven-eighths of all privately owned new housing are built with the aid of lump-sum public subsidies of £100 to £275. The cash contribution is useful, but because it is a once-for-all subsidy, recipients are not considered subsidized tenants, nor do they have a public agency as a landlord. Public housing is politically controversial for two reasons. The first is the charge that sites of housing–particularly in the City of Londonderry–have been chosen to maintain Unionist power in the constituencies, by confining new Catholic houses to wards that already elect Nationalist or Republican representatives. Survey evidence cannot confirm or reject this charge. It is, however, relevant to test

292

The Political Salience of Economic Differences

charges of systematic and widespread discrimination against Catholics in the allocation of council houses by local authorities. The custom of a councillor influencing housing allocations within his ward could easily lead to discrimination against Catholics, because of the disproportionate number of Protestant councillors in Northern Ireland.[34]

If discrimination against Catholics in housing were systematically practised in all parts of Northern Ireland, then the proportion of Catholics in receipt of subsidized housing would be virtually nil. To test this, each respondent was asked whether he owned his house or, if a tenant, who his landlord was (Table IX.5). The figures show that *in aggregate* Catholics are more likely than Protestants to be living in council houses. Aggregate figures do not necessarily evidence the

Table IX.6   Types of housing by local authority areas

	BELFAST (Unionist)		ELSEWHERE (Unionist)		ELSEWHERE (Nationalist)	
	Prot	*Cath*	*Prot*	*Cath*	*Prot*	*Cath*
	%	%	%	%	%	%
Home-owner	44	27	47	48	60	35
Private landlord	41	47	15	16	17	16
Local authority house	9	19	25	24	15	39
N.I. Housing Trust	3	6	12	11	6	8
Not classified; lodgers	3	1	1	1	2	2
Numbers in group	187	124	523	310	47	100
	D.I. = 19%		D.I. = 2%		D.I. = 26%	

absence of any discrimination. Protestant-dominated councils could discriminate on behalf of Protestants, and Catholic-dominated councils discriminate in the opposite direction. To test for this possibility, patterns of tenancy were analysed by the political pattern of control. As it is most unusual for the party governing a local authority to change, there has been ample time for discrimination to be cumulatively effective. Here again the survey found no evidence of systematic discrimination against Catholics. The greatest bias appears to favour Catholics in that small part of the population living in local authorities controlled by Catholic councillors (Table IX.6). Systematic discrimination cannot be found when patterns are examined in each of the six counties and two county boroughs, all controlled by Unionists. In five of the eight instances, a larger proportion of Catholics than Protestants were living as subsidized

The Political Salience of Economic Differences

tenants. The greater number of Protestants in the Province means that when an even proportion of each religion receives a housing subsidy, the majority of recipients will be Protestants. None the less, the survey found that in four of the eight areas studied – Belfast, Derry City, Armagh, and Tyrone – a majority of respondents in public housing were, in fact, Catholics (cf. Table III.1). A corollary of this is that both Protestants and Catholics can be found in slum housing. Significant evidence on this point was collected by the Building Design Partnership in a study of central Belfast prior to the 1969 disorders. In the 100 per cent Catholic ward of Cromac at least 90 per cent of the houses lacked an indoor toilet, a hand basin, a fixed bath or hot water. In the overwhelmingly Protestant Sandy Row and Shankill Road districts, a similar proportion also lived in housing described as 'grossly deficient in the provision of standard amenities'.[35]

The provision of public housing proportionately by religion is not conclusive evidence of non-discriminatory policies. A non-discriminatory housing policy would lead to a disproportionate number of needy people in subsidized housing. If more Catholics live in slum conditions than Protestants, then the need of the former would be greater. One way to test this possibility is to examine the incomes of Protestant and Catholic tenants in public and in private housing. If housing is allocated primarily in regard to need, then the proportion of Protestants and Catholics in each income bracket receiving subsidized housing should be equal. In fact, in all but one income category, the proportion of Catholics in subsidized housing is slightly *higher* than that of Protestants. The difference, while consistent, averages only four per cent. Income is not the only indicator of need. People with large families will also have greater need of subsidized housing because earnings must be divided among more people. Family size differs between Protestants and Catholics, and large Catholic families are a point of contention in Northern Ireland. Protestant councils determine whether applicants for housing with large families have demonstrated need or social irresponsibility. An analysis of housing provision by family size shows that there is a 12 per cent difference against Catholics in the proportion of families with more than six children assigned public housing. But because large families are five times more numerous among Catholics than among Protestants, Catholics still constitute 78 per cent of all large families in public housing.

To acquit the Unionist regime of blanket charges of discrimination

294

in public housing is not to assert the absence of any religious discrimination. At a minimum, religion tends to influence the assignment of individuals to Protestant or Catholic housing estates. The copious files of civil rights organizations, moreover, indicate that individual instances of blatant discrimination can and do occur, e.g., the assignment of a house to a Protestant couple without children, while a large Catholic family remains in a slum suited only for demolition. The Stormont regime has implicitly admitted defects in housing administration by taking housing powers from local authorities and local councillors, and vesting them in a Central Housing Authority, employing a points scheme as an objective measure of need in assessing qualification for public housing. James Callaghan, the British Home Secretary who encouraged use of the scheme, estimated without citing evidence that 'perhaps ten per cent of the local authorities had been allocating houses on a basis of discrimination'.[36] (No distinction was made between Catholic and Protestant controlled authorities.) The Commissioner for Complaints has reported that housing causes more complaints than any other subject. The Commissioner states that many grievances arise from the general shortage of good housing in Northern Ireland, but others concern discretionary powers of local authorities outside his terms of reference.[37] From an economist's point of view, the problem is limited, especially if bias is only shown in a fraction of the cases coming before the biased authorities. But from a civil rights point of view, *each individual case* of discrimination is a matter for protest.

The effect of public housing upon individual recipient's political outlooks is marginal. Among subsidized Catholic tenants, 39 per cent support the Constitution, as against 25 per cent of persons living in private tenancies. One cannot say whether this figure reflects a change of attitude by tenants in subsidized housing, or a tendency for authorities to give loyal Catholics subsidized housing. There is no relationship between subsidized tenancy and willingness to comply with basic political laws in either community. In short, the amount of support for the Constitution gained by housing policies is very limited, and does not affect rebellious acts. This is consistent with the fact that residence in a subsidized house does not give Catholics immunity from political problems. The prelude to the August, 1969 disorder was the harassment of Catholics living in Belfast Corporation's ironically named Unity Flats. Violence not only affected Catholics living in aged, sub-standard terrace houses, but also Catholics in the modern, council-built Divis Towers. In the Bogside of Londonderry, the roof of the tallest new council flat was used as a lookout point, and new flats and maisonettes were in the line of fire for teargas and stones.[38] The IRA operates on council estates as in slum areas.

Public employment is the second economic area in which discrimination is most often alleged. In a land of high unemployment, the security of a post on the public payroll compensates for any marginally lower earnings. Moreover, in a low-wage economy, civil service pay rates are relatively high. For example, one attraction of service in the RUC has been the rate of pay. A total of eight per cent of Protestants and seven per cent of Catholics said that they or someone in the family was currently publicly employed; another eight per cent of Protestants and six per cent of Catholics said that someone had formerly held a public job. There are a multiplicity of public jobs; employers include the Northern Ireland civil service, local authorities, and the Westminster civil service and nationalized industries. In Northern Ireland jobs, 69 per cent of employees interviewed were Protestants, ten per cent higher than their proportion among all survey respondents. In the United Kingdom posts, the proportion of Protestants was 63 per cent. This limited degree of over-representation is no different in magnitude from that found for Catholics in housing.

As a further test of the possibility of aggregate discrimination, public employment patterns were separately analysed for six counties and two boroughs. Because of the size of sampling error, given small numbers in many counties, it would be misleading to draw highly specific conclusions from figures for a single county. What is striking is that while Protestants are more numerous in the public services in five of the eight areas, Catholics are more numerous in two, and equal in a third. As a test of job status, family incomes were analysed in relation to public employment. In the small number of cases available (Protestants=59; Catholics=34), the median Protestant and Catholic public servant each have household incomes of £21 to £25 a week; 82 per cent of these Protestants and 80 per cent of the Catholics said they were at least fairly satisfied with their earnings. There is, moreover, no tendency for public authorities to favour unqualified Protestants; 56 per cent in public jobs have at some time obtained a qualification by examination; among Catholics, the proportion is 46 per cent. In sum, the survey evidence indicates that there is no great *aggregate* discrimination in public employment. The data cannot, however, be cited to deny or prove charges of discrimination in individual instances, or in particular local authorities.[39] The Commissioner for Complaints notes the difficulty of proving discrimination in public employment.[40]

The effect of a public job upon political outlooks is very limited. Catholics in public employment are more likely to support the regime, but only by a margin of 11 per cent. A majority in this group still withhold approval of the Constitution. One would expect that Protestants in public jobs would be readier to fight to keep the regime Protestant to protect their jobs. This is not the case; the proportion prepared to endorse political violence is below average, 43 per cent, suggesting if anything greater respect for procedural legality. Catholics on the public payroll are as ready as others to endorse demonstrations against the regime that pays their wages.

As the great bulk of people in Northern Ireland work for private employers, discrimination in this sector of the economy is potentially of greater significance than discrimination by public authorities. In small shops and firms, a tendency to employ relatives will inevitably result in a religious bias in employment. An explicit religious qualification for employment may also occur when relatives are not being hired. For instance, in November, 1959, when Terence O'Neill was Minister of Finance, his wife inserted an advertisement in the *Belfast Telegraph* stating, 'Protestant girl required for housework. Apply to the Hon. Mrs. Terence O'Neill, Glebe House, Ahoghill, Co. Antrim.'[41]

When a disproportionately high number of Protestants is employed in a large firm, then a *pattern* of bias is evidenced, whether or not it is consciously articulated by the company's management. For example, Harland & Wolff's shipyard in Belfast, with 10,000 employees the largest firm in Northern Ireland, has a workforce which is about 95 per cent Protestant. The Orange Order has always been strong among workers in the shipyard. The pattern has not been affected by the provision of about £20 million of public money in loans and subsidies.[42] Sirocco engineering works in Belfast has similarly been accused of discrimination, since the firm, with 1,500 employees, has only a handful of Catholics on its payroll. The chairman of the company said, in reply to the charge, that he had no idea of the exact number of Catholics on the staff, adding 'Catholics probably do not feel at home in a Protestant atmosphere'.[43]

The Political Salience of Economic Differences

From the perspective of the victim of discrimination, it makes little difference whether he is denied a job by a public or a private employer. Without regard to jurisdiction, he may feel aggrieved against 'the system'. To test for overt grievances about discrimination in employment, each person was asked the non-directive question: Do you think there are any difficulties for a person like yourself in finding a job in Northern Ireland today? A total of 39 per cent of persons interviewed said yes, with Catholics seven per cent more numerous. The obstacles to employment most often cited, however, had nothing to do with religion, but concerned old age or a lack of a skill. Only five per cent of persons interviewed mentioned religious discrimination as an obstacle to finding a job. Among this group, seven-eighths were Catholics. There is no tendency for Protestants worried about employment to be distinctive in their regime outlooks. This is also true about Catholic attitudes toward the Constitution. Catholics worried about finding a job are more likely to favour demonstrations against the regime than secure co-religionists by a margin of 13 per cent.

Unemployment is another cause of deprivation. In the Loyalty survey, seven per cent said the head of the household was then unemployed. The unemployment rate among Protestants was four per cent; among Catholics, it was 11 per cent.[44] In absolute terms, Catholic unemployment is very high, by comparison with any other region within the United Kingdom. Catholic unemployment is also more than two and one-half times that of Protestants. Two-thirds of all unemployed are Catholics, almost double what would be expected from the proportion in the population. Here again, the only basic attitude affected by unemployment is Catholic readiness to endorse demonstrations. Among the Catholic unemployed, 63 per cent favour illegal parades by Republican groups. These demonstrations on non-economic issues are also endorsed by 47 per cent of Catholics in work.

Any deprivation suffered within Northern Ireland may be discounted by comparison with the deprivation that might be involved if Ulster merged with the Republic. Just as the living standard in Northern Ireland is below that of Great Britain generally, so that of the Republic is below Ulster. An economic situation that appears relatively deprived from a Westminster point of view may look relatively advantaged, viewed from Dublin, Cork or the Gaelic West. The gross national income *per capita* of the Republic is substantially lower than that in Britain and every other Western nation.[45] Welfare standards are much higher in Northern Ireland than in the Republic. The population of Ulster is about half that of its southern neighbour, but annual expenditure on education is slightly higher, and on social services and health more than half again higher.[46] In 1958, an economic development programme began in the Republic, seeking to raise living standards; appropriately, it was blessed by a Catholic bishop. Living standards in the Republic have subsequently risen.[47] But as economic growth has occurred in the North too, the economic differential between the two has remained. Unionists have never hesitated calling attention to this. For instance, Terence O'Neill would ask, 'Why are our schools and universities, roads and motorways, our housing estates and our levels of social benefit outstanding in Ireland? Because as British citizens we enjoy these high standards as of right.'[48]

Table IX.7   The economic effect of abolishing the Border

	Protestant	*Catholic*	*Total*
	%	%	%
Make conditions better	3	13	8
No difference	32	44	37
Make conditions worse	48	24	38
Don't know	17	19	17
		D.I.	= 24%

Given the amount of travel across the Border, there is good reason to believe that Ulstermen have some first-hand familiarity with living conditions on both sides of the Border. Whatever the 'facts' of the situation – and economic data are always subject to more than one interpretation – their political significance will be mediated by the values used to interpret what is seen. Individuals who believe in a United Ireland may discount any objective evidence of poverty in the Republic, just as Protestant Ultras may discount evidence of prosperity there. To measure the political significance of these perceptions, each person was asked to say what difference, if any, he thought getting rid of the Border would make to his standard of living (Table IX.7). The replies show less of a Protestant fear of lower living standards than might be expected: for every three Protestants who think abolishing the Border would be harmful, two think it would make no difference. Among Catholics, the median person thinks that abolishing the Border would have no economic

The Political Salience of Economic Differences

effect. Ironically, the difference index between the two religions is less than that for the European Common Market issue.

Empirically, there is no true or false answer to a question about the future consequences of a hypothetical action: the uniting of Ireland. Politically, one would expect that persons who thought that a United Ireland would lower their standard of living would be most ready to support the existing regime. Survey evidence tends to support this hypothesis. Among Protestants who think abandoning the Border would lower living standards, 63 per cent are Ultras. Of those who think the Border makes no economic difference, 42 per cent are also prepared to resort to force. Among the quarter of Catholics who think abolishing the Border would cost them money, 43 per cent support the existing Constitution, and 63 per cent are against illegal Republican demonstrations. These relationships also mean that a majority of Catholics who see ending the Border as economically harmful none the less refuse to support the Constitution and a substantial minority endorse illegal demonstrations against it.

The disturbances since 1969 have not fundamentally altered the economic relations between Northern Ireland and a better off Britain. Northern Ireland's prospects for attracting new industrial investment have been unfavourably affected by political disorder. But the disorder has also been used by the Unionist regime to show the need for more British subsidies for capital and current expenditure in Northern Ireland. Against this must be charged the cost of property destroyed and the incalculable cost of human injury, death and suffering.[49]

The politician's theory that Catholic allegiance can be bought with economic benefits is refuted by the evidence of this chapter. The increase in support and compliance resulting from higher income or the receipt of welfare and patronage benefits is limited or non-existent. The theory of buying allegiance fails because it assumes that individual aspirations are solely satisfied by the provision of private goods, i.e., personal economic benefits. It appears that the most important political concerns of individuals are collective goods.[50] The pattern of replies to questions about discrimination, viewed in the light of widespread popular support for civil rights demonstrations, implies a concern with collective wellbeing, that is, the wellbeing of the Catholic community. Catholics offered benefits by the regime will readily accept them but not give allegiance in return, in so far as

300

they believe that there remain other Catholics who are discriminated against or suffer unemployment because of the regime. It hardly matters whether the regime or its supporters among private employers are viewed as the cause of grievance. To the person aggrieved, the intensity of his complaint is more important than its source. Moreover, reaction against the regime is not proportionate to the incidence of complaints. It is disproportionately greater. Catholics are not concerned with the quantity of complaints or the cash value of their deprivations, but rather, with *any* evidence of discrimination. Just as members of a large union will endure a prolonged strike for the sake of a small number of workers, so the majority of Catholics in work and in receipt of benefits 'strike' against the regime that makes unemployment disproportionately the experience of Catholics, and excludes Catholics from sharing the powers of the regime.

Ironically, the man who tried hardest to buy Catholic support for the regime, Terence O'Neill, provided a perfect illustration of why his efforts failed. He did this in a radio interview a few days after resigning as Prime Minister. Replying to a question–Why do Protestants fear Catholics?–he unwittingly showed how non-economic and economic attitudes intertwine:

> The basic fear of the Protestants in Northern Ireland is that they will be outbred by the Roman Catholics. It is as simple as that. It is frightfully hard to explain to a Protestant that if you give Roman Catholics a good job and a good house, they will live like Protestants, because they will see neighbours with cars and television sets.
> They will refuse to have 18 children, but if the Roman Catholic is jobless and lives in a most ghastly hovel, he will rear 18 children on national assistance.
> It is impossible to explain this to a militant Protestant, because he is so keen to deny civil rights to his Roman Catholic neighbours. He cannot understand, in fact, that if you treat Roman Catholics with due consideration and kindness they will live like Protestants, in spite of the authoritative nature of their church.[51]

Conceivably, Terence O'Neill and his supporters might some day convince their fellow Protestants of the rightness of this analysis. It does not follow that the repetition of these arguments, in media that Catholics as well as Protestants can hear, would make the former wish to exchange their religion, nationality and politics for all the cars and television sets that Stormont can offer.

X · The Structure of Communalism

Then we have people genuinely trying to be helpful who advocate a kind of reciprocal emasculation. No National Anthem or Loyal Toast to offend one side: no outward signs or symbols of Nationalism to offend the other. This approach, too, I believe to be misconceived; it is rather like trying to solve the colour problem by spraying everyone a pale shade of brown.

TERENCE O'NEILL

Politics is a social phenomenon, even when the actions and aims of political groups are considered anti-social. This is true because politics is much more concerned with relationships between people than with subjective feelings within each subject. However important it is to social scientists to study the configuration of an individual's attitudes and what things influence them, government is much too complex a phenomenon, even in a small country, to think in terms of individuals. Some sort of structure must be found or imposed upon social relationships in order to make them manageable, intellectually or politically.

There are several contrasting ways in which communities of Northern Ireland people might be structured. Geographical distinctions are convenient, not least to politicians elected by geographically small constituencies. Such analysis will not find that every place is politically unique, because of the existence of political differences common to Protestants and Catholics wherever they live. It might find that there are ecological differences from place to place, arising from special characteristics of local societies. But sociologists tend to think in terms of communal groups differentiated by class, religion, national identity and other characteristics deemed worthy of inclusion in the social structure. Another group of social scientists is less concerned with social or geographical characteristics and much more with clusters of attitudes that form relatively coherent and comprehensive ideologies. Such attitudes create a community of outlook between individuals adhering to the same ideology. This approach would seem particularly relevant in Ulster, given the great importance of politics and religion, fields in which ideologies abound.

302

The Structure of Communalism

Politically, the presence or absence of structured groups in society is extremely important. In a highly structured society, individuals with many political views and social characteristics in common would form distinctive and separate communities, and political parties would be based upon them. Even if these parties disagreed about many of the means and ends of government, the very clarity of their differences and the cohesion of their support would make it possible for the leader of each communal group to gain recognition for his position and strength. This could lead to a bargain among communal leaders, sharing out benefits among the groups, or, at worst, isolating one segment. While political or social isolation has many drawbacks, it does permit the maintenance of distinctive outlooks and activities. Separation from the rest of society also permits insulation from the influence of the regime. In such circumstances, a regime may fail to gain the full compliance of the isolated group; disaffection is, however, confined by the very characteristics that give it cohesion.

In a society in which political outlooks are relatively independent of social structure, the very dispersion of friends and opponents of the regime will require indiscriminate 'blanket' policies much the same for all. If a regime has majority support and the members of the minority have their views eroded by contact with opponents, then dispersion can become a means to the end of full legitimation. The point is often implicit in arguments against housing segregation, whether in Ulster or the United States. It is assumed that frequent contact will reduce differences occurring with physical separation. Yet, in so far as dispersion does not lead to amelioration, it can increase friction. Moreover, opponents of the regime will no longer be contained in recognizable places or easily distinguished by their social characteristics. The disaffected will be found almost everywhere in society, and the potentiality for rebellion too. This situation is best described as 'dispersion at bi-polar extremes'.

Ecological theories of political behaviour posit that the influences upon the behaviour of an individual are not a constant, but vary according to environment.[1] For example, in a community in which nearly all male Protestants march on the Twelfth of July and nearly all male Catholics turn out on Easter Monday, it would take an abnormally strong commitment to a deviant position to stand apart from one's co-religionists. In a complementary fashion, in societies where religious ties are weak, it is more difficult for religious groups to organize activities in the face of communal secularism. Those most influenced by their social environment are likely to be those who are least involved in politics or else most strongly attached to their immediate community. To hypothesize the existence of ecological influences is not to suggest that they can override the influence of religion, party or class but rather that they can operate independently of individual social characteristics. For instance one not only wishes to know what proportion of Catholics favour illegal demonstrations against the regime, but also, how much, if any, the proportion rises in localities that are predominantly Catholic, and how much it falls among Catholics in predominantly Protestant communities.

The proportion of Protestants and Catholics in a community would seem, in theory and in practice, the most important of all potential ecological influences upon political outlooks. In the extreme case of a village composed exclusively of Protestants or Catholics, there is no minority to react against or influence. Where a minority does exist but is not large, the majority has little objective grounds to fear being 'swamped', and the minority is subject to pressures to conform to the majority view. Studies of race relations in the American South have found a clear relationship between the proportion of black people in a county and its degree of political discrimination.[2] The 'minority' effect might operate differentially upon Protestants and Catholics. Where Catholics are in a minority in a community, they are exposed to pressures to conform both to local and to Northern Ireland norms. Where Protestants are in a minority locally, they may move toward an Ultra position, because a Protestant monopoly of power in Northern Ireland becomes a guarantee of local dominance. It is possible that the greatest pressures to extremes are found in communities where the proportions of Protestants and Catholics leave most grounds for uncertainty about long-term power relationships, either because of numerical equality, or because gerrymandering at local elections has maintained a Protestant council against a Catholic majority.

In stratifying the population for the Loyalty survey, a special effort was made to classify by religious composition each town or village in order to distribute interviews among areas reflecting the various proportions in which Protestants and Catholics are mixed. Each primary sampling unit was an urban polling station or a district electoral division in the countryside; this corresponds to each person's immediate face-to-face community, in which he meets others regularly in a variety of contexts, whether friendly or aggressive. Using census data, church locations and first-hand observation, each sampling unit was classified as predominantly Protestant, predominantly Catholic, or mixed in religion. The majority of respondents – 64 per cent of Protestants and 52 per cent of Catholics – live in localities where their own kind are predominant; 30 per cent of Catholics and 14 per cent of Protestants live where they are clearly in the minority.[3] The balance of the religions has, however, no significant influence upon political outlooks. There was only a slight tendency for Catholics to be less in favour of illegal demonstrations where they are in the minority than where they are in the majority. In other words, prudential considerations of local numbers neither encourage nor discourage anti-regime outlooks.

Table X.1   Changes in communal relations by type of community

	Change for better	No change	Worse	D.K.
Protestants in:	%	%	%	%
Mostly Protestant area	57	34	7	2
Mixed area	51	34	7	9
Mostly Catholic area	57	38	5	1
Catholics in:				
Mostly Protestant area	60	32	6	2
Mixed area	74	22	2	2
Mostly Catholic area	66	26	4	4
Total Protestants	56	35	7	3
Total Catholics	65	27	4	3

D.I. $= 10\%$

The quality of local relationships between Protestants and Catholics is potentially more important than the quantity of each group. Given the large number of small communities in Northern Ireland, there is ample opportunity for substantial variations to occur between communities, arising from the local importance of a past incident, such as an IRA raid, or the influence of an individual Orangeman, priest or exponent of harmony between religions. To assess the quality of Protestant-Catholic relations, each person was asked whether he thought they were better, about the same, or worse than five years ago. This covered exactly the period in which Terence O'Neill had then been Prime Minister (Table X.1). The replies show that O'Neill's 'era of good feelings' was not a myth. A majority of Protestants and Catholics in all kinds of localities agreed that relations were improving in the period and very few anywhere thought they were getting worse. This suggests that Protestants and Catholics regard better inter-faith relations as mutually beneficial, and not a situation in which improvements for Catholics mean worse conditions for Protestants. There is nothing irreversible in such a trend. Some places selected for interviews were subsequently scenes of illegal demonstrations and disorder.

Improving community relations was a major means by which Terence O'Neill sought full legitimation of the regime.[4] The survey indicates that improved community relations had very little effect upon political outlooks. Among Catholics who felt that community relations had improved only 36 per cent supported the Constitution, and 44 per cent still favoured illegal demonstrations. Improvements in community relations were associated with a tendency for Protestants to reject Ultra tactics; these were endorsed by 46 per cent of Protestants who thought relations had improved, by 61 per cent of those who thought they had remained the same, and by 71 per cent of the small group that thought they had worsened.

Instead of regarding ecological influence as the reflection of a single condition, the ratio of Protestants to Catholics, it may be cumulative in character. The greater the extent to which people live within the confines of their own religious group, then the more likely it is that they will conform or overconform to communal norms. Face-to-face relationships with kin, friends and those at work not only lead to the exchange of ideas and values, but also form strong emotional bonds, adding extra strength to communal ties. Such ties are particularly likely to be important because small towns, villages and rural areas predominate in Northern Ireland. People there have few choices of companions and no expectation that their choice of company will change much from one decade to the next. To deviate from group standards in such circumstances is thus to risk isolation in a peculiarly severe way. Yet, to avoid contact with people of the opposite religion when neither linguistic nor class barriers exist and all live near[5] each other also requires an ideology for justification. Ideologies exist that justify living in a back-to-back relationship in a face-to-face community.

To measure the extent to which Protestants and Catholics keep themselves to themselves in social relations, each person interviewed was asked the proportion of co-religionists he met in a variety of contexts inside and outside the home (Table X.2). The pattern of replies shows that only in marriage is there strict segregation by religion; even there, 30 per cent of all respondents reported at least one relative by marriage of the opposite religion.[6] There is, however, a marked religious difference concerning acquaintanceship with people in politics; many Catholics do not know anyone in this disproportionately Protestant group. Given conditions in Ulster, one might expect that self-selection plus random clustering would particularly cause Protestants to lack contact with Catholics in social

Table X.2   Religious segregation in primary groups

Proportion same religion	*All*	*Most*	*Half*	Less than *half; none*	*D.K.*
	%	%	%	%	%
Relatives by marriage					
Protestants	74	17	3	2	4
Catholics	65	22	5	4	4
Friends					
Protestants	32	46	18	1	2
Catholics	25	32	35	7	1
Neighbours					
Protestants	28	40	22	6	4
Catholics	33	24	27	13	3
People self/husband works with					
Protestants	20	24	34	9	13
Catholics	16	16	38	18	12
Community leaders; people in politics					
Protestants	29	38	9	2	21
Catholics	15	17	16	16	36

relations. This is not the case. Protestants are almost as likely to have some contact with Catholics as Catholics are to have some contact with Protestants. Politically, there is no clear tendency for segregation on any of these measures to affect support for the regime. There is a limited but consistent tendency for those with contacts exclusive to their own religion to refuse compliance with basic political laws. This is most noticeable for Protestants whose friends are all Protestants: 66 per cent endorse political violence, if necessary. Among Catholics, this tendency is highest among those who know only Catholic political leaders; 56 per cent endorse illegal demonstrations against the regime.

The Structure of Communalism

Even though social relations are not strictly segregated, by choice or chance there will always be some people who have little contact with people different from themselves. One could hypothesize that these would most likely be Ultras or disaffected from the regime, for people who live among their own kind would have no stimulus to consider other points of view when making political judgments: they might even think all of Ulster was like their own constricted world. In so far as they tried to take the views of the other community into account, they would not be able to do so accurately, because of lack of knowledge. Reciprocally, exposure to a multiplicity of different points of view may lead to trust, understanding and a willingness to compromise because of an understanding of the other man's view.

To test the hypothesis that communal exclusiveness leads to anti-regime views, a communalism scale was created from the replies of each individual to the questions about social relations reported in Table X.2. A person completely among his own kind would score 20 points, and a person completely isolated from his co-religionists would score 0.[7] The overall profile of social relationships shows a bias toward co-religionists, but not to the point of exclusiveness. The median and modal Protestant had a communal score of 15, reflecting on average that 'most' of his social relations were with co-religionists. The median and modal Catholic had a score of 14, showing a very similar situation (Table X.3). Only ten per cent of Catholics and three per cent of Protestants were consciously in the religious minority in most of their social relationships. The pattern of contact across religious lines does not suggest a society in which political differences are matched by social segregation.

The extent to which an individual is segregated among his own kind has little influence upon his readiness to support the Constitution; such fluctuations as appear are usually within the limits of sampling error (Table X.3). Social segregation does increase Protestants' readiness to defy basic political laws. The proportion of Ultras rises from 28 per cent in the least segregated group to 64 per cent in the most segregated. The same trend appears much more weakly among Catholics; 39 per cent endorse demonstrations among the least segregated, and 50 per cent among the most segregated. Ironically, the implication of this finding is that the best way to reduce violent anti-regime views is to place Protestants in a predominantly Catholic environment. Yet this type of mixing cannot be done on a large scale in Northern Ireland.[8] Given population ratios, many

308

Northern Ireland Protestants must live among a majority of their own kind. Protestants are sufficiently numerous to set limits upon their social dispersion.

The character of party activity in a community is another potential source of ecological influence. Political parties not only reflect individual attitudes but also may stimulate them. This is particularly likely to occur in Northern Ireland, because the pattern of party competition is not constant from constituency to constituency. Moreover, in constituencies where only one party nominates candidates, then pressures to conform to the majority might be unusually strong. Among the 30 constituencies represented in the Loyalty survey, five patterns of party competition occurred in the three

Table X.3 Social segregation in relation to political outlooks

Segregation	Least		(Degree of social segregation)					Most
	5–6	7–8	9–10	11–12	13–14	15–16	17–18	19–20
Protestants								
Supports Constitution %	*	*	60	65	69	70	71	63
Rejects compliance %	*	*	28	45	51	52	65	64
Total %	1	1	4	11	25	33	19	7
Catholics								
Supports Constitution %	*	25	42	31	36	26	33	38
Rejects compliance %	*	39	39	48	49	51	55	50
TOTAL %	2	4	12	21	24	25	12	2
COMBINED TOTAL	1	2	7	15	24	29	16	5

* No percentages calculated: 10 or less cases.

Stormont general elections of the 1960s. In 11 constituencies, Unionists were unopposed in at least two of the three contests; in six, Unionists were opposed by Labour candidates, and in another six, Unionists were usually opposed by candidates of a Green tendency. Nationalist candidates were usually returned unopposed in six of the seats, and in North Down, a Liberal usually challenged the Unionist MP. The character of party competition does not influence support for the Constitution in a constituency, but it does correlate with attitudes towards compliance. In seats held uncontested by Unionists, 40 per cent of Catholics favour illegal demonstrations as against 59 per cent in constituencies that Nationalists had held unopposed. In seats held uncontested by Nationalists, the Ultra position was taken by 47 per cent of Protestants, as against 62 per cent holding this view where Unionists fought Nationalists. With the bulk of numbers on their side in the Province, Protestants may feel confident that they have a basic advantage in competitive situations. By contrast the Catholic minority feel more need for overwhelming numbers in an area when demonstrating against the regime.

Local political patronage in Northern Ireland is often a source of political controversy. Civil rights demonstrators have sought one man, one vote, one value in local government to give Catholics control where they are a numerical majority. The Cameron Report justified this demand by documenting patterns of discrimination against Catholics in communities that were the scene of civil rights protests.[9] Yet the Loyalty survey in spring, 1968 found very little sign of grievance directed specifically against local council activities. When asked whether fair treatment was expected in dealings with people from the local council, 91 per cent of Protestants and 81 per cent of Catholics said yes (D.I.=10%). Only ten per cent of Catholics and four per cent of Protestants said they did not expect fair treatment. As replies elsewhere showed a much higher level of general Catholic concern with discrimination and rejection of the Constitution, this indicates that local government activity was not the sole source of disaffection from the regime.

The effect of differences in council control is difficult to assess, because so few councils have been governed by Catholic majorities. At the time of the survey, all the county borough and county councils were Unionist, as were the nine borough councils; seven of the 24 urban district councils and four of the 27 rural district councils were Nationalist.[10] Of the 11 per cent of respondents found living in Nationalist local authorities, two-thirds were Catholic. Such Catholics are not more anti-regime than their co-religionists 'beleaguered' in Unionist areas; in fact six per cent more favoured the Constitution, and two per cent less favoured illegal demonstrations. Among Protestants in Catholic-run local authority areas, support for the Constitution was very high: 89 per cent voiced positive views and only six per cent were apathetic. But Protestants were no more likely to be Ultras than elsewhere. In other words, experience of Catholics controlling the local council does not encourage extremism; if anything, it tends slightly to increase allegiance among both religions.

Growing recognition of the administrative faults of historic units of local government in all parts of the United Kingdom stimulated a decision to review Northern Ireland local government, beginning in March, 1966. The review was primarily concerned with questions of administration: what population, what geographical size and what rateable value does a local authority require to be efficient? Inevitably this meant reconsidering the desirability of devolving major powers to small country and urban councils, given the population of the Province and its limited resources. Yet administrative considerations were not the only matters of significance. In Western Ulster, where Catholics are sufficiently numerous to expect to control many local authorities, given one man, one vote, one value, there are important political questions at stake. Protestants were concerned that they would be ruled by Catholics to their disadvantage. The West Ulster Unionist Council was formed, with Ultras prominent in its membership, to lobby for a 'careful' drawing of new local authority boundaries, i.e., boundaries that would maximize Protestant control of the reformed authorities. Simultaneously, Catholics feared that the reduction of local authority powers, however justified on administrative grounds, would leave the civil rights campaign a hollow victory: control of reformed local councils after their major powers were gone. The withdrawn powers, if transferred to Stormont, would not be susceptible to Catholic influence as long as the regime remains in Unionist hands. In the event, the Northern Ireland government chose reforms intended to neutralize local government politically by centralization of most powers in Stormont, or in bodies such as the Central Housing Authority, reporting to Stormont. In doing this, it followed the lead of a Review Body on Local Government, chaired by Patrick Macrory. Catholics reacted to the proposal with mixed views.[11] It promised to reduce the powers of local Unionist councillors, but also meant that Catholics too would have less hope of sharing in the power of the regime.

Centralization of decision-making in Northern Ireland had already been an issue, because Stormont's economic development programme of the 1960s has been followed by a concentration of development in Belfast. This policy is justified by the argument that only the Belfast region has the manpower, administrative services, communications and commercial resources required by modern industries, especially industries not already committed to Northern Ireland.[12] Critics allege that development projects are concentrated

The Structure of Communalism

around Belfast because the regime is unwilling to invest in Catholic areas in the rural west of Ulster. Politically, the poorer part of Ulster is defined as west of the River Bann, an area including all of Fermanagh and Tyrone and most of Armagh and County Londonderry, including Derry City. Catholics living east of the Bann are, however, no readier to support the Constitution than those living in the west. There is a slight tendency for Protestants west of the Bann to be readier to use violence; 61 per cent endorse such action, as against 52 per cent to the east. Similarly, there is a slight tendency for Catholics there to endorse illegal demonstrations; 53 per cent do so, as against 45 per cent in the east. While the figures show a little hardening of conflict in the west, there is no softening of outlooks east of the Bann.

As a test of perceived regional discrimination, each person was asked whether he thought the Northern Ireland government was giving his part of the country its fair share of economic help. Among Protestants, 72 per cent said yes; among Catholics, the proportion is 48 per cent (D.I.=24%). While satisfaction is high among Protestants everywhere, among Catholics a sense of discrimination was strongest in Derry City, where 75 per cent felt the government had been unfair, and in County Tyrone, where 61 per cent expressed a similar view. The proportion of Protestants voicing complaints was relatively high in the west, but still much lower than that of Catholics. Among Catholics who perceived the government as helping their region, 42 per cent supported the Constitution, compared to 26 per cent among those who felt their region was treated unfairly. Similarly, in the former group, 54 per cent opposed illegal demonstration; among those with a sense of regional discrimination, 54 per cent favoured such protests. These differences suggest that the aid Stormont provides in the prosperous east tends to benefit both Protestants and Catholics. In the west, however, where need is greater and aid less, it increases discord, for Protestants are regarded as the chief beneficiaries by both Protestants and Catholics.

One reason why people east of the Bann may show a slightly higher level of allegiance is that the urban population of Ulster is concentrated there. In cities and towns, people are free from the constraints of face-to-face rural communities. They are exposed to more cosmopolitan outlooks characteristic of modern industrial society. This might increase levels of allegiance, or, at the least, decrease defiance of basic political laws. To test for this, individuals were grouped according to the level of urbanization of their community, with Belfast in a class by itself because of its size and Londonderry because of its political history. Degree of urbanization has no effect upon readiness to support the Constitution. Protestant Ultras were strongest in the smaller towns of Ulster, and weakest in Belfast, but the difference is not more than five per cent. Among Catholics, support for illegal demonstrations is most often found in Derry and Belfast, where mass demonstrations are politically most significant. Sufficient dispersion exists so that the potential for illegal demonstrations or Ultra reaction can be found in dozens of places in Ulster.

Belfast, as the capital, may exert a special influence upon those frequently in the city. As it is convenient by modern transport to all parts of the Province, regular visitors can come from anywhere in Ulster. A variety of theories of modernization propose that such 'cosmopolitans' should be most likely to be fully allegiant, or least opposed to illegal political action. Each person living outside Belfast was asked how often he visited there. Among Protestants, 38 per cent of non-residents came into Belfast at least weekly, and 21 per cent of Catholics; Catholics were more likely to avoid the big city than Protestants (D.I.=17%). Undoubtedly Dublin is more attractive to those who feel themselves Irish on cultural as well as political grounds; in certain areas it is also as easy of access.[13] There is no support for the hypothesis that those avoiding the city are more inclined to reject the regime. If anything, the tendency is the opposite among Catholics, for 38 per cent of those who avoid Belfast support the Constitution, as against 33 per cent of Catholic residents of the city. People who live in Belfast are slightly readier to support illegal demonstrations than those who occasionally or never visit it. In short, rebellion in the capital city cannot be blamed on 'outsiders', for the predisposition to violate basic political laws is strongest among those who make their homes there.

The prominence of the Border in Northern Ireland politics suggests that people who live closer to the Border might be more likely to adopt anti-regime views. Protestants could do this in reaction to the threat of IRA-type attacks at the vulnerable perimeter of Ulster, and Catholics because of a belief that rebellion could change the border to their advantage. The evidence, however, rejects this hypothesis. Neither Catholic nor Protestant attitudes toward the regime are significantly affected by closeness to the Border. This is specially noteworthy inasmuch as more than three-fifths of the people in

Border areas are Catholics. The absence of a 'front-line' effect is probably best explained by the fact that no part of Northern Ireland is as much as 100 miles from the Border and most parts are less than two hours by fast automobile from it. Belfast, for example, is 49 miles by road from Dundalk in the Republic.

The character of a community may be less significant an influence upon political outlooks than the strength of an individual's attachment to it. A man or woman who has lived all his life in a terrace house in the Shankill or Falls Road or in an isolated rural area may be so committed to it that he literally cannot conceive of being without the friends and customs that he has known for a lifetime. A cosmopolitan person, by contrast, can conceive of alternatives to his present place of residence; such awareness may make him 'choosy' in evaluating his immediate environment. Epigrammatically, the localist adapts himself to his community, whereas the cosmopolitan adapts his community to suit himself.

In Northern Ireland, the community to which a Protestant adapts is one in which the political inferiority of Catholics has long been taken for granted. To alter this would be to change an integral part of the society he knows and cleaves to. Thus, one would expect a Protestant with strong local ties to be rigidly Ultra in his political outlook. Among Catholics, the situation is very different. The development of community attachments may be prevented by discrimination. The greater the rejection, then the greater the likelihood that an individual might emigrate. A person who is totally committed to a community has every incentive to avoid noting or considering seriously any arguments that would make him dissatisfied with his lot. This would only cause him tension. Reducing political expectations provides a simple means of avoiding tension.

One measure of localism is the portion of his life that a person has lived in the same place. A total of 54 per cent of Northern Ireland people said that they had lived in the same place all their lives; another 25 per cent were there for most or all of their adult lives; If they remain in Ulster, Catholics are more likely to stay put than are Protestants; 61 per cent have never moved as against 49 per cent of Protestants. The length of time that a person has lived in a community has no significant effect upon his attitude toward the regime. A localist can also be defined as a person with strong kinship ties to his place of residence. When family and kin are part of a community, an individual is intimately and emotionally embedded in it. There is much contact with kin in Northern Ireland; about one-quarter see relatives outside their house daily, another quarter see them several times a week, and another quarter see them at least weekly. By contrast, only 40 per cent in England see relatives at least weekly.[14] There is very little difference between Protestants and Catholics in ties to kin (D.I.=7%). The extent to which kin and community are intermingled also has no effect upon an individual's willingness to give allegiance to the regime.

Ultimately, attachment to place is a very subjective matter. For this reason, each person was asked: How do you feel about this area as a place to live in? Are you glad that you live here? The replies were much the same from both religions (D.I.=6%). Two-thirds of the people said they liked their home area very much and another 19 per cent gave unequivocally positive replies, and only two per cent disliked it very much. In all, 14 per cent indicated mixed or negative feelings about where they live. There was no tendency for liking of place to affect Protestant political outlooks or Catholic support for the Constitution. There was a tendency for Catholics very much satisfied with their community to be less likely to favour disrupting it: 58 per cent opposed illegal demonstrations. Asking people how they would feel if they had to leave Northern Ireland is another way to assess attachment to place. Replies show some differences of opinion, but not along religious lines (D.I.=8%). A total of 56 per cent say they would be very unhappy or somewhat unhappy to leave, and 39 per cent say they would have mixed feelings about leaving or regard departure with pleasure. This distribution suggests that emigration is not a potent emotional issue to people in Ulster; it is a matter of fact occurrence which has been going on for generations. This interpretation is reinforced by finding no clear association between feelings about having to leave Ulster and attitudes toward its regime.

Asking people what they like and dislike most about living in Northern Ireland further illuminates the character of the subjective world in which they live. One might expect that Protestants would frequently refer to their political position as a source of satisfaction, just as Catholics would nominate sectarian conflict as a thing disliked. The chief characteristics that people like about Northern Ireland are surprisingly general–the people, the countryside and scenery, the way of life, and all things familiar to them. Such answers could equally well be given about any society, whether in

The Structure of Communalism

England, America, Africa or Asia. These simple, even primordial likes have little to do with politics, religion, or even wages and welfare conditions. The average number of Protestant likes, 1·5, was nearly matched by Catholics, 1·4 likes, and the pattern of replies is much the

Table X.4   The things liked most about Northern Ireland

	Protestant	Catholic	Total
	%	%	%
The people, family and friends	52	46	50
The countryside and scenery	36	27	33
The way of life	22	18	20
Habit, where I was born	21	18	20
Good wages, welfare benefits	9	11	10
'Better than others'	4	6	5
Political regime	4	2	3
Religious atmosphere	2	1	2
Nothing; don't know	4	8	6

D.I. = 16%

same too (Table X.4). In view of the failure of the majority of Catholics to support the regime, one would expect that politics would frequently be mentioned among things disliked about Ulster life. In fact, the modal Protestant and Catholic each said that there was nothing to dislike about Ulster life (Table X.5). Only one person in five refers to a grievance about religion. The weather is about as often

Table X.5   The things disliked most about Northern Ireland

	Protestant	Catholic	Total
	%	%	%
Religious controversies	22	22	22
The weather, physical geography	20	8	16
Economic difficulties	13	16	14
Political controversies	7	8	7
People, way of life	6	7	6
Nothing; don't know	44	47	45

D.I. = 10%

a cause of complaint as are economic or political controversies. References to religious controversies are mixed, with some people disliking the actions of the other community, some blaming both sides, and a few even criticizing their own co-religionists. It is noteworthy that the average number of complaints voiced was slightly less by Catholics than by Protestants: 0·6 as against 0·7.

In all, the judgments of Ulster people upon their society are favourable, with likes outweighing dislikes by a margin of more than two to one among both Catholics and Protestants. Moreover, the pattern of replies shows community attachments insulated from political issues, for political outlooks do not affect individual views of the society as a whole. People do not evaluate their lives principally in terms of political conditions, but by such things as family and friendship, the countryside, the way of life, habit, and even the weather.

Table X.6   Dispersion in the social structure

		Protestants		Catholics	
		Urban	Rural	Urban	Rural
		%	%	%	%
Middle class	*British	12·5	3·7	1·9	0·5
	Irish	3·0	1·1	4·5	1·6
Working class	*British	21·1	9·4	4·6	3·0
	Irish	5·5	2·3	14·7	10·4

* This category includes Ulster and hyphenated identities, as well as the all non-Irish responses.

In view of the absence of strong, simple correlations between single communal characteristics and basic political outlooks, it is desirable to consider the combined effect of a multiplicity of social conditions upon political outlooks. The Lipset-Rokkan framework for analysing multiple social differences can assess the extent to which individuals are influenced by their composite position in society. Religious, urban-rural and industrial class differences are all salient in Northern Ireland. Moreover, the lack of a single national identity also creates a 'centre-periphery' problem, or contrast between two peripheries: those who look to Dublin or to London as the centre. When these dichotomized distinctions are combined, then there are sixteen possible permutations of individual characteristics. This theoretical complexity need not be matched by an equivalent complexity in the society. For instance, a similar analysis of British society places 61 per cent of the population in two groups: middle-class or working-class English urban Protestants.[15] By contrast, in Northern Ireland the two largest categories in the social structure contain 35·8 per cent of the population. Problems of coalition building are illustrated by the fact that the four largest groups, constituting more than half the population, are very disparate: they are the Protestant British urban middle class and working class, and the Catholic Irish urban and rural working class. The aggregate profile clearly emphasizes the dispersion of society into a large number of small groups (Table X.6).

The Structure of Communalism

The dispersion of political outlooks can be measured by seeing to what extent each of the eight Protestant and eight Catholic groups varies from the average in their attitude to the Constitution and compliance with basic political laws. In so far as political outlooks do not differ between each of these social categories, then conflicts about the regime are dispersed and that much harder for politicians to predict or contain. In so far as each of the groups is cohesive in outlooks and differs from the communal average, then class, urban-rural or national identity differences can become crucial in building a majority coalition among Protestants or among Catholics. Cohesion makes political management of allies or opponents much easier. The distributions in Table X.7 emphasize the extent to which

Table X.7   Social structure and basic regime outlooks

			Protestants		Catholics	
			Urban	Rural	Urban	Rural
			%	%	%	%
Middle class	British	Support	72	75	60	(—)
		Non-compliance	49	54	25	(—)
	Irish	Support	63	(57)	21	43
		Non-compliance	39	(40)	52	60
Working class	British	Support	70	69	42	54
		Non-compliance	58	56	32	44
	Irish	Support	59	60	29	29
		Non-compliance	55	46	56	45

(—)=Less than ten cases: ( )=less than 20 cases.

outlooks are bi-polar, differing between religions. Among Protestants the median level of support in seven cells deviates only five per cent from the Protestant average; among Catholics, the deviation is ten per cent, and the greatest difference–the unusually high support given by British middle-class urban Catholics–comes from a cell with less than two per cent of the Northern Ireland population. By contrast, the difference between all Protestants and all Catholics in support for the regime is 35 per cent. Similarly, the median deviation from the communal average level of non-compliance is four per cent among Protestants and eight per cent among Catholics. The contrast between Ultras and disaffected Catholics is much greater than this. Thus, in terms of the Lipset-Rokkan framework, conflict about the regime is pervasively dispersed among many little groups.

The inability of *a priori* hypotheses to locate social characteristics other than religion that influence regime outlooks is not conclusive evidence that discord is found independently of social structure. It may simply be a reflection of the invalidity or inappropriateness of theoretical assumptions in the hypotheses. To guard against this, one can inductively try to locate social characteristics associated with distinctive political outlooks by using multivariate statistical techniques to see whether other sources of disaffection and Ultra views can be found by such searching. If multiple social influences do exist, then multivariate statistical analysis can uncover these, and will attribute a relatively high degree of explanatory power to them. In so far as the statistical analysis explains only a relatively low proportion of the total variation in society then as John Sonquist, an expert statistician notes, this provides 'convincing evidence that a particular variable of interest does *not* have any effect on the phenomenon under consideration when theory predicts that it should'.[16] This would further buttress the conclusion that discord is pervasive rather than confined to a few defined *and* confinable groups. If only religion and its immediate political and sectarian correlates appear as the most important influences, this would further substantiate the picture of dispersion at bi-polar extremes.

A statistical technique known as Automatic Interaction Detector (AID) analysis is particularly appropriate for detecting social categories relatively homogeneous in political outlooks.[17] A high-speed computer can readily test all possible combinations of social characteristics relating to support for the Constitution or compliance with basic political laws. Then, at each stage of the analysis, the population is divided by that characteristic which best differentiates people in terms of their political views. Each of the resulting pairs is then analysed again in the same way, until only trivial variations are found in subdivisions and/or only trivial numbers remain in each group. The successive subdivisions are like branches of a tree; hence the technique is often known as tree analysis. As the name implies, the statistical procedures take into account interaction effects, that is, circumstances in which outlooks change substantially if two social characteristics occur together, but fail to change at all if only one occurs. In order to maximize the opportunity of locating meaningful social structure influences, a total of 23 different social characteristics were included in the AID analysis. The measures ranged from sex and education through place of residence and class to church attendance.

The Structure of Communalism

The importance of religion in relation to support for the Constitution is demonstrated by the fact that it is the most important differentiating influence. It accounts for 35 per cent of the variance; the remaining eight branchings together account for an additional 5·6 per cent of the variation to be explained. The homogeneity of the Protestant community is reflected by the fact that 88 per cent are placed in the first branch of the tree after religion, an end group that could not be further subdivided: this category consists of Protestants who support the Unionist Party. Differences within the Catholic community are reflected by the appearance of seven end groups in the several branches of the Catholic side of the tree. In addition to religion, friends' religion, income, constituency location and party preference all differentiate Catholics at least a little from each other. There is, however, no politically meaningful pattern in these subdivisions nor is any statistically strong.[18] While the Catholic community is dispersed into many parts, it is also polarized in relation to the Protestant community, for only one of its ten groups had a higher mean support score than one of the Protestant groups.

As a further exploration of the relative importance of social characteristics, views on the Constitution[19] were also analysed by a second multivariate technique—Multiple Classification Analysis.[20] This test, involving 10 major variables, also showed the same pattern of influences: religion, party, church attendance and the religious character of the immediate area are the most important influences taken singly, and class and trade union membership are of very little importance (Table X.8). The pattern of dispersion is emphasized by the fact that the multiple correlation explained only 15·9 per cent of the variance. When the analysis is run separately for Protestants and Catholics, to see what besides religion influences support for the Constitution, the proportion of variance explained is very low, 4·8 per cent for Protestants and 5·1 per cent for Catholics. Politically, the consequences of these findings are equally difficult. The bunching of Protestants reflects the fact that both Ultras and fully allegiant people give verbal endorsement to the Constitution. The dispersion of Catholics presents politicians of that community with a particularly difficult job of brokerage.

In analysing compliance with basic political laws, Protestant Ultras and Catholic rebels were placed at opposite ends of a continuum and Ulstermen prepared to obey all laws in a single intermediate category, to make it possible to combine Protestant and

Catholic replies to different but comparable questions. The importance of religion for the aggregate pattern of compliance is shown by the fact that the tree analysis again found it the most important differentiating influence. Religion accounts for 48·3 per cent of the variance; the other seven branchings together account for an additional 5·3 per cent of the total variation of attitudes toward compliance.[21] Of these secondary influences, membership in the Orange Order, party preference and the religious character of friends are directly linked to religion. Among Protestants, it is particularly striking to note that members of the Orange Order could not be subdivided by any other socio-economic variable; they form an end group in the tree, without any further differentiation within the Order. Among Catholics, the same was true of those who lived in East and West Belfast and in Fermanagh and South Tyrone, areas where anti-regime parties have done well among Catholic voters. In all, nine end groups result. In theory, this number of groups could form a variety of coalitions–but for the fact that religion is such a barrier to coalition across communal lines.

Table X.8   Social characteristics influencing regime outlooks

	Support		Compliance	
MCA coefficients for	*Eta*	*Beta*	*Eta*	*Beta*
Religion	·361	·250	·711	·562
Party identification	·370	·190	·636	·194
Age	·097	·089	·079	·074
Urban residence	·118	·079	·174	·073
Have lived away from N.I.	·097	·074	·086	·063
Church attendance	·163	·067	·377	·014
Trade union membership	·069	·066	·045	·028
Class	·080	·048	·101	·033
Pass examination	·054	·025	·079	·052
Religion in neighbourhood	·152	·022	·329	·029

(In Multiple Classification Analysis, the square of the eta statistic indicates the proportion of the total sum of squares explained by the variable concerned. The value of the beta coefficient measures the explanatory power of a variable after adjusting for the effects of all other predictors. For a discussion, see Frank Andrews *et al.*, *Multiple Classification Analysis*, p. 22 and p. 110.)

Mutual Classification Analysis explains 52·9 per cent of the variance in attitudes toward compliance with basic political laws.The most important single influence of the ten examined is again religion;

The Structure of Communalism

party preference is the second most important influence. By comparison, all other socio-economic characteristics have little weight (Table X.8). This point is emphasized when attitudes of Protestants and Catholics are analysed separately, thus controlling for religion. In such circumstances, the proportion of variation explained among Protestants is 5·7 per cent, and among Catholics, 7·5 per cent. This underscores the extent of dispersion at bi-polar extremes.

If maximizing statistical correlation were an end in itself, then there would be much to be said for randomly correlating political, social and economic attitudes with basic political outlooks. This will not be done here, because of the risk that correlations between two separate questions concerning opinions may reflect nothing more than a single underlying attitude. If, for instance, one found a correlation between views about the Catholic Church in the Republic and views about the regime in the Republic, one could not conclude from this whether the people giving this pair of responses were against the regime because of the church or vice versa. Equally plausibly, they might be against everything to do with the Republic, with church and state but two aspects of the object of their dislike.

The important point to establish here is the extent to which basic political outlooks form part of a generalized ideology or are independent of any specifiable cultural outlook. A reading of the history of Northern Ireland would suggest that people have two coherent and opposing sets of views about this world and the next world, explaining and justifying the political discord within their society. In such circumstances, it would be meaningless to write about political culture in the singular, for the very nature of politics would reflect a conflict between a Protestant-Unionist culture and a Catholic-Republican culture. To describe two sets of doctrines involving mutually exclusive political views as sub-cultures of an overarching set of beliefs is to imply a unity of outlooks that need not be present. In so far as two very distinctive cultures or ideologies exist, then discord about the regime can be seen as a conflict between two sets of true believers, each with minds and hearts closed to the values, beliefs and emotions of their opponents. It would follow from this that a decline or change in ideological thinking would also lead to a decline in Ultra and disaffected political outlooks, if the latter are part of some general *weltanschauung*. Yet contemporary survey research in England, America and other countries has found that only a limited fraction of the population hold a general political

322

philosophy that is articulated in a reasonably coherent ideological manner.[22] In so far as articulated ideologies are not found in society, this would mean that pro- and anti-regime views are independent of other values and beliefs. This autonomy would make them impervious to change when other views changed. It would also mean that differences about the regime need not inhibit agreement about many other issues. As far as the vast bulk of issues are concerned, politics could be conducted harmoniously. Politics would become discordant only when unique issues arose concerning the regime.

Statistically a straightforward way to test for the existence of underlying attitudinal dimensions is to do a factor analysis of responses to attitude questions, thus identifying the extent to which replies to individual items reflect common considerations. Because the Loyalty survey focused on a relatively narrow range of issues related to Constitutional questions, there is much reason to expect coherent attitude dimensions to be discernible. In so far as a general cultural outlook exists in Northern Ireland, then in a factor analysis a relatively high proportion of the total variance in attitudes would be explained, a relatively large number of attitudes would be affected by each factor, and there would be a limited number of separate underlying factors. The reverse would indicate that no general ideology or conflicting ideology existed among Ulster people.

To discern the extent of ideological coherence, 36 different attitudes about politics, religion, economic matters, local community, national identity, and personality matters were subjected to factor analysis. The results once again confirm the extent of dispersion in cultural outlooks, for the four factors together explain only 25 per cent of the total variance, a surprisingly low figure.[23] Of the 144 factor loadings calculated, only four were higher than ·60, and another six higher than ·50. Each of the four factors explained about the same amount of variance. Two concerned religion. One of these factors loaded high in terms of strength and certainty of religious belief, and attachment to Northern Ireland; the other loaded high in relation to ecumenism and breaking laws conflicting with religious principles. Another factor isolated four measures of interest in politics as a cluster. The final factor emphasized approval of big business and a belief that some people are born to rule.[24] The distinctive importance of a few religious and political concerns is again demonstrated by the fact that the attitudes having the highest proportion of variation accounted for by the factors (i.e., commonality scores of more than ·40) are three religious measures and two concerning political involvement. The low scores of economic, local community, personality and national identity measures emphasize, in a complementary fashion, the extent of dispersed bi-polarization in general cultural outlooks, notwithstanding the existence of long-established, comprehensive and clearly articulated ideologies in Northern Ireland.[25]

From a politician's point of view, the aggregate distribution of political attitudes is more important than the configuration of views within an individual. In aggregate, congruence, a form of consensus, will exist, notwithstanding differences of opinion between individuals, if the profiles of attitudes within the Protestant and Catholic communities are identical or nearly so. Similarly, dissensus will prevail if there is no overlap in attitudes among individual Catholics and Protestants on an issue, even if there is a considerable amount of disagreement within each community. The latter model describes a situation of dispersion at each end of a polarized conflict situation, and the former a society in which differences of opinion about issues do not parallel the major social difference. One can also distinguish a situation in which there is some overlapping and some disagreement between Protestants and Catholics.[26] In reality, it is unlikely that either pure consensus or pure dissensus will be approached, yet there is no *a priori* reason why opinions should divide so as to produce an equal proportion of members in agreement and disagreement with each other within and between the two communities.

Culture conflict would be pervasive if Protestant and Catholic views approached dissensus on a wide range of attitudinal questions. The preceding chapters have shown that this is not the case. The difference index, which would register 100 per cent in a situation of complete dissensus between the two communities, has tended toward 0, showing a very high degree of consensus in aggregate between Protestants and Catholics. The existence of much similarity about so many aspects of Ulster life provides an explanation for the persistence of civil society simultaneously with political discord and disorder. Political differences are confined to one part of life. Moreover, in so far as a person's life is not primarily concerned with political affairs, then the scope for overt clashes with those of the other religion is thereby lessened.

The chief values and beliefs of the *political* culture show a very different profile. Two contrasting outlooks exist. A review of the different indices for each of the attitude questions in the survey shows that the most dissensual values (i.e., a difference index of more than 25 per cent) are about constitutional and related sectarian matters. In the distinctive circumstances of Ulster, dissensus is also relatively high in matters concerning Christian ecumenicism. One of the highest difference index ratings—61 per cent—concerns a factual [*sic*] matter: discrimination against Catholics. This is extremely appropriate, inasmuch as it was this issue that stimulated the civil rights demonstrations of 1968, which by action and subsequent reaction has shown the intensity of discord. The fragmentation of Unionists when confronted with civil rights challenges, and the fragmentation of Catholics when confronted with Protestant resistance jointly emphasize that polarization on matters concerning the regime does not mean that those at each extremity are united. Instead, they are dispersed. In aggregate this fragmentation carries autonomy to the point of confusion. It characterizes armed political groups as well as non-violent parties. As Ultra and IRA groups have demonstrated, fragmentation is no obstacle to sporadic, localized and intense expression of anti-regime views.

Because conflicts about basic political values can coexist with otherwise friendly relationships, one must conclude that bringing Protestants and Catholics together more—whether in housing, in schools or in a host of ways—will *not* lead to a reduction in political discord. Such measures may well be recommended on non-political grounds, in the hope that their political consequences would be neutral. It is possible that social mixing may have negative political effects. This is most evidently the case in housing, for the religious minority in a locality will have to live with affronts to their political views, whether expressed on the Twelfth or Easter Monday. In times of crisis, particularly in Belfast, people may prefer to abandon their homes and retreat to a totally segregated area where they can be safer from the peril of riot, fire and bullet.[27]

The spatial and social dispersion of opponents of the regime makes full coercion as difficult to achieve as full legitimacy or full repudiation. Spatial dispersion is specially important inasmuch as the regime risks challenge at literally hundreds of points within its 5,206 square miles. Defending and preventing every potential object of anti-regime attack is impossible, however large the police or army.

XI · Socialization into Conflict

I sometimes dream about Members of Parliament falling off a mountain top with a dagger in their backs, and sometimes they are drowning in the Laggan.

Essay, 9-year-old CATHOLIC BOY

If the R.C. school beside us was the only school in the world I wouldn't go to it. There's a chapel just beside us too and Fenians have fired shots off the roof there. But my big brother has two guns and ammunition at home.

Essay, 10-year-old PROTESTANT BOY

The most important feature of political socialization is what a person learns, not how he learns it. In a fully legitimate regime, virtually everyone develops an allegiant outlook. But in a regime lacking full legitimacy, such as Northern Ireland, the process of learning about politics involves contingent and mutually exclusive alternatives; an individual learns to accept *or* reject the regime. In the first instance, a young person unselfconsciously adjusts to the existing authority; in the other, he learns that the regime should be adjusted (i.e., overthrown) to fulfil the values of those who shape his outlook. American and English social scientists studying the development of political outlooks stress the extent to which values and beliefs are constant from generation to generation. For example, one explanation for the full legitimacy of the regime in England today is the resolution of problems of civil war and mass enfranchisement in previous centuries.[1] But pattern maintenance is a neutral process. In a regime lacking full legitimacy, the tendency of each generation to reflect views from the past means that discord about the regime persists through time, as one generation of Orangemen and Republicans is succeeded by another.

A model of political socialization emphasizing the persistence of political attitudes from generation to generation is *prima facie* relevant in a land where 'Remember 1690' is a contemporary political slogan. Carried to an extreme, such a model posits that no change in political outlooks can ever occur. Yet the history of Irish politics shows that significant, even revolutionary changes have occurred in the lifetime of many people living in Ulster today. No greater change can be imagined than that which followed the Troubles in the 1920s – the abolition of the old Dublin Castle regime and the institution of new regimes in both Dublin and Belfast. Such disjunctions with the past challenge an individual to think again about his habitual political outlook. It does not follow that he will necessarily alter his views to fit the claims of the new regime. While regimes can be started afresh, in terms of constitutional theory if not political genealogy, an individual can only respond to a new set of political institutions in the light of what he has learned under the old regime. Thus, in Northern Ireland, political learning is socialization into discord not harmony.

The process is best conceived as an accumulation of individual experiences, beginning in early childhood and continuing into adult life. It includes conventional political experiences, such as exposure to election campaigns, and for some, unconventional experiences, e.g., being burned out of one's house during a riot. Neither the experiences nor the results will be the same for everyone. The question is: are they complementary? In England, experiences cumulatively prepare persons for complementary roles as political leaders exercising authority, or as subjects of authority. A small proportion, for example, a working-class boy at Oxford, will be subjected to conflicting pressures in the process.[2] In Northern Ireland, ideal-type models are alternative and discordant. The ideal-type Protestant, from his birth into a strong Unionist family to adult membership in the Orange Order, is differentiated in his regime outlook from an ideal-type Irish Catholic, moving through the local Catholic school to adult participation in Gaelic sports and Republican parades on Easter Monday. Variations from ideal-type experiences may also explain deviations from ideal-type outcomes. In so far as the causes of contemporary variations can be found in influences relatively amenable to change, e.g., the schools or the mass media, then the possibility of altering political discord is proportionately increased. In so far as the most important influences must be taken as unalterably given in the short run, e.g., prior childhood experience, then prospects are proportionately reduced for changing basic regime outlooks except in the very long run.

The significance of religion in socialization is great and unalterable because it is ascribed at birth by derivation from the infant's parents. While Catholicism and Protestantism are not inherited genetically, they can have all the force of an inherited distinction in a society in which religious identification is important to others, even if it is not to the individual so labelled. Those who forswear religious beliefs are still labelled by others by their former religion. In the Northern Ireland vernacular, a non-believer must be either a Protestant atheist or a lapsed Catholic, just as a Jewish convert to Christianity is considered an ex-Jew and not a gentile. The claim of religion as an inalienable birthright (or curse) is advanced by the Catholic Church, since any person baptized a Catholic is reckoned a Catholic for life.

In so far as gross religious identification is important and ascribed at birth, then one could hypothesize that the chief influence upon political outlooks was not gradual exposure to social institutions, whether the schools, the mass media or the church, but rather precursive: the religion of a person's parents. Just as one may explain a child giving allegiance to the British regime if born of English parents, or to the Swedish Crown if born of Swedish parents, so one might hypothesize that birth as a Protestant or catholic is the primary determinant of regime outlooks in Northern Ireland. The experiences that follow in childhood and adulthood can reinforce or alter this basic predisposition, but only to a limited extent. Inasmuch as 96 per cent of persons interviewed reported that both parents were of the same religion, transmission of a Protestant or Catholic identity almost always occurs unambiguously at birth. Existence of variations in outlooks within both the Protestant and Catholic communities is sufficient to emphasize that the primacy of religion at birth is relative and not absolute. One might expect that deviations would most likely be found among the small proportion of people born of parents with different religions, and thus exposed within the home to tensions of the larger society. The regime outlooks of these offspring today are, however, no different in profile from those who grew up in religiously homogeneous homes. Children of mixed marriages have a clearcut adult religious identity with all its political consequences.

Families may differ in the interpretation that parents give to the religious divisions of Northern Ireland. To assess this, each respondent was asked what sort of attitude his parents had toward mixing between Protestants and Catholics when he was a child. The replies show a high degree of recollected goodwill. A total of 40 per cent said their parents were actively friendly, and another 43 per cent said they had a live-and-let-live attitude; only 13 per cent said that parents were against mixing with the other religion. The views reported were slightly more friendly among Catholics; the difference index is 13 per cent. Even allowing for some error in recall, the basic point is clear: the majority of people in Northern Ireland today were not raised by parents who actively opposed their meeting people of the other religion on a live-and-let-live or friendly basis. These recollections also imply that good relations between Protestants and Catholics extend back to times before the Troubles.

Sex is another ascriptive characteristic potentially able to influence attitudes toward the regime. In nearly every society, women are expected to be less inclined to hold political office than men. For example, in Northern Ireland at the time of the Loyalty survey, two of the 52 members of the House of Commons were women, and no woman held a senior administrative post at Stormont. Moreover, nearly all the persons who have died in the violence of the 1960s have been men; this is also true of individuals sentenced to jail for participation in political demonstrations. The reasons for female abstention from politics is not difficult to surmise. Responsibilities in rearing families, especially large families, will restrict the activities of women outside the home; working women will still retain their domestic duties. The concern of many women with things about the house might make them apathetic about the Constitution. The concern of women with the family might make them oppose illegal demonstrations and, *a fortiori*, violence. A man may achieve glory by fighting and dying for his country, whichever one it is. But in life, as in an O'Casey play, a woman can only achieve widowhood.

The survey data show less rebellion and Ultra views among women than men; 26 per cent of Protestant women and 42 per cent of Catholic women have no opinion about the Constitution. In total, 33 per cent of women as against 19 per cent of men have no views about the Constitution. There is no similar sign of apathy about questions concerning basic political laws. Protestant men are ten per cent more likely than their women to express a willingness to fight to keep Northern Ireland Protestant; 48 per cent of Protestant women also endorse Ultra views. Among Catholics, 53 per cent of the men and 43 per cent of women endorse illegal demonstrations against the regime. The difference in outlooks is in the expected direction, but the degree is limited and of little aggregate political importance. The similarity in outlooks does not reflect wives adopting the views of their husbands, for unmarried women have much the same outlook as women who are married.

330

Socialization into Conflict

The failure of sex to differentiate political outlooks is consistent with studies elsewhere that show sex is of little importance for party allegiance. The finding is surprising, in so far as membership in the Orange Order, a major institutional base of the Ultras, is confined to men, and in so far as Republican mythology stresses the man's role as the warrior fighting for Cathleen ni Houlihan. The fact that women are almost as ready as men to oppose the regime has important consequences for maintaining discord from generation to generation. In so far as disaffected women have husbands with similar views, then children will be raised in a household in which *both* parents display attitudes undermining the regime. It is much easier for children to accept such views than would be the case if fathers often advocated extreme political action, while mothers were bemoaning such opinions and their consequences. The permeation of whole families by anti-regime outlooks puts very strong and immediate emotional sanctions behind attitudes of disaffection and defiance.

The community in which childhood is spent exerts an influence independently of the immediate family. A child is reared not only by his parents but also by playmates and the adults in his immediate surroundings. The most extreme example of environmental effect should be a childhood spent outside Northern Ireland; this is determined by parents and not by the child himself. Of people interviewed, 92 per cent had spent most of their childhood within Northern Ireland; another four per cent had been raised in other counties of Ireland. There was no significant difference between Protestants and Catholics on this point. Only four per cent of respondents had come from England or further away;[3] of this small group, nearly three-quarters are Protestant. Potentially, Protestant migrants to Northern Ireland represent a force for change, because free of traditional predispositions to Ultra values. In so far as they adopt the outlooks of the natives, however, this would argue that an Ulster upbringing, while sufficient, is not a necessary condition of Ultra views. The survey found that Protestants coming into Northern Ireland as adults tend to adopt the outlook of fully allegiant subjects: 81 per cent support the Constitution, and 62 per cent reject the use of any measures to keep the country Protestant. While these outsiders are less ready to adopt an Ultra outlook than native-born Ulster Protestants, they are by no means impervious to it. Given the small proportion of immigrants, their aggregate influence in favour of full legitimation is very slight.

Socialization into Conflict

Within Northern Ireland, considerable local variations exist in religious milieu. Among Protestants, 57 per cent said they were brought up in a primarily Protestant area, and seven per cent in one primarily Catholic. Among Catholics, 38 per cent were brought up in a predominantly Catholic area and 14 per cent in a predominantly Protestant area. The median Catholic was raised in a mixed environment. The character of the area shows no influence upon attitudes toward the regime. As a further test, each person was also asked to describe what relations were like between Protestants and Catholics in the area in which he grew up. Among Protestants, 81 per cent said they were very good or fairly good, a judgment also endorsed by 83 per cent of Catholics. Notwithstanding the historical proximity of war, childhood was not recollected in an atmosphere of civil war tension between the communities. Only eight per cent of Protestants and seven per cent of Catholics said relations were 'not good' or 'bad'. Among the small group of Protestants who said relations were 'not good' (N=32), 72 per cent endorse Ultra views. However, among those who had grown up where relations were described as actively bad (N=25), only 28 per cent endorsed violence. For Catholics, a similar tendency appeared. This suggests that while sectarian bitterness will make people fighting mad, some who see its consequences in bloodshed and disorder will react against it.

Studies of the way in which American children learn about politics often suggest support for the hypothesis that if a child's earliest political awareness is benign, then as an adult he will have a positive attitude to the regime.[4] The illustration most frequently cited is the transfer of affection from the figure of the President or the Queen to the regime generally. In Northern Ireland, a child has two heads of state, two flags, two sets of patriotic songs and two symbols of heroism–the British Army and the IRA–to learn about. Pilot studies of Belfast children in 1970, following two years of demonstrations and killings in the city, emphasize how varied and intense are the elements that enter into political outlooks at an early age. Remarks made in essays and in classroom discussions by the very young emphasize limited or confused knowledge of politics.[5] 'My grandmother has a record of King Billy singing "The Sash My Father Wore". I've heard it often' (10-year-old Protestant boy). 'The Queen helps keep Britain tidy and she goes and sees disasters and sends the troops to help people who are being burned out' (8-year-old Catholic girl). The first remark shows the boy unaware of the chronology of Ulster history, for King Billy (i.e., William of Orange) died centuries before Orange songs could be recorded. Both remarks indicate a positive emotional response to misunderstood political figures.

The importance of value-laden emotions for political outlooks is explicitly illustrated by a dialogue between two 11-year-old Protestants. A boy comments, 'I don't like Paisley. He makes too much noise. When you go to his church he stands up and goes "Yah! Yah! Yah!" all the time. I don't like it.' A girl classmate replies, 'No. That's not true. He's a very nice man and very kind to children.' Emotions need not focus upon major symbolic figures. For example, a 12-year-old Catholic boy reports, 'We're frightened all the time. Even when we go to mass we can't think to pray right we're so frightened they're going to attack the chapel.' The political values and beliefs of young children often have a high emotional content too. A 10-year-old Protestant boy believes, 'Fenian shop-keepers sell poisoned things to Protestants to kill them off. I found poison in a lemonade bottle I got from one of them.' Similarly, a 7-year-old Catholic boy believes that a citizen is 'somebody in Belfast who drives his car with a gun beside him' and a 9-year-old Catholic, 'If our Lord tried to stop a street fight the Protestants would kill him.'

Values are sometimes expressed in a very straightforward way. A 10-year-old Protestant states that if she were writing a letter to the Prime Minister it would read, 'Dear P.M. I'm backing Britain.' Similarly, an 8-year-old Catholic boy matter of factly explains his view of Ulster, 'I don't like Northern Ireland 'cause it's got dirt and Proddy dogs and too many bombs and things.' But many childish comments appear to express fantasies. For instance, a 10-year-old Protestant boy boasts, 'To change what the Government is doing I'd hit them in the face and throw bombs at them and burn the Ormeau bakery and keep the trouble running.' A 14-year-old Catholic boy asserts, 'I'd like to get all the members of the government in one plane and then hi-jack it and take them off.' In an Ulster context, however, it would be historically inaccurate to describe accounts of bombings, shootings and fighting as fantasies. After all, the adults who fight and bomb and kill were not long ago children like those quoted here. In a land in which nearly every form of political violence has been used, no security officer of the regime would dismiss as fantasy a youngster's claim that he will some day hi-jack an airplane with the Prime Minister on it.

Socialization into Conflict

The accounts that Northern Ireland children give of politics after two years of recurring disorder need not be typical of the experience of previous generations of Ulster people, or such early memories may not persist into adulthood. Yet the frequent recurrence of disorder means that no generation is completely free from some exposure to such events. To explore this, each adult interviewed in the Loyalty survey was asked to recall the earliest political event that he could remember from his own lifetime (Table XI.1). The modal Protestant

Table XI.1 Earliest political memories

Type of event:	Protestant %	Catholic %	Total %
Violence and insurrection	25	28	26
Orange or Republican activities	11	7	10
World Wars	18	16	18
British affairs: elections, Coronations, etc.	13	6	10
Economic phenomena, e.g., depression	1	1	1
Can't recall; don't know	31	41	35
		D.I. =	13%

or Catholic was first introduced to politics in explicitly violent terms, e.g., the rising in Dublin, gun battles with the police, or by Orange parades or Republican rallies, recalling violent events. The most dramatic recollection of all was from the respondent who said his first political memory was 'being shot in Lisburn'. In the context of Northern Ireland, a memory such as the heavy bombing of Belfast in 1941 is non-violent, i.e., destruction unconnected with a campaign by or against local rebels. Only one-tenth of persons recalled events that were peaceful as well as potentially benign, such as a Coronation or a British general election. The failure of one-third of the population to voice any early political recollection does not mean that such persons have no political awareness. Such an inference is rejected by the very few don't know replies to other political questions. Instead, it suggests that many adults have difficulty in recollecting which of so many major political events came first to their consciousness in a society in which the past has so many landmarks.

Where early political memories are malevolent, then individuals should be less inclined to give full allegiance. Memories of violence, insurrection, or Orange and Green events might be considered malevolent by an outside observer, because threatening disorder or death. Yet, to an Ulsterman, such events may be as reassuring and positively benign as the stories that American children hear about the Revolution of 1776 or that English children learn about the Battle of Waterloo. One might therefore hypothesize that such recollections will make those exposed to them more likely to be Ultra or disaffected, according to their religion. There is a slight tendency for Catholics with such memories to be more likely to disapprove of the Constitution and for Protestants to endorse it; the difference in each instance is less than ten per cent. A similar slight tendency occurs regarding compliance with basic political laws. If anything, familiarity with violence in childhood hardens political outlooks. In view of the great exposure of many young people to Ultra and rebel activities in 1969–70, the tendency, while small, is no comfort to officials of the regime.

As a child grows he is increasingly exposed to education, important in itself and as a means to many valued adult goals. Schooling can influence people by the amount and sophistication of instruction, by its content, and, not least, by social relations with classmates. In Northern Ireland, a clearcut division in the educational system separates state schools and Catholic schools. The state schools provide non-denominational religious instruction, as in England. The hierarchy of the Catholic Church regards such instruction as inadequate for Catholic children, and maintains its own system of schooling for Catholics. Thus, the absence of Catholic pupils turns the state schools into Protestant schools. Only at Queen's University, Belfast, the New University of Ulster and in technical colleges does the hierarchy willingly accept co-education of Protestants and Catholics. The justification of separate schools–often described as segregated by Protestants–is religious, not academic. In the words of the Catholic Bishop of Down and Connor, Dr. William Philbin:

> It is by the standards of the Gospel, not by those of the current wave of secularism that we must judge ourselves. In these days, particularly when anti-religious influences are growing in strength, we feel we can protect the faith of the next generation only through our schools.[6]

Protestants often complain that the existence of separate schools causes or helps maintain political conflict in Northern Ireland. Many Catholics reject this argument. As a matter of historical fact, political discord in Ulster antedates by centuries the introduction of separate and compulsory education. Dr. Philbin has also argued that the teaching of the Catholic Church works 'in the direction of restraint and patience, a refusal to return injury for injury',[7] that is to say, it does not encourage disaffected Catholics to turn to rebellion.

Existing educational structures are not popular with Northern Ireland people. Surveys show that a clear majority–64 per cent of adults and 65 per cent of youths–favour educating Protestant and Catholic children together. Among Catholics, 69 per cent approve of integrated education, as against 26 per cent endorsing separation. The fact that parents as well as young people favour mixed education indicates that this disapproval is not a consequence of the educational unrest of the late 1960s, but a considered judgment.[8] A further indication of popular support for education without regard to denominational issues is shown by the fact that 64 per cent of the Protestants approved the idea that as much public money should go to Catholic schools as to Protestant schools; 23 per cent expressed disapproval. Under legislation prevailing at the time, Catholic schools received more than two-thirds of their funds from the state, a position far more favourable than that in the United States. In 1968, legislation was passed increasing very substantially state aid to Catholic schools; the law now provides funds on much the same basis as in England.[9]

Notwithstanding the preference of Northern Ireland people for mixed schools, five-sixths have been educated solely in Protestant or Catholic schools. Among people born and educated in Northern Ireland the difference index is extreme–83 per cent. Among Ulster residents born outside Northern Ireland, segregated education is also the rule. The two per cent of respondents who had been educated in a denominational school opposite to their present religion reflect the incidence of religious conversion. In view of the stress that the Catholic Church lays upon the conversion of Protestants in the case of a mixed marriage, it is hardly surprising that three-quarters of the very small number of conversions are to Catholicism. Non-denominational education in Northern Ireland, like desegregation of schools in America, is often valued because mixed schools are expected to encourage friendliness between groups. Proponents also expect non-denominational schooling to reduce political discord. There are sufficient persons with a mixed education to measure how such exposure affects political outlooks. The surprising conclusion is that, while attendance at mixed schools tends to reduce Ultra and rebel views, it does so only to a very limited extent (Table XI.2). The finding is the more striking, because those in mixed education are disproportionately not born in Ulster. The limited effect of separate education is consistent with a variety of studies elsewhere of Catholic and state schools.[10]

The failure of mixed schooling to have more influence upon political outlooks may be explained in at least two ways. Education is but one among a multitude of formal and informal influences upon political attitudes. Inasmuch as a child's school is effectively determined by his parents' ascribed religion, then schooling can do little about differences that exist before a child commences education. Another possible explanation is that a better understanding of the opposite religion gained by integrated education will not necessarily lead to greater trust. A Catholic in a mixed school may learn that

Table XI.2 The effect of mixed schooling upon political attitudes

| | Protestant | | Catholic | |
	Protestant schools %	*Mixed* %	*Catholic schools* %	*Mixed* %
Constitution				
Supports	67	72	32	31
Disapproves	10	5	36	21
Don't know	22	23	33	40
	D.I. = 5%		D.I. = 11%	
Basic political laws				
Refuses compliance	55	47	48	36
Favours compliance	45	52	52	64
	D.I. = 7%		D.I. = 12%	

when Protestants say 'Not an inch' they mean it, just as a Protestant may learn that his Catholic classmates refuse to regard the Union Jack as the flag to which they give allegiance. The very limited extent to which mixed education affects attitudes is not sufficient to justify its introduction on the ground that political discord can be ended by integrating schools. This would require years of negotiation about existing institutions and to establish new schools. Then, it would literally take generations before the bulk of the adult population of Northern Ireland had been exposed to the weak ameliorating influence of mixed education.

Denominational differences in schools may be unimportant because of wide variations among Protestant or among Catholic schools, arising from a headmaster's influence, or local considerations affecting the school's informal norms. Bernadette Devlin, for

Socialization into Conflict

example, gives particular weight to the influence of the headmistress of her convent school, Mother Benignus, a fanatical Republican and Gaelic enthusiast.[11] To test local influences, respondents were asked whether their teachers were mostly Unionists, Nationalists or politically indifferent. Among Protestants, 41 per cent said their teachers were Unionists, one per cent Nationalist, and nine per cent reported they were mixed in views. Among Catholics, 46 per cent recall having Nationalist teachers, eight per cent teachers with mixed views, and three per cent Unionist teachers (D.I.$=45\%$). One would expect that those aware of the political views of their teachers would be most likely to support the regime if Protestant, and to reject it if Catholic. There is a slight tendency in this direction among Protestants, for among those with strong Unionist teachers, 75 per cent positively voice support for the regime as against 61 per cent who did not know their teachers' politics. In addition, 60 per cent with strong Unionist teachers endorse violence for political ends, as against 49 per cent without. Among Catholics, no significant difference is discernible.

Another indication that nationalist sentiments are important is that pupils are taught the Irish language at school. Among Catholics taught the Irish language, 29 per cent still endorse the Northern Ireland Constitution. There is only a very slight tendency to favour illegal demonstrations among Catholics taught Irish. This finding is striking, inasmuch as Irish language classes can be a recruiting ground for the IRA and other Republican groups. The very limited strength of these influences again emphasizes the influence of factors outside the school upon political outlooks.

Conventionally, social science theories emphasize that the amount of education of a young person is a major determinant of social and political attitudes. This assumes that the more a person is exposed to formal instruction, the more understanding he has of all kinds of complex phenomena. In a society in which a regime lacks full legitimacy, it is uncertain what the political consequences of further education might be. In so far as educational values favour the regime or lead people to jobs which give them a stake in the system, then it could increase support for the Constitution and for peaceful forms of political action. Yet, in so far as it increases understanding, it might lead Catholics or Protestants to the conclusion that only by refusing compliance with basic political laws could they attain desired ends.

To test for the effect of education, respondents were divided into

338

three groups: those with the minimum education required by law, leaving school at age 15 or before;[12] those with secondary education between the ages of 16 to 18, and those with higher education at university, teachers' training college or similar institutions.[13] Among Protestants, level of education has no effect upon support for the Constitution. It also has no effect among Catholics except among the five per cent with higher education; 54 per cent of the most educated Catholics actively disapprove of the Constitution. Among Protestants with higher education, 30 per cent endorse Ultra views, as against 49 per cent with secondary education and 57 per cent with minimum education. Among Catholics, the relationship is in the opposite direction. The most educated are the most likely to endorse illegal demonstrations: 58 per cent take this view, as against 43 per cent of those with a secondary education and 49 per cent with a minimum education. None of the Catholics with higher education endorsed the use of violence to Republican ends. Perhaps educated Catholics note the instrumental advantage of a minority challenging authority by non-violent means it finds difficult to suppress. As the most educated Catholics are also most explicit in their disapproval of the Constitution, this makes them specially predisposed to take part in demonstrations against the regime.

While the survey data show that higher education is a constraint upon violence, the finding has different implications for social scientists and for men in politics. To the former it demonstrates that even in a society where legitimacy is lacking, education encourages people to believe in settling disputes by reasonable means – especially if an illegal civil rights march may be considered 'reasonable' action. The bulk of professionally trained people – teachers, doctors, lawyers and such – are not inclined toward revolutionary violence or armed insurrection. But such a finding, while statistically impressive, is politically depressing, because this group constitutes only seven per cent of the Northern Ireland population. Given the limitation of resources for higher education, it would take generations for the majority of Northern Ireland people to reach this most educated stratum. In consequence, politicians working in the here and now face three immediate dangers. The educated Catholic civil rights movement, endorsing illegal but non-violent protests, is numerically smallest. More numerous are groups of Catholics with limited education endorsing the traditional Republican resort to violence, and Protestants with minimum education endorsing violence in opposition to them. At a time of political crisis, the leaders of the regime must appeal in simple terms capable of being understood and accepted by the two-thirds of the population with minimum education. But the arguments for avoiding force are not always simple in a land where the regime itself was founded in consequence of a popular civil war. Opponents of the regime have the advantage of expressing their appeals in simple, often dramatic language. Ultras can point to an illegal flag and urge a crowd to tear it down. Noncompliant Catholics can point to a line of police and urge a crowd to stone them, or build barricades against the police. The appeal of the educated politician for moderation will be fully understood by a small proportion of the population. The educational gap between politicians and followers handicaps leaders in communicating nuances and subtleties to agitated and agitating supporters.[14] For example, a man accustomed to the rhetoric of Parliament may regard the statement 'We must fight the enemy' as a metaphor. A person less versed in such sophisticated distinctions may take the injunction literally, with stark, even fatal consequences.

In late adolescence, British military service can claim two years or more of a young man's life. At this very formative stage, army service exposes a youth to extreme demands for loyalty to the regime he defends. But it also gives training in techniques of violence. Northern Ireland has never effectively had national military service. The British attempt to make conscription compulsory throughout Ireland in the First World War was a stimulus to rebellion. During the Second World War, volunteer recruits were raised in Northern Ireland, for the open border with a neutral Republic meant that any attempt at compulsion would have been of little avail. In consequence, the fraction of the population with experience in the British Army is limited; one-sixth of all men, of whom three-quarters are Protestants. Among Protestants with military experience, there is no particular readiness to apply military training on behalf of Ultra groups. The proportion endorsing violence to keep Ulster Protestant is 46 per cent, slightly lower than the national average. The small group of Catholic ex-soldiers, despite their previous service to the Crown, approximate a cross-section of Northern Catholics in their political outlooks.

Of all adult experiences, marriage can be the most central and enduring influence upon all kinds of social outlooks. Marriage often unites like-minded people whose views will reinforce each other, as well as creating bonds of trust and common concern encouraging one partner to adopt the views of the other. One would particularly expect that women would be predisposed to adopt the political views of their husbands, if they entered marriage with little or no political awareness. The proportion of the married Ulster population is high and rising, thus increasing the potential significance of the conjugal home. Divorce is rare, although legal, as divorce is not in the Irish Republic.[15] Endogamy reflects and helps perpetuate religious differences. Because the numbers who marry across religious lines is so small, four per cent,[16] one cannot analyse their political outlooks–nor would they have much significance in aggregate. The degree of family unity in political matters is indicated by the finding that only four per cent recalled that their parents supported different political parties, and in only three cases in 1,291 did parents differ across the divide of Orange and Green.

In adulthood, some people will substantially alter their life-styles, whether rising above the level of their parents, or falling below that status. Some political sociologists have argued that upward or downward mobility has important, even traumatic consequences for political opinions. Mobile individuals are assumed to project into politics tensions that might arise from changes in social status; people who do not experience such mobility are assumed to be stable in their political outlooks. It is also argued that support for anti-regime politics comes disproportionately from downwardly mobile individuals who are trying to compensate for their *déclassé* status, and/or from people who have risen in the world, yet in consequence of social mobility have difficulties in gaining acceptance in old-line status groups because they are 'upstart' in origin or manners.[17] In Northern Ireland, Protestants who have experienced substantial mobility would be expected to endorse Ultra views, as an extreme reaction. Catholics who are downwardly mobile might be most anti-regime, because of their increasingly disadvantaged position. Upwardly mobile Catholics would be more pro-regime, because they had prospered. Since these hypotheses combine sociological and social psychological assumptions about class, they provide a more sophisticated test of very general theories than do many hypotheses reviewed in Chapter IX.

Social mobility in Ulster can be experienced in at least three different ways. In the first instance, a man may rise to a better job than his parents or a woman may marry a man of a higher status than her father. But inter-generational mobility is experienced by only a limited fraction of the population. When respondents are classified into three[18] social strata–the business and professional middle class; the lower middle class and the working class–59 per cent of Protestants and 55 per cent of Catholics show no change in status from that of their parents; in addition, another nine per cent of Protestants and 13 per cent of Catholics gave insufficient evidence for firm classification. The maximum movement is up or down two strata; movement across one stratum could make a substantial change in life-style. Notwithstanding this, there is no consistent tendency for upward or downwardly mobile Catholics to have their views toward the Constitution altered by mobility, or to differ in their attitudes toward illegal demonstrations.

Another form of inter-generational mobility in Northern Ireland is movement from farming into the industrial or service sectors of the economy. This shift has been substantial in the twentieth century, because of the decline of agriculture. The Loyalty survey found that of those whose fathers were farmers, only 38 per cent are themselves still farmers. The movement from the farm has been more marked among Protestants than Catholics, perhaps reflecting greater opportunities for Protestant youths or greater ambition to get ahead. Leaving the farm to take a job in industry is a major change, for it removes a person from an intensely personal and family-centred job to a place where an individual works in an impersonal environment, independent of family and meeting people with a wide spectrum of views. Notwithstanding the extent of changes in living conditions arising from such shifts, they do not correlate consistently or strongly with differences in political outlooks.

In a lifetime of work, a man may rise or fall in his class standing. To assess the extent to which people have gone up or down during their working lifetime, questions were asked about the job of each person at age 21 and at the time of interview. The replies of women had to be excluded, because so high a proportion have been housewives at one time or at both. Among men providing full information, 77 per cent have not changed class in their adult life, 17 per cent have risen, usually a single stratum, and five per cent had fallen, almost invariably, a single stratum. (The proportion of upwardly mobile Catholics is consistent with their numbers in the population.) There is no significant association between mobility up or down and regime outlooks. The high proportion of the population that has been stable in class means that both defenders and opponents of the regime are secure in their place in Northern Ireland.

The mass media may challenge political attitudes of adults at any time by the presentation of varied news and views. This is particularly true of broadcasting, for the BBC and Ulster Television have licences requesting them to balance political viewpoints in their very public channels of communication. Watching television news and current affairs programmes exposes Ulster people to opinions that they might not hear, or not hear discussed neutrally or sympathetically, in their immediate environment. It could be hypothesized that awareness of a variety of political views would make an individual more likely to be fully allegiant, because of a recognition of the complex problems facing the regime.

In the period up to the outbreak of civil rights demonstrations, political programmes on television and radio implicitly accepted the regime as an inevitable consequence of publicizing legal and parliamentary forms of political activities that took the regime for granted. They could hardly do otherwise, because the alternative was to give equal time to illegal organizations, such as the IRA and the UVF. Officials of such organizations could not appear regularly on television without incriminating themselves and risking arrest. The values of public service broadcasting were also congenial to the political ethos of the O'Neill administration. Moreover, many parliamentary politicans welcomed the opportunity to present their views and their faces before wider audiences. The political heterogeneity of the audience provided an incentive to moderate views for politicians accustomed to speaking to an Orange Lodge or in a Catholic parish hall. In the Loyalty survey, 74 per cent said that they usually made a point of following such programmes (D.I.$=7\%$). These interested viewers used the medium to reinforce and not to modify their views, for they did not differ from non-viewers in attitudes toward the Constitution or in willingness to comply with basic political laws.

The potential influence of the press is different, for newspapers are not licensed to give news favouring many points of view, nor is there any political censorship restricting what they do print. Religious differences are an incentive for newspapers to concentrate their readership appeal, and both Belfast morning newspapers do this. The *News-Letter* focuses upon events of interest to the Protestant community, including Unionist activities; 87 per cent of its readership is Protestant. Similarly, the *Irish News* appeals to Catholic readers

Socialization into Conflict

with coverage of Gaelic sports, Catholic parochial news, and Republican activities. Its readership is 93 per cent Catholic. The Province's largest and only afternoon newspaper, the *Belfast Telegraph*, attempts to give wide coverage to all manner of political and social affairs in its news columns. The editorial line in the 1960s was liberal Unionist, with very strong support given Terence O'Neill. Its readership reflects the population of the Province: 68 per cent are Protestants and 32 per cent Catholic.

Newspaper readers in Northern Ireland have a wide choice beyond the local press, for they can also conveniently buy newspapers edited in Britain or in Dublin. Only five per cent report reading a Dublin daily paper, and another 32 per cent read a British paper. A slightly higher proportion of Catholics than Protestants read the British papers, suggesting that *The Mirror* and the *Daily Express* are read for their entertainment value and not for political news. Analysis of political outlooks by newspaper readership, controlling for religion, shows that there are no substantial differences about political outlooks among the major readership groups. For example, among Protestants reading the *Belfast News-Letter*, 56 per cent endorse Ultra views; but so do 52 per cent of Protestants reading the liberal Unionist *Belfast Telegraph*. Similarly, among Catholics reading the *Irish News*, 55 per cent endorse illegal demonstration, as do 48 per cent of Catholics reading the *Telegraph*. The absence of stronger correlations is evidence that those who take political news from the press evaluate what they read in terms of outlooks formed independently of their newspaper, and are not influenced by the paper's political position.

In times of political disorder, the mass media are often accused of 'creating' the troubles that they publicize. This is particularly true of television, which gives a visual and sometimes on the spot picture of disorder. Yet the supposed intimacy of television is a poor substitute for first-hand experience of trouble–until television can emit the smell of teargas, and occasionally scatter a hail of stones at its viewers. Moreover, broadcasters and journalists can prove that street fighting occurred in Northern Ireland long before the invention of the cathode tube or the rotary printing press.

The alternative to public reporting of political disorder is not popular ignorance, but rather, popular knowledge based on word-of-mouth information. News of discord can hardly be suppressed when riots occur in major cities in full sight of thousands of people. The dissemination of political information by word-of-mouth provides a field day for rumours to spread without verification or refutation. Reliance upon word-of-mouth knowledge in preference to public media betokens deep distrust of the honesty of established authorities. The Loyalty survey found that the public media are the most trusted source of news: 55 per cent said they thought TV and radio broadcasts the best source and another 24 per cent put the press first. Only four per cent named private conversations as the best source of information about Ulster politics (D.I.=9%). This emphasizes the extent to which Northern Ireland people have confidence in the freedom of the media to report the major news of the day.

The failure of so many major institutions of socialization to influence political outlooks casts further doubt upon efforts to relate social structure deterministically to political attitudes. Perhaps the chief determinants of basic political outlooks are not in the social structure but social attitudes. For example, the attitudes that people have toward political authority might be determined by the attitudes that they previously developed toward non-political authority figures such as parents or teachers. While social attitudes are related to social structure, they can be independently important as intervening variables influencing political outlooks. The attitudes of an individual toward other people may be described as his social personality. A variety of social scientists have stressed the importance of a good fit between the predominant social personality of a society and its form of government.[19] Because such theories concern general social predispositions, they are easier to test empirically with survey data than are statements about deep unconscious psychological drives, or about that familiar but vague abstraction 'national character'.

Diffuse attitudes toward authority, learned in such extra-political contexts as the home, school and work, are often hypothesized to be of major importance in the development of attitudes toward the authority of the regimes.[20] In Northern Ireland this would imply that individuals who accept[21] authority in extra-political concepts will be most inclined to give full political allegiance, and those who reject authority will be most likely to be Ultras or disaffected. Stated baldly, such a proposition ignores the fact that every individual goes through stages in his life in which he is dominated, e.g., as a child, or dominant, e.g., as a parent. This objection can be met by defining acceptance of authority in terms of the recognition of limited and role-specific

Socialization into Conflict

claims to obedience. From this, Harry Eckstein has developed a theory of stable democracy which postulates that the crucial determinant of full legitimacy is the extent to which there is a 'graduated resemblance' between political and extra-political authority patterns. Eckstein thus recognizes that a greater degree of hierarchy will occur in some aspects of social life than others. He also recognizes that regimes may vary in the extent to which they are organized in a hierarchical or egalitarian way. As long as the political style fits the extra-political style of authority, then there will be little basis for conflict about the regime, Eckstein asserts.[22]

To test the importance of diffuse authority patterns, individual respondents were asked how important they thought it that obedience should be given to agents of authority in six disparate areas of life—the family of origin, school, the conjugal home, at work, at church and in politics. Concentrating attention upon present attitudes avoids the risk that people asked to recollect events from their childhood will err in their recall. In so far as early socialization experiences are important, moreover, they should influence present attitudes. The question about the authority of parents over children was omitted, after piloting showed that nearly everyone thought it very important that children should obey their parents.

Table XI.3 Importance of obedience to authority figures

Very important for:	Protestant %	Catholic %	Total %	D.I. %
Pupils to obey teachers	73	77	75	4
Workers to obey employers	62	67	64	5
Church members to obey priest/minister	30	62	44	32
Citizen to obey government	38	41	39	4
Wife to obey husband	20	27	23	8

The result, by almost any set of expectations, was surprising (Table XI.3). Contrary to what was hypothesized, Protestants who think it very important to obey the government are disproportionately Ultra in their views; 66 per cent endorse non-compliance with basic laws, as against 47 per cent among those who do not think it at all important to obey government. In other words, those who say they are most obedient expect that the regime will order them to do what they want to do anyway. If it doesn't, it can be resisted. Among Catholics who think it is not at all important to obey the government,

346

19 per cent more endorse illegal demonstrations than among those who think it very important to obey government. The readiness of Catholics to respect directives of the priest is unrelated to views about illegal political demonstrations. This suggests that within the Catholic community there is no perception that the hierarchy is opposed to non-violent demonstrations deemed illegal by the Stormont regime. In areas more remote from politics, such as pupil-teacher and employer-employee relations, no association exists between respect for authority and regime allegiance. But the minority of Protestants who feel strongly about the rights of husbands to give commands to wives are also disproportionately Ultras.

Table XI.4   Diffuse obedience and political compliance

		Compliance with basic laws		
Obedience score		Protestant	Catholic	Total in category
		%	%	%
10	Highest	32	54	11
9	↑	44	60	9
8		36	55	15
7		38	50	14
6		41	46	16
5		52	52	13
4	↓	56	52	10
1–3	Lowest	61	50	12

To assess the political significance of a general predisposition to obey authorities, each person was assigned a place on a ten-point scale[23] reflecting his answers to each of the five questions listed in Table XI.3. Those scoring highest think it most important to obey all kinds of authorities; persons with the lowest scores give least emphasis to social obedience. The median score for Protestants is six, and for Catholics, seven. A total of 45 per cent of all Catholics think it very important to obey at least four of the five authority figures referred to, as do 29 per cent of all Protestants. In short, there is no tendency toward the diffuse rejection of authority by Ulster people. This is especially true among Catholics, who are most disaffected from political authority. One would hypothesize that the greater the general predisposition to obedience, the greater the level of compliance with basic political laws (Table XI.4). The relation is the reverse for Protestants, and nil for Catholics. Among the most generally obedient Protestants, only 32 per cent are fully allegiant, and 68 per cent endorse an Ultra outlook. Among the least obedient

Socialization into Conflict

Protestants, 61 per cent are fully allegiant, and 39 per cent endorse an Ultra outlook. The Protestant is not a rebel in the conventional social sense.[24] His willingness to take up arms reflects a rigid political outlook that cannot accept any compromise of the principle of Protestant rule. In conventional democratic politics, such inability to compromise is usually a liability, because it leads to political isolation. In civil war situations, it is an asset, because it increases the credibility of a threatened resort to arms, as well as making disaffected opponents unable to see any alternative but rebellion.

Table XI.5 Bases of political deference

Agree with statement:	Protestant	Catholic	Total	D.I.
	%	%	%	%
Some people are born to rule	70	59	65	11
People with the best education are best to govern	64	66	65	5
Gentlemen are the best to govern	40	34	37	8

Many studies of political authority in England assert the importance of deference to people with distinctive social attributes. Deference is not only assumed to affect voting, but also support for a regime led by men with upper-class social mannerisms. The major studies of deference in England have compounded two different claims to authority–deference to persons of noble birth and to persons educated in a gentlemanly manner at an elite public school, Eton.[25] In the process of trying to adapt these measures to Northern Ireland, where symbols of status are different in form, it became apparent that at least three bases for deference must be distinguished –birth, gentlemanly manners, and education. The first attribute is ascriptive: some people are born to rule and others are not. Gentlemanly manners mark the public schoolboy, inasmuch as training in a specific style of deportment is stressed in boarding schools, independently of intellectual training. In Northern Ireland, such manners are also a mark of Anglicization, since gentlemen speak with an Oxford not an Ulster accent. Education can command respect independently of birth and breeding. While educational achievements are highly valued by social scientists, popular attitudes toward those with 'book-learning' may be deferential, ambivalent, or openly antagonistic. In aggregate, birth is most deferred to (Table XI.5). It does not follow that those born to rule are necessarily those of the highest social status. The fact that gentlemen receive least deference suggests

Socialization into Conflict

that, at least for a portion of the respondents, it is Protestants rather than Anglo-Irish gentry that are the class reckoned born to rule. This interpretation is further supported by the difference in Protestant and Catholic ratings on this point. Catholics defer first of all to education.

Politically, one would expect that those readiest to defer would also be most likely to comply with basic political laws. Among Protestants, the reverse is the case. Those who are rated most deferential on a three-item scale[26] are also more likely to endorse an Ultra position: 60 per cent take this stand. But among Protestants who consistently reject any of these three claims to deference, 28 per cent endorse the use of violence. There is no correlation of deference and regime outlooks among Catholics. As in the case of attitudes described in Table XI.3, Protestants who show most regard for obedience outside the realm of politics are also most assertive and unyielding in their political views.

Willingness to defer to other people implies trusting others to take one's own concerns into account when decisions are made. In a divided regime, such trust might be low, as proponents and opponents of the regime have good reason to view sceptically the political actions of others. To assess the general feeling of trust, each person was asked whether he thought most people can be trusted or that one must watch out for other people. The responses show that 55 per cent are inclined to watch out and 39 per cent to trust. Catholics and Protestants have much the same view: the difference index is four per cent. The level of trust is lower by 16 per cent than that found in America and ten per cent lower than that found in Britain in a cross-national survey. The trusting group is also 20 per cent higher than that in Germany, and 32 per cent higher than that in Italy.[27] The political experience of Northern Ireland people has not made them as suspicious as Germans or Italians. There is no tendency for trusting attitudes to correlate with views about the Constitution. Untrusting Protestants were only eight per cent readier to endorse Ultra views and trusting attitudes were unrelated to Catholic readiness to demonstrate.

Attitudes toward change are another personality trait of potential political significance in Northern Ireland. People who believe that change is often for the better, or that they can direct the course of the future are very different in temperament from those who are pessimistic or fatalistic. In Northern Ireland, 58 per cent endorse trying

349

new things, as against 37 per cent who favour sticking by what they know. Protestants and Catholics are equally ready to trust in change (D.I.=4%). One might hypothesize that those who challenge the regime are readiest to trust in change. There is a very slight tendency for this to be true among Catholics. Among Protestants, a complementary tendency was found: 61 per cent of those fearful of change also endorse Ultra resistance to change. One reason why people may fear change is that they doubt their ability to influence the direction it takes. Yet most Ulster people show a high degree of confidence in their ability to control their own conditions of life: 78 per cent of Protestants and 67 per cent of Catholics agreed that a person can do a lot to change his way of life. (It is noteworthy that two-thirds of Catholics endorse what might be considered this very 'Protestant' assumption about individual responsibility.) Among Catholics feeling powerless, there is a slightly greater tendency to endorse illegal demonstrations: 56 per cent take this view, as against 44 per cent among Catholics who feel a person can influence his own future.

Beleaguered officials trying to defend a regime against disorder often argue that those who reject political authority are lawless hooligans. In social science terms, one would hypothesize that individuals who violate basic political laws are also inclined to disobey other kinds of laws, whether they concern walking on the grass, assault, robbery or arson. The hypothesis implies that the same conditions that cause anti-social crimes also cause anti-regime crimes. By defining opponents as pathologically anti-social, the regime can justify treating the demands made by these opponents as of no political consequence. To admit that those who attack the regime differ from anti-social criminals is to recognize the disaffected as political criminals, a label with important and disturbing implications. Yet, the hypothesis is inconsistent with certain known features of Ulster history. For instance, among the signers of the defiant Ulster Covenant were prominent Protestant lawyers and community leaders. Similarly, members of the IRA are expected to lead exemplary lives; many are teetotallers. Their major conventional crime is bank robbery. The robberies are not for personal gain, but to finance the purchase of arms.

To test the degree of support for lawless behaviour generally, each respondent was asked whether there were any laws or government regulations that a self-respecting person wouldn't necessarily have to obey. The pattern of replies shows that Northern Ireland people generally respect laws: 83 per cent of Protestants could name no law that they thought could be broken, and 71 per cent of Catholics took the same view. By comparison a similar question asked in the English community of Stockport found that 46 per cent of respondents could think of a law that might be broken.[28] Ironically, the laws that Ulster Protestants most often countenance violating concern Sunday observance, laws passed because of the influence of Sabbatarian Protestants. Among Catholics, the laws most mentioned as suitable to violate are political, especially the Special Powers Act. In Stockport, by contrast, the laws most likely to be violated had no political over-tones. A comparison of crime statistics in Northern Ireland with those for Scotland and England and Wales provides further confirma-tion of the generally law-abiding character of Northern Ireland people.[29]

Table XI.6   Attitudes toward law violations, Northern Ireland and England

	N.I. Prot %	N.I. Cath %	English town* %	D.I. Prot-Cath %	D.I. N.I.– England %
It is all right to:					
Fiddle income tax	13	18	11	7	9
Steal food in need	8	15	20	8	11
*Break law against religion/conscience	28	46	27	20	17

* In Northern Ireland, 'law against religion'; in Stockport, 'law against conscience'.

Sources: Loyalty survey: 1964 Stockport survey, reported in R. Rose and H. Mossawir, 'Voting and Elections', p. 190.

Further confirmation of the law-abiding morality of Ulster people is given by their replies to a series of questions asking specifically whether they approve of fiddling the income tax, stealing food when in need or breaking a law against one's religion. The answers again can be compared with those obtained in the survey of an English community (Table XI.6). The replies show that in intent both Protes-tants and Catholics are generally as law-abiding as their English neighbours. Significantly, the chief difference has political overtones, laws going against religion (D.I.=20%). A plurality of Catholics in Northern Ireland unambiguously endorse violating such laws.

The assertion that opponents of the regime are generally lawless

Socialization into Conflict

implies that people who favour violating basic political laws will also be ready to condone the violation of non-political laws. In fact, no such relationship exists. The great majority of Protestants and Catholics who reject compliance with basic political laws also reject the idea of fiddling their income tax, or stealing food if in need. Those who are potentially political criminals show the same readiness to accept non-political laws as do those who are ready to comply with the regime. The one exception is easily understood. Catholics prepared to endorse breaking laws going against their religion are 16 per cent more likely than those who do not to endorse illegal Republican demonstrations. The conclusion is clear and important. Both Protestant and Catholic opponents of the regime are strongly predisposed to obey the laws. They do not condone income tax violation or even the theft of food when personal survival may be at stake. Their disobedience is selective: they only endorse breaking a few laws. But these are just the laws that the regime deems crucial for its survival.

Another commonly voiced complaint about Northern Ireland by those who advise from the outside is that Ulster people are always bringing up the past. Proponents of a purportedly 'better' future can well argue that if Ulster people start thinking of the past then all is lost. Reciprocally, an Ultra or a Republican rebel may think, 'If we start forgetting the past, we are lost.' To test the evaluation placed upon past history, each person was asked whether he thought it was better to forget the past, or to accept that the troubles of the past cannot be ignored. Among Protestants stressing the importance of the past, 70 per cent actively endorse the use of force to keep the regime Protestant. Among Catholics emphasizing the past, 62 per cent endorse holding illegal demonstrations and 55 per cent stressing past events disapprove of the Constitution. But the aggregate effect of such commitment to the past is limited, inasmuch as only 15 per cent of Ulster people wish to conserve such memories; 82 per cent wish to look only to the future. This means that most who challenge the regime, whether Protestant or Catholic, do not stand upon past grievances, but rather, upon present grievances or fears of the future.

The desire to forget the past and look to the future may arise from a sense of historical fatalism, and not from confidence. Where past events have been benign, belief in predestination by past events will be reassuring or even provide a sense of over-confidence: 'There will always be an England', or more flamboyantly, 'God looks after fools, drunkards and Americans'. When the story of the past is one of travail, as in Northern Ireland, then consciousness of it may make an individual feel trapped by history, thus reducing his readiness to support or challenge the regime. To measure the extent of political fatalism within Northern Ireland, each person was asked three questions. The first was about the biggest problem 'troubling' the people of Northern Ireland: both Protestants and Catholics named economic issues. Spontaneous references to religious and constitutional difficulties came second in frequency, and were more often cited here than in reply to a question about things the government should do something about.[30] Each person was then asked: How would you say this first came about? Among those giving some reason, 36 per cent of Protestants and 43 per cent of Catholics explicitly referred to causes in the past.[31] Some reached back centuries to account for today's ills: 'It goes back to the Reformation!' 'The siege of Derry.' 'Cromwell and Britain caused it.' Moreover, many of the replies classified as contemporary references named conditions that have persisted for generations: bigotry, population increase, or even, perhaps, incompetent leaders. To conclude, each person referring to a problem was asked what, if anything, he thought the government could do about it. Surprisingly, only 17 per cent of all respondents said that nothing could be done about the country's biggest problem. By contrast, 59 per cent showed a positive faith in remedial action by government; the remainder were content or apathetic. Those expressing complete hopelessness were not particularly inclined to reject the regime, nor to endorse violation of basic political laws because of their frustration.

The absence of a widespread sense of fatalism in Northern Ireland has important political implications. It means that there is no large, apathetic group in society whose support for a regime might be mobilized by initiatives from political leaders. The faith that people have in their ability to influence their future is an encouragement to action, not apathy or political passivity. Individuals who feel aggrieved by the policies of the regime do not feel helpless. This is true whether the aggrieved are Ultras, Republicans, or fully allegiant subjects. If such persons decide to act, they act self-confidently, hoping for a better future to be gained by taking the law into their own hands.

Because the great bulk of people interviewed do not articulate consciously an awareness of the past does not mean that past events

Socialization into Conflict

are of no significance in their political socialization. To explain discord about the regime in terms of the ascription of religious differences at birth is not to prove that parents have caused this discord. It only raises the question: How did their parents come to think this way about religion? Any reply to this question must then consider phenomena extending back centuries in time to the Reformation politics of Henry VIII, because the chief institutions related to discord–the Catholic and Protestant churches–institutionalize ideologies that long antedate the foundation of the Stormont regime.

Ideologies of discord survive in Northern Ireland today because they are relevant to the present as well as to the past. This arises from their content and not from particular forms of political socialization.[32] Relevance can be illustrated in many different ways. Protestants have no trouble in equating IRA activities in the present with the successful rebellion against the Crown in Dublin in 1916. A political rally by the Rev. Ian Paisley consciously seeks to evoke the atmosphere of an Ulster Covenant meeting in 1912, with threats of Rome rule and betrayal from over the water, i.e., London. Similarly, Catholics confronted with an Orange parade and RUC policemen relate these circumstances to previous marches, when they were subjected to intimidation and assault. A group of Republicans manning machine-guns at a street corner in West Belfast may see themselves as reaffirming, as in every generation, 'their right to national freedom and sovereignty'.[33]

Londonderry on August 12, 1969, aptly illustrates how time past and time present can fuse together in an explosive way. Protestants there that day were commemorating the 280th anniversary of the liberation of the besieged Protestant bastion within the old walled city from Catholic hordes surrounding it.[34] As they looked over Derry's walls, the marchers could see that Catholics, as in Jacobite times, were present in great numbers in the Bogside just below their fortifications. Catholics did not have to turn their minds further back than the previous twelve months to anticipate what might happen next. In that period, the Royal Ulster Constabulary several times entered the Bogside in large numbers, assaulting Catholics on the streets and in their homes in ways that official enquiries could later amnesty but not excuse. The Catholics began to build barricades to prevent a recurrence of this. This recalled Protestants from ancient history to the present. The barricades were interpreted as the beginning of yet another Catholic insurrection. The approach of the

354

police to the barricades was seen by Catholics behind the lines as yet another instance in which Protestants sought, in the words of an eighteenth-century Irish song, to make 'Croppies lie down'. In such circumstances, it hardly matters whether an individual interpreted events in seventeenth-, eighteenth-, or twentieth-century terms. In Northern Ireland, the conclusions drawn – for or against the regime – are much the same in one century as in the next.

Part Three

XII · Change and Resistance to Change

> *Then came the great war. Every institution, almost, in the world was strained. Great Empires have been overturned. The whole map of Europe has been changed. The position of countries has been violently altered. The modes of thought of men, the whole outlook on affairs, the grouping of parties, all have encountered violent and tremendous changes in the deluge of the world. But as the deluge subsides and the waters fall short, we see the dreary steeples of Fermanagh and Tyrone emerging once again. The integrity of their quarrel is one of the few institutions that has been unaltered in the cataclysm which has swept the world.*
> WINSTON CHURCHILL, House of Commons, 1922

In every political situation two equal and opposite assumptions compete for favour–the belief that everything will always continue as it has been, or that trends already immanent will make the future different from the past. Political discord has persisted for enough centuries in Ulster to support the assumption that fundamental change will not occur soon. Yet the twentieth century has seen great political transformations everywhere, not least in Ireland, where Covenanters and Republicans changed their form of rule by free-will commitments to insurrection. The very intensity of discord in Ireland encourages optimists and pessimists to think that discord cannot be interminable; however bright, awful or improbable, there must be a final solution.

Within society, the turnover of generations gradually offers an opportunity for political outlooks to form free of past disagreements, in so far as socialization into conflict is less than perfect. In Ulster, social change can also occur from the imbalance between emigration and immigration; in all but the very best of times, more people leave the Province than enter it. In so far as emigration is not random, it can indirectly alter the balance of political forces. Political pressures to change are never absent, where groups are as fragmented as in Ulster. Competition between political leaders is an incentive for the outs to try to upset whatever *status quo* prevails. The popular endorsement of extra-constitutional activities means that politicians

359

Change and Resistance to Change

need not limit their challenges to occasional elections. Political institutions outside Ulster also have significance, for the regimes in Dublin and London both claim the right to intervene in Northern Ireland politics, though neither has shown an eagerness for involvement. A religious person might even pray for an act of God–or acts by those who claim to speak with divine sanction–to increase harmony.

The slowest but potentially the most effective source of political change arises from the turnover of generations. Generational change can alter the aggregate level of support for the regime in so far as the outlooks of younger people differ from their seniors, because of differences in historical situations and socialization. For example, young people without experience of economic depression may value economic policies differently from those who have suffered a decade or more of unemployment. A second source of change is indirect. In so far as social characteristics influence political outlooks, then if social structure changes, aggregate profiles of political attitudes will also change.[1] For example, a rise in the proportion of university graduates in Ulster's population would indirectly lead to a decline in the proportion of Protestant Ultras.

The preceding chapter supports the null hypothesis, i.e., there is little difference in basic political outlooks in Northern Ireland from generation to generation. Yet theories of social change (e.g., increasing secularism) and of political modernization (e.g., increasing rationalism) imply that significant and unilinear change will differentiate the oldest and the youngest generations of Ulster people. As the crisis of the foundation of Stormont and the Irish Republic recedes further into the past, so the significance of discord about the regime might also be expected to recede. In short, the younger a person is, the greater the likelihood that he will be fully allegiant or reject Ultra and rebel alternatives. A variant theory is the 'three-generations' cycle of change. It is propounded in America to account for variations in religious and ethnic loyalties among American immigrants and their descendants.[2] The first generation has its outlook formed by traumatic experience; for the new American it is immigration, and for the Ulsterman, civil war. The second generation reacts against the values of the parents, in part because they appear irrelevant and in part because they are a handicap in getting ahead in the only world they know. The third generation reacts against the second; because the heritage of the past cannot be ignored or dismissed as

360

inconsequential, they accept it. Because the worst of the past is now remote in time, hardships can be discounted or even gain romantic appeal.

In practice the boundaries of generations are never clearcut. Within a cohort of adults labelled young, middle-aged or old, individuals will be widely dispersed. The mid-point of any age cohort by definition contains only a small fraction of the group. For example, if people in their 20s are defined as young, this constitutes a group in which an equal proportion are likely to be nearing middle age (i.e., 30) as are close to adolescence. The tendency toward heterogeneity is complicated by the fact that there is no simple formula to stipulate the age at which basic political outlooks will be fixed for life. For this reason, it seems simplest to test hypotheses about inter-generational change by dividing the population into cohorts by decades (Table XII.1).

Table XII.1 Generational variations in attitudes toward the regime

Age	20s	30s	40s	50s	60s	70s+
Born	(Post-1938)	(1928–37)	(1918–27)	(1908–17)	(1898–1907)	(Pre-1898)
Supports Constitution	%	%	%	%	%	%
Protestants	65	70	70	66	71	67
Catholics	31	35	26	38	45	28
Refuses compliance						
Protestant	57	47	52	45	66	67
Catholics	60	36	52	46	44	49
% in each cohort	19	20	20	19	13	8

The data from age cohorts clearly reject the hypothesis that there has been a steady change across generations in views of the regime. When regression lines are plotted to measure secular trends in regime outlooks for each decade of respondents, the rates of change are very low: an average of 1·2 per cent per decade; there is no consistency in their direction.[3] Any extrapolation of aggregate change would thus require a half-century or more to accumulate substantial change. Moreover, there is no assurance that inter-generational changes in attitudes will necessarily be convergent. The young in both communities are inclined to endorse illegal actions against the regime. There is also no support for a hypothesis of a cycle of three generations, for in none of the four tests are there statistically significant differences in the predicted direction between those aged 20–39,

Change and Resistance to Change

40–59, and 60 plus. The rejection of the hypothesis is reasonable, inasmuch as every generation in Northern Ireland in the past century has had some exposure to political disorder.[4]

In projecting future trends from the youngest generation of Ulstermen, it is important to consider the extent to which parents consciously seek to inculcate their children with their own views. To explore the climate in which the next generation is being raised, adults were asked how important they think it is to bring up children with the same views as their parents about religion, the Border and party politics (Table XII.2).

Table XII.2   Importance of children following parental views

Very/fairly important:	Protestant	Catholic	Total	D.I.
	%	%	%	%
About religion	82	89	85	7
About the Border	28	17	23	11
Supporting same party	25	16	21	9

Overwhelmingly, parents believe it important that their children follow them in religion, but they do not self-consciously think 'keeping the faith' important politically. Among Protestants who think religion very important, 62 per cent endorse an Ultra position. Among those who think it very important to raise children with their views about the Border or party politics, 77 per cent are Ultras. Catholics show only a slight relationship between their views as parents and their political views. The aggregate influence of consciously extremist parents is limited by their relatively small numbers. Moreover, there is little need for overt parental indoctrination into regime outlooks. Parents give their children a sufficient sense of religious identification to orient most for or against the regime. In addition, some opponents of the regime adopt this position because of adult experiences.

The preconditions of inter-generational change exist in so far as younger people differ from their elders in their involvement in activities that sustain political discord. Four measures of religious commitment can be used. There is no difference in church attendance among different Catholic age groups: 95 per cent of those age 60 or above went to church at least weekly, as did 95 per cent of those in their 20s. Among Protestants too, there was no substantial trend: 47 per cent in the oldest age group went to church at least weekly, as did 42 per cent in their 20s. Among Protestants, men under the age of

40 were slightly less likely to be members of the Orange Order: 27 per cent were in the Order, as against 35 per cent of their elders. When those who say they are 'very sure' that religion provides the best guide to life are analysed by age, no increase in scepticism is found among younger groups. A fourth measure of change is the comparison that each respondent made between his own religious commitment and that of his parents at the same age. A majority said that they were just as religious as their parents (D.I.=5%). Those who reported that they were less religious than their parents, 29 per cent, were average in their likelihood to withhold full allegiance from the regime. In other words, as long as any religious identification is transmitted–regardless of strength–generations are relatively un-affected in their political outlooks by their degree of religiosity.

Another inter-generational change of potential political significance concerns national identity. Individuals were asked to recall what nationality their parents usually considered themselves. The significance of national identity is shown by the fact that only seven per cent of those interviewed could not recall this identity, and only two per cent reported that their parents were mixed in national loyalties. The tendency for parental loyalties to be retained by children is most marked among those who think of themselves as Irish, for 85 per cent describe themselves as sharing exactly their parents' identity, as do 76 per cent of those from families where parents were self-consciously British. Very few people change sides completely in their national identity. Only seven per cent of persons from Irish homes now think of themselves as British, and only eight per cent from British homes now think of themselves as Irish.

Party identification also shows very limited differences between generations. Among those with Unionist parents, 87 per cent are also Unionists; the proportion able to recall their parents' party is 71 per cent–ten per cent greater than in Britain.[5] Similarly, 79 per cent with Nationalist parents are also Nationalist, and 72 per cent from Northern Ireland Labour homes are also Labour in their party identification. Reciprocally, only one per cent have switched between generations from Unionism to Nationalism, or vice versa. The major defections from parental loyalty at the time of the Loyalty survey were in the direction of the Northern Ireland Labour Party; this is logical, in view of its re-formation in the 1940s. The accession of support relatively recently is an ambiguous advantage, for it also implies that Northern Ireland Labour supporters are less firmly

Change and Resistance to Change

attached to this party and could more easily go back to the sectarian party of their community.

Conceivably, while individuals may retain the same community identifications as their parents, younger people may differ in their attitudes toward particular issues of great importance in maintaining discord about the regime. The views of each decade of respondents about four major political issues show far greater contrasts between the two religions than they do between the young and old within them (Table XII.3). There is no evidence of a convergence of

Table XII.3 Age cohort variations in attitudes

Age	20s %	30s %	40s %	50s %	60s %	70+ %
Catholics treated unfairly						
% Protestants agree	25	23	21	19	4	5
% Catholics agree	83	73	77	71	69	59
Church unity good in principle						
% Protestants agree	27	28	36	26	20	25
% Catholics agree	73	71	66	67	66	69
Church unity possible						
% Protestants agree	19	17	19	19	11	8
% Catholics agree	52	48	38	42	37	39
Orange Order						
% Protestants approve	54	47	56	57	68	66
% Catholics approve	3	9	9	9	14	9

attitudes along age rather than communal lines.[6] The most noteworthy and consistent trend concerns belief in discrimination against Catholics. Younger people are readier to say discrimination exists than are older people. This provides an impetus for Catholics to reject the regime, but still leaves the great majority of Protestant youths opposed to them in opinions and, prospectively, in the streets.

Given the importance of religion in differentiating attitudes toward the regime, it is reasonable to hypothesize that any increase in the Catholic proportion of the population will increase the challenge to the regime. This is *a fortiori* true in so far as Protestants react to such an increase with anxiety about their position, and turn to extra-constitutional measures to keep from being 'swamped'. Given the strength of Protestant Ultras, a Stormont regime would be under more pressure to repress a potential Catholic majority than to treat it in a conciliatory fashion. The differential birth-rate of Protestants and Catholics is therefore potentially the most important inter-generational influence upon politics in Northern Ireland. In the nineteenth century and earlier this was of little consequence, because large families were the rule among both religions, and consistent with the way of life of a predominantly rural society. The diffusion of inexpensive methods of birth control among all classes has created a difference in recent decades, inasmuch as Catholics have been inhibited from restricting family size by Papal encyclicals.[7] The consequence can be seen in the fact that the proportion of Catholics among babies enumerated in the last pre-war census of 1937 was 38·0 per cent of total births, and 43·7 per cent in 1961. Survey evidence confirms the existence of a religious differential in family size. The median Protestant parent interviewed had three children, and the median Catholic four children. Of married persons, ten per cent of Protestants had yet had no children as against six per cent of Catholics. Moreover, among Catholics with children, 31 per cent reported families of six or more, as against eight per cent of the Protestants. Of all children born to those interviewed, 55 per cent were Catholic and 45 per cent Protestant, notwithstanding the fact that Protestants outnumbered Catholics by 18 per cent among the respondents. This discrepancy arises because one Catholic parent of nine children will make a contribution to the population equal in number to that of three Protestant parents.

In spite of a high birth-rate, the Catholic community is handicapped in maintaining a supply of leaders by the rule of celibacy in the priesthood. This forestalls the creation of lay leaders who are sons or grandsons of the manse, a group prominent among Protestants in many Anglo-American societies.[8] The lack of offspring among this group is made more important by the relatively small size of Ulster's population. Were the number of Catholics in Ulster as great as in France or Italy, then the loss of potential leaders could easily be compensated for by other professional groups in society. But in a society with about 100,000 Catholic families, then problems of numbers become crucial. This is especially so inasmuch as the fragmentation of Catholic political groups inflates the demand for able leaders without increasing the supply.

It is dangerous to project birth-rates into the future, especially to a date sufficiently distant to give a conjectural Catholic majority in Ulster. Projections usually assume 'all other conditions remain constant'. Specifically, it is assumed that attitudes toward birth control will continue to differ by religion. The 1968 *Belfast Telegraph* survey of Ulster youth found that 38 per cent of Catholic youth actively disapproved of the Papal encyclical against birth control, and 64 per cent endorsed birth control methods disapproved by their Church if birth control was desirable on health grounds.[9] If Protestants begin to have larger families for any reason whatsoever, this too would reduce the Catholic advantage in 'cradle' politics.

Notwithstanding the higher birth-rate of Catholics, the overall proportion of Catholics to Protestants in Northern Ireland has remained virtually constant for generations. Catholics were 34·8 per cent of the population in the 1901 census, and 34·9 per cent at the 1961 census. In so far as can be inferred from census data, the proportions of Protestants and Catholics in the population are unaffected by differential life expectancies. In the absence of direct measures, the life expectancy of the two groups can only be estimated by comparing the proportions of Protestants and Catholics in older age cohorts at two successive decennial censuses. Assuming that emigration is virtually nil among those aged 50 or above, then a decline in the absolute numbers of persons in each cohort should still show the proportion of Protestants to Catholics constant–unless Catholics have a shorter life expectancy. A comparison of the religious composition of older age groups as recorded in the 1951 and 1961 censuses shows no consistent tendency for Protestants to live longer than Catholics.

Emigration is the most significant regulator of the proportion of Catholics to Protestants in Northern Ireland. Barritt and Carter calculate that from 1951 to 1961 there was a net emigration of about 51,000 Catholics and 41,000 Protestants from Northern Ireland. This means an outflow during the decade of nine per cent of Catholics born or resident in the Province, as against the departure of four per cent of Protestants.[10] Catholic emigration from Northern Ireland has, incidentally, been less than from the Republic of Ireland; between 1926 and 1966 about 45 per cent of the people born there had left the Republic.[11] Because emigration is a by-product of difficulties that the young and mobile have in obtaining a job in Northern Ireland, it specially affects people in late adolescence, about the time they come of voting age. While Catholics formed 40·2 per cent of the population under the age of 25 in 1961, their numbers fell to 32·1 per cent among those aged 25 to 49.[12]

In conditions of full employment in England, emigration sets a limit upon the amount of indigenous unemployment within Ulster, because many without work will leave the Province. From a Republican point of view, more or less forced emigration can be seen as an extreme deprivation of the right to live in the land of one's birth. Yet, from an economic perspective, moving to England or America gives a higher standard of living to those leaving their homeland. Politically, the disproportionate emigration of Catholics tends to alleviate Protestant fears of being 'swamped' by their traditional opponents. The creation of full employment in Northern Ireland, while removing economic grievances among Catholics, could also stimulate political fears among Protestants, by reducing the outflow of Catholic emigration. Inasmuch as the data in Chapter IX indicate that jobs and higher earnings will not increase allegiance among Catholics, this would result in an increase in the total proportion of disaffected and Ultra subjects in Northern Ireland.

Emigration can act as a political safety valve, in so far as the people most ready to reject the regime are those most likely to leave. By this reckoning, the strongest opponents of the Stormont regime would not be at home but in London, Birmingham, Boston and New York. Except when Northern Ireland's Constitution temporarily becomes an international diplomatic issue, their departure would strengthen the regime by leaving behind the most politically satisfied or passive Catholics. Alternatively, it could be argued that emigration is a sign of indifference to Ulster life, and that those who remain behind are those who are most involved emotionally in the life of the Province in all respects. One could even reason that Catholics unwilling to emigrate would be specially ready to adjust to the Stormont regime, in order to reduce the emotional conflict that would otherwise arise. By definition, a survey within Northern Ireland cannot study the attitudes of people who have left. It can, however, measure the extent to which emigration is attractive to Ulster people. Among all respondents, 36 per cent said that they had at some time thought of emigration. There is no association between thoughts of emigration and attitudes toward the regime, thus suggesting that political problems are not consciously a motive for emigration.

In view of the slight or nil rates of political change implied in social change, it is important to consider the extent to which popular attitudes themselves show demands for change. In a society in which the majority of people wish major policies to change, a conventional

Change and Resistance to Change

liberal model of politics implies that changes would occur consistent with these opinions. Alternatively, where majority views are opposed to change, then a regime would uphold the status quo. Neo-elite theories of politics emphasize the importance of situations in which the absence of strongly held or clearly stated popular preferences give politicians considerable leeway within which they can manœuvre without repudiation at elections or in the streets. Applying such models to Northern Ireland calls attention to the fact that such simple models do not take into account the problems of a society divided into two unequal and opposing groups. In such circumstances a simple majority is not a guarantee of a concurring majority in both of its parts. A simple majority may demand changes that would intensify discord between Protestants and Catholics. Yet waiting for Catholics to concur with a Protestant majority before acting would mean that politicians gave the minority a veto power in government. In other words, how a Northern Ireland politician responds to demands for change is not only a function of popular opinions, but also of his preference for simple majority or concurring majority rules.[13]

To assess the profile of popular demands concerning the Border, the power of the Unionist Party, and relations between Protestants and Catholics, each person interviewed was asked what changes *if any* he would like to see on each of these points. The answers to each question can be classified under one of four headings–maintain the status quo, ameliorate political conflict, polarize political differences, or don't know. For example, if a Protestant said that he thought there should be more friendship or freer trade across the Border, this would be an ameliorative answer because it endorsed more contacts. Reciprocally, if he gave an answer such as 'close the Border completely', this would be classified as a preference for polarization, because it would intensify differences. Table XII.4 shows that there is a majority within and between religions on only one of the three basic issues–better relations between Protestants and Catholics. The difference index is substantial between the two communities regarding the future of the Unionists and the Border. Equally important is the fact that a plurality of Protestants show satisfaction with their position of dominance by endorsing the status quo for party politics and the Border. Reciprocally, Catholics show dissatisfaction by endorsing a change in the Border that Protestants would overwhelmingly reject, and by rejecting Unionist government at a time when the party was under the relatively liberal leadership of Terence O'Neill. The

368

instability of popular views in aggregate about the Border and the Unionist Party is illustrated by the fact that the median view, favouring the status quo, is *not* the majority view within society as a whole or within either religious community. The status quo is the middle way only because the majority are divided about the direction they wish to go, with substantial numbers desiring polarization and others endorsing ameliorative measures. In such circumstances, the leeway of political leaders is no more than the option of choosing between minority policies, or trying to shift between the status quo and opposing alternatives in ways that minimize popular reaction against them.

Table XII.4   Changes desired in basic political conditions

		Ame-liorate %	Status quo %	Polarize %	Don't know %
BORDER					
Protestants		33	55	1	11
Catholics		11	23	55	12
	Total	24	42	23	11
					D.I. = 55%
UNIONIST POWER					
Protestants		30	42	10	18
Catholics		27	15	28	30
	Total	29	31	18	23
					D.I. = 30%
PROTESTANT–CATHOLIC RELATIONS					
Protestants		79	14	5	2
Catholics		89	6	3	2
	Total	83	11	4	2
					D.I. = 10%

People who desire change do not necessarily expect changes to follow. This is particularly likely in politics, where popular lore suggests that politicians will promise much and do little. In so far as people think that there is little likelihood of change, then they might be less likely to act to further their desires. To assess expectations of political change, each person was asked how likely he thought it would be that the change he wished would be realized. The degree of optimism shown by Protestants and Catholics desiring change is substantial. On all three issues, the largest single group thought it likely that the change they desired would, in fact, come about; very few saw little or no chance for the future to satisfy their political desires.

Change and Resistance to Change

Those who expect to be satisfied by future events have much less incentive to act outside conventional political channels than those who expect that their wishes will be frustrated. This proposition is particularly reasonable in a society in which extra-constitutional action is both recognized and frequent. The replies given to the Loyalty survey show that in Northern Ireland attitudes are much more complex than this. Among Protestants, there is no significant relationship between regime outlooks and the likelihood that desired changes would come about. Among Catholics, those who thought it likely that there would be changes in the strength of the Unionist Party were also readiest to support the Constitution: 48 per cent took this view, as against 25 per cent of those who thought changes in the party situation unlikely. The strength of this correlation probably results from the fact that Catholics expecting that the Unionists' position will change are, in effect, anticipating a major change in the Constitution of a one-party regime. Surprisingly, in two of the three tests of attitudes toward demonstrations, Catholics optimistic about change were slightly readier to demonstrate. The relationship was not, however, a strong one. The results suggest that in the ranks of a dominant majority, the anticipation of future disappointment is not sufficient to encourage people to adopt anti-regime positions in the present. Among the minority, optimism about the future may be a positive encouragement to extra-legal activities. Optimism can even arise from the belief that extra-constitutional measures will bring about desired changes.

In the last resort, every politician must take initiatives that chance public support for his actions, whether he is a British Army officer secretly meeting a group of Republicans, or a civil rights organizer calling a demonstration without knowing whether 20 or 2,000 people will turn out. In so far as popular opinion is prepared to endorse more than one alternative policy – or at least, a majority is not actively opposed – then the leeway for leaders is enlarged. The complex process of aggregating opinions gives additional room for manœuvre to politicians seeking support for their actions. In a regime lacking full legitimacy, the range of political alternatives is much wider than in a regime with full legitimacy. Measures inconceivable in the latter, involving violation of basic political laws, the overthrow of a regime or the internment of opponents, are matter-of-fact possibilities.

To test popular reactions toward possible leadership initiatives,

Protestant and Catholic respondents were asked to express approval or disapproval of four alternative policies concerning the Border, Protestant-Catholic relations and party politics. One alternative was maintaining the status quo; another, amelioration of differences; a third, greater polarization; and the fourth, chosen to test the outer limit of acquiescence, a policy that would transform relations in an unexpected direction, e.g., the assent of the Unionist Party to a United Ireland. The presentation of a long list of policy options to respondents might, of course, stimulate a fixed pattern of unthinking response among some. The low proportions endorsing policies of transformation is evidence that this occurred infrequently. Moreover, in so far as individuals are predisposed to acquiesce to ideas offered in an interview situation, this suggests that they might similarly acquiesce if the policy were offered with the full weight of the regime's authority behind it.

From the responses that each individual gives to the full range of twelve alternative policies for three major issues, one can construct a scale indicating the political leeway allowed by popular attitudes. The greater the number of alternative policies that an individual does not reject, then the more malleable he is *vis-à-vis* political leaders. The more an individual is inclined to disapprove alternatives set before him, then the less leeway he allows his leaders. The profile of respondents shows that both Protestant and Catholic politicians have backers who are inclined to allow considerable tolerance. Only one-fifth have views so well formed that they would reject three of the four policy alternatives put before them concerning Protestant-Catholic relations, and only one-tenth reject three out of four alternative policies about Border and party politics. The median Protestant and Catholic will only reject one of the four alternatives put before him concerning party politics. When replies to all twelve questions are cumulated, the median Protestant and Catholic disapprove of four of the twelve alternatives to which they are asked to react. The extent of the leeway that politicians enjoy is a source of instability, however, when politicians compete against each other by stressing policies that differ in the extreme. The moderate favouring an ameliorative policy has considerable hope of a positive response or only passive opposition to his initiative. But so too does a politician seeking to polarize conflict.

The policy alternatives put before Ulster people in the Loyalty survey inevitably were affected by the political circumstances of the period shortly before the commencement of civil rights demonstrations. Thus, the specific content of the alternatives endorsed is less significant than their direction. Whatever the situation, there is always the option of maintaining the status quo or else seeking to change it by polarizing, ameliorating or transforming actions. Table XII.5 shows that both Protestants and Catholics reject policies that would transform and thus deny their historic commitments.[14] Especially given the extent of popular support for extra-constitutional activities, this establishes outer limits for manœuvre by Ulster politicians. To note that Ulster people would react strongly against fundamental changes by their leaders is not to say that they endorse the status quo. A striking feature of Table XII.5 is the very

Table XII.5   Popular reaction to policy initiatives

	BORDER		RELIGION		PARTY	
	Prot	*Cath*	*Prot*	*Cath*	*Prot*	*Cath*
	(% approving minus % disapproving)					
Polarization	+6	+8	−2	+28	+16	−3
Status quo	+58	+9	+25	−10	+36	+5
Amelioration	+66	+14	+41	+34	+34	+19
Transformation	−78	−16	−46	−57	−30	−8

(For details of questions and replies, see Appendix: Qs. 8, 9, 10; 13, 15, 16.)

limited approval that Catholics give to the status quo–a plurality positively disapprove of the current state of Protestant-Catholic relations. By contrast, Protestants consistently approve the status quo. The lack of fit between Protestant and Catholic views is further emphasized by the fact that a majority in both religions only endorse one of the twelve initiatives, the amelioration of Protestant-Catholic relations. Ironically, in this case, an absolute majority of Roman Catholics said they would favour 'integration' of schools, flatly contradicting the views of their bishops. Protestant endorsement of giving financial grants to Catholic schools on the same basis as Protestant schools thus favours an ameliorative action not fully supported by the Catholic hierarchy.

In dynamic terms, the profile of views implies that Catholic politicians have been under strong popular pressure to take initiatives to alter conditions. On the other hand, Protestant leaders have constituents who approve of the status quo, thus encouraging negative reactions to Catholic initiatives. The fact that the majority of Protestants approved ameliorative policies explains the early support for Terence O'Neill evidenced in the November, 1965 general election. The fact that ameliorative policies are concessions *in the direction of* transforming policies–even though only a little bit–disturbed some Protestants. The commencement of Catholic civil rights demonstrations, polarizing opinions by their demands, was undoubtedly interpreted by many Protestants as a threat that ameliorative measures would lead to the transformation of the Ulster they knew and wished to preserve. So stimulated, Protestants opposed amelioration. Because change had already commenced, the status quo they sought to uphold was now the status quo *ante*. Hence, efforts to 'stabilize' the situation in Protestant eyes required reversing the direction of policies, an object far more difficult to achieve when inertia is in the opposite direction.

Because Northern Ireland lacks the formal status of an independent state, its politics are most obviously subject to influence by powers outside its territory, above and beyond those customarily affecting small states with large neighbours. Britain, the Republic of Ireland and other outside parties, such as the Vatican or the European Common Market, might intentionally or accidentally affect the security of its regime.

The formal sovereignty of the United Kingdom government provides a legal basis for London to intervene in Northern Ireland affairs. The intervention of the British Army in August, 1969, dramatically illustrates how Westminster can make its influence felt in extreme circumstances. Yet it is important to recognize that British intervention need not be an agent of change; it may support the status quo. This is true whether the status quo is defined as a reformed regime or a strictly Protestant one. There is nothing inevitably liberalizing, let along revolutionary, in the influence that Westminster might exert.

Ever since the signature of the Treaty ending the Anglo-Irish war in 1921, successive British governments have sought to avoid entanglement in the domestic politics of Ireland, North and South.[15] As long as thousands of British soldiers are present in Northern Ireland, there is the possibility that Westminster may increase the extent of its influence upon civil government, in order to protect its military commitment, or in an attempt to veto any Stormont policies that British civil and military advisers regard as 'indefensible'. As long as British troops guarantee security, then London could also be an agent of change by withdrawing troops. The withdrawal of British responsibility for security might occur in circumstances in which the Northern Ireland regime no longer needed such formidable defence against rebellious subjects. Alternatively, withdrawal might occur in troubled times, when the indigenous partners in a civil war were too strong, singly or collectively, to be coerced by Britain's military strength.

The Republic of Ireland might influence Northern Ireland politics in either of two very different ways. At one extreme, its leaders could abandon a long-standing Protestant grievance, namely the Republic's formal claim to sovereignty in Ulster. (The fact that successive Prime Ministers of the Republic have stated they desire 'reunification' by peaceful means, not force, hardly alleviates the grievance.) The Protestants of Ulster, like the Jews of Israel, think it both unreasonable and suspicious that an enemy defeated in the field should persistently refuse to recognize the state that vanquished him. At the other extreme, the Republic could directly or indirectly support an armed attack upon the Stormont regime. Historically, Dublin has not countenanced this. The Irish Civil War made the IRA and kindred groups as much opposed to the pro-Treaty regime in Dublin as to Stormont. The indictment of leading Cabinet members in Dublin in May 1970 showed that a regime founded by force and insurrection contains within it politicians who will accept that what their elders did yesterday their cousins in the North may not do tomorrow. If, for example, a pogrom were launched against Catholics, any government in Dublin would be subject to pressure to 'do something'; armed intervention across an international border is one possibility.[16] The British Army might think it beneath its dignity to fight the small and ill-equipped Army of the Republic. Yet any fighting across international boundaries would be politically important, for it would justify a Dublin appeal for the United Nations to intervene, to maintain order in Northern Ireland, and incidentally, undermine the Stormont regime. Intervention need not be taken by authority of the full Dail, or even of the Cabinet. The Taoiseach could take a unilateral initiative. Or, equally consistent with Irish history, units of the regime's Army – or of the Irish Republican Army – could intervene independently of or contrary to the wishes of the legally constituted regime.

The Roman Catholic Church lacks the formal status of a regime. None the less, its claims to authority over adherents and its peculiar significance in Northern Ireland give it substantial scope for exerting influence from outside. This is particularly true in so far as Irish bishops simply endorse policies laid down in Rome for Catholics in many different lands.[17] Protestants cite three things that could not be altered by the Catholic Church in Ireland, but could readily be altered by Vatican decrees. If the Vatican rescinded its prohibitions against the simplest means of birth control, Protestant fears of being 'outbred' by Catholics would have less substance, as would their resentment of welfare state payments made to Catholic parents of large families. (What effect such a measure would have upon Catholics in Ulster is less certain.) Another initiative with special significance would be the abandonment of Catholic schools. Survey data indicate that this would not remove discord between Protestants and Catholics. Yet, arguably, by bringing the two groups together, it would increase understanding of the *real* areas of disagreement between the two communities. A third and lesser change would be repeal of the *Ne Temere* decree, which directs that a Catholic marrying a non-Catholic should insist that the latter agree to have their children raised as Catholics. There is no reason why decisions made in the Vatican should be taken with the problems of Northern Ireland in mind. Any Pope has many problems, without adding Northern Ireland to his list. The changes in the Catholic Church begun in the pontificate of John XXIII have resulted in major challenges to the authority of the Vatican within the international body of the Catholic Church. Thus, it is possible that conflicts outside Ireland may so disrupt or alter the Roman Catholic Church that Irish bishops will be confronted with problems of allegiance and religious authority unknown to them for centuries. In such circumstances, it is well to remember that both clerics and laymen will be forced to decide for or against the Vatican's historic authority, as well as for or against specific measures of reform.

A secular European phenomenon of potential significance to Northern Ireland is the growth of free trade areas, such as the European Common Market. In so far as these institutions are dedicated to reducing the significance of international boundaries, they have a peculiar relevance to the Border issue in Ireland. Moreover, the European Common Market is significant as a union of predominantly Catholic countries, with pro-Catholic parties much stronger than Protestant-based parties.[18] Given these circumstances, it is hardly surprising that nearly twice as many Ulster Catholics as Protestants favour joining the Common Market. A successful

Change and Resistance to Change

British application to join the European Six, especially if accompanied by a successful Dublin application, would inevitably arouse both hopes and fears of change in Northern Ireland.

While the number of potential sources of change is great, this of itself promises neither full legitimation nor repudiation of the Stormont regime. The possible changes catalogued are unlikely to affect both Protestants and Catholics equally and in the same direction. Dublin initiatives could even increase the distance between the two communities. Moreover, openness to change, a sign of adaptability in a fully legitimate regime, may be regarded in a divided regime as yet another token of instability. For example, the leeway that followers give leaders permits politicians to compete with alternative policies that affect the very authority of the regime; each may reckon that he has some chance of success, whether propounding ameliorative, Ultra or rebel views.

The variety of divisions within both the Protestant and Catholic communities results in a situation in which coalitions of support can be built in many different ways. Yet the vulnerability of Ulster to outside influences, as well as to extra-constitutional influences within, means that any coalition, whether supporting the regime or attacking it, is liable to collapse under the pressure of events. Subconsciously, if not consciously, Ulster politicians formulate hypotheses about what will happen if they adopt one tactic rather than another. As the analysis of survey data illustrates, many hypotheses are falsified in the event. The difference between the politician's hypothesis and that of the social scientist is not the extent to which it is valid or invalid, but rather the consequences of rejection. A social scientist's hypothesis risks no more than the integrity of a theory about social relations. By contrast, a politician in a divided regime not only risks his own political future upon his assumptions, but also puts at hazard the survival of the regime.

XIII · The Limits of Leadership

> *Because I helped to wind the clock*
> *I come to hear it strike.*
> THE O'RAHILLY, Easter Monday, 1916

> *Each Sub-District [of the Ulster B Specials] remains and*
> *rightly so, more or less of a private army, proud of its own*
> *particular way of doing things.*
> WALLACE CLARK, *Guns in Ulster*

In any political situation, some see conflict in terms of personalities: *who* is to be master, that is all. Others see it as the opposition of impersonal forces: *which* class, religion or nationality is to be master, that is all. The history of Ireland, including Ulster, offers copious examples of the importance of political leadership, from the time of Cú Chulainn and Cromwell to the era of Carson and Craigavon. Yet the same annals record the downfall of many men who strove for greatness, because the forces against them proved insurmountable in the event. The doom of The O'Rahilly is a reminder of the price that strong men have paid for failure, or even, success.

In analysing the importance of leadership in Northern Ireland, one must first of all understand the character of the political problems that leaders must master or face defeat. One must also consider the leaders' outlooks, their institutional position and the extent to which nominal followers share their views. Examining followers as well as leaders is specially important, for without followers reputed leaders have a weak or anomalous status.[1] Given this, one can then consider the scope for political leadership in terms of the courses of action open to them and the constraints that limit their choice of alternatives.

Every new political movement, whether revolutionary, counter-revolutionary or ameliorative, must start some time, whether in a time as seemingly auspicious as 1798, when the United Irishmen raised their standard, or as seemingly inauspicious as those confronting the Ulster Volunteer Force and the Irish Republican Brotherhood early in this century. In time present, it is never possible to refute the argument that a policy, whatever its goals, will *never* succeed. The longer the time perspective, then the greater the possible difference between the goals of political leaders and the present political outlooks of the population. It follows from this, however, that the shorter the time perspective, then the less the difference possible between the goals of political leaders and followers on matters as important as the survival of the regime. To note that at a given moment in time politicians must take people's values as they find them is not to say that they need be passive. As long as there is more than one possible combination of views that can provide a majority large enough for governing, then there will also be more than one way in which politicians can successfully respond.

Combining the views that individuals have about the Constitution and about compliance with basic political laws displays the extent of dissensus which confronts every Ulster politician (Table XIII.1).

Table XIII.1   An aggregate profile of allegiance

	Compliant	*Uncertain*	*Non-compliant*
Support	FULLY ALLEGIANT 25%	INTERMITTENTLY ALLEGIANT 3%	ULTRAS 26%
Protestant	30%	1%	38%
Catholic	18%	6%	10%
Uncertain	PARTIALLY ALLEGIANT 12%	DIVIDED 3%	ALIENATED 11%
Protestant	11%	—	11%
Catholic	15%	6%	11%
No support	REPRESSED 7%	SEMI-COERCED 2%	REBELS 11%
Protestant	5%	—	4%
Catholic	10%	5%	19%

Notwithstanding the dichotomous force of communal civil war, respondents are distributed in most of the nine logically possible combinations of replies. *There is no majority—for or against the regime.* The largest groups are far apart—fully allegiant citizens, Protestant Ultras and Catholic rebels. No single group contains more than one-quarter of the whole population. Five of the nine categories—including all three of the most strongly non-compliant groups—contain at least one-tenth of the respondents. The dispersion of the population is primarily the result of differences among Catholics; six of the nine possible categories contain at least one-tenth of their respondents. This is also true of four of the Protestant categories. The composite picture implies no single, simple direction for Protestant or Catholic politicians to follow.

Ambivalence in aggregate does not imply an equivalent amount of uncertainty among individual Ulstermen. The opposite is the case: two-thirds of all respondents give clear yes or no answers to questions about the Constitution and about rejecting basic political laws. Protestants are more likely than Catholics to be sure of their views on both issues, suggesting greater rigidity in the dominant community. Only three per cent of the great majority of persons interviewed were don't knows on both major issues. The fact that a greater majority of people were willing to give a clear answer to questions about violating basic political laws than about the Constitution emphasizes the intensity of differences. Ulster politicians have little to gain by winning over people who are don't knows about the regime.

The basic choice for a wouldbe Unionist political leader is whether he wishes to align himself with those who would use force to keep the regime Protestant. Among those who endorse the use of force, there are degrees of rejection of the regime, ranging from the conditional allegiance of the Ultra to the openly rebellious Protestant who may reckon that Stormont has already 'sold out' to the Catholics. Among Protestants who reject force, there are also significant differences about the Constitution. Two-thirds, but no more than that, positively affirm their support; among the remaining third there are some who are less in favour of the Constitution than they are against the use of force. Catholic politicians face more widely dispersed potential supporters. They are guaranteed the support of some of their co-religionists–and the opposition of others–whatever constitutional position they adopt. The two largest groups of Catholics are at opposite corners of Table XIII.1–the fully allegiant Catholics and the rebels. In addition, those with no opinion about one or two basic issues form 43 per cent of the Catholics. The potential rebel leader cannot count on majority support from his co-religionists, but since demonstrations do not require majority support, he has enough support to act. A demonstration backed by 19 per cent of the Catholic population would produce a turnout of thousands in Londonderry and tens of thousands in Belfast. There are enough Catholics willing to endorse the use of force to meet the needs of several IRAs.

The compliant and the non-compliant are so evenly balanced that the median Ulsterman is literally and symbolically a don't know when it comes to giving obedience to basic political laws. This middle ground is not the position where most people cluster, but rather where fewest are found.[2] Even if all who do not actively

379

disapprove of the Constitution or endorse disobedience to its basic political laws are regarded as in the 'zone of allegiance' (i.e., inclined to behave as allegiant subjects whatever their verbal reservations), one still does not obtain a majority. The group is slightly outnumbered by those who fall in the 'zone of rebellion', i.e., persons who positively endorse non-compliance with basic political laws. When popular outlooks are so divided, then there is no programme that an individual politician can endorse, secure in the knowledge that he will agree with the overwhelming majority of his fellow citizens. Instead, he is offered the opportunity to choose his friends, certain that this will also give him numerous enemies.

Whatever the pattern of popular outlooks, there is no assurance that political leaders will inevitably reflect the views of those whom they claim to represent. In Northern Ireland, there could be substantial differences between leaders and followers, in the absence of the unambiguous popular preferences that impose practical and normative constraints upon everyone in a fully legitimate regime. While an Ulster politician's claim to speak for all the people cannot be accepted at face value, there is good reason to believe that there will be *some* support for almost any view, whether that of a Republican, a Paisleyite, or something in between. The question is: How similar or dissimilar are the views of political leaders from those whom they claim as followers?

The views of politicians and their putative followers might be related in any one of four major ways.[3] The first pattern is that in which the outlooks of leaders and followers are much the same. In such circumstances, the activities of leaders will simply reinforce existing discord within society. The politician is truly representative; he can act as an honest broker because he and his client want the same thing. A second pattern is that of leaders with more extreme views than their followers; for example, the proportion of Ultras or rebels among leaders would be greater than among those in whose name they claim to speak. In such circumstances, politicians, in so far as they lead, would intensify discord about the regime. Alternatively, those who are politically prominent may hold views less extreme than their followers, moderating the extent of conflict about the regime. For example, both Terence O'Neill and Eddie McAteer held views more moderate than many who voted for them. In 1969 the gap between leaders and followers became so wide that McAteer was defeated in seeking re-election in Londonderry, and O'Neill resigned as Prime Minister. Many issues of importance to those who govern excite little interest among those who are governed. For example, reform of the civil service is an issue of greater interest to civil servants and politicians than it is to most subjects. When the majority are don't knows, then political matters can be disposed of with little friction between leaders and led, because leaders have much leeway.

The extent of fit or misfit between leaders' and followers' outlooks is of special significance in a divided regime. Politicians from different groups may negotiate with each other without knowing the extent of their own support or the support of those who sit opposite them. At times of disorder and change, uncertainty arises about the numbers represented by newly emergent leaders. Their ability to create political issues promises some following, but their recent and often incoherent state of organization makes it uncertain how much support they have or how long their support will last. In such circumstances, a group of politicians may negotiate with each other, only to find that those with whom they have just reached agreement are repudiated, or that they themselves are repudiated. The most famous instance of this in Irish politics occurred in 1921 when Arthur Griffith and Michael Collins agreed a Treaty with Britain that kept the new Irish Free State nominally under the Crown. Some followers rejected their leadership to the point of civil war.

Defining, locating and generalizing about political leaders presents both practical and conceptual difficulties. If a leader is defined as someone who has been followed by the majority, then such individuals can only be studied after the event. To make success the sole test of a following is arbitrarily narrow, since 'failed' leaders can have substantial followings too. Defining leaders by their office in formal organizations is reasonable inasmuch as politicians, trade unionists and others claim the right to speak on behalf of organized groups. Such claims can then be empirically tested by comparing the views of representatives and those they claim to represent. Another alternative is to define leadership with reference to persons who are respected in face-to-face informal groups. This definition is unusually relevant in Northern Ireland, because the population is clustered in so many small towns and villages. In so far as the line between leaders and followers is not clearcut, then it is also desirable to consider persons actively involved in politics, although lacking official standing. Such activists are potential leaders pressing upon those directly above them. The more formalistic the definition, the easier it is to locate those regarded as leaders. Fortunately, survey techniques permit the identification of informal leaders as well as *ex officio* ones. The narrower the definition, the harder it is to generalize about leaders, because the cases involved are so few. The wider the definition, the less the study of leadership becomes a study of the actions of individual politicians of national repute and the more it becomes a study of many who are active in politics.[4]

In Northern Ireland, there is no doubt about the antiquity or importance of formal organizations. The churches, the Orange Order, trade unions, and the Unionist Party all have a history antedating the foundation of the regime. A Republican group can echo the past when announcing 'a new departure'. The persistence of institutional support for political outlooks from the past is particularly significant. Institutions tend to be conservative, because the values that they institutionalize are derived from the past, even if nominally concerned with some future state of this or the next world. The passing of generations affords an opportunity for a turn-over in the national profile of attitudes. But there is no equivalent among organizations. In Northern Ireland, major institutions long antedate the birth of their current members. Even if an individual were to join an organization to change it, the balance of influences would favour the organization changing the individual more. Among both Protestants and Catholics, the intersection of political, religious and nationality issues means that organizations can be relevant in several areas of social life. For example, a Gaelic Athletic Association hurley team can become politically active without dropping their hurley sticks! And a church parade–especially one with a Protestant flute band–can switch from a religious to a politician procession as easily as its musicians can change from a hymn to a 'party' tune.

The definition of organizational leadership used by many social scientists is leadership in voluntary associations. In so far as any body other than the state or a conscript army has an element of voluntariness in it, then this definition is unusually broad. If one regards a church as a voluntary organization, then nearly every Catholic and most Protestants in Northern Ireland are active in at least one such group. The high level of trade union affiliation in Northern Ireland assures that many employed persons belong to at least two voluntary associations. Yet these types of associations differ substantially from sports clubs, musical societies or social and drinking clubs. The latter are not primarily intended to exert political influence. Yet they give active individuals status and visibility, thus making it possible for them to call upon others for help in times of political crisis. Some social scientists would argue that it is the potential of voluntary associations to support or oppose the regime from a basis independent of politics that makes them particularly important.[5]

The level of involvement in voluntary associations in Northern Ireland is high by Western standards. A total of 32 per cent said that they belong to some sort of club or organization exclusive of church and trade union membership. By comparison, in the United States, 51 per cent reported themselves members of similar groups, in Britain 33 per cent, in Germany 34 per cent, and in Italy 25 per cent.[6] If trade union membership and/or church attendance is reckoned as participation in a formal organization, then Northern Ireland is a land of joiners far more than Britain or America. Among Protestants, 90 per cent are regular church attenders or belong to a trade union or another form of voluntary association; among Catholics, 98 per cent belong to a group.[7] The role of the Catholic Church as the central institution in its community is demonstrated by the fact that only 19 per cent of Catholics belong to a voluntary association other than the Church or a trade union; among Protestants, 41 per cent are members of such associations. The fact that many people do not belong to a voluntary association does not mean that they are socially isolated, but rather, that *religion is sufficient* to provide them with a network of social relationships. Among members of clubs and voluntary associations, 46 per cent are in organizations consisting solely of co-religionists, and 34 per cent in very mixed groups; the remainder are in associations that have a religious bias in their membership, but are not strictly sectarian. Only two per cent of all club members said they didn't know the religious bias of their organization.

In so far as voluntary organizations favour the regime, then the greater the level of an individual's involvement in them, the greater the likelihood that he will be fully allegiant. In so far as organizations oppose the regime, then the highest levels of disaffection or Ultra views should be found among the most involved. These hypotheses can be tested for officers, members and non-members of most clubs and organizations. Where numbers are smaller, the hypotheses can be tested between members and non-members. Tendencies for or against moderation are not all important, if the median person in all

383

strata still withholds approval from the regime. Thus it is also important to see whether officials and organization members are above or below a threshold of majority support. Small numbers decrease reliability of these estimates.

Table XIII.2   Organizational involvement and regime outlooks

| | Protestant | | | | Catholic | |
	Sup-port* %	Non-com-pliant %	T %	T %	Sup-port* %	Non-com-pliant %
All organizations						
Officers	91	49	21	9	27	44
Members	89	54	20	11	57	48
Non-members	86	54	59	80	51	48
Unions						
Officers	80	48	6	6	27	36
Members in family	87	51	45	42	39	54
Non-members	90	56	50	52	61	43
Business and Professional						
Members, past or present	90	36	9	6	44	51
Orange Order/Hibernian						
Members	91	75	19	3	33	69
Non-members	87	48	81	97	50	47
Church organization						
Officers	86	49	10	3	—	—
Members	92	51	14	10	37	63
Non-members	87	54	76	87	51	46

* Because don't knows are disproportionately large among the least involved, they have been eliminated in calculating support as well as non-compliance percentages.

Ex officio leaders are not a moderating influence in Northern Ireland politics. Among Protestants, there is no significant difference between leaders, members and the uninvolved in views about the Constitution. Moreover, Protestants in most strata divide evenly in their readiness to reject or comply with basic political laws. The greater readiness of professional men to comply is more than offset numerically by the inclination of members of the Orange Order to favour the use of any means to keep Northern Ireland Protestant. Among Catholics, those involved in community life are strongest in disapproving the Constitution. This relationship is consistent and substantial in each of the five tests of Table XIII.2. Only officers and members of church groups disproportionately favour illegal demonstrations; endorsement of demonstrations is substantial at all levels of Catholics. If those defending the regime call upon society's *ex officio* leaders to 'give a political lead', more likely than not this lead would *intensify* discord about the regime.

The visibility of officials and organization members does not assure that their influence will be equally tangible. A variety of social scientists have argued that persons whose personal influence rests upon their status in informal groups are collectively as influential or more influential than those identified by title and membership cards.[8] The theory emphasizes the importance of status in face-to-face groups, whether in an office, a pub, at a launderette, a housing estate, or at a building site. The absence of formal titles within such groups does not mean that each member exercises equal influence. There is good reason to argue that their very intimacy will make it easier for one person to emerge as a political leader, because those to whom he speaks will trust him and can question him more easily than they can a person who is, except for vicarious appearances in the media, an absent leader. The significance of informal leadership is specially important in times of civil disorder, for the first man with a following who throws a stone or who takes an initiative to end disorder exerts an 'on-the-spot' authority of immediate importance to the regime.

There are two ways to identify informal political leaders by survey data. The first is to rely upon an individual's own account of seeking to influence others. This method has the disadvantage that individuals may claim to be more influential than they are or that they may not wish to think they are politically influential in a land where politics is often trouble. Therefore it is also useful to consider those who are most involved in politics – the most interested, informed and understanding – as informal leaders, either *in potens* or *in esse*. They constitute a 'slack potential';[9] in crisis situations, they are likely to become politically active and by weight of their additional numbers, they may alter outcomes. Terence O'Neill, for example, sought to mobilize this group with a broadcast appeal to Ulster in December, 1968, at the beginning of the civil rights crisis. In response to his explicit appeal, 150,000 people expressed support for his policies.[10] The fact that O'Neill resigned five months later is a reminder that the political outlooks of those who write letters are not always representative. In so far as survey data are valid, informal political leadership in Northern Ireland is less than in Britain or the United States.

The Limits of Leadership

For example, 73 per cent of Northern Ireland people report that they have no interest or not much interest in politics, as against 48 per cent of British survey respondents. Ulster people also are less likely to talk politics, according to their own reports. In the Loyalty survey, 51 per cent said they never talked politics, as against 24 per cent in the

Table XIII.3   Political involvement and regime outlooks

	Protestants				Catholics	
	Sup-port*	Non-com-pliant	T	T	Sup-port*	Non-com-pliant
	%	%	%	%	%	%
Asked political views						
More likely than friends	80	41	3	2	20	73
Average	88	55	45	35	46	52
Less likely	88	53	51	62	54	43
Talks politics						
Three groups or more	89	51	24	15	45	61
Two contexts	91	54	17	11	30	54
One context	85	58	15	12	46	52
Not at all	86	53	43	62	57	42
General conversation						
Good	87	48	34	29	35	54
Average	88	55	44	44	56	48
Poor	90	58	22	27	65	42
Interest in politics						
A lot, some	90	54	31	19	31	52
A little, none	86	54	69	80	55	47
Understands public affairs						
Very, fairly well	89	54	44	32	43	51
Not very well	86	54	40	40	49	47
Not at all	90	50	16	27	61	37
Estimate of political influence						
A lot, some	93	64	23	12	61	36
A little, none	86	51	77	88	47	49

* Before percentaging, don't knows have been eliminated in order to control for their greater proportion among the least involved.

United States, and 29 per cent in Britain.[11] The hypothesis that informal leaders exert a moderating influence in Northern Ireland politics is rejected (Table XIII.3). Among Protestants, support for the Constitution is high at all levels of political involvement. Endorsement of Ultra views is higher among those who think they have a lot of political influence than among those who feel less efficacy. Other indicators show substantial support for Ultra sentiments both

386

among potential leaders and potential followers. As might be expected, the most politically involved Catholics are least likely to support the Northern Ireland Constitution.The only exception consists of that small proportion of Catholics who think they have at least some political influence. Those who are most involved politically tend to be readiest to endorse political demonstrations too. This pattern is consistent with recent Ulster history.

The profile of regime attitudes among organization and informal leaders shows clearly that the minimum condition for political bargaining–a consensus among leaders favouring the survival of the regime–does not exist. The divisions in Northern Ireland, if anything, are more intense among those most involved in politics. Leading Catholics disproportionately tend to disapprove of the Constitution and approve illegal demonstrations. Many Protestants in the leadership strata endorse the Ultra position. Because differences about the regime exist at all levels of the Protestant and Catholic communities, one can find some adherents of every outlook in any group of leaders.

Because the principal conflict of Ulster policies is vertical within each major social institution, members are divided about the most fundamental of issues. This is true even of the Orange Order, for one-quarter show themselves fully allegiant, in opposition to the majority of their Ultra brethren. In such circumstances, ambitious politicians are encouraged to compete against one another, because of the relatively even balance of forces within their organizations. In the Unionist Party, the competition between Terence O'Neill and his opponents reflected the division between fully allegiant and Ultra viewpoints. It also reflected personal ambitions, but ambitious men need to use an issue to gain their ends. The result of competition is also predictable: factional disputes that encourage the break up of the organization as a unified body. This was most vividly demonstrated in the competition between Unionists for votes at the 1969 Stormont election (cf. Table VII.1). The consequences of competition can also be seen in the ranks of the Republicans, both armed and unarmed. The history of the IRA has been a history of breakaway groups, as individuals find themselves in disagreement about how to repudiate the Stormont regime and to what end.[12]

Leaders may avoid taking sides politically to preserve from disruption organizations not solely concerned with defending or repudiating the regime. Those who disagree about the regime can remain united on points that they have in common. Political influence is thus sacrificed for non-political ends. In a less than totalitarian society, such a course is both recognized and accepted. This policy of aloofness is one that has most notably been followed by the churches, both Catholic and Protestant. The Cardinal and the Catholic bishops have ostentatiously avoided supporting the regime *or* those who publicly urge illegal actions to overthrow it. Similarly, the Protestant churches, while issuing denunciations of lawlessness in general, have not had clergymen use their influence against Ultra parishioners in their congregations. (The absence of hierarchical authority or the penalty of excommunication in Protestant churches limits their potential influence by comparison with the Catholic Church.) The Catholic Church is diverse enough to have priests who denounce the IRA from the pulpit, and those who will have a good word to say for it, privately if not in public. Similarly, Protestant churches provide some clergymen for ecumenical groups and others as chaplains of Orange lodges. The most ambitious goal for an Ulster leader would be to break the existing impasse by changing the chief dimension of political differentiation. As E. E. Schattschneider aptly notes, when people are in disagreement it is easier to create a new basis of disagreement than to get people to alter views along traditional lines.[13] For example, if politics in Northern Ireland divided people along class lines, then Protestants and Catholics currently in different parties might come together in parties as familiar and peaceable as those prevailing in Britain. A wide variety of politicians have sought to introduce such a transformation, from the time of James Connolly to the Prime Ministership of Terence O'Neill. To see how much scope politicians have for such major acts of leadership, one can compare the strength with which Ulster people say they identify with their religion, nationality, party, and class. The findings are clear (Table XIII.4). The people of Northern Ireland–both Protestant and Catholic–most often identify strongly with their religion and nationality. Only one-eighth consider themselves strong members of either the working class or middle class. There is thus little scope for politicians to lead people along class lines.

In many times past, politicians have transformed problems by altering the numbers of persons involved in disputes. The liberal democratic assumption is that the gradual expansion of the franchise and the creation of representative institutions will inevitably lead to political harmony. In Irish history, this led to increasing discord, as

The Limits of Leadership

the Nationalists used their electoral majority in Ireland to seek independence from Britain. The 1968 civil rights campaign sought to expand the range of participation in local government by introducing one man, one vote, one value. The local government reforms announced in 1970 met these claims, although simultaneously reducing the powers of local authorities *vis-à-vis* Stormont. Inasmuch as the Stormont franchise grants one vote to each adult, then expansion of the electorate cannot be a means of reducing discord. There remains, however, the possibility of altering the effect of universal suffrage, by changing the form of the electoral system. Catholics and Republicans interested in electoral politics advocate this. A proportional representation system of election would reduce the preponderance of Unionist MPs in the Stormont Commons, although it would not necessarily end their majority.

Table XIII.4 The strength of social identifications

	Protestant	Catholic	Total
	(per cent 'strong' identifiers)		
Religion	45	38	42
Nationality	45	28	38
Party	28	16	23
Class	13	10	12

Faced with this impasse, the ordinary liberal is tempted to abandon any desire to understand, let alone change Ulster politics. The desire of successive British governments to avoid knowledge of what happens in Northern Ireland shows that even great powers with great experience prefer to pretend that the problem does not exist. The people of Northern Ireland are not so fortunately placed. They cannot abandon all concern with their form of government – if only from fear of what would come after if vigilance were relaxed. Moreover, the longevity of the Stormont regime demonstrates that it *is* possible to govern without consensus. The measures taken by the regime, its Ultra watchdogs and its disaffected opponents show that survival does not come easily, or by means that are always comforting. The failure of successive Republican groups to bring down the regime by insurrection, by demonstration or by ballot suggests that the only thing harder than defending the regime is repudiating it.

The basic problem confronting all politicians in Northern Ireland is how to build and maintain a majority for *any* regime. The use of the language of electoral politics is metaphorical not absolute. Terence

389

The Limits of Leadership

O'Neill's experience with Unionist MPs demonstrates that it is of little avail to win a series of votes for the regime by a majority of one. What is needed is a substantial majority, i.e., support by something more than 50·1 per cent of the population. Inevitably, this will be support by something less than 100 per cent of the population. For the present (and the present situation has lasted for generations in Northern Ireland), given the distribution of outlooks displayed in Table XIII.1, there are only a limited number of potential governing coalitions including some improbable ones.[14] The range and character of these possible coalitions are the chief limitation upon those who seek to lead in Northern Ireland politics.

(1) The traditional basis for government in Northern Ireland has been a coalition of Ultra Protestants and fully allegiant subjects. Not only has this provided weight of numbers in support of the regime, but also, it has assured that those most inclined to political violence –the Ultras–would not attack the regime. This did not guarantee the security of those 'disloyal' to this coalition. For better or for worse– and Irish historians will inevitably provide at least two judgments– Terence O'Neill disrupted that alliance. He did not destroy its constituent parts. Whatever the distance between the two groups, such a coalition remains practicable in terms of numbers.

(2) The only other durable coalition that might be possible, given basic outlooks as they are, is a coalition between fully allegiant and compliant Protestants, and fully allegiant and repressed Catholics. Such a government could, at a maximum, hope to attract the support of about half the Protestants and all Catholics, except for those exclusively committed to rebellion on behalf of a Republican ideal. The creation of a bi-confessional government would depend upon the willingness of some Protestant politicians to hold office with Catholics, and of some Catholic politicians to take an office under the Crown. As neither community is completely monolithic, politicians of this sort might be found. A coalition could only be formed with the break up of the historic Unionist Party. It would also become less improbable if proportional representation were reintroduced. This would be a major departure from conventional English forms of government.[15] As the existing Stormont regime is already a departure from English practice, this is not an argument in principle against a bi-confessional government. A very different objection is that a bi-confessional government would stimulate an Ultra rising

against the regime – and that the Ultras might prove the stronger in a trial at arms.

(3) The argument that Ultras could and would overthrow a bi-confessional government implies that the Ultras are potentially, if not in fact, a majority in Northern Ireland. If events since the 1968 Loyalty survey have turned half the fully allegiant Protestants into Ultras, then this would just make Ultras a majority in Northern Ireland. Whether this has happened is a moot point. The general election in February, 1969, showed that the Ultras were not then dominant among Unionists. An Ultra takeover of the regime need not occur with the drama of a formal coup or a leadership crisis. It could even happen without any change of political personnel. All that need occur is that Unionist politicians already in office give increased attention to Ultra wishes by introducing new measures and amending or modifying other policies by administrative fiat. A take-over of this sort need not involve any formal change of constitutional relations with Great Britain; the first four decades in the history of Stormont show that a Protestant monopoly of power in Ulster is in no way incompatible with the Constitution of the United Kingdom. Such a tactic would succeed as long as fear of the Ultras' guns and will to resist intimidated Westminster.

(4) In logic, a majority coalition could be made up of Protestant Ultras and disaffected Catholics. Alliances of rebellious Protestants and Catholics are not unknown in Irish history. The classic example, the rising led by Wolfe Tone's United Irishmen in 1798, failed. Today, such an alliance is improbable, in so far as the *raison d'être* of the Ultras is opposition to any Catholic participation in government. One could envision circumstances in which a temporary *de facto* alliance might exist between Ultras and rebels, for the sake of over-throwing the Stormont regime and/or expelling the British Army. In 1969, for example, both groups were out in Belfast, making dynamite attacks to discredit the Stormont regime. For one night in June, 1970 at Ballymacarret in East Belfast, Protestant and Catholic forces fired their weapons at British soldiers whenever the soldiers sought to interpose themselves between two groups anxious to carry on with their own local war. Such co-operation can only be temporary, inasmuch as the overthrow of Stormont would be followed by a struggle for succession.

The Limits of Leadership

(5) In theory, one might conceive of a 'non-party' government, led by individuals not associated with any of the groups displayed in Table XIII.1. The very small proportion of those who occupy apathetic cells in that table emphasizes that there is no apathetic mass ready to tolerate politicians who wish to avoid commitment for or against the Constitution. Politicians, like atheists, are not expected to specify what they favour, but in Northern Ireland, they are always expected to make clear what they are against.

(6) As long as a group of politicians enjoy possession of office, then it can try to govern with only minority support. The mechanics of the British parliamentary system make this entirely practicable, for a Prime Minister need only win a majority of votes in the private caucus of the majority party to claim the votes of the whole majority party in a subsequent vote of confidence in Parliament. James Chichester-Clark was elected by the slimmest of margins–one vote. In a Commons where the majority party commands up to three-quarters of all seats, then the support of half of this group need not represent more than the support of one-third to two-fifths of the Commons. Such parliamentary support can provide a 'working minority' for an indefinite period in the House of Commons, but not in the country as a whole. Because Northern Ireland is a society with a tradition of extra-parliamentary as well as parliamentary opposition, government by a minority coalition is especially vulnerable.

The weight of Westminster is difficult to assess in this calculus because it has no votes at Stormont. Yet, as long as the British Army has responsibility for the day-to-day security of the Stormont regime, it is a uniquely placed pressure group. But if London leaves civil authority in the hands of a regime responsible to the Parliament at Stormont, its role in constituting government is limited: it can but support or repudiate whatever coalition the Commons throws up. A Stormont government dependent upon two masters–its Commons and British civil-military advisers–will try to keep both groups happy. But if it cannot, then under the rules of the regime it must give priority to the views of its parliamentary supporters, even if this means flatly opposing British wishes. To go against its parliamentary majority means sure ejection from office. To go against British wishes has a less certain set of consequences. At such a juncture, a

British government will either redefine its wishes to accede to the Stormont majority or choose one from a limited number of options open to it.

(7) In a situation of great crisis, with a multiplicity of forces engaged in killing, arson, intimidation and anti-regime demonstrations, then a British government might place responsibility for day-to-day government in the hands of the British Army commander in the field. Government by martial law requires vast resources in terms of manpower, judging by what was required to place one small area under curfew for two days in Belfast. The British Army does not have the infantry strength to suppress civil disorder simultaneously at a large number of places in the Province. In so far as the British Army could contain and suppress disorder, such action does no more than provide a necessary precondition of civil government. The Army cannot itself constitute a civil regime.[16]

(8) With or without an interim period of military rule, Britain could create a new form of coalition government and suspend or abolish the Stormont House of Commons. The new executive—whether called a Committee, a Commission or a Cabinet—would then be solely responsible to the British government through its authorized representative.[17] The resulting executive, using Stormont administration personnel, could be constituted along the lines of any coalition alternative cited above. There is a precedent for suspension of an elected authority in Northern Ireland, for the Unionist government suspended the elected council of Londonderry following the civil rights demonstrations there in 1968, placing responsibility for governing Derry in the hands of an appointed Commission. A number of civil rights and Republican groups have urged the suspension of Stormont.[18]

(9) In formal terms, the problem of coalition government at Stormont would disappear if this Parliament within a unitary state were abolished, and Northern Ireland governed as an integral part of the United Kingdom. While local government elections would remain of some importance, the parliamentary majority governing Northern Ireland would be determined overwhelmingly by the votes of English electors. Northern Ireland would contribute something like three per cent of the MPs at Westminster. In such circumstances,

a measure of executive devolution justifiable on the grounds of history, distance and special local problems might be provided along the lines of administrative devolution in Scotland or Wales. In both instances, the chief executive in the Scottish or Welsh Office sits in the British Cabinet and is immediately answerable to Parliament in Westminster for his actions. Such a change would evoke memories of the fateful and ultimately unsuccessful British effort to govern Ireland by an Irish Office at Dublin Castle. The proposal to swamp Ulster by governance from Westminster has been opposed at Westminster on the ground that it would pollute British politics by introducing an alien [*sic*] part of the United Kingdom into the mainstream of British politics. Republicans would see this as a further extension of alien rule in Ireland, whereas civil rights demonstrators might see it as responding better to their demands. Protestants would approach such an arrangement wondering whether it would be 'neutral on the Protestant side' or 'neutral against'.

(10) The opposite of integration is for Northern Ireland to splinter off from the United Kingdom by any one of several very different means. Since the time of the Anglo-Irish Treaty and the debate on Home Rule, London has never seriously entertained the possibility of ceding its claim to sovereignty in Northern Ireland. Yet withdrawal, out of deference to local wishes or in admission of the ungovernability of Ulster, remains at least a theoretical possibility. During the Home Rule controversy the prospect of secession in defiance of the United Kingdom Parliament helped lay the foundations for the present Stormont regime. In the aftermath of reforms introduced to placate civil rights demonstrators, a few Protestant Ultras made speeches raising the possibility of a Unilateral Declaration of Independence. The 1968 Loyalty survey showed that a substantial proportion of Protestants would endorse 'any measures necessary' to keep power out of Catholic hands. In population, location and resources, an independent Ulster would be neither the strongest nor weakest of states. Moreover, because the planters and their descendants (i.e., the Protestants) are a majority, and the descendants of the native Gaels (i.e., the Catholics) a minority, an independent Ulster would be *prima facie* more viable than a regime such as Southern Rhodesia, where a minority of settlers seeks to rule permanently a large native majority.[19]

(11) With or without an alteration in the contribution that Britain

makes to the balance of power in Northern Ireland, groups in the Republic of Ireland might independently seek to use their numbers to swing the coalition balance. From the point of view of Republicans, this would do no more than assure that fundamental right: majority rule. In their eyes, politicians in Ulster should compete for influence with politicians from Leinster, Munster and Connacht in a 32-counties Republic. It is known Catholics would be a majority in such a state by a margin of almost three to one. Some Protestants fear that their position as a minority would be no different politically than that of Catholics in Northern Ireland today. Catholics and Republicans deny that this would be the case. An unsuccessful military campaign to reunite Ulster and the Republic would almost certainly strengthen Protestants in the North, not only by virtue of their victory, but also by the voluntary or involuntary exodus of Catholics that would result.

(12) The balance of power could also be altered if the government of Northern Ireland became an international problem, with nations other than the Republic and the United Kingdom joining to resolve its difficulties. The Republic of Ireland has from time to time sought to internationalize the Northern Ireland problem by raising it at the United Nations. UN members have refused the invitation to add their weight to the balance, out of deference to Britain and out of deference to the intractable nature of Ulster.

As things stand, governing Northern Ireland is an insoluble problem for anyone who can think only of government by a fully legitimate regime. But it is also insoluble for those who like to think of governing a fully coercive regime. Anyone seeking to govern Ulster must accept the limitation that he governs without consensus. Because there is no consensus and any majority is problematic, great areas of choice are open. The alternative coalitions are numerous, and vast is the distance between them. Politicians are not limited to debating the relative merits of pensions schemes or the intricacies of foreign exchange controls. Instead, they can dispute the relative merits of regimes as different as a 'hard-line' Protestant regime; a rural Gaelic Republic; a bourgeois Catholic representative democracy; rule by a conservative or liberal middle-class Protestant ascendancy: or a Marxist Irish workers' soviet. A politician could even advocate something as different and improbable as a twentieth-century liberal secular state! Each choice implies opposition by the majority of Ulster people, as well as support by a minority of some size. Confronted with such problems, an Ulster leader cannot escape from the burden of choice—even if he chooses to fall between the horns of the dilemma.

Because no choice is easily sustained and all are uncertain, long-term alternatives differ greatly. Yet in a society which can quickly approach civil war, short-term questions of alliance or isolation are pressing and grave. Those who are isolated can be pushed to the wall in the grimmest sense of that metaphor. Those in alliance may find themselves dependent upon partners whose ends as well as means are repugnant to them. Social science analysis cannot tell a man which choice to make: it identifies the hard alternatives. Whether a politician is a proud man, like many who ride grandly through Irish history, or a hard man, like many whose stern features have left their mark on Ulster, or a prudent, even sly man, every politician at the end of the day has the freedom and the responsibility of deciding which choice will be his fate.

XIV · Bargaining Amidst Discord

The Constitutional position of Northern Ireland is not a matter on which there can be any compromise, now or in the future.

TERENCE O'NEILL

Two guns are better than one.

IRISH REPUBLICAN at trial, Belfast, 1969

Discord about the regime can be understood in terms of the issues that are the substance of controversy or in terms of the procedures that contain or sustain discord. The first approach emphasizes the extent to which issues in dispute cannot be made to disappear by recourse to institutional engineering. For example, in a divided regime free elections will reproduce in the national assembly disagreements in the country. The second approach emphasizes the extent to which the procedures by which men manage discord may increase or decrease conflict about the regime. For example, the challenge of a socially distinctive and geographically concentrated minority will affect a regime differently if its procedures are those of a federal system or a unitary state. In this chapter the substance of issues will be considered first, and procedures of conflict management second.

In so far as political discord arises from substantive issues, then the crucial question is the extent to which the chief issues are bargainable. Peaceful bargaining is possible, if the matter in dispute permits negotiations that can lead to an outcome acceptable to all. An issue is not bargainable if there is no way in which all concerned can be sufficiently satisfied to accept the outcome – or at least not be so dissatisfied that they will wish to repudiate the regime that fixes the terms. Whether or not an issue is bargainable is reflected by three characteristics: whether it involves a zero-sum conflict; whether it involves private or collective goods, and whether competing claims are stated as absolute values or advanced as demands for more or less of something. An issue involves zero-sum conflict if the sum of what one group can gain equals the sum of what other groups would thereby lose. For instance, if two races differ about the desirability of integration and segregation, then victory for one would entail loss for the other. A collective or public good is something that must be equally available to everyone in a society. As Mancur Olson notes, 'There is no necessity that a public good to one group in a society is necessarily in the interest of the society as a whole.'[1] A regime is a collective good, since its authority 'not only *can* but *must* be made available to all.'[2] When an issue concerns a private good, a settlement need not be on the same terms for everyone. For example, a dispute about public provision for university education will not result in an 'all or nothing' decision in which everybody is compelled to go to university or nobody goes, but rather, a decision about what proportion of youths will have university places provided by the state. A third characteristic of issues is whether claims are advanced as absolutes or with recognition that other claims may be balanced against it. For example, liberal theories of government do not regard the powers of a regime as absolute; they are meant to be restrained by a variety of competing loyalties and institutions. By contrast, militant civil rights groups may demand justice as an absolutely overriding claim: *fiat justitia, ruant coeli* – let justice be done though the heavens fall.

The great advantage of analysing issues in terms of their bargainability or non-bargainability is that it avoids treating all demands made upon a regime as equally important to its authority. As any government will have many demands made upon it, and as differences arise where demands are greater than the resources to meet them, then regime leaders seeking to survive must give special priority to those issues most difficult to settle. Demands that concern absolutely valued collective goods that can only be distributed in zero-sum ways will cause greatest discord. By contrast, demands for relative adjustments in private goods that can be distributed without anyone being worse off are least likely to create political discord. The social differences stressed in the Lipset-Rokkan analysis are those with the potential to create non-bargainable issues.

Conventionally, social scientists describe the issues that arise from economic differences as the stuff of class conflict. Such a vague term obscures more than it clarifies. Northern Ireland demonstrates that economic differences are not necessarily the most important source of political differences, even when economic hardships are real to many people. In spite of ubiquity, economic issues are bargainable. Typically, these differences are stated in terms of money, a commodity that it is very easy to bargain about. When economic growth prevails or where productivity and profitability can be increased, then industrial disputes can be settled by a non-zero outcome, in which both workers and employers benefit. Rising real standards of living in society provide a margin of discretionary income that can further increase economic satisfactions in the population. Moreover, the infinite divisibility of national income means that economic benefits are typically private goods, rather than collective goods. State welfare benefits need not be granted to all subjects or none. For instance, the provision of state subsidized housing for slum dwellers need not mean removing other people from their houses, just as the provision of unemployment compensation does not threaten those in work with a loss of job. Once the right of trade unions to organize is established, economic differences are rarely advanced in absolute terms. For instance, the nationalization issue is not discussed in absolute but in incremental terms in Western societies today; it has become a question of more or less state control of major segments of a mixed economy welfare state. The issue is literally marginal, that is, it concerns the point at which state intervention should stop. Even social status differences theoretically associated with occupation can be altered from a zero-sum relationship of Them vs. Us to a situation in which a substantial or infinite series of status gradations dissipate any basis for simple, bi-polar conflict.[3] The increasing number of status distinctions salient to some groups in society prevents absolute conflicts, in so far as groups value different things – money, education, gentlemanly manners or moral qualities.[4] The relative nature of status deprives it of the fixity and universality of differences based upon race. To note all this is not to suggest that there are no grounds for disagreement about economic issues in a modern Western society. The point is that existing economic differences – whether a cause of dispute within the economic system, the political system or both – are bargainable issues. For this reason, they need not challenge the survival of the regime.

Urban-rural differences may involve contrasting ways of earning a living within a market economy or contrasting ways of life differing far beyond economic issues. Viewed from an urban economist's perspective, the differences between people in the countryside and in cities are but one example of the eternal disagreement between buyers and sellers about the price at which they exchange their goods. Farmers have an interest in high prices for their products, and in cheap credit and supplies. Urban dwellers have an interest in cheap food, whether grown at home or abroad. Stated thus, the dispute is relative, not absolute, because it is capable of infinite marginal adjustment in formulae fixing subsidies for farmers and food prices in cities. The result will appear non-zero sum to subjects if subsidies are 'lost' in the general burden of taxation, and not seen as money transferred from one segment of society to another. It will truly be non-zero sum, if a declining number of farmers, by increasing productivity, average larger incomes while total subsidy costs remain constant. The dispersion of agriculture into a number of specialized types of production – grain, meat, dairy products and vegetables – makes it possible to disaggregate issues and benefits into smaller units, rather than compelling a collective solution.[5]

Differences between urban and rural dwellers are non-bargainable only when they involve a non-economic issue: the contrast between an urban industrial way of life and a traditional rural way of life. Within a traditional rural community, subsistence farming sustains kinship ties, and religious or cultural values that it would be absolutely unthinkable to abandon. Features of urban industrial life such as electricity, farm machinery and household amenities are private goods. The whole of an agricultural community does not have to accept them. In such circumstances, there is little ground for an absolute defence of the 'traditional' way of rural life. The challenge to a rural way of life becomes absolute only when changes concomitant with modernization threaten to force some or all of a community to leave the land because it no longer gives them a subsistence living, and the local village offers no alternative work. To a farmer who sees his work less as a source of income and more as a means of maintaining a subsistence livelihood for his extended family *near at hand*, this is an absolute threat.[6] The resulting protest can produce violent reactions against agents or symbols of change, e.g., warehouses, factories or government offices. The Luddite protest in early nineteenth-century England against the introduction of factory-based power looms that destroyed the domestic weaving industry is a classic example of this.[7] Such protests, while violent, are not necessarily threats to the regime, for they can be directed at economic instead of political targets. Even if a regime intervenes with decrees and troops, it is not the immediate party to an absolute conflict. A regime may reduce conflict by providing cash subsidies to protesting sub-marginal farmers, or by encouraging people to change jobs yet retain their distinctive way of life. Modern methods of transport make it possible for people to remain based in rural society, yet commute on a daily, weekly or long-term basis to areas where work is plentiful. By such means, the absolute conflict is not resolved, but it is forestalled or dissipated. The pressure upon those committed to an absolute defence of traditional ways is reduced, and successive generations are less likely to give an absolute value to traditional ways. The survey data on attitudes toward emigration in Northern Ireland emphasize a further point: some people forced to leave for work elsewhere see this as a positive advantage.[8]

Religion, by contrast, often raises issues based upon a non-bargainable absolute value, the assertion by churches of a supernatural sanction for their distinctive claims against a regime. The history of the Roman Catholic Church and of various Protestant denominations illustrates the impossibility of compromise when transcendental and worldly values are in conflict. These conflicting claims put severe strains upon those who are both subjects and believers; for them, there is no escape from disobeying one set of commands, with the consequence of punishment in this world or the next. While the Erastian Church of England has shown that much toleration is consistent with religion, there is a point at which nearly every religion will maintain requirements of faith and acts. Beyond that point, there is, to use an Ulster motto, 'No surrender'. A religious dispute can be zero-sum, if both sides agree about the importance of Christian doctrine but disagree about which is the follower of Christ and which is the follower of the anti-Christ. It will be absolute if one church insists that its way is the *only* way to salvation. Churches concern themselves with collective goods as well as private salvation. Of special political concern are religious views of education and morality. In so far as education is regarded as important in integrating individuals into society, then the claim of a church to control education is unlikely to be bargainable. If a church claims the right to provide religiously oriented education to all members of society, then everyone must share this, whether it is regarded as a collective good or a collective 'bad'. If a church claims the right to educate its own believers separately from unbelievers, the claim is zero-sum, inasmuch as a separate, clerically dominated education system prevents the integration of all children in a single network of schools. Questions of morality, such as the censorship of books or divorce, may be treated by a church as a collective good, with regulations that will be legally binding on everyone – non-believers as well as believers – as has happened in the Republic of Ireland and in Italy. The decision to raise a non-bargainable religious issue is not taken by a regime, but by clerical authorities.

'Centre-periphery' questions of language and national identity concern collective goods rather than private goods. A national identity has no meaning if an individual is not allowed to share his identification with his fellow nationals. If one group claims the right of official recognition for their language or nation, then this will compel adaptation by those outside the group. In so far as bilingualism becomes a prerequisite for public appointments, then the advantage is zero-sum, for what the minority group gains will be matched by the disqualification of those members of the majority group who are not bilingual.[9] Where those who have different languages tend to be segregated in different regions of a state, then linguistic conflict can be diminished. Disputes literally become marginal: where shall the language boundary be drawn? In Canada, the fact that 86 per cent of the population lives and works in a monoglot environment does not mitigate confrontation where boundary questions arise.[10] Moreover, the existence of clearcut spatial boundaries between groups can encourage demands for political autonomy, whether within the boundaries that the regime controls or by disrupting them. Where the balance of advantages to a minority do not favour maintenance of the regime's boundaries, there can be no expectation that its people will give absolute allegiance to the regime rather than to their linguistic or national identity. Ireland illustrates that distinctiveness in language is not a necessity for making nationalist demands, for most Irish Republicans are monoglot English-speakers by birth. Switzerland demonstrates that a multilingual society is not sufficient to challenge a regime. Historically, disparate language or national groups have most easily coexisted by insulation within a state. The increased contacts between centre and periphery arising from modernization can intensify identity crises and conflicts, where regimes do not govern nation-states.

To list social differences that can exist within Western societies is not to assert that each and every difference must be translated into a major political issue, whether consistent or inconsistent with the authority of the regime. One way to measure the relative importance of these differences is to see to what extent political parties draw their support from social groups defined in class, urban-rural, religious or national terms. With this one can test the extent to which the chief non-bargainable issues identified above–religion and language or nationality problems–sustain parties that challenge regimes and, conversely, whether regimes tend to be fully legitimate where parties are primarily based on bargainable class issues. A systematic review of 17 Western countries with 76 parties shows class and religion are almost equally important in providing electoral support.[11] A total of 35 parties are based upon churchgoing or secular groups and 29 parties cohesive in class terms. Urban-rural differences have been the basis of agrarian parties in each of four Scandinavian nations, but they are altering their labels, if not their sources of support, to attract urban as well as rural voters. The incidence of parties with a nationalist or linguistic following is limited: seven such parties of more than trivial size occur outside Northern Ireland. In ten of the 17 countries there is no linguistic or national minority substantial enough to sustain a significant peripheral party.

The challenge that bargainable and non-bargainable issues present to regimes can best be tested in relation to religious and class differences. The countries where parties based only on class receive the great bulk of the vote–the four Scandinavian lands of Denmark, Norway, Finland and Sweden–are also countries which have fully legitimate regimes. Finland is exceptional in that it appears to have overcome the consequences of civil war sufficiently to admit the Communist Party, one of the protagonists in that battle, into coalition government. In Britain, Australia and New Zealand, where class parties compete with parties drawing support from heterogeneous sources, the regimes are also notable for full legitimacy. By contrast, where parties based on religious or secular followings are strongest, challenges to regimes are substantial. This is clearly the case in Northern Ireland, Belgium, France and Italy; it was the case in Austria too until the *anschluss* with Germany created abnormal political conditions there. It is important to note that even though the chief challenge to authority in France and Italy comes from Marxist parties today, discord about the regime originated in conflict between clerical and secular groups. The Communist and Socialist parties in both countries have remained anti-clerical, as well as being 'left' on economic issues. In three societies where religious and secular parties do not disrupt the regime–the Netherlands, Germany and Switzerland–there are tripartite rather than bi-polar differences of religion, with secular, Protestant and Catholic groups all significant politically.

Bargaining Amidst Discord

The association of religious and anti-clerical parties with discord about the regime follows from the non-bargainable character of religious issues. This is not to deny the existence of politically salient economic differences, but rather to emphasize that these disagreements do not challenge the authority of the regime. One reason for this is that economic interest groups are not dependent upon political decision-makers to resolve their differences; they can also turn to the market-place to secure satisfaction. The characteristic institutions of economic interests are the labour union, the corporation, the professional association and the interest group, rather than the political party or the insurrectionary force. The most parsimonious assumption is that economic differences in the first instance lead to economic disagreements. These may be pursued by economic means, such as labour-management bargaining, strikes, lockouts, price wars, etc. Only when workers or employers cannot secure their ends in the market-place will they seek redress from the state. The institutional prominence and resources of economic interest groups are an incentive to avoid challenging the regime, inasmuch as rebellious action would make resources forfeit to the regime, should efforts fail. Communist parties are exceptional in maintaining a 'combat' wing in their parties. It does not follow that such parties will overtly challenge a regime when the opportunity arises, as the restraint of the PCF showed in France in the events of May, 1968.

The failure of national and linguistic differences to match religion in disruptive strength is striking, inasmuch as nineteenth-century European history is full of accounts of non-bargainable nationalist claims against regimes. The reason for this shift in the source of discord is that the great majority of European states are now virtually homogeneous in ethnic terms. Belgium and Switzerland are the major exceptions in Western Europe. National and linguistic homogeneity makes it impossible to have ethnic conflict; there is literally nothing to differ about. The settlement of nationalist problems did not come about by peaceful bargaining. In 1900 there were seven populous states in Europe: the United Kingdom, France, Germany, the Austro-Hungarian Empire, Italy, the Ottoman Empire and the Russian Empire. Of these, each had a nationality problem. In the case of France and Italy, numbers were small but the location of the minority—on the border of another great power—was important in two world wars. The United Kingdom solved its chief nationality problem by the secession of Ireland after a civil war. The problems of the Austro-Hungarian and Ottoman Empire were resolved by the repudiation of both regimes and states at the end of the First World War. The difficulties of nationalities subject to Germany and Russia were only resolved by the movement of troops back and forth across disputed territories in two major land wars. The Second War provided a 'final solution' of the most gruesome sort for German and East European Jewry. In twentieth-century Europe, only Norway provides an example of the peaceful creation of a succession state free from duress, after its grant of independence by Sweden in 1905.[12] Only Switzerland has survived as a multi-national state without challenge to the authority of the regime. If the character of nationalist issues be at all proportionate to the force required to remove them, then nationalism must be accounted a social difference potentially as strong as religion, and much stronger than class.[13]

In sum, this review of Western nations shows that discord about the regime in Northern Ireland is within the mainstream of modern European politics *because* it is based upon non-bargainable differences about religion and nationality. These are the issues that have disrupted regimes elsewhere in Europe in this century and in the past. The unimportance of class and urban-rural differences for regime discord is also confirmed by this comparative review. For a regime to be faced with industrial and agricultural problems does not *ipso facto* present a challenge to its authority. This was particularly demonstrated in Anglo-American lands in the 1930s, when the Great Depression created massive unemployment in all parts of society, disrupting existing parties, yet did not present any significant challenges to the regime. Because of this, economic problems cannot be considered a sufficient cause of the repudiation of the regimes in Europe then.[14]

The least bargainable form of political disagreement might appear to be a demand to change the regime as an end in itself. Yet, this is not necessarily the case. Constitutional arrangements are uniquely the prerogative of the regime. Politicians are better able to change political institutions than social institutions. Moreover, unless all regimes are conceived as static, each must be allowed the possibility of altering its fundamental arrangements by recognized constitutional means. Any theory of politics that takes time into account must allow for a regime adapting its institutions in part. The relative ease with which this can be done is illustrated by reviewing the history of the expansion of suffrage. In principle and in practice, the claim of the disenfranchised for a vote was a bargainable demand. The most important franchise reform groups rarely claimed the franchise as a universal and absolute right that had to be granted immediately, notwithstanding other considerations. Instead, franchise reform typically became the subject of incremental adjustment, with each successive stage of reform resulting in the qualification of more subjects for the vote; universal suffrage was thus reached as the last stage in a long process.[15] In Britain, for example, 86 years elapsed between the first reform of 1832 and universal male suffrage in 1918. Only in France was universal suffrage advanced as an absolute claim–and there it was resisted in absolute terms, with subsequent disorder for successive nineteenth-century regimes. Rarely did franchise reform involve zero-sum conflict. In most lands, the result was an increase in the number of people eligible to vote, without the elimination of pre-existing franchise rights. In this way, a larger proportion of the population was given a stake in electoral politics. In so far as the newly enfranchised turned to electoral, not insurrectionary politics, this led to increased allegiance to the regime, rather than discord. In Ireland, for example, early nineteenth-century franchise reforms made the ballot the pre-eminent instrument of political protest for three-quarters of a century. It was only abandoned when it demonstrated failure. Where the expansion of the franchise meant the abolition of the right of an individual to sit in Parliament or to nominate a member from a pocket borough, then change involved identifiable losses. But the numbers of beneficiaries so outnumbered those deprived of nomination rights that the result was not zero-sum but in aggregate a positive gain. The crucial good– control of the powers of the regime–was not altered drastically by franchise reform. In England, for example, inertia and institutional factors so inhibited change that the partisan consequences of the 1867 reforms did not become fully apparent until the Liberal government of 1906, and the first Labour majority did not occur until 78 years after the reform.[16] This gradualness greatly dampened reactions among those adversely affected by reforms.

In the twentieth century, non-bargainable demands to change the regimes in whole rather than in part have been advanced by several different types of parties. Nationalist parties threaten a regime by seeking to destroy the state that it governs. Religious or anti-clerical parties question the allocation of authority between governmental and transcendental authorities, but the decline in religious involvement and the creation of nation-states has therefore reduced the scope of challenge to regimes. In contemporary Western politics, Communist parties most often overtly threaten regimes. Yet the challenge to authority expressed by Communists is also a means to an ulterior end: the advance of the working class. The success of parliamentary Socialist parties suggests that the repudiation of the regime is not the only way in which working-class groups can advance their interests. Fascist parties are exceptional, in that they have advocated repudiation of a regime as a political end in itself.[17] In a complementary fashion, resistance to Fascism was often organized as a coalition to repudiate the Fascist regime, rather than as a coalition to advance a social interest. Once the Second World War was over, these coalitions collapsed.[18] So, too, did Fascist parties.

*

Whatever the source of challenge to a regime, its leaders must devise some strategy to cope with the discord that confronts them, if they wish to avoid repudiation. The analytic framework outlined in Chapter I identified two alternative strategic objectives—full legitimacy or full coercion. Both promise a fully effective solution to political discord. In Northern Ireland the tactics most often recommended to secure full legitimacy have shown no evidence of success. An increase in material prosperity for individuals does not increase individual allegiance to the regime. The institutions of electoral competition likewise do not strengthen the regime. National identity is a subject of disunity, and churches too express the lack of moral solidarity within the boundaries of the regime.

The achievement of full coercion is easier said than done, not least in a society as historically resistant to coercion as Ireland, both North and South. Coercion by intimidation, by incarceration, exile or execution promises a final solution—only if it can be made to work. The obstacles to full coercion in Northern Ireland are both philosophical and practical. The philosophical aversion to coercion runs very deep in Anglo-American liberal thought. The use of force in domestic politics is the negation of a claim to government by consent. When individuals and groups arise that refuse consent to a liberal regime, those challenged are often confused as to how to respond. The use of coercion will violate libertarian assumptions concerning freedom of speech and association. By refusing to recognize signs of disaffection or rebellion, politicians may avoid the problem of coercion by denying that enemies of the regime exist. Failure to act may be followed by the exhaustion or dissipation of the challenge. But it may also be followed by the repudiation of the challenged regime.[19]

In Northern Ireland, neither regime officials nor leaders of the disloyal opposition doubt the existence of challenges to the regime. Yet managing coercion, like managing the economy, requires skill and luck, as well as very tangible resources. The greater the mass support for rebels, the more difficult coercion becomes, since a mass cannot be executed or imprisoned. It can only be deprived of its leaders, or have members punished more or less randomly; both strategies are likely to increase opposition among those not coerced. Moreover, the use of fully armed soldiers to maintain a regime is uneconomical in political as well as material resources. The British Army and the Royal Ulster Constabulary lack the men to coerce compliance with basic political laws. They can only 'police' the disaffected population, i.e., arrest individuals caught in flagrant violation of basic political laws, yet leaving at large many who could, would and have expressed their rejection of the regime. Coercion typically requires a full-time and specially trained para-military force, accustomed to control civilian crowds without resort to weapons, yet sufficiently armed to overcome resistance by petrol bomb, gunfire or gelignite. This work is best performed by full-time para-military forces, like the French *Compagnie Républicaine de Sécurité* (CRS) and the French *Gendarmerie*.[20] No such force exists in Northern Ireland, nor would it be easy to recruit and train such a force, especially on a bi-confessional basis. In short, after the 1969 Hunt Committee reforms, the Stormont regime still finds itself with security forces inadequate to coerce those who challenge it.

In a divided regime, where neither full legitimacy nor full coercion is possible, politics–'attending to the arrangements of a set of people'–does not cease. Instead, the relationship between governors and governed takes a special form; bargaining about the unbargainable. From the point of view of the leaders of the regime, adaptation of institutions can be accepted, as long as this will increase the authority of the regime. But the survival of the regime is not a matter for concession.[21] Yet the relationship between defenders and

challengers of the regime is not that of protagonists in a civil or international war, where there are no constraints upon the level of force
to be used against the enemy. It is best regarded as a bargaining
relationship, inasmuch as the parties to negotiations try to adjust
their actions to others in the 'market-place of discord'.[22] Bargaining
in such circumstances is very different from bargaining about private
goods in a peaceful market situation. The proponents of the regime
seek to calculate what price must be paid to get their opponents into
the system, just as the challengers must calculate the price that they
will have to pay if they break off negotiations and turn to overt
rebellion. All sides retain the option of a resort to force as an alternative to bargaining.

In such bargaining situations the immediate issue to those who
govern and to rebels is whether the regime will survive. Repudiation
of the regime will result in a *political* revolution,[23] whether intended
as a means to other ends or as an end in itself. While such an event
may not have immediately noticeable consequences for most members of a society, it will have immediate consequences for those who
have been governing. The immediate concern of the regime's defenders is not the maintenance of social or cultural advantages,
but rather, political advantages. Reciprocally, the first priority of
their opponents is to take political power from those they are
against.[24]

Leaders of divided regimes often refuse to accept the assertion that
their problems are political. This is particularly likely when the
government is endorsed by free elections. While elections will not
legitimate the regime in the minds of rebels, it will legitimate it *in the
eyes of those who rule*.[25] Thus, in moral terms as well as in terms of
entrenched interests, those who lead such regimes are likely to be in-
sensitive to rebel demands. They see no fault within themselves or
their institutions. The trouble is diagnosed as 'something wrong' with
the disaffected. Disaffected persons may thus be ignored or treated as
propagators of alien as well as inimical doctrines, since no subject is
expected to think like that. In Northern Ireland, this was the traditional response to Catholic grievances until months *after* the civil
rights marches began.

Terence O'Neill adopted a new tactic: he assumed that the reason
why Catholics protested about justice and power was that they
lacked houses and jobs. (The same assumption is implicit in many
American diagnoses of the black man's position in America.) Thus,

men who are hardly economic determinists but moderate and liberal in their professed values may try to meet a political problem with an economic solution. People asking for police protection–or protection from the police–will be shown plans for new houses or new factories. People asking for political power in their own hands will be shown the benefits that other hands are providing for them. People who protest that the rules of the game are biased politically will be told that the game is not about political power but about economic wellbeing. In the 'prosperity' game, everyone can win cash prizes, even if their sum political gain is nil.

From the perspective of the defenders of a regime, such misperception, whether intentional or unconscious, has much to recommend it. In an economy of growth, the aggregate benefits available for distribution or redistribution to subjects will increase.[26] Progressive taxation can raise additional sums of money as an insurance premium from well-to-do supporters of a regime. Yet, in so far as grievances and satisfactions cannot be substituted as between economic and political realms, such a policy is wasteful and ineffective. It is ineffective inasmuch as many people will take benefits without reflecting upon the source. The nearer people are to subsistence, the less likely they are to think of exchanging political allegiance for material benefits. They will do or say almost anything to secure such goods–and undo and unsay it the next day for the same reason. In the short run, material benefits can be used tactically, e.g., to secure the cancellation of a protest march. Those who have threatened a protest will then have something in hand as part compensation for their grievances, but only as part. Leaders of a regime may think their disaffected subjects 'ungrateful' to take these benefits while withholding political support. Opponents of a regime may reciprocally think that politicians who offer them material benefits are either naïve or trying to solve their problems 'on the cheap', by giving something of less value than what they ask for. A marginal increase in public expenditure is, after all, of little value compared to something priceless: the institutions by which a group sustains its power.

In so far as money can affect allegiance, then it might be spent more economically if it is offered to leaders of anti-regime movements, rather than divided out among multitudes of followers.[27] The idea of 'buying off' extra-constitutional opposition leaders is best understood metaphorically, for the objects offered will include the symbols or substance of power and status, as well as financial rewards. The tactic assumes that individuals are much more easy to negotiate with than are collectivities of people. Not only is it possible to talk clearly and confidentially to individuals, but also, it is possible to observe closely whether those who are willing to do a deal stick to their side of the bargain. From the perspective of anti-regime leaders, any offer to negotiate raises a question about the relative value of entry to the system to advance demands and make bargains, as against remaining outside the exit in a non-negotiable position.[28] Few protesters embrace the diehard alternative, for this means they must live the hard lives of professional revolutionaries. From afar, an organization such as the IRA may appear glamorous or amusing, but there is nothing attractive about living or dying rough in a bog, or long periods of incarceration in British or Irish prisons. Generations of Republicans can testify to this.[29]

The medium- and long-term consequence of a strategy of co-option depends primarily upon the relationship between opposition leaders and those whom they call their followers. In so far as these relationships are institutionalized and the aggrieved groups have several points of social cohesion, then followers are likely to stick together with defined aims and predictable responses. By contrast, people who claim to speak in the name of large categoric entities, e.g., American blacks or 'the Irish nation since time immemorial', are less closely and certainly linked with their nominal followers. In the event, the followers may act independently of those who claim to represent them. Yet the organization of disaffection does not necessarily mean that those who stick together will follow their *ex officio* leader. While leaders have much leeway, any decision to co-operate with the enemy calls into question the very purpose for which the disaffected have organized. (In so far as it meets the terms of the disaffected, then it will undermine the leaders of the regime with its Ultras.) Whether followers repudiate their leader depends greatly upon how the terms of the bargain are perceived. The leaders of the disloyal opposition must not only strive to convince officials of the regime that their demands are right, but also convince their followers that the settlement is right.

In such circumstances, a leader is often a marginal man caught between those who defend the regime and those who oppose it as rebels or as Ultras. If pressures in two directions exist within his own organization, this threatens the repudiation of his institutional authority. A protest leader can avoid such risks by refusing negotiation with the defenders of the regime, since any bargain he makes may threaten his own repudiation. Yet to oppose without negotiation is to achieve little, unless some new tactic of extra-constitutional opposition otherwise gains concessions from the regime. In so far as the most innovative anti-regime techniques emerge independently of institutionalized leaders perpetuating 'accepted' means of legal or illegal demonstrations, then new techniques of opposition will also result in new leaders. Thus, whether a politician speaking for the disaffected strikes a bargain with regime leaders or not, he is vulnerable. This helps explain why such leaders often have short periods of office or prominence, and then become established or *passé*. In the Northern Ireland civil rights movement, as in America, a generation can last only a year or two, as status depends upon the successful exploitation of a technique of disaffection. Ironically, the successful refusal of defenders of the regime to bargain can stabilize leadership among the disaffected by making all of them unsuccessful.

The conditions just described are conditions of high uncertainty. When decisions about the regime's future must be made, they are also conditions of high anxiety. Politicians may prefer at a given time to act *as if* the above arguments are not valid; they can succeed as long as the arguments are not *overtly* invalidated. A good illustration is the visit to Northern Ireland by the British Home Secretary, James Callaghan, shortly after the killings of August, 1969. Callaghan acted as if the partners in discord – both killers and victims – were not in fundamental opposition about the regime. He tried to bring together prominent Protestants and Catholics to discuss values and goals that Northern Ireland people held in common. The immediate response was peaceable, and the visit was written up in the British press as 'successful'. Within a year, the temporary character of the success was evident, for by that time British troops had been shot and were shooting at Protestants and Catholics opposed to the Stormont regime. The appearance of unanimity created in conditions of high uncertainty and anxiety could not be sustained.

When defenders and opponents of a regime meet to negotiate realistically about the basic causes of conflict, this moment of truth is likely to increase tension rather than lessen it. The defenders of the regime cannot claim that the distribution of political power is outside their ability to alter. To say that a regime has the power to mollify the disaffected is not to say that it has the will to do so, or that to do so would necessarily assist survival. The problem is that political and legal rights are collective goods. The regime that governs one part of a society must govern other parts too. People who have the same wants in terms of private goods, such as food, shelter and television sets, do not necessarily share the same taste in forms of government.[30] For Catholics to benefit from the right to vote in Londonderry, then Protestants must also participate in the election, and collectively share the outcome–victory for one and defeat for the other. Securing justice for those wronged or killed means that those who are at fault must go to jail. The fact that everyone shares in power does not mean that everyone benefits from such sharing. What one side regards as a gain, the other side can regard as a loss; the conflict is zero-sum. Moreover, the conflict necessarily gives all sides perfect information about what is happening, since a general election can hardly be held in private.

The dilemma facing the defender of a divided regime, attacked by disaffected and Ultra subjects, is how to devise a strategy that will deal with both. The problem can easily be stated diagrammatically.

Figure XIV.1   The dynamic tensions in a divided regime

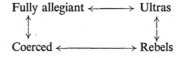

A movement toward coalition with Ultras will increase the distance of the regime from the coerced. If the coerced move in reaction to this strategy, they will then move toward the rebel category, further increasing the distance between themselves and the regime. The dynamics of the situation are the same in the opposite direction if the leaders of the regime move toward the coerced. Where the two groups are approximately equal in size, as in Northern Ireland, then prudential calculations will not identify one of the strategies as much more likely to be rewarding. Yet failure to move can also be a source of discontent or risk. At this juncture a regime can be challenged from two sides, as in the case of the discord generated in Northern Ireland, or in the case of the civil rights *and* the Wallace movements in the United States.

In such circumstances, challenged leaders often fall back upon the twin tactics of conciliation and coercion.[31] The problem still remains:

XV · The Social Consequences of Discord

We cannot stress too strongly the catastrophe which must befall any society which ceases to respect the rule of law or takes the law into its own hands.

THE HUNT COMMITTEE ON THE POLICE, 1969

What difference does it make to people if they live under a regime that lacks full legitimacy? What is the character of the catastrophe to which the Hunt Committee points? In so far as conditions are different, is this true in most countries where there is political discord or is it something peculiar to Northern Ireland? A social determinist would argue that politics has little independent influence upon social conditions; to him, the actions of a regime are a consequence, not a cause, of social conditions. A political determinist would argue the contrary. Only by the intervention of the state can the living conditions of the people alter greatly. A third alternative, rarely argued but equally plausible, is that a regime has little or no effect upon the economic wellbeing or social status of a people; instead, its most important consequences are specific to politics.

Questions stated in such general terms do not permit a meaningful answer, for the words do not indicate what specific conditions a regime does or ought to influence. The only clear implication is that regimes are to be evaluated for their effects upon individuals, and/or their aggregate achievements. The two are not identical.[1] For instance, economic growth, conceived as an increase in the gross *national* product, implies nothing about the advantages that individual subjects may derive from such growth. If the extra resources gained by growth are used to equip an army, a secret police or to institute the compulsory teaching of a dead language, fewer benefits will accrue directly to individuals than would result if the economic dividend of growth were used to improve welfare service for individuals. Similarly, advantages that accrue to individuals are not *ipso facto* advantages to a regime. For example longer life for an individual in retirement is technically counter-productive, for it greatly increases claims on national pension funds, without increasing national economic resources.

Given that one wishes to study the living conditions of individuals, what particular conditions require measurement? Is a regime to be evaluated for its effect upon individual economic conditions, social welfare, intellectual understanding, spiritual wellbeing or athletic skills? Without some *a priori* framework specifying conditions of relevance, it is impossible to begin to answer such a question, and identify the kinds of evidence – quantifiable or non-quantified – that would be most useful. Neither national nor international compilations of statistics contain within themselves criteria of relevance. Moreover, the kinds of social conditions readily amenable to quantification are a biased sample of all conditions; one American study has found that the proportion of social conditions conveniently measured in quantified form has been declining in recent decades.[2]

Constitutional pronouncements are of little help in the particular circumstances of Northern Ireland, for the written Constitution that the regime possesses was not drafted in Ulster, but by the United Kingdom Parliament prior to the foundation of the regime. The provisions are not accepted unanimously within the society. (The Constitution has been described by a Justice in the Irish Republic as, 'A statutory abortion of December, 1920, sardonically entitled "An Act to provide for the better government of Ireland".'[3]) The nearest Northern Ireland approximation to a declaration of independence – the Ulster Covenant of 1912 – is also vague; it is a commitment to nothing beyond United Kingdom citizenship. There are no criteria that can be borrowed from the English Constitution for there is no such written document. Incidentally, some of the most important measures reckoned part of Constitutional lore, such as Magna Carta and the Bill of Rights of 1688, are markedly anti-Papal. The 1937 Constitution of the Republic of Ireland refers vaguely in its first article to the hope that the Irish nation 'develop its life, political, economic and cultural, in accordance with its genius and traditions'. Such a statement cannot be applied to Northern Ireland, for it posits a unique Irish genius that Protestants do not wish to share. The preamble to the United States Constitution offers a multiplicity of objectives that might be used to evaluate the effects of government. Three of these – providing a more perfect Union, ensuring domestic tranquillity and a common defence – refer to collective goods not individual benefits. Three are applicable to individuals: the enjoyment of justice and liberty, and the maintenance of general welfare. Only one of these six objectives, the general welfare clause, refers even by implication to socio-economic conditions; the remainder are overtly political. A bias toward political objectives is also found in other Western constitutions, such as those of Germany and the Fifth French Republic. A global review emphasizes the heterogeneity of aims that individual states proclaim.[4]

From a plethora of social science writings concerning the relationship of regimes and living conditions, the most immediately relevant to the evaluation of Northern Ireland is that of T. H. Marshall in *Citizenship and Social Class*.[5] Marshall distinguishes three elements of citizenship–civil, political and social rights. (These rights are, in effect, claims upon the state for services or benefits ensuring desirable living conditions.) Civil rights concern individual freedom and equality before the law. Voting and the right to participate in government are the chief political rights. Marshall uses the term social rights to refer to a wide range of conditions, some of which are explicitly economic, such as employment, and some of which are not, e.g., education. The advantages of this framework are several. The first is that the criteria are historically meaningful, for Marshall shows how modern English history can be analysed in terms of a progression from civil through political to social rights. It is apt to compare Northern Ireland with England, if only to measure the extent of deviation. A second advantage of the framework is that each of these criteria immediately relates to powers of government. The administration of civil and criminal law and the determination of qualifications for political participation are among the defining characteristics of government. Acceptance of responsibilities for education, employment and other socio-economic conditions are often cited as defining conditions of a 'modern' government. Because the framework covers both social welfare and political measures, there is no *a priori* commitment to socio-economic *or* political-legalistic approaches. It becomes an empirical matter what kind of conditions are most highly correlated with political discord. While the criteria are of considerable normative relevance, they yet avoid specific endorsement of particular methods for ensuring these rights; for example, full employment, freedom of speech or legal equality could be enjoyed under a Socialist or a capitalist regime. The application of criteria derived from Anglo-American experience to Continental

The Social Consequences of Discord

European nations can provide a check of the extent to which they reflect 'culture-bound' assumptions.[6]

The general relevance of criteria derived from English history is confirmed by comparing them with those elucidated by contemporary American social scientists. The most obvious point of comparison is with *Toward a Social Report*, a study published on behalf of the United States Department of Health, Education and Welfare in 1969, with the explicit intention of developing measures of the quality of American life.[7] The conditions surveyed there include health, social mobility, the environment, income and poverty, public order, learning and the arts, participation and alienation. As the title implies, the report was a preliminary attempt to assess the conditions of the American people. There was no theoretical or historical rationale for the subject matter chosen, beyond that of convenience and immediate political interest. It is none the less noteworthy that the resulting product covers much the same interests as does Marshall. A framework devised by Gabriel Almond, viewing governmental consequences as primarily relevant to evaluating the capability of regimes, also covers much of the same ground as does Marshall.[8] Almond and Powell do add one criterion of considerable potential significance: the symbolic gratification or deprivation that a regime affords citizens, through various 'priceless' activities such as parades, symbolic ceremonies or, in the case of the Irish Republic, restoring the Gaelic language. As Bagehot long ago pointed out, emotional gratification is not the least condition important in a fully legitimate regime.[9] As Almond's criteria are additive rather than logically integrated, it is entirely appropriate to incorporate emotional rights as a fourth standard for evaluating the consequences of divided regimes.

The significance of these criteria is confirmed by considering them by four standards basic in measuring the magnitude of a public policy: the scope of the population affected, the intensity of impact, the frequency of influence, and the probability that a given individual will be affected.[10] The four rights are all universal in the scope of application within a society. There is a high probability that the legal, political and emotional rights of individuals will be affected periodically, e.g., at election time. For most people, these rights are of intermediate intensity – except when they are deprived of them. Social rights are usually matters of medium or high intensity, and often they are of continuing importance. Moreover, in a modern

418

society there is a virtual certainty that everyone will be influenced by the regime's welfare policies. Noting the significance of these activities is not to assert that a regime is solely responsible for all that happens in such policy areas, but rather, to call attention to their intrinsic importance. Moreover in many Western societies, regimes are pledged to maintain minimum conditions, for example, a number of years of compulsory schooling.

Cross-national comparison gives every measure of living conditions more meaning, for few can be interpreted solely in absolute terms. For example, statistics of life expectancy or *per capita* national income can theoretically assume an infinity of values. In order to judge Northern Ireland conditions, one wants to know how life expectancy or income there compares with that in other countries: is it greater, less, or about the same as that elsewhere? In so far as political discord depresses living conditions, then Northern Ireland should rank below countries with fully legitimate regimes. Comparison also provides a safeguard against generalizing wrongly from a single case. For instance, if one only examined Northern Ireland the coexistence of divided authority and the use of English might make one infer that English was a language used to express political discord. Comparing all English-speaking countries shows that there is no necessary correlation between use of English and divided authority.

The question then arises: With what country or countries is Northern Ireland at all comparable? Politically, Northern Ireland is characterized not only by political discord but also by the presence of competitive parties and free elections. By world standards, Northern Ireland is a relatively prosperous industrial nation. In short, it meets the two criteria usually employed to define Western nations: free elections and a modern, industrial economy. By confining comparison to Western nations, one can control for the influence of many other influences. This is desirable inasmuch as the conditions assessed here are culture-bound, i.e., derived from Western experience. They would not necessarily be appropriate for Oriental, Arab or African countries. The universe of 18 nations includes three distinct groups within it – Scandinavia, Continental Europe and the Anglo-American world.

The general hypothesis to test can best be stated in a null form – there is no relationship between political authority and the living conditions of subjects in Western countries. The hypothesis is a statement of probabilities, not an iron law. No general relationship

The Social Consequences of Discord

will occur if, for example, living conditions are below average in some divided regimes, and above average in others. Conceivably, Northern Ireland is a deviant case, above or below the general norm. Some variation is almost certain to exist, inasmuch as many things affect living conditions besides the authority of the regime.

To test this hypothesis it is first necessary to measure, as well as one can, the authority of each regime. Ideally, this requires statistical data about levels of support and compliance derived in a manner that has the same literal and functional meaning in all 18 countries. In democratic societies, support for the regime can be consistently measured by referring to the proportion of the voters casting ballots for parties that favour rather than oppose the regime. In this analysis, parties will be considered in favour of the regime unless they advocate one of the following: non-compliance with basic political laws (e.g., the American Independent Party of George Wallace); transformation of the regime by whatever measures are necessary, whether or not constitutional (e.g., Communists); rejection of the existing regime by whatever measures necessary, without regard to what follows (e.g., Poujadists); the dissolution of the state or major alterations in its existing boundaries, by whatever measures are necessary (e.g., nationalist parties). Election results provide a convenient and comparable source of data for all Western nations[11] except Northern Ireland, where the absence of contests in many constituencies precludes meaningful aggregation of vote totals. Measures of non-compliance with basic political laws or a predisposition to disobey are more difficult to obtain. The most wide-ranging comparative studies have not concentrated upon non-compliance *per se*, but rather, upon the incidence of civil strife and political violence.[12] Disorder has been treated as a challenge to the regime without regard to political intent, and orderly but illegal acts have been ignored. Moreover, these indices were primarily developed for measuring strife in non-Western nations. In the absence of survey data about individual predisposition to refuse compliance with basic political laws in 18 nations, there is much to be said for using support for anti-regime parties as an indirect indicator of non-compliance. The choice can be justified theoretically on the grounds that in societies where coercion is least used and party competition exists, then individuals are encouraged to act in defiance of basic political laws by the anti-regime organizations they endorse. While it does not follow that everyone who votes for the French Communist Party or the American Independence Party is *ipso facto* ready to act illegally, it is reasonable to infer that societies where such parties obtain support are in aggregate likely to have more non-compliant subjects than societies where anti-regime parties secure only a trivial number of votes. The point is illustrated by conditions in France and Italy. As the vote for anti-regime parties rises, then the level of division about authority can also be said to rise. Use of this single measure for the two components of authority incidentally avoids the problems that would arise in efforts to combine separate and possibly incommensurable measures of support and compliance.

The general hypothesis refers to present political conditions and present social conditions. However, a strong relationship between two variables observed at the same point in time provides no guidance about cause and effect. To introduce an element of causality into the analysis, the measure of regime authority has been derived from the first post-war general election in each country and all other measures from a date in the 1960s, thus ensuring a gap of about 20 years between the two observations. Logically, a correlation between later data about living conditions and the earlier data about regimes cannot prove the influence of living conditions upon prior political events. If anything, it would be evidence of the influence of the regime upon social conditions. There is, of course, an infinite regression back in time to search for the first cause, since pre-war living conditions may have affected the post-1945 regime, just as pre-1914 regimes may have affected inter-war living conditions. The choice of 1945 as a starting point can be justified by the war's role as a political watershed: for example, there is virtually no correlation between the anti-regime vote in each society at the last competitive election before the Second World War and at the first afterwards.[13] Moreover, the post-1945 Western world has seen a steady growth in national prosperity, whereas the inter-war period was a time of prolonged depression.

Two correlation statistics provide convenient summary measures of the association between regime allegiance and living conditions. Pearson's product moment correlation (abbreviated as r) is suited to normally distributed[14] characteristics conveniently measured numerically, such as data on life expectancy. The value of r can range from $+1\cdot00$ to $-1\cdot00$, according to the extent and direction of the association between two measures. If, for example, *per capita* national income and anti-regime outlooks both tend to rise and fall together,

The Social Consequences of Discord

then the score approaches $+1\cdot00$; where one figure rises as the other falls, then the score approaches $-1\cdot00$. As the value approaches $\pm0\cdot00$, the degree of association is progressively weaker or nil. Because the available measures of social conditions are not perfectly reliable for cross-national comparison, the extent of association has also been calculated by ranking countries in terms of pairs of variables, and computing the rank order correlation value of Kendall's Tau (abbreviated as T). This statistic assumes that it may be easier and more accurate to rank countries, e.g., as more or less fully legitimate, than it is to make a precise numerical estimate of the degree of allegiance. Kendall's Tau varies from $+1\cdot00$ to $-1\cdot00$; values near $\pm0\cdot00$ reflect that no association exists between items measured.[15] Because of the small number of nations available as cases for testing the hypothesis, it is desirable to employ statistical significance tests to indicate that the null hypothesis is not true in a given case. When the probability is greater than 19 chances in 20 that a correlation is not due to chance, then it will be regarded as significant and the hypothesis accordingly rejected.

Marshall's definition of social rights is broad rather than precise. He does not define social rights in terms of a single abstraction but by illustration. These illustrations embrace 'the whole range from the right to a modicum of economic welfare and security to the right to share to the full in the social heritage and to live the life of a civilised being according to the standards prevailing in the society. The institutions most closely connected with it are the educational system and the social services.'[16] The multiplicity of examples is an advantage, in so far as it requires a multiplicity of specific tests of the general hypothesis. If a wide variety of tests confirm the hypothesis, this should increase confidence in it more than the outcome of a single test. Three different kinds of claims upon the regime are implied in Marshall's statement. One is a claim for a national minimum where virtually 100 per cent achievement could be attained, e.g., in literacy or full employment. The second set of social conditions involves open-ended commitments, where more is always possible, and more means better. This is true of education and economic wellbeing, for there is virtually no ceiling on the amount of education or *per capita* income that subjects might enjoy. Thirdly, the emphasis upon sharing in a social heritage implies a measure of individual integration with fellow citizens in a community that provides satisfactory social relationships for each within it.

The Social Consequences of Discord

The number of tests is restricted by the availability of reliable and comparable data. For example, while it is possible to test the association between unemployment and other factors within a single country at two points in time, it is not practicable to do so between countries at the same point in time, because five different conventions for estimating unemployment are used in the 18 countries.[17] Similarly, figures on old age pensions are not included because the content, scope and value of such pensions differ in such a combination of ways that figures cannot easily be reduced to a common denominator for multi-national comparisons. It is not even possible to measure modern housing conditions by noting the proportion of houses with a bath. Saunas are used in place of baths in Finland and where showers are installed in modern flats, the flats appear insanitary on a 'bathtub' index.[18] The indicators employed in these tests are not perfect measures for national or cross-national purposes. As the label 'indicator' suggests, they provide evidence relevant to the condition that it is desired to measure.[19] Wherever possible, effort has been made to obtain two sets of indicators for each living condition.

Four comparative measures are available for standards of individual and environmental health. Northern Ireland ranks second from the bottom among 18 nations in its infant mortality, and exactly in the middle for overall male life expectancy (Table XV.1). There is no significant correlation between these conditions and the level of political discord. One traditional measure of environmental health – tuberculosis due to poor housing conditions – is derived from data about individual living conditions, and therefore is reliable for cross-national comparison. Northern Ireland's tuberculosis rate is ninth among 18 nations, the same as that for England and Wales. It also ranks in the middle on a second measure of poor housing: the number of individuals in a room. There is a statistically significant positive correlation between political discord and poor housing, and death by tuberculosis.

In every Western society since the war, the regime has accepted responsibility for education and for the performance of the economy. (The Republic of Ireland is exceptional in that the Catholic Church has retained responsibility for secondary education, and conscious economic management policies were not introduced until the late 1950s.) One measure of the provision of education is the number of years of compulsory fulltime schooling. Northern Ireland, with Britain and France, ranks second to the United States. In every

423

Sources:

1. Anti-regime vote at first election post VE Day, 1945. From Derek W. Urwin, *Elections in Western Nations, 1945–1968.*

2. Infant mortality in the first year of life per 1,000 live births. *Statistisches Jahrbuch der Schweiz, 1969* (Bern: Eidgenossischen Statistischen Amt, 1969), p. 572. Data for year 1967.

3. Male life expectancy at birth in years. *Statistisches Jahrbuch der Schweiz, 1969*, pp. 570–1. Data for various years in the 1960s.

4. Tuberculosis deaths per 100,000 inhabitants. Data for various years in the late 1960s. *Statistisches Jahrbuch für die Bundesrepublik Deutschland 1969* (Wiesbaden: Statistisches Bundesamt, 1969), p. 36*.

5. Persons per room. *United Nations Statistical Yearbook, 1969* (New York: UN, 1970), pp. 678ff. Data from early 1960s.

6. Years of compulsory fulltime education. *UNESCO Statistical Yearbook, 1966* (Paris: UNESCO, 1966), pp. 39–46.

7. Adjusted school enrolment ratio for primary and secondary education, c. mid-1960s. *UNESCO Statistical Yearbook, 1966*, pp. 59–77. These ratios for some countries are only estimates; the Belgian figure is particularly questionable.

8. Gross national product *per capita* in 1968 US dollars. *United Nations Statistical Yearbook, 1969* (New York: UN, 1970), pp. 563ff.

9. Per cent rate of growth in gross national product, 1958–68. *National Accounts of O.E.C.D. Countries, 1958–68* (Paris: OECD, no date), pp. 360ff.

10. Church attendance. Percentage of persons who report that they attend church frequently or fairly often (i.e., monthly or are practising Christians, in a variety of national surveys in the 1960s. Because attendance measures are not identical in all surveys some estimates and adjustments have been made. The majority of the sources used are cited in Richard Rose and Derek Urwin, 'Social Cohesion, Political Parties and Strains in Regimes'.

11. Union membership as a proportion of non-agricultural employees. Data on union membership principally from *Europa Yearbook, 1969* (London: Europa Publications, 1969). Data on non-agricultural employment in 1965 calculated from UN Food and Agricultural Organization, *Production Yearbook*, Vol. 22 (Rome: FAO, 1969), Table 5, p. 21.

12. Strikes: the ratio of work days lost on average, 1965–67, in relation to persons employed in non-agricultural work, as derived in Source Note 11. For strike statistics, see *Statistisches Jahrbuch für die Bundesrepublik Deutschland 1969*, p. 47*.

13. Suicides per 100,000 inhabitants, usually 1966 data. See *Statistisches Jahrbuch für die Bundesrepublik Deutschland 1969*, p.39*.

14. Violent deaths known to the police per 100,000 people. Data from the mid-1960s, calculated as a five-year average, from figures in the appropriate national statistical yearbooks.

country, a proportion of youths stay on at school beyond the minimum leaving age. The proportion of children staying on at school to complete secondary education is a measure of the level of educational benefits received. Cross-national variations in the age of commencing secondary education and its standard and content mean that any figures are 'rough' indicators, and should be treated cautiously in comparisons. To increase accuracy UNESCO figures are adjusted for differences in national elementary and secondary systems. These place Northern Ireland third, behind only the United States and Belgium, in the amount of education received by young people. There is no apparent association between the degree of a regime's legitimacy and the extent of education it provides its youths.

Studies of economic conditions usually emphasize two measures of wellbeing – gross national product *per capita* and the rate of economic growth. Gross national product figures are not conventionally calculated for Northern Ireland on its own, because its economy is integrated so closely with that of Britain. As the *per capita* gross national product of Britain is thirteenth among the nations surveyed, and as Northern Ireland is poor relative to Britain (cf. Table II.6) then it will inevitably rank low by Western standards, above only the Republic of Ireland, and perhaps Austria and Italy. Northern Ireland has, however, had its economy expand at a rate about one-fifth faster than that of Britain in the past two decades.[19] This would still make its growth rate below average by Continental standards (cf. Table XV.1). In the group of nations as a whole, the slowest rates of economic growth have been experienced by those nations with the highest levels of political allegiance. This statistically significant finding may reflect the joint influence of wartime invasion and defeat upon levels of discord and growth rates in the period prior to that measured here. It could also result from the fact that the regimes with greater discord have a slightly lower level of *per capita* income, as indicated by the negative correlation for this indicator. At a minimum, the findings show that discord did not inhibit economic growth in the period 1958–68.

Unless one is committed to an exclusively materialist definition of social wellbeing, then it is important to consider the effect of political discord upon an individual's psychological wellbeing and his relationships with others around him. The advance of welfare state legislation and the rise in economic prosperity in Western nations provide ample reminders that material change does not, *ipso facto*, guarantee social or political harmony. Social scientists have no single measure of desirable social relations comparable to the economist's concept of gross national product. Mancur Olson Jr. has suggested that the appropriate theoretical conception would be a society seeking 'the minimization of alienation'.[20] Stated positively, this would mean measuring the maximization of social integration, using the term integration in its broadest sense. An individual's integration in social groups is also regarded as significant in a number of theories of fully legitimate government.[21] The very breadth of this criterion is both an advantage and a weakness in application. The relationship of regimes to social integration might be tested in many different contexts. The availability of comparable cross-national data fortuitously limits tests, yet provides them in several very different areas of social life.

Membership in voluntary associations is one important indicator of integration or, at the least, of the absence of alienation. Many organizations can mediate between an individual and the regime as well as provide companionship near home. The two organizations for which comparative data are available are ones which regimes are likely to be concerned about, churches and trade unions. Church attendance is significant inasmuch as churches not only concern man's relation with the supernatural, but also provide an immediate community of believers who can support a wide variety of social relationships locally within a parish or community. The corporateness of worship can extend through the week. Alternatively, one might hypothesize that church attendance would be inversely related to legitimacy. In countries where regimes lack full legitimacy, individuals might turn to religion in an attempt to transcend worldly political problems. The data on church attendance summarized in Table XV.1 are drawn from a variety of survey sources, and the definition of 'regular' attendance is not constant from country to country, because of variations in phrasing questions. Northern Ireland ranks second among Western nations in church attendance; only the Republic of Ireland is ahead of it. There is no significant association between church attendance and challenges to regimes. In view of the relatively high level of church attendance among Roman Catholics, an additional test was made of the relationship between the proportion of Catholics in a country and allegiance to the regime. There is a positive correlation between political discord and the proportion of Catholics in a country, significant at the ·10 level in the product moment correlation (r=·41; T=·21). The relationship is not caused by Catholic parties challenging regimes, but rather, by anti-clerical Communist parties challenging both church and state in Continental countries.

Trade unions integrate individuals into groups with very different values from churches. Their social functions are comparable, in that unions are an intermediary between individuals and their regime, and also join people together in face-to-face local groups to achieve common ends. Reciprocally, a low rate of union organization might indicate substantial obstacles to co-operation within a society. The most appropriate national indicator of unionization is the ratio of union members to workers employed outside agriculture. This avoids distortions arising from the differing importance of farming cross-nationally. Judged by this indicator, Northern Ireland once again ranks satisfactorily in the willingness of its people to come together for collective purposes. It is tied at eighth among 18 nations, ahead of Britain, America and Ireland. There is no significant relationship between the degree of unionization in a society and the authority of its regime.

Examining social disintegration has particular relevance in studies of divided regimes, in so far as a 'bad' regime is likely to drive people to act in an anti-social fashion. In particular, it might be hypothesized that the frustrations of repressed and rebellious subjects might lead them to displace political aggressions elsewhere. Such a hypothesis calls attention to the potential value of evidence about small, even deviant groups, as an indication of pervasive social conditions.

Displacement of aggressive feelings at work could lead to frequent industrial disputes and strikes, as workers and employers faced at work questions of authority which could not be resolved by regimes lacking full legitimacy. The plausibility of this hypothesis is further strengthened if one assumes that anti-regime trade unionists will encourage strikes, not only for economic gain but also as a sign of protest against the regime. The measure of strikes–days lost on average per annum for each worker outside agriculture–shows Northern Ireland ranking fifth among Western nations, ahead of Great Britain in the years under review, but behind Ireland and America. There is no relationship between strikes and political discord.

Suicide is another indicator used by sociologists since Durkheim to measure integration within a society. It is an extreme form of aggression, albeit directed against oneself. The exact significance of suicide in a culture has been much disputed, and the classification of deaths as suicide undoubtedly varies cross-nationally.[22] Bearing these qualifications in mind, it is none the less interesting to note that suicide rates in Northern Ireland are third lowest among 18 nations, and, except for the Republic, lowest in the Anglo-American world. The low suicide rate in Northern Ireland is not an artifact of its large Catholic population, for Northern Ireland has a lower such rate than seven of the nine other countries that have at least as large a proportion of Catholics. In so far as a low suicide rate indicates a high degree of social integration, then in Northern Ireland it might reflect good relations within each religious community, if not always between the two communities. One might even suggest that the need to unite against 'the enemy' gives both Protestants and Catholics a higher degree of social integration than would otherwise be expected.[23] There is no cross-national support for such an hypothesis in the overall correlations.

Another indicator of aggressiveness is crime against the person. American studies have particularly emphasized the extent to which blacks, in reaction to their political status, have vented their aggressive feelings by physical assault, traditionally against other members of their race. Crime statistics, even more than suicide rates, are subject to many problems of measurement error. These difficulties are compounded cross-nationally. Hence, to assure as high a degree of comparability as possible, the data used here refer only to actions known to the police resulting in the loss of life, whether classified as murder or manslaughter. It is assumed that in Western societies violent deaths will more likely become known to the police than other forms of crime and that they will be most likely to be classified similarly. Northern Ireland conditions are exceptional. The rate of violent deaths was 0·3 per 100,000 people for the five-year period 1963–67, ranking lowest among 18 Western nations. This finding is particularly striking, inasmuch as political violence causing death has been a recurring feature of Irish and Ulster politics. It shows that Ulster people can distinguish between lethal assault with a political purpose and what might be called politically meaningless manslaughter. Violent deaths are twice as common in Britain, and 18 times so in the United States. Only the Republic of Ireland has a death by violence rate so low. Cross-nationally, there is no tendency for violent deaths to occur more frequently in divided regimes; if anything, they occur slightly less often.

Consideration must be given to the possibility that third factors may influence both the degree of legitimacy and particular social conditions. This would mask a real relationship or create a spurious correlation. On theoretical grounds, the crucial third factor might possibly be gross national product *per capita* or the degree of urbanization, defining this in two different ways – the proportion of people in towns of more than 20,000 and the proportion of the employed population in agriculture. Consistently, these controls further reduce the existing limited degrees of correlation. In only one instance did stronger relationships appear when the effect of these influences was controlled for.[24]

The ranking of countries by social conditions shows that Northern Ireland people enjoy average conditions by the standards of the Western world. Among 18 nations, they have an average rank of 8·2 on the 13 measures of social wellbeing for which data are available. If the mean ranking for all 18 countries on each of the measures is taken, then Northern Ireland is placed tied for fourth with three other countries on its aggregate score. Northern Ireland ranks tied with Britain, and ahead of the United States. Within the United Kingdom, Northern Ireland is not unusual with some social conditions slightly less favourable than those in England. The same is also true of Wales, Scotland and English regions relatively distant from London.[25] It is equally noteworthy that Northern Ireland consistently ranks ahead of the Republic of Ireland in its social conditions, for the average position of the Republic is 10·2, and its aggregate rank ties at 13th among 18 nations. The disparities between rankings as between indicators emphasize the importance of the country and the criteria chosen for comparison. By the standards of Britain, Northern Ireland is less prosperous, but it is more prosperous than the Republic. The Republic of Ireland, by comparison, may claim that its subjects are better integrated into one community, for they have a higher rate of church attendance and a lower suicide rate than Britain or Northern Ireland. Ulster people can look down on the British for their much higher suicide rate and much lower level of church attendance. In such ambiguous circumstances, international comparisons of social conditions are unlikely to alter the views of Northern Ireland subjects toward the Stormont regime.

The foregoing 13 tests of the general hypothesis consistently support the conclusion that there is no relationship between the degree of authority of the regime and the social conditions of its people. Only three from the thirteen of the Pearson's r correlations are statistically significant: those concerning tuberculosis, over-crowding and growth rate of the economy, 1958–68.[26] These correlations perhaps reflect the extent to which regimes lacking full legitimacy govern countries that were battlefields in the Second World War. They do not appear to be theoretically significant. It would be wisest to emphasize that 12 of the 13 rank-order correlations showed nil relationship between regime authority and social conditions. Moreover, some correlations show, if anything, relationships to be the reverse of expectations; for example, there is a negative association between deaths by violence and political discord.

Testing the relationship between a regime's authority and civil and political rights requires a shift from quantitative to qualitative evidence, for deprivations of individual civil rights are often not easily quantified. Marshall defines civil rights as follows:

> The civil element is composed of the rights necessary for individual freedom – liberty of the person, freedom of speech, thought and faith, the right to own property and to conclude valid contracts, and the right to justice.[27]

These conditions are logically independent of the right to vote: they were general in England before the majority had the ballot. While the chief civil rights are clearly stated in Marshall's statement, there are substantial practical problems in applying them. One difficulty is proving a negative – that there are *no* restraints on liberty of the person or freedom of speech. Where infringements of civil rights are claimed, the regime in power often rejects the allegation; there is thus no standard international compilation of statistics on the denial of civil rights. In view of these difficulties, no general test can be undertaken of the correlation between political authority and the civil rights of subjects. The review of evidence will concentrate on Northern Ireland; references to other countries will be made where appropriate information is at hand.

Liberty of the person is explicitly infringed in Northern Ireland by the Civil Authorities (Special Powers) Act, introduced at the foundation of the regime as a temporary measure and subsequently re-enacted and extended with amendments. The Act empowers the Minister of Home Affairs to detain persons without trial or the relief of habeas corpus for activities specified in the Act *or* for matters not specified therein but 'calculated to be prejudicial to the preservation of the peace or maintenance of order in Northern Ireland' (Sec. 2.4). Under this Act, a variety of organizations such as the IRA have been declared illegal. Members or suspected members of these groups have been arrested and interned indefinitely without trial or charge. The power of internment has been used principally when IRA activity was substantial. At the height of the IRA campaign in the 1950s as many as 187 persons were interned without trial at one time, some individuals for several years.[28] Internment without trial has subsequently been avoided because of the resulting political criticism; it was noteworthy that the regime did *not* use its internment powers in 1968–70 notwithstanding Protestant demands that this be done.

Whatever is decided about the need of the regime to intern enemies or potential enemies, there is no doubt that Stormont's powers derogate from the liberty of the individuals so interned. Harry Calvert, author of a standard study of constitutional law in Northern Ireland, notes, 'The Special Powers Act certainly does evidence a radical departure from the procedural safeguards traditionally and justifiably regarded as desirable for the preservation of civil liberties.' It is, for instance, contrary to the European Convention on the Protection of Human Rights and Fundamental Freedoms.[29] The only other place in the Anglo-American world where similar legislation is known is the Republic of Ireland. Its Offences Against the State Act of 1939 was passed to meet the same problem that confronted the Stormont regime – armed groups pursuing a policy intended to unite Ireland – and its provisions are much the same. The conditions of internment policy in the Republic have often appeared draconian by comparison with conditions of imprisonment in Northern Ireland.[30] The suspension of habeas corpus is justified in the words of an Irish Supreme Court opinion on the ground that detention 'is not in the nature of punishment but of preventive justice, being a precautionary measure'.[31]

Freedom of speech, thought and faith is unchallenged in Northern Ireland. Freedom of religious practice is explicitly protected in entrenched clauses of the Government of Ireland Act, 1920;[32] unlike England and Scotland, there is no established church. Freedom of thought is not infringed in Northern Ireland. It could be argued that the extent of controversy about the regime and the variety of participants in the controversy puts a freer and wider range of views in front of Northern Ireland people than would occur were the regime fully legitimate. Openness to ideas is further facilitated by the free circulation within Northern Ireland of periodicals from the Republic and Britain. Efforts are made to infringe freedom of speech from time to time by discretionary order of the Minister of Home Affairs. For instance, sale of the Republican newspaper, *The United Irishman*, was subject to legal harassment in an order of December 23, 1968, but the inability of the RUC to enforce the ban led to the virtual abrogation of the order subsequently. The Prevention of Incitement to Hatred Act, passed in June, 1970, formally provides a curb on the speech of anti-Catholic propagandists. The Rev. Ian Paisley protested strongly against its passage, alleging that it was part of a deal with Opposition MPs. The Stormont regime has not, however, shown any eagerness to use the Act against persons making inflammatory statements or displaying slogans such as 'To Hell with the Pope' on the outside walls of their homes. More censorship exists in the Republic. It primarily concerns morality rather than political issues.[33]

Freedom of association, omitted by Marshall from his catalogue of civil rights, is a necessary corollary of freedom of speech, for an individual who can only express his thoughts in isolation can have little influence in political society. The principal restrictions placed upon freedom of association in Northern Ireland arise from discord about the regime; they do not occur in industrial relations.[34] Restrictions upon armed, quasi-military and uniformed political organizations are not unique to Northern Ireland. For instance, Finland, a land where private para-military organizations have fought for and against the regime, has legislation prohibiting military training except under the auspices of the Ministry of Defence.[35] In Northern Ireland, this ban is primarily directed against the IRA; the Ulster Volunteer Force is similarly proscribed. The practical effect of the ban on IRA training is limited by the use made of training facilities in the Republic. The ban on military training has been held not to cover the organization of gun clubs formed by ex-members of the B Special Constabulary,[36] nor does the ban on uniformed political organizations apply to the Orange Order. Its distinctive regalia is not regarded as that of a political association under the terms of the Act. Republican clubs have been deemed prohibited associations.[37] The proscription of anti-regime associations is not unique to Northern Ireland. It has also been practised since the Second World War in the Republic of Ireland, in France, Germany, the United States, and abortively in Australia, against the Communist Party.

The Social Consequences of Discord

From time to time since the start of the civil rights demonstrations, the Minister of Home Affairs has issued proclamations banning all public processions for a stated period of time. The issuance of such a proclamation in late July, 1970, was primarily a restriction upon the freedom of association of Protestants, for major Protestant parades were scheduled for August 12th. In 1970, as in the nineteenth century, government bans did not stop marches. Another technique occasionally used by the Northern Ireland courts to restrain freedom of association is a court order binding an individual over to keep the peace for a stated period of time. The Rev. Ian Paisley has twice preferred to serve short prison sentences rather than accept any restrictions upon his activities.

The right to own property and to conclude valid contracts is uninfringed by statute law in Northern Ireland. There is no body of law on the statute book that still reflects the penal laws against Catholics of the late seventeenth century. In recognizing freedom of contract and property ownership, Northern Ireland is consistent with other Western nations. There is, however, an informal inhibition upon freedom to own property, for in times of trouble Catholics living in predominantly Protestant areas have recurringly been subject to intimidation, reinforced by guns and by arson, to make them leave their homes. Intimidation has been a recurring feature of life in Belfast for a century. In 1935, an estimated 500 Catholic families were driven from their homes by mobs threatening violence; a small number of Protestant families were also forced from their homes.[38] In August, 1969, intimidation and burning once again occurred in Belfast. The Northern Ireland government estimates that approximately 200 houses were destroyed then, and another 500 damaged. In all, more than 9,000 persons were rehoused, because they felt unsafe as members of a minority in high tension areas. Ghetto residences are safer than integrated housing when a community is dis-integrating. The worst of the arson was directed against Catholics and they formed the bulk of those leaving homes they rented or owned. The Ardoyne area, where dozens of families were burned out, has since been a stronghold of the Provisional IRA. Protestants too have suffered from intimidation.[39] After Easter, 1970, more than 100 Protestant families on the New Barnsley council estate in West Belfast abandoned their homes because of insecurity. By autumn, enrolment at the school on the estate had dropped from 500 to 20 Protestant children.[40]

434

The right to justice is described by Marshall as of central importance because 'it is the right to defend and assert all one's rights on terms of equality with others and by due process of law'.[41] Justice can be given two very different kinds of definitions. One definition emphasizes the intrinsic 'rightness' of what is done, however right may be defined morally and empirically. The other regards justice as actions that are 'correct' according to statutory laws and procedures as interpreted by judges. There is no assurance in any land that legal processes will in every instance give an outcome consistent with substantive ideas of what is morally right. One does not have to read Franz Kafka[42] to appreciate that the regulations and conventions of the legal process so emphasize procedural concerns that they may at times conflict with substantive concerns, thus increasing rather than decreasing political discord.

The importance of procedural constraints in relation to substantive justice is illustrated by the activities of the Northern Ireland Commissioner for Complaints. The office was established in December, 1969 to investigate citizens' complaints of unfair treatment by local authorities and other Northern Ireland public bodies. It was one of a number of reforms announced in May, 1969, in response to the civil rights campaign. The terms of reference were not confined to cases of religious discrimination, for maladministration can occur between members of the same religion as well as across communal lines. None the less, it was expected that the Commissioner would settle many complaints alleging sectarian bias. In the words of a Stormont white paper, 'This should enable any genuine grievances to be settled.'[43] Promptly upon the passage of the Act establishing the office, a senior Stormont civil servant, J. M. Benn, was appointed to the post. By October, 1970, he had a staff of 47.

The Unionist regime's claim that the Commissioner could ensure substantive justice by settling 'any genuine grievance' is meaningless. In law, the Commissioner can only investigate those cases that lie within his statutory responsibilities, take into account evidence consistent with his prescribed responsibilities, and arrive at conclusions that are within the terms of his statutory powers. The Commissioner's Second Report, based upon ten months' experience in working the law, draws attention to the limitations as well as the strengths of his office in securing redress of all citizens' grievances. Of the first 970 complaints filed, nearly one-third, 307, were outside the Commissioner's powers of jurisdiction. The most important exclusion, given the emphasis upon charges of job discrimination, is the absence of any statutory power to investigate discrimination in private employment in Northern Ireland.[44]

In enquiring into the validity of complaints, the Commissioner, as a bureaucratic official, must use procedures involving delay as well as care. Moreover, complaints may be incomplete in details, malicious, frivolous or poorly grounded in law or in fact. The allegation of unfair treatment is not, *ipso facto*, proof that substantive injustice has occurred. Reciprocally, a formal finding by the Commissioner that maladministration has not occurred is no assurance that substantive injustice has not been done. At best, it increases the probability that the matter concerned did not involve a substantive wrong to a citizen. The reason for this is that the procedures governing the determination of maladministration exclude from the Commissioner's consideration matters that could be considered crucial to a determination of fact by an historian or a social scientist. For example, in the absence of maladministration, the Commissioner may not review the use that a local or public authority makes of its discretionary powers in evaluating candidates applying for a job. Yet in many employment situations, especially in a land where those seeking work heavily outnumber the vacancies, choosing one among several qualified applicants is the most important decision in the employment process. As the Commissioner notes:

> It is not difficult for a body if it is so inclined to profess policies of impartial selection and to point to ostensibly proper procedures whilst yet following discriminatory practices. It can, for example, find plausible reasons for placing at the top of the list a candidate whom it prefers for a quite different reason.[45]

As long as the local authority has not violated any of its procedural rules (e.g., appointing a person outside its age limits or lacking the educational qualifications advertised) then it may continue to exercise discretion in a way that an aggrieved subject could regard as discriminatory in fact even if not so under the terms of the Commissioner for Complaints Act (Northern Ireland) 1969.

The Commissioner's experience in attempting to gather information about possible patterns of discrimination in employment increases the probability that discretionary powers may be abused. American investigations of employment practices have often taken the proportion of minority group personnel hired as an indicator of the consistent use of discretionary powers in a discriminatory manner. In Northern Ireland, a job applicant's statement of schooling almost invariably testifies to his religion too, given the maintenance of separate and distinctively named Catholic schools. The Commissioner found it 'unconvincing' that some officials in small Northern Ireland bodies claimed they neither knew the religion of their staff members nor had means of finding this out.[46]

Within the scope of his powers and procedural constraints, the Commissioner seeks to arrive at settlements acceptable both to the complainant and the authority against which the complaint is lodged. In the extreme instance, the authority is appreciative of attention being called to its administrative error and promptly satisfies the complainant. A finding that an individual has been the victim of maladministration does not of itself resolve the problem of what, if anything, will be done to redress his substantive injustice. At a minimum, the 'considerable concern' expressed by the Commissioner about the length of time taken in processing cases may leave the injured person without benefit of a house or job while the complaint is being investigated. More importantly, the Commissioner has no mandatory powers to assure substantive redress; he cannot issue positive orders that the aggrieved individual be forthwith given a house or appointed to a specific job. If the public authority wishes to resist the course of action suggested in the Commissioner's findings, it is free to do so. The individual favoured by the finding must then go to a conventional court with a civil action for damages or repair of his rights, a procedure that can be costly as well as lengthy.[47]

By comparison with citizens elsewhere in the United Kingdom or in the American federal system, individuals resident in Northern Ireland have more legal restrictions upon their activities, and fewer procedural safeguards. Consistently, the Stormont Parliament has used its power to refuse to follow Westminster in passing permissive legislation concerning matters such as sabbath observance, divorce, homosexuality, abortion and drinking. In Ulster, liberty of the individual remains constrained by the regime's desire to enforce particular moral standards universally.[48] Individuals are also handicapped in securing redress of grievances through the courts. There is, for example, no statutory bill of rights and the judicial review of executive acts is based upon the archaic procedure of the prerogative writs. The Home Office confirmed to the Campaign for Social Justice in 1964 that there was no means by which an individual Catholic

The Social Consequences of Discord

could get a court to hear complaints of discrimination.[49] In the United States, by contrast, the Supreme Court has gradually broadened the interpretation of the due process clause of the Constitution to give individuals many legal channels by which they can seek to defend or advance claims to substantive justice.

In so far as any set of judicial proceedings and legal statutes will some times fall short of what the perfectionist or the man in the street may mean by justice, then civil rights becomes a question of assessing whether individuals have an equal probability of obtaining justice or avoiding injustice in contacts with the law. If departures from justice form a pattern rather than occurring randomly, then the loss of justice will be greater. At the most elemental level of equal protection of life, person and property, substantial departures from justice have existed for decades in Northern Ireland, yet few persons are ever tried or convicted for causing deaths in political disorder. The same is true of individuals causing bodily injury, whether demonstrators or policemen. It is even more true for the individuals engaged in burning houses and intimidating inhabitants from their homes. From October, 1968 until Easter, 1970, Catholics were a disproportionate number of those killed, injured or intimidated from their homes. There is little solace for Protestants in noting that in the subsequent nine months there was a move toward greater equality, as more Protestants became the victim of attacks by organized and unorganized Republican and Catholic action groups in Belfast. For both communities equally to *lack* protection from political violence is hardly a civil good.

The absence of equal protection of the laws was especially evident in 1969, when members of the Royal Ulster Constabulary failed to apprehend Protestants harassing, stoning or clubbing disaffected Catholic demonstrators.[50] In August, 1969, RUC men were responsible for directing automatic weapons fire at Catholics. Evidence to the Scarman Tribunal conveys very clearly the police belief that their job was to protect Protestants from assault by Catholic demonstrators, without regard to what Protestant groups were simultaneously doing to Catholics.

Immediately after the British Army became established in Belfast, the situation changed abruptly. Catholics still were unequally protected, but in autumn, 1969, they were the favoured group. The RUC was 'expelled' from the Bogside of Londonderry and the Falls Road area of West Belfast. Barricades were established to keep police–

438

especially police in armoured cars–from entering the areas. The British Army stood sentry near Catholic barricades. Their efforts were supplemented by vigilante groups, with armed Republicans available for defence in the last resort. The establishment of this 'No go' land for the police became the subject of a steady stream of complaints from Protestants who viewed it as an unpunished rebellion against the regime. Complaints increased when it became evident that arms were being stored in the 'No go' areas. In spring, 1970, the Army and the RUC began to co-operate closely in covering the two areas. The Army-RUC arms raid and curfew in the Lower Falls in July, 1970, demonstrated that these Catholic areas were no longer privileged. Later in the month the Prime Minister announced that policemen would begin returning to 'Free' Belfast and 'Free' Derry in increasing numbers till normality was restored. By September, 1970, the Falls Road Citizens' Defence Committee was complaining that the security forces were engaged in 'one-sided' searches for arms in Catholic districts. It asked for an 'equality of searching' in Protestant and Catholic districts. It did not specify whether it wished the security forces to search an equal number of Protestant and Catholic homes, or search until they found an equal or proportionate amount of arms on each side.[52] By February, 1971, some Catholics in Belfast felt the hand of Republican 'courts', established by IRA groups to mete out summary punishment in areas where civil authorities were not welcome. Sentences ranged from tarring and feathering to death.

Decisions to prosecute–or not to prosecute–also raise questions about the regime's ability or desire to apply laws equally to all individuals. The matter became specially serious in June, 1970, with the adoption of an Act providing stiff minimum mandatory sentences for a wide variety of activities, ranging from shouting insults to hurling stones or petrol bombs or marching in illegal parades. An early test of the new legislation and its use came in Londonderry on August 12, 1970, when thousands of Apprentice Boys sought once again to hold their annual parade notwithstanding the official ban. The *Belfast Telegraph* that day headlined, 'Thousands Join Defiance Walk'. An Army spokesman at the scene explained the absence of thousands of arrests by stating that the activities of the 3,000 or so men in parade regalia were the movements of 'an orderly football type crowd' and not an illegal parade.[53] Subsequently, the Stormont regime has used a policy of selectively prosecuting some Protestants and Catholics in illegal parades, but not prosecuting all who are present on such occasions. Because the Derry ban was announced by the Minister of Home Affairs under the Special Powers Act and not under the Public Order Act or any of its amendments, Protestant marchers prosecuted for violating the order have been fined and not subject to a mandatory prison sentence of six months. This would have been the case if Stormont had used against Ultras legislation passed *a propos* civil rights demonstrations.[54]

The most egregious failure of the regime to prosecute on a basis of equality is the indictment of Bernadette Devlin *and no one else* for involvement in the rising in the Bogside in August, 1969. There is no doubt that Miss Devlin participated in building the Bogside barricades.[55] The point here is that she did not singlehandedly cause the rising. Yet no other Catholic defender of the Bogside was indicted along with Miss Devlin. Undoubtedly, the names of others involved in the rising were known. (The RUC has justified its inability to indict policemen guilty of crimes of assault on the Bogside by saying that it does not know who the criminals are.) The failure of the regime to indict all the leaders indicates that it was less interested in the equal application of the laws than in imprisoning a particular political opponent.

A catalogue of statutes, court cases and discretionary administrative decisions that avoided court cases could be continued *ad infinitum*. It would include complaints voiced by the Rev. Dr. Ian Paisley on behalf of 'loyalists' who have come into legal conflict with the Stormont regime,[56] as well as complaints voiced by civil rights groups and Republicans. Sufficient illustrations have been cited here and in Chapter IV to reject the null hypothesis, and conclude that there is a relationship between political discord and civil rights, especially equal protection by the law. The finding is not unique to Northern Ireland, although the extent of deprivation is unusual in the Western world today. It could equally well be applied to the administration of justice in parts of the United States, where both courts and police have systematically deprived black Americans of civil rights, not least in those Southern states where American Ultras are politically strong.[57]

Marshall's definition of political rights is clearly and succinctly stated, 'The right to participate in the exercise of political power as a member of a body invested with political authority or as an elector of the members of such a body.'[58] The definition comprises two separate criteria–the right to vote and the right to hold office. Both of these rights concern conditions for which regimes are explicitly responsible.

The elements of a democratic election are several, not singular. They include the right to vote, to vote secretly, to have ballots counted fairly, and to determine major offices in the regime. Notwithstanding the many controversies surrounding politics in Northern Ireland, the conduct of elections results in relatively little controversy. This does not mean that the elections are free from all suspicion of fraud, for there are cases of personation leading to court convictions at Stormont elections. But it is unusual for an individual to allege that malpractices have influenced results in a marginal constituency. There is no evidence to suggest that any Stormont election has fit any of the categories of pathological elections–the muddled, stolen or made.[59]

The great predominance of Unionist representation in the Stormont House of Commons is not an infringement upon political rights of a citizen, unless only a proportional representation electoral system is assumed to assure this right. The electoral system used in Northern Ireland, the first-past-the-post plurality system, is customary in the Anglo-American world. Wherever used, such a system favours the strongest party. In Northern Ireland, the fact that opposition is divided into several parties, all very much weaker than the Unionists, accentuates the Unionist strength. Comparative analysis of inequalities in the proportion of MPs to a party's share of the vote shows no significant correlation with the strength of anti-regime parties.[60]

The chief limitation upon the right to vote in Northern Ireland has occurred in local government election. In part this arose from the retention in Northern Ireland of franchise laws restricting voting to persons with statutory qualifications as property-owners or tenants. In consequence, about one-quarter of persons eligible to vote in Westminster elections were not eligible to vote in their local authority, and plural votes could be claimed by people with multiple property qualifications. At one time the legislation was not unique to Northern Ireland; it prevailed in England until the end of the Second World War.[61] It is estimated that a disproportionate number of persons ineligible to vote in local elections were Catholics, though disfranchisement affected a substantial number of Protestants too. The greater denial of franchise rights arose from gerrymandering procedures in towns where Catholics formed the majority. The most extreme example was the borough of Londonderry, where Catholics out-number Protestants in the population by a ratio of two to one, and the Unionists outnumbered Nationalists on the council by almost the same ratio. In 1969 the Cameron Commission found that the limited franchise and gerrymandering enabled Unionists to hold a majority on four of five local authorities studied where adult Catholics were a majority in the population. In response to civil rights demands, the Stormont regime has introduced a new franchise law, giving one man one vote in local elections and pledged that electoral districts will be 'impartially' drawn in future. Moreover, it suspended local authority elections in 1969 pending the implementation of the recommendations of the Macrory Report on local government reform. These recommendations will substantially alter local authority boundaries and reduce their powers.[62]

Voting is a necessary but not a sufficient political right. Marshall emphasizes that individuals must also have a share in executive power. In Northern Ireland, the chief executive authority of government is the Cabinet. The House of Commons has even less influence in Northern Ireland than in other British-style regimes, because of the permanent strength of the Unionist Party. When an Opposition MP does succeed in securing passage of a bill, it may be one like the Wild Birds Act of 1931.[63] In no country does the choice of political leaders operate strictly as a random process. Women, for example, are disproportionately represented in the political executive in every Western country. Hence, a degree of under- or over-representation of a group in government would prove less than the total exclusion or virtual exclusion of a group from a share in executive powers of the executive.

There is no *de jure* exclusion of Catholics from executive office in Northern Ireland, but there is a consistent pattern of *de facto* exclusion and under-representation. No Catholic has held Cabinet office since the founding of the state in 1921. The possession of a monopoly of the political executive has meant that any Catholics in appointive offices have had to depend upon the endorsement of Unionists, a circumstance not likely to encourage an independence of outlook among individuals from a minority. In the senior civil service, approximately six per cent of senior appointments are held by Roman Catholics. Catholic appointees to a range of part-time government advisory bodies are as many as two out of twelve on the Milk Marketing Board, down to nil on the National Assistance

442

Board.[64] About 11 per cent of the membership of the RUC was Catholic prior to the Hunt Committee reforms; they were principally men with family connections with the police. The B Special Constabulary was an exclusively Protestant organization.[65] In such circumstances, it is hardly surprising that there is a substantial difference between Catholics and Protestants in the influence they reckon that people like themselves have upon government (D.I.= 21%), and an even greater difference–40 per cent–between Americans and Ulster Catholics.[66] The 1969 reforms in response to civil rights demonstrations have increased the number of government boards with Catholic appointees. In every instance, however, Catholics sit as nominees of the Unionist government, and not as representatives chosen by Catholic electors.

The exclusion of Catholics from sharing executive power in Northern Ireland is matched nowhere else in the Western world. The nearest equivalent was the exclusion of American blacks from senior posts in American federal government. At the time of the 1961 census, blacks constituted 11 per cent of the population but held no senior executive appointment in the Kennedy Administration; Congressional committee posts were the most senior positions held. In the subsequent decade, however, changes have occurred. Robert Weaver was appointed to a Cabinet post in 1966 and Thurgood Marshall to the United States Supreme Court in 1967. In Northern Ireland, no such change has occurred, nor have the leaders of the Unionist regime given any public sign of wishing to share any executive power with Catholics.

The extent to which a regime's activities provide symbolic gratification is, as Almond and Powell note, 'difficult to measure'. They suggest that symbolic gratification might be provided by such things as official 'displays of flags, troops and military ceremony; visits by royal or high officials' and by a variety of culturally specific activities.[67] The difficulty in measuring symbolic gratifications (or symbolic deprivations) does not make their character any less significant. Symbols can be a source of emotional gratification to individuals. Subjects may in certain circumstances respond more strongly to symbolic gratifications than to material inducements. This is particularly true in wartime, when patriotic symbols encourage men to sacrifice their lives.

In a divided regime such as Northern Ireland, the symbols of the regime gratify some subjects but enrage others. Each of the indicators

The Social Consequences of Discord

cited by Almond and Powell as a source of gratification is a source of political disorder if displayed where both Protestants and Catholics can express their conflicting emotions. The most obvious example of this is the flag. The official flag of Northern Ireland is the Union Jack. Catholics prefer to fly the tricolour of the Irish Republic. (Some Republicans, such as Bernadette Devlin, prefer the Plough and the Stars of James Connolly's Irish Citizens' Army, thus showing their rejection of both regimes.) The Flags and Emblems (Display) Act of 1954 makes it an offence to interfere with the display of the Union Jack or to display a flag or emblem, e.g., the tricolour, in circumstances considered by the police likely to cause a breach of public order. The Union Jack is so much used by Unionists and the Orange Order in their parades and processions that Catholics regard it as a partisan emblem. For example, a Catholic woman testified to the Scarman Tribunal that in August, 1969, she was awakened by a group pushing a petrol bomb and a Union Jack inside her house, a symbol that she was being burned out by loyalists. When a Catholic in County Tyrone sought to remove a Union Jack from an Orange Hall on the eve of the Twelfth in 1970, he was apprehended by local men. The culprit was sentenced to six months for his action. The judge told him he was 'lucky to be alive'. The police will at times act to remove tricolours. During the 1964 Westminster election the display of the Irish tricolour from a Republican party office in the Falls Road area of West Belfast became the subject of repeated public protests by the Rev. Ian Paisley. After several nights of disorders the RUC removed the flag; thirty people required hospital treatment for injuries suffered in the resulting disorder. In 1970, two Belfast Catholics were given six-month prison sentences after police found them painting a tricolour and slogan on a house.[68]

Royal symbols are much used by Protestants in Northern Ireland to signify their rejection of the Republic in the South. Reciprocally, Republicans have always desired to avoid association with symbols of the British crown, even when the Irish Free State was legally still a part of the Empire with dominion status.[69] The 'national' anthem in law and in the eyes of fully allegiant subjects is 'God Save the Queen', as in Britain. Catholics, however, prefer to sing the national anthem of the Republic, 'The Soldier's Song', composed for the Republican movement in 1907 as a song to encourage guerilla soldiers to fight against the Crown. In October, 1970, a Catholic youth received a six-month sentence for singing the Republican

444

anthem after a policeman ordered a crowd to stop.[70] As Republicans may enrage Protestants by deriding royalty, so Protestant demonstrators may enrage Catholics by making derogatory or obscene references to the Pope. A journalist supporter of Orange outlook aptly sums up the gulf by noting, *a propos* a display of political slogans on a Belfast house, 'No Pope here. No surrender. God save the Queen. The three standard slogans of Protestant Ulster.'[71] In these circumstances, it is hardly surprising that Opposition MPs should protest about the requirement that an oath of allegiance to the Crown must be taken by an estimated 66,000 persons in jobs in public employment in Northern Ireland. Austin Currie protested that one of his constituents was required to take an oath of allegiance 'to shovel muck out of a sheugh'. (A sheugh is a ditch.) In reply to this protest, the Minister of Finance asked, 'Is it too much to ask persons paid by the state to express their loyalty to the state?'[72]

The evidence used in testing the association between political authority and social conditions is variable in its quality, given the range of countries surveyed. None the less, findings are consistent in direction, and the general conclusion is clear. There is no tendency for subjects in regimes lacking full legitimacy to suffer deprivation of social rights, whether these are measured in relation to minimum standards of health or maximum economic benefits. Nor does social integration decline where regimes are divided. The finding applies specifically to Northern Ireland as well as to the other 17 Western countries included in the survey. The evidence of Northern Ireland shows that the chief deprivation in a divided regime is political.[73] People lose freedom of speech and association, equal protection of the law, a share in power and emotional satisfactions. The deprivations incurred are not suffered by all the population, for a substantial number of subjects inevitably benefit politically from the actions taken against the disaffected.

If one assumes that things as different as housing conditions and justice are not interchangeable, then it follows that satisfying one of these wants will not affect the sense of deprivation concerning the other. In short, offering jobs and houses to people who are also asking for power and justice will not meet all their demands. Houses and jobs are relatively easy to offer–especially if subsidized by Britain– because they are private goods. Moreover, providing social benefits for Catholics need not deprive Protestants of their benefits. Meeting political demands with political solutions is more difficult. Power and

XVI · Through Irish Eyes

The Irish do more to us than we to them.
J. BOWYER BELL

In a literal sense, no place else on earth is the same as Northern Ireland. This is as true of Leinster, Munster and Connacht in the Republic, as it is of Sweden or Switzerland. To note the uniqueness of a land is not to assert that it is unique in every respect. It would be very odd if a people who so easily fit into English and American life when they emigrate had nothing in common with the two leading nations of the Anglo-American world. One of the great challenges in any study of politics is to specify what things in a society are unique to it, and what things are sufficiently comparable with other lands to support or reject general propositions of the social science. Because managing conflict is of the very essence of politics, the study of a divided regime should, at a minimum, help delimit generalizations drawn from lands in which politics has had a more peaceful course than Northern Ireland.

In a wide-ranging survey of political oppositions, the editor, Robert Dahl, notes that loyal oppositions, a *sine qua non* for fully legitimate regimes, are found at most in only one-quarter of the member states of the United Nations.[1] Because it lacks full legitimacy, Northern Ireland is thus like most other countries in the world. Yet, loyal oppositions are usually found in Western regimes, so that Northern Ireland is atypical of this smaller universe. Within the world of Western nations, Northern Ireland might be compared and contrasted with three very disparate groups. One point of comparison is with Continental nations having major differences about religion or about regimes. The second comparison is with the Republic of Ireland and other nations now or formerly within the British Commonwealth. Of all of the ex-colonial nations, the United States is particularly suited for comparison with Northern Ireland, not only because of historic ties between the two lands but also because American political history has had its share of violence and civil war.

*

Through Irish Eyes

Among fully legitimate European regimes, the Netherlands, super-ficially at least, appears to have much in common with Northern Ireland. Within Dutch society religious differences are of major political and social importance: in addition to a Catholic party, there are two Protestant parties–one fundamentalist and one middle-of-the-road–and two secular parties–one liberal and one Socialist. Each of these three major *zuilen* (literally, pillars)–the Catholic, Protestant and secular–has its own schools, newspapers, television stations and other institutions. These are meant to segregate individuals in each group from their fellow subjects. Yet, instead of resulting in political discord, modern Dutch politics is a record of peaceful, if sometimes incessant, bargaining about political differences among politicians who give full allegiance to the regime.

In his appropriately entitled *The Politics of Accommodation*, Arend Lijphart demonstrates that political differences are settled peacefully in the Netherlands by negotiations among leaders of the three major *zuilen*. The existence of these well-organized groups within society helps make the regime work. As long as the leaders of the groups can settle differences by bargaining on terms that do not create disaffection among their own followers, then the sense of solidarity among each provides assurance that the settlements so made will be accepted. (In France, by contrast, the absence of such strong organization means that nominal leaders are not able to rely upon the assent of their wouldbe followers; bargains, when struck, have no similar guarantee of acceptance or durability.) Because the different groups co-operate through intermediaries, rather than by coalescence into large and heterogeneous parties, Lijphart describes this form of government as consociational democracy; he argues it is just as viable and fully legitimate as the more conventional Anglo-American pluralist model. Reciprocally the decline in attachment to *zuilen*, evident in the 1960s, presents the chief potential challenge to the regime.[2]

From his study of the Netherlands, Lijphart abstracts a set of six conditions favourable to the development of fully legitimate consociational regimes.[3] Of the six conditions, Northern Ireland and the Netherlands appear to be similar on only one: both have distinctive and multiple social differences.[4] Yet this similarity is misleading, for the two societies differ in that the Netherlands has a multiple balance of power, whereas Northern Ireland is divided into two communities.

448

The consequence is extremely important. As Daalder notes in his historical analysis of the Netherlands:

> The divisive effects of segmentation are softened by the circumstance that none of the subcultures has much chance of acquiring an independent majority, while there is at the same time little advantage to any two of them in forming a lasting coalition against the third.[5]

In consequence of the necessity of coalition government, even that most controversial of issues – the relationship of church and state in education – was capable of compromise in the Netherlands. The two Christian groups combined to assure state subsidies to separate denominational schools. Either group, in combination with the secular *zuil*, could prevent the monopoly of the other sectarian groups. In a complementary fashion, the secular *zuil* secured the creation of a secular school system, paralleling the sectarian ones. By contrast, the division of Northern Ireland people into two groups, with one permanently in the majority, removes the need or possibility of coalition government with an alternation of groups in power. Lijphart describes permanent one-party rule in a competitive party system as 'majority dictatorship'.[6]

Because it is rare for the two parties in a two-party system to dispute the very existence of a regime, the particular form of party competition known in Britain and America is sometimes treated as a factor making for a fully legitimate regime. The consequences of two-party politics are contingent rather than certain.[7] The history of modern Austria demonstrates this even more clearly than Northern Ireland, for Austria has had two-party politics cause discord about the regime between the wars, yet help maintain it as fully legitimate since 1945.

Austria and Northern Ireland, improbable as it may seem, have much in common. Both were created after the end of the First World War as a byproduct of settling the nationality claims of their former compatriots. The citizens of the First Austrian Republic did not see themselves as a separate nation-state, but rather as a dominant group within the multi-national Austro-Hungarian Empire or as a part of the German people. The uncertainty about national identity has remained after the Second World War, to an extent matched only among Protestants in Northern Ireland. A survey in Austria in 1964 found that only 47 per cent of respondents believed that Austria is a nation; the median respondent thought that a sense of national consciousness in Austria did not begin to develop until after 1945. The findings show no change from a study in 1956, in which 49 per cent of those interviewed said that Austrians are a separate nation (*eigenes Volk*) whereas 46 per cent thought that they were a group of the German nation.[8] Differences about national identity caused much discord in inter-war Austrian politics, because of Pan-Germanism in many parts of society. Even though a merger with Germany was forbidden by the peace treaty of St. Germain in 1919, the Border issue was as real an issue in Austria as in Northern Ireland.

The intensity and extent of social and political differentiation in the First Austrian Republic is indicated by the fact that the major political groupings were described as *lager*, i.e., armed camps.[9] The dominant camp (cf. the Dutch *zuil*) was pro-clerical as well as Catholic and anti-Socialist. One of the Christian Social Premiers of the First Republic was a Catholic priest. Support for a restoration of the Habsburg monarchy was great, for the Christian Social *lager* was not committed to representative democracy. The second *lager*, almost equal in size, was that of the Marxist-oriented Socialist Party. It was strongly anti-clerical, and against the restoration of a monarchy. Its leaders were prepared to use the rhetoric of Socialist revolution, and, given the level of discord about the regime, such words had more than emotive relevance. The third *lager*, far smaller than the first two, consisted of advocates of Pan-Germanism; they were usually anti-clerical as well as anti-Socialist. Together, the clerical and the Socialist *lagers* dominated the politics of discord in the First Republic.

In the First Republic, as in Northern Ireland, the political groups fought each other in the streets and in the countryside, as well as in Parliament.[10] Because Austria was a defeated nation, the peace treaty restricted the size of its Army. This restriction weakened the public forces available to the regime to secure compliance with its basic laws. Simultaneously, this gave encouragement to the *lager* to form their own armed groups privately, to assist or oppose the regime. The Christian Socials had the *Heimwehr*, in addition to the use of the regime's police and army. The Socialists maintained a *Republikanischer Schutzbund*. During the 1930s, Pan-German and Nazi armed groups became prominent too. These private armed forces differed from the IRA and Protestant Ultra groups in that the Austrian forces were well organized and disciplined. This discipline not only made them more effective as fighting units, it also made it much easier for the groups to be controlled. While these forces were sufficiently strong to maintain discord about the regime and to fight pitched street battles, they were no match for external forces and in 1938 were buried in the *Anschluss* with Hitler's Germany.

Because Northern Ireland and the First Republic of Austria have so much in common, the contrast between the Stormont regime and the Second Austrian Republic is remarkable. Since the withdrawal of the four Allied military powers from Austria in 1955, there has been harmony not discord. Force has not been of any consequence in domestic politics. Catholic priests withdrew from politics under Cardinal Innitzer's orders in 1945, and in 1958 the Socialists declared an end to their *Kulturkampf* with the Church. From 1949 until 1966, the country was governed by a coalition between the pro-Catholic Austrian People's Party and the anti-clerical Socialist Party of Austria. Since that time, control of government has peacefully passed from the coalition to the People's Party and then to the Socialists, confirming beyond doubt the full legitimacy of the regime. Co-operation in coalition recognized the major differences between the two major *lager*.[11] In the distribution of ministerial portfolios each partner was expected to dominate the ministries assigned to it by patronage appointments. Thus, during the Coalition, the People's Party dominated the Army, and the Socialists the police. In government corporations and nationalized industries, appointments were made by proportional representation. The *Proporz* meant the sharing of power within a given sector of the regime. In both instances, the regime was run on an explicitly bi-confessional basis. (Historically, Austrian Socialism has been just as much a 'confessed faith' as Austrian Catholicism.) The resolution of conflict by a *Proporz* system of bargaining between leaders resembles the consociational form of government that developed in the Netherlands.[12] It also has clear relevance to Northern Ireland, inasmuch as a Protestant-Catholic *Proporz* coalition can be easily visualized in theory, though not in fact.

The question then arises: Why is politics in Northern Ireland so different from that in the Second Austrian Republic? This is best answered by explaining the circumstances that changed Austria from an intensely divided regime to a fully legitimate one. The principal force making for change was 17 years of military occupation, first under the Germans, and then by Russian, American, British and

French forces. In the concentration camps of Nazi Germany politicians who had previously opposed each other in principle found that they had some common interests, if only antipathy to subjugation in a German *Reich*. The decision of the four Allied occupying forces to permit free elections throughout Austria in November, 1945, quickly established a representative framework of government.[13] The holocaust of war and double occupation gave highest priority to the simplest needs: finding food, housing and jobs for people, and negotiating the withdrawal of occupation armies to secure the independence of the state. These positive goals, where unity was an asset, confirmed a coalition outlook induced by the Nazi *Anschluss*. While Northern Ireland has known insurrection and civil war, it has never had the experience of military occupation and rule by forces regarded as alien by both Protestants and Catholics. A second way in which Austria differs from Northern Ireland is in the duration of the conflict between Socialist and clerical *lager*. Prior to the First World War, discord within the Austro-Hungarian Empire concerned nationality groups, and the relative merits of authoritarian or elective regimes. The two parties in opposition in the First Austrian Republic were only formed in 1889. By contrast, the groups in opposition in Ulster can trace their lineage back to the seventeenth century. The Fenian movement antedates the creation of the Austrian state by half a century and the Orange Order by a century and one-quarter. A third point of contrast is the very even balance in the electoral strength of the People's Party and the Socialists in the Second Republic. In four elections since the removal of the occupation armies, the two parties have differed by an average of 2·8 per cent of the vote. The presence of minor parties in proportional representation elections has only once allowed either party to obtain an absolute majority of seats in the *Nationalrat*. In such circumstances, coalition was a necessary condition of any government being formed. In Northern Ireland, by contrast, the predominance of the Protestants, reinforced by the over-representation of the stronger group in a British-type electoral system, has always given a united Unionist Party having a large majority at Stormont.

*

The contrast between Northern Ireland and Continental societies may be explained by very different cultural traditions and institutional features of Continental as against Anglo-American societies. These explanations would not, however, apply to a comparison of Northern Ireland with regimes within the Anglo-American world. Comparing the authority of the regime in Northern Ireland and the Republic of Ireland is particularly useful as a means of testing the proposition that there is something in the political culture of people in Ireland that makes them 'ungovernable', that is, unwilling to comply with basic political laws. The charge is often made, casually and sometimes with malice, by those who wish to draw a contrast between the Irish and the English, to the advantage of the latter. It is also a statement that would seem a fair summary of a central theme in Irish history, whatever the century chosen for careful analysis. Yet the fact of violence does *not* establish that political disorder is valued *as an end in itself*, nor does it make disorder the normal way of conducting politics.

In so far as the people of Ireland – North and South – turn naturally to disorderly and extra-constitutional politics, then the history of the Irish Republic should show coercion and disaffection to be as prominent as it is in the North. A superficial look at the history of the Republic might seem to substantiate this view. The signing of the Treaty was followed by a bloody civil war. Since then, IRA groups have actively challenged the authority of the Republic, as well as of Stormont. Yet these incidents, significant as they are, do not substantiate the argument that Irish people are predisposed to reject all political authority. A careful look at the history of the Irish Republic leads to the opposite conclusion. There is no challenge to the legitimacy of the regime, *except* with regard to the unity and independence of Ireland. In so far as this objective is achieved, the great majority of Irish people appear ready to give both support and compliance to the regime. Unlike American politics, in Ireland there is no general predisposition to violence.[14] The Irish have shown themselves as ready to comply with laws as their ancestors have been rebellious. The point is vividly demonstrated by the very swift transition from civil war to the peaceful alternation of parties in government. Republican forces gave the order to dump arms in 1923 and de Valera led a group of ex-Republicans into the Dail in 1927. By 1932, de Valera was Prime Minister. A peaceful exchange of office between a government and loyal opposition had occurred.[15]

The subsequent record of both the Fianna Fail and Fine Gael governments has emphasized the commitment to constitutional politics of the overwhelming majority of the Irish people. The record of the regime is particularly noteworthy in view of the failure of the Republic to provide those benefits of a modern economy that are sometimes thought to be a concomitant or cause of fully legitimate regimes.[16] In fact, one of the classic complaints about Irish politics – both before the Rising and since – is that men who have at one time espoused idealistic causes have been only too ready to turn to the machinations of machine politicians, and adopt policies showing too much regard to their personal and private fortunes.[17]

The response in the Republic to the killings of August, 1969, illustrates the extent to which the regime seeks to avoid going outside the limits of constitutional politics. A public opinion survey in May, 1970, found that only 17 per cent of respondents approved of moving the Irish Army into the North in the event of a repetition of the events of August, 1969; 76 per cent unambiguously disapproved. Similarly, only 14 per cent are willing to endorse the use of force to remove the Border, almost exactly the same proportion as among Catholics in the North (cf. Table V.5).[18] The minority status of Republican elements in the South, whether working through Sinn Fein or the IRA, further underscores popular avoidance of anything that implies a resort to violence to resolve a major political issue. The Republican minority is large enough to challenge the regimes in Dublin and Stormont. But whatever its consequences for political institutions, it is *not* representative of a predisposition to political violence among the bulk of the population.

In both parts of Ireland, violence is accepted as a necessary means to political ends in clearly specified and limited purposes. To reject the use of force, even in a last resort, is the mark of an absolute pacifist. No government is completely pacifist anywhere in the world. The leaders of the Dublin regime are distinctive in that they regard the land border with Northern Ireland as their major foreign policy issue rather than some great divide in Europe or Asia. By the standards of twentieth-century aggrandizing regimes, the circumstances in which the Republic would authorize the use of force are circumscribed indeed. It is undoubtedly the case that in 1970 officials of the Dublin regime were prepared to import arms for use in Northern Ireland in circumstances of last resort. But two other points are also true. The efforts of very prominent people in the regime to run arms were 'betrayed' by others in the regime. Even while offering military assistance to Catholics in the North, the Dublin regime confined most of its activities to the Republic, rather than concentrating upon offensive activities in the North.

Except for the issue of the Border and, before that, the independence issue, there is no evidence of Irish people withholding compliance with basic political laws, or resorting to political violence for its own sake. The exception is a major one; this volume is devoted solely to it. None the less, to argue that the Irish are naturally violent in asserting their independence opens the door to the complementary argument that the English are naturally violent in maintaining the United Kingdom. One does not have to be George Bernard Shaw to emphasize that for eight centuries the government of Ireland has borne witness to the readiness of the English Crown to use force to maintain sovereignty within one part of the British isles.

Comparing the institutions of parliamentary government at Stormont with those elsewhere in the British Commonwealth can indicate whether these institutions of government lead to the full legitimacy of a regime, or are neutral or negative in their consequences. At the end of the Second World War, there were five Dominions in the Empire, and 42 major dependencies.[19] In four of the five Dominions (including Ireland as a Republic) parliamentary institutions continue to work. In the Republic of South Africa, they have helped to keep a minority group permanently in power. Of the 29 dependencies that have since become independent without merging with other non-British territories, 27 had British-style forms of government at independence. Of these, 17–slightly more than half–still have parliamentary forms of government as of 1970. This indicates that British parliamentary institutions are not specially subject to repudiation or survival, when transferred to foreign environments. They are probably of little importance in maintaining a regime.

The most relevant point to emerge from a review of the evolution of Empire into Commonwealth is the fragile nature of the state boundaries that British authority established and defended. In many parts of the world, both before and after the Second World War, the Colonial Office actively encouraged the creation of relatively large states by bringing together a number of contiguous colonies. The federations of Canada and Australia are nineteenth-century examples of this policy. The Indian Empire and Nigeria are early examples from the non-Western world. After the Second World War, federations were also established in Malaya, East Africa, Central Africa and the British West Indies. None of these British-sponsored states has survived peacefully and intact the transition to independence. The partition of India into two states divided along religious lines is particularly relevant for comparison with Ireland. The ability of the British government to fit state boundaries to groups of people has been imperfect outside as well as within the British isles.

Three territories of the former Empire have had histories particularly relevant for comparison with Northern Ireland. Both Cyprus and the old Palestine mandate were territories which contained two peoples with mutually exclusive, non-bargainable political objectives. In Cyprus, Greeks sought union with Greece, and Turks opposed it. Both Palestinian Arabs and Jews claimed Palestine as their own homeland. In both instances the British could claim that their presence was necessary in a mediating role. Yet the status of middle-man is ambiguous, not least in a society polarized by civil war. It may confer the advantages of impartial arbiter, or it may place the third force in a position of being literally shot at by both sides. In Palestine, the British found themselves so much caught in a cross-fire that the Army withdrew, leaving the people to partition themselves by land war. In Cyprus, Britain gave a grant of independence to a new regime, but it is a regime that Turks reject because they are a permanent minority.

Events in Southern Rhodesia in the 1960s illustrate yet a third way in which conflicts have been resolved between London and its dependencies. Southern Rhodesia, by virtue of its late foundation and large proportion of settlers from Britain, contains a white population much closer to the cultural values of England than most dependencies. Once there, English settlers found themselves very much in a minority, as against the native population. They then proceeded to use the institutions of parliamentary government to maintain the form of British politics, while enjoying the substance of one-party white rule.[20] In the 1960s, both Conservative and Labour governments sought to invoke British allegiance and Britain's constitutional sovereignty as the sanction for reforms bringing more African participation in government. This test showed that the Ultras were much more numerous than fully allegiant white Rhodesians. As fervently as any Ulster Covenanter, they proclaimed loyalty to the Queen, and issued a Unilateral Declaration of Independence. The test also showed that Britain preferred to allow *de facto* independence to a rebel regime, rather than use force to sustain a claim to be a sovereign power over 220,000 white people.

*

A comparison of the United States and Northern Ireland is justified, notwithstanding the gross difference in size, by many similarities in history. Both lands were settled as colonies of the English crown in the seventeenth century. James I of England chartered a settlement in Virginia a few months before he chartered the Plantation of Ulster. In that century, the colonization of the east coast of America moved ahead more peaceably than the colonization of Ulster. American Indians were less numerous and less fierce in their opposition to new arrivals than were the 'mere Irishry'. The latter's Continental allies made them an even more formidable force. The success of the American plantation was confirmed before the Treaty of Limerick in 1691 confirmed the security of English and Scottish settlers in Ulster. The motive that led colonists to Ulster and to America was often the same, a search for a better life, whether this was defined in terms of freedom of worship, economic prosperity, or escape from conditions of the homeland. In the eighteenth century, economic and religious pressures encouraged tens of thousands of Ulster migrants, especially Scots, to try their fortune a second time by moving on to America. The Scotch-Irish American became almost the prototypical White Anglo-Saxon Protestant.[21] The Irish Catholic immigrants that followed a century later failed to qualify as Protestants, but showed themselves ready and able to assimilate to American customs and life.

The most parsimonious way to compare America and Northern Ireland is to review the extent to which the major social differences emphasized in the Lipset-Rokkan framework have presented challenges to the authority of the American regime. In doing this, it is necessary to remember that the extent of violence found is not necessarily evidence of a challenge to authority. It may reflect the absence of constraints against violence in non-political contexts, as might be expected in a land where primitive frontier conditions meant that social controls and law enforcement differed from more settled lands. Violence is politically significant only when it is employed in defiance of basic political laws. The lynching of a horse-thief represents no challenge to the regime, but there is a challenge in the lynching of an ex-slave, in defiance of protections enshrined in the Constitution.

American history demonstrates that the balance of political power between rural and urban sectors of society can be transformed without challenging the authority of the regime. The United States in 1790 was 94 per cent rural in its population. In 1860, 74 per cent of the population lived on isolated farms or in towns of 2,500 people or less. By 1960, the proportion of Americans in rural areas had fallen to 30 per cent.[22] A nation founded upon agriculture and a wealth of natural resources had become a nation of industry and urban dwellers. Politically, the change is of major importance because it removed the structural basis for the Jeffersonian ideal of a democratic, agrarian society. Latterday historians have emphasized the great cultural changes involved in the transition from a rural to an urban America. Rural areas were typically Anglo-Saxon and Protestant, whereas cities have attracted masses of Catholic and Central and East European immigrants, with very different life-styles and *weltanschauung*. Notwithstanding the very great differences in outlook, there has been a striking absence of overt challenge to the regime by declining agricultural interests. Events such as Shay's Rebellion of 1786–7 and the Whisky Rebellion of 1794 were shortlived and localized. The absence of sustained and large-scale challenges to authority is noteworthy, in view of the great and immediate economic differences between farmers and middlemen – the brokers and the railroads – about divisions of profits, as farming changed from subsistence agriculture to production for distant or overseas markets during the nineteenth century. Instead of resorting to violence, farmers organized in third parties or switched allegiance abruptly between the major parties. This tradition of rapid and independent partisan realignment has persisted into the present, yet remained within the confines of the constitutional party system.[23]

American history demonstrates that political differences between workers and employers can be settled in an industrializing society without challenging the authority of the regime. The absence of a Socialist or Labour party is usually cited as evidence of the non-revolutionary or non-radical nature of American working-class political activity. It is not conclusive evidence, however, since Socialist or Labour parties in Western nations have often given allegiance to their regime. The strongest evidence for the fully allegiant outlook of American workers is that they have never used force to challenge the regime, notwithstanding the willingness of working-class groups to resort to violence to challenge the authority of employers. The violence, occurring at points in time ranging from the 1870s through the 1930s, was localized and not endorsed as a matter of policy by union headquarters. It was directed against the claim of employers to be free of union 'interference' in industrial relations.[24] The chief attempt to generalize this opposition–the Industrial Workers of the World movement before the First World War–failed for lack of popular working-class support. The employers had no need to challenge the regime, because they were able to call upon mobile groups of strike-breakers and the National Guard to protect their interests. Notwithstanding this, workers still refused to 'politicize' their greatest industrial disputes. The Depression of the 1930s, with up to one-third of the labour force unemployed, also passed without anti-regime challenges, notwithstanding the activities of the Communist Party in some unions. The enactment of a National Labour Relations Act by the New Deal helped bring to an end the resort to violence in industrial disputes.

Historically, religious issues were important in leading immigrants to America in rejection of allegiance to European regimes, including the English Crown. At the time of the foundation of the United States, no religious denomination was dominant, but collectively, the new country was overwhelmingly Protestant. There were only about 25,000 Catholics among the land's 4,000,000 subjects. By the time that the first Catholic immigrants began to arrive in numbers–the Irish in the first half of the nineteenth century–the native American tradition was established as Protestant, rather than British. The original settlers were ready to incorporate newcomers as citizens without regard to language or land of origin–hence the very vague identification with Anglo-Saxon stock–but not without regard to religion. Historians differ about the extent of anti-Catholicism. Father John Tracy Ellis claims that it was substantial from the founding of Jamestown, whereas Ray Billington claims that it grew in intensity–not least after the arrival of Protestants from Ulster.[25] Attacks upon Catholics reached a climax in the period shortly before the American Civil War, involving riots and arson on a scale permitting comparison with Northern Ireland. The attacks were justified on the ground that Irish Catholics, notwithstanding their common language and British background, were undesirable or incapable of assimilation as Americans. The Know Nothing Party, which gave national significance to the debate on Catholic citizenship, split on the issue of slavery. Anti-Catholic attitudes did not disappear, but were redistributed among Republicans and Democrats. Anti-Catholicism still persisted a century later in the presidential election of 1960. The nomination of a Catholic candidate for President caused some Protestants and Catholics to shift their votes to accord with their attitude toward the Catholic Church. The bloc voting of American Catholics has been exceeded by the bloc voting of American Jews. The attachment of Jews to the Democratic Party is noteworthy, not only for strength and persistence, but also because by virtue of their occupation, income and education levels, American Jews should be disproportionately Republican.[26]

In the United States today, there remain differences about authority that echo historic conflicts between secular and spiritual authorities. The First Amendment to the Constitution, by erecting barriers between church and state, removed potential grievances between Protestant denominations by giving none a privileged position. However, it has become a major source of contention between Protestant clergymen and the Catholic hierarchy, if not always of great concern to adherents of these faiths. The disagreement arises because the Catholic hierarchy has claimed the right and duty to create and manage a variety of institutions providing welfare services for its adherents. Because schools, hospitals and similar institutions are owned by a Church, they have been ineligible for public subsidy. The conflict of interest has been most apparent in the field of education. In the words of Mr. Justice Frankfurter in a 1948 decision on the issue, 'The non-sectarian public school was the means of reconciling freedom in general with religious freedom.' The Catholic hierarchy in America has viewed religious freedom as implying a right to maintain separate schools for Catholics and receive tax funds for this purpose. The claim for concurrent endowment has nowhere been met, although the principle of non-subsidy has been breached in some states by subsidizing peripheral costs of education. In a generation that has seen school desegregation begun between black and white, there has been no similar move in the United States to end the separation of Protestants and Catholic pupils. The issue has not led to challenges to the regime, because both politicians and priests are anxious to avoid clearcut and open discord on this issue.[27]

Because America was founded as a nation of immigrants, national identity has been contingent. The relative fewness of Indians in relation to settlers, and the Indians' propensity to retreat or fight to extermination when confronted by settlers, eliminated the difficulties that faced Protestant Ulstermen in coming to terms with the native population.[28] The varieties of immigrants meant that the making of a common American identity, overriding both European origins and local or state patriotism, has been a very lengthy process. This was especially true for Catholics and Jews, differentiated by religion as well as national origin from the historically prototypical American identity. From a *political* perspective, what is most striking is that even though ethnic groups can be differentiated in their political behaviour in many ways, persisting ethnic loyalties to European homelands have *not* created challenges to the regime.[29] The potentially strongest challenges to the regime arose in the two World Wars of the twentieth century, because of the presence of large numbers of aliens and citizens with close family ties with enemy countries. At the time of the Second World War, about 10,000,000 Americans were either German or Italian born, or the children of parents born there. There were also hundreds of thousands of Japanese-Americans. Notwithstanding family connections and, in some cases, harassment because of their alien origins, these groups of Americans were overwhelmingly loyal to the United States.[30]

The greatest challenge to the full legitimacy of the regime in America, historically and today, arises from controversies about the relationship of blacks and whites. The controversy concerns the definition of the rights and duties of citizens. Historically, American blacks have demonstrated their allegiance to the regime, rather than their rejection of it. This claim to full citizenship has divided whites, who have disagreed about whether to accept black Americans as fellow citizens or reject their claims. Politically, blacks have worked through existing political institutions. The Supreme Court, as interpreter of the constitutional rights of citizenship, was the chief governmental agency used by blacks from the 1930s to the 1960s, and the Democratic Party the chief electoral agency. Congressional support was sought and obtained for measures increasing black integration in the political system and, more generally, in American society. The dominant white response outside the South has been to bargain with black politicians about their claims. Only in the 1960s did some black activists begin to gain prominence by advancing non-bargainable demands that explicitly repudiated the regime.

Notwithstanding the vocal nature of black nationalists, the majority of the black community in America has continued to endorse the Constitution and express confidence in securing their aims by constitutional means.[31] The position of American blacks is fundamentally different from that of Catholics in Northern Ireland. Even though both are minorities, Ulster Catholics can claim that a revision of the boundaries of the state would make them a majority in a 32-counties Ireland, or argue that the abolition of the Stormont regime and full integration into the United Kingdom would make Orangemen a very small minority within the resulting regime. Northern Ireland Catholics have more in common with the 'unredeemed' part of a European nationalist group than with blacks in America.

The Second Reconstruction

The most appropriate comparison within the Anglo-American world is between Northern Ireland and the states of the American South. Each is a 'fragment' society, having broken away from a larger society of which it was once an integral part.[32] The people of the South formed part of a United States from 1789 until the approach of the Civil War. Similarly, the people of Ulster were a part of Ireland from the seventeenth century until the Treaty of 1921. The 'peculiar institution' of slavery gradually led to great sectional discord within the United States, just as the 'peculiar institutions' of anti-Popery and Republicanism have differentiated Ulster. Because of population change, the South has become an increasingly smaller part of the federal Union. At the time of the first census in 1790, the South constituted 50 per cent of the population of the nation; in 1860, at the outbreak of the Civil War, 36 per cent, and in 1960, 30 per cent of the population. More importantly, the character of the South has changed, so that the area most differentiated from the rest of the Union by virtue of outlooks on race, has contracted to about five states – Alabama, Mississippi, Louisiana, South Carolina and Georgia – with 8·5 per cent of the country's population.[33] Ireland too has contributed a steadily declining part of the population of the United Kindgom since 1801 (cf. Table II.8). Yet in absolute terms, both Northern Ireland and the American South have been growing in size. The former has increased its population by one-half, and the five states of the Deep South have a population greater than many European states, and two-thirds of the countries in the United Nations.

Viewed from a distant perspective, the American South and Northern Ireland appear peripheral in relation to their central governments in Washington and Westminster. Social distinctiveness compounds geographical isolation. In the red hills of Georgia or the canebrakes of Northern Mississippi a New Yorker would feel as alien–and be regarded as alien–as a merchant from the City of London would feel estranged in Londonderry. Viewed from the perspective of people who live in these so-called peripheral areas, there need be no sense of remoteness. People can regard their own Province or state as central to their lives and loyalties. Richmond or Montgomery may be their centre, and the capital at Washington, D.C. or a federal space agency at Huntsville, Alabama peripheral. The partition of authority explicit in American federalism and the Government of Ireland Act, 1920, further confuses the location of political institutions central to a peripheral people.

In the Deep South, as in Northern Ireland, patriotism is strong. The question is: What is *la patrie*? In America the settlement of Southern states before the Revolution or by the offspring of pre-Revolutionary settlers has given Southerners an indubitable claim to be among the first Americans. This, in turn, has encouraged nativism, i.e., a suspicion of later immigrants of different national origins from the primarily British and Protestant settlers of the South. The relatively small proportion of these Continental immigrants settling in the South has further strengthened this distinctive identity.[34] In Northern Ireland, by contrast, Protestants could not claim to be the original inhabitants, but they could and did come to think of themselves as having a right to the land they settled, and belonging no place else. In Northern Ireland, the question of identity has been masked by Protestants calling themselves 'British' while identifying most strongly with their own local institutions. Protestants simultaneously proclaim their 'Britishness' and their readiness to resort to arms in defiance of the British Parliament. In the American South, the institutions of federalism permit dual patriotism as well as dual citizenship. This is stronger in the South than west of the Mississippi, because so many of the Southern states antedated the founding of the United States. Allegiance to Virginia or South Carolina came first in time for these Americans. As long as no discord existed between the two, then nothing threatened the regime.

Through Irish Eyes

But conflict came. In the American South, the secessionist movement forced a choice upon each state. Secession votes were taken in 14 state legislatures, and carried in 11.[35] The conflict between loyalty to the state or the Union was poignantly expressed by Robert E. Lee, a believer in the maintenance of the Union. He resolved it thus:

> With all my devotion to the Union and the feeling of loyalty and duty of an American citizen, I have not been able to make up my mind to raise my hand against my relatives, my children, my home.[36]

In both societies, conflicts of loyalties led to Civil War, as Ultras took up arms. The American Civil War was bloody; about two-fifths of men of military age were under arms, and more than one-quarter died or were wounded.[37] More Americans lost their lives in that war than died in the First or Second World Wars. In Northern Ireland, the readiness of Protestants to bear arms in support of 'their' regime was attested in the raising of the Ulster Volunteer Force. The Republican rising had the incidental effect of making the Ulster Protestants defenders of lawful authority, by making their enemy also the enemy of the English Crown.

The history books tell us that both wars were finished long ago. In a sense, this is true. The Confederate armies recognized the military victory of the North in 1865, and representatives of Sinn Fein signed a treaty of peace in 1921. Yet neither Lee's surrender at Appomatox nor the Anglo-Irish treaty of Downing Street has provided a final solution. These incidents only changed the terms in which the struggle was carried on. The emancipation of slaves and the establishment of Reconstruction governments under the eyes of an occupying Army required white Southerners to adopt new tactics to regulate their relationship with free blacks and with the federal government. Similarly, the Stormont regime had to face the question: How will we live with our Catholic neighbours? How will we live with Westminster? In both instances, the answer was the same: We shall live by dominating our opponents and remain at arm's length from those who claim nominal sovereignty in our land. The South, with more than one-third of its population black, remained a white man's land politically, just as Northern Ireland, with one-third of its population Catholic, became an exclusively Protestant regime.

Settlement of the civil war required the voluntary or involuntary collaboration of three groups—the peripheral majority, the peripheral minority and the nominally sovereign central authority. In both situations the central authority was far readier to relax its claim to authority than was the peripheral majority. London washed its hands of responsibility for the government of Northern Ireland, except in financial matters. Ironically, London was far more concerned with developments in the new Irish Free State, involving symbolic issues concerning Commonwealth allegiance and substantive issues of access to naval ports. In both instances, Dublin gained its objectives. London had no wish to test the determination of Dublin by using force. After decades of having the Irish problem run its sometimes disruptive course through their deliberations, Parliament welcomed a period of silence on this matter. The Speaker's initial interpretation of the respective powers of Westminster and Stormont resulted in many subjects being declared outside the competence of the Westminster Parliament to discuss or debate. In the five years preceding the disorder of 1969, the Commons devoted less than one-sixth of one per cent of its time to discussions of Northern Ireland questions; most of this talk concerned matters of trade, not the matters that affected allegiance to the regime.[38] Free from the constraints of distant politicians with neither the understanding nor the will to dictate terms, Stormont's leaders had no difficulty in securing the compliance of Ulster Catholics, even though they could not obtain their support.

In America, the victorious Union sought to reconstruct the South both politically and socially, as a necessary prelude to the return of the secessionist states to full membership in the Union. As W. G. Brock aptly notes:

> At the heart of the Reconstruction crisis was a momentous question about the character of national existence. It was framed most often with reference to the vexed question of loyalty. What did it mean to be a loyal American?[39]

The resolution of Reconstruction was pragmatic, not ideological. The efforts of agents of the federal government to construct a new form of government in the South, consistent with the Constitution as interpreted by Congressional radicals in the North, were of little avail, against the determination of Southern whites and growing apathy in the North. The South could no more be reconstructed peacefully than Ulster could have peacefully become part of an independent 32-counties Ireland. Northern determination to change the

South quickly gave way to a desire to accommodate the peripheral majority there. White Southerners were anxious to return to the Union–on their own terms. The accident of a contested Presidential election in 1876 gave the supporters of the Republican, Rutherford B. Hayes, the opportunity to complete the withdrawal of federal troops in return for Southern support of their dubious claims to electoral victory. The result was the Compromise of 1877, described by C. Vann Woodward as:

> ... the withdrawal of federal troops from the South, the abandonment of the Negro as a ward of the nation, the giving up of the attempt to guarantee the freedman his civil and political equality, and the acquiescence of the rest of the country in the South's demand that the whole problem be left to the disposition of the dominant Southern white people.[40]

With the reconciliation of two of the three partners, Southern whites had no difficulty in assuring the compliance of blacks with the regime that rapidly evolved after the withdrawal of federal troops. The extent of legally enforced domination was infinitely greater in the American South than in Northern Ireland. The adoption of Jim Crow laws segregating blacks from whites in many aspects of social life had no counterpart in Ireland after the decline of the penal code in the seventeenth century. In Ulster, the parties to violence, if not evenly matched, were both armed and numerous. In the South, violence often took the form of a mass of whites intimidating or lynching defenceless blacks. From 1882 to 1900, an average of more than 90 blacks were annually reported lynched.[41] Politically, the passage of restricted franchise measures in the South not only deprived blacks of the vote, but also effectively disfranchised many poor whites. Agitation of the race issue was also important in breaking or preventing the emergence of any political alliance of poor whites and poor blacks. Northern politicians, having known civil war, accepted these developments as a necessary price of peace. Woodward comments:

> Since the Negro was the symbol of sectional strife, the liberals joined in deprecating further agitation of his cause and in defending the Southern view of race in its less extreme forms ... Such expressions doubtless did much to add to the reconciliation of North and South, but they did so at the expense of the Negro.[42]

The relationship of autonomous peripheries and distant, formally powerful central regimes has been asymmetrical in both America and in the United Kingdom. The Stormont regime and the states of the Deep South retained the right to secede or 'contract out' on those things that most concerned their political power, such as franchise laws and the maintenance of internal security. In the late nineteenth century, Congress even repealed a series of Reconstruction laws meant to safeguard elections.[43] Yet both regimes remained, for purposes of public international law, subordinate parts of a larger regime. On many occasions, the peripheral power was ready to participate fully in the duties and privileges of the central government. This was true in wartime, when contributions were costly in lives, as well as in peacetime, when participation has brought benefits. In Northern Ireland, assistance has taken the form of British Treasury payments to the Province. In America, Southerners benefited from New Deal and post-New Deal legislation. Moreover, because of the relative strength of the one-party South in the Democratic Party, its politicians have enjoyed great influence, both as Congressional committee chairmen and in the executive. In the twentieth century, three of the five Democratic presidents have been Southerners, and four of the seven Democratic vice-presidents.[44]

The justification for these arrangements lay in the pattern of allegiance found in the periphery. In the American South, white citizens were loyal to the United States – but only on conditions. They wished to maintain a monopoly of local political power, and were prepared to adopt all measures necessary to prevent their black fellow citizens from enjoying rights that the 13th to 15th Amendments to the Constitution meant them to have. When the federal government sought to enforce these Amendments, Southern whites showed their Ultra outlook, seeking to void federal influence by legal means, or by intimidation through such organizations as the Ku Klux Klan.[45] The tradition of Ultra loyalty – first to states rights and to federal rights secondarily – has continued for a century. It showed itself following the desegregation decisions of the United States Supreme Court in 1954. Massive resistance to integration by state officials in the Deep South employed laws as well as private and public instruments of coercion to maintain political institutions in defiance of Court orders. In Northern Ireland, until the late 1960s the Protestant Ultras had no occasion to defy the lawful regime, because its policies and theirs were never in opposition.

The peripheral regimes governed by consent of the central government and a dominant local majority. Bi-lateral agreement did not assure consensus, for neither Southern blacks nor Ulster Catholics were consulted about the political institutions which they were expected to give compliance to. The emergence of civil rights movements in the American South and in Northern Ireland has shown to the world that these regimes are governing without consensus. The demands of the groups have not resolved discord, but they have greatly altered the way in which authorities try to manage discord. In the United States, civil rights groups have sought to advance the rights of blacks in two ways. The first is by using federal institutions to alter practices of state governments. The existence of a federal system with a carefully articulated set of responsibilities and privileges has made it possible for blacks to secure substantial advances, particularly in the North and Border states, where the proportion of white Ultras has been politically inconsequential. The federal courts were the chief institution where aid was sought, and for several decades this constitutional instrument of change was the place of first resort. The courts consistently sustained claims of blacks to civil rights, albeit they could do little themselves to control the consequences of their decisions, because of their separation from administrative agencies. The courts continued to rule on behalf of black claims after civil rights workers took to the streets, breaking state and local laws but not, the courts ruled, violating federal laws.[46] In Northern Ireland, by contrast, Catholics had neither inclination nor hope in turning to the courts. Republicans argued that force, not legal argument, was all that would impress a British Parliament. Peaceful and disaffected Catholics could find no means by which they could take cases of discrimination to the courts, because of the absence of judicial review throughout the United Kingdom, and the failure of the Government of Ireland Act to provide meaningful legal remedies to aggrieved Catholics. While American blacks were beginning to exert influence upon Congressmen by organizing bloc votes, in Northern Ireland there was no way in which Catholics could achieve legislative influence, given the permanent Protestant majority at Stormont.

Successive Presidents of the United States maintained public detachment from the struggle between blacks and whites in the South. President Dwight Eisenhower had sent federal troops to Little Rock, Arkansas to intervene in a school dispute there in 1957. This was not part of an interventionist policy, but rather, a decision in the *last* resort to uphold federal courts in the South. John F.

Kennedy and his brother, Robert, after two years in office privately felt that they were 'constitutionally impotent' to protect blacks in the American South and end what the United States Civil Rights Commission had already described as 'the subversion of the Constitution'.[47] The Kennedys were hesitant to become engaged in a fully-fledged civil rights campaign not only because of the strength of Southern states in the federal system, but also because of their political desire to avoid issues that might make even more difficult Congressional approval of their other domestic and foreign policy aims. Finally, in the spring of 1963, a series of police attacks upon black demonstrators in Birmingham, Alabama, followed by bomb attacks by Ultras, gave President Kennedy the necessary stimulus to act. Since then, both peaceful and violent events have made his successors accept responsibility for civil rights in the South and in the North. In Northern Ireland, too, it took violence and the eight deaths of August, 1969, to make the British government accept responsibility for sovereignty in Northern Ireland. The British government became once again involved in Irish politics with one advantage that American presidents have lacked: legislative power to abolish the Constitution of its most troublesome area. Much of this apparent advantage has been lost, however, because the Westminster Parliament gave Stormont exclusive powers in most areas of political concern, rather than claiming concurring powers, as happens in America. The scope of powers exclusively delegated to Stormont is far greater than that held by the American states in the 1960s.

Now, both the United States and the United Kingdom are engaged in a Second Reconstruction. The federal government of the United States seeks to reconstruct its authority in the Deep South, after acquiescing in the lapse of crucial powers at the end of the First Reconstruction. The task of the Second Reconstruction is different from that of the first, for the problem of black-white relations is no longer confined exclusively to the South. In 1870, only 10 per cent of American blacks lived outside the South. In 1960, the proportion had risen to 35 per cent, and blacks are disproportionately numerous in the major cities of America. Hence, the federal government not only meets resistance from white Southerners with Ultra inclinations, but also feels pressures from Northern urban blacks with possible rebel inclinations. If the strength of Alabama's George Wallace is taken as an indicator of Ultra inclinations, then in 1968 this group of citizens formed a plurality in five Southern states, and had some degree of support almost everywhere. The Westminster government approaches Ulster relatively free from the electoral pressures that affect an American President. The migration of Protestant and Catholic people from all Provinces of Ireland has not brought into the centre of Britain the discord of the periphery. The relatively small size of Northern Ireland and its political insulation from the rest of the United Kingdom provide less incentive to attempt reconstruction. As of 1970, the British government's ideal of Reconstruction has been the defence and reform of an autonomous Stormont regime.

At such a juncture, the first question is not technical but substantive: reconstruct to what end? The solution sought inevitably depends upon how the problem is defined. This, in turn, reflects the values and interests of the parties to the conflict.

The white Southerner, like the Ulster Protestant, tends to define the problem as a black or a green problem. The minority is made the source of the difficulty. The white Southerner sees things this way because the black man refuses to accept the place that the white man assigns him. The black man's rejection is a sign of contrariness or worse. The white man sees little wrong with the *status quo* or the *status quo ante*, that is, the regime before the campaign for a Second Reconstruction began. It withstood the ravages of civil war, Northern occupation and successive economic depressions. In the North, some whites also define the problem as that of the black man. If only the black would change his ways and act more like a white man, then he could be treated like a white man. These whites assume that it is within the power of blacks to change the way they act; failure to do so is evidence of their unruliness.[48] In Northern Ireland, Protestants believe that the Catholic minority is the cause of the regime's difficulties. The majority of Catholics refuse allegiance to the regime. In Protestant eyes, their complaints of discrimination are unfounded, and are but the work of trouble-makers. The discord would be resolved, as far as Protestants are concerned, if only Catholics abandoned their symbolic commitment to a United Ireland and stopped complaining about their treatment by the Stormont regime. The refusal of the minority to agree with the majority's definition of the problem only increases the resentment of the latter.

The black Southerner, like the Northern Ireland Catholic, sees the difficulty as a white or Orange problem. They argue that as they seek no more than their rights as subjects of a powerful, albeit distant central government, those who resist their demands are the cause of the problem. The moderate demands of blacks in the American South are stated in terms consistent with the federal Constitution: equality before the law, equity in public services and, not least, a share in political power. Similar demands are made by civil rights groups in Northern Ireland; their justification is a doctrine of natural rights. The doctrines invoked are consistent with those prevailing elsewhere in the United Kingdom. The two minorities differ in that Catholics have also been willing to resort to force in efforts to change the boundaries of the state. In the American South, there is no comparable tradition of a black resort to arms.

Because the problem is confined to a peripheral part of the state, the leaders of the central regime stand aside from the prime combatants. Yet they cannot disclaim all concern with discord at the periphery, for it still remains a part of their territory and responsibility. In theory, this test of will and strength between central sovereignty and a technically subordinate jurisdiction might be resolved by force. Yet forcing compliance by another political jurisdiction is even more difficult than compelling compliance from individuals, for the peripheral jurisdiction has powers of administration that are often crucial. For example, in the South and in Ulster, police powers, many judicial powers and control of education is in the hands of the peripheral regime. In the event of defiance of central authority, neither the United States nor the United Kingdom has sufficient military means to compel compliance from masses of recalcitrant subjects, and to administer the rebel territory thereafter. If central sovereignty could be enforced effectively on a 'cost free' basis, then in all likelihood it would have been done generations ago.

Given such constraints, the leaders of the central regime are likely to define their goal as managing or containing conflict. As the third party in a localized dispute, the most attractive role is that of 'honest broker', seeking to define and extend areas of agreement and accommodation. Yet this strategy is not practicable when discord is so pervasive that no potential area of agreement can be found, unless fundamental political differences are simultaneously resolved. Moreover, the claim to neutrality of any broker will be impugned, in so far as the policies recommended are perceived as benefiting one side more than the other. This will necessarily occur where zero-sum conflicts are at issue. The central regime hardly needs to intervene on the side of the local majority; they are usually strong enough and determined enough to manage local affairs to the satisfaction of themselves, if not to the satisfaction of all who live under their jurisdiction. To intervene on behalf of the local minority is to challenge the local regime's *status quo*. As Graham and Gurr note in their review of American history, 'The historical and contemporary evidence of the United States suggests that popular support tends to sanction violence in support of the *status quo*.'[49] If conflict cannot be managed, then it may be contained by actions that avoid discord spreading from the periphery to other parts of the regime. The peripheral majority have no wish to involve others, as this would only jeopardize their power. Left alone, they can maintain a 'stable equilibrium' indefinitely, even if this is done in ways that the peripheral minority unsuccessfully oppose. It follows from this that the simplest way for the central regime to contain its difficulties is to maintain an open or tacit alliance with the peripheral majority.

Any political solution requires two things that are usually conspicuous by their absence: time and goodwill. When discord has been institutionalized for centuries, as in Northern Ireland and the American South, one may have to wait a very long time indeed for time to heal such wounds. The intensity of discord also implies that force is unlikely to provide a prompt and easy solution. The existence of Stormont today is a monument to the failure of Irish Republicans to force a solution to the Northern Ireland problem. The problems of the Second Reconstruction in the Deep South testify to the inability of the Union's armies to secure a political as well as military settlement in the era of the First Reconstruction. The immediate question is not how long the problem will last, but what shall be done in the here and now. To do nothing is to make a contribution to discord, as Westminster and Washington have shown. Yet action is full of uncertainty. There is some consolation in noting that those engaged in the First Reconstruction were in the same predicament.

When Abraham Lincoln came to make his Second Inaugural address in the closing days of the American Civil War, there was no hint of blame in his description of the two parties: 'Both read the same Bible, and pray to the same God; and each invokes His aid against the other.' The two groups showed a determination that would do credit to Ulstermen: 'One of them would *make* war rather than let the nation survive; and the other would *accept* war rather than let it perish.' With the end of a bloody war near, the President turned his attention to what might come after. A month before an assassin's bullet struck him down, Lincoln could only suggest how the divided land might proceed:

> With malice toward none: with charity for all: with firmness in the right, as God gives us to see the right, let us strive on to finish the work we are in; to bind up the nation's wounds; to care for him who shall have borne the battle, and for his widow, and his orphan.

Appendix · The Loyalty Questionnaire

The text of the major questionnaire analysed in this book follows here. Minor alterations have been made to assure clarity and comprehension on the printed page, and the format is altered to save space. Wherever possible, percentage distributions of replies have been given separately for Protestants, Catholics and for their collective total. This is not done for Questions 7a–17a, as these were not asked of both religions. Replies given to open-ended questions have not usually been reported, because of space limitations. For instance, the initial classification of answers to the question about earliest political memories employed 82 categories.

In every instance, the total number of replies have been percentaged in relation to 757 Protestants, 534 Catholics and a total sample of 1,291. Where very simple yes/no questions are involved, e.g., readership of a particular newspaper, only positive answers have been recorded. The following conventions are used here and elsewhere in the volume in reporting survey findings:

1. All percentages have been calculated to an extra decimal place, then rounded off to a two-digit figure.
   (a) Columns may not total 100 per cent precisely because of rounding-off adjustments.
   (b) The Difference Index was calculated prior to rounding off. When the index ended in 0·5 per cent, it was rounded down.
2. The Don't Know category includes individuals for whom no reply was recorded or ascertainable. Occasionally, the abbreviation 'NA' occurs. This indicates a person for whom the question was not appropriate or whose answer was not ascertained because of a clerical error or another fault.
3. An entry of 0 indicates that no replies were given in this category. A dash (—) indicates that 0·5 per cent or less of all replies are in this category.
4. Where totals in tables in the book are substantially larger than 100 per cent, this is because respondents could and did give more than one answer to a question, e.g., what they think a political party stands for.
5. Where two phrases are given, e.g., Minister/Priest in Q.29e, only the term appropriate to the respondent is used in the oral interview.

Good morning/afternoon. I am conducting a public opinion survey for an American University Professor. He is trying to find out what people think about life in different countries today. (His name is Professor Richard Rose.)

474

	Protestant %	Catholic %	Total %
1a. How long have you lived in this community?			
All my life	49	61	54
Since childhood	4	3	4
Since marriage	11	10	10
Most of adult life	12	11	11
Part of adult life	19	9	15
Arrived in last two years	5	5	5
1b. How do you feel about this area as a place to live in? (That is, are you glad that you live here?)			
Like it very much	68	65	67
Like	17	21	19
Mixed views	12	8	10
Dislike	2	3	2
Dislike very much	1	3	2
1c. Have you ever lived outside Northern Ireland?			
Yes	27	31	29
IF YES: (ca) Where did you live?			
Republic	5	7	6
Scotland	4	5	4
England and Wales	17	22	19
North America	3	3	3
OTHER	6	2	5
1d. Have you ever taken trips outside Northern Ireland?			
Yes	87	87	87
IF YES: (d–i) Where was that to?			
Republic	73	78	75
Scotland	44	22	35
England and Wales	58	48	54
Continent of Europe	18	12	16
North America	7	5	6
OTHER	7	3	5
1e. What are the things that you *like* most about living in Northern Ireland?			
1f. What are the things that you *dislike* most about living in Northern Ireland?			
1g. Have you ever thought about emigrating?			
Yes	40	30	36
1h. How would you feel if you *had to leave* Northern Ireland?			
Very unhappy	37	43	39
Somewhat unhappy	18	17	17

	Protestant %	Catholic %	Total %
Mixed feelings	35	27	32
Somewhat glad	4	6	5
Very glad	2	2	2
Depends	3	2	3
Don't know	1	2	2

1i. Apart from people in this house how often do you see any of your relatives?

Daily	23	28	25
Several times a week	23	25	24
Weekly	30	25	28
Monthly	10	10	10
Less than once a month	12	10	11
Never	2	2	2

1j. For NON-BELFAST Respondents ONLY:

How often do you go to Belfast?

Daily	7	3	5
Weekly	8	5	7
At least once a month	12	8	10
Occasionally	29	31	30
Hardly ever–never	15	29	21
N.A.	29	24	27

2. Aside from your work and your family, what are the activities that interest you most? (That is, how do you like to spend your free time?)

2a. Do you belong to any clubs or organizations?

Yes	41	19	32

IF YES:
(1) What kind of clubs are they?
(2) Have you ever been on a Committee or held office in any of these clubs?

Yes	21	9	16

(3) Would you say that the members of this/these clubs are all Protestant, all Catholic, mostly Protestant, mostly Catholic or mixed?

All Protestant	22	—	13
All Catholic	—	5	2
Mostly Protestant	7	1	4
Mostly Catholic	—	4	2
Mixed	11	8	10
D.K.	1	—	1
N.A.	59	81	68

3. And what is your religion?

Presbyterian			27

	Protestant %	Catholic %	Total %
Free Presbyterian			—
Church of Ireland			22
Methodist			5
Other Protestant			3
Roman Catholic			41
Other			1
None			—

IF OTHER/NONE:
(i) Do you feel closer to either the
    Protestant or Catholic Community?

3a. Would you say that relations between
    Protestants and Catholics are better
    than they were five years ago, worse,
    or about the same now as then?

Better	56	65	60
About the same	35	27	32
Worse	7	4	6
D.K.	3	3	3

4. Do you think that religion will ever make
   no difference in the way people feel about
   each other in Northern Ireland?

Yes	23	34	27
No	64	49	58
Depends	4	4	4
D.K.	10	13	11

   (1) Why would that be?

5. There has always been a lot of controversy about the Constitutional position
   of Northern Ireland. On balance, do
   you approve or disapprove of it?

Approve	68	33	54
Disapprove	10	34	20
D.K.	22	32	26

   (IF APPROVES)
   (1) And why would you say that?

   (IF DISAPPROVES)
   (2) Why do you say that?
   (3) And what would you like to see in
       its place?

5a. Do you think that in the next ten years
    or so there will be any big changes in
    the situation concerning the Border?

Yes	33	35	34
No	50	45	48
Depends	4	3	4
D.K.	12	17	14

	Protestant %	Catholic %	Total %
5b. What changes, if any, would *you* like to see concerning the Border?			
IF CHANGE MENTIONED:			
(1) How likely do you think this is to come about?			
Definitely	4	8	6
Very likely, probably	22	32	26
Not likely	15	17	16
Definitely not	2	3	2
D.K.	6	7	6
N.A.	51	33	44
5c. Do you think that in the next ten years or so there will be any big changes in relations between Protestants and Catholics in Northern Ireland?			
Yes	43	57	49
No	41	27	35
Depends	5	4	4
D.K.	11	12	12
5d. What changes, if any, would *you* like to see in relations between Protestants and Catholics in Northern Ireland?			
IF CHANGE MENTIONED:			
(1) How likely do you think this is to come about?			
Definitely	5	9	6
Very likely, probably	48	54	50
Not likely	20	16	18
Definitely not	2	3	2
D.K.	8	9	8
N.A.	18	9	14
5e. Do you think that in the next ten years or so there will be any big changes in the power of the Unionist Party in Northern Ireland?			
Yes	25	22	24
No	49	41	46
Depends	3	2	3
D.K.	21	35	27
5f. What changes, if any, would *you* like to see in the power of the Unionist Party in Northern Ireland?			
IF CHANGE MENTIONED:			
(1) How likely do you think this is to come about?			
Definitely	2	3	2
Very likely, probably	20	24	21
Not likely	13	18	15

	Protestant %	Catholic %	Total %
Definitely not	1	4	2
D.K.	4	5	5
N.A.	60	46	55

5g. Some people say that we should try to forget the troubles of the past in Northern Ireland and look only to the future. Others say that, like it or not, we cannot ignore what has happened here in the past. What do you think?

Try to forget; look to the future	77	89	82
Can't ignore the past	20	9	15
D.K.	3	2	3

6. HOW IMPORTANT WOULD YOU SAY IT IS:

6a. For pupils to do whatever their teachers tell them

Very important	73	77	75
Fairly important	21	20	21
Not very important	4	1	3
Not at all important	1	—	1
D.K.	1	—	—

6b. For workers to do whatever their employers tell them

Very important	62	67	64
Fairly important	31	26	29
Not very important	6	4	5
Not at all important	1	1	1
D.K.	—	—	—

6c. For members of a church to do whatever their Minister/Priest tells them

Very important	30	62	44
Fairly important	27	25	26
Not very important	27	7	19
Not at all important	14	3	10
D.K.	2	—	1

6d. For a wife to do whatever her husband tells her

Very important	20	27	23
Fairly important	35	36	35
Not very important	24	21	23
Not at all important	18	12	16
D.K.	2	1	2

6e. For a citizen to do whatever his government tells him

Very important	38	41	39
Fairly important	38	39	38
Not very important	17	13	15

	Protestant %	Catholic %	Total %
Not at all important	5	4	5
D.K.	2	1	2

If **PROTESTANT**, continue with
Q. 7a–11a

If **CATHOLIC**, JUMP to Q. 12a–17a

PROTESTANTS ONLY

	Protestant %

7a. Do you think that it was right about 50 years ago, for people in the North to take up arms and stand ready to fight to keep Northern Ireland British?

Yes	82
No	6
Other	1
D.K.	11

7b. Sometimes you hear people say today that it would be right to take any measures necessary in order to keep Northern Ireland a Protestant country. Are you inclined to agree or disagree with this view?

Agree	52
Disagree	45
D.K.	4

7c. Why would that be?

7d. Sometimes you hear of the government banning meetings or parades planned by Protestant groups. When this happens, do you think it is still all right for these to be held?

Yes	20
No	67
Depends	11
D.K.	2

Now I would like to ask you about different decisions that public leaders might some day take about the Border problem. After I describe each decision could you tell me whether you would approve, disapprove, or have no opinion?

HOW WOULD YOU REACT:

8a. If the Government announced it was in favour of a United Ireland governed from Dublin?

Approve	6
Disapprove	84
D.K.	10

8b. If the Government increased co-operation across the Border with people in the South?

Approve	78

| | *Protestant* |
| | % |

Disapprove — 12
D.K. — 9

8c. If the Government continued its present policy on the Border?
    Approve — 71
    Disapprove — 13
    D.K. — 16

8d. If the Government took stronger measures to defend the Border?
    Approve — 42
    Disapprove — 36
    D.K. — 22

9. Would you say that the opinion that Roman Catholics have of what the Government does is:
    Very important — 24
    Fairly important — 39
    Not very important — 27
    Not at all important — 7
    D.K. — 3

9i. In dealings with Catholics, do you think that a Protestant should usually
    Stand up strongly for his own religion — 32
    Ignore religious differences — 25
    In view of past troubles make a special effort to be friendly — 40
    Other — 2
    D.K. — 1

Now I would like to ask you about different decisions that a Government might some day take about relations between Protestants and Catholics.

HOW WOULD YOU REACT:

9a. If the Government passed a law making it illegal to refuse a job or rent a house to a Catholic because of his religion?
    Approve — 23
    Disapprove — 69
    D.K. — 7

9b. If the Government gave as much public money to Catholic schools as to Protestant ones?
    Approve — 64
    Disapprove — 23
    D.K. — 13

9c. If relations between Catholics and Protestants remained as they are?
    Approve — 57
    Disapprove — 32
    D.K. — 11

Appendix

Protestant
%

9d. If the Government took measures to keep Catholic
   influence from growing stronger?

Approve	38
Disapprove	40
D.K.	22

Now, how about different things that might be decided about
party politics.

HOW WOULD YOU REACT:

10a. If the Unionists went into Opposition for a while, and a
   Labour-Liberal-Nationalist Coalition governed instead?

Approve	22
Disapprove	52
D.K.	26

10b. If the Unionists sought more members and candidates
   from the Catholic community?

Approve	57
Disapprove	23
D.K.	20

10c. If the Unionists kept the present arrangements in party
   politics as they are?

Approve	57
Disapprove	21
D.K.	22

10d. If the Unionists paid more attention to criticism from
   people who are strong loyalists?

Approve	47
Disapprove	31
D.K.	22

11. If a Protestant decided to change his politics and vote
   Nationalist, what difference, if any, do you think this
   would make to his relations with friends and family?

Big difference	35
Difference to some	28
Not much difference	16
No difference	11
Depends	6
D.K.	4

11a. Would you happen to be a member of the Orange Order?

Yes	19
No	80
Refused to answer	—
D.K.	1

CATHOLICS ONLY

Catholic
%

12a. Do you think that it was right, about 50 years ago, for people in the South to take up arms and fight in order to make the Republic?

Yes ... 60
No ... 21
D.K. ... 18

12b. Sometimes you hear people today say that it would be right to take any measures necessary in order to end Partition and bring Ulster into the Republic. Are you inclined to agree or disagree with this view?

Agree ... 13
Disagree ... 83
D.K. ... 4

12c. Why would that be?

12d. Sometimes you hear of the Government banning meetings or parades planned by Republican groups. When this happens, do you think it is still all right for these to be held?

Yes ... 40
No ... 43
Depends ... 14
D.K. ... 3

Now I would like to ask you about different decisions that public leaders might some day take about the Border problem. After I describe each decision, could you tell me whether you would approve, disapprove, or have no opinion?

HOW WOULD YOU REACT:

13a. If Nationalists agreed to stop debating Partition and accepted the present Border as final?

Approve ... 30
Disapprove ... 46
D.K. ... 24

13b. If the Nationalists talked less about the Border issue?

Approve ... 45
Disapprove ... 31
D.K. ... 24

13c. If Nationalists continued their present stand against the Border?

Approve ... 39
Disapprove ... 30
D.K. ... 31

13d. If Nationalists started campaigning harder to end Partition?

Approve ... 41
Disapprove ... 33
D.K. ... 25

Appendix

14a. Would you say that the opinion that Protestants have of
Nationalist political activities is:

Very important	19
Fairly important	25
Not very important	32
Not at all important	17
D.K.	6

14b. In dealings with Protestants, do you think that a Catholic
should

Stand up strongly for his own religion	29
Ignore religious differences	21
In view of past troubles make a special effort to be friendly	45
Other	4

Now I would like to ask you about different decisions that a
Government might some day take about relations between
Protestants and Catholics.

HOW WOULD YOU REACT:

15a. If Catholics said publicly that there was no problem
about religious discrimination in Northern Ireland?

Approve	14
Disapprove	71
D.K.	15

15b. If a campaign started to mix Catholics and Protestants
together in state schools?

Approve	62
Disapprove	28
D.K.	10

15c. If relations between Catholics and Protestants remained
as they are?

Approve	40
Disapprove	50
D.K.	10

15d. If Catholics began protesting very strongly against cases
of religious discrimination

Approve	55
Disapprove	27
D.K.	18

Now, how about different things that might be decided about
party politics.

HOW WOULD YOU REACT:

16a. If Nationalists split on economic issues, and some joined
the Conservative Party and others the Labour Party?

Approve	25
Disapprove	33
D.K.	41

	Catholic %
16b. If Nationalists tried harder to demonstrate that they were loyal, as well as the Opposition?	
Approve	40
Disapprove	21
D.K.	39
16c. If the Nationalists kept their present attitude toward the other political parties?	
Approve	30
Disapprove	25
D.K.	45
16d. If Nationalists encouraged more active support for the Republican cause?	
Approve	32
Disapprove	35
D.K.	33
17. If a Catholic decided to change his politics and vote Unionist, what difference, if any, do you think this would make to his relations with friends and family?	
Big difference	26
Difference to some	25
Not much difference	19
No difference	21
Depends	3
D.K.	6
17a. Would you happen to be a member of the Hibernians? (A.O.H.)	
Yes	3
No	97
Refused to answer	—
D.K.	—

ALL RESPONDENTS AGAIN

	Protestant %	Catholic %	Total %
18a. Which of these terms best describes the way you usually think of yourself?			
British	39	15	29
Irish	20	76	43
Ulster	32	5	21
Sometimes British–sometimes Irish	6	3	5
Anglo-Irish	2	1	1
Other	1	—	1
18b. Would you say that you are a strong (Irishman/Ulsterman/British, etc.) or average?			
Strong	45	28	38
Average	53	71	60
D.K.	1	1	1

Appendix

	Protestant %	Catholic %	Total %
18c. Why do you think of yourself as ... British/Irish/Ulster, etc.			
18d. Would you say that in general people in England are much different or about the same as people in Northern Ireland?			
Different	66	63	65
About the same	29	30	29
D.K.	5	7	5
18e. Would you say that in general people in the Republic are much different or about the same as people in Northern Ireland?			
Different	46	48	47
About the same	45	44	45
D.K.	9	7	8
19a. What would you say are the most important things that the Orange Order stands for?			
19b. On balance, do you approve or disapprove of the Orange Order's influence on life in Northern Ireland?			
Strongly approve	36	3	22
Somewhat approve	21	6	15
Mixed views	18	12	16
Somewhat disapprove	8	17	12
Strongly disapprove	5	34	17
No opinion–D.K.	12	28	18
19c. What would you say are the most important things that the Hibernians stand for?			
19d. On balance, do you approve or disapprove of the Hibernians' influence on life in Northern Ireland?			
Strongly approve	1	8	4
Somewhat approve	5	13	8
Mixed views	12	11	12
Somewhat disapprove	11	7	10
Strongly disapprove	17	9	13
No influence	—	3	2
No opinion–D.K.	54	49	51
20a. Which would you say are the political parties that are now active in Northern Ireland?			
Number of parties mentioned.			
One	16	9	13
Two	27	28	27

	Protestant %	Catholic %	Total %
Three	29	27	28
Four	14	15	14
Five	4	5	4
Six	1	1	1
Seven	—	1	—
D.K.	9	15	12

20b. What would you say the UNIONIST Party stands for?

20c. What would you say the NATIONALIST Party stands for?

20d. What would you say the NORTHERN IRELAND LABOUR Party stands for?

21a. Generally speaking, how interested are you in politics?

Very interested	8	6	7
Somewhat interested	23	13	19
Not much interested	36	27	32
No interest	33	53	41

21b. And how would you say you feel about the way the country is governed?

Very proud	21	6	15
Fairly proud	53	37	46
Not very proud	20	34	26
Ashamed	3	13	7
Other	2	6	4
D.K.	1	3	2

22a. When there is an election for Parliament at Stormont, do you usually vote or not?

Usually	79	70	75
Sometimes	4	5	5
Usually not	4	6	4
Never	6	12	9
Spoil ballot	—	—	—
Uncontested seat	—	—	—
Not eligible	1	2	1
Too young previously	6	4	5

22b. Why would that be? (That is, why do you usually–)

22c. At elections, do you think that all (RESPONDENT'S RELIGION) should vote for the same party?

Yes	26	25	26
No	57	55	56
Depends	10	11	10
D.K.	7	8	7

	Protestant %	*Catholic* %	*Total* %
23a. Have you ever personally done anything to try and get the local council or the Stormont Government to deal with a problem?			
Yes	13	15	14
No	86	85	86
23b. With regard to the national and international issues facing Northern Ireland, how well do you think you can understand them?			
Very well	5	5	5
Fairly well	39	27	34
Not very well	40	40	40
Badly, can't understand	15	26	20
23c. How much influence do you think people like yourself have on what the government does?			
A lot	9	4	7
Some	14	8	12
A little	39	28	34
None	38	58	46
D.K.	1	2	1
24. Generally speaking, what party do you usually think of yourself as supporting?			

IF NAMES A PARTY:

(1a) Would you call yourself a strong ... or average?

Strong	28	16	23
Average	59	65	62
Other	1	2	1
N.A.–No party named	12	17	14

IF DOESN'T NAME A PARTY:

(1b) Do you think of yourself as a little closer to *one* of the parties than to the others? (Which party is that?)

ALL RESPONDENTS

(2) If the party you supported (or, feel closest to) didn't have a candidate at the next election here, which of the other parties would you consider voting for? (List in order of preference)

1st ....
2nd ....
3rd ....

(3) Is there any party you would *never* vote for?

		Protestant	*Catholic*	*Total*
		%	%	%

25. When the last Stormont election was held in 1965, do you recall if you voted?

	Protestant	Catholic	Total
Yes, voted	75	61	69
Uncontested seat	1	1	1
No, didn't vote	15	26	20
Too young	7	6	6
D.K.	1	4	2
N.A.	1	2	1

IF YES:
(1) Which party did you support?

26. When you think of your own situation and that of your family, what problem concerns you most?

   (1) And who is most able to help you with this?

27a. Do you think it would be a good idea for this country to join the European Common Market?

	Protestant	Catholic	Total
Yes	30	56	41
No	36	14	27
D.K.	34	30	32

27b. Do you think that state welfare benefits are too high, too low, or about right?

	Protestant	Catholic	Total
Too high	34	19	28
Too low	11	18	14
About right	41	56	47
Other	8	4	7
D.K.	6	2	4

27c. Do you approve or disapprove of the influence of trade unions on life in Northern Ireland?

	Protestant	Catholic	Total
Approve	41	41	41
Disapprove	25	21	24
Mixed views	17	15	16
D.K.	17	23	19

27d. Do you approve or disapprove of the influence of big businesses on life in Northern Ireland?

	Protestant	Catholic	Total
Approve	54	39	48
Disapprove	13	23	17
Mixed Views	16	11	14
D.K.	17	27	21

28a. Do you think that the Northern Ireland Government is giving this part of the country (the Belfast area) its fair share of economic help?

	Protestant	Catholic	Total
Yes	72	48	63

Appendix

	Protestant %	Catholic %	Total %
No	17	41	27
Other	—	—	—
D.K.	11	11	10

28b. What do you think is the most important problem that the government ought to do something about?

28c. Are there any other problems you can think of?

29a. Do you read a daily newspaper?

	Protestant	Catholic	Total
None	13	19	16
One	50	35	44
Two	26	32	29
Three	9	10	9
Four	2	3	2
Five or more	—	1	—

READS:

	Protestant	Catholic	Total
Belfast Telegraph	61	39	52
Belfast News Letter	34	7	23
Irish News	3	49	22
Dublin Paper	1	11	5
British Paper	32	33	32
Other	4	6	5

IF READS NEWSPAPER:
(1) Do you usually make a point of reading stories about politics in the paper?

	Protestant	Catholic	Total
Yes	34	27	31
No	52	54	53
Doesn't read papers	14	19	16

29b. Do you usually make a point of listening to news and current events programmes on radio or television?

	Protestant	Catholic	Total
Yes	77	70	74
No	11	17	14
No radio or TV	11	13	12

29c. Do you ever talk about politics and public affairs with other people, such as:

	Protestant	Catholic	Total
One 'yes' response	15	12	14
Two	17	11	15
Three	15	9	13
Four or five	9	6	8
None	43	62	51

TALKS TO:

	Protestant	Catholic	Total
Relatives Yes	45	28	38
People at work Yes	30	21	26

	Protestant %	Catholic %	Total %
Friends and neighbours Yes	35	27	32
Community leaders, people in politics Yes	14	9	12
People at church Yes	12	6	9

29d. When Catholics and Protestants are together, do you think it is a good idea to let talk flow freely, or to avoid controversial subjects such as politics?

Flow freely	58	58	58
Depends	33	32	33
Avoids politics, controversy	8	9	9

29e. Do you think that your MINISTER/ PRIEST ought to speak his views on public matters that he thinks important?

Yes	67	64	66
No	24	26	25
Depends	3	4	3
D.K.	5	5	5

29f. Does he ever do this?

Often	7	5	6
Occasionally	43	42	42
Never	32	46	38
D.K.	18	7	13

30a. Compared with most people you know, would you say that you were more likely or less likely to be asked your views on politics, or would you be about average?

More likely	3	2	3
Average	45	35	41
Less likely	51	62	55

30b. If you wanted some advice on a political question, who would you go to for help?

One answer	82	75	79
Two	10	12	11
Three	1	1	1
D.K.	—	4	2
N.A.–None	6	8	7

WOULD GO TO:

Friends	18	18	18
Relatives	18	20	19
Neighbours	2	4	3
People at church	1	1	1
Politicians/Community leaders	51	42	47
Minister/Priest	15	16	15
Other	3	4	3

Appendix

		Protestant %	Catholic %	Total %
30c.	Generally speaking, what would you say is the best source of information about what is happening in Northern Ireland politics?			
	Newspapers	27	21	24
	TV/Radio	53	58	55
	Talking with people	4	4	4
	Church talks, sermons	1	—	1
	Public meetings	4	2	3
	Other	10	9	9
	D.K.	1	5	3
31a.	Do you think that a person can do a lot to change his way of life, or that he can't do much to change it?			
	Can change	78	67	73
	Can't change	18	25	21
	Other	1	2	2
	D.K.	3	6	4
31b.	How much effect do you think the activities of the Stormont government have on your life?			
	A lot	24	25	24
	Some	26	15	22
	A little	31	28	30
	None	17	31	23
	D.K.	1	2	2
	IF ANY EFFECT:			
	(1) Do you think that its actions usually make your life better or worse?			
	Better	43	25	35
	Worse	6	12	9
	Depends	14	10	12
	Don't know	4	7	5
	N.A.–No effect	33	47	39
32a.	Would you happen to know the name of the person who represents this constituency in the Parliament at Stormont?			
	Mentions name–correct	52	49	51
	Mentions name–incorrect	14	18	16
	D.K.	33	33	33
32b.	Which PARTY represents this constituency at Stormont?			
	Mentions party–correct	78	65	74
	Mentions party–incorrect	6	13	9
	D.K.	13	22	17

492

	Protestant %	Catholic %	Total %
32c. Would you happen to know the name of the person who represents this constituency in the British Parliament in London?			
Mentions name—correct	49	35	44
Mentions name—incorrect	7	7	7
D.K.	44	58	49
32d. How about the Republic? Would you know the name of the Prime Minister there?			
Jack Lynch	62	68	65
Other	10	9	10
D.K.	27	22	25
32e. And would you know which PARTY is in charge of the government of the Republic?			
Fianna Fail	29	48	37
Other name	3	2	3
D.K.	67	50	60

33. Many things are often said in support of the way this country is governed. What do you think are the most important reasons for supporting the government in what it does?

34. Now I'd like to read you a few things that people sometimes say in favour of our system of government. After each statement, can you tell me whether you agree, disagree, or have no opinion?

	Protestant %	Catholic %	Total %
It's good because it is traditional			
Agree	51	23	40
Disagree	31	46	37
No opinion	18	31	23
It usually provides lots of benefits for people			
Agree	85	75	81
Disagree	9	18	13
No opinion	6	7	6
It keeps things peaceful here			
Agree	82	58	72
Disagree	12	29	19
No opinion	6	13	9
It is good because it gives us a Queen to rule over us			
Agree	82	37	63
Disagree	12	36	22
No opinion	6	27	15

Appendix

	Protestant %	Catholic %	Total %
Its goals are usually good ones			
Agree	86	52	72
Disagree	6	28	15
No opinion	8	19	13
It is in the hands of men who are good leaders			
Agree	73	47	62
Disagree	14	32	22
No opinion	12	21	16
It is good because it is what the people vote for			
Agree	74	37	59
Disagree	14	36	23
No opinion	11	27	18
We've got to accept it whatever we think			
Agree	67	74	70
Disagree	27	12	21
No opinion	6	14	9

35a. Are there any laws or government regulations that you think are really wrong, laws that a self-respecting person wouldn't necessarily have to obey?

35b. Do you think it is all right if:

	Protestant %	Catholic %	Total %
People do a bit of fiddling on their income tax			
All right	13	18	15
Wrong	73	66	70
Depends	11	11	11
D.K.	3	5	4
A person who doesn't have any work or money steals food			
All right	8	15	11
Wrong	77	71	75
Depends	13	11	12
D.K.	2	3	2
A person doesn't obey a law that he feels is deeply against his religion			
All right	28	46	36
Wrong	46	32	40
Depends	18	12	16
D.K.	8	10	8

36a. Some people think that in Northern Ireland we ought to take notice of what is said about us in other countries.

494

	Protestant	Catholic	Total
	%	%	%

But others say there's no point in worrying about opinions elsewhere. What do you think?

	Protestant	Catholic	Total
Don't bother	39	36	38
Pay attention	55	54	54
D.K.	6	10	8

36b. What do you think is the biggest problem troubling the people of Northern Ireland?

IF NAMES A PROBLEM:

(1) How would you say this first came about?
(2) What, if anything, do you think that the government can do about this?

37. Some people think that it's better to stick by what you have than to be trying new things you don't really know about. What do you think?

	Protestant	Catholic	Total
Stick with what we have	36	38	37
Try new things	59	55	58
D.K.	5	6	5

38a. Would you say that you are a strong (CATHOLIC/PROTESTANT) or average?

	Protestant	Catholic	Total
Strong	45	38	42
Average	53	60	56
D.K.	2	2	2

38b. If a person with the same religion as yourself decided to turn (OPPOSITE TO RELIGION OF RESPONDENT), what difference do you think it would make, if any, to his friends and family?

	Protestant	Catholic	Total
Big difference	47	43	45
Difference to some	34	38	36
Not much difference	12	10	11
No difference	5	7	6
D.K.	1	2	1

38c. Some say that people with the same religion ought to stick together and do a lot to help each other. But others disagree. What do you think?

	Protestant	Catholic	Total
Ought to stick together	60	54	58
Disagree	33	40	36
D.K.	6	6	6

Appendix

		Protestant %	Catholic %	Total %
39.	How often do you go to church for services or prayer?			
	Daily	1	8	4
	More than once a week	6	25	14
	Weekly	39	62	48
	At least monthly	18	1	11
	Occasionally/Hardly ever	30	2	18
	Never	5	1	4
	N.A.	1	1	1

IF ATTENDS CHURCH:

	Protestant	Catholic	Total
(1) Do you belong to any kind of organization connected with your church?			
Yes	22	11	17
N.A.	8	2	5

IF YES:

	Protestant	Catholic	Total
(1) Have you ever held any office in the organization?			
Yes	10	3	7

40a. What would you say are the most important things that you *like* about the Protestant churches in Northern Ireland?

40b. And what things, if any, do you *dislike* about the Protestant churches?

40c. What would you say are the most important things that you *like* about the Catholic Church in Northern Ireland?

40d. And what things, if any, do you *dislike* about the Catholic Church?

	Protestant	Catholic	Total
41. Would you say that in general (OPPOSITE RELIGION OF RESPONDENT) are much different or are about the same as people of your own religion?			
Much different	28	14	22
About the same	67	81	73
D.K.	4	4	4

	Protestant	Catholic	Total
42. Thinking of the people you know in each of the following groups, what proportion would you say are also (SAME AS RESPONDENT) Protestant/Catholic?			
(1) *Friends*			
All	32	25	30
Most	46	32	40

	Protestant %	Catholic %	Total %
Half	18	35	25
Less than half	1	7	4
None	—	—	—
D.K.	2	1	1

(2) *Neighbours*

	Protestant %	Catholic %	Total %
All	28	33	30
Most	40	24	33
Half	22	27	24
Less than half	6	11	8
None	—	2	1
D.K.	4	3	4

(3) *Relatives by Marriage*

	Protestant %	Catholic %	Total %
All	74	65	70
Most	17	22	19
Half	3	5	4
Less than half	2	3	2
None	1	1	1
D.K.	4	4	4

(4) *People you/your Husband work with*

	Protestant %	Catholic %	Total %
All	20	16	19
Most	24	16	21
Half	34	38	36
Less than half	7	15	10
None	2	3	2
D.K.	13	12	12

(5) *Community leaders, people in politics*

	Protestant %	Catholic %	Total %
All	29	15	23
Most	38	17	29
Half	9	16	12
Less than half	1	12	6
None	1	4	2
D.K.	21	36	27

43. People sometimes say that in parts of Northern Ireland Catholics are treated unfairly. Do you think this is true or not?

	Protestant %	Catholic %	Total %
Yes	18	74	41
No	74	13	48
D.K.	8	13	10

IF YES:
(1) Do you have personal knowledge of such discrimination or have you just heard people talk about it?

	Protestant %	Catholic %	Total %
Personal knowledge	4	36	17
Only heard/Read about it	15	38	24

(2) What, if anything, do you think can be done to reduce discrimination here?

Appendix

	Protestant %	Catholic %	Total %
IF NO:			
(1) Why do you think Catholics sometimes complain about discrimination?			
(2) Do you think these complaints should be ignored or investigated?			
Ignored	26	7	18
Investigated	49	26	39
Other	1	—	1
D.K.	4	3	4

Now I would like to read you a few statements about beliefs that some people hold. After I read each statement could you tell me whether you agree or disagree?

	Protestant %	Catholic %	Total %
44a. Everything that happens must be accepted as God's will.			
Agree	56	68	61
Disagree	39	28	35
D.K.	4	4	4
44b. The more active you are in politics, the harder it is to be a good Christian.			
Agree	41	38	39
Disagree	43	36	40
D.K.	16	26	20
44c. The miracles in the Bible happened just as they are described there.			
Agree	72	78	74
Disagree	16	10	13
D.K.	12	12	13
44d. Men whose religious doctrines are false should not be allowed to preach in this country.			
Agree	62	60	62
Disagree	27	28	27
D.K.	11	11	11
45. How sure are you that your religion provides the best guide to life?			
Very sure	54	71	61
Fairly sure	31	23	28
Uncertain	11	4	8
D.K.	4	2	3
46a. Do you think most people can be trusted, or that you have to watch out for other people?			
Can trust	41	38	39
Watch out	53	57	55
Depends	4	3	3
D.K.	2	2	2

	Protestant %	Catholic %	Total %
46b. Generally speaking, would you expect to be treated fairly in dealings with people from the local council?			
Yes	91	81	87
No	4	10	6
Depends	2	2	2
D.K.	3	7	5

47a. Is there anything in particular that you *like* about the government in the Republic?

47b. Is there anything in particular that you *dislike* about the government in the Republic?

47c. What do you think of the position of the Catholic Church in the Republic?

48a. Where did you live most of the time as a child?			
Belfast	27	19	24
Antrim	15	5	11
Down	20	19	19
Armagh	7	10	9
Borough Londonderry	2	8	4
County Londonderry	11	11	11
Fermanagh	3	3	3
Tyrone	7	18	11
Republic	3	4	3
Britain	5	1	3
Other	1	1	1

48b. Was this area mostly Protestant, mostly Catholic, or fairly evenly mixed?			
Mostly Protestant	57	14	39
Mostly Catholic	7	38	20
Mixed	34	46	39
D.K.	2	1	2

48c. What were relations like between Protestants and Catholics in that area?			
Very good	47	53	49
Fairly good	34	31	32
Not good	4	4	4
Bad	3	3	3
Only one religion	9	7	8
D.K.	3	2	3

48d. When you were growing up, what kind of work did your father usually do? (If father was not household head, re-phrase question to fit, e.g., uncle, grandfather, etc.)

(PROBE for EXACT description)

	Protestant %	Catholic %	Total %

IF FARMER: About how many acres did he farm?
IF LABOURER: What kind of industry did he work in?

49a. When your *(FATHER/MOTHER)* was about your present age, was (he/she) more religious than you are now, about as religious or less religious than you are now?
*(Use same sex as respondent)

	Protestant %	Catholic %	Total %
More	28	31	29
Same	52	54	53
Less	7	3	5
D.K.	13	12	13

49b. What sort of attitude did your parents (or head of household) have about mixing between Protestants and Catholics?

Favourable, friendly	35	47	40
Live and let live	45	40	43
Against	16	9	13
D.K.	4	3	4

49c. Did both of your parents (or heads of household) support the same political party?

Yes	82	72	78
No	4	4	4
D.K.	14	24	18

IF YES: Which party was that?
IF NO, D.K.: Which did your father (or male head of household) support?

And your mother? (or aunt, grandmother, etc.)

50a. How old were you when you finished your fulltime education?

11 years old	1	2	1
12 years old	2	4	3
13 years old	4	6	5
14 years old	39	46	42
15 years old	21	17	19
16 years old	13	10	12
17 years old	6	5	6
18 years old	4	3	4
19 years +	9	4	7
No education or under 11	1	1	1

50b. Did you ever pass any kind of examination—for school leaving, the Civil Service, secretarial work, or a diploma of any kind?

	Protestant %	Catholic %	Total %
Yes	34	19	27
No	66	80	72
N.A.	1	1	1

50c. What is the earliest political event that you can remember happening in your own lifetime?

50d. Did you go to a (PROTESTANT/ CATHOLIC) school, or a mixed school, or to both kinds?

	Protestant	Catholic	Total
Always Protestant	82	3	50
Always Catholic	1	80	34
Always mixed	12	12	12
Part mixed–Part Protestant	1	—	1
Part mixed–Part Catholic	—	1	1
Other	3	2	2

50e. Were you taught the Irish language at school?

	Protestant	Catholic	Total
Yes	4	39	18
No	96	60	81
N.A.	1	1	1

50f. Were most of your teachers Unionists, Nationalists or what?

	Protestant	Catholic	Total
Unionists	41	3	26
Nationalists	1	46	20
Mixed in views	9	8	9
D.K.	48	42	46

IF RESPONDENT MALE:

51a. What kind of job did you have when you were 21?

51b. Were you ever in the services?

	Protestant	Catholic	Total
Yes	9	4	7

IF YES:
Did you like being in the services?

	Protestant	Catholic	Total
Yes, liked it	8	4	6
Mixed view	1	—	1
Disliked it	1	—	—

51c. What kind of job do you have now?

IF RESPONDENT FEMALE:

52a. What kind of job did you have when you were 21?

52b. What kind of job do you have now?

52c. What kind of job (does/did) your husband (head of household) have?

Appendix

	Protestant %	Catholic %	Total %
ALL RESPONDENTS			
53. Have (YOU/HE) ever worked in the civil service, or for some kind of public agency?			
Yes, at present	8	7	8
Yes, formerly	8	6	7
IF YES: What kind of public employer is that?			
N. Ireland Civil Service	7	4	5
Local Authority	6	4	5
Westminster Civil Service	3	2	2
Nationalized Industry	—	1	—
Other	1	1	1
N.A.	83	88	85
53a. IF RETIRED: What kind of work did (YOU/HE) do before retiring?			
53b. IF UNEMPLOYED: What kind of work do (YOU/HE) usually do?			
53c. IF FARMER: (1) Do you own your farm, rent it, or work for a wage on it?			
Own	9	10	10
Rent	—	—	—
N.A.	91	89	90
(2) About how many acres do you have here?			
54. Do you think there are any difficulties for a person like yourself in finding a job in Northern Ireland today?			
Yes	36	43	39
No	50	43	47
Depends	4	2	3
D.K.	6	7	7
N.A.	3	4	4
IF YES OR DEPENDS: What kind of difficulties?			
55. Does your (head of household's) work bring you (him) into contact with people living outside Northern Ireland?			
Yes, a lot	11	12	12
Yes, occasionally	24	21	22
No	58	61	59
D.K.	6	6	6
55a. Number of places ringed			
One	11	13	12

	Protestant %	Catholic %	Total %
Two	9	6	8
Three	7	6	7
Four	3	3	3
Five	3	3	3
Six	1	1	1
Seven	—	—	—
D.K.	1	1	1
N.A.–No contact	65	67	66

IF YES:
Where are these people from?

	Protestant	Catholic	Total
Republic	17	18	18
Scotland	18	15	16
England/Wales	30	26	28
Continent of Europe	8	6	7
North America	7	8	7
Other	3	1	2

56a. How about your standard of living?
Would you say that your (your family's)
earnings at present are:

	Protestant	Catholic	Total
Very satisfactory	16	10	14
Fairly satisfactory	62	58	60
Not very satisfactory	18	25	21
Poor	3	4	4
D.K.	1	2	1

56b. Will you please look at this card and
tell me which of these groups comes
closest to your total family income
during recent weeks?

	Protestant	Catholic	Total
Up to £5 per week	3	4	3
£6–£10	13	17	14
£11–£15	18	23	20
£16–£20	19	22	21
£21–£25	16	13	15
£26–£30	9	8	9
£31–£38	8	4	8
More than £2,000	10	4	8
D.K.	4	4	4
Refused to answer	1	—	1

56c. Do you own your house or do you
rent it?

	Protestant	Catholic	Total
Own	45	37	42
Rent	53	59	54
Lodger	1	2	1
Other	2	2	3

IF RENT:
Do you have a private landlord or what?

	Protestant	Catholic	Total
Private	21	23	22
Council	20	26	23

Appendix

	Protestant %	Catholic %	Total %
N.I. Housing Trust	10	9	9
Other	2	1	1
N.A.	47	41	44

56d. What difference, if any, do you think getting rid of the Border would make to your standard of living?

	Protestant	Catholic	Total
Make it better	3	13	8
Worse	48	24	38
No difference	32	44	37
D.K.	17	19	17

57. Have you (or the head of your household) ever belonged to a trade union?

	Protestant	Catholic	Total
Yes	48	43	46

IF NO: Has anyone in your household ever belonged to a trade union?

	Protestant	Catholic	Total
Yes	8	9	8

IF THERE IS A TRADE UNION MEMBER:
(1) Are you (is he) a very strong or an average trade union member?

	Protestant	Catholic	Total
Strong	10	11	10
Average	40	36	38

(2) Have you (he) ever held an office in the trade union?

	Protestant	Catholic	Total
Yes	6	6	6

(3) Are the members of your (his) union mostly Protestant, mostly Catholic or fairly mixed?

	Protestant	Catholic	Total
Protestant	4	2	3
Roman Catholic	1	3	2
Mixed	42	40	41
D.K.	4	3	3

IF NO TRADE UNION MEMBER:
(4) Have you (or has the head of household) ever been a member of any kind of business or professional association:

	Protestant	Catholic	Total
Yes (now)	9	5	7
Yes (past)	3	1	2
No	32	41	36

IF YES:
(a) Are you (is he) a strong or average association member?

	Protestant	Catholic	Total
Strong	2	1	2
Average	10	5	8

(b) Have you (or this member) ever held office in the Association?

	Protestant	Catholic	Total
Yes	3	1	2

	Protestant %	Catholic %	Total %
(c) Are the members of your (his) association mostly Protestant, mostly Catholic, or fairly mixed?			
Mostly Protestant	2	1	2
Mostly Catholic	—	1	—
Mixed	9	4	7
D.K.	1	—	1
N.A.	87	94	90

58a. There's quite a lot of talk these days about different social classes. If you had to make a choice, what class would you call yourself?

58b. IF GIVES A CLASS:
And do you consider yourself a strong member of that class or average?

Strong	13	10	12
Average	66	68	66
D.K.	7	7	7
N.A.–no class given	14	15	14

ALL RESPONDENTS

58c. What other classes would you say there are in Northern Ireland today?
Number of classes given:

One	10	13	11
Two	21	25	23
Three	51	40	47
Four	6	6	6
Five	1	1	1
D.K.	3	6	5
N.A.–no classes	7	8	8

58d. How would you describe people in the (1st named) class?

58e. And people in the (2nd named) class?

58f. How about people in the (3rd named– IF ANY) class?

58g. And in the (4th named–IF ANY) class?

58h. Do you think that the interests of different classes are in conflict, or that the different classes of people get along well together?

Conflict	19	23	21
Depends	13	11	12
Get along	57	51	54
D.K.	11	14	12

Appendix

		Protestant %	Catholic %	Total %
58i.	Do you think that you have more in common with a person of the same class as yourself, but a different religion, OR with a person of a different class but the same religion?			
	Same class	39	39	39
	Same religion	17	12	15
	No difference	33	39	36
	Depends	2	1	2
	D.K.	9	9	8
59a.	There are those who say that some people are born to rule. Others disagree. What do you think?			
	Agree	70	59	65
	Disagree	20	26	22
	Depends	3	4	3
	D.K.	7	1	9
59b.	Some say that those who are gentlemen are the best to govern a country. Others disagree. How do you feel about this?			
	Agree	40	34	37
	Disagree	41	45	43
	Depends	10	8	10
	D.K.	9	12	10
59c.	Some say that people with the most education are best to govern the country. Others disagree. What do you think?			
	Agree	64	66	65
	Disagree	25	21	23
	Depends	8	7	7
	D.K.	3	6	5
60a.	Where was your Father born			
	Co. Down	17	17	17
	Belfast	18	15	17
	Antrim	17	6	12
	Armagh	8	10	9
	County Londonderry	9	10	10
	Borough Londonderry	1	7	4
	Fermanagh	3	3	3
	Tyrone	8	15	11
	Monaghan	4	4	4
	Republic	7	10	8
	Britain	9	4	7
	Other	1	1	1
	Where was your Mother born?			
	Co. Down	19	17	18
	Belfast	18	15	17

Appendix

	Protestant %	Catholic %	Total %
Antrim	16	6	12
Armagh	8	9	8
County Londonderry	9	9	9
Borough Londonderry	2	8	4
Fermanagh	2	3	3
Tyrone	8	14	11
Republic	6	11	8
Britain	9	6	7
Other	1	2	1

60b. Were both of your parents of the same religion?

Same	94	91	93
Different	3	6	4
N.A.	2	2	2

61a. When you were growing up, did your parents (or head of household) think of themselves as British, Irish, Ulster, or what?

British	46	10	31
Ulster	27	3	17
Irish	18	75	41
Sometimes British, sometimes Irish	—	1	1
Anglo-Irish	1	—	—
Other	1	—	—
Parents mixed	1	3	2
D.K.	5	7	7

IF MIXED, D.K.:
(1) What about your Father (or Male head of household)?

British	1	2	1
Irish	1	1	1
D.K.	4	3	4

(2) and your Mother (Aunt, Grandmother, etc.)?

British	1	1	1
Irish	—	—	1
D.K.	3	3	3

61b. How old are you?

61c. Are you married?

Yes	71	63	68
Widower	10	10	10
Separated/Divorced	1	1	1
No	18	25	21
N.A.	1	1	1

IF MARRIED:
(1) And is (was) your Husband/Wife also a Protestant/Catholic?

	Protestant %	Catholic %	Total %
Same	75	68	72
Different	2	2	2
N.A.	23	29	26

(2) How many children do you have?
(3) What age is your youngest child?
   (If any)

ALL RESPONDENTS:

62a. How important would you say it is for children to be brought up with the same religious views as their parents?

Very important	67	79	72
Fairly important	15	10	13
Not very important	4	3	3
Let them make up their own minds	14	7	11
D.K.	1	1	1

62b. How important would you say it is for children to be brought up with the same views as their parents on the Border question?

Very important	16	10	13
Fairly important	11	7	10
Not very important	11	15	13
Let them make up their own minds	60	67	63
D.K.	1	1	1

62c. How important would you say it is for children to be brought up to vote for the same party as their parents do?

Very important	17	8	13
Fairly important	8	8	8
Not very important	7	11	9
Let them make up their own minds	67	71	68
D.K.	1	1	1

63. There's a lot of talk these days about uniting the Protestant Church and the Roman Catholic Church into one. What do you think of this idea?

Let me make sure I have this clear:

(1) Do you think that *in principle* uniting the Protestant and Catholic Churches is:

Desirable	27	69	45
Undesirable	60	16	42
Depends	6	7	7
D.K.–no opinion	7	8	7

(2) Do you think that *in practice* uniting the churches is

Possible	17	43	27

	Protestant %	Catholic %	Total %
Impossible	72	41	59
Depends	6	7	7
D.K.–no opinion	5	9	7

THAT ENDS THE INTERVIEW. THANK YOU VERY MUCH FOR YOUR TIME AND CO-OPERATION.

TO BE COMPLETED BY INTERVIEWER ALONE

	Protestant %	Catholic %	Total %
1. Interviewer's Name			
2. Time interview begun			
Time interview completed			
3. Briefly evaluate the respondent in terms of:			
Conversation			
Good talker	34	29	32
Average	43	44	43
Poor	22	27	24
Way home is kept			
Clean, tidy,	76	65	71
Fair	18	24	21
Poor, shabby, dirty	5	10	7
Level of prosperity			
Definitely prosperous	10	4	7
Average middle class	32	22	28
Average working class	50	59	54
Poor	6	13	9
N.A.	2	2	2

4. Was anyone else present at the interview?
   One group (person)
   Two groups and so on
   No one

   Pre-School children

   Older Children

   Husband/Wife

   Other relatives

Appendix

	Protestant %	Catholic %	Total %
Other			

IF someone else present: what part, if any,
played in the interview.
      Very influential
      Somewhat influential
      Slightly influential
      Not at all influential/none
      D.K.–can't judge
      N.A.

5. Respondent's attitude at beginning of
interview:

	Protestant	Catholic	Total
Very interested	23	18	21
Interested	46	49	47
Not very interested	22	25	23
Antagonistic	1	—	1
Nervous, uncertain	6	6	6

IF antagonistic, nervous, please explain:

6. Respondent's attitude at end of interview:

	Protestant	Catholic	Total
No change	63	61	62
More interested, helpful	26	26	26
Less interested, helpful	5	5	5
Hurrying to get it over	6	6	6

7. Were there any particular sections of the
questionnaire that the respondent had
difficulty with?
      Politics
      Religion
      Class
      Open-ended questions
      Many questions
      N.A.

8. Were there any particular sections of the
questionnaire that the respondent was
hesitant to answer, or where he was
suspiciously vague?
      Politics
      Religion
      Class
      Income
      Open-ended questions
      Many questions
      N.A.

Any other comments helpful in interpreting this interview:

Notes

Introduction

1. Sir Keith Feiling, *Life of Neville Chamberlain* (London: Macmillan, 1947), p. 372.
2. See James G. Leyburn, *The Scotch-Irish: a Social History* (Chapel Hill: University of North Carolina Press, 1962), pp. 148, 180; R. T. Berthoff, *British Immigrants in Industrial America, 1790–1950* (Cambridge, Massachusetts: Harvard, 1953); George McBride, *American Presidents of Ulster Descent* (Bangor, Co. Down, 1969), p. 5; and E. R. R. Green, editor, *Essays in Scotch-Irish History* (London: Routledge, 1969).
3. See e.g., George W. Potter, *To the Golden Door: The Story of the Irish in Ireland and America* (Boston: Little, Brown, 1960). Cf. Nathan Glazer and D. P. Moynihan, *Beyond the Melting Pot* (Cambridge, Massachusetts: MIT, 1963).
4. Quoted in C. Vann Woodward, *The Burden of Southern History* (New York: Vintage edition, 1961), p. 169. Woodward's discussion of history is also relevant to Northern Ireland.
5. *Ibid.*, p. 170.
6. An earlier but still relevant phase of Irish politics is magnificently related to European trends by Nicholas Mansergh in *The Irish Question, 1840–1921* (London: Allen & Unwin, revised edition, 1965).
7. The case for studying political variations among nations modern in socio-economic terms is presented in Richard Rose, 'Modern Nations and the Study of Political Modernization', Stein Rokkan, editor, *Comparative Research Across Cultures and Nations* (Paris: Mouton, 1968).
8. For a detailed argument, see Harry Eckstein, *Division and Cohesion in Democracy: a Study of Norway* (Princeton: University Press, 1966), p. v, and Joseph LaPalombara, 'Macrotheories and Microapplications in Comparative Politics: a Widening Chasm', *Comparative Politics* I:1 (1969).
9. The author was also teargassed by the Chicago police while attending the Democratic National Convention in August, 1968. Comparatively, Ulster teargas is nicer; Chicago teargas is more powerful. Being hit by a stone is far more unpleasant and dangerous than being teargassed.
10. Paraphrasing the familiar saying of the Christian, one might argue that the trouble with Voltaire's prescription for civil peace is that it has never been tried. Cf. his remark in a letter to a friend in 1761. *Est-ce*

Notes

que la proposition honnête et modeste d'étrangler le dernier jésuite avec les boyaux du dernier janséniste ne pourrait amener les choses à quelque conciliation? In the Ulster context, Presbyter might be substituted for Jesuit.

Chapter I

1. Cf. *The History of Violence in America*, edited by H. D. Graham and T. R. Gurr (New York: Praeger, 1969), J. H. Plumb, *The Growth of Political Stability in England, 1675–1725* (London: Macmillan, 1967), and various studies of George Rudé, e.g., *The Crowd in History, 1730–1848* (New York: Wiley, 1964).
2. See e.g., Robert Peabody's article on the subject in the *International Encyclopedia of the Social Sciences* (New York: Macmillan and Free Press, 1968).
3. This definition is thus much simpler than that of David Easton, who conflates cultural values, procedural norms and institutional features. Cf. *A Systems Analysis of Political Life* (New York: Wiley, 1965), Ch. 12.
4. See e.g., H. H. Gerth and C. Wright Mills, editors, *From Max Weber* (London: Routledge, 1948), p. 78; David Easton, *The Political System* (New York: Knopf, 1953), pp. 130ff.; G. A. Almond and J. S. Coleman, editors, *The Politics of Developing Areas* (Princeton: University Press, 1960), pp. 5ff., and Robert A. Dahl, *Modern Political Analysis* (Englewood Cliffs, N.J.: Prentice-Hall, 1963), Ch. 2.
5. See e.g., Ghita Ionescu, *The Politics of the European Communist States* (London: Weidenfeld & Nicolson, 1967).
6. The characteristics of primitive political groups lacking fixed territorial locales, such as African tribes, are not within the ambit of this study. For a discussion of their significance for political systems theory, see W. J. M. Mackenzie, *Politics and Social Science* (Harmondsworth: Penguin, 1967), Ch. 13.
7. See chapters 4 and 5 by Joe Frantz and Richard Maxwell Brown in H. D. Graham and T. R. Gurr, editors, *The History of Violence in America*.
8. Dorothy Emmet, *Function, Purpose and Power* (London: Macmillan, 1958), p. 23.
9. The definition is found in *From Max Weber*, p. 183.
10. See e.g., Bernard Akzin, *State and Nation* (London: Hutchinson, 1964), p. 33, and D. A. Rustow's article on Nation in *International Encyclopedia of the Social Sciences* (New York: Macmillan and Free Press, 1968).
11. Typically, definitions of legitimacy imply only a single measure or a multiplicity of measures. The latter are difficult to apply empirically because of their complexity. The single-attribute definition may err by being too simple. Cf. S. M. Lipset, *Political Man* (New York: Doubleday, 1960), Ch. III and the discussion in Brian Barry, *Sociologists,*

Economists and Democracy (London: Collier-Macmillan, 1970), pp. 63ff.

12. Cf. the similar though not idential phrases 'primary rules' and 'secondary rules', as used by H. L. A. Hart, *The Concept of Law* (Oxford: Clarendon Press, 1961), Ch. 5.

13. James Q. Wilson, *Varieties of Police Behavior* (Cambridge, Massachusetts: Harvard, 1968), p. 49. For a similar English analysis, note Michael Banton, *The Policeman in the Community* (London: Tavistock, 1964).

14. See Allan Silver, 'Official Interpretations of Racial Riots', in *Urban Riots: Violence and Social Change* (New York: Proceedings of the Academy of Political Science, XXXIX:1, 1968).

15. For the role of judicial decisions in the political process, see the seminal study by Jack W. Peltason, *Federal Courts in the Political Process* (New York: Random House, 1955). For popular attitudes, see Walter F. Murphy and Joseph Tanenhaus, 'Public Opinion and the United States Supreme Court', in *Frontiers of Judicial Research*, edited by Joel B. Grossman and Joseph Tanenhaus (New York: Wiley, 1969).

16. Cf. Richard Rose, *Politics in England* (London: Faber, 1965), Ch. 10.

17. The point is very well developed in H. L. Nieburg's *Political Violence* (New York: St. Martin's Press, 1969), especially pp. 56ff.

18. See e.g., Angus Campbell and Howard Schuman, *Racial Attitudes in Fifteen American Cities* (Ann Arbor: Institute for Social Research, 1968), p. 52.

19. For a review of evidence justifying this assumption, see Richard Dawson and Kenneth Prewitt, *Political Socialization* (Boston: Little, Brown, 1969).

20. Cf. Bruce Russett, J. David Singer and Melvin Small, 'National Political Units in the Twentieth Century: a Standardized List', *American Political Science Review* LXII:3, 1968.

21. See Val R. Lorwin, 'Belgium: Religion, Class and Language in National Politics' in Robert A. Dahl, editor, *Political Oppositions in Western Democracies* (New Haven: Yale, 1966).

22. See Martin Needler, *Political Development in Latin America* (New York: Random House, 1968), p. 65.

23. Cf. H. Herring, *A History of Latin America* (New York: Knopf, 1963 edition), and Martin Needler, 'Political Growth and Military Intervention in Latin America', *American Political Science Review* LX:3, 1966.

24. See Harry Eckstein, editor, *Internal War* (New York: Free Press, 1964), p. 3 and T. R. Gurr, 'A Comparative Study of Civil Strife', pp. 628–30 of H. D. Graham and T. R. Gurr, editors, *The History of Violence in America*.

25. 'Succession in the Twentieth Century', *Journal of International Affairs* XVIII:1 (1964), p. 107. See also Fred R. von der Mehden, *Politics of the Developing Nations* (Englewood Cliffs, N.J.: Prentice-Hall, 1964), p. 65.

26. Walter Bagehot, *The English Constitution* (London: World's Classics edition, 1955), p. 40.

27. A more detailed discussion of causes of changes in authority patterns

Notes

is contained in the article on which this chapter is based, 'Dynamic Tendencies in the Authority of Regimes', *World Politics* XXI:4 (1969), pp. 612ff.

28. On the concept of inheritance, in the transition from one regime to another, see J. P. Nettl and R. Robertson, *International Systems and the Modernization of Societies* (London: Faber, 1968), Part II.

29. See T. R. Gurr with Charles Ruttenberg, *The Conditions of Civil Violence: First Tests of a Causal Model* (Princeton: Center for International Studies, Research Monograph No. 28, 1967), p. 107.

30. Cf. Lucian W. Pye, *Aspects of Political Development* (Boston: Little, Brown, 1966), Ch. 3.

31. The ideas are set out in the introduction by S. M. Lipset and Stein Rokkan, editors, *Party Systems and Voter Alignments* (New York: Free Press, 1967). See also, Stein Rokkan, 'The Structuring of Mass Politics in the Smaller European Democracies', *Comparative Studies in Society and History* X:2 (1968).

32. See *Presidential Power* (New York: Wiley), p. 155.

33. See Richard Rose, 'Dynamic Tendencies in the Authority of Regimes', pp. 624ff., and more generally S. P. Huntington, *Political Order in Changing Societies* (New Haven: Yale University Press, 1968).

34. For a good critical discussion of the confusion surrounding the use of these associated terms in much social science literature, see Brian Barry, *Sociologists, Economists and Democracy*, especially Chs. 3–4.

Chapter II

1. 'The British Political System', in S. H. Beer and A. Ulam, editors, *Patterns of Government* (New York: Random House, 2nd edition), p. 84. See also S. H. Beer, *Modern British Politics* (London: Faber, 1965).

2. 'Great Britain', in Roy Macridis and Robert Ward, editors, *Modern Political Systems: Europe* (Englewood Cliffs, N.J.: Prentice-Hall, 2nd edition), 1968, p. 42; J. Blondel, *Voters, Parties, Leaders*, p. 21.

3. For a discussion of the political connotations of the terms Ulster as used in Unionist and Irish circles, see House of Commons *Debates*, Vol. 792, Cols. 980ff. (December 1, 1969).

4. For typologies of intergroup relations, see Milton M. Gordon, 'Assimilation in America', *Daedalus* XC:2 (1961) and Charles Price. 'The Study of Assimilation' in J. A. Jackson, editor, *Migration* (Cambridge: University Press, 1969).

5. See Leslie Wolf-Phillips, *Constitutions of Modern States* (London: Pall Mall, 1968).

6. Robert Alford, *Party and Society* (Chicago: Rand, McNally, 1963), pp. 170–1.

7. Note the generalizations about British culture in G. A. Almond and Sidney Verba, *The Civic Culture* (Princeton: University Press, 1963).

In fact, the data from their survey did not provide sufficiently large numbers of Scottish and Welsh respondents to permit generalization about non-English parts of Britain.

8. Cf. Karl W. Deutsch *et al.*, *Political Community and the North Atlantic Area* (Princeton: University Press, 1957), W. G. Runciman, *Relative Deprivation and Social Justice* (London: Routledge, 1966), and John E. Schwarz, 'The Scottish National Party: Non-violent Separatism and Theories of Violence', *World Politics* XXII:4 (1970).

9. See D. Elliston Allen, *British Tastes* (London: Panther edition, 1969), pp. 66, 89f., 162f., 169f.

10. The point is well put in Michael Hechter, 'Images of National Integration' (Washington, D.C.: Paper presented to the American Sociological Association Annual Meeting, 1970).

11. See e.g., A. H. Birch, *The British System of Government* (London: Allen & Unwin, 1967), p. 16, and Jean Blondel, *Voters, Parties and Leaders* (Harmondsworth: Penguin, 1963), p. 21.

12. Because of limits of space, no attention will be given to the political status of the 'offshore' parts of the British isles, such as the Isle of Man and the Channel Isles. Cf. D. G. Kermode, 'Legislative-Executive Relationships in the Isle of Man', *Political Studies* XVI:1 (1968).

13. Sir Reginald Coupland, *Welsh and Scottish Nationalism* (London: Collins, 1954), p. xv.

14. See Ada C. Kopec, 'Blood Groups in Great Britain', *Advancement of Science* XIII:51 (1956).

15. Cf. M. W. Heslinga, *The Irish Border as a Cultural Divide* (Assen, Netherlands: Van Gorcum, 1962), pp. 105ff., and Joseph Raftery, editor, *The Celts* (Cork: Mercier Press, 1964).

16. See Arnold Schrier, *Ireland and the American Migration, 1850–1900* (Minneapolis: University of Minnesota Press, 1958), p. 4. See also, M. W. Heslinga, *The Irish Border as a Cultural Divide*, and Stanley Johnson, *Emigration from the United Kingdom to North America* (London: Routledge, 1913), p. 351.

17. See the data in Michael Hechter, 'Regional Inequality and National Integration in the British Isles, 1801–1921' (San Francisco: American Sociological Association Annual Meeting, 1969), Tables 9a and b.

18. For Northern Ireland data see 1968 Loyalty survey, for Wales, see *Readership Survey of Wales* (London: Thomson Organization, 1961).

19. Cf. Colin Seymour-Ure, *The Press, Politics and the Public* (London: Methuen, 1968) and James Kellas, *Modern Scotland* (London: Pall Mall, 1968), pp. 13–16.

20. Cf. B. R. Mitchell, *Abstract of British Economic Statistics* (Cambridge: University Press, 1962), p. 52; J. A. Jackson, *The Irish in Britain* (London: Routledge, 1963), p. 191, Julius Isaac, *British Post-War Migration* (Cambridge: University Press, 1954), Chs. 5–6.

21. See e.g., H. J. Hanham, *Scottish Nationalism* (London: Faber, 1969), p. 30.

22. Dr. John Beddoe, a Victorian ethnologist concerned with 'racial colour-types', calculated that the Irish had an index of 'nigrescence' of

Notes

65 per cent, compared with 28 per cent for an English sample. E. A. Freeman, Regius Professor of History at Oxford, eschewed scientific methods when asserting his views on racial types. *A propos* America, he wrote a friend from New Haven, Connecticut, in 1881: 'This would be a grand land if only every Irishman would kill a negro, and be hanged for it.' Both points are found in L. P. Curtis Jr., *Anglo-Saxons and Celts: a Study of Anti-Irish Prejudice in Victorian England* (Bridgeport, Connecticut: Conference on British Studies, 1968), pp. 81 and 136n.

23. See *Report on a Study of Certain Aspects of Nationalism* (London: Market Information Services, 1968).

24. See 'Support Soars for Home Rule Causes in Britain', an Opinion Research Centre survey reported in the *Belfast Telegraph*, November 21, 1967.

25. Figures are accurately and conveniently presented by national groups in F. W. S. Craig, *British Parliamentary Election Statistics, 1918–1968* (Glasgow: Political Reference Publications, 1968), pp. 1ff. Note also D. E. Butler and J. Freeman, *British Political Facts 1900–1967* (London: Macmillan, 1968 edition), p. 145.

26. See David Butler and Donald Stokes, *Political Change in Britain* (London: Macmillan, 1969), pp. 140ff.

27. It is noteworthy that legal anomalies positively favour citizens of the Irish Republic. By comparison, non-white British nationals have been subjected to a variety of forms of legal discrimination, culminating in 1968 with measures against Kenyan Asians with British passports. Cf. E. J. B. Rose *et al.*, *Colour and Citizenship* (London: Oxford University Press, 1969).

28. Cf. Sir Reginald Coupland, *Welsh and Scottish Nationalism*, p. 212; and Kenneth Morgan, *Wales in British Politics, 1868–1922* (Cardiff: University of Wales Press, 1963), p. 312. The decennial statistics for Wales and Scotland contain figures about Welsh and Gaelic speakers.

29. See Sir Reginald Coupland, *Welsh and Scottish Nationalism*, pp. 188ff.

30. Data from Northern Ireland Loyalty survey, 1968; Opinion Research Centre survey of social life in Wales, 1968; and University of Strathclyde, Glasgow Monarchy survey, 1968.

31. See 1 Will. & Mary Sec. 2, ch. 2. Note also, Geoffrey Wilson, *Cases and Materials on Constitutional and Administrative Law* (Cambridge: University Press, 1966), p. 13.

32. G. I. T. Machin, *The Catholic Question in English Politics 1820 to 1830* (Oxford: Clarendon Press, 1964), p. 9.

33. See George Rudé, *The Crowd in History, 1730–1848*, pp. 59ff.

34. See e.g., E. R. Norman, *Anti-Catholicism in Victorian England* (London: Allen & Unwin, 1968), Ch. 3, and D. Cresap Moore, 'The Other Face of Reform', *Victorian Studies* V:1 (1961).

35. Quoted in E. R. Norman, *Anti-Catholicism in Victorian England*, p. 169.

36. *Ibid.*, pp. 215–16.

37. See e.g., Elie Halévy, *Imperialism and the Rise of Labour* (London: Benn Paperback edition, 1961), pp. 163–210.

38. See W. S. F. Pickering, 'The 1851 Religious Census–a Useless Experiment?', *British Journal of Sociology* XVIII:4 (1967), and K. S. Inglis, *Churches and the Working Classes in Victorian England* (London: Routledge, 1963).
39. In addition to Irish census data, see K. O. Morgan, *Wales in British Politics*, pp. 307ff.; James Kellas, *Modern Scotland*, p. 264n., and John Highet, 'The Churches' in A. K. Cairncross, editor, *The Scottish Economy* (Cambridge: University Press, 1954), p. 305.
40. Cf. K. W. J. Alexander and A. Hobbs, 'What Influences Labour MPs?' in Richard Rose, editor, *Studies in British Politics* (London: Macmillan, 1969 edition).
41. Bryan Wilson, *Religion in Secular Society* (London: Watts, 1966), pp. xivff.
42. E. R. Norman, *The Conscience of the State in North America* (Cambridge: University Press, 1968), p. 18
43. See David Butler and Donald Stokes, *Political Change in Britain*, p. 125.
44. Cf. Peter Laslett, *The World We Have Lost* (London: Methuen, 1965).
45. See Phyllis Deane and W. A. Cole, *British Economic Growth, 1688–1959* (Cambridge University Press, 2nd edition, 1967), pp. 142–3.
46. Asa Briggs, *The Age of Improvement* (London: Longmans, 1960), p. 182.
47. See B. R. Mitchell, *Abstract of British Economic Statistics*, pp. 24–7, and Sir Reginald Coupland, *Welsh and Scottish Nationalism*, p. 171.
48. See Richard Rose, 'Class and Party Divisions: Britain as a Test Case', *Sociology* II:2 (1968), Table 7.
49. See William Gwyn, *Democracy and the Cost of Politics* (London: Athlone Press, 1962) and Richard Rose, *Influencing Voters* (London: Faber, 1967), Ch. 1.
50. For the problem of nineteenth-century Irish immigrants, see J. A. Jackson, *The Irish in Britain*. For comparison, note mid-twentieth-century coloured immigration, as described, for example, in E. J. B. Rose *et al.*, *Colour and Citizenship*.
51. Riots are conveniently summarized in Andrew Boyd, *Holy War in Belfast* (Tralee: Anvil Press, 1969).
52. See George Dangerfield, *The Strange Death of Liberal England* (London: Constable, 1935).
53. See J. N. Toothill, *Report on the Scottish Economy* (Edinburgh: Scottish Council, 1962), Appendix 20.
54. No information about the Republic of Ireland is given about earnings and unemployment, because of the radical difference between its still heavily peasant and agricultural economy and that of the United Kingdom.
55. See *Abstract of Regional Statistics, 1969* (London: HMSO), Table 54.
56. See Edwin Hammond, *An Analysis of Regional Economic and Social Statistics* (Durham University: Rowntree Research Unit, 1968), Table 2.2.1, and *Digest of Statistics* No. 31 (Belfast: HMSO, 1969), Table 11.
57. Market Information Services, *Report on a Study of Certain Aspects of Nationalism*, Q. 2 & 4.
58. Data from the Sample Census of 1966 for England, Wales, and Scotland,

Economic Activity Tables, Table 30, and for Northern Ireland, from the comparable *1961 Census: General Report*. All data concern economically active and retired males only. The 'middle class' is here defined as Classes I and II of the Registrar-General's five-point stratification scheme.

59. Figures from a 1964 Gallup Poll survey of Great Britain, and from the 1968 Northern Ireland Loyalty Survey.

60. No consideration is given here to significant regional differences within Scotland, Wales and Northern Ireland. The existence of major differences within a nation is independent of major differences between nations.

61. Both points of view are reflected in the terms of reference of the Royal Commission on the Constitution, established with Lord Crowther as chairman in 1969.

62. On this point, see Chs. IV and VII *infra*, and Basil Chubb, *The Government and Politics of Ireland* (Stanford: University Press, 1970), especially Ch. 13.

63. See Sir Ivor Jennings, *Party Politics: Volume I* (Cambridge: University Press, 1960), pp. 6–7.

64. See the *Census of Ireland 1841* (Dublin: Thom for HMSO, 1843), p. viii; E. R. R. Green, 'The Great Famine', in T. W. Moody and F. X. Martin, editors, *The Course of Irish History* (Cork: Mercier Press, 1967). For a traveller's impression in 1835, see Alexis de Tocqueville's *Journeys to England and Ireland* edited by J. P. Mayer (London: Faber, 1958), Ch. 4.

Chapter III

1. For a discussion of fragment societies, see the studies in Louis Hartz, editor, *The Founding of New Societies* (New York: Harcourt, Brace, 1964). Unfortunately, Northern Ireland is not included in that volume.

2. See Andrew Boyd, *Holy War in Belfast*.

3. See e.g., E. Estyn Evans, *The Irishness of the Irish* (The Irish Association for Cultural, Economic and Social Relations, no place of publication, 1967); Joseph Raftery, editor, *The Celts*, and the contributions by G. F. Mitchell and Francis J. Byrne to T. W. Moody and F. X. Martin, editors, *The Course of Irish History* (Cork: Mercier Press, 1967).

4. *The Irish Border as a Cultural Divide*, p. 113.

5. See Brian O Ciuv, 'Ireland in the Eleventh and Twelfth Centuries', in T. W. Moody and F. X. Martin, editors, *The Course of Irish History*, pp. 115ff., and A. G. Donaldson, *Some Comparative Aspects of Irish Law* (London: Cambridge University Press, 1957), p. 38.

6. The figure is that of F. H. Newark, cited in M. W. Heslinga, *The Irish Border as a Cultural Divide*, p. 126.

7. 'The Anglo-Norman Invasion', in T. W. Moody and F. X. Martin, editors, *The Course of Irish History*, pp. 142–3.

8. See R. J. Dickson, *Ulster Emigration to Colonial America, 1718–1775* (London: Routledge, 1966), p. 3.
9. Gilbert Camblin, *The Town in Ulster* (Belfast: Mullan, 1951), p. vii and Ch. 3.
10. See James G. Leyburn, *The Scotch-Irish*, Part III.
11. J. C. Beckett, *The Making of Modern Ireland, 1603–1923* (London: Faber, 1966), pp. 35 *et seq.*
12. See Aidan Clarke, 'The Colonisation of Ulster and the Rebellion of 1641', in T. W. Moody and F. X. Martin, editors, *The Course of Irish History*, p. 201. See also J. C. Beckett, *The Making of Modern Ireland*, Chs. 4–5. Cf. Benignus Millett, D.F.M., *Survival and Reorganization* (Dublin: Gill, A History of Irish Catholicism, 1968), Vol. III.
13. The date is given New Style. J. G. Simms, *Jacobite Ireland, 1685–1691* (London: Routledge, 1969), p. 144, states that no evidence exists for the story that the Pope ordered a *Te Deum* sung in St. Peter's to celebrate the defeat of France's allies. He grants that Catholic powers such as Spain and Austria applauded the victory of the Protestant William over their common enemy.
14. For a systematic discussion of the position of the Irish 'natives' in a quasi-colonial situation, see e.g., E. Strauss, *Irish Nationalism and British Democracy* (London: Allen & Unwin, 1951), and Liam de Paor, *Divided Ulster* (Harmondsworth: Penguin, 1969).
15. See the estimates discussed in James G. Leyburn, *The Scotch-Irish*, p. 180. For specific details, consult R. J. Dickson, *Ulster Emigration to Colonial America*.
16. An eyewitness description, quoted in J. G. Simms, *Jacobite Ireland*, p. 198. A skein is a dagger.
17. Quotations from an early oath of membership, cited in Hereward Senior, *Orangeism in Ireland and Britain, 1795–1836* (London: Routledge, 1966), p. 21. Italics supplied.
18. For documentary evidence concerning agrarian troubles and the 1798 rising in Ulster, see *Aspects of Irish Social History 1750–1800* (Belfast: HMSO for the Public Record Office of Northern Ireland, 1969).
19. See N. Mansergh, *The Irish Question*, p. 53, and L. P. Curtis Jr., *Anglo-Saxons and Celts*, especially p. 122n.
20. See the comparative analysis by Oliver MacDonagh in Ch. 2 of his study, *Ireland* (Englewood Cliffs, N.J.: Prentice-Hall, 1968).
21. See Galen Broeker, *Rural Disorder and Police Reform in Ireland, 1812–36* (London: Routledge, 1970), p. 237, and J. C. Beckett, *The Making of Modern Ireland*, p. 310.
22. The point is emphasized in a number of contexts by Conor Cruise O'Brien, *Parnell and his Party, 1880–1890* (Oxford: Clarendon Press, 1964 edition).
23. See E. R. Norman, *The Catholic Church and Ireland in the Age of Rebellion* (London: Longmans, 1965), Ch. 3. The condemnation resulted from representations of the British government to the Vatican. The place of parliamentary and violent means in Fenian politics is a

Notes

major theme in T. W. Moody, editor, *The Fenian Movement* (Cork: Mercier, 1968), pp. 37ff. and 101ff.

24. See Donal McCartney, 'From Parnell to Pearse' in T. W. Moody and F. X. Martin, editors, *The Course of Irish History*, p. 301.

25. See Thomas Wilson, editor, *Ulster Under Home Rule* (London: Oxford University Press, 1955), pp. 208–9. The Constitution of the Fianna Fail Party, adopted in 1953, emphasizes the restoration of the Irish language and way of life, and the maintenance of Ireland as a rural society. See Basil Chubb, editor, *A Source Book of Irish Government* (Dublin: Institute of Public Administration, 1964), p. 215.

26. See *General Report: Census of Population 1961* (Belfast: HMSO, 1965), pp. xvii–xviii and J. C. Beckett and R. E. Glasscock, *Belfast: Origin and Growth of an Industrial City* (London: BBC, 1967), p. 118.

27. See Hereward Senior, *Orangeism in Ireland and Britain*, Ch. 11.

28. Andrew Boyd, *Holy War in Belfast*, provides a convenient summary of eyewitness and official reports of nineteenth-century riots in Belfast.

29. Cf. D. C. Savage, 'The Origins of the Ulster Unionist Party, 1885–86', *Irish Historical Studies* XII:47 (1961), and J. W. Boyle, editor, *Leaders and Workers* (Cork: Mercier Press, c. 1965) especially the chapter on William Walker.

30. Quoted in J. W. Boyle, 'Belfast and the Origins of Northern Ireland', in J. C. Beckett and R. E. Glasscock, editors, *Belfast: Origin and Growth*, p. 138.

31. Quoted in Dorothy Macardle, *The Irish Republic* (London: Corgi edition, 1968), p. 85. See also, Ian Colvin, *The Life of Lord Carson: Volume II* (London: Gollancz, 1934), p. 206.

32. See Robert Blake, *The Unknown Prime Minister* (London: Eyre and Spottiswoode, 1955).

33. A. T. Q. Stewart, *The Ulster Crisis* (London: Faber, 1967), pp. 244ff. On the effects of the crisis on the British Army, see A. P. Ryan, *Mutiny on the Curragh* (London: Macmillan, 1956) and Sir James Fergusson, *The Curragh Incident* (London: Faber, 1964).

34. See A. T. Q. Stewart, *The Ulster Crisis*, p. 241.

35. Quoted from Liam de Paor, *Divided Ulster*, p. 93. For Dillon's comment, see F. S. L. Lyon's chapter in F. X. Martin, editor, *Leaders and Men of the Easter Rising* (London: Methuen, 1967), p. 35.

36. See Wallace Clark, *Guns in Ulster* (Belfast: Constabulary Gazette, 1967), especially p. 68; D. Barritt and C. F. Carter, *The Northern Ireland Problem* (London: Oxford University Press, 1962), p. 128; J. J. Campbell, 'Between the Wars', in J. C. Beckett and R. E. Glasscock, *Belfast: Origin and Growth*, p. 147.

37. The arrangements are succinctly set out in Nicholas Mansergh, *The Government of Northern Ireland* (London: Allen & Unwin, 1936). For another view, see Frank Gallagher, *The Indivisible Island* (London: Gollancz, 1957).

38. A statement by Viscount Craigavon (then Sir James Craig), writing as Prime Minister of Northern Ireland; italics in the original. Quoted in Nicholas Mansergh, *The Irish Question*, p. 213.

Notes

39. Quoted in J. W. Boyle, 'Belfast and the Origins of Northern Ireland', p. 143.
40. See Nicholas Mansergh, *The Government of Northern Ireland*, pp. 118–119.
41. Figures from T. P. Coogan, *Ireland Since the Rising* (London: Pall Mall, 1966), p. 47. See also Desmond Williams, editor, *The Irish Struggle 1916–1926* (London: Routledge, 1966).
42. 'A General Survey' in T. W. Moody and J. C. Beckett, editors, *Ulster Since 1800: A Political and Economic Survey* (London: BBC, 1955), p. 133.
43. For an account of de Valera's diplomacy, see Nicholas Mansergh, 'Ireland: External Relations 1926–1939', in Francis MacManus, *The Years of the Great Test 1926–1939* (Cork: Mercier Press, 1967).
44. For details of the Border settlement see *Report of the Irish Boundary Commission* (Cork: Irish University Press, 1970) and J. L. McCracken, 'The Political Scene in Northern Ireland 1926–37' in F. MacManus, editor, *The Years of the Great Test*, pp. 150–1.
45. See Nicholas Mansergh, *The Government of Northern Ireland*, p. 240. Cf. the epigraph quoting de Valera at Ch. VIII, *infra*.
46. No figures for party strength in terms of votes can be given, because many and sometimes the majority of seats have been uncontested at general elections.
47. Quoted in Nicholas Mansergh, *The Government of Northern Ireland*, p. 240.
48. See *For Members of Parliament Only* (Belfast: privately printed, *c.* 1936). On the period generally, see 'The Real Case Against Partition', *The Capuchin Annual* (1943).
49. Unpreparedness made it vulnerable to a series of surprise German air raids in 1941. See John W. Blake, *Northern Ireland in the Second World War* (Belfast: HMSO, 1956).
50. For a discussion of the intricacies of the period, see e.g., chapters in Kevin Nowlan and T. Desmond Williams, editors, *Ireland in the War Years and After, 1939–51* (Dublin and London: Gill and Macmillan, 1969); J. Bowyer Bell, *The Secret Army* (London: Blond, 1970) and R. M. Smyllie, 'Unneutral Neutral Eire', *Foreign Affairs* XXIX (1946).
51. Cited and discussed in Harry Calvert, *Constitutional Law in Northern Ireland* (London: Stevens, 1968), Ch. 1. For the political background, see F. S. L. Lyons's chapter in Kevin Nowlan and T. Desmond Williams, editors, *Ireland in the War Years and After*.
52. The most detailed history of this IRA campaign is contained in J. Bowyer Bell, *The Secret Army*.
53. *Ulster Under Home Rule*, p. 208. Cf. Wallace Clark, *Guns in Ulster*, especially p. 24.
54. *The Making of Modern Ireland, 1603–1923*, p. 461.
55. The impact of O'Neill's personality was frequently overrated by visiting journalists, and the daring nature of his policies underrated. No questions about the Prime Minister's personality were included in the 1968 Northern Ireland Loyalty survey because an extensive pilot

study in Belfast in 1967 had found that respondents did not have a very detailed or clear picture of Terence O'Neill as a promoter of policies.

56. Cf. the *Hall Report*, Cmnd. 1835 (London: HMSO, 1962), and the Wilson Report, *Economic Development in Northern Ireland*, Cmd. 479 (Belfast: HMSO, 1965). For a review of the political sentiments behind these changes, see the former Prime Minister's speeches, reprinted as *Ulster at the Crossroads* (London: Faber, 1969). Cf. Barry White, 'A memo to Ulster's nice guys', *Belfast Telegraph*, January 29, 1970.

57. All figures from *Digest of Statistics*, No. 31, March, 1969 (Belfast: HMSO). Later figures are subject to influence from subsequent political demonstrations in the Province.

58. Dr. Conor Cruise O'Brien has claimed that the Republic's government had already shown its lack of interest in the Border issue by refusing to raise the issue at the United Nations. See Andrew Boyd, *The Two Irelands* (London: Fabian Research Series, No. 269, 1968), p. 8.

59. See *Orange and Green* (Sedbergh, Yorkshire: Northern Friends Peace Board, 1969), pp. 33ff.

60. Cf. 'Clear Lundy's out of Stormont, urges Paisley', *Belfast Telegraph*, June 16, 1966, and Terence O'Neill's speech of the previous day in Northern Ireland House of Commons *Debates*, Vol. 64, Cols. 386ff.

61. The Northern Ireland regime's official *Commentary* on events of this period (Belfast: HMSO, Cmd. 534, 1969) makes this point by implication. All the reforms catalogued up to the outbreak of the 1968 demonstrations (paragraphs 7–16) are economic; those afterwards refer primarily to civil rights.

62. For accounts of the foundation, see e.g., Lord Cameron's Report, *Disturbances in Northern Ireland* (Belfast: HMSO, Cmd. 532, 1969), paragraphs 185ff.

63. *The Cameron Report*, paragraph 51.

64. *Ibid.*, paragraphs 80, 83. See also, Barry White, 'Shame and fear of club wielders on loose', *Belfast Telegraph*, December 2, 1969.

65. See Terence O'Neill, *Ulster at the Crossroads*, pp. 139–46.

66. See 'The day B-Specials joined civil rights ambush', *Sunday Times*, April 27, 1969; Bowes Egan and Vincent McCormack, *Burntollet* (London: LRS Publishers, 1969), and Bernadette Devlin, *The Price of My Soul* (London: Pan, 1969), pp. 120ff.

67. *The Cameron Report*, Ch. 9. The remark by a policeman is quoted from a British eyewitness.

68. See Bernadette Devlin, *The Price of My Soul*, p. 150, and Bowes Egan and Vincent McCormack, *Burntollet*, pp. 15–16.

69. 'Derry's riot bill for past year £1,733,169–Commission man', *Belfast Telegraph*, November 14, 1969, and Scarman Tribunal Hearings (Londonderry: Xerox (1970), Day 32, pp. 31, 34.

70. Max Hastings, *Ulster 1969* (London: Gollancz, 1970), p. 143.

71. See 'Sinister elements blamed', *The Times*, August 18, 1969. Cf. testimony to the Scarman Tribunal, especially that of Chief Inspector Cushley, November 6, 1970, and Mr. Justice Scarman's cross-examination.

72. The most useful guide to the reform programme is the regime's own *Commentary*, Cmd. 534, 1969.
73. 'Cheer Up, Ulster!', *Belfast Telegraph*, March 6, 1970.
74. 'Policy IS mailed fist in "moderation" glove–Clark', *Irish News*, October 23, 1970. Cf. House of Commons *Debates*, Vol. 803, Col. 206 (July 3, 1970) and 'Callaghan and Hogg–what they say', *Belfast Telegraph*, June 16, 1970.
75. 'Arms case man cleared', *Belfast Telegraph*, January 8, 1970.
76. See e.g., Edmund Curran, 'Ballymurphy . . . Why did it happen?', *Belfast Telegraph*, April 10, 1970.
77. See 'GOC warns "Get a move on to settle your own problems" ', *Belfast Telegraph*, April 7, 1970, and 'UVF join in death threats', *ibid.*
78. Cf. *Law (?) and Orders: the Story of the Belfast 'Curfew'* (Belfast: Central Citizens' Defence Committee, 1970), and 'No Evidence of Excessive Force by Army–Freeland', *Belfast Telegraph*, September 15, 1970, and Max Hastings, *Ulster 1969*, p. 157.
79. See 'CS gas thrown in Commons to cry of "Belfast" ', *The Times*, July 24, 1970. See also 'Ulster: Facts of death', *Sunday Times*, February 28, 1971.
80. Ian Colvin, *The Life of Lord Carson: Volume II*, p. 299.

Chapter IV
(Where no footnote reference is made to a source, information was obtained privately.)

1. *Census of Population 1961: County Borough of Belfast*. The scale of events is often well reflected in journalism. See e.g., John Bayley and Peter Loizos, 'Bogside off its Knees', *New Society*, August 21, 1969.
2. Cf. R. B. McDowell, *The Irish Administration 1801–1914* (London: Routledge, 1964) and H. J. Hanham, 'The Creation of the Scottish Office 1881–87', *The Juridical Review* X:3 (1965).
3. See e.g., Oliver MacDonagh, *Ireland*, Ch. 2 and Basil Chubb, *The Government and Politics of Ireland*.
4. The most comprehensive albeit formalistic description of governmental institutions is in *The Ulster Year Book* (Belfast: HMSO, 1970).
5. Harry Calvert, *Constitutional Law in Northern Ireland*, p. 33.
6. R. J. Lawrence, *The Government of Northern Ireland: Public Finance and Public Services, 1921–1964* (Oxford: Clarendon Press, 1965), p. 14.
7. See the relevant discussion in *The Times*, August 14, 1970, 'The key to direct rule in Ulster'.
8. See Harry Calvert, *Constitutional Law in Northern Ireland*, pp. 96ff. For later events, see Paul Rose, 'The smashing of the convention', a two-part article in the *Irish Times*, February 3–4, 1970.
9. See *The Development Programme, 1970–75* (Belfast: HMSO, 1970), pp. 33ff. The standard discussion of Westminster-Stormont relationships in this field is R. J. Lawrence, *The Government of Northern Ireland*.

10. Cf. Ulster Office statement (London: mimeograph, September 26, 1969); Terence O'Neill, *Ulster at the Crossroads*, p. 143: 'Ulster's Economy', *The Economist*, August 23, 1969 and John Simpson, 'That £100m. subsidy: fact or fiction', *Fortnight* (Belfast), October 23, 1970

11. Cf. *A Scottish Budget* (London: H.M. Treasury, 1969) and 'S.N.P. allege the Scottish budget was cooked', *Glasgow Herald*, November 6, 1969.

12. See Professor Thomas Wilson, 'Memorandum submitted to the Royal Commission on the Constitution' (Glasgow: University, 1969), p. 15.

13. A detailed text of the Ulster Unionist Council position appears in a story entitled 'Rights inequality major cause of unrest–NILP', *Irish News*, February 13, 1970.

14. *House of Commons Debates*, Vol. 751, Cols. 1681ff. (October 25, 1967). The epigraph of Ch. II is quoted from this debate. For a back-bench view, see Paul Rose, 'The smashing of the convention'.

15. See events documented in *A Commentary to Accompany the Cameron Report*.

16. See particularly 'Devenney death probe negative', *Belfast Telegraph*, December 15, 1969; 'Devenney family awarded £375 total', *ibid.*, March 13, 1970; and *House of Commons Debates*, Vol. 797, Cols. 981–92; Vol. 798, Col. 1202; Vol. 799, Col. 240 (March 23–24 and April 7, 1970).

17. See 'The silent conspiracy', *Belfast Telegraph*, November 4, 1970.

18. Harry Calvert, *Constitutional Law in Northern Ireland*, Ch. 1 questions whether the United Kingdom Parliament in London can unilaterally alter the Constitution of Northern Ireland. Calvert holds that as the initial Union was created by a Treaty between the Parliaments in Dublin and London in 1800, it can only be altered by the bilateral agreement of London and Stormont.

19. 'Maudling warns of dangers of backtracking', *Belfast Telegraph*, August 11, 1970. Cf. the reaction of John Taylor, Ulster Unionist MP in charge of Home Affairs, *ibid.*, August 12, 1970.

20. *Labour Party Annual Conference Report 1970* (London: Labour Party, 1970); *Sunday Times*, March 7, 1971.

21. 'Memorandum Submitted to the Royal Commission on the Constitution', pp. 15–16.

22. Otto Kirchheimer, *Political Justice* (Princeton: University Press, 1961), p. 177. The whole book is relevant to this chapter.

23. 'Text of Father Faul's Dungannon Lecture', *Irish Times*, December 2, 1969. Cardinal Conway issued a statement disagreeing with Father Faul. Cf. *Irish News*, November 18, 1969. See also, Tom Hadden and Kevin Boyle, 'The Hunt Report–Convincing Justice', *New Law Journal*, December 18, 1969.

24. See *House of Lords Debates*, Vol. 312, Col. 922 (November 17, 1970), a reply by Lord Windlesham to a question by Lord Brockway. Note also C. E. B. Brett, 'Memorandum of Evidence to the Royal Commission on the Constitution'.

25. See Harry Calvert, *Constitutional Law in Northern Ireland*, p. 383; *House of Commons Debates*, Vol. 784, Col. 667 (May 22, 1969).

26. *The National Council For Civil Liberties Report of a Commission of Inquiry* (London: NCCL, 1936), reprinted in 1969.

27. *The Cameron Report*, Ch. 4, especially paragraph 44; see also Appendix VI.

28. 'Newsman in curfew case cleared', *Irish News*, July 28, 1970; 'Freeland right in imposing curfew, Magistrate rules', *ibid.*, September 9, 1970.

29. 'You may be shot warning to missile throwers', *Irish News*, November 2, 1970.

30. '6 month sentence for "no tea" man', *Belfast Telegraph*, August 13, 1970.

31. See 'Minister says he broke march ban but RUC disagree', *Irish News*, July 27, 1970.

32. '1221 arrests in Ulster', *The Times*, September 12, 1970.

33. 'Youth gets jail term after incidents when passing Unity Flats', *Belfast Telegraph*, September 15, 1970.

34. Cf. *The Prosecution Process in England and Wales* (London: Justice, 1970), *The Hunt Report*, paragraph 142, and the Magistrate's remarks quoted in 'Curfew-breaking charges against 66 withdrawn', *Irish News*, November 24, 1970.

35. See e.g., 'No Hatred Act prosecutions yet, says A–G', *Irish News*, November 6, 1970.

36. See 'All five found not guilty in blast case', *Irish News*, February 21, 1970.

37. See 'MPs walk out as Taylor refuses to give court facts', *Irish News*, December 17, 1970.

38. 'Reluctant judge: I'll still try Haughey', *Belfast Telegraph*, July 30, 1970.

39. Cf. 'Security net in seconds after blast at courthouse', *Irish News*, February 11, 1970, and the article cited in footnote 36, *supra*.

40. Cf. 'Judge quashes £2,200 award to trustees of hall', *Belfast Telegraph*, October 8, 1970; 'Troops cleared of Falls charges', *ibid.*, September 17, 1970. 'Man sentenced for attack on Arbuckle witness', *ibid.*, January 5, 1971.

41. See the cases cited in footnotes 30, 40, and 44.

42. Cf. Kevin Boyle, 'The "Minimum Sentences" Act', *Northern Ireland Legal Quarterly* XXI:4 (1970), and 'New Bill to end some mandatory jail sentences', *Irish News*, November 25, 1970.

43. 'Amnesty will clean slate for 230, say police', *Belfast Telegraph*, May 7, 1969.

44. 'Malachy Grogan starts a new life', *Belfast Telegraph*, March 21, 1970; '3,000-strong army of women help', *Irish News*, July 6, 1970.

45. The judgments here cannot reflect a response to the Tribunal's Report, which was not in print when the above paragraph was written.

46. 'Troops now acting as judges and executioners too', *Irish News*, August 10, 1970.

Notes

47. See especially the testimony to the Scarman Tribunal by the B Specials taken in Armagh, December 14–17, 1970.
48. See *House of Commons Debates*, Vol. 803, Col. 206 (July 3, 1970).
49. See Kevin Boyle, 'Police and Police Reforms in Northern Ireland' (Cambridge: Fourth National Conference on Research and Teaching in Criminology, mimeograph, 1970), pp. 4–8. After the killings of 1969, non-political crime appears to have risen. Cf. a report in the Belfast *News-Letter*, December 1, 1970.
50. See the Scarman Tribunal testimony about the RUC position during the attack on Unity Flats, Belfast on August 3, 1969, reported in the *Irish News*, January 3, 1970.
51. See 'Bullets only alternative: PM', *Belfast Telegraph*, March 11, 1970.
52. See *The Hunt Report*, Chs. 8–9.
53. See the generally favourable picture of the RUC that emerges in J. Bowyer Bell's *The Secret Army*.
54. 'B-men were not trained for riots', a statement by Major James Chichester-Clark, *Belfast Telegraph*, May 1, 1970 and a memoir of the B Specials by his relative, Wallace Clark, *Guns in Ulster*.
55. On the discretionary powers of the police, see e.g., James Q. Wilson, *Varieties of Police Behavior*.
56. *The Cameron Report*, paragraph 172.
57. *The Cameron Report*, paragraph 181.
58. This paragraph draws upon the author's observations at the scene from both sides of the barricades.
59. *Ulster 1969*, p. 145.
60. See 'Sinister elements blamed', *The Times*, August 18, 1969.
61. *The Hunt Report*, paragraphs 80–3.
62. *Ibid.*, Ch. 4.
63. *Ibid.*, paragraph 19.
64. See e.g., 'UDR has 3869 on the strength', *Belfast Telegraph*, November 27, 1970, and 'Barrage of questions about UDR from Unionist MPs', *ibid.*, May 8, 1970. For criticisms of the Hunt recommendations, see e.g., *House of Commons Debates*, Vol. 792, Cols. 980–1255 (December 1, 1969).
65. 'Now Craig drops a new bombshell', *Belfast Telegraph*, August 10, 1970.
66. 'RUC doves gain a close win on guns', *Belfast Telegraph*, September 15, 1970.
67. 'RUC will never again be armed force – Sir Arthur', *Irish News*, November 4, 1970. See also, Edmund Curran, 'The always controversial Sir Arthur', *Belfast Telegraph*, November 12, 1970.
68. See e.g., Barry White, 'In Enniskillen it was more like a funeral than a political march', *Belfast Telegraph*, December 3, 1970.
69. See especially the comments of the CCDC in 'RUC go back to a cool reception', *Belfast Telegraph*, August 1, 1970.
70. See *Statistical Abstract for the United Kingdom* (London: HMSO, No. 75, 1932), p. 89.
71. See Wallace Clark, *Guns in Ulster*, pp. 61ff.

72. Quoted in a 'This Ulster' column of *The New Statesman*, August 29, 1969. The figure for licensed guns in Northern Ireland was 67,558 as of October, 1969. See 'Fitt triggers off discussion on guns', *Belfast Telegraph*, December 16, 1970.
73. See Wallace Clark, 'Memorandum on the functions of the Ulster Special Constabulary' (Upperlands, County Londonderry: mimeograph, 1970), p. 2; 'CCDC "concerned" at formation of Specials' gun clubs', *Irish News*, December 12, 1970.
74. 'Murder court is told of collection in street for guns', *Belfast Telegraph*, October 1, 1970.
75. Cf. *The Cameron Report*, paragraph 221. See also 'Irish Unity? We'd rather join Russia!' interviews with J. McQuade and J. McKeague, *Irish Press*, February 11, 1971.
76. See 'Cardinals and Bishops issue C.R. statement', *Irish Times* January 20, 1969.
77. See *The Cameron Report*, paragraph 186.
78. *Ibid.*, Ch. 15 and appendixes X–XII give the Constitution of the CRA and chronicle its development.
79. *Ibid.*, Ch. 4.
80. 'CRA priorities wrong, says Miss Devlin', *Irish News*, December 7, 1970. See more generally, Bernadette Devlin, *The Price of My Soul*.
81. 'People's Democracy: a discussion on strategy', *New Left Review*, No. 55 (1969), p. 17. The article contains the views of several prominent PD members. Cf. the comments on the PD in *The Cameron Report*.
82. See e.g., 'Top C.R. trio quit executive over alleged drift to left', *Irish News*, February 16, 1970 and 'Communication to Civil Rights Association Members' (Dungannon: Mrs. B. Rodgers, John Donachy and Conn McCluskey, duplicated, 1970).
83. Quoted from Liam de Paor, *Divided Ulster*, p. 83.
84. The quotations are from Galen Broeker, *Rural Disorder and Police Reform in Ireland 1812–1836*, p. 7.
85. See especially Roy Hodson, 'Divided leadership behind the barricades of Free Belfast', *Financial Times*, September 17, 1969, and Tony Geraghty, 'Army and IRA in secret talks as barriers go down', *Sunday Times*, September 7, 1969.
86. See 'Probation Act for 7 young Derry men on firearms charge', *Irish News*, January 9, 1970.
87. *The Cameron Report*, paragraph 188. See also, 'IRA in CR says Goulding', *Belfast Telegraph*, February 10, 1969.
88. The discussion of the IRA in the late 1960s draws upon a series of two two-part interviews by Jack Dowling with Cathal Goulding, Ruairi O'Bradaigh and a spokesman of the Provisional Army Council, in *This Week* (Dublin), July 31–August 21, 1970. For historical background, see J. Bowyer Bell, *The Secret Army*.
89. Testimony to the Scarman Tribunal, Monday, October 5, 1970.
90. Quoted from 'IRA faction wages war of terror in Ulster streets', *The Times*, April 7, 1970 and Stephen Fay, 'The five faces of the IRA', *Sunday Times*, August 23, 1970.

Notes

91. See Stephen Fay, 'The five faces of the IRA'.
92. Quoted from a statement by Capt. James Kelly, 'Distress fund used for guns', *Belfast Telegraph*, October 16, 1970.
93. *This Week*, December 17, 1970, pp. 9ff.
94. See 'Operation Doomsday plan by Eire government', *Belfast Telegraph*, January 13, 1971.
95. Testimony as reported in the *Belfast Telegraph*, October 15, 1970.
96. See Captain James Kelly's statement, reported in 'Abolish Stormont was Lynch's aim', *Belfast Telegraph*, December 8, 1970. Lynch's views are set out for Northern consumption in a two-part interview with John Rooks in the *Belfast Telegraph*, July 16–17, 1970. An official enquiry into the Dublin regime's activities commenced after this book went to press.
97. A comment by a spokesman for the Provisional Army Council, quoted in *This Week*, August 21, 1970, p. 32.
98. See the CCDC advertisement, 'Stop! Stop! Stop!' *Irish News*, November 18, 1970; italics supplied. Cf. 'Bernadette Devlin: What I learned in prison', *The Observer*, October 25, 1970, and 'Belfast: Why three young soldiers died,' *Sunday Times*, March 14, 1971.
99. For general discussion of the question, see Richard Rose, *People in Politics* (London: Faber, 1970), Ch. 7.
100. Quoted in *The Times*, February 5, 1971.
101. For CCDC efforts to have these parades re-routed, see *Law (?) and Orders*, pp. 7–9. The pamphlet omits mention of the Protestants and Catholics killed in consequence.
102. On the Army's lack of manpower to cover the area, see the remarks by Deputy Commissioner Samuel Bradley to the Scarman Tribunal, as reported in the *Irish News*, November 17, 1970.

Chapter V

1. Excluding posts at the Scottish and Welsh offices, in the period 1957–1970, only five Scottish MPs—Sir Alec Douglas-Home, Tom Fraser, Michael Noble, George Thomson, and the Edinburgh born Viscount Kilmuir—held Cabinet posts, and two Welsh MPs, Jim Callaghan and Cledwyn Hughes. The combined population of the two nations is more than five times that of Northern Ireland.
2. As of January, 1971. These figures exclude one member of the Senate with non-departmental responsibilities in the government.
3. 'Cheer Up Ulster!', *Belfast Telegraph*, March 6, 1970.
4. See Basil Chubb, ' "Going About Persecuting Civil Servants": The Role of the Irish Parliamentary Representative', *Political Studies* XI:3 (1963).
5. The average population per constituency in Northern Ireland is 29,000 persons, whereas in seven of the nine largest American cities it is greater

than this per ward, rising to 71,000 per constituency in Chicago and 311,000 in New York City. Cf. Edward Banfield and J. Q. Wilson, *City Politics* (New York: Vintage Books, 1963), pp. 89ff.

6. See Philip Converse, 'The Nature of Belief Systems in Mass Publics' in David Apter, editor, *Ideology and Discontent* (New York: Free Press, 1964), especially pp. 234ff. For Congressmen-constituency relations, see Warren E. Miller and Donald Stokes, 'Constituency Influence in Congress', *American Political Science Review* LVII:1 (1963).

7. The relation of the views of leaders and followers is lucidly examined in Robert A. Dahl, *Who Governs?* (New Haven: Yale University Press, 1960).

8. During the August, 1969 troubles, the respondent was forced to evacuate his wife and children to the Republic and patrol at the barricades, because of the imminent threat of a Protestant attack upon his street.

9. The lengthy interviews were also a tribute to the patience and care of the field staff of Ulster Opinion Surveys, under the direction of Mrs. George Davis.

10. The number of parliamentary constituencies in Northern Ireland has always been 52. Until February, 1969, however, four MPs represented a non-geographical constituency, consisting of graduates of the Queen's University, Belfast.

11. Sampling procedures used in Northern Ireland are discussed in detail in Leslie Kish, *Survey Sampling* (New York: Wiley, 1965). See particularly pp. 398ff. for a description of the technique for selecting an individual respondent from within a single household.

12. See D. Barritt and C. F. Carter, *The Northern Ireland Problem*, pp. 6ff.

13. If the 1971 census figures show any Catholic over-representation in the 1968 sample, it would be a simple matter technically to weight responses by religion to correct for such a sampling fluctuation. For 1961 religious figures, see *Census of Population 1961: General Report* (Belfast: HMSO, 1965), p. 29.

14. Cf. M. Axelrod, D. R. Matthews and J. W. Prothro, 'Recruitment for Survey Research on Race Problems in the South', *Public Opinion Quarterly* XXVI:2 (1962). This study of Southern whites and blacks produced a response rate of 85 per cent and, as the authors note, 'not one interviewer was insulted, threatened or "run out of town" '. Cf. Donald R. Matthews and James W. Prothro, *Negroes and the New Southern Politics* (New York: Harcourt, Brace & World, 1966), p. 492.

15. Cf. David Butler and Donald Stokes, *Political Change in Britain*, p. 453.

16. See Appendix A of G. A. Almond and Sidney Verba, *The Civic Culture*.

17. Cf. David Butler and Donald Stokes, *Political Change in Britain*, p. 96 and p. 449. The number of Catholics interviewed is larger than the *total* number of persons interviewed in a major American community power study, Robert A. Dahl, *Who Governs?* pp. 338–9. It obtained 525 interviews from 818 names selected from a list of registered voters in New Haven.

18. All Northern Ireland tabulations are from the 1968 Loyalty survey unless otherwise stated.

Notes

19. The full text of all questions and percentage replies, reported separately for Protestants, Catholics and the total sample, is contained in the Appendix.
20. The don't knows were twice as high among Protestants with no success in educational examinations and half again as high among Catholics by comparison with the answers of their more educated co-religionists.
21. *The Cameron Report, passim.*
22. An Opinion Research Centre Survey Number 372, undertaken on behalf of the *Sunday Times*, found that 47 per cent of Catholics approved more demonstrations, 26 per cent disapproved and 27 per cent were don't knows. Among Protestants, 4 per cent approved.
23. The relevant statistics were calculated as a byproduct of the computer programme. When inspection showed a finding of interest, or the logic of a table in this book provides space for analysis, the figures are presented in the text.
24. See H. D. Graham and T. R. Gurr, editors, *The History of Violence in America*, especially the contributions by Gurr and by Ivo Feierabend *et al.*
25. The number of cases in each analytic category is not constant, because of differences in those excluded for uncertainty. Among Protestants, all 757 can be classified for their views on the Constitution, and 729 for views on basic political laws. Among Catholics, 534 can be classified for views on the Constitution, and 443 for views on illegal demonstrations. Figures are calculated to sum to 100 per cent on the basis of these totals.
26. See especially Chs. X and XIII *infra.*
27. A. J. Ayer, *Philosophy and Politics* (Liverpool: University Press, 1967), pp. 9–10. The empirical approach that Ayer recommends on commonsense grounds at pp. 20ff. is broadly consistent with the approach used in this book.
28. Cf. Fred Greenstein, *Personality and Politics* (Chicago: Markham, 1969), pp. viii–ix, and Richard Rose, *People in Politics* (London: Faber, 1970), pp. 41ff.
29. In 'The Island of Ireland: a Psycho-Analytical Contribution to Political Psychology', 1922, reprinted in Ernest Jones, *Essays* (London: Hogarth Press, 1951).
30. The conventional Gini index of inequality is not suitable for this purpose, since it presupposes that data are ordinal. Gini himself proposed an index of this sort in an early publication. (See Corrado Gini, 'Sulla Misura della Concentrazione e della Variabilita dei Caratteri', *Atti Reale Ist. veneto sci. lettere ed arti*, Vol. 73 (1913–14), Part 2.) I am indebted to William L. Miller for this citation.
31. Kruskal and Goodman's Tau-Beta test of association was calculated for many of the relationships hypothesized in the subsequent chapters. As the calculations almost invariably showed the influence was very low, trivial, or nil, it was decided not to clutter the text with the resulting figures. When a text reference is made to nil or very low statistical association, the measure used is Tau-Beta. Cf. Leo A. Goodman and

William H. Kruskal, 'Measures of Association for Cross Classifications', *American Statistical Association Journal* (December, 1954).

32. For a discussion of this fallacy, see Erwin Scheuch, 'Cross-National Comparisons Using Aggregate Data' in Richard L. Merritt and Stein Rokkan, *Comparing Nations* (New Haven: Yale University Press, 1966).

Chapter VI

1. This and related definitions can be found, with a list of sources, at pp. 26ff., *supra.*
2. *Nationalism* (London: Hutchinson, 3rd edition, 1966), p. 18.
3. T. W. Moody, 'The Fenian Movement in Irish History', in *The Fenian Movement*, p. 104. For a comparative discussion of the national question in Ireland, see Nicholas Mansergh, *The Irish Question, 1840–1921.*
4. See Basil Chubb, editor, *A Source Book of Irish Government*, Ch. 1, especially Article 3 of the 1937 Constitution at p. 21. Cf. Harry Calvert, *Constitutional Law in Northern Ireland*, pp. 142–3.
5. For the mutual antagonism between Anglo-Saxon and Celtic labels at the time of Irish independence, see L. P. Curtis Jr., *Anglo-Saxons and Celts.*
6. See James G. Leyburn, *The Scotch-Irish*, Appendix I.
7. See remarks in the Westminster debate on the Ulster Defence Regiment, *House of Commons Debates* (London: December 1–2, 1969), Vol. 792, Col. 980ff.
8. Retranslated and quoted in Northern Ireland House of Commons *Debates*, Vol. 75, Col. 325 (February 17, 1970).
9. 'The Minister with an unenviable task', *Irish News*, November 12, 1970.
10. Italics supplied. 'Dublin study group can learn a lot from Ulster', *Ulster Commentary*, September, 1970, pp. 10–11.
11. *Ibid.*
12. See *The Irish Tourist Board Report* (Dublin: Bord Fáilte Éireann, 1968), p. 24.
13. See David Butler and Donald Stokes, *Political Change in Britain*, p. 475, Q. 55–6.
14. Only eight in 1,291 respondents volunteered the opinion that the Border was the most important issue. Cf. Chs. VII and XII.
15. See the introduction by Fredrik Barth, editor, *Ethnic Groups and Boundaries* (London: Allen & Unwin, 1969).
16. The largest Tau-Beta value for nine tests of association is ·02.
17. If those who cause disorder live somewhere in Northern Ireland, the most parsimonious assumption is that they do not travel great distances to engage in violence.
18. For an extreme argument about the importance of national identity for personal security, see Lucian W. Pye, *Politics, Personality and Nation-Building* (New Haven: Yale, 1962).

Notes

19. See e.g., *Putting PEP into the Local Community* (Belfast: HMSO, c. 1967).
20. 'Political Development: Time Sequences and Rates of Change', *World Politics* XX:3 (1968), p. 507.

Chapter VII

1. On temporal developments, see Fred Greenstein, *Children and Politics* (New Haven: Yale University Press, 1965). In a survey undertaken by the author in Stockport, England in 1964, when a Conservative government was in office, the proportion of Conservative voters positively disapproving the system of government was five per cent, and of Labour voters, nine per cent.
2. See Enid Lakeman, *How Democracies Vote* (London: Faber, 1970 edition), p. 239.
3. Cf. Derek Urwin, *Elections in Western Nations, 1945–1968* (Glasgow: Strathclyde Occasional Paper No. 4/5, 1969). In the Netherlands, where multipartyism is also combined with a relatively small legislature, the ratio of parties to seats is 1 to 13·6 MPs. After the 1969 Stormont election, it was 1 party to 7·4 MPs.
4. See returns and party labels given in the *Belfast Telegraph*, November 26, 1965.
5. Cf. F. W. S. Craig, *British Parliamentary Election Statistics, 1918–1968*, p. 46, for figures from previous elections.
6. See Barry White, 'A test of the parties', *Belfast Telegraph*, February 13, 1969.
7. See e.g., an interview with Edward Heath on Northern Ireland affairs, printed in two parts in the *Belfast Telegraph*, October 3–4, 1967, and an interview with the chairman and vice-chairman of Ulster Unionists at Westminster, L. P. S. Orr and Robin Chichester-Clark, *ibid.*, March 25, 1966. Edward Heath has also supported publicly the 1969 reform proposals.
8. See 'Unionist MP quits Orange Order', *Belfast Telegraph*, August 22, 1969. The candidate adopted by the Unionists in his place was an Orangeman and critic of Terence O'Neill, W. J. Morgan. Morgan was defeated in the ensuing by-election by the Rev. William Beattie, a Paisleyite clergyman.
9. Cf. 'Louis Boyle quits the Unionist Party', *Belfast Telegraph*, July 8, 1969; 'Catholics welcome in party: PM', *ibid*, November 21, 1969, and 'PM defends right to be an Orangeman', *ibid.*, December 3, 1969.
10. The analytical model outlined by the author in 'Parties, Factions and Tendencies in Britain', *Political Studies* XII:1 (1964) is also appropriate to the analysis of Unionists and Unionism in Ulster.
11. A part of the West Ulster Unionist Council's concern has been the protection of Protestant control of local government in areas where Catholics might gain control following franchise reform. Cf. *It Matters to You* (Enniskillen: West Ulster Unionist Council, 1970). For a

general policy statement, see 'Not rebels; not extremists; not break-aways–Harry West', *Ulster Times*, September, 1970.

12. Quoted from a news story in the *Belfast Telegraph*, November 29, 1968.

13. 'I am a man prepared to stand my ground–Craig', *Belfast Telegraph*, September 29, 1969.

14. See the NUM press statement and list of supporters in an advertisement in *Belfast Telegraph*, February 7, 1969.

15. The quotations are from party leaflets. See also, 'The making of a party', *Belfast Telegraph*, April 28, 1970, and Barry White, 'The Alliance Party', *Fortnight*, October 23, 1970.

16. 'Paisley tells Bishop what loyalty means to him', *Belfast Telegraph*, October 10, 1969.

17. Article 17. The text of the constitution of the group is printed as Appendix IX of *The Cameron Report*.

18. Quoted in Barry White, 'Are the politicians leading or being led?', *Belfast Telegraph*, February 9, 1969.

19. See the story with that headline, *Belfast Telegraph*, May 23, 1966. On the movement into official opposition and out again after the 1969 killings, cf. 'Nationalists to take active role', *ibid.*, December 13, 1965, and 'Nationalists: we won't be foolish', *ibid.*, November 25, 1969.

20. 'Have patience, delegates told by McAteer', *Belfast Telegraph*, June 24, 1968.

21. See e.g., 'Tri-colour must be respected', *Belfast Telegraph*, April 10, 1969; 'Nationalists stand by a separate identity', *ibid.*, November 24, 1969; and an interview with McAteer in the *Irish News*, January 19, 1970.

22. For details see 'New opposition party is formed–states its aims', *Irish News*, August 22, 1970, and Barry White, 'SDLP', *Fortnight*, September 25, 1970.

23. See 'Split widens as "true Sinn Fein" group is formed', *Belfast Telegraph*, October 26, 1970.

24. See e.g., David Thornley, 'The Development of the Irish Labour Movement', *Christus Rex* (Dublin) XVIII (1964).

25. See 'Labour Party backs CR campaign', *Belfast Telegraph*, May 24, 1969.

26. See e.g., 'Storm of protest over Labour sacking of McCann', *Irish News*, November 21, 1970. On Paddy Devlin, see 'Devlin tells Scarman of IRA "split" in the Falls', *Belfast Telegraph*, November 18, 1970.

27. See 'Labour no-go to opposition unity plea', *Irish News*, August 19, 1970, and 'Ulster dilemma for Labour', *The Times*, October 1, 1970.

28. Pilot interviews showed that asking people what a party stands for produced different kinds of replies than questions about likes and dislikes. The former question appears to get at the underlying image of the party, which is little modified by transitory things liked and disliked, such as the personality of a leader, or a particular topical policy.

29. Cf. Richard Rose and Derek Urwin, 'Social Cohesion, Political Parties and Strains in Regimes', pp. 27ff.

Notes

30. Cf. Richard Rose and Harve Mossawir, 'Voting and Elections: a functional analysis', *Political Studies* XV:2 (1967), pp. 174ff.
31. See e.g., Richard Rose and Derek Urwin, 'Social Cohesion, Political Parties and Strains in Regimes', Table 1.
32. The Tau-Beta association is ·37.
33. See Philip Converse, 'The Problem of Party Distances in Models of Voting Change', pp. 185ff. in M. Kent Jennings and L. Harmon Zeigler, editors, *The Electoral Process* (Englewood Cliffs, N.J.: Prentice-Hall, 1966).
34. See *The Cameron Report*, Ch. 12.
35. Sweden is the nearest competitor, where the Labour Party has not been out of office since 1932. It has, however, at times ruled by a coalition.
36. For the influence, see Douglas Rae, *The Political Consequences of Electoral Laws* (New Haven: Yale University Press, 1967), pp. 70ff.
37. See Nicholas Mansergh, *The Government of Northern Ireland*, Ch. 7 and Enid Lakeman, *How Democracies Vote*, pp. 235ff. For a statement indicating some Unionists might consider a return to proportional representation, see 'It's one man, one vote–and no more delay', *Belfast Telegraph*, October 30, 1970.
38. Quoted in *The Times* story 'O'Neill seeks to bridge gap between the communities', February 15, 1969.
39. See e.g., *A Systems Analysis of Political Life*.
40. Cf. G. A. Almond and S. Verba, *The Civic Culture*, p. 80.
41. The Tau-Beta association is ·09, between Catholic perceptions of regime benefits and support for the Constitution.
42. See especially Max Weber, *The Theory of Social and Economic Organization*, pp. 115ff. and 324ff.
43. See Richard Rose and Harve Mossawir, 'Voting and Elections: a functional analysis'.

Chapter VIII

1. See Harry Calvert, *Constitutional Law in Northern Ireland*, pp. 253ff., for a thorough discussion of the legal situation. The 1922 Constitution of the Irish Free State was much more like the Northern Ireland Constitution in its formal commitment to non-sectarianism. See R. Dudley Edwards, 'Church and State in Modern Ireland', in K. B. Nowlan and T. Desmond Williams, *Ireland in the War Years and After*, pp. 110ff.
2. *Census of Population* 1961 : General Report, Table XIX, p. 29.
3. The remaining four were assigned to the two major religious groups on the basis of other answers. This is consistent with the Northern Ireland convention that even an atheist must be a Protestant or a Catholic atheist, in order to have a status in the society.
4. Cf. D. Barritt and C. F. Carter, *The Northern Ireland Problem*, Ch. 1.

The 'two views' are daily evident in the press too, as a comparison of the *Belfast News-Letter* (Protestant) and the *Irish News* (Catholic) illustrates.

5. E.g., *See Ulster at the Crossroads*, p. 114, and 'Cross denominational barriers, P.M. appeals to all', *Belfast Telegraph*, February 20, 1968.

6. See especially Gerhard Lenski, *The Religious Factor* (New York: Anchor, 1963 edition) and Charles Y. Glock and Rodney Stark, *Religion and Society in Tension* (Chicago: Rand McNally, 1965). English studies utilizing survey data include David Martin, *A Sociology of English Religion* (London: Heinemann, 1967) and Michael Argyle, *Religious Behaviour* (London: Routledge, 1958).

7. Cf. G. Lenski, *The Religious Factor*, p. 171 and cross-tabulations from the Stockport survey reported in Richard Rose and Harve Mossawir, 'Voting and Elections: a Functional Analysis'.

8. See '1916–Revolution and Religion', p. 215 in F. X. Martin, editor, *Leaders and Men of the Easter Rising*. For historical background, note also E. R. Norman, *The Catholic Church and Ireland in the Age of Rebellion*.

9. For a general discussion of this problem, see Stanley Rothman, 'The Politics of Catholic Parochial Schools: an Historical and Comparative Analysis', *Journal of Politics* XXV:1 (1963).

10. See 'O'Neill remark criticized by the Cardinal', *Belfast Telegraph*, April 27, 1966.

11. For details on the position, see relevant chapters in the *Ulster Yearbook* and for background D. Barritt and C. F. Carter, *The Northern Ireland Problem*, pp. 114–16. For comparisons, note E. R. Norman, *The Conscience of the State in North America* (Cambridge: University Press, 1968), Ch. 4.

12. See e.g., 'R.C. hierarchy holds the key', *Belfast News-Letter*, March 1, 1969 and 'Withers tells of one big sorrow', *Belfast Telegraph*, June 3, 1969.

13. See 'The Catholic Bishops *have* recognized the Constitution', from a two-part interview with Cardinal Conway by John E. Sayers, *Belfast Telegraph*, March 27, 1969.

14. *Roman Catholic Priests and Local Politics in Northern Ireland* (Glasgow: University of Strathclyde M.Sc. dissertation, 1969), pp. 71–3.

15. 'Conflict of hate saddens the Pope', *The Times*, August 18, 1969 and 'Let justice be done and leave the rest to history', *Belfast Telegraph*, March 28, 1969.

16. 'Don't be betrayed–Cardinal', *Belfast Telegraph*, May 22, 1970.

17. *Belfast Telegraph*, March 28, 1969.

18. For an unflattering picture of this connection, see 'The Churches During the Crisis', *Nusight* (October, 1969), pp. 38–9.

19. *The Price of My Soul*, p. 72.

20. Cf. 'Catholic districts invaded by armed mobs–Cardinal', and 'Hierarchy's statement one-sided–Bradford', *Belfast Telegraph*, August 25, 1969.

21. See especially *Law (?) and Orders*.

Notes

22. See e.g., profiles by David Kemp, *Glasgow Herald*, February 5, 1969 and John Chartres and Innis Macbeth, *The Times*, January 29, 1969.

23. These findings come from National Opinion Polls survey 2577, conducted in 1967 on behalf of the *Belfast Telegraph*. The number of Protestants interviewed was 526.

24. See John Whyte, *Church and State in Modern Ireland* (Dublin: Gill, 1971).

25. Cf. *Orangeism* by the Rev. M. W. Dewar, the Rev. John Brown, and the Rev. S. E. Long (Belfast: Grand Orange Lodge of Ireland, *c*. 1967).

26. Letter in the *Belfast Telegraph*, July 16, 1969. In Londonderry, the same function is performed by the parade of the Apprentice Boys, commemorating the lifting of the Catholic siege of the city on August 12, 1690.

27. Quoted in an interview with Barry White, 'The grand master tells of discipline maintained with dignity', *Belfast Telegraph*, July 8, 1969.

28. Cf. Barry White, 'Shock and confusion, so more and more are joining', *Belfast Telegraph*, July 7, 1969; 'Membership of Order has not influenced me', a statement by the Attorney-General, *ibid.*, November 14, 1969, and 'Paisleyism threat to Orangeism', *ibid.*, January 4, 1971.

29. These figures are complicated by the fact that the Order does not admit women. Among men in the Order, 73 per cent endorse the Ultra position and among men outside the Order, 50 per cent.

30. See *The Ancient Order of Hibernians* (Dublin: AOH, 1967).

31. See Charles Y. Glock and Rodney Stark, *Religion and Society in Tension*, Ch. 5.

32. See *Television and Religion in Northern Ireland* (London: Opinion Research Centre, duplicated report of Survey 307, 1968), Table 28.

33. *The Religious Factor*, p. 206. Italics in the original.

34. See e.g., Bryan Wilson, *Religion in Secular Society* (London: Watts, 1966), Chs. 8–10.

35. Charles Y. Glock and Rodney Stark, *Religion and Society in Tension*, p. 118.

36. Calculated from David Martin, editor, *A Sociological Yearbook of Religion in Britain* (London: SCM Press, 1968), p. 180.

37. Cf. G. Lenski, *The Religious Factor*, pp. 23ff.

38. See *Television and Religion in Northern Ireland*, Table 33.

39. For a range of international comparisons, see the appendix of Richard Rose and Derek Urwin, 'Social Cohesion, Political Parties and Strains in Regimes'.

40. See *Census of Population 1966: General Report*, Table 16, occupational category XXII:875 and *Television and Religion in Northern Ireland*, Tables 23–4. On the ambivalent position of a clergyman in a community, see also Rosemary Harris, 'The Selection of Leaders in Ballybeg'.

41. *Roman Catholic Priests and Local Politics in Northern Ireland*, Part II.

42. The four items were selected on the basis of a factor analysis of the type described in Chapter X. They employ Questions 38a, 38b, 38c and 41 in the appendix. Positive responses were scored 3, negative 1, and

don't knows and ambiguous replies were scored 2. The most clannish are those scoring 11 or 12, and the least clannish, 4 or 5.

43. A question about discrimination against Protestants was used in the pilot studies but dropped from the final survey because so few persons referred to this type of discrimination.

44. See 'Ex-PM does not favour 1 man, 1 vote', *Belfast Telegraph*, February 18, 1969.

45. *Ibid.*

46. Calculated from Table 29 in *Television and Religion in Northern Ireland*. In Britain, 48 per cent said they thought it 'very important' that their their country should be 'Christian'.

Chapter IX

1. The best source for visitors' perspectives is in Nicholas Mansergh's classic study, *The Irish Question 1840–1921*. The epigraphs to this chapter are taken from there, at pp. 104–5.

2. Cf. *Belfast: Origin and Growth of an Industrial City* and Andrew Boyd, *Holy War in Belfast*.

3. Mansergh notes, 'History has shown the Marxist analysis and conservative statemanship alike to have been misconceived', *The Irish Question 1840–1921*, p. 103. Ch. 3 of his book is particularly relevant for an appreciation of the general significance of Irish nationalism for theories of economic determinism. Contrast E. Strauss, *Irish Nationalism and British Democracy*.

4. See *Abstract of Regional Statistics No. 5* (1969), Table 13.

5. See e.g., *Trade Union Information* (Dublin: Irish Congress of Trade Unions, September, 1970).

6. For a convenient summary, see *Development Programme 1970–75* (Belfast, HMSO, 1970), Part I, especially p. 4.

7. *Ulster at the Crossroads*, p. 142.

8. *Struggle in the North* (Belfast: People's Democracy, 1969), p. 33.

9. 'People's Democracy: a Discussion on Strategy', *New Left Review*, No. 55 (1969), p. 6.

10. James Chichester-Clark, 'We must lift our eyes to these bigger issues', *Ulster Commentary*, December, 1970, p. 5.

11. The preference for economic analysis but the awareness of political-military problems is aptly reflected in James Callaghan's speech to the Labour Party Annual Conference, October 2, 1970.

12. See 'Stormont must take new look at spending, MPs told', *Belfast Telegraph*, November 19, 1970.

13. See 'Bernadette Devlin: What I learned', *The Observer*, October 25, 1970.

14. For a discussion of various definitions of 'modern' societies and their political relevance to England, see Richard Rose, 'England: a Traditionally Modern Culture', in Lucian Pye and Sidney Verba, editors,

Notes

Political Culture and Political Development (Princeton: University Press, 1965).

15. See *Development Programme, 1970–75*, especially Ch. 14 and the report by Professor Thomas Wilson, *Economic Development in Northern Ireland*, Ch. 9.

16. See Northern Ireland Economic Council, *Area Development in Northern Ireland* (Belfast: HMSO, 1969), p. 6. The level of agricultural employment in Northern Ireland today is thus that prevailing in England in the 1880s. Cf. Phyllis Deane and W. A. Cole, *British Economic Growth, 1688–1959* (Cambridge: University Press, 2nd edition, 1967), p. 142.

17. *The Statistical Abstract of Ireland* (Dublin: Stationery Office, 1968) does not employ a social class scale comparable to that of Britain.

18. *The Northern Ireland Problem*, p. 140. See also a three-part series on the trade unions by Barry White in the *Belfast Telegraph*, September 20–22, 1967.

19. See Andrew Boyd, *The Two Irelands* (London: Fabian Research Series, No. 269, 1968), pp. 20–1.

20. Similarly, among members of business and professional associations, 71 per cent said their group mixed the two religions. This data is not further analysed because of the limited proportion with someone in the family belonging to such an organization, seven per cent.

21. Cf. Tables II.14 and XV.1. Wives of union members are here analysed with male members, given the propensity of husbands and wives both to show the influence of union affiliation. Cf. Richard Rose, 'Class and Party Divisions: Britain as a Test Case', p. 146.

22. Cf. Richard Rose and Derek Urwin, 'Social Cohesion, Political Parties and Strains in Regimes'.

23. The proportion approving of both business and unions is 24 per cent, of business and not unions 12 per cent, and of unions but not business seven per cent. A total of seven per cent disapprove of the influence of both groups; the remainder give indefinite replies to at least one of these two questions.

24. Cf. J. Blondel, *Voters, Parties and Leaders* (Harmondsworth: Penguin, 1963), p. 78.

25. For replies to a slightly different phrasing, see David Butler and Donald Stokes, *Political Change in Britain*, p. 478, Q. 65a. See also, W. G. Runciman, *Relative Deprivation and Social Justice*, pp. 158ff. and Joseph Lopreato, 'Class Conflict and Images of Society', *Journal of Conflict Resolution*, XI:3 (1967), p. 284.

26. Cf. Elizabeth Bott, *Family and Social Network* (London: Tavistock, 1957).

27. See David Butler and Donald Stokes, *Political Change in Britain*, p. 479, Q. 73.

28. Cf. Richard Rose, 'Class and Party Divisions', pp. 151f.

29. See *Political Man* (New York: Doubleday, 1960), pp. 50ff. Lipset tends to confound democracy and all fully legitimate regimes.

30. Confirmation of the accuracy of the profile of self-reported income is provided by reports of interviewers on the level of prosperity of

respondents. The difference index for the interviewers' rating–16 per cent–is almost identical to that for subjective assessments.

31. Figures on expenditure are calculated from *Monthly Digest of Statistics*, No. 31 (Belfast: HMSO, 1969), Tables 119 and 122. Here and elsewhere economic figures are cited for the last year prior to the civil rights demonstration in order to avoid the possibility of the measures being affected by the demonstrations.

32. It can be argued that religion is itself a response to an individual's sense of deprivation. See e.g., Charles Glock, 'The Role of Deprivation in the Origin and Evolution of Religious Groups', in Robert Lee and Martin E. Marty, editors, *Religion and Social Conflict* (New York: Oxford University Press, 1964). This would not, however, account for abnormally high Protestant religiosity in Northern Ireland.

33. Cf. the theories of Karl W. Deutsch in e.g., *Nationalism and Social Communication* (Cambridge, Massachusetts: MIT Press, 2nd edition, 1966) and W. G. Runciman, *Relative Deprivation and Social Justice*.

34. Cf. *Ulster Yearbook*, 1970, Ch. 7; *Development Programme, 1970–75*, Ch. 5; Frank McBrien, 'How good is our housing record?', *Fortnight*, September 25, 1970; and *The Cameron Report*, paragraphs 128ff.

35. See *People and their Houses* (Belfast: Building Design Partnership, 1967), Tables 5 and 12. Some of these houses are no longer standing; they were destroyed in the 1969 disorders.

36. See *House of Commons Debates*, Vol. 788, Col. 57, October 13, 1969. For details and discussion of the Northern Ireland scheme, still being debated as this book was written, see relevant entries in the *Debates* of the Northern Ireland House of Commons.

37. See *Second Report of the Northern Ireland Commissioner for Complaints* (Belfast: HMSO, H.C. 2048, 1970), pp. 4ff. Cf. pp. 435ff., *infra*.

38. For details, see press reports at the time and hearings of the Scarman Tribunal.

39. Cf. *The Cameron Report*, paragraph 138, and *The Plain Truth* (Dungannon: Campaign for Social Justice, 1969, 2nd edition), pp. 4ff.

40. *Second Report of the Northern Ireland Commissioner for Complaints*, pp. 11, 13.

41. See the advertisement reproduced in the *Sunday Times*, March 2, 1969.

42. See Vincent Hanna, 'Belfast: the shadow on the shipyards', *Sunday Times*, July 5, 1970; 'Shipyard Catholics told to name intimidators', *Irish News*, July 1, 1970.

43. 'Dr. Philbin accuses city firm of bias against Catholics', *Belfast Telegraph*, May 27, 1966.

44. If unemployment percentages are calculated after removing the retired and dependent heads of households from calculations, then the unemployed Catholics are 13.6 per cent of those seeking work, and unemployed Protestants, 4·6 per cent, in the Loyalty survey.

45. Cf. Table XV.1.

46. See e.g., 'Ulster's Economy; the fight that was lost on the barricades?', *The Economist*, August 23, 1969; *Trade Union Information* (September and October, 1970) and 'Poverty in Ireland', *Nusight* (November, 1969).

Notes

47. See *Economic Development* (Dublin: Stationery Office, Pr. 4803, 1958), p. 9.
48. 'Unionists alone can guarantee a happy life', *Belfast Telegraph*, August 30, 1968.
49. See e.g., 'Bradford counts up the cost of strife', *Belfast Telegraph*, July 9, 1970.
50. The theme of the deprivation of collective goods is further elaborated in Chs. XIV–XV, *infra*.
51. Quoted from 'Ex-P.M. puts blame on extremists', *Belfast Telegraph*, May 5, 1969. O'Neill here accepts that Catholicism or Irish nationality need not inhibit economic success. For American evidence to the same effect, see Norval Glenn and Ruth Hyland, 'Religious Preference and Worldly Success', *American Sociological Review* XXXII:1 (1967).

Chapter X

1. See e.g., Mattei Dogan and Stein Rokkan, editors, *Quantitative Ecological Analysis in the Social Sciences* (Cambridge, Massachusetts: MIT Press, 1969).
2. See D. R. Matthews and J. W. Prothro, *Negro Political Participation in the South*, pp. 115ff. and Thomas F. Pettigrew, 'Continuing Barriers to Desegregated Education in the South', *Sociology of Education* XXXVIII:2 (1965).
3. The difference index is 16 per cent if one treats as similar people who live with a majority of their co-religionists, and also treats as similar those in a minority position.
4. See, for example, *Putting PEP into the Local Community*.
5. 'Nearness' here is used in its geographical sense.
6. Cf. G. A. Almond and S. Verba, *The Civic Culture*, pp. 132ff.
7. A score of four was assigned each time a person said all his contacts were within his religion, three for responses indicating most contacts within his religion, down to a score of 0 where no contacts were within the group. Those giving a don't know reply were given the median score of two.
8. Among those Protestants who remained as a minority in the Republic following the Anglo-Irish Treaty, there have been no signs of refusing full allegiance to the regime there.
9. See *The Cameron Report*, Ch. 12. For a detailed statement of the civil rights case, see *The Plain Truth*.
10. I am indebted to Denis Barritt for assistance in classifying local authorities by their party complexion.
11. See e.g., the Macrory Committee report, *Review Body on Local Government in Northern Ireland*, 1970 (Belfast: HMSO, Cmd. 546); 'CRA divided on Macrory Report plan', *Irish News*, November 16, 1970 and 'Ulster Prime Minister puts proposals for five area boards answerable to Stormont', *The Times*, December 18, 1970. Proposed

boundaries and powers were not settled by legislation at the time this book went to press.

12. See e.g., *Belfast Regional Survey and Plan* (Belfast: HMSO, 1963, Cmd. 451); *Economic Development in Northern Ireland*, and *Development Programme, 1970–1975*, especially pp. 21ff.

13. Cf. the Ulster joke in which a Dubliner remarks, when asked how he likes Belfast, 'I don't like it, it's cold and wet and full of Protestants.' 'Then go to Hell,' his questioner responds. 'It's warm and dry and full of Papists.'

14. *Community Attitudes Survey: England* (London: HMSO, Royal Commission on Local Government Research Studies 9, 1969), pp. 45–7.

15. Cf. Richard Rose and Derek Urwin, 'Persistence and Change in Western Party Systems Since 1945', *Political Studies* XVIII:3 (1970), pp. 308–9.

16. 'Simulating the Research Analyst', *Social Science Information* VI:4 (1967), p. 212.

17. For details of the technique, see John A. Sonquist and J. N. Morgan, *The Detection of Interaction Effects* (Ann Arbor, Michigan: Monograph No. 35, Survey Research Center, 1964). For an illustration of its use in political analysis, see e.g., Klaus Liepelt, 'The Infrastructure of Party Support in Germany and Austria', Mattei Dogan and Richard Rose, editors, *European Politics* (Boston: Little, Brown, 1971).

18. The branches in the Catholic part of the tree additional to religion account for only 1·6 per cent of the variation to be explained.

19. In the AID analysis, which requires the dichotomization of the dependent variable, Protestant don't knows are classified as supporting the Constitution, and Catholic don't knows as against the Constitution. It seemed better to assign them to modal groups, rather than classify both don't know groups together. In the MCA analysis, which does not require dichotomization, those favouring the Constitution were scored one; don't knows of both religions, two; and against, three. The difference in scoring does not alter the substantive interpretation.

20. For details of this technique, see Frank Andrews, James Morgan and John Sonquist, *Multiple Classification Analysis* (Ann Arbor, Michigan: Survey Research Center, 1969). The analysis omitted a number of socio-economic variables included in the AID runs because of the risk that some of these would be closely inter-correlated, creating difficulties in MCA but not in AID analysis.

21. In the analysis of compliance, the BSS/TSS ratio for the second and third best candidates for the first branch in the tree are party, 33·4 per cent, and church attendance, 11·1 per cent. The *proxime accesserunt* in the support run are also party, 25·3 per cent, and church attendance, 7·4 per cent.

22. See especially, Philip E. Converse, 'The Nature of Belief Systems in Mass Publics', and David Butler and Donald Stokes, *Political Change in Britain*, pp. 200–14.

23. When the analysis was done separately by religion, the total variance

Notes

explained for Protestants was 24·5 per cent and for Catholics, 25·1 per cent.

24. The items loading at ·50 or higher on each of the factors, with reference to their place in the questionnaire in the appendix, are the following: *Factor I.* Political Involvement: Q. 21a, Interest in politics. Q. 23b, Understanding of politics. Q. 31b, Effect of Stormont. *Factor II.* Religious Cohesion: Q. 38a, Strength of religious identification. Q. 45, Sure of faith. *Factor III.* Ecumenicism: Q. 63.1, Principle of church unity. Q. 63.2, Practicability of church unity, and Q. 3, Religion. *Factor IV.* Q. 27d, Approval of big business. Q. 59a, Some are born to rule.

25. After drafting this chapter, the author came across Norman R. Luttbeg's analysis with a comparable intent, 'The Structure of Beliefs among Leaders and the Public', *Public Opinion Quarterly* XXXII:3 (1968). The factor scores reported for supposedly uninvolved citizens are much higher than those obtained in Northern Ireland. In Luttbeg's terms, p. 409, Northern Ireland displays a 'fragmented, low-constraint belief system'.

26. One could conceivably have a complete identity of views within a group without variation. In such circumstances, the alternative *vis-à-vis* the other group would be pure consensus if it had an identity of outlooks *and* the same value, or complete dissensus if an identity existed but did not take the same value.

27. See e.g., 'Healthy society not marked by forced consensus', *Irish News*, March 23, 1970, and 'Belfast's riot-hit families won't mix', *Belfast Telegraph*, December 20, 1969.

Chapter XI

1. Cf. Richard Rose, 'England, a Traditionally Modern Culture', pp. 83ff., Philip E. Converse, 'Of Time and Partisan Stability', *Comparative Political Studies* II:2 (1969) and David Butler and Donald Stokes, *Political Change in Britain*.

2. See e.g., Richard Rose, *Politics in England*, Ch. 3 and Brian Jackson and Dennis Marsden, *Education and the Working Class* (London: Routledge, 1962).

3. Only five per cent reported a father born in England or further away, and five per cent a mother from remote parts. In this context, it is assumed that Scotland is not outside the cultural ambit of Northern Ireland, given close historical ties and Protestant-Catholic relations there.

4. See e.g., David Easton and Jack Dennis, *Children in the Political System* (McGraw-Hill, 1969), Fred I. Greenstein, *Children and Politics* and for a general view, Richard Dawson and Kenneth Prewitt, *Political Socialization* (Boston: Little, Brown, 1969), pp. 45ff. Research in this area has not been conducted long enough to permit direct testing of the hypothesis by studying the same person in childhood and then a decade or two later.

5. All quotations from children used in the pilot stage of a study of Ulster children are from interviews conducted by J. L. Russell of the Politics Department of the University of Strathclyde in 1970–71.
6. 'No hate in our schools', *Belfast Telegraph*, March 7, 1967.
7. *Ibid.*
8. Data from National Opinion Polls surveys for the *Belfast Telegraph* NOP/2577, Q. 11 (1967) and NOP/3150 (1968), Q. 22, a special survey of Ulster youth. These findings are confirmed by data from the Loyalty survey.
9. On basic institutional arrangements, see *Ulster Yearbook, 1970*, section 6. Protestants have also had their grievances with the Stormont regime from 1923 until 1949. See Rev. S. E. Long, 'The Union: Pledge and Progress 1886–1967', in the Rev. M. W. Dewar *et al.*, *Orangeism*, pp. 174–85.
10. See e.g., Andrew Greeley and Peter Rossi, *The Education of Catholic Americans* (Chicago: Aldine, 1966) and E. R. Tapper, *Secondary School Adolescents* (Manchester: Faculty of Economics Ph.D., 1968).
11. *The Price of My Soul*. It is relevant to note that Mother Benignus's pupil had already imbued Republicanism from her parents and earlier associates. At most, the headmistress reinforced Miss Devlin's views.
12. In fact, the minimum age for school leaving was raised from 14 to 15 in the 1947 Act. The outlooks of those who had been educated to age 15 before this was compulsory do not differ significantly from their younger counterparts.
13. As a further check on the extent of education, each respondent was asked whether he had ever succeeded in passing an examination on leaving school or as a vocational qualification; 34 per cent of Protestants and 19 per cent of Catholics had done so. Political outlooks among people in these categories were of a similar pattern to those classified by age at leaving school.
14. Cf. Basil Bernstein, 'Some Sociological Determinants of Perception', *British Journal of Sociology* IX:2 (1958).
15. Cf. *The 1961 Census*, p. xliii.
16. Estimated from replies to questions about type of schooling.
17. For a variety of arguments to this effect, see Daniel Ball, editor, *The Radical Right* (New York: Doubleday, 1963). See also Ioan Davies, *Social Mobility and Political Change* (London: Macmillan, 1970).
18. The number of classes specified by the researcher greatly affects the incidence of social mobility, for the more classes specified, the greater the likelihood of movement across class lines. The three used here are obtained by collapsing in pairs the first six of the Registrar-General's occupational class categories; category VII, a residual group, is excluded. The definition thus provides a measure of mobility within the middle class from lower to upper middle, as well as a measure of distance travelled up from the working class.
19. In a British context, see especially Eric A. Nordlinger, *The Working-Class Tories* (London: MacGibbon & Kee, 1967).

Notes

20. See e.g., G. A. Almond and S. Verba, *The Civic Culture* and Harry Eckstein, *Division and Cohesion in Democracy*, Appendix B.
21. An authority relationship can be accepted by an individual in a superordinate or a subordinate position.
22. See *Division and Cohesion in Democracy*, Appendix B. Since this statement was written but after the Northern Ireland fieldwork was completed, Eckstein has greatly elaborated his ideas and the criteria for testing them. This means that what follows is not to be considered a test of Eckstein's theory of government performance. Support and compliance are two of the five component indicators of performance as he defines it. Cf. Harry Eckstein, 'Authority Relations and Governmental Performance', *Comparative Political Studies* II:3 (1969), especially p. 287.
23. A person saying it is very important to give obedience was given a score of two, and a score of one for saying it is fairly important to give obedience. All other responses were scored 0.
24. Conventional authoritarian scales were not employed in the Ulster survey. Quite apart from general controversy about their validity, there are particular problems arising in cross-cultural transference. For instance, neither anti-Semitism nor attitudes toward blacks are relevant in Ulster.
25. See Eric A. Nordlinger, *The Working-Class Tories*, and Robert McKenzie and Allan Silver, *Angels in Marble* (London: Heinemann, 1968) especially Appendix B.
26. Agreement with each measure of deference was scored three, disagreement one, and a depends or don't know answer, two. The resulting scale thus had seven points; the difference index for it is eight per cent, with Protestants tending to be slightly more deferential in their political values.
27. Figures from G. A. Almond and S. Verba, *The Civic Culture*, p. 267.
28. Richard Rose and Harve Mossawir, 'Voting and Elections: a Functional Analysis', p. 190.
29. Cf. *Annual Abstract of Statistics*, No. 106 (1969), Tables 64–84.
30. Cf. pp. 240ff., *supra*.
31. By contrast, when a British sample was asked what was liked and disliked about the Conservatives, Labour or Liberals, no more than 1·5 per cent of the respondents referred to historical events. See detailed codes in the codebook for the Butler-Stokes survey, 1963, issued by the Inter-University Consortium for Political Research, Ann Arbor, Michigan.
32. For the forms of socialization to be important, they would have to account for greater variations in regime outlooks than is found in the data reported earlier in Ch. XI.
33. A quotation from the Proclamation of the Republic in Dublin, 1916, a document redolent with historical reference.
34. J. G. Simms, *The Siege of Derry* (Dublin, APCK, 1966) and his *Jacobite Ireland, 1685–91, passim*. Cf. the testimony to the Scarman Tribunal about events in Derry (and Belfast) in 1969.

Chapter XII

1. An excellent illustration of this form of analysis is found in David
   Butler and Donald Stokes, *Political Change in Britain*. It should be
   noted, however, that the very marginal alterations in divisions of
   opinion that are crucial in electoral contests are not so important in
   differences about the regime. A more relevant comparison is with
   studies of the inter-generational persistence of attitudes. See e.g.,
   Philip Abrams and Alan Little, 'The Young Voter in British Politics',
   British Journal of Sociology XVI:2 (1965).
2. See especially Will Herberg, *Protestant, Catholic, Jew* (New York:
   Anchor Books, 1960).
3. The regression coefficient for Protestant support is $+0.2\%$ per decade,
   and for approval of 'any measures' $+2.9\%$. Among Catholics, for
   Constitutional support it is $+0.7\%$ per decade and -1.1% for endorsing illegal demonstrations.
4. An Opinion Research Centre survey conducted in February, 1969, five
   months after civil rights demonstrations began, found that 46 per cent
   of Catholics under the age of 35 endorsed resuming demonstrations
   after the Stormont election, as did 52 per cent of those above the age of
   50. The chief contrast is not by age, but by religion; the difference index
   between Protestants and Catholics is 61 per cent.
5. The comparison is with figures for father's party preference reported
   for the 1963 Butler-Stokes British Survey (Inter-University Consortium
   for Political Research, Ann Arbor, Michigan) Variable 61. Recall was
   better among Protestants, 78 per cent, than among Catholics, 60 per
   cent, reflecting the greater fragmentation of Green parties in Ulster.
6. Cf. the Northern Ireland youth survey done by National Opinion Polls
   for the *Belfast Telegraph*, October–November, 1968.
7. One Paisleyite preacher has even alleged that birth control is a Popish
   plot. The Roman Catholic Church is said to propagate the spread of
   birth control in order to reduce the proportion of young Protestants,
   while Catholics continue to multiply.
8. Conceivably, such national losses could be offset in so far as the Catholic Church is able to give opportunities for leadership, via the priesthood, to youths who would otherwise not have found them.
9. See the *Belfast Telegraph*'s report, November 4, 1968.
10. *The Northern Ireland Problem*, pp. 107–8. A similar pattern was found
    for the period 1937–51.
11. See R. C. Geary and J. G. Hughes, *Certain Aspects of Non-Agricultural
    Unemployment in Ireland* (Dublin: Economic and Social Research
    Institute, No. 52, 1970), pp. 11–12.
12. *The 1961 Census*, p. lii.
13. The problem of majority rule formulae is discussed elegantly in Robert
    A. Dahl, *A Preface to Democratic Theory* (Chicago: University Press,
    1956). The significance that Dahl attributes in his study to 'intensity'
    can be mitigated if those in both groups are equally intense in their
    outlooks.

Notes

14. The rejection is less among Catholics, where a substantial minority was prepared to endorse the break up of the Nationalists and their replacement by Conservative and Labour parties. Evidence in Ch. VII makes clear that this would not imply abandoning Republican sentiments.
15. See Ch. IV.
16. The testimony of the defence and prosecution in the Dublin arms trial of September–October, 1970, not only evidences 'misunderstandings' between individuals about the policies of the Republic, but also, the avoidance of an unequivocal rejection of using arms in the event of a 'doomsday' situation in Northern Ireland.
17. Cf. the discussion of the Irish bishops and the Vatican in 'The Church in Turmoil', *Nusight*, May, 1970.
18. Cf. Murray Forsyth, 'European Assemblies' in PEP *European Political Parties* (London: Allen & Unwin, 1969).

Chapter XIII

1. For a discussion of leader-follower relations in a British context, see Richard Rose, 'Complexities of Party Leadership', *Parliamentary Affairs* XVI:3 (1963).
2. This model of party competition differs in three ways from that used by Anthony Downs in his *An Economic Theory of Democracy* (New York: Harper, 1957). First, the smallest proportion of supporters are in the middle and the largest at the extremes. Secondly, more than two groups compete for support. Thirdly, the parties will not necessarily accept the verdict of the ballot box, but may resort to force.
3. There is a vast American literature on this subject. For a summary, see Norman R. Luttbeg, editor, *Public Opinion and Public Policy* (Homewood, Illinois: Dorsey, 1968). For a Northern Ireland village study, see Rosemary Harris, 'The Selection of Leaders in Ballybeg'.
4. During the period of research the author interviewed at length a wide variety of public officials and those opposed to the regime, often more than once. An application for funds to interview a systematic sample of politicians and clergymen was turned down by the British SSRC in autumn, 1968 on the grounds that it would be a separate research project.
5. See e.g., William Kornhauser, *The Politics of Mass Society* (London: Routledge, 1960), G. A. Almond and S. Verba, *The Civic Culture* and Norman H. Nie *et al.*, 'Social Structure and Political Participation', *American Political Science Review* LXIII:2–3 (1969).
6. Cf. G. A. Almond and S. Verba, *The Civic Culture*, p. 302. Results calculated from the original survey data.
7. If the criterion of church attendance is made weekly rather than 'at least monthly' the proportion of involved Protestants is 85 per cent and the Catholic figure remains at 98 per cent.
8. For a discussion, see e.g., Paul Lazarsfeld, B. Berelson, and H. Gaudet, *The People's Choice* (New York: Columbia University Press, 1968,

3rd edition) and Elihu Katz, 'The Two-Step Flow of Communication: an up-to-date Report on an Hypothesis', *Public Opinion Quarterly* XXI:1 (1957) and Sidney Verba, *Small Groups and Political Behaviour* (Princeton: University Press, 1961).

9. Cf. Robert A. Dahl, *Who Governs?*, Part V.
10. See his *Ulster at the Crossroads*, pp. 145–6.
11. Data from the Loyalty survey, the British Electoral Survey, 1963 and *The Civic Culture* data files.
12. See J. Bowyer Bell, *The Secret Army*.
13. *The Semi-Sovereign People* (New York: Holt, 1960).
14. By definition, a 'charismatic' leader would resolve the difficulty by destroying differences strongly institutionalized in Northern Ireland. Such charismatic figures are few in modern Western history and some, e.g., Charles de Gaulle or Adolf Hitler, are ambivalent or evil in Anglo-American eyes. The history of Ireland in the past century suggests that anyone casting himself in such a role may have a glorious life–but it will also be a short one.
15. Cf. pp. 449ff., *infra* and sources cited there for an illustration of bi-confessionalism in Austria.
16. See the discussion in S. E. Finer, *The Man on Horseback* (London: Pall Mall, 1962).
17. For a discussion of the Governor's position, see 'The key to direct rule in Ulster', *The Times*, August 14, 1970. Note also Harry Calvert, *Constitutional Law in Northern Ireland, passim.*
18. Cf. an interview with John Hume by Harold Jackson, 'Instead of Stormont . . .?', *The Guardian*, August 14, 1970.
19. For a pre-UDI study of Southern Rhodesia, where exclusion of one group from power was also a premise of many active in politics, see Colin Leys, *European Politics in Southern Rhodesia* (Oxford: Clarendon Press, 1959).

Chapter XIV

1. *The Logic of Collective Action* (New York: Schocken Books edition, 1968), p. 15, n. 22. Olson uses the terms 'collective' and 'public' goods interchangeably. The former usage will be employed here to emphasize that no attempt is made to apply the whole of the economic theory of public goods to this discussion.
2. Cf. J. G. Head, 'Public Goods and Public Policy', *Public Finance*, XVII:3 (1962), pp. 204–5.
3. See Elizabeth Bott, *Family and Social Network*, pp. 159ff. Note also Ch. IX, *supra.*
4. See W. G. Runciman, *Relative Deprivation and Social Justice.*
5. The point emerges with particular clarity in J. Roland Pennock, 'Responsible Government, Separated Powers and Special Interests: Agricultural Subsidies in Britain and America', *American Political Science Review* LVI:3 (1962).

Notes

6. The concept of a peasantry oriented toward maintaining a domestic economy, not a market economy, is taken from S. H. Franklin's brilliant conceptualization in *The European Peasantry* (London: Methuen, 1969).

7. Cf. E. P. Thompson, *The Making of the English Working Class* (Harmondsworth: Pelican Books, 1968) and Neil Smelser, *Social Change in the Industrial Revolution* (London: Routledge, 1959).

8. Cf. pp. 315ff., *supra*.

9. In so far as the majority are disadvantaged because they do not know the minority language, then the balance of gain and loss may even have a negative sum. Cf. Walter Simon, 'Linguistic Pluralism as a Source of Cleavages and Conflict' (Varna, Bulgaria: VIIth World Congress of the International Sociological Association, mimeograph, 1970).

10. John Meisel reports that in Canada Francophones are less ready to endorse compliance with laws than are Anglophones. See 'Language Continua and Political Alignments: the case of French and English-Users in Canada' (Varna, Bulgaria: VIIth World Congress of the International Sociological Association, mimeograph, 1970), note 14.

11. The following paragraphs draw upon data and definitions discussed and reported fully in Richard Rose and Derek Urwin, 'Social Cohesion, Political Parties and Strains in Regimes'.

12. Iceland detached itself from Denmark peaceably too, but it is worth noting that the decision was ratified in May, 1944, when Denmark was still under German occupation. The vote was 70,725 for complete independence and 370 against.

13. For a survey of nationalist ideologies stated in absolute terms, see Elie Kedourie, *Nationalism* (London: Hutchinson, 1960).

14. See Derek Urwin and Richard Rose, 'Persistence and Disruption in Western Party Systems Between the Wars' (Varna, Bulgaria: VIIth World Congress, International Sociological Association, 1970).

15. See especially Stein Rokkan, *Citizens, Elections, Parties* (Oslo: Universitetsforlaget, 1970), p. 33.

16. The phenomenon is discussed and an explanation offered in Richard Rose, 'Class and Party Divisions', pp. 130ff.

17. The point is endorsed by an author who apparently would prefer to think in economically determined categories. See T. W. Mason, 'The Primacy of Politics – Politics and Economics in National Socialist Germany', in S. J. Woolf, editor, *The Nature of Fascism* (New York: Vintage, 1968).

18. See D. W. Urwin, *Western Europe Since 1945* (London: Longmans, 1968), Ch. 1.

19. The problems that Western regimes have in using force for defence against repudiations are discussed in Juan Linz, 'The Breakdown of Democratic Politics' (Varna, Bulgaria: VIIth World Congress, International Sociological Association, 1970).

20. See Edward Luttwak *Coup d'Etat*, pp. 90ff. More generally, see Brian Chapman, *Police State* (London: Macmillan, 1970).

21. Undoubtedly, some employees of a regime will benefit by its over-

throw. Such individuals, even if officers of the regime, should be conceived of as among the challengers.

22. Cf. the discussion of bargaining as a form of relatedness, even when conflict is involved, in H. L. Nieburg, *Political Violence*, pp. 75ff. The idea of a market-place of discord may thus be viewed as a special illustration of a situation of partisan mutual adjustment. Cf. C. E. Lindblom, *The Intelligence of Democracy* (New York: Free Press, 1965).

23. For useful reviews of the varying meanings of the term revolution, with the emphasis upon its political content, see e.g., Peter Calvert, 'Revolution: the Politics of Violence', *Political Studies* XV:1 (1967) and Lawrence Stone, 'Theories of Revolution', *World Politics* XVIII:2 (1966).

24. Concern with political power for its own sake explains why such politicians will not sell out, whether for or against the regime, in exchange for non-political goods. They are only interested in political advantages. Hence, offers of political benefits must be made to get a person to change sides.

25. Cf. the response to the question about elections in Table VII.10.

26. This assumes that changes in the structure of the population do not absorb the product of economic growth.

27. Cf. Mancur Olson Jr., *The Logic of Collective Action*.

28. The concepts of 'entry' and standing outside the exit are an extension of the analysis in Albert O. Hirschman's *Exit, Voice and Loyalty* (Cambridge, Massachusetts: Harvard, 1970). Hirschman's study does not deal with problems of allegiance in *divided* regimes.

29. See J. Bowyer Bell, *The Secret Army* and interviews reported in T. P. Coogan, *The IRA*.

30. Cf. Mancur Olson Jr., 'Economics, Sociology and the Best of All Possible Worlds', *Public Interest*, No. 12 (1968).

31. Cf. L. P. Curtis Jr., *Coercion and Conciliation in Ireland, 1880–92* (Princeton: University Press, 1963).

32. *The Federalist*, No. 51: authorship attributed to Alexander Hamilton or James Madison.

Chapter XV

1. Cf. Erwin Scheuch, 'Cross-National Comparisons Using Aggregate Data: Some Substantive and Methodological Problems' in Richard Merritt and Stein Rokkan, *Comparing Nations* (New Haven: Yale University Press, 1966).

2. See Albert Biderman, 'Social Indicators and Goals', pp. 85ff., in Raymond Bauer, editor, *Social Indicators* (Cambridge, Massachusetts: MIT Press, 1966).

3. Quoted in Harry Calvert, *Constitutional Law in Northern Ireland*, p. 41.

4. Cf. the Constitutions reprinted in Leslie Wolf-Phillips, *Constitutions of Modern States* (London: Pall Mall, 1968).

5. *Citizenship and Social Class* (Cambridge: University Press, 1950).

Notes

6. For their historical application to Continental nations, particularly with reference to industrial organization, see Reinhard Bendix's study, with Stein Rokkan, *Nation-Building and Citizenship* (New York: Wiley, 1964), pp. 74–104.

7. *Toward a Social Report* (Washington: Government Printing Office, 1969), p. 97.

8. G. A. Almond and Bingham Powell Jr., *Comparative Politics: a Developmental Approach* (Boston: Little, Brown, 1966), pp. 199ff.

9. *The English Constitution* (Original edition, 1867; London: Oxford University Press edition, 1955), pp. 3ff.

10. See Richard Rose, *People in Politics*, pp. 195ff.

11. The basic source of figures is Derek W. Urwin, *Elections in Western Nations, 1945–1968*. For Northern Ireland, the proportion of Catholics in the population in the 1961 census was used instead of a vote total. This avoids making the anti-regime vote a majority of the population, as could be done by referring to Table XIII.1.

12. See e.g., H. D. Graham and T. R. Gurr, editors, *The History of Violence in America*.

13. Pearson's r for the association is ·12. The rank-order of nations in terms of discord is more consistent, for Kendall's Tau for the relationship of anti-regime vote before the Second World War and immediately after is ·60. Correlations between the total anti-regime vote at the first post-war election and at the latest election in the 1960s are $r = ·75$; $T = ·58$; with the average in the post-war years, $r = ·92$ and $T = ·70$; and with the highest anti-regime vote in each country since the war, $r = ·93$ and $T = ·71$.

14. To ensure normal distribution, the raw figures given in Table XV:1 have been standardized before computing r.

15. See Maurice Schaeffer and Eugene Levitt, 'Concerning Kendall's Tau, a Nonparametric Correlation Coefficient', *Psychological Bulletin* LIII: 4 (1956).

16. *Citizenship and Social Class*, p. 11.

17. Moreover, the base for calculating employed workers also varies; hence, the ratio of unemployed to employed workers, i.e., the per cent unemployed, can vary even more widely in meaning. Cf. *UN Statistical Year Book 1969*, p. 85.

18. I am grateful to members of a 1969–70 postgraduate seminar at the University of Strathclyde for applying their specialized knowledge of a range of Continental societies to an evaluation of these data sources: Keith Hill, Christopher Hull, Tom Mackie, John Madeley and Alastair Thomas. Our joint efforts added several variables for inclusion here and eliminated many others.

19. See *Development Programme, 1970–75*, p. 4.

20. 'Economics, Sociology and the Best of all Possible Worlds', *The Public Interest*, No. 12 (Summer, 1968), p. 112.

21. See e.g., William Kornhauser, *The Politics of Mass Society*.

22. Cf. the three articles in the *International Encyclopedia of the Social Sciences*.

23. Cf. the low rate of suicide as against homicide in the American South, as reported in Sheldon Hackney, 'Southern Violence', in H. D. Graham and T. R. Gurr, editors, *The History of Violence in America*, pp. 507ff.
24. There was a slight rise in the negative correlation of church attendance with anti-regime votes when controls were introduced for gross national product and urbanization.
25. Cf. Edwin Hammond, *An Analysis of Regional Economic and Social Statistics.*
26. The significance levels range from ·05 for the Pearson's r correlation with tuberculosis death to ·001 for the r correlating anti-regime vote with change in gross national product.
27. *Citizenship and Social Class*, p. 10.
28. D. Barritt and C. F. Carter, *The Northern Ireland Problem*, pp. 133ff.
29. See e.g., Harry Calvert, *Constitutional Law in Northern Ireland*, p. 381; 'Human Rights in Northern Ireland', *The Review of the International Commission of Jurists*, No. 2 (June, 1969), pp. 18–19; J. L. J. Edwards, 'Special Powers in Northern Ireland', *Criminal Law Review* (1956). For the case for the Act, see *supra*, pp. 128f.
30. See J. Bowyer Bell, *The Secret Army*, passim.
31. Cited from a 1949 Supreme Court opinion in Basil Chubb, editor, *A Source Book of Irish Government*, p. 67. Cf. the reactions to the proposal to reintroduce internment in 1970: *This Week* (December 17, 1970).
32. See Harry Calvert, *Constitutional Law in Northern Ireland*, pp. 253ff.
33. See Northern Ireland House of Commons *Debates*, Vol. 76, Col. 1581 (June 30, 1970). Cf. Basil Chubb, *The Government and Politics of Ireland*, p. 126.
34. The Stormont regime, however, has been less forward than Conservative governments in Westminster in extending recognition to the unions. Cf. D. Barritt and C. F. Carter, *The Northern Ireland Problem*, pp. 138–42. In divided democratic regimes, trade unions are not particularly the subject of legal inhibitions. Cf. Reinhard Bendix with Stein Rokkan, *Nation Building and Citizenship*, pp. 74ff.
35. See *The Statesman's Yearbook 1969/1970* (London: Macmillan, 1969), p. 895.
36. See Ch. IV.
37. Cf. Tom Hadden, 'Special Powers North and South', *This Week* (December 17, 1970).
38. See *For Members of Parliament Only*, pp. 9ff., 48.
39. Figures from the Government Information Service, Stormont Castle. Fuller details will appear in the Report of the Scarman Tribunal.
40. Cf. '140 RC pupils go to State school', *Belfast Telegraph*, September 7, 1970.
41. *Citizenship and Social Class*, pp. 10–11.
42. The original German title of *The Trial* is particularly relevant – *Der Prozess.*
43. *A Commentary to Accompany the Cameron Report*, paragraph 27.

Notes

44. *Second Report of the Northern Ireland Commissioner for Complaints*, paragraphs 5–6.
45. *Ibid.*, paragraph 51.
46. *Ibid.*, paragraphs 52–5.
47. If a case involves a second offence of the same sort by the same authority, then the Attorney-General may seek a court injunction to prevent the body from persisting in maladministration.
48. See C. E. B. Brett's 'Memorandum of Evidence to the Royal Commission on the Constitution'.
49. See *Why Justice Cannot be Done* (Dungannon: Campaign for Social Justice, 1964).
50. See *supra*, pp. 104ff. and 143ff., and sources cited there.
51. See especially the testimony to the Scarman Tribunal of Chief Inspector David Cushley, RUC on November 5–6, 1970. Note also the testimony of Head Constable James Seay, as reported in 'Hooker St. homes burned by civilians, says RUC officer', *Belfast Telegraph*, April 29, 1970.
52. 'Falls–Bogside to have rapid police build-up, PM', *Belfast Telegraph*, July 24, 1970 and 'RUC go back to a cool reception', *ibid.*, August 1, 1970. See also, 'Search for arms is one sided, says CCDC', *ibid.*, September 1, 1970.
53. 'Thousands join defiance walk', *Belfast Telegraph*, August 12, 1970.
54. See Kevin Boyle, 'The "Minimum Sentences" Act', pp. 432–3.
55. See press accounts of evidence and pleas at the Devlin trial, December, 1969.
56. See the files of the *Protestant Telegraph* for these complaints.
57. See the five-volume *Report* of the 1961 United States Commission on Civil Rights, especially on the police, and the *Report of the National Advisory Commission on Civil Disorders* (The Kerner Commission).
58. *Citizenship and Social Class*, p. 11.
59. Cf. W. J. M. Mackenzie, *Free Elections* (London: Allen & Unwin, 1958), Ch. 20.
60. Pearson's r = ·12 and Kendall's Tau = ·11. The index of unrepresentativeness is as calculated by C. J. Hull, 'Inequalities in Electoral Systems and Regimes' (Glasgow: University of Strathclyde seminar paper, 1970).
61. Cf. Bryan Keith-Lucas, *A History of the English Local Government Franchise* (Oxford: Blackwell, 1952).
62. Cf. *The Cameron Report*, Ch. 12 and items cited in Ch. X, note 11.
63. The statement is made by Fergus Pyle, 'Stormont: What chance for the future?', *Fortnight*, November 20, 1970.
64. *Orange and Green*, p. 33. See also D. Barritt and C. F. Carter, *The Northern Ireland Problem*, pp. 116–18.
65. Cf. *The Hunt Report*, paragraphs 119ff.
66. The American data, collected in 1966, are reported in John P. Robinson *et al.*, *Measures of Political Attitudes* (Ann Arbor, Michigan: Institute for Social Research, 1968), p. 648.
67. See G. A. Almond and Bingham Powell Jr., *Comparative Politics*, p. 199.

68. See Harry Calvert, *Constitutional Law in Northern Ireland*, p. 389 and 'Prison terms for painting tri-colours', *Irish News*, July 23, 1970. ' "Lucky to be alive" youth is jailed', *Irish News*, July 28, 1970.
69. See e.g., A. C. Donaldson, *Some Comparative Aspects of Irish Law*, Ch. 3.
70. See 'Youths sang "Soldier's Song" court is told', *Belfast Telegraph*, October 20, 1970. On the origins of the flag and anthem, see Appendices F and G of James D. O'Donnell, *How Ireland is Governed* (Dublin: Institute of Public Administration, 1967). The words of the Anthem were written by Peader Kearney, Brendan Behan's uncle.
71. Avro Manhattan, *Religious Terror in Ireland* (London: Paravision Books, 1970), p. 147.
72. See the Commons debate reported in 'Muck shovelling is only for those loyal to State', *Irish News*, November 5, 1970. Pride in the regime is lower among Catholics than Protestants (D.I. = 30%). See Appendix, Q. 21b.
73. The absence of any systematic testing of the hypothesis with materials from Continental Europe, e.g., Italy and France, makes this finding less conclusive than the negative findings derived from statistical analysis in the first part of the chapter.

Chapter XVI

1. Robert A. Dahl, editor, *Political Oppositions in Western Democracies* (New Haven: Yale University Press, 1966), p. xi.
2. Cf. *The Politics of Accommodation* (Berkeley: University of California Press, 1968) and 'Consociational Democracy', *World Politics* XXI:2 (1969).
3. 'Typologies of Democratic Systems', *Comparative Political Studies* 1:1 (1968), pp. 25ff.
4. The extent of *verzuiling* in Northern Ireland is less than anticipated, as the data in Ch. X show. Lijphart's Dutch evidence does not permit precise comparison with the Northern Ireland data. In fact, his fragmentary survey evidence concerning social differences indicates that the degree of *verzuiling* is often less than complete. Cf. the tables in *The Politics of Accommodation*.
5. Hans Daalder, 'The Netherlands: Opposition in a Segmented Society', in Robert A. Dahl, editor, *Political Oppositions in Western Democracies*, p. 219.
6. Arend Lijphart, 'Social Heterogeneity and Political Instability: the Case of Northern Ireland' (Varna, Bulgaria: VIIth World Congress, International Sociological Association, 1970), p. 1.
7. See Robert A. Dahl, editor, *Political Oppositions in Western Democracies*, pp. 371ff., for the conditions in which two-party competition can create discord in a regime.
8. The survey data are quoted from Rodney Stiefbold *et al.*, editors,

Notes

Wahlen und Parteien in Osterreich (Vienna: *Osterreichischer Bundesverlag*, 1966, Vol. II, Part B), pp. 575ff.
9. See F. C. Engelmann, 'Austria: the Pooling of Opposition', in Robert A. Dahl, editor, *Political Oppositions in Western Democracies*, p. 262.
10. For a contemporary description, see C. A. Macartney, 'The Armed Formations in Austria', *International Affairs* VIII (1929), pp. 617ff.
11. For the distinctiveness of the party profiles, see Richard Rose and Derek Urwin, 'Social Cohesion, Political Parties and Strains in Regimes', p. 52. For a variety of points of view about the Coalition and Coalition practices, see Rodney Stiefbold *et al.*, editors, *Wahlen un Parteien in Österreich*, Vol. II, Part B, pp. 774ff.
12. On Switzerland, a state which has some similarities with both the Netherlands and the *Proporz*-regime of Austria, see Gerhard Lehmbruch, *Proporzdemokratie* (Tübingen: Mohr, 1967) and Jurgen Steiner, 'The Principles of Majority and Proportionality', *British Journal of Political Science* 1:1 (1971).
13. See F. C. Engelmann, 'Haggling for the Equilibrium', *American Political Science Review* LV:3 (1962), pp. 652ff.
14. Cf. H. D. Graham and T. R. Gurr, editors, *The History of Violence in America*.
15. The transition is carefully examined in Frank Munger, 'The Legitimacy of Opposition: the Change of Government in Ireland in 1932' (New York: American Political Science Association, duplicated, 1966).
16. Cf. Table XV.1 and the deviant position of Ireland, high on stability in relation to socio-economic characteristics, as shown in Phillips Cutright, 'National Political Development', *American Sociological Review* XXVIII:2 (1963).
17. Cf. William Butler Yeats, 'September, 1913'; the quotation from Patrick Pearse, at p. 161 *supra*, and the aftermath of the Dublin arms trial of 1970.
18. See *A Survey of Public Opinion for This Week Magazine* (Dublin: Irish Marketing Surveys, May, 1970), Tables 6a and 9a.
19. The numbers are as of September 15, 1946. I am indebted to T. T. Mackie for checking out the details of institutional history.
20. See Colin Leys, *European Politics in Southern Rhodesia*, pp. 173ff.
21. See especially, James G. Leyburn, *The Scotch-Irish*.
22. See *Historical Statistics of the United States, Colonial Times to 1957* (Washington, D.C.: U.S. Bureau of the Census, 1957), p. 14, and *The World Almanac, 1969* (New York: Newspaper Enterprise Association, 1968), p. 601.
23. The conditions of rural voters as described by Angus Campbell *et al.*, *The American Voter* (New York: Wiley, 1960), Ch. 15, according to some social science theories, would make them particularly prone to extra-constitutional political acts.
24. See e.g., Philip Taft and Phillip Ross, 'American Labour Violence; Its Causes, Character and Outcome', in H. D. Graham and T. R. Gurr, editors, *The History of Violence in America*.

Notes

25. See John Tracy Ellis, *American Catholicism* (Chicago: University Press, 1955), pp. 19ff. and Ray A. Billington, *The Protestant Crusade, 1800–1860* (New York: Macmillan, 1938), p. 1.
26. See Angus Campbell *et al.*, *The American Voter*, Ch. 12, and Philip E. Converse, 'Religion and Politics: the 1960 Election', in Angus Campbell *et al.*, *Elections and the Political Order*.
27. See E. R. Norman, *The Conscience of the State in North America* (Cambridge: University Press, 1968), pp. 141ff. For a review of persisting differences, see Richard E. Morgan, *The Politics of Religious Conflict* (New York: Pegasus, 1968).
28. *Historical Statistics of the United States*, p. 9 contains what official data are available on the American Indian population, cf. the notes at p. 3 of the same volume.
29. The point is brought out by the attempt of Michael Parenti to demonstrate the importance of ethnic politics, at levels below regime conflict. See 'Ethnic Politics and the Persistence of Ethnic Identification', *American Political Science Review* LXI:3 (1967).
30. For the hostile reception of some categories of immigrants, especially those differentiated by religion (i.e., Catholics and Jews), see John Higham, *Strangers in the Land* (New York: Atheneum edition, 1963). For statistics, see *Historical Statistics of the United States*, pp. 65–6. For the positive loyalty of immigrants, even rejected Japanese-Americans, see Morton Grodzins, *The Loyal and the Disloyal* (Chicago: University Press, 1956).
31. See e.g., the very relevant findings of a survey by the Gallup Poll, reported in *Newsweek*, June 30, 1969.
32. Cf. Louis Hartz, editor, *The Founding of New Societies*.
33. *Historical Statistics of the United States*, pp. 12–13.
34. Low rates of foreign immigration have continued to the present. See *The World Almanac, 1969*, pp. 599, 602.
35. A detailed breakdown of votes is contained in *The World Almanac, 1969*, p. 387.
36. As quoted in Morton Grodzins, *The Loyal and the Disloyal*, p. 143.
37. For details, see *The World Almanac, 1969*, p. 751.
38. Calculated as a ratio of columns reported by *Hansard* index as related to Northern Ireland, as against total columns of debates, 1964–8 inclusive.
39. W. G. Brock, *An American Crisis* (London: Macmillan, 1963), p. 13.
40. C. Vann Woodward, *The Strange Career of Jim Crow* (New York: Oxford University Press, 1955), p. 6. For more detail, see Woodward's *Reunion and Reaction* (New York: Anchor edition, 1956).
41. Figures quoted in *Freedom to the Free: Century of Emancipation* (Washington, D.C.: U.S. Commission on Civil Rights, 1963), p. 71.
42. C. Vann Woodward, *The Strange Career of Jim Crow*, pp. 52–3.
43. See *Freedom to the Free*, p. 55.
44. In addition, one Republic President, Dwight D. Eisenhower, was born in Texas and held many states' rights views.
45. See W. G. Brock, *An American Crisis*, especially pp. 250, 269.

Notes

46. Two particularly relevant studies of the courts and American civil rights are Clement Vose, *Caucasians Only* (Berkeley: University of California Press, 1959) and J. W. Peltason, *Fifty-Eight Lonely Men* (New York: Harcourt, 1961).
47. See the sympathetic account in Arthur M. Schlesinger Jr., *A Thousand Days* (London: Deutsch, 1965), Chs. 35–6.
48. Cf. Howard Schuman, 'Sociological Racism', *Trans-Action* VII:2 (1969).
49. H. D. Graham and T. R. Gurr, *A History of Violence in America*, p. 813.

List of Tables, Figures and Maps

List of Tables, Figures and Maps

List of Tables, Figures and Maps

Index

Act of Union, 1707, 53
Act of Union, 1800, 82
Albania, 36
Algeria, 33
Alliance Party, 226
Almond, Gabriel, and Powell, B., 418, 443f.
America, 18ff., 49, 52, 56, 62, 78f., 89, 95ff., 106, 112, 157, 179ff., 196, 221, 234, 241, 248ff., 258, 261, 277, 303, 322, 327, 332ff., 360, 367, 383ff., 409ff., 423ff., 438ff., 453ff.,
American South, 17f., 35, 181, 304, 440, 447, 459, 462ff.
Amery, L. S., 42
Andrews, Frank, 321
Angles, 48
Anglicization, 45, 65
Anglo-American world, 18f., 25, 126, 157, 171, 242, 365, 405, 407, 417, 419, 429, 441, 447f., 453, 462
Anglo-Irish Treaty, 1921, 90
Antrim, West, 79, 90
Appalachia, 17
Appomatox, 464
Arabs, 456
Armagh, 81, 90, 100, 103, 135, 138, 170, 249, 251, 267, 294, 312
Army, British, 97, 107ff., 121f., 129ff., 145ff., 163ff., 252, 332, 370, 373f., 391ff., 408, 438f., 456
Asquith, H. H., 88
Attorney-General of Northern Ireland, 133, 259
Aughrim, Battle of, 18
Australia, 17, 52, 117, 403, 424, 433, 455
Austria, Republic of 264, 403, 424, 426, 449ff.
Austro-Hungarian Empire, 404ff.
Ayer, A. J., 198f.

Bagehot, Walter, 42, 418

Balfour, A. J., 275
Ballymacarrett, 175, 391
Ballymurphy, 110
Bann, River, 312
Bannside, constituency of 105, 226
Barritt, D., and Carter, C. F., 281, 366
Beckett, J. C., 97
Belfast *News Letter*, 343f.
Belfast *Telegraph*, 220, 258, 297, 344, 366, 439
Belgium, 36, 403f., 424, 426
Bell, J. Bowyer, 447
Benn, J. M., 435
Bentham, J., 198
Bill of rights, 1689, 58, 416, 439
Billington, Ray, 459
Blacks in America, 461ff.
Blaney, Neil, 168f.
Blondel, Jean, 43
Blood groups, 48
Bob Jones University, 254
Bogside, 104ff., 121, 131, 143f., 159ff., 252, 278, 296, 354, 439f.
Border, The (of Northern Ireland and the Republic), 111ff., 141f., 167, 231, 299f., 313, 362, 368ff.
Boru, Brian, 76
Bosanquet, B., 198
Boundary Commission, 1921, 92
Boyle, Kevin, 104, 161
Boyle Louis, 224
Boyne, Battle of, 18, 75, 79, 181, 327
Bradford, Roy, 108
Bretons, 48
Briggs, Asa, 64
B.B.C., 54, 247, 343
British West Indies, 456
Brock, W. G., 465
Brookeborough, Viscount 95ff., 179, 203, 242, 273
Building Design Partnership, 296

Index

Bulgaria, 36
Burntollet Bridge, 131, 194
Burroughs, Ronald, 122, 171
Butler, D. E., 94, 186

Callaghan, James, 107f., 122, 125, 134, 295, 412
Calvert, Harry, 129, 432
Cameron Commission, 129, 137, 143, 154, 164, 310, 442
Cameron, Lord, 107, 136, 271
Campaign for Democracy in Ulster, 121
Campaign for Social Justice, 102, 160, 437
Canada, 52, 117, 402, 424, 455
Cardiff, 50, 52
Carson, Sir Edward, 86, 88, 112, 120, 377
Catholic Emancipation Act, 59
Cavan, county, 43, 90
Celtic, Glasgow, 140
Celts, 17, 48, 54, 75, 191
Central Citizens Defence Committee, 138, 163, 169f., 175, 252f.,
Centre and periphery, 40, 45ff., 317ff., 402ff.
Chamberlain, Neville, 17
Channel Isles, 119,
Churchill, Lord Randolph, 86
Churchill, W. S., 359
Civil Rights movement 31, 102f., 110, 121, 123, 134, 136, 152, 157ff., 165, 229, 251, 278, 310, 373, 440, 442, 468f
Clark, Major James D. Chichester-, 105ff., 121, 136, 153, 173, 179, 207, 225, 277, 392
Clark, Wallace, 153, 377
Class, as an influence, 45, 65–9, 231, 279ff., 318ff., 341f., 398f.
Clydeside, 65, 85
Coleraine, 98, 158
Collins, Michael, 381
Communism, 32, 37, 58, 237, 242, 273, 281, 403ff., 420, 428, 433, 459
Communist Party, the British, 25, 108
Complaints, Commissioner for, Northern Ireland, 295, 297, 435ff.
Connacht, 49, 80f., 88, 395, 447
Connolly, James, 84, 106, 159, 164, 203, 231, 277, 388, 444

Conservative (Party), 55, 61, 65, 85ff., 124, 128, 222f., 277, 285, 456
Conway, William Cardinal, 249ff.
Cooper, Ivan Lee, 105, 230
Cork, 95, 298
Cornish people, 48
Craig, Sir James (Lord Craigavon) 90ff., 242, 377
Craig, William, 103, 129, 136, 147, 225f.
Craigavon (town of) 98
Cromwell, Oliver, 18, 58, 73, 79, 377
Council of Ireland, 98, 116
Courts and Law, 125ff., 434ff.,
Crown, the English 31, 58, 80, 116, 119, 132ff., 151, 198, 204f., 227, 340, 354, 390, 444f., 455, 459
Cú Chulainn, 377
Curran, Lord Justice, 135
Currie, Austin, 102, 133, 154, 230, 445
Cushley, Chief Inspector David, 106
Cyprus, 456
Czechoslovakia, 17, 32, 35

Daalder, Hans, 449
Dahl, Robert, 447
Daily Express, The, 344
Deference, 348f.
Denmark, 36, 403, 424
Derry, *see* Londonderry
Desertmartin, 152
Devenney, Samuel, 123f., 131
Devlin, Bernadette, 105, 110, 124, 159 170, 180, 221, 233, 252, 278, 337 440, 444
Devlin, Joe, 93
Devlin Paddy, 165, 230, 233
Dillon, John, 88
Disreli, B., 82
Donegal, 43, 74, 90ff., 102, 154, 168
Dowling, Samuel, 110
Down, County, 90
Down, North constituency, 309
Dublin, 30, 50ff., 63ff., 75, 80ff., 110, 115f., 126, 149, 162, 165f., 169, 183, 298, 313, 317, 328, 344
Dunadry, 134
Dundalk, 165, 168, 314
Dungannon, 101f., 127, 160, 251
Durkheim, Emile, 428

Easton, David, 239
Eckstein, Harry, 37, 43, 346

Index

Index

Ulster B Special Constabulary, 97, 104ff., 138ff, 163, 433, 443
Ulster Covenant, 87, 153f., 192, 350ff., 416, 456
Ulster Protestant League, 95
Ulster Television, 343
Ulster Unionist Party, 19, 27, 120
Ulster Volunteer Force, 86, 92, 133, 153f., 161, 170, 193, 233f., 343, 377, 433, 464
Ultras, 33, 86, 103ff., 121, 124, 127, 134, 147ff., 173, 191, 197, 205ff., 226, 236, 245ff., 267ff., 279ff., 289ff., 299ff., 360ff., 376ff., 410, 413, 440, 450, 456, 464ff.
Union Jack, 17f., 56, 153, 217, 243, 273, 337, 444
Unionist Party, 86ff., 132, 134, 152ff., 171ff., 200, 207, 211, 219ff., 258f., 267, 281ff., 292ff., 309ff., 320ff., 338, 344, 362, 368, 370f., 382, 387ff., 435, 441ff., 451
United Irishmen, 30, 81, 377, 433
United Nations, 374, 395, 426, 447, 463
United States Civil Rights Commission, 469
United States Constitution, 30, 35, 416, 438, 465

Valera, Eamon de, 92f., 247, 453
Vietnam, South, 34

Wales, 35, 43ff., 116, 124, 179, 206, 276
Wallace, George, 413, 420, 469
Weaver, Robert, 443
Weber, Max, 242f.
Wellington, Duke of, 64
Welsh language, 48, 56, 61, 65
Welsh Nationalist Party, 33, 64, 70
Wessex, 27
West, Harry, 225
West Ulster Unionist Council, 225, 311
Western nations, 17ff., 26, 32, 37ff., 159, 219, 234, 237, 262ff., 275, 282, 299, 383, 399, 402ff., 419ff., 440ff., 458
Whyte, John, 246
William of Orange, 59, 73, 79, 332
Williams, Walter, 258
Wilson, Harold, 73, 121, 124, 129, 141, 179
Wilson, Thomas, 84, 97f., 126
Wolf-Phillips, Leslie, 45
Woodward, C. Vann, 466
World Council of Churches, 100
Wright, Oliver, 108, 122, 179

Yeats, W. B., 25, 74
Young, Sir Arthur, 146f.
Yugoslavia, 36

Zionists, 28